A Concepts-Based Introduction to Financial Accounting

FOURTH EDITION

David L Kolitz
B Com (Natal), B Com (Hons) (SA), M Com (Wits)
Associate Professor, School of Accountancy
University of the Witwatersrand

Alan B Quinn
B Com, B Acc (Wits)
Registered Accountant & Auditor
Joint Managing Director, Core People (Pty) Ltd

Gavin McAllister
B Com (Hons) (Wits), CA(SA), ACA, CFA
Associate in Financial Sector Transaction Services
KPMG, London

JUTA

First published 1997
Second impression 1999
Second edition 2001
Third edition 2005
Fourth edition 2009
Reprint 2011

PO Box 14373, Lansdowne 7779

ISBN: 978-0-70217-749-1

Project management: Marlinee Chetty
Copy editing: David Kolitz
Proofreading: Rae Dalton
Permissions co-ordinator: Natasha Talliard
Design and typesetting: Ashley Richardson
Cover design: Jacques Nel
Printed and bound by Bevan Group

Contents

Dedication

To

Maeve and Dylan

To

Jennie, Nikolá, Aidan and Ronin

To

Roy, Lindy and Taryn

Preface

Pedagogical philosophy

The literature refers to the procedural and conceptual approaches in the teaching of an introductory accounting course. The procedural course is usually described as being mainly concerned with the techniques of double-entry bookkeeping, while the conceptual approach in its pure form moves away from the techniques of accounting for transactions and uses a decision-making approach as the foundation for explaining the need and role of accounting in society.

It is submitted that the procedural approach places too much emphasis on how to perform various techniques rather than why these techniques are performed. It is proposed that this may not develop the student's ability to apply the techniques to practical situations. On the other hand, the application of the pure conceptual approach places little emphasis on the techniques of double-entry bookkeeping.

The *concepts* model integrates the conceptual and procedural approaches to the teaching of introductory accounting by teaching students to understand the concepts that underpin the application of accounting theory in the solution of accounting problems. This impacts on both the order of teaching of the topics and the way in which the various topics are taught.

Changes made for the fourth edition

The broad outline, as described below, has been maintained. The requirements and terminology of the new IAS 1 have been incorporated throughout the book. The statement of comprehensive income is introduced and used where appropriate – otherwise the income statement is used. The statement of financial position is used throughout instead of the balance sheet.

Extensive changes have been made to the pedagogical style of the book. Each chapter now begins with an extract from the financial statements of a listed company related to the material covered in that chapter. This adds a real life relevance to the chapter contents. In addition, key definitions are now highlighted in each chapter. This enables students to focus on those definitions when reading the text and is useful for revision purposes. A further enhancement is 'pause and reflect' insertions throughout each chapter. These are short scenarios, both narrative and numerical, designed to confirm understanding, illustrate a specific point or to make the reader think about the meaning and implication of the preceding paragraphs.

Chapter 1, 'The role of accounting in business' has been updated to incorporate the impact of IFRS on standard setting and financial reporting in South Africa. In addition, reference is made to proposed changes to the conceptual framework as set out in the 2008 exposure draft. The comprehensive example used to explain the accounting process throughout Chapters 2 to 7 has been changed to a retailer of computer equipment, but the structure of the example remains.

Chapter 8, now entitled 'The recording of purchase and sale transactions' has been completely rewritten. The focus of the chapter is now on the recognition and measurement of revenue from sales and purchases of inventory, in other words, the treatment of settlement, cash and trade discounts. The perpetual system is used as the main teaching example with a comparison to the periodic system included at the end of the chapter. As the conceptual principle of measuring revenue from sales and purchases of inventory was explained in detail in Chapter 8, it was felt unnecessary to incorporate discounts into the examples in Chapter 9, 'The Analysis Journals'. The focus of Chapter 9 would have been lost if discounts were incorporated. Instead, certain questions in Chapter 9 of the accompanying text, '*Questions, Exercises and Problems in Financial Accounting: Introductory*', include the treatment of discounts in the recognition and measurement of revenue from sales and purchases of inventory. Chapter 10, 'Value Added Tax', has been extended to incorporate the VAT implications of discounts.

In Part 5, '*Entity Forms*', Chapter 18 now deals with companies before Chapter 19 which now is a shortened chapter on close corporations. The Companies Act of 1973 is still used as the basis for teaching companies. However, reference is made, where appropriate to the draft Companies Bill of 2008.

The only changes to the sundry topics in Part 6 are the pedagogical changes to this 4th edition.

Outline

The *entity* concept (separation of the business entity and the owner from an accounting perspective) is emphasised as being essential to the understanding of how transactions affect owner's equity. The *accrual* basis of accounting is described in detail and is used as the basis to explain how an income statement and a statement of financial position are prepared. Complete, albeit simple, financial statements are drawn up based on the conceptual introduction without any reference to debits and credits or the double-entry bookkeeping system.

The accounting equation in the form of 'Assets = liabilities + owner's equity' is introduced next and transactions are analysed by examining the effect that the transaction has on the assets, liabilities or owner's equity. If the transaction affects owner's equity, it is analysed further into income, expense or other items affecting owner's equity (investments or distributions to the owner). Emphasis is placed on an appreciation of the impact of transactions on owner's equity. The change in owner's equity is analysed, and after reversing the effect of investments and distributions, the profit for the period can be established. The income statement is drawn up by extracting the income and expense items from the analysis of owner's equity and the statement of financial position is drawn up by including the balances on each asset, liability and the owner's equity column from the accounting equation. There is still no reference at this stage to debit or credit rules and the double-entry system.

Part 2, 'The Accounting Process', introduces double-entry bookkeeping as a direct outgrowth of the conceptual framework and the accounting equation. Debits and credits are taught as a form of recording changes in the components of the accounting equation and extensive emphasis is placed on understanding debits and credits in the context of the conceptual framework and the accounting equation before teaching the procedural aspects of recording transactions in a journal and posting to a ledger.

Adjusting entries are introduced conceptually as part of the accrual basis of accounting and the income statement and statement of financial position effect of adjusting entries are taught by reference to the conceptual framework definitions.

The accounting equation worksheet is then used to explain further the impact of adjusting entries on the income statement and statement of financial position before finally considering the debits and credits involved.

Closing entries are then taught as a procedural exercise after the preparation of the financial statements.

A unique feature of this book is the use of a common example to explain the accounting process throughout Chapters 2 to 7. The transactions of a computer retailer, Simon Smart, who operates under the name of Smart Concepts, are used. Using the concepts model, students learn how to analyse transactions and prepare an income statement, statement of financial position and statement of changes in equity in Chapter 2 using the principles of a conceptual framework only. The same transactions are analysed in Chapter 3 using an accounting equation worksheet and students recognise that the financial statements prepared are the same as in Chapter 2. In Chapter 4 the same transactions are processed again, this time through a bookkeeping system where the transactions are entered in a journal and posted to a ledger, and a trial balance is extracted. The resultant financial statements are identical to those prepared using the principles of the conceptual framework in Chapter 2 and the accounting equation in Chapter 3. When considering the adjusting entries in Chapter 5, students understand the reasons for the adjustments having been exposed to these transactions on a conceptual level in earlier chapters.

Icons used in text

The following is a list of the icons used throughout the text to assist in teaching, learning and understanding:

Highlights key definitions. This enables the reader to focus on important definitions when reading the text and is useful for revision purposes.

Pause and reflect. These are short scenarios, both narrative and numerical, designed to confirm understanding, illustrate a specific point or to make the reader think about the meaning and implication of the preceding paragraphs.

This indicates an explanation to an example.

This appears at the end of each chapter where a summary of concepts and applications is provided.

Part 3 expands the accounting process by addressing specific issues relating to the recognition and measurement of revenue from sales and purchases of inventory. Further procedural aspects concerning the use of cash, sales and purchases journals are covered as well as introduction to accounting for VAT.

Part 4 entitled 'Recognition and Measurement of the Elements of Financial Statements' includes sections on property, plant and equipment and depreciation, inventory and cost of sales, accounts receivable and bad debts, cash and bank, non-current and current liabilities as well as owner's equity. Emphasis in teaching is on the conceptual framework definitions of assets and liabilities and on the impact of relevant transactions on the accounting equation.

Part 5 is entitled 'Entity Forms' and introduces partnerships, companies and close corporations. The emphasis is placed here on how profit is distributed to the owners in the various entity forms and on the composition of owner's equity in each entity form. No statutory disclosure is discussed. Conversion of one entity form to another entity form concludes the discussion of different forms of business entity

Part 6 deals with various topics often found in an introductory accounting course such as statements of cash flow, analysis of financial statements, accounting for non-business entities and incomplete records.

Supplements

A complete set of over 300 teaching transparencies is available from the publishers to academic institutions that prescribe this book. These transparencies closely follow the order of each chapter and include selected diagrams from the book as well as solutions to the main examples.

This textbook has an accompanying tutorial/assignment book by Kolitz, *Questions, Exercises and Problems in Financial Accounting: Introductory*. The chapters in both books correspond for ease of reference when the books are used together.

Acknowledgements

We are forever extremely grateful for the support, encouragement and suggestions of many people over almost two years devoted to the planning, thinking, developing, writing, reviewing and editing of the first edition of this book, published in 1997.

The fourth edition proved to be an enormous challenge. The amendments to the comprehensive example, as well as the incorporation of the changes to accounting standards, posed a number of conceptual issues, which resulted in many hours of debate.

A number of Wits BAccSc students have been involved in amending the text and the examples as well as with proofreading. A big thank-you, for assisting with this edition, and under immense time pressure, goes to a team of talented students from the University of the Witwatersrand, who dedicated part of their vacation to the clarification of accounting standards for the sake of future students – Stephen Carew and Justin Cousins for amending the text and examples; Daniel Lutrin, Jessica van Aarle and Claire Zajac for proofreading.

To the team at Juta Academic, Glenda Younge, Melanie Wagner, and Marlinee Chetty, thank you for your co-operation in making this project happen. Also, a word of sincere appreciation to the designer and typesetter, Ashley Richardson, for enduring his first accountancy text book.

Thank-you also to Pam Townsend of the School of Accounting at Wits for continuously suggesting changes and improvements.

The chapters on VAT and Analysis of Financial Statements were written by Maeve Kolitz.

We welcome comments from lecturers, tutors and students to assist us in improving future editions.

Dave Kolitz
Alan Quinn
Gavin McAllister

December 2008

Part 1

A Conceptual Overview

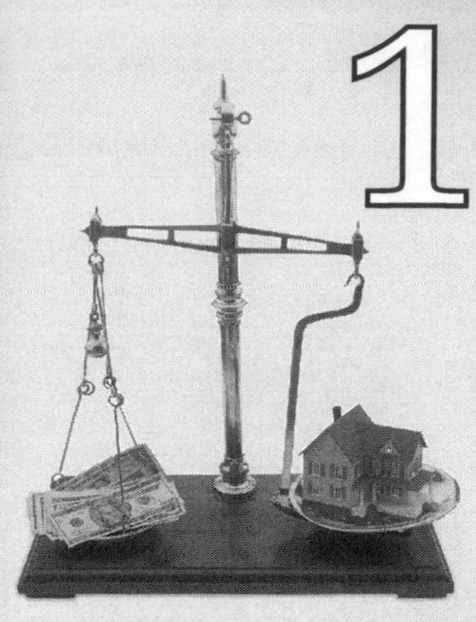

1 The Role of Accounting in Business

'By inspection of a merchant's books, by a man that hath skill, one may soon find out his wisdom and success, as well as his real worth.'
(North, 1714)

Outcomes

- Describe the value of information in the commercial decision-making process.
- Recall the various forms of ownership of business entities and the different types of business.
- Describe the nature of accounting, the users and their information needs and the areas of accounting activity.
- Discuss the development of accounting standards.
- Explain internal control in a business entity.

Chapter outline

1.1 Decision making and information
1.2 Introduction to business and business enterprises
1.2.1 Forms of business ownership
1.2.2 Types of business entities
1.3 The nature of accounting
1.3.1 The accounting information system
1.3.2 Users and their information needs
1.3.3 Qualitative characteristics of financial statements
1.4 Accounting standards
1.4.1 Background
1.4.2 Application
1.4.3 Development of accounting standards
1.5 Fields of accounting activity
1.5.1 Financial accounting
1.5.2 Management accounting
1.5.3 Auditing
1.5.4 Taxation
1.6 Internal control

Pick 'n Pay Stores Limited
Income Statement for the year ended 29 February 2008

	Retained Earnings (R Millions)
Revenue	45 381
Cost of sales	(37 411)
Gross profit	7 970
Expenses	(6 445)
Profit before tax	1 525
Tax	(558)
Net profit	967

When Raymond Ackerman started Pick 'n Pay in 1965 he could never have imagined that Pick 'n Pay would become one of Africa's largest retailers that employs over 50 000 people. But how is such a large company managed and evaluated? This is where the role of the accountant comes in.

1.1 Decision making and information

In general, accounting is concerned with the preparation and presentation of the **financial information** needed to make **economic decisions**. A decision is a choice between two or more alternatives, and can be rational only when sufficient information is available. Every individual or group in society makes decisions about the future. Students make decisions about which university to attend and what courses to study and whether to apply for a bank loan. A bank manager decides whether to advance funds to a student or any other individual or business enterprise applying for a loan. The management of a business enterprise decides how to finance operations of the enterprise, in other words whether to borrow funds from a lender such as a financial institution or to obtain the funds from the owners. Individuals or organisations with cash available decide on the type of investment they wish to make.

Accounting contributes to these decisions by identifying what information will assist the various decision makers, how it should be measured and how it should be communicated to them. Accounting provides information about various types of ***entities*** to a wide variety of ***users*** for decision-making purposes. It is often described as the language of business.

A **business entity** is an organisation or enterprise that uses economic resources for the primary goal of maximising profit. Non-business entities are concerned with providing a service to members.

Users of financial information may be broadly categorised as *primary and other users* or as *management.*[1] Primary and other users are sometimes referred to as external users and management is sometimes referred to as internal users.

- Primary and other users are users who lack the ability to prescribe all the financial information they need from an entity and therefore must rely on the information provided in financial reports.
- Management is responsible for preparing financial information.

Primary users are interested in financial reporting because it provides information that is useful for making decisions. When making those decisions, primary users are interested in assessing the entity's ability to generate net cash inflows and management's ability to protect and enhance their investments.[2] Management, while being responsible for preparing financial information, also is interested in financial information about the entity. Thus financial reporting information for primary and other users is also useful to management. In addition, management has the ability to access financial information to meet its unique needs.[3]

Consider an investor who wishes to buy shares in a company listed on the JSE Securities Exchange. The investor would require information about the company's resources, performance and the risk of variability in its performance. A large part of this information is contained in the company's financial reports. The investor, who is not involved in the company's activities *per se*, but wishes to obtain information about the company, is a primary user of that information. Detailed information concerning the company's activities is available only to management.

Accounting thought and practice can be classified according to the user group to whom it is directed.

- Financial accounting is concerned with providing useful information about business entities for primary and other users.
- Management accounting is concerned with providing useful information related to the deployment of resources and exploitation of opportunities for management.

The financial statements provide information about an entity's financial position and performance for external decision makers. They are prepared by both small and large entities.

The emphasis in this text is on financial accounting for primary and other users.

1.2 Introduction to business and business enterprises

Entrepreneurs are individuals who provide goods or services in response to demand from potential customers. They use their entrepreneurial skill together with the other factors of production (resources, labour and capital) to produce goods or services. They also take the risk that the income generated from the goods or services may or may not exceed the expenses incurred. Business activities take place within a business entity.

A business entity can be defined as an organisation composed of one or more individuals, capital goods and other resources directed towards the purpose of producing specific goods or services for sale at a profit.[4]

In the business world, there are many different forms of ownership of a business entity and many different types of business entities. No matter what the form or type of business, accounting information is required for the successful running of the business and the making of decisions.

1.2.1 Forms of business ownership

Four forms of business ownership currently exist in South Africa. These are

- a sole proprietorship
- a partnership
- a company
- a close corporation.

Entrepreneurs wishing to form a business entity consider a number of factors in deciding which of the entity forms to choose. These factors include the number of owners, access to funding, tax considerations and whether to operate as an ***unincorporated*** entity or as an ***incorporated*** entity.

As you will see in the following paragraphs, a sole proprietorship and a partnership are unincorporated entities whereas a company and a close corporation are incorporated entities. The reason for this distinction lies in the legal form of the entity associated with each type of entity.

A sole proprietorship and a partnership are not formed or incorporated as legal entities through legislation and are thus known as unincorporated entities. On the other hand, a company and close corporation are formed or incorporated as separate legal entities apart from the owners and are thus known as incorporated entities.

At the time of writing this text, the Companies Act is undergoing a comprehensive transformation. We will therefore make reference to the existing Companies Act (the Companies Act, 1973) and the draft Companies Bill (the Companies Bill, 2008). One of the consequences of the proposed new legislation will be to change the nature of the comparative relationship between the entity forms.

Sole Proprietorship

This type of business entity is owned by one person. For small entities this is a popular form of ownership since there are no formal procedures required to set up the entity. Expansion in the sole proprietorship is limited by the funding available to the owner.

The sole proprietorship or sole trader, as it is often referred to, is not a separate legal entity apart from its owner. It cannot be involved in any legal relationship or activity except in the name of the owner.

For normal tax purposes, the sole proprietor is not a separate taxable entity. Therefore the owner is taxed on the activities of the business entity in his or her personal capacity.

Partnership

A partnership is widely used for comparatively small business entities that wish to take advantage of combined financial capital, managerial talent and experience. This form of entity is also frequently found amongst the professions, such as doctors, dentists, lawyers and accountants. However, some of the large audit, tax and advisory practices have chosen to incorporate. There are specific provisions in the existing Companies Act and draft Companies Bill to cater for this.

A partnership is a legal relationship which arises as a result of an agreement between two or more persons, but not exceeding twenty. The membership of organised professions which are designated by the Minister of Trade and Industries may, however, exceed twenty.

No legislation exists in South Africa to control partnerships. The principles of common law are therefore applicable. A partnership is also not a legal entity and it has no legal standing apart from the members who constitute it. The individual partners are the joint owners of the assets and are jointly and severally liable for the liabilities of the partnership. In other words, each partner could incur unlimited liability for all the debts and obligations of the partnership.

A partnership is not taxed in its own right; that is, it is not a taxable entity. The profits are taxed in the hands of the individual partners.

Company

A company is a legal entity distinct from the persons who own it. The shareholders as a group own the company through ownership of the shares issued by it. They do not personally own its assets. They have no direct claim on the profit of the company which becomes due to them only if it is distributed by way of dividends. The shareholders appoint a board of directors to conduct the activities of the company. A company, being a separate legal entity, is liable to pay tax on its profits.

The two most important types of companies (both in the Companies Act of 1973 and the Companies Bill of 2008) are known as the public company and the private company. The Companies Act of 1973, as amended, does not distinguish between the reporting requirements of large public companies and small private companies. For public companies, this is appropriate as owners and management are different groups of people. The shareholders are the owners of the company and management manages the company on behalf of the shareholders. For most private companies, this is not appropriate as owners and management are usually the same group of people and thus have access to all the information that they require without complying with onerous reporting requirements.

The requirement to prepare annual financial statements and to appoint an auditor is often an onerous and costly task for smaller companies. As such, many small business entities operate as close corporations. The Companies Bill proposes that private companies will not be required to appoint an auditor and will also not be required to prepare financial statements if one person holds all the shares in the company or if every shareholder is also a director of the company. These types of shareholdings are typical of many small business entities and thus the recognition of this fact does away with the need for close corporations. As such, the Companies Bill, while allowing existing close corporations to continue in existence, does not permit the formation of new close corporations. These issues will be discussed in more detail in Chapter 18, Accounting for Companies and Chapter 19, Accounting for Close Corporations.

Pause and reflect...

Do you think that small private companies with one shareholder will not prepare annual financial statements under the proposed new legislation?

Response

It is unlikely that annual financial statements will not be prepared. Users such as lenders and the taxation authorities will require financial statements to be prepared. However, it is likely that a different, simplified set of accounting standards will apply to certain private companies.

Close Corporation

In 1984 an additional form of business ownership was introduced into South African law when the Close Corporations Act No 69 of 1984 was passed by parliament. As mentioned above, this ownership structure was included to provide a legal entity which is less complex and more easily administered than a company.

A close corporation enables smaller undertakings to acquire corporate status with a legal personality distinct from its members, as well as providing limited liability and perpetual succession. The Act, however, sets out circumstances in which the members may lose their limited liability.

As with a private company, there is no distinction envisaged between owners and management of a close corporation. The close corporation is used by different types and sizes of business entities as their trading vehicle.

The profits made by a close corporation belong to the corporation and not to the members until properly declared as a distribution.

The close corporation is a taxpayer in its own right, and pays tax at the company rate.

As mentioned above, the draft Companies Bill allows existing close corporations to continue in existence but does not permit the formation of new close corporations.

1.2.2 Types of business entities

Business entities engage in different business activities. From an accounting point of view, it is important to understand the different activities that these businesses enter into in order to account for those activities.

The table below summarises the main types of business, illustrating for each type of business the activity performed, the nature of the income earned and an example of that type of business

Type of business	Activity	Income	Example
Service enterprise	Provides a service to clients	Fees	Lawyers, accountants
Merchandising enterprise or retailer	Buys and sells goods to the public	Sales	Supermarket
Wholesaler	Buys and sells goods to the retailer	Sales	The fresh produce market
Manufacturer	Manufactures goods for resale	Sales	Car manufacturer
Agent	Performs services on behalf of someone else	Commission	Estate agent
Financial institution	Advances funds to individuals and business enterprises and accepts funds for investment	Fees, interest	Bank

Diagram 1.1: Types of business entities

1.3 The nature of accounting

1.3.1 The accounting information system

Accounting is an information system which **selects data**, **processes that data** and **produces information** about an economic entity. Information is central to the operation of effective capital markets. Accounting, and more specifically financial reporting, has the unique role of reducing the risks and uncertainties that investors and lenders must deal with by providing relevant and reliable information about transactions and events. The input, processing and output of the system is governed by accounting principles, theory and concepts.

From a plethora of information in the economy, **data is selected** which has an economic impact upon the reporting entity. This can take the form of the receipt of cash, the payment of cash, the purchase of goods and services or the sale of goods and services.

The **data is processed** through the accounting process. This activity is referred to as bookkeeping. Bookkeeping must not be confused with accounting, as, in fact, accounting involves much more than bookkeeping. Bookkeeping is that part of accounting that records transactions and other events, traditionally by entering the transactions into a book of original entry referred to as a journal and from there transferring the details into a list of accounts called a ledger. This will be described in Chapter 4. However, before looking at the bookkeeping procedures to process data, Chapter 2 will introduce the concepts and definitions which underpin the preparation of financial information. You will be shown how to process data on a conceptual level and produce information in the form of an income statement, a statement of financial position and a statement of changes in equity. In Chapter 3 you will be introduced to the concept of the accounting equation and be shown how to process data using the accounting equation.

Whether the data is processed on a conceptual level, through the accounting equation or via a formal bookkeeping system, the same **information** is produced. The International Accounting Standards Board (IASB) has issued a document entitled 'Framework for the Preparation and Presentation of Financial Statements'. It is a framework which sets out the concepts that underlie the preparation and presentation of financial statements and will be referred to in this book as the conceptual framework.

The conceptual framework states that the objective of financial statements is to provide information about the financial position, performance and changes in financial position of an enterprise that is useful to a wide range of users in making economic decisions.[5]

The economic decisions that are taken by users of financial statements require an evaluation of the ability of an entity to generate cash and of the timing and certainty of its generation. This ultimately determines, for example the ability of an entity to pay its employees and suppliers, meet interest payments, repay loans and make distributions to its owners. Users are better able to evaluate this ability to generate cash if they are provided with information that focuses on the financial position, performance and changes in financial position. Information about financial position is primarily provided in a statement of financial position, while information on performance is primarily provided in an income statement. Information about cash flows is provided in a statement of cash flows.

A detailed discussion about the determination of the financial position and performance is provided in Chapter 2. In addition, there is further elaboration in Chapter 2 and in Chapter 6 on a financial statement component referred to as the statement of comprehensive income, that incorporates the information about performance in the income statement as well as additional information. For the moment, you should understand that the statement of financial position is a representation of the financial position of an entity at a particular point in time and that the income statement is a measure of the performance of an entity over a period of time.

This can be represented diagramatically as follows:

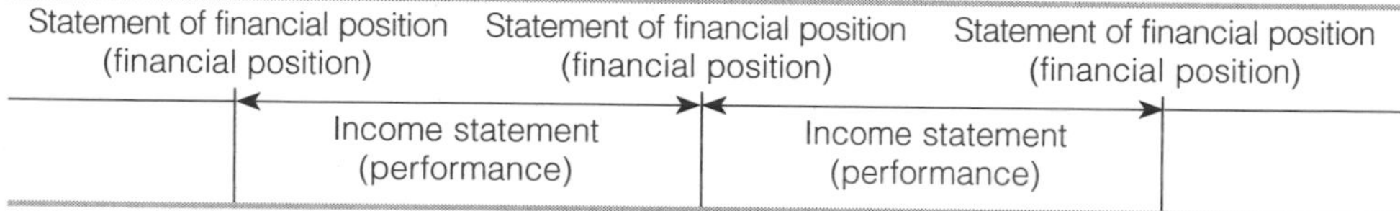

Diagram 1.2: Relationship between financial position and performance

During 2008, the IASB issued a draft of the first phase of a new conceptual framework. The new conceptual framework is a joint effort of the IASB and the U.S. Financial Accounting Standards Board (FASB). Draft documents issued by standard setters such as the IASB and FASB are known as exposure drafts.

The exposure draft states that the objective of general purpose financial reporting is to provide financial information about the reporting entity that is useful to present and potential equity investors, lenders, and other creditors in making decisions in their capacity as capital providers. Information that is decision-useful to capital providers may also be useful to other users of financial reporting who are not capital providers.[6]

Pause and reflect...

What differences can you notice between the definition in the existing conceptual framework and the definition in the proposed new conceptual framework?

Response

The existing conceptual framework refers to financial statements whereas the proposed new conceptual framework refers to financial reporting. Financial statements are part of the broader financial report. Thus, the objective pertains to financial reporting as a whole, not just to financial statements.

The proposed new conceptual framework also emphasises general purpose financial reporting stemming from the common information needs of users.

1.3.2 Users and their information needs

General purpose financial reporting is directed towards the needs of a wide range of users rather than only towards the needs of a single group. General purpose financial reporting stems from the information needs of users who lack the ability to prescribe all the financial information they need from an entity and therefore must rely, at least partly, on the information provided in financial reports.

Let us now examine the information needs of the users of financial information. As already described in section 1.1, users of financial information may be broadly categorised as *primary and other users* or as *management*.

Primary and other users [7]

The ***primary users***, or capital providers are the *equity investors, lenders* and *other creditors*. An entity obtains economic resources from capital providers in exchange for claims to those resources. By virtue of those claims, capital providers have the most critical and immediate need for general purpose financial information about the economic resources of an entity. The information provided by general purpose financial reporting focuses on the needs of all capital providers, not just the needs of a particular group.

Equity investors are those with an ownership interest in the business, typically through the holding of shares. Equity investors generally invest economic resources, in the form of cash, in an entity with the expectation of receiving a return *on*, as well as a return *of*, the cash provided. In other words, they expect to receive more cash than they provided in the form of cash distributions, known as dividends and increases in the prices of shares. Therefore, equity investors are directly interested in the amount, timing, and uncertainty of an entity's future cash flows and also in how the perception of an entity's ability to generate those cash flows affects the prices of their shares. Equity investors often have the right to vote on management actions and therefore are interested in how well the directors and managers of the entity have discharged their responsibility to make efficient and profitable use of the assets entrusted to them.

Lenders are those with a financial but not an ownership interest in the business. They provide financial capital to an entity by lending it economic resources, in the form of cash. Lenders generally expect to receive a return in the form of interest and repayments of borrowings. Like equity investors, lenders are interested in the amount, timing, and uncertainty of an entity's future cash flows. Lenders also may have the right to influence or approve some management actions and therefore also may be interested in how well management has discharged its responsibilities.

Other creditors also have a financial but not an ownership interest in the business. They provide resources as a consequence of their relationship with an entity, even though the relationship is not primarily that of a capital provider. For example, *employees* provide human capital in exchange for a salary or other compensation, some of which may be deferred for many years. *Suppliers* may extend credit to facilitate a sale. *Customers* may prepay for goods or services to be provided by the entity. To the extent that employees, suppliers or customers make decisions relating to providing capital to the entity in the form of credit, they are capital providers.

The ***other users*** who have specialised needs are *suppliers, customers*, and *employees* (when not acting as capital providers), as well as *governments and their agencies*, such as the South African Revenue Service) and *members of the public*, also may find useful the information that meets the needs of capital providers. However, financial reporting is not primarily directed to these other groups because capital providers have more direct and immediate needs.

Management [8]

The board of directors and managers of an entity, often referred to simply as management, also are interested in financial information about the entity. However, management's primary relationship with the entity is not that of a capital provider. As already mentioned, management is responsible for preparing financial reports; management is not their intended recipient.

1.3.3 Qualitative characteristics of financial statements

You have already learnt that the objective of financial reporting is to provide financial information about the reporting entity that is useful to a wide range of users in making decisions. In order to be useful to users, information needs to possess certain attributes. Qualitative characteristics are the attributes that make the information provided in financial statements useful to users. The existing conceptual framework identifies four principal qualitative characteristics identified in the accounting framework:[9] relevance, reliability, comparability and understandability. It is not our intention here to give a detailed exposition of the qualitative characteristics, but rather to give an overview and to highlight certain important aspects. A summary is provided in diagram 1.3.[10]

Before turning to the four principal qualities and their ingredients, it is necessary to look at the threshold quality of materiality and the constraints of timeliness and cost/benefit.

Information is **material** if its omission or misstatement could influence the economic decisions of users. Information which is not material cannot be useful. Materiality thus provides a threshold or cut-off point.

The constraint of **timeliness** suggests that if there is undue delay in the reporting of information it may lose its relevance. Management needs to balance the relative merits of timely reporting and the provision of reliable information.

The **cost/benefit** constraint seeks to ensure that the benefit derived from information should exceed the cost of providing it.

Accounting information is useful if it is relevant and reliable.

Relevance

Information is relevant when it influences the decisions of users by virtue of its **predictive** value or its **feedback** value. Relevant information can assist users to make

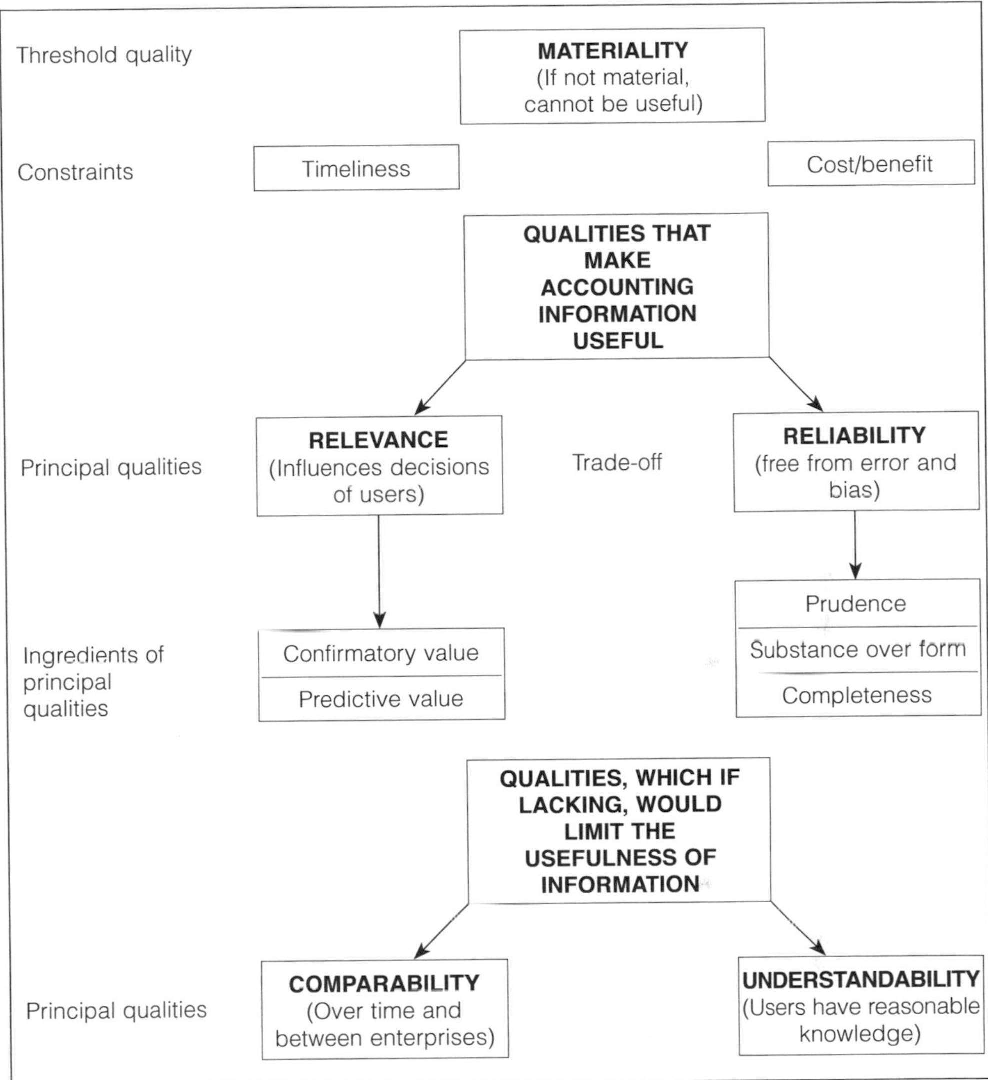

Diagram 1.3: Qualitative characteristics of financial statements

predictions about the outcomes of past, present or future events or to confirm their previous evaluations.

Reliability

Information is reliable when it is free from error and bias and when users can rely on the financial statements to be a **truthful representation** of the economic events which underly them.

If the information is to be depended upon by users as a valid description of the underlying transactions, it is necessary that the transactions be accounted for and presented in accordance with their substance and economic reality and not merely their legal form. The **substance over form** concept would require, for example, an enterprise which leases an asset for the majority of its useful life to report the asset and the corresponding liability on the balance sheet.

The preparers of financial statements have to contend with the uncertainties which inevitably surround many events. Prudence is the inclusion of a degree of caution in the exercise of judgements needed in making the estimates required in accounting for events and transactions.

To be reliable, information must also be **complete** within the bounds of materiality and cost.

Relevance and reliability require a trade-off – more of one may mean less of the other. The other two principal or primary qualities identified in the accounting framework are comparability and understandability. These qualities, if lacking, would limit the usefulness of the information.

Comparability

Information in the financial statements may satisfy the qualities of relevance and reliability, but its usefulness is limited if it is not comparable with information provided in previous years or by other enterprises.

Understandability

The usefulness of the information provided in the financial statements depends partly on the extent to which it is understood by users. Users are, however, assumed to have a reasonable knowledge of business and accounting. It would be expected, for example, for users to know that the net profit reported on the income statement does not represent the increase in cash and bank balances over the period.

The 2008 draft of the new conceptual framework has revisited the structure of the qualitative characteristics and has proposed that it is helpful to distinguish the qualitative characteristics as either ***fundamental*** or ***enhancing*** depending on how they affect the usefulness of information. The following is a brief summary of the proposed new structure.

Fundamental qualitative characteristics

Fundamental qualitative characteristics distinguish useful financial reporting information from information that is not useful or is misleading. For financial information to be useful, it must possess the two fundamental qualitative characteristics – **relevance** and **faithful representation**. Relevant information is capable of making a difference in decision-making by virtue of its predictive or confirmatory value. Financial reporting information is a faithful representation if it depicts the substance of an economic phenomenon completely, neutrally, and without material error.

Enhancing qualitative characteristics

Financial reporting information may have varying degrees of usefulness to different capital providers. Enhancing qualitative characteristics distinguish more useful information from less useful information. They enhance the decision usefulness of financial reporting information that is relevant and faithfully represented. Enhancing qualitative characteristics (**comparability**, **verifiability**, **timeliness**, **and understandability**) should be maximised to the extent possible. However, the enhancing qualitative characteristics, either individually or in concert with one another, cannot make information useful for decisions if that information is irrelevant or not faithfully represented.

Comparable information enables users to identify similarities in, and differences between two sets of economic phenomena. **Verifiable** information lends credibility to the assertion that financial reporting information represents the economic phenomena that it purports to represent. **Timeliness** provides information to decision-makers when it has the capacity to influence decisions. **Understandability** is the quality of information that enables users to comprehend its meaning.

Providing useful financial reporting information is limited by two *pervasive constraints*, **materiality** and **cost**. Information is material if its omission or misstatement could influence the decisions that users make on the basis of an entity's financial information. The benefits of providing financial reporting information should justify the costs of providing that information.

1.4 Accounting standards

1.4.1 Background

You have seen a number of times in this chapter that the objective of financial reporting is to provide financial information about the reporting entity that is useful to users in making decisions. Accounting standards have evolved over a number of years in an attempt to establish practices and principles for the communication of information to users. More specifically, accounting standards govern how the financial data of a business entity is recognised, measured and reported.

This resulted in the development of sets of standards, both internationally and in South Africa. Internationally, the International Accounting Standards Board (IASB) publishes its standards as a series of pronouncements known as International Financial Reporting Standards (IFRS).

In 1999, SAICA took a decision to harmonise South African statements of GAAP with IFRS. This involved amending existing standards and issuing a number of new standards. By the end of 2003, local statements of GAAP were harmonised with IFRS issued by the IASB. At that point, the Accounting Practices Board (APB) of SAICA took a decision to, in future, issue the text of IFRS in South Africa, without any amendments.

Accounting standards are developed in accordance with the conceptual framework, which is a theoretical foundation of fundamental accounting concepts. You will learn much more about the framework in Chapter 2, entitled 'The Conceptual Framework'. Without accounting standards, business entities could present accounting information in a variety of ways. This would seriously hinder the ability of users to make comparisons between different entities and of the same entity over a period of time. The IASB is committed to narrowing these differences by seeking to harmonise regulations, accounting standards and procedures relating to the preparation and presentation of financial statements. Much has been achieved since the IASB's predecessor body was formed in 1973 and since the IASB was formed in 2001. More than one hundred countries, including South Africa, the United Kingdom, Australia, New Zealand and the entire European Union now require or permit the use of IFRSs or are converging with the IASB's standards. Notable exceptions are the United States, Canada and most of South America.

1.4.2 Application

International Financial Reporting Standards refers to the entire body of IASB pronouncements. IFRSs manifest themselves as a numbered series of pronouncements labelled International Accounting Standards (IAS), issued by its predecessor as well as a new numbered series of pronouncements labelled International Financial Reporting Standards (IFRS). All references in this book are to the relevant IAS or IFRS.

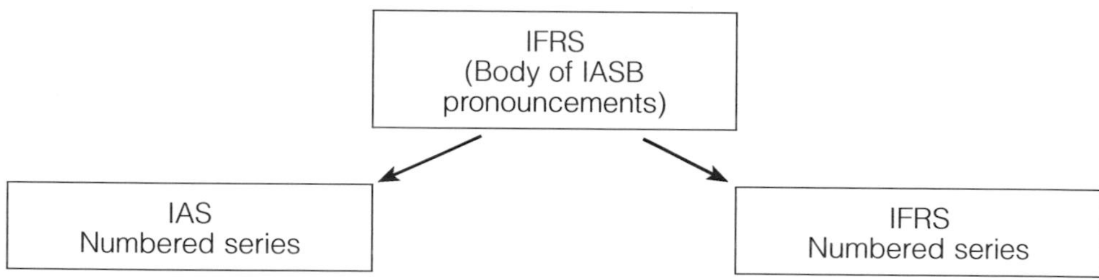

Diagram 1.4: IFRS and the distinction between IASs and IFRSs

1.4.3 Development of accounting standards

International Financial Reporting Standards are developed through a formal system of due process and international consultation that involved accountants, analysts, the business community, stock exchanges, regulatory authorities, academics and interested parties around the world.

1.5 Fields of accounting activity

Accountants perform work in four main areas. These fields of activity are financial accounting, management accounting, auditing and taxation.

1.5.1 Financial accounting

Financial accounting provides information to users who are not involved in the daily operations of the entity. These would include all of the primary, and other users described above. The information is distributed through the financial statements. Such financial statements are prepared and presented at least annually, and as described above, are directed toward the common information needs of a wide range of users.

Financial statements form part of the process of financial reporting. A set of financial statements normally includes a statement of financial position, an income statement and a statement of cash flows. These will be described in the following chapter.

1.5.2 Management accounting

Management accounting provides information to the management of an entity. Management accounting statements include much of the same information that is reported in financial accounting. However, management accounting goes further and includes a great deal of information that is not reported outside the company.

As mentioned above, management is also interested in the information contained in the financial statements even though it has access to additional management and financial information that helps it carry out its planning, decision-making and control responsibilities.

1.5.3 Auditing

In terms of the Companies Act of 1973, as amended, every company is required to appoint an auditor. The Companies Bill proposes to relieve private companies of the requirement.

It is the responsibility of the board of directors to have financial statements prepared which fairly present the company's financial position, performance and cash flows. The role of the auditor is to express an opinion on the fair presentation of the information and whether or not it has been prepared in accordance with International Financial Reporting Standards.

An audit is carried out by a firm of independent auditors and, as such, adds credibility to the financial statements.

1.5.4 Taxation

Accountants who are specialists in taxation assist their clients in planning their affairs in order to minimise taxes payable. The taxes may include any of the following taxes, depending on the nature of the transaction: income tax, donations tax, estate duty, VAT and transfer duty.

Tax specialists may also assist clients with the rendering of tax returns, the checking of assessments, objections to assessments with which the client disagrees and generally assisting with any tax-related problems which might arise.

1.6 Internal control

A sound system of internal control is important to ensure that the business organisation is effectively and efficiently run, that the assets are safeguarded, and that the financial statements faithfully present the information which they purport to present.

A system of internal control ensures that:

- the information the directors need to make decisions is available
- the delegated authorities are properly exercised
- the data needed for the control of costs is accurate and complete
- the data needed for the preparation of financial statements is accurate and complete.

The internal control system is integral to ongoing business operations and is as important to the continuation of the business as are market opportunities and cash flows.

Summary of concepts and applications

1. Accounting prepares and produces financial information about various types of entities to a wide variety of users for decision-making purposes. A business entity is an enterprise that uses economic resources for the primary goal of maximising profit.
2. There are four forms of ownership of business enterprises, namely sole proprietorship, partnership, company and close corporation, and several different types of businesses may be operated, each performing different activities and earning income of different natures.
3. Accounting is an information system which selects data, processes that data and produces information about an economic entity. The objective of financial reporting is to provide information about the financial position, performance and changes in financial position of an enterprise that is useful to a wide range of users in making economic decisions. Users can be divided into two groups – primary and other users as well as management. There are four fields of activity in which accountants perform work, namely financial accounting, management accounting, auditing and taxation.
4. A sound system of internal control is important to ensure that the business enterprise operates effectively and efficiently, that the assets are safeguarded and that the financial statements faithfully present the information which they purport to present.

Notes

1. Conceptual Framework for Financial Reporting, Financial Accounting Series Exposure Draft, *Financial Accounting Standards Board*, (2008), p. OB3–OB8.
2. Conceptual Framework for Financial Reporting, (2008), p. OB9.
3. Conceptual Framework for Financial Reporting, (2008), p. BC1.33.
4. Mueller, G. G. and Kelley, L., (1991), p. 6.
5. Framework for the Preparation and Presentation of Financial Statements, *The International Accounting Standards Board*, (2005), paragraph 12.
6. Conceptual Framework for Financial Reporting, (2008), p. OB2.
7. Conceptual Framework for Financial Reporting, (2008), p. OB6–8.
8. Conceptual Framework for Financial Reporting, (2008), p. OB8.
9. Framework for the Preparation and Presentation of Financial Statements. (2004), paragraph 24.
10. Arnold, J., Hope, T., Southworth, A. and Kirkham, L., *Financial Accounting*, London: Prentice Hall Inc., (UK) Limited, (1994), p. 78

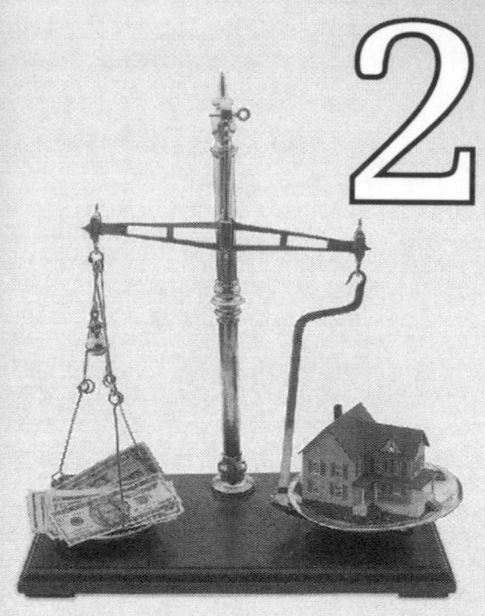

2 The Conceptual Framework

'The beginning of wisdom is, get wisdom; therefore use all your means to acquire understanding.'
(Proverbs 4: 7)

Outcomes

- Explain the importance of cash in the decision-making process.
- Define and recall the concepts relating to the financial statements of a business entity, including the entity concept and the elements of the financial statements.
- Recall the general features relevant to the preparation and presentation of financial statements.
- Analyse transactions using the conceptual framework and prepare a set of financial statements.
- Explain the differences between an income statement prepared using the cash basis of accounting and one prepared using the accrual basis of accounting.

Chapter outline

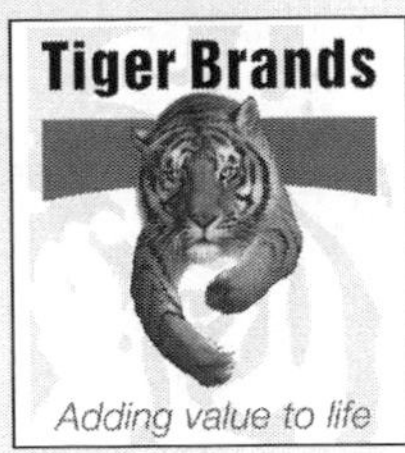

Tiger Brands Limited
Income Statement for the year ended 30 September 2008

	(R Millions)
Revenue	20 126
Cost of sales	(13 241)
Gross profit	6 885
Expenses	(4 225)
Profit before tax	2 260
Tax	(826)
Profit for the period	834

Statement of cash flows for the year ended 31 March 2008

	(R Millions)
Cash flows from operating activities	620
Cash flows from financing activities	459
Cash flows from investing activities	(2 241)
Net decrease in cash and cash equivalents	(1 162)

Tiger Brands produces products that we are exposed to every day; from Black Cat to Koo! From the above income statement it is evident that the business is very profitable. However, the statement of cash flows reports a net outflow of cash. This chapter explains how this is possible.

2.1 Information for decision-making

2.1.1 Forecasting cash flows

In section 1.3.1 of the previous chapter you were briefly introduced to the information output of the accounting information system. You learnt that information about the financial position is primarily provided in a statement of financial position, while information on performance is primarily provided in a statement of comprehensive income. The statement of financial position represents, as its name implies, the financial position of the entity *at a specific point in time*, while the statement of comprehensive income reflects the performance of the entity *over a period of time* as well as certain other items of income and expense. Both the statement of financial position and the statement of comprehensive income will be discussed in more detail later in this chapter. The information presented thus relates to the *present* (the statement of financial position) and to the *past* (the statement of comprehensive income).

External users need to predict the entity's *future* performance and more specifically, future cash flows. Cash flows in and out of a business enterprise are fundamental to its operations. If the business does not generate enough cash, it may be unable to distribute cash to its owners. Cash is needed to pay interest on borrowings, to pay suppliers and also to repay amounts borrowed. When the owner decides to sell part or all of his ownership interest, potential investors will look to future cash flow in valuing the business.[1]

Future cash flows are therefore important information to users of financial statements. This leads us to ask how users can obtain this information. Management, as an *internal* user has this information, but is reluctant to provide forecasts of future cash flows for strategic reasons and because the forecast might prove to be inaccurate. External users, for example, investors and lenders, do not have access to the data needed to generate cash forecasts.

As a result, external users need to analyse and interpret the information about the *current* financial position and *past* performance presented in the statement of financial position and statement of comprehensive income in order to assess the entity's *future* financial position and performance. By so doing, we assume the continuity of business activities. Although many aspects change over time, other important aspects remain constant.

One possible way of providing information to users for decision-making purposes is the ***cash basis*** of accounting. The next section examines the cash basis of accounting, followed by a discussion of the accrual basis in the sections that follow. We will then consider which basis provides the best information for external users' decision-making purposes.

2.1.2 Cash basis of accounting

The cash basis of accounting measures performance by subtracting cash outflows from cash inflows to arrive at a net cash flow for the period. You will learn much later in this book (Chapter 21) that cash flows can be analysed into three categories, namely cash flows from operating, investing and financing activities. Operating activities are the primary revenue-producing activities of the enterprise, including cash received from the sale of goods and services, as well as cash paid to suppliers for the purchase of goods and services. Investing activities incorporate the acquisition and disposal of long-term assets; in other words, cash flows relating to resources used to generate future profits and cash flows. Financing activities, on the other hand, relate to cash flows from owners and lenders.

We will exclude cash flows from financing activities when determining the performance of the enterprise. This means that cash investments by owners are excluded, as are cash distributions to owners. We will consider the conceptual reasons for this later in this chapter, but for now it is sufficient to understand that the *performance* of the business entity could not be assessed if the transactions with owners are included with operating transactions. In the same way, cash proceeds from borrowings, and cash repayments of amounts borrowed do not affect the *performance* of the business entity. The cost of the borrowings, that is, interest, does affect the financial performance; however, the amounts borrowed and repaid only affect the financial position.

Example: Cash basis of accounting

This example introduces you to the activities of Simon Smart, a computer retailer, operating under the name of Smart Concepts. The example will be used throughout parts 1 and 2 of this book to introduce the conceptual aspects of accounting and to explain the accounting process. The following is a record of the transactions of the business for the three-month period from 1 January to 31 March 20X5.

External transactions

1. On 2 January, Simon Smart started a business as a computer retailer. He drew R950 000 from a savings account and opened a bank account in the name of Smart Concepts into which he paid R950 000.
2. On 2 January, Smart Concepts negotiated a loan from Techno Bank for an amount of R600 000. The loan is repayable in four equal annual installments, beginning on 31 December 20X5. The interest rate is 12% per annum, payable quarterly in arrears.
3. On 2 January, Simon located premises from which to operate in Rosebank. The monthly rent for the premises is R12 000. Smart Concepts paid four months rent in advance on 2 January.
4. On 2 January, Simon transferred R120 000 from the bank account into a fixed deposit account earning interest at 5% per annum.
5. On 2 January, Smart Concepts purchased furniture and fittings for R240 000. This was paid for from funds in the bank account. The expected useful life of the furniture and fittings is five years.
6. On 5 January, Smart Concepts purchased supplies of stationery for R5 000 as well as supplies of computer parts for R12 000. All the supplies were paid for in cash.
7. On 7 January, Smart Concepts opened an account with Computer World, the supplier of its inventory.
8. On 10 January, Smart Concepts purchased inventory of sixty computers from Computer World at a cost of R10 000 each. The total amount owing is to be paid by 25 March.
9. On 12 January, Smart Concepts paid a service provider R750 in respect of a data bundle for internet access.

10. On 25 January, Smart Concepts sold fifteen computers on account to a customer for R12 500 each. An amount of R125 000 is due by 15 March and the balance by 15 April.
11. On 1 February, Smart Concepts employed a computer technician at a salary of R8 000 per month.
12. On 8 February, Smart Concepts paid R7 000 for an advertisement in a newspaper, advertising the computers available for sale.
13. On 12 February, Smart Concepts sold thirty computers, to customers, for R12 500 each. The customers paid cash for the computers.
14. On 25 February, Smart Concepts received cash of R48 000 in respect of technical support contracts taken out by customers. The contracts are for a two year period.
15. On 28 February, Smart Concepts paid the computer technician his salary for February.
16. On 4 March, Smart Concepts purchased inventory of a further seventy-five computers from Computer World at a cost of R10 000 each. The total amount owing is to be paid by 25 May.
17. On 5 March, Smart Concepts paid a service provider R750 in respect of a data bundle for internet access.
18. On 15 March, Smart Concepts received R125 000 from the customer in transaction 10.
19. On 25 March, Smart Concepts paid Computer World an amount of R600 000.
20. On 29 March, Smart Concepts sold thirty computers, to customers, for R12 500 each. The customers paid cash for the computers.
21. On 30 March, Smart Concepts paid the computer technician his salary for March.
22. On 30 March, Smart Concepts paid the interest on the loan from Techno Bank for the three month period.
23. On 30 March, Simon authorised a distribution to himself of R60 000 for personal use.

You are required to:

prepare an income statement on the cash basis of accounting for Smart Concepts for the three-month period ended 31 March 20X5.

Solution: Cash basis of accounting

Each transaction needs to be examined in order to determine whether cash has been received or paid. If a transaction involves an inflow or outflow of cash, the amount is included with an appropriate description on the cash basis income statement.

Transaction 1 is an investment of funds by the owner. Although R950 000 cash is being received by the business entity, investment of funds by the owner does not represent income earned from operations and does not appear on the statement. Similarly, transaction 23 is a distribution of cash to the owner. The R60 000 is a cash outflow, but also does not appear on the statement.

Transaction 2 is the cash proceeds from borrowings which do not affect the performance of the entity and also do not appear on the statement.

Transactions 13, 14, 18 and 20 are transactions involving the receipt of cash. Transactions 13 and 20 relate to the sale of computers for cash and are included as cash inflows. Transaction 14, where customers pay R48 000 in respect of technical support contracts relating to the next two years, results in a cash inflow on the cash basis of accounting. Transaction 18 records the receipt of cash amounting to R125 000 from a customer for the computers sold on account in transaction 10, where no cash inflow was recorded.

Transactions 3, 5, 6, 9, 12, 15, 17, 19, 21 and 22 are transactions comprising an outflow of cash. In transaction 3, the full R12 000 rent paid is shown as a cash outflow, as is the total of

R240 000 paid for furniture and fittings in transaction 5, even though the business premises had been occupied and the furniture and fittings used for only three months. The R17 000 paid for the supplies and parts in transaction 6 is shown as a cash outflow, as opposed to the cost of inventory purchased of R600 000 in transaction 8 and R750 000 in transaction 16, which is not shown as a cash outflow, as the inventory was purchased on account. It is only the payment for the inventory in transaction 19 that leads to an amount of R600 000 being shown as a cash outflow. The R7 000 paid for advertising in transaction 12 and the R8 000 paid for the technician's salary in transactions 15 and 21 as well as the R750 paid for internet acess in transactions 9 and 17 all give rise to a cash outflow on the cash basis of accounting. In transaction 22, the R18 000 interest paid is shown as a cash outflow in determining performance on the cash basis. You will learn in Chapter 6 to identify finance costs as a *separate* line item in determining *performance*.

The transactions that do not affect the cash basis income statement, other than those mentioned above (transactions 1 and 23, 10, 8 and 16) are numbered 4, 7 and 11. The transfer of R120 000 from the bank account to a fixed deposit account in transaction 4 is simply a movement of cash resources from one account to another, while transactions 7 and 11 do not have any economic impact on the entity.

SMART CONCEPTS
CASH BASIS INCOME STATEMENT
FOR THE PERIOD ENDED 31 MARCH 20X5

		R
Cash inflows		923 000
Sales	(125 000 + 375 000 + 375 000)	875 000
Service		48 000
Cash outflows		(947 500)
Inventory	(10 000 x 60)	600 000
Rent	(12 000 x 4)	48 000
Furniture and fittings		240 000
Advertising		7 000
Computer parts & stationery supplies		17 000
Salaries		16 000
Interest		18 000
Internet		1 500
Net cash flow		(24 500)

The cash basis income statement reports a net cash outflow of R24 500 for the period. This does not represent a true measure of performance for the period. The full R48 000 received for the technical support contracts is included as a cash inflow, yet the work is to be performed over a two-year period. The cash outflows include R240 000 paid for furniture and fittings (in transaction 5) which will be used for five years. Also included is R48 000 paid for rent up to the end of April 20X5.

We need to apply a basis for measuring income and expenses which provides a more useful measure of the firm's performance. The accrual basis of accounting is introduced in the next section. It attempts to relate more properly the firm's performance with activities during the period.

2.2 Financial statements

2.2.1 The entity concept

As mentioned in the previous chapter, the sole trader and partnership can be referred to as unincorporated entities, while the close corporation and company can be referred to as incorporated entities.

The owner of the sole trader and the partners of the partnership are separate accounting entities apart from the business entity, but from a legal viewpoint they are the same legal entity.

The members of the close corporation and the shareholders of the company are separate accounting and legal entities apart from the business entity. The close corporation and the company are incorporated as separate legal entities in terms of statute.

Financial statements are prepared from the perspective of the business entity, utilising the entity concept.

The entity concept entails:

- identification of the business enterprise
- separation of the recording of transactions relating to the business entity as an accounting entity and the owner as the proprietor of the entity.

In other words, irrespective of the form of entity, the transactions of the business entity must be accounted for separately and distinctly from its owner or owners. The financial statements of the business entity should not mix the owner's personal transactions with the business transactions. If the entity concept is not followed, the information reported in the financial statements of the business entity will not be useful to the users in making their decisions.

The practical application of the entity concept is summarised below:

Transaction	Recording of transaction
Transactions of the business entity with external parties	Recorded as transactions of the business entity
Transactions carried out by the owner on behalf of the business entity	Recorded as transactions of the business entity
Transactions carried out by the owner on his own behalf	Not recorded as transactions of the business entity

Diagram 2.1: Application of entity concept

2.2.2 Basis for presentation of financial statements

The International Accounting Standards Board (IASB) has issued an International Financial Reporting Standard (IFRS), IAS 1, entitled 'Presentation of Financial Statements'.

This standard prescribes the basis for presentation of general purpose financial statements in order to ensure comparability both with the entity's financial statements of previous periods and with the financial statements of other entities.[2] You have already learnt in Chapter 1 that *comparability* is one of the qualitative characteristics or attributes that make financial statements useful to users.

The standard sets out the general features for the presentation of financial statements (to be dealt with in this chapter), guidelines for the structure of the financial statements (to be covered in Chapter 6) as well as minimum requirements for the contents of the financial statements (included with the relevant sections in Chapters 11 to 16).

2.2.3 The purpose of financial statements

Financial statements are a structured representation of the financial position and the financial performance of an entity.

IAS 1 confirms that the objective of general purpose financial statements is to provide information about the financial position, performance and cash flows of an entity that is useful to a wide range of users in making economic decisions.[3] This is consistent with the objective stated in the Accounting Framework and referred to in Chapter 1.

General purpose financial statements are those intended to meet the needs of external users, that is, users who are not able to demand reports specifically for their needs.

Financial statements also show the results of management's stewardship of the resources entrusted to it.

 **Pause and reflect...**

What do you understand by the term, management's stewardship?

Response

In large listed companies management and shareholders are different groups of people. The shareholders are the owners of the company and management manages the company on behalf of the shareholders. The stewardship function refers to the relationship that exists between the management and the shareholders and the responsibility of management to the shareholders.

2.2.4 Components of financial statements

To meet the objective of financial statements stated above, IAS 1 requires that a complete set of financial statements includes the following components:[4]

- a statement of financial position (which provides information about the entity's assets, liabilities and equity)
- a statement of comprehensive income (which provides information about the entity's income and expenses)

- a statement of changes in equity (which reflects change in wealth)
- a statement of cash flows (which provides information about cash flows)
- notes (comprising accounting policies and other explanatory notes)

IAS1 requires an entity to present items of income and expense either in two separate statements:

- The income statement (displaying items of profit and loss) and
- The statement of comprehensive income (displaying components of other comprehensive income),

or in a single statement, referred to as the statement of comprehensive income (displaying items of profit and loss as well as components of other comprehensive income).

IAS 1 identifies five specific items of income and expense that comprise the components of other comprehensive income. Most of the components of other comprehensive income are beyond the scope of this book. In fact, you will be exposed only to one such component, known as a revaluation. You will be introduced to the concept of a revaluation later in this chapter, and will revisit revaluations in more detail in chapter 11 (dealing with property, plant and equipment) and Chapter 18 (dealing with companies).

The statement of financial position (also known as the balance sheet) provides, as its name implies, information about the *financial position* of the entity at the end of a period. The income statement (as a separate statement) or that part of the single statement of comprehensive income that displays components of profit and loss provides information about the *performance* of an entity.

Now let us turn our attention specifically to the statement of financial position (incorporating the assets, liabilities and equity) and the statement of comprehensive income (incorporating the income and expenses).

Assets, liabilities and equity as well as income and expenses are known as the elements of the financial statements. This is discussed in detail in the next section.

2.2.5 The elements of financial statements

Financial statements portray the financial effects of transactions and other events by grouping them into broad categories according to their economic characteristics. These categories are termed the elements of financial statements. The elements directly related to the measurement of the financial position in the statement of financial position are assets, liabilities and equity. The elements directly related to the measurement of profit or loss and of other comprehensive income in the statement of comprehensive income are income and expenses.[5] Note that the accrual basis of accounting (to be described more fully in section 2.3 below) is an underlying assumption in the preparation of financial statements.

The statement of financial position

The elements directly related to the measurement of the financial position in the statement of financial position are assets, liabilities and equity.

An **asset** is:
- a resource controlled by the enterprise
- as a result of past events
- from which future economic benefits are expected to flow to the enterprise. [6]

For a *resource to be controlled* by the enterprise, physical form and right of ownership are not essential. Many assets, for example, property or equipment, have a physical form and are associated with the right of ownership. However, intangibles such as patents and copyrights may have no physical form other than a certificate of registration. They are, however, assets if they are controlled by the enterprise and future economic benefits are expected to flow from them. Property held on a lease is not legally owned by the lessee, but the substance of the agreement may give the lessee control over the benefits which are expected to flow from the property.

Financial assets, such as accounts receivable, are also a resource controlled by the enterprise. In the case of accounts receivable, when the entity has sold goods or provided a service to customers on account, the resource controlled is the right to collect cash from the customers.

In addition to tangible assets, intangible assets and financial assets, there are other assets, for example, rent paid in advance, which also represents a resource controlled by the enterprise, namely, the right to occupy the property.

Pause and reflect...

a) A business entity sells goods *on credit* or on account to its customers. Selling on credit means that the customer agrees to pay the business entity for the goods at a later date. These customers are known as *accounts receivable* or *debtors* of the business. Are the accounts receivable a resource controlled by the entity?

b) A business entity takes out an insurance policy and pays the premium in advance for a one year period. Is the insurance paid in advance a resource controlled by the enterprise?

Response

a) The accounts receivable are a resource controlled by the enterprise as the enterprise has the right to collect the amounts owing from the customers.

b) By paying cash in advance for a service, in this case, the insurance cover, the entity has the right to receive that service in the future. It is a resource controlled by the enterprise, referred to as an insurance asset or insurance paid in advance.

The assets of an enterprise result from *past transactions or events*. Enterprises normally obtain assets by purchasing or producing them. Events expected to occur in the future do not in themselves give rise to assets; for example, an intention to purchase a vehicle does not, in itself, meet the definition of an asset.

The *future economic benefit* embodied in an asset is the ability to contribute, directly or indirectly, to the flow of cash to the enterprise. An enterprise uses its assets to produce or purchase goods or services wanted or needed by customers. As these goods or services meet the customers' wants or needs, they are prepared to pay for them and thus contribute to the cash flow of the enterprise. Cash itself embodies future benefits because of its command over other resources.

The future economic benefits embodied in an asset may flow to the enterprise in a number of ways.[7] The asset may be:

- used in the production of goods or services sold by the enterprise
- exchanged for other assets
- used to settle a liability
- distributed to the owners of the enterprise.

Pause and reflect...

Do accounts receivable meet the definition of an asset?

Response

The accounts receivable are a resource controlled by the enterprise (the right to collect the amounts owing from the customers), as a result of past events (the sale of goods on credit), from which future economic benefits are expected to flow to the enterprise (cash will be received from the customers).

A **liability** is:

- a present obligation of the enterprise
- arising from past events
- the settlement of which is expected to result in an outflow from the enterprise of resources embodying economic benefits. [6]

A fundamental characteristic of a liability is that the enterprise has a *present obligation*. Obligations may be legally enforceable or may arise from normal business practice or custom. A legally enforceable obligation arises, for example, when the enterprise has purchased goods or services from suppliers on account. The amounts owing are referred to as accounts payable. In addition, a legally enforceable obligation may arise when customers have paid for goods or services in advance, for example, subscribers paying for magazine subscriptions in advance. The present obligation of the enterprise is to provide those goods or services in the future. On the other hand, if an entity decides to rectify defects in its products after the warranty period has expired, there is no legally enforceable obligation, but the amounts that are expected to be expended in respect of goods already sold are liabilities.

Pause and reflect...

a) A business enterprise buys goods *on credit* or *on account* from its suppliers. Buying on credit means that the business enterprise agrees to pay the supplier for the goods at a later date. These suppliers are known as *accounts payable* or *creditors* of the business enterprise. Are the accounts payable an obligation the enterprise?

b) A daily newspaper offers subscribers one year subscription agreements to have a newspaper delivered to the subscriber's home every week day. The newspaper receives R1 200 cash from a subscriber for a one year subscription agreement. Is the cash received from the subscriber an obligation of the enterprise?

Response

a) The accounts payable are an obligation of the enterprise as the enterprise has an obligation to pay cash to the suppliers.

b) By receiving cash in advance for a service, the enterprise has an obligation to provide that service in the future. It is an obligation of the enterprise, referred to as a subscription liability or subscription received in advance or unearned subscription income.

Liabilities result from *past transactions or events*. As mentioned above, the purchase of goods gives rise to accounts payable and the receipt of a loan gives rise to an obligation to repay the loan.

The settlement of an obligation involves the enterprise giving up *resources embodying economic benefits* in order to satisfy the claim of the other party. Settlement of a present obligation may occur in a number of ways.[9] These include:

- payment of cash
- transfer of other assets
- provision of services
- replacement of that obligation with another obligation.

A distinction needs to be drawn between a present obligation and a future commitment. A decision to acquire assets in the future does not, of itself, give rise to a present obligation.

Pause and reflect...

Do accounts payable meet the definition of a liability?

Response

The accounts payable are an obligation of the enterprise (the obligation to pay the amount owing to the suppliers), as a result of a past event (the purchase of the goods on credit), the settlement of which is expected to result in an outflow from the enterprise of resources embodying economic benefits (cash will be paid to the suppliers). Accounts payable do meet the definition of a liability.

Equity is the residual interest in the assets of the enterprise after deducting all its liabilities.[10]

It is often referred to as the net assets or net wealth of the business. Assume that a business entity has assets of R10 000 000 and liabilities of R4 000 000. The assets of R10 000 000 are resources controlled by the business and the liabilities of R4 000 000 represent the obligation of the business to outside parties. The residual of R6 000 000 is the equity or the owner's interest in the entity.

Commercial, industrial and other business activities can be undertaken by sole proprietorships, partnerships, close corporations or companies. Although equity in each of these entity forms will have different sub-classifications, the definition is appropriate for all such entities. A detailed discussion of the sub-classifications of equity appears in Chapter 16.

Using the above amounts, a simple statement of financial position could be drawn up as follows:

STATEMENT OF FINANCIAL POSITION
AT 31 DECEMBER 20X5

	R
Assets	10 000 000
Equity	6 000 000
Liabilities	4 000 000
	10 000 000

The statement of comprehensive income

The elements directly related to the measurement of profit or loss or other comprehensive income in the statement of comprehensive income are income and expenses.

Income is defined as increases in economic benefits during the accounting period in the form of:

- inflows or enhancements of assets, or
- decreases in liabilities

that result in increases in equity, other than those relating to contributions from equity participants.[11]

Various kinds of *assets may be received* by earning income, such as cash or receivables received in exchange for goods and services supplied. Income may also be earned by the *settlement of a liability*; for example, a publisher may earn income by distributing magazines to subscribers who have paid for them in advance.

The definition of income encompasses both revenue and gains.[12] Revenue arises in the course of the ordinary activities of an entity and includes sales, fees, interest and royalties. Gains represent increases in economic benefits and do not arise in the course of the ordinary activities of an entity, for example, profit on the sale of property, plant or equipment.

Pause and reflect...

On 1 April 20X5, a daily newspaper receives R1 200 from a subscriber for a 12 month period, from 1 April 20X5 to 31 March 20X6. The year end of the newspaper entity is 31 December 20X5. Discuss whether any income is recognised for the year ended 31 December 20X5, and if so, what is the amount of the income?

Response

The cash received of R1 200 refers to the contract period from 1 April 20X5 to 31 March 20X6. Income of R900 (R1 200 x 9/12) is recognised as earned for the year ended 31 December 20X5. There is a decrease in liability (the unearned income that was recognised when the cash was received) that results in an increase in equity (income earned increases equity) and it is not a contribution from an equity participant.

Expenses are defined as decreases in economic benefits during the accounting period in the form of:

- outflows or depletions of assets, or
- incurrences of liabilities

that result in decreases in equity other than those relating to distributions to equity participants.[13]

An *asset may be given up* by the incurral of expenses, such as the payment of cash for goods and services received. Expenses may also result in the *incurral of a liability*, for example, wages owing for services performed in the current period.

The definition of expenses encompasses losses as well as those expenses that arise in the ordinary course of activities of the entity.[14] Expenses that arise in the course of the ordinary activities of the entity include, for example, cost of goods sold, cost of supplies used, rent, wages and the consumption of benefits embodied in property, plant and equipment. Losses represent decreases in economic benefits, which do not arise in the ordinary activities of the entity, for example, a loss from flood damage.

Pause and reflect...

On 1 October 20X5, an entity pays R1 200 for an insurance policy for a 12 month period from 1 October 20X5 to 30 September 20X6. The year end of the entity is 31 December 20X5. Discuss whether an expense is recognised for the year ended 31 December 20X5, and if so, what is the amount of the expense?

Response

The cash paid of R1 200 relates to the contract period 1 October 20X5 to 30 September 20X6. An expense of R300 (R1 200 x 3/12) is recognised for the year ended 31 December 20X5. There is an outflow of assets (the prepaid insurance asset that was recognised when the cash was paid), that results in a decrease in equity (expenses decrease equity) and it is not a distribution to an equity participant.

You will recall from the discussion in earlier paragraphs that the income and expenses in the statement of comprehensive income measure both *profit or loss* and *other comprehensive income*. It is now important to understand which items of income and expense are recognised in profit or loss and which items are recognised in other comprehensive income, and how these are reported on the statement of comprehensive income.

Profit or loss is defined as the total of income less expenses, excluding the components of other comprehensive income.

The profit or loss measures the *performance* for the period. In other words, the profit or loss, or performance, is measured by the income earned from business activities less the expenses incurred from business activities.

Other comprehensive income is defined as items of income and expense that are not recognised in profit or loss.

In other words, other comprehensive income are items of income and expense that do not relate to the measure of performance for a period.

The profit or loss and other comprehensive income are then combined to give the total comprehensive income.

Total comprehensive income comprises all components of profit or loss and all components of other comprehensive income.

As we mentioned briefly earlier in this chapter, IAS 1 identifies five components of other comprehensive income. We are going to consider one such component, a revaluation of an item of property, plant and equipment. Assume that a business entity buys a property for a cost of R1 000 000. After a period of say, two years, an independent valuer assesses the property to be worth R1 200 000. We can then say that the *fair value* of the property is R1 200 000 and that there has been an increase in the value of the property of R200 000. If the business entity chooses to measure the property at its fair value, this is referred to as a *revaluation.* (The choice between measurement at cost or at revaluation will be discussed in detail in Chapter 11.)

An important question to now consider is whether the revaluation of R200 000 represents income. There is an increase in economic benefits during the period, in the form of an enhancement of an asset (the value of the property has increased), that results in an increase in equity (the revaluation, you will see, does increase equity), other than a contribution from equity participants (there is no contribution of capital). The revaluation therefore does represent income.

Pause and reflect...

Is the revaluation of R200 000 an income item that is included in profit or loss for the period or is it an item of other comprehensive income?

Response

Profit or loss measures performance for a period. The R200 000 does not represent income earned from business activities during the period. It is therefore an item of other comprehensive income as it does not relate to the measure of performance for the period.

You will recall that IAS1 requires an entity to present items of income and expense either in two separate statements

- ❑ The income statement (displaying components of profit or loss) and
- ❑ The statement of comprehensive income (displaying components of other comprehensive income),

or in a single statement, referred to as the statement of comprehensive income (displaying components of profit and loss as well as components of other comprehensive income).

Assume, during a period, a business entity earns income from business activities of R1 500 000, incurs expenses from business activities of R1 000 000 and revalues a property by R200 000.

If two separate statements are presented, a simple income statement and statement of comprehensive income could be drawn up as follows:

INCOME STATEMENT
FOR THE PERIOD ENDED 31 DECEMBER 20X5

	R
Income	1 500 000
Expenses	(1 000 000)
Profit for the period	500 000

STATEMENT OF COMPREHENSIVE INCOME
FOR THE PERIOD ENDED 31 DECEMBER 20X5

	R
Profit for the period	500 000
Other comprehensive income	
Revaluation	200 000
Total comprehensive income	700 000

If a single statement is presented, a simple statement of comprehensive income could be drawn up as follows:

STATEMENT OF COMPREHENSIVE INCOME
FOR THE PERIOD ENDED 31 DECEMBER 20X5

	R
Income	1 500 000
Expenses	(1 000 000)
Profit for the period	500 000
Other comprehensive income	
Revaluation	200 000
Total comprehensive income	700 000

The statement of changes in equity

Changes in an entity's equity between two reporting dates reflect the increase or decrease in its net assets during the period.[15] There are no categories or elements unique to the statement of changes in equity (as assets, liabilities and equity are related to the statement of financial position and as income and expense are related to the statement of comprehensive income). Rather, it reports the effect of transactions during the period that have increased or decreased equity.

IAS 1 requires the statement of changes in equity to present changes in equity separated into

- ❑ Owner changes in equity
- ❑ Non-owner changes in equity

Owner changes in equity are changes in equity arising from transactions with owners in their capacity as owners. This incorporates contributions to capital by owners (which increases equity) and distributions to owners (which decreases equity).

Non-owner changes in equity are changes in equity arising from income and expense transactions. You learnt in the previous section that income increases equity and expenses decrease equity. Thus, the profit for the period (income less expenses from business activities) or, the total comprehensive income (if there are items of other comprehensive income) is included on the statement of changes in equity as a line item.

Assume the business entity referred to above had a balance of equity at the beginning of the period of R4 400 000. Contributions to capital by owners amounted to R1 000 000 and distributions to owners amounted to R100 000. The income, expense and other comprehensive income amounts are the same as in the above example. A simple statement of changes in equity could then be drawn up as follows:

STATEMENT OF CHANGES IN EQUITY
FOR THE PERIOD ENDED 31 DECEMBER 20X5

	Capital R	Revaluation R	Total R
Equity at 1 January 20X5	4 400 000	-	4 400 000
Contributions by owners	1 000 000		1 000 000
Distributions to owners	(100 000)		(100 000)
Total comprehensive income	500 000	200 000	700 000
Equity at 31 December 20X5	5 800 000	200 000	6 000 000

2.2.6 The purpose, components and elements of financial statements summarised

Objective	Components	Elements
(To provide useful information about)		
Financial position	Statement of financial position	Assets, liabilities, equity
Profit or loss and total comprehensive income	Statement of comprehensive income	Income, expenses
Cash flows	Statement of cash flows	Operating, investing & financing activities

- The statement of changes in equity provides information about the movements in equity.
- The accounting policies and explanatory notes are necessary to assist in understanding the financial statements. You will remember that *understandability* is another one of the qualitative characteristics or attributes that make financial statements useful to users.

2.2.7 Presentation of income and expenses

Section 2.2.5 above has explained and illustrated the alternative presentations of income and expenses, that is, as two separate statements (income statement and statement of comprehensive income) or as a single statement (statement of comprehensive income). IAS 1 allows a choice between the two alternatives. In this textbook, a single statement of comprehensive income will be used when there are items of other comprehensive income. Where there are no items of other comprehensive income, and for the purposes of illustrating concepts, a separate income statement will be used.

2.3 General features

The **General features** listed in IAS 1 are a combination of underlying assumptions relating to the measurement of financial statement items and the reporting of those items. The features dealt with in IAS 1 relate to the accrual basis of accounting, fair presentation, going concern, consistency of presentation, comparative information, materiality and aggregation, offsetting, and finally frequency of reporting.

Both the accrual basis of accounting and the going concern assumption are listed as underlying assumptions in the preparation of financial statements according to the accounting framework. An understanding of the accrual basis of accounting is essential for the preparation of even the most elementary financial statements.

2.3.1 Accrual basis

When the accrual basis of accounting is used, items are recognised as assets, liabilities or equity and as income or expenses when they satisfy the definitions and recognition criteria for those elements in the accounting framework.[16] The definitions of the elements have already been described in this chapter. The recognition criteria will be addressed in Chapter 6.

The implication of the accrual basis is that the effects of transactions are recognised when they occur and not when cash is received or paid, and they are recorded in the accounting records and reported in the financial statements of the periods to which they relate.

Only amounts that are **earned** in, or relate to a period are recognised as income and included in the statement of comprehensive income. Goods or services may be provided for cash; in other words the provision of the goods or services and the receipt of cash occur in the same period and the amount received is recognised as income. If the goods or services have been provided and cash is not received the amount is still regarded as earned and is recognised as income. Conversely, cash received in the current period for goods or services provided in a previous period is not recognised as income when received. The relevant amount would have been recognised as income in the period when the goods or services were provided.

Turning our attention to expenses, only amounts that are **incurred** in, or relate to a period are recognised as an expense and included in the statement of comprehensive income. When dealing with expenses, it is only goods or services that are **used** in the period under review that are recognised as expenses. The use of the goods or services and the payment of cash may occur in the same period and the amount paid is recognised as an expense. If the goods or services have been used and cash is not paid the amount is still regarded as incurred and is recognised as an expense. Conversely, cash paid in the current period for goods or services used in a previous period is not recognised as an expense when paid. The relevant amount would have been recognised as an expense when the goods or services were used.

Consider a legal practice that consults with one hundred clients in a financial period of one month. If the practice charges each client R500, the income earned for the period should be R50 000. All the clients might pay the practice in the current month, in which case the income earned of R50 000 will equal the R50 000 cash received (scenario 1). Two other scenarios could exist – the practice could receive less than R50 000 in the current month, say R30 000, because some clients have not yet paid their accounts (scenario 2); or the practice may receive more than R50 000, say R70 000, as certain clients decide to pay in advance for future consultations (scenario 3). In both of these cases the statement of comprehensive income will still reflect R50 000 as income from fees as that is the amount which has been earned in the period from services provided. The recognition of income on the statement of comprehensive income is a measure of *accomplishment* for the period and is not dependent on the cash received.

Think about the rent the practice has to pay for its office space. If the landlord charges the practice rent of R10 000 per month, the practice's rent expense should be R10 000. The practice might pay the landlord the full R10 000 in the current month in which case the expense incurred of R10 000 will equal the cash paid of R10 000 (scenario 1). Again, two other scenarios could exist – the practice could neglect to pay the R10 000 in the current month (scenario 2) or it may pay R20 000 by paying the following month's rent in advance (scenario 3). In both of these cases the statement of comprehensive income will reflect R10 000 as rent expense as that is the amount which has been incurred in the period and which needs to be matched with the income earned. The recognition of expenses on the statement of comprehensive income is a measure of *sacrifice* for the period and is not dependent on the cash paid.

The three scenarios described above, together with the statement of financial position implications of each scenario are set out in diagram 2.2 below.

Scenario 1

	R
Cash received from clients	50 000
Cash paid for rent	10 000

INCOME STATEMENT			**STATEMENT OF FINANCIAL POSITION EFFECT**
	Cash **R**	**Accrual** **R**	
Income			
Fees	50 000	50 000	No statement of financial position effect.
Expenses			
Rent	(10 000)	(10 000)	No statement of financial position effect.
Profit for the period	40 000	40 000	

Scenario 2

	R
Cash received from clients	30 000
Cash paid for rent	0

INCOME STATEMENT			**STATEMENT OF FINANCIAL POSITION EFFECT**
	Cash **R**	**Accrual** **R**	
Income			
Fees	30 000	50 000	Asset of R20 000 representing a *resource controlled* by the entity, in respect of the amount owing by clients.
Expenses			
Rent	(0)	(10 000)	Liability of R10 000 representing an *obligation* of the entity, in respect of the amount owing to the landlord.
Profit for the period	30 000	40 000	

Scenario 3

	R
Cash received from clients	70 000
Cash paid for rent	20 000

INCOME STATEMENT			**STATEMENT OF FINANCIAL POSITION EFFECT**
	Cash	**Accrual**	
	R	**R**	
Income			
Fees	70 000	50 000	Liability of R20 000 representing an *obligation* of the entity, in respect of the fees received in advance from clients.
Expenses			
Rent	(20 000)	(10 000)	Asset of R10 000 representing a *resource controlled* by the entity, in respect of the rent paid in advance to the landlord.
Profit for the period	50 000	40 000	

Diagram 2.2 Income statement and statement of financial position effect of the accrual basis

2.3.2 Fair presentation

A requirement of IAS 1 is that the financial statements should fairly present the financial position, performance and cash flows of an entity.[17] This is consistent with the requirement of section 285(3) of the Corporate Laws Amendment Act, 2006 which requires financial statements to fairly present the financial position and results of operations in accordance with financial reporting standards.

According to IAS 1,[18] fair presentation requires the faithful representation of the effects of transactions, other events or conditions in accordance with the definitions and recognition criteria for assets, liabilities, income and expenses as set out in the Accounting Framework.

The above requirement is presumed to be achieved by the application of appropriate International Financial Reporting Standards.

2.3.3 Going concern

Financial statements are normally prepared on a going concern basis, which assumes that the enterprise will continue in operation for the forseeable future. Financial statements should be prepared on this basis unless management either intends to liquidate the entity or to cease trading or has no alternative but to do so.[19]

The statement of financial position therefore does not report liquidation values of assets. Rather, assets are reported on the statement of financial position at cost. The going concern assumption has important implications for the treatment of property, plant and equipment as well as inventory. These will be discussed in Chapters 11 and 12 respectively.

The going concern principle is ignored if the business is expected to be liquidated and assets are reported on the statement of financial position at estimated market values.

2.3.4 Consistency of presentation and comparative information

One of the four qualitative characteristics is that of *comparability*. Users need to be able to compare different enterprises when making investment decisions and also compare the financial statements of a particular enterprise over time.

As such, IAS 1 requires a consistent presentation and classification of items in the financial statements from one period to the next.[20]

IAS 1 further requires comparative information to be reported in respect of the previous period for all amounts reported in the financial statements.[21] As the focus of this book is on a conceptual introduction to financial accounting and not on disclosure, comparative information has not been incorporated.

2.3.5 Materiality and aggregation

An item is regarded as being material if it can affect users' decisions. IAS 1 requires each material class of similar items as well as items of a dissimilar nature to be presented separately.[22] Immaterial items should be aggregated with similar items and need not be presented separately.

2.3.6 Offsetting

It is important that assets and liabilities as well as income and expenses, are reported separately. Offsetting in the income statement or the statement of financial position detracts from the ability of users both to understand the transactions, events and conditions that have occurred and to assess the entity's future cash flows.

2.3.7 Frequency of reporting

IAS 1 requires an entity to present a complete set of financial statements at least annually.[23]

2.4 Example: Analysing transactions and preparation of financial statements from concepts

The following is a record of the transactions of Simon Smart, a computer retailer, for the three-month period from 1 January 20X5 to 31 March 20X5. Transactions 1 to 23 are the same as in the previous example and transactions 24 to 29 are now included to take into account the accrual basis of accounting.

External transactions

1. On 2 January, Simon Smart started a business as a computer retailer. He drew R950 000 from a savings account and opened a bank account in the name of Smart Concepts into which he paid R950 000.

2. On 2 January, Smart Concepts negotiated a loan from Techno Bank for an amount of R600 000. The loan is repayable in four equal annual installments, beginning on 31 December 20X5. The interest rate is 12% per annum, payable quarterly in arrears.
3. On 2 January, Simon located premises from which to operate in Rosebank. The monthly rent for the premises is R12 000. Smart Concepts paid four months rent in advance.
4. On 2 January, Simon transferred R120 000 from the bank account into a fixed deposit account earning interest at 5% per annum.
5. On 2 January, Smart Concepts purchased furniture and fittings for R240 000. This was paid for from funds in the bank account. The expected useful life of the furniture and fittings is five years.
6. On 5 January, Smart Concepts purchased supplies of stationery for R5 000 as well as supplies of computer parts for R12 000. All the supplies were paid for in cash.
7. On 7 January, Smart Concepts opened an account with Computer World, the supplier of its inventory.
8. On 10 January, Smart Concepts purchased inventory of sixty computers from Computer World at a cost of R10 000 each. The total amount owing is to be paid by 25 March.
9. On 12 January, Simon paid a service provider R750 in respect of a data bundle for internet access.
10. On 25 January, Smart Concepts sold fifteen computers on account to a customer for R12 500 each. An amount of R125 000 is due by 15 March and the balance by 15 April.
11. On 1 February, Smart Concepts employed a computer technician at a salary of R8 000 per month.
12. On 8 February, Smart Concepts paid R7 000 for an advertisement in a newspaper, advertising the computers available for sale.
13. On 12 February, Smart Concepts sold thirty computers, to customers, for R12 500 each. The customers paid cash for the computers.
14. On 25 February, Smart Concepts received cash of R48 000 in respect of technical support contracts taken out by customers. The contracts are for a two year period.
15. On 28 February, Smart Concepts paid the computer technician his salary for February.
16. On 4 March, Smart Concepts purchased inventory of a further seventy five computers from Computer World at a cost of R10 000 each. The total amount owing is to be paid by 25 May.
17. On 5 March, Smart Concepts paid a service provider R750 in respect of a data bundle for internet access.
18. On 15 March, Smart Concepts received R125 000 from the customer in transaction 10.
19. On 25 March, Smart Concepts paid Computer World an amount of R600 000.
20. On 29 March, Smart Concepts sold thirty computers, to customers, for R12 500 each. The customers paid cash for the computers.
21. On 30 March, Smart Concepts paid the computer technician his salary for March.
22. On 30 March, Smart Concepts paid the interest on the loan from Techno Bank for the three month period.
23. On 30 March, Simon authorised a distribution to himself of R60 000 for personal use.

Internal transactions

24. On 31 March, Simon examined the records of the business and established that technical support in respect of contracts to the value of R6 000 had been provided to customers.
25. On 31 March, Smart Concepts accounted for the interest on the fixed deposit earned for the period.
26. On 31 March, Smart Concepts recognised the rent expense incurred for the period.
27. On 31 March, the telephone account for R1 500 and the electricity account for R2 500 had been received but not paid.

28. On 31 March, Simon counted stationery supplies on hand costing R2 000 and also determined from the records that computer parts costing R8 500 had been used.
29. On 31 March, Smart Concepts accounted for the usage of the furniture and fittings for the period.

You are required to:

prepare, for Smart Concepts, the income statement and the statement of changes in equity for the three months ended 31 March 20X5, and the statement of financial position at 31 March 20X5. You should develop the answer using the concepts taught in this chapter, and applying the accrual basis of accounting.

Solution: Analysing transactions and preparation of financial statements from concepts

Each transaction needs to be analysed bearing in mind the entity concept, the elements of the financial statements, the general features and the qualitative characteristics. We suggest that you set up an outline of the income statement and statement of financial position and enter each item, or components of that item, on the financial statements as the transaction is analysed.

External transactions

1. Remember that the financial statements are prepared from the perspective of the business entity, utilising the entity concept. When Simon Smart withdraws R950 000 from his personal savings account, the business entity is not affected. When R950 000 is paid into the bank account of the business entity, Smart Concepts, the first transaction takes place. The cash in the bank embodies future benefits because of its command over other resources. Each transaction must affect at least two elements of the financial statements, or classifications of the same element twice. As the R950 000 is an amount contributed by the owner, it is entered as an increase in owner's equity.
2. The granting of the loan increases the asset, bank, by R600 000. The amount owing to Techno Bank is recognised by increasing the liability, borrowings, by the same amount. The borrowing is a liability as it is a present obligation of the enterprise (an amount owing to an outside party) arising from a past event (the loan transaction) and is expected to result in an outflow of resources on settlement (cash will be paid to the bank in settlement of the loan).
3. By paying four months' rent in advance, the business has a right to occupy the premises for the months of January, February, March and April. This right is an asset, as it is a resource controlled by the enterprise (the right of occupation) as a result of a past event (the rental agreement with the landlord) and from which future economic benefits are expected to flow (income will be earned by selling computers from the premises). The item, rent asset, is therefore increased on the statement of financial position. The amount of R48 000 has been paid and therefore the asset, bank, is decreased by the same amount. You will notice that items on the financial statements that are affected by more than one transaction have brackets behind the narration simply to expedite the calculation of the final balance.
4. The transfer of funds from the bank account to a fixed deposit account results in the decrease of one asset, bank, and the increase of another asset, fixed deposit investment. Interest is earned on a time proportion basis and will be recognised as income at the end of the period.
5. The furniture and fittings are assets and have been paid for in cash from the funds in the bank. Therefore the asset classification, furniture and fittings, is increased and the asset, bank, is decreased.

6. Supplies comply with the definition of an asset, and are recorded as such on purchase. The supplies are a resource controlled by the enterprise (ownership of the supplies rests with Smart Concepts) as a result of a past event (the purchase transaction) and from which future economic benefits are expected to flow (the supplies will be used in the operations of the enterprise). Only when the supplies are used will an expense be incurred. The assets, stationery supplies and computer parts, are increased by R5 000 and R12 000 respectively, while the asset, bank, is decreased by R17 000.
7. The opening of the account with the supplier is a transaction that has no economic impact on the enterprise and therefore the financial statements are not affected.
8. The asset, inventory, is increased when inventory is purchased. The inventory is a resource controlled by the enterprise (the risks and rewards of ownership have been transferred) arising from a past event (the purchase transaction) and from which future economic benefits are expected to flow (the inventory will be sold to customers). The amount owing to Computer World is represented by an increase in the liability, accounts payable. It is a present obligation of the enterprise (the amount owing to the supplier) arising from a past event (the purchase transaction) and is expected to result in an outflow of resources upon settlement (cash will be paid to Computer World).
9. Purchase of a data bundle gives rise to an expense. It is a decrease in an economic benefit in the form of, in this instance, the decrease of an asset, bank (the amount paid to the service provider). An asset is not created, bearing in mind the threshold quality of materiality and the cost/benefit constraint.
10. Smart Concepts earns income by selling computers to customers. This sale is on account and the customer is going to pay part of the purchase consideration before the end of the period and the remainder during the next period. Income, in the form of revenue from sales, must be recognised immediately in terms of the accrual basis. Remember that the accrual basis requires income to be recognised as it is earned and not when it is received. An asset, accounts receivable, is increased and the sales revenue included as income on the income statement. Note that there has been an increase in an economic benefit in the form of, in this case, the increase of an asset (the amount owing by the customer as accounts receivable).

    An expense must also be recognised, as there has been a decrease in economic benefits in the form of, in this case, an outflow of an asset (the inventory sold). An expense, cost of sales, is increased and the asset, inventory, is decreased.
11. The employment of the technician is also a transaction that has no economic impact on the enterprise and the financial statements are not affected.
12. Inserting an advertisement into the publication gives rise to an expense. It results in a decrease in economic benefits in the form of, in this instance, the outflow of an asset (the cash paid to a newspaper).
13. The sales in this transaction are for cash. The customers pay immediately and the asset, bank, is increased. Income, in the form of revenue from sales, must be recognised as earned on the income statement, as there has been an increase in an economic benefit in the form of, in this case, the enhancement of an asset (the cash in the bank). The accrual basis of accounting supports the recognition of income, as the cash has been received in the same period as the income has been earned.

    As in transaction 10, the cost of sales must be recognised at the time the sale is made.
14. This transaction requires a careful examination of the accrual basis. Cash has been received and the asset, bank, must clearly be increased. The provision of technical support, however, is going to take place partly in the current period and partly in future periods. The accrual basis requires income to be recognised only when it is earned and as the technical support will be provided over a two-year period, the income for the current period can only be recognised at the end of the period when the value of the work that has been performed is known. In the meantime, a liability is created representing the obligation of Smart Concepts to provide customers with technical support.

15. Payment to the technician gives rise to an expense for the same reason as the payment for the advertisement. The expense has been incurred through a decrease in the asset, bank. Note that the incurral of the expense and the payment of the cash have taken place in the same period.
16. This is identical to transaction 8.
17. This is identical to transaction 9.
18. The customer to whom the computers were sold in transaction 10 now pays part of the amount owing by him. If you look back at transaction 10, you will notice that in terms of the accrual basis, the income was recognised at the time the sale was made. Income cannot be recognised again now that the cash has been received. The asset, bank, is increased and the asset, accounts receivable, is decreased by R125 000.
19. This transaction involves the settlement of a liability. The asset, bank, is decreased and the liability, accounts payable, is also decreased. Note that no expense is created here as the expense (in this case, cost of sales) is recognised when the inventory is sold and not when the liability is settled.
20. Thirty computers have been delivered and the customers have paid the amount owing in cash. The asset, bank, is increased by the R375 000 received and the income item, sales revenue, is also increased by the same amount. As in the previous sales transactions (10 and 13), the cost of sales of R300 000 must also be recognised by increasing the expense, cost of sales, and decreasing the asset, inventory.
21. This is identical to transaction 15.
22. The interest is payable quarterly in arrears, which means that the interest payments are made at the *end* of each three-month period. The payment of the interest gives rise to an expense, as there is a decrease in an economic benefit in the form of, in this instance, the outflow of an asset, bank.
23. The definition of an expense refers to decreases in economic benefits that result in decreases in equity other than those relating to distributions to equity participants. The R60 000 distributed to Simon decreases the asset, bank, but no expense is shown on the statement of comprehensive income, as the amount is distributed to the owner. The entity concept also applies here, as an amount distributed to the owner cannot create a business expense. Hence, the owner's equity is reduced by R60 000.

Internal transactions

24. When Smart Concepts received cash of R48 000 in respect of technical support contracts taken out by customers (see transaction 14), a liability was established representing an obligation of the enterprise to provide a service in the future. At the end of the period, the service records show that R6 000 of the work has been performed. The accrual basis of accounting requires this amount to be recognised as income in the period when earned. Hence, income is recognised by a decrease in the service liability on the statement of financial position and an increase in the service revenue on the income statement.
25. The transfer to the fixed deposit investment was made at the beginning of January. No interest has been received from the bank, but interest for three months has been earned. As mentioned previously, interest is earned on the time apportioned basis. Therefore interest revenue of R1 500 (R120 000 x 5% x 3/12) is recognised as income on the income statement and an interest asset is shown on the statement of financial position representing the amount of interest owing to Smart Concepts.
26. When Smart Concepts paid R48 000 in transaction 3, a rent asset was created representing the right to occupy the premises from January to April. At the end of March, the rent expense for the period of R36 000 needs to be recognised. A rent expense item is included on the income statement and the rent asset on the statement of financial position is reduced by R36 000.

27. The telephone and electricity accounts have been received, but will only be paid in the following month. However, both are expenses incurred in the current period. The fact that the cash will only be paid in the following month is irrelevant in terms of the accrual basis. A telephone and electricity expense therefore appears on the income statement and a corresponding liability appears on the statement of financial position representing the amount owing to Telkom and to the municipality. You will notice that the same items, telephone and electricity, appear on the income statement as an expense and on the statement of financial position as a liability.
28. When the supplies were purchased in transaction 6, an amount of R5 000 was recorded as a stationery supplies asset and an amount of R12 000 as a computer parts asset. At the end of the period, R2 000 of the stationery supplies is still unused, implying that R3 000 has been used during the period. The amount used must be shown as a stationery supplies expense and the balance unused must be reflected as a stationery supplies asset. This is effected by including R3 000 on the income statement as an stationery supplies expense and reducing the stationery supplies asset on the statement of financial position to R2 000.

    Similarly, at the end of the period, Simon determined from the service records that parts costing R8 500 had been used. Again, the amount used must be shown as a computer parts expense and the balance unused must be reflected as a computer parts asset. This is effected by including R8 500 on the income statement as a computer parts expense and reducing the computer parts asset on the statement of financial position to R3 500. Note that the same items, stationery supplies and computer parts, appear on the income statement as expenses and on the statement of financial position as assets.
29. The furniture and fittings are expected to have a useful life of five years. Even though the full purchase price of R240 000 was paid in cash during the current period, the cost of the asset needs to be expensed over the periods when the asset is used. An amount of R12 000 (R240 000/5 x 3/12) is thus included as an asset usage expense on the income statement and the carrying amount of the furniture and fittings is reduced by R12 000.

SMART CONCEPTS
INCOME STATEMENT
FOR THE THREE MONTHS ENDED 31 MARCH 20X5

			R
INCOME			945 000
Sales revenue	(187 500 + 375 000 + 375 000)	937 500	
Service revenue		6 000	
Interest revenue	(120 000 x 0.05 x 3/12)	1 500	
EXPENSES			(856 000)
Cost of sales	(150 000 + 300 000 + 300 000)	750 000	
Internet expense	(750 + 750)	1 500	
Advertising		7 000	
Salaries	(8 000 + 8 000)	16 000	
Interest expense	(600 000 x 0.12 x 3/12)	18 000	
Rent expense		36 000	
Telephone & electricity expense	(1 500 + 2 500)	4 000	
Stationery supplies expense	(5 000 – 2 000)	3 000	
Computer parts expense		8 500	
Asset usage expense		12 000	
PROFIT FOR THE PERIOD			89 000

SMART CONCEPTS
STATEMENT OF FINANCIAL POSITION
AT 31 MARCH 20X5

		R
ASSETS		2 375 000
Furniture and fittings	(240 000 – 12 000)	228 000
Fixed deposit investment		120 000
Inventory	(600 000 – 150 000 – 300 000 + 750 000 – 300 000)	600 000
Accounts receivable	(187 500 – 125 000)	62 500
Stationery supplies asset	(5 000 – 3 000)	2 000
Computer parts asset	(12 000 – 8 500)	3 500
Rent asset	(48 000 – 36 000)	12 000
Interest asset		1 500
Bank	(950 000 + 600 000 – 48 000 – 120 000 – 240 000 – 17 000 – 750 – 7 000 + 375 000 + 48 000 – 8 000 – 750 + 125 000 – 600 000 + 375 000 – 8 000 – 18 000 – 60 000)	1 345 500
		2 375 000
OWNERS EQUITY		979 000
LIABILITIES		1 396 000
Borrowings		600 000
Accounts payable	(600 000 + 750 000 – 600 000)	750 000
Service liability	(48 000 – 6 000)	42 000
Telephone and electricity liability	(1 500 + 2 500)	4 000
		2 375 000

SMART CONCEPTS
STATEMENT OF CHANGES IN EQUITY
FOR THE PERIOD ENDED 31 MARCH 20X5

	R
Balance at 1 January 20X5	-
Profit for the period	89 000
Distributions	(60 000)
Contribution to capital	950 000
Balance at 31 March 20X5	979 000

2.5 Cash basis compared to accrual basis of accounting

It is appropriate at this stage to compare the income statement prepared under the cash basis of accounting and the income statement prepared under the accrual basis of accounting in order to assess which provides a better measure of performance.

The cash basis income statement shows cash inflows of R923 000 compared to R945 000 recognised as income on the accrual basis. The differences are caused partly by the R48 000 cash received in respect of the service plans, of which only R6 000 is reported as income on the accrual basis income statement, and partly by the R187 500 sales to a customer and recognised as income, of which cash of R125 000 has been received. Also contributing to the difference is the R1 500 reported as interest earned on the accrual basis income statement, in respect of which no cash has been received.

SMART CONCEPTS
COMPARATIVE INCOME STATEMENTS ON THE CASH BASIS AND ACCRUAL BASIS

	Cash **R**	**Accrual** **R**
CASH INFLOW/INCOME	923 000	945 000
Sales	875 000	937 500
Service	48 000	6 000
Interest	–	1 500
CASH OUTFLOW/EXPENSES	(947 500)	(856 000)
Cost of sales	600 000	750 000
Internet	1 500	1 500
Advertising	7 000	7 000
Salaries	16 000	16 000
Interest	18 000	18 000
Rent	48 000	36 000
Telephone & electricity	–	4 000
Computer parts & stationery supplies	17 000	11 500
Furniture and fittings	240 000	12 000
NET CASH FLOW/PROFIT	(24 500)	89 000

The cash outflow on the cash basis income statement amounts to R947 500 compared to R856 000 reported as expenses on the accrual basis. Where the cash paid coincides with the expense incurred, the same amount is shown on the cash and accrual basis income statements, for example, the R7 000 paid for advertising, the R16 000 paid for salaries and the R18 000 paid for interest. On the other hand, where cash is paid for an asset which will be used to earn income over a number of periods in the future, the cash basis income statement shows the total amount paid as a cash outflow in the current period, whereas the accrual income statement will recognise as an expense only that portion of the asset used in the current period. The R48 000 paid in respect of four months' rent and the R240 000 paid for the purchase of the furniture and fittings are shown as cash outflows on the cash basis, whereas the accrual basis reports a R36 000 rent expense and R12 000 for the usage of the furniture and fittings. Consider also the amounts reported for cost of sales and supplies on the cash basis compared to the accrual basis. A total of 135 computers, at a cost of R10 000 each were purchased during the period. Cash was paid in respect of 60 of the computers while 75 computers were sold. Therefore, an amount of R600 000 (60 x R10 000) is reported as cost of sales on the cash basis compared to an amount of R750 000 (75 x R10 000) on the accrual basis. Turning our attention to the supplies, the total amount purchased of R17 000 is shown as a cash outflow as the supplies were paid for in cash. However, supplies costing only R11 500 were used and thus shown as accrual basis expenses. The cash basis will also not take into account those expenses incurred in the current period but only paid for in a later period, such as the telephone and electricity. In our example, R4 000 is recognised as an expense when incurred, that is, the three months from January to March, even though the cash will be paid in the following period.

The accrual basis income statement provides information on the results of an entity's operations, or *performance* for the relevant period. Income earned by the entity for goods or services provided is included as a measure of *accomplishment* in the period when the goods are sold or the service provided and not when the cash is received (unless the goods or services are provided for cash). The expenses incurred by the entity are included as a measure of *effort* in the period when used or consumed and not when the cash is paid (unless the expenses are paid in cash).

The advantage of the cash basis of accounting is that it is factual, and cash flows, particularly the prediction of future cash flows, are of interest to investors.

On the other hand, there are some major disadvantages to consider. When measured over short periods of time, the cash basis may seriously misrepresent the long-run cash-generating ability of the enterprise. For example, many business enterprises encounter large cash outflows in one period to acquire resources such as property and equipment that will be used to produce goods and services in future periods. It might be appropriate to allocate a portion of the cost of these items to future periods. In addition, the entity may acquire or use resources in the current period which were paid for in a previous period or which may be paid for only in a future period. Similarly, the entity may provide goods and services in the current period in respect of which the cash was received in a previous period or for which the cash will be received only in a future period.

The R89 000 profit on the accrual basis better reflects the result of the period's activities compared to the R24 500 net cash outflow on the cash basis. We can conclude that information provided on the accrual basis provides a superior measure of performance than information provided on the cash basis.

2.6 Exam example

Miss Dilly Olebagge owns and operates a boarding house just off Empire Road. She started the business two years ago when she stumbled across an old house in desperate need of renovation and fell in love with it immediately. She signed a lease for R7 200 per year, payable in advance in equal instalments on 1 January and 1 July each year.

The landlord, thankful that Miss Olebagge had rented the house, agreed to do certain renovations, which included a new kitchen, new bathrooms, edge-to-edge carpets and a coat of paint, for which he paid R15 000.

On her side, Miss Olebagge had to buy both furniture and food preparation equipment. The furniture cost R7 200 and will probably need replacing in six years' time. The food preparation equipment cost a total of R6 000 and she estimates that this equipment will serve her purpose for five years, after which it could be sold for R900.

The house accommodates 15 students for both room and board at a monthly rate of R200 each, in arrears, and provides meals only to another 10 students at R80 per month each, in arrears. One of the 10 students lost his DP for Accounting I during May 20X8 and disappeared without trace at the end of the month before he paid for his meals.

During May 20X8, she purchased food for R1 940 on account and paid R2 340 for the purchases for April. She estimated that she had R480 worth of food on hand at the end of April and R380 worth of food on hand at the end of May.

She employs two staff members, one for cleaning and one for meal preparation. The domestic worker is paid R3 840 per annum and the cook receives R6 000 per annum. The cook has had his May salary held back for a week pending proof of boarders' allegations of discovering items of biological interest in their dinner.

The electricity and water account from the City Council (which was paid just before the end of May) reflected an amount owing of R200. This included R54 still owing in respect of April 20X8.

Miss Olebagge is currently re-evaluating the profitability and wisdom of entering into such a venture. She knows that you, as one of her tenants, are a first-year Accounting student and approaches you to assist her in her dilemma.

You are required to:

(a) prepare an income statement for May 20X8 using the cash basis of accounting;
(b) prepare an income statement for May 20X8 using the accrual basis of accounting;
(c) decide which statement you think will be more useful for Miss Olebagge's decision. Support your answer with reasons.

Suggested solution: Exam example

(a) MISS DILLY OLEBAGGE'S BOARDING HOUSE INCOME STATEMENT ON CASH BASIS FOR THE MONTH OF MAY 20X8

		R
Cash receipts (inflows)		3 720
Room and board (15 x 200)	3 000	
Meals only (9 x R80)	720	
Cash payments (outflows)		(2 860)
Payment for April's food purchases	2 340	
Salaries (320 + 0)	320	
Electricity and water	200	
Net cash flow		860

(b) MISS DILLY OLEBAGGE'S BOARDING HOUSE INCOME STATEMENT ON ACCRUAL BASIS FOR THE MONTH OF MAY 20X8

		R
Income		3 800
Room and board (15 x 200)	3 000	
Meals only (10 x 80)	800	
Expenses		(3 871)
Rent (7 200/12 months)	600	
Cost of food used (480 + 1 940 – 380)	2 040	
Asset usage expense – furniture (7 200/72 months)	100	
– equipment (6 000 – 900)/60 months)	85	
Salaries (320 + 500)	820	
Electricity and water (200 – 54)	146	
Bad debts expense	80	
Loss for the period		(71)

(c) The income statement prepared on the accrual basis of accounting is a better indicator of performance as it recognises income earned and expenses incurred during the period, irrespective of the timing of the receipts and payment of cash. The income statement prepared on the cash basis of accounting takes into account only cash received and paid during the period. It does not attempt to allocate cash receipts and payments to the periods when earned or incurred.

Although the current net loss implies that the business as presently operated is not viable in the long run, it is important to look at the reasons for the net loss. These are the bad debts, as well as the possibility that the charge for board and lodging is too low.

Summary of concepts and applications

1. Cash flow forecasts enable primary and other users of financial statements to predict an entity's future performance and future cash flows. The cash basis of accounting measures performance by subtracting cash outflows from cash inflows to arrive at a net cash flow for the period.
2. The entity concept advocates that the transactions of the business entity must be accounted for separately from its owners. IAS 1 prescribes the basis for presentation of general-purpose financial statements in order to ensure comparability. The objective of these general-purpose financial statements is to provide information about the financial position, performance and cash flows of an entity that is useful to a wide range of users in making economic decisions. In order to meet this objective, IAS 1 requires that a complete set of financial statements include a statement of financial position, statement of comprehensive income, statement of cash flows, statement of changes in equity and notes. Financial statements portray the financial effects of transactions and other events by grouping them into elements according to their economic characteristics. The elements related to the measurement of financial position in the statement of financial position are assets, liabilities and equity and the elements related to the measurement of performance in the statement of comprehensive income are income and expenses.
3. The general features are listed in IAS 1 and are a combination of underlying assumptions relating to the measurement of financial statement items and the reporting of those items. The considerations relate to the accrual basis of accounting, fair presentation, going concern, consistency of presentation and comparative information, materiality and aggregation and offsetting.
4. Transactions are analysed bearing in mind the entity concept, the elements of the financial statements, the general features and the qualitative characteristics. An outline of the statement of comprehensive income and statement of financial position is set up, and each item, or component of that item, is entered on the financial statements as the transaction is analysed.
5. The income statements prepared in the Smart Concepts example under both the cash and accrual basis of accounting indicate that there are significant differences between these two methods. The accrual basis income statement provides information on the results of an entity's operations for the relevant period. The cash basis provides factual information that is useful in the prediction of future cash flows. However, the cash basis may misrepresent the long-run cash-generating ability of the enterprise and distort the relationship between the inflow or outflow of resources and the receipt or payment of cash.

Notes

1. Mueller, G. G. and Kelley, L., *Introductory Financial Accounting*, New Jersey: PrenticeHall Inc., (1991), p. 36.
2. IAS 1, Presentation of Financial Statements, *The International Accounting Standards Board*, (2007), paragraph 1.
3. IAS 1, paragraph 9.
4. IAS 1, paragraph 10.
5. Framework for the Preparation and Presentation of Financial Statements, *The International Accounting Standards Board*, (2001), paragraph 47.
6. Framework for the Preparation and Presentation of Financial Statements (2001), paragraph 49(a).
7. Framework for the Preparation and Presentation of Financial Statements (2001), paragraph 55.
8. Framework for the Preparation and Presentation of Financial Statements (2001), paragraph 49(b).
9. Framework for the Preparation and Presentation of Financial Statements (2001), paragraph 62.
10. Framework for the Preparation and Presentation of Financial Statements (2001), paragraph 49(c).
11. Framework for the Preparation and Presentation of Financial Statements (2001), paragraph 70(a).
12. Framework for the Preparation and Presentation of Financial Statements (2001), paragraph 74.
13. Framework for the Preparation and Presentation of Financial Statements (2001), paragraph 70(b).
14. Framework for the Preparation and Presentation of Financial Statements (2001), paragraph 78.
15. IAS 1, paragraph 109.
16. IAS 1, paragraph 28.
17. IAS 1, paragraph 15.
18. IAS 1, paragraph 15.
19. IAS 1, paragraph 25.
20. IAS 1, paragraph 45.
21. IAS 1, paragraph 38.
22. IAS 1, paragraph 30.
23. IAS 1, paragraph 36.

3 The Accounting Equation and the Analysis of Transactions

"The first appearance of the double entry system of accounting in Europe coincided with the introduction of algebra during the early 13th century ... mathematicians ... may well have developed the concept of double entry accounting which, after all, is based on an equation.'
(Hain, 1970)

Outcomes

- Distinguish between internal and external transactions.
- Explain the logic of the accounting equation.
- Analyse the effects of transactions on the accounting equation.
- Analyse transactions using the accounting equation and prepare a set of financial statements.
- Reconcile the profit for the period.

Chapter outline

The Bidvest Group Limited
Statement of financial position for the year ended 30 June 2007

	(R Millions)
Assets	32 843
Capital and Reserves	10 825
Liabilities	22 018
Total Equity and Liabilities	32 843

The Bidvest Group is an investment company that owns more than 250 other companies, operates on four continents, and employs 104 000 people. Accounting for it is as complex as it can get, yet the basic premise of A = OE + L still applies.

3.1 Transactions

In Chapter 2, we analysed the transactions or events of Smart Concepts for the period from 1 January 20X5 to 31 March 20X5. For each transaction we determined whether an asset, liability or the owner's equity was affected, and whether income was earned or an expense incurred. Remember that assets, liabilities, owner's equity, income and expense are the elements of the financial statements.

Transactions are therefore economic events which have an impact on the financial position of an entity. Transactions can be categorised as either external transactions or internal transactions.

External transactions are economic events that occur between the entity and another business entity or person. *Internal transactions* are internal adjustments made to the financial position of an entity in order to apply the accrual basis of accounting.

When we revisit Smart Concepts later in this chapter we will identify the external and internal transactions.

Pause and reflect...

Think about some of the transactions that we processed in the Smart Concepts example in Chapter 2:

a) The owner, Simon Smart, invested R950 000 in the business entity (Transaction 1).
b) Smart Concepts paid R48 000 in respect of four months rent in advance (Transaction 3).
c) Smart Concepts recognised the rent expense incurred for the period (Transaction 26).

Can you identify and explain which of the above transactions are external transactions and which are internal transactions?

Response

a) This is an external transaction because the owner and the business entity are separate accounting entities.
b) This is an external transaction because the landlord is another business entity or person.
c) This is an internal transaction because it takes into account the accrual basis of accounting by recognising an expense of R36 000 (R12 000 X 3 months) for the period from 1 January 20X5 to 31 March 20X5.

3.2 The accounting equation

A business entity is financed from two primary sources – investors (owner's funds) and lenders (borrowed funds). Owner's funds are known as owner's equity and the investment of funds into a business entity by an owner is known as the investment of ***capital***. Borrowed funds are known as liabilities.

Source of financing	Known as
Owner's funds – Investors Borrowed funds – Lenders	Owner's equity Liabilities

These funds are used to purchase assets to enable the entity to operate. Both the investors and the lenders are separate accounting entities apart from the business entity (the investors because of the entity concept discussed in Chapter 2, and the lenders because they are independent entities in their own right). Remember that the owner's equity represents the owner's interest in the entity, and the liabilities represent the obligations of the entity, or the amounts that the entity owes to lenders. In other words, the owner's funds and borrowed funds (sources of financing of an entity) represent the claims on the assets of the entity.

We can therefore develop an equation to measure the financial position of a business entity as follows:

Sum of assets	=	Claims on assets
Sum of assets	=	Total source of finance
Assets	=	Funds provided by lenders and investors
Assets	=	Borrowed funds and owner's funds
Assets	=	Liabilities + owner's equity
A	=	L + OE

The elements of the financial statements that appear on the *statement of financial position* are assets, liabilities and owner's equity. The equation 'Assets = liabilities + owner's equity' (A = L + OE) is known as the accounting equation. The accounting equation is a simple representation of the statement of financial position of a business entity. We are going to use this equation to help us analyse transactions that take place in a business.

3.3 Effects of transactions on the accounting equation

The accounting equation has two sides, which we can label the *left* side and the *right* side. Incorporating these labels, we can begin to develop an accounting equation worksheet which we can use to analyse transactions. Each transaction needs to be analysed to determine its effect on the accounting equation. The accounting equation must always be in balance.

Left	=	Right
Assets	=	Claims on the assets
Assets	=	Liabilities + Owner's equity

It is possible to identify four sets of transactions, all of which maintain the equality of the accounting equation. These are transactions that:

- increase the left side (assets) and increase the right side (claims on the assets) of the equation
- decrease the left side (assets) and decrease the right side (claims on the assets) of the equation
- increase the left side (assets) and decrease the left side (assets) of the equation
- increase the right side (claims on the assets) and decrease the right side (claims on the assets) of the equation.

We will now examine some typical external and internal transactions that occur in a business entity to determine the effect that they have on the elements of the accounting equation. The transactions are listed in diagram 3.1.

Transaction	**Effect on accounting equation**				
	A	=	L	+	OE
External transactions					
a. Owner invests funds in the entity	+	=			+ **C**
b. Entity borrows funds from lender	+	=	+		
c. Entity buys assets for cash	±	=			
d. Entity buys assets on credit	+	=	+		
e. Entity sells goods/provides a service for cash	+	=			+ **I**
f. Entity sells goods/provides a service on credit	+	=			+ **I**
g. Recognition of cost of goods sold	−	=			− **E**
h. Entity receives cash from a customer/client	±	=			
i. Entity pays expenses in cash	−	=			− **E**
j. Entity pays lender/supplier in cash	−	=	−		
k. Cash received in advance of earning income	+	=	+		
l. Cash paid in advance of incurral of expense	±	=			
m. Distribution of funds to owner	−	=			− **D**
Internal transactions					
n. Recognition of unearned income		=	−		+ **I**
o. Income earned and cash receipt outstanding	+	=			+ **I**
p. Recognition of pre-paid expenses	−	=			− **E**
q. Expense incurred and cash payment outstanding		=	+		− **E**
r. Recognition of usage of an asset	−	=			− **E**

Capital invested by owner	**C**
Income earned	**I**
Expense incurred	**E**
Distribution	**D**

Diagram 3.1: Effect of transactions on the accounting equation

(a) Owner invests funds in the business

As mentioned in chapter 2, cash is a resource controlled by the entity because of its command over other resources. Therefore the asset column is increased on the left side of the equation to reflect the inflow of cash. Cash introduced is a source of financing for the business. The other side of the transaction is to increase the owner's equity column on the right side of the equation. The owner's equity column represents the claim the owner has against the assets of the entity or the owner's interest in the entity.

(b) Entity borrows funds from lender

The funds borrowed from the lender represent cash under the control of the entity. Again, the asset column is increased on the left side of the equation to reflect the inflow of cash. The other side of the transaction is to increase the liability column on the right side of the equation. The liability column represents the claim the lender has against the assets of the entity, or the amount the entity owes the lender.

(c) Entity buys assets for cash

The asset purchased is a resource controlled by the entity. The asset column is firstly increased on the left side of the equation to reflect the asset purchased. The asset purchased is financed from cash funds within the entity, therefore the other side of the transaction is then to decrease the asset column, also on the left side of the equation. The overall effect of this transaction is an increase and a decrease in the asset column by the same amount.

(d) Entity buys assets on credit

Again, the asset purchased is a resource controlled by the entity and the asset column is increased on the left side of the equation to reflect the asset purchased. The asset purchased is financed by a lender or supplier, therefore the other side of the transaction is to increase the liability column on the right side of the equation.

(e) Entity sells goods/provides a service for cash

This transaction results in income being earned. You learnt in the previous chapter that income gives rise to increases in economic benefits during the accounting period in the form of *inflows or enhancements of assets* or *decreases of liabilities* that result in increases in equity, other than those relating to contributions from equity participants.

On the left side of the equation we increase the asset column due to the inflow of cash. The other side of the transaction is to increase the owner's equity. Income is a measurement of accomplishment, and income earned increases the owner's interest in the business. Thus income is recognised as an increase in owner's equity in the same period that we recognise the increase in cash.

(f) Entity sells goods/provides a service on credit

The only difference between this transaction and the previous one is that the transaction in (e) was concluded for cash whereas this transaction is on credit. Remember that the definition of income refers to the inflow or enhancement of assets.

On the left side of the equation we increase the asset column due to an increase in the right to claim the amount owing from a customer. It is important to note that income is recognised when the goods are sold or the service provided and not when the cash is received from the customer. The other side of the transaction is to increase the owner's equity. As mentioned above, income is recognised in the same period that we recognise the increase in the right to claim an amount from the customer.

(g) Recognition of cost of goods sold

When an entity sells goods, as opposed to providing a service, the cost of the goods sold must be recognised as an expense. You also learnt in the previous chapter that expenses give rise to decreases in economic benefits during the accounting period in the form of outflows or depletions of assets or incurrances of liabilities that result in decreases in equity, other than those relating to distributions to equity participants.

On the left side of the equation we will decrease the asset column due to the outflow of inventory. The other side of the transaction decreases owner's equity, recording the expense, cost of sales. Just as owner's equity is increased to record income earned, it must be decreased to record expenses incurred.

(h) Entity receives cash from a customer/client

The receipt of cash from a customer or client does not give rise to income being earned as the income was recognised as earned when the goods were sold or the service was provided.

On the left side of the equation we increase the asset column due to the inflow of cash. In this instance, we also decrease the asset column representing a decrease in the right to receive an amount owing from a customer.

(i) Entity pays expenses in cash

This transaction results in an expense being incurred. Expenses are defined as decreases in economic benefits during the accounting period in the form of *outflows or depletions of assets* or *incurrences of liabilities* that result in decreases in equity, other than those relating to distributions to equity participants.

On the left side of the equation we will decrease the asset column due to the outflow of cash. The other side of the transaction decreases owner's equity, recording the expense incurred.

(j) Entity pays lender/supplier in cash

The paying of cash to a lender/supplier does not give rise to an expense being incurred since an obligation is being settled.

On the left side of the equation we decrease the asset column due to the outflow of cash. The outflow of cash in this instance will decrease the liability column on the right side of the equation.

(k) Cash received in advance of earning income

When cash is received in advance of earning income, a liability is created at the time of receipt of the cash, representing the obligation of the entity to provide goods or services in the future. At the end of the period, an internal transaction is needed to recognise that part of the liability earned during the period. (See transaction n.)

On the left of the accounting equation we increase the asset column due to the inflow of cash. The other side of the transaction is to increase the liability column on the right side of the equation.

(l) Cash paid in advance of incurral of expense

When cash is paid in advance of incurral of expenses, an asset is created at the time of payment of the cash, representing the right of the entity to receive goods or services in the future. At the end of the period, an internal transaction is needed to recognise that part of the asset that is used or expired during the period. (See transaction p.)

On the left of the accounting equation we increase the asset column representing the right to the goods or services in the future and also decrease the asset column due to the outflow of cash.

(m) Distribution of funds to owner

The distribution of funds to the owner results in an outflow of resources from the entity. This decreases owner's equity as it reduces the owner's interest in the entity. It is, however, important to remember that the distribution of funds to the owner does not result in the incurral of an expense. This is because of the entity concept which separates the activities of the entity and the owner.

On the left side of the equation we decrease the asset column due to the outflow of cash. The other side of the transaction is to decrease the owner's equity column.

(n) Recognition of unearned income

When cash is received prior to the goods or services being provided (see transaction k), a liability is established representing the obligation of the entity to provide the goods or services in the future. At the end of a period, part of the liability will be earned as income (based on the goods sold or service provided) and part will remain a liability to be recognised as income in future periods. The accrual basis of accounting requires the amount earned to be recognised as income in the period when the goods or services are provided.

On the right side of the accounting equation the liability column is decreased by the amount of income earned. The other side of the transaction is to increase the owner's equity column representing an increase in the owner's interest in the business.

(o) Income earned and cash receipt outstanding

Income needs to be recorded when earned, which may occur before the cash is received. If, at the end of the period, earned income is unrecorded because payment has not been received, an internal transaction is needed to record the income earned during the period.

On the left side of the equation the asset column is increased, representing the right to receive the amount owing in the future. The other side of the transaction is to increase the owner's equity column on the right side of the equation. Owner's equity is increased because income earned increases the owner's interest in the entity.

(p) Recognition of pre-paid expenses

When cash is paid prior to goods or services being received or used (see transaction l), an asset is established representing the right of the entity to the goods or services in the future. At the end of a period, part of the asset will be incurred as an expense (based on the goods or services received) and part will remain an asset to be recognised as an expense in future periods. The accrual basis of accounting requires the amount incurred to be recognised as an expense in the period when the goods or services are received or used.

On the left side of the accounting equation the asset column is decreased by the amount of the expense incurred. The other side of the transaction is to decrease the owner's equity column, representing a decrease in the owner's interest in the entity.

(q) Expense incurred and cash payment outstanding

Expenses need to be recorded when incurred, which may occur before the cash is paid. If, at the end of the period, incurred expenses are unrecorded because payment has not been made, an internal transaction is needed to record the expense incurred during the period.

On the right side of the equation the liability column is increased, representing the obligation to pay the amount owing in the future. The other side of the transaction is to decrease the owner's equity column, also on the right side of the equation. Owner's equity is decreased because expenses incurred decrease the owner's interest in the entity.

It is important to note that the expense is recognised and owner's equity decreased irrespective of whether cash has been paid (see transaction i) or the amount is owing and a liability created (this transaction).

(r) Recognition of usage of an asset

The assets of a business may be classified as either current or non-current. When cash is paid to acquire a current or non-current asset, the item is treated as an asset on purchase. The cost of these assets must be recognised as an expense as they are used to produce income. Once an asset has been used it becomes an expense.

On the left of the accounting equation the asset column is decreased by the portion of the asset used. The other side of the transaction is to decrease the owner's equity column representing a decrease in the owner's interest in the entity.

3.4 Analysis of transactions and preparation of financial statements using the accounting equation

In Chapter 1 we mentioned that accounting is an information system which selects data, processes that data and produces information about an economic entity. We mentioned further that data is processed through the accounting process. In Chapter 2 you learnt how to process data and prepare financial statements through a conceptual analysis of the transactions. We will now build on this by seeing how the accounting equation can help us process the data and produce information in the form of a statement of comprehensive income and statement of financial position.

3.4.1 Use of the accounting equation worksheet

The elements of the accounting equation need to be broken down into different classifications known as ***accounts***. We need a separate column on the accounting equation worksheet for each account. Assets are typically classified into accounts such as cash, accounts receivable, inventory, motor vehicles, computer and office equipment and supplies. Liabilities are typically classified into accounts such as accounts payable and borrowings. The individual accounts are used to classify the transactions in a useful manner and assist in the preparation of the financial statements.

3.4.2 Principles learnt from the accounting equation

The financial statements can be prepared with the use of the accounting equation. The accounting equation is set up as a worksheet showing the elements broken down into the different columns or accounts. Each transaction is entered into the worksheet after determining the effect it has on the entity's financial position. At the end of the accounting period a new financial position is determined, taking into account all the transactions that have taken place. The ***statement of financial position*** of the entity can then be prepared from the summarised information in the accounting equation. The total of each column represent the amounts of each asset, liability and the owner's equity for the statement of financial position.

		Assets			=		Liabilities		+	Owner's equity
Cash	+	Accounts receivable	+	Motor vehicles	=	Accounts payable	+	Borrowings	+	Owner's equity

Diagram 3.2: Columns in the accounting equation worksheet

You may have noticed while working through the transactions on the previous pages that owner's equity is affected by four types of transactions only:

C	Investment of **c**apital by the owner *increases* owner's equity
I	Earning of **i**ncome *increases* owner's equity
E	Incurral of **e**xpenses *decreases* owner's equity
D	**D**istribution of funds to the owner *decreases* owner's equity

Ignoring for the moment, items of other comprehensive income, only *income* and *expense* items affect profit. Funds invested by the owner do not represent income. Distributions to the owner do not represent expenses. Therefore to determine profit on the statement of comprehensive income from the information in the accounting equation, the owner's equity column needs to be analysed to identify those transactions that result in income being earned and expenses being incurred.

To assist in the preparation of the ***statement of comprehensive income***, the accounting equation worksheet can be modified with specific columns further analysing owner's equity. When a transaction is analysed and entered into the worksheet, it is very important to understand which transactions affect owner's equity, and whether it is a capital investment, the earning of income, the incurral of an expense or a distribution of funds. The statement of comprehensive income can then be prepared taking the information from the *income* and *expense* columns in the accounting equation worksheet.

Owner's equity						
Capital investment	+	Income	–	Expenses	–	Distributions
Investment	+		Profit		–	Distributions

Diagram 3.3: Components of owner's equity

The movement in owner's equity for a period can therefore be summarised as shown in the diagram below. It is very important that you fully understand the impact that each component has on the ending balance in owner's equity.

Owner's equity	
Balance at beginning of period	Bal BOY
Add capital investment	+ C
Add income	+ I
Less expenses	– E
Less distributions	– D
Balance at end of period	Bal EOY

Diagram 3.4: Movement in owner's equity

The statement of changes in equity, which was introduced in Chapter 2, is prepared to provide information to users about the changes in an entity's wealth during the period. You will recall from Chapter 2 that the statement of changes in equity presented both *owner* and *non-owner* changes in equity. The owner changes in equity included the contributions to capital by owners as well as the distributions to owners. The non-owner changes in equity comprised the income earned and expenses incurred, as represented by the total comprehensive income. You should therefore realise that the statement of changes in equity provides information about the four types of transactions that affect equity.

 **Pause and reflect...**

If a property was revalued during an accounting period, how would this affect owners equity and the statement of changes in equity?

Response

The revaluation of a property represents income as defined in the Accounting Framework. It therefore increases owners equity. Furthermore, the revaluation is an item of other comprehensive income and is included in total comprehensive income. It is therefore reported on the statement of changes in equity as part of total comprehensive income.

3.5 Example: Analysis of transactions using the accounting equation worksheet and the preparation of financial statements from the worksheet

The following is a record of the transactions of Smart Concepts, a computer retailer, for the period from 1 January 20X5 to 31 March 20X5. These are the same transactions that we analysed on a conceptual level in Chapter 2. You must not forget the concepts taught in the previous chapters when analysing transactions using the accounting equation. The explanation which follows this example incorporates the conceptual framework with the explanation of each transaction on the accounting equation worksheet, and with the preparation of the statement of comprehensive income, statement of financial position and statement of changes in equity.

External transactions

1. On 2 January, Simon Smart started a business as a computer retailer. He drew R950 000 from a savings account and opened a bank account in the name of Smart Concepts into which he paid R950 000.
2. On 2 January, Smart Concepts negotiated a loan from Techno Bank for an amount of R600 000. The loan is repayable in four equal annual installments, beginning on 31 December 20X5. The interest rate is 12% per annum, payable quarterly in arrears.
3. On 2 January, Simon located premises from which to operate in Rosebank. The monthly rent for the premises is R12 000. Smart Concepts paid four months rent in advance.
4. On 2 January, Simon transferred R120 000 from the bank account into a fixed deposit account earning interest at 5% per annum.

5. On 2 January, Smart Concepts purchased furniture and fittings for R240 000. This was paid for from funds in the bank account. The expected useful life of the furniture and fittings is five years.
6. On 5 January, Smart Concepts purchased supplies of stationery for R5 000 as well as supplies of computer parts for R12 000. All the supplies were paid for in cash.
7. On 7 January, Smart Concepts opened an account with Computer World, the supplier of its inventory.
8. On 10 January, Smart Concepts purchased inventory of sixty computers from Computer World at a cost of R10 000 each. The total amount owing is to be paid by 25 March.
9. On 12 January, Smart Concepts paid a service provider R750 in respect of a data bundle for internet access.
10. On 25 January, Smart Concepts sold fifteen computers on account to a customer for R12 500 each. An amount of R125 000 is due by 15 March and the balance by 15 April.
11. On 1 February, Smart Concepts employed a computer technician at a salary of R8 000 per month.
12. On 8 February, Smart Concepts paid R7 000 for an advertisement in a newspaper, advertising the computers available for sale.
13. On 12 February, Smart Concepts sold thirty computers, to customers, for R12 500 each. The customers paid cash for the computers.
14. On 25 February, Smart Concepts received cash of R48 000 in respect of technical support contracts taken out by customers. The contracts are for a two year period.
15. On 28 February, Smart Concepts paid the computer technician his salary for February.
16. On 4 March, Smart Concepts purchased inventory of a further seventy five computers from Computer World at a cost of R10 000 each. The total amount owing is to be paid by 25 May.
17. On 5 March, Smart Concepts paid a service provider R750 in respect of a data bundle for internet access.
18. On 15 March, Smart Concepts received R125 000 from the customer in transaction 10.
19. On 25 March, Smart Concepts paid Computer World an amount of R600 000.
20. On 29 March, Smart Concepts sold thirty computers, to customers, for R12 500 each. The customers paid cash for the computers.
21. On 30 March, Smart Concepts paid the computer technician his salary for March.
22. On 30 March, Smart Concepts paid the interest on the loan from Techno Bank for the three month period.
23. On 30 March, Simon authorised a distribution to himself of R60 000 for personal use.

Internal transactions

24. On 31 March, Simon examined the records of the business and established that technical support in respect of contracts to the value of R6 000 had been provided to customers.
25. On 31 March, Smart Concepts accounted for the interest on the fixed deposit earned for the period.
26. On 31 March, Smart Concepts recognised the rent expense incurred for the period.
27. On 31 March, the telephone account for R1 500 and the electricity account for R2 500 had been received but not paid.
28. On 31 March, Simon counted stationery supplies on hand costing R2 000 and also determined from the records that computer parts costing R8 500 had been used.
29. On 31 March, Smart Concepts accounted for the usage of the furniture and fittings for the period.

You are required to:

- ❑ enter the above transactions in the accounting equation worksheet
- ❑ prepare for Smart Concepts, an income statement and statement of charges in equity for the three-month period ended 31 March 20X5 and a statement of financial position at 31 March 20X5.

Solution: Analysing transactions and preparation of financial statements using the accounting equation.

Each transaction is analysed and explained with an extract of the relevant line of the accounting equation worksheet. On page 75 the complete worksheet is provided, before preparing the income statement and statement of financial position.

1	Assets	=	Liabilities	+	Owner's equity
	Bank				Capital
	950 000	=			950 000 (C)

On 2 January, the owner, Simon Smart, invested funds into the business entity. The funds introduced to the entity increase the bank column on the left side of the equation by R950 000. The owner introduced the funds; therefore the owner's equity column on the right side of the equation is increased by R950 000.

2	Assets	=	Liabilities	+	Owner's equity
	Bank		Borrowings		
	600 000	=	600 000		

On 2 January, Smart Concepts negotiated a loan of R600 000 from Techno Bank. The loan will increase the bank column on the left side of the equation by R600 000. The funds are under the control of Smart Concepts which will derive future economic benefits from their use. The other side of the transaction is to increase the borrowings column by R600 000 on the right side of the equation. This is an obligation which will result in an outflow of resources in the future.

3	Assets			=	Liabilities	+	Owner's equity
	Bank		Rent asset				
	(48 000)	+	48 000	=			

On 2 January the entity paid four months' rent in advance. Prepaid rent is an asset because, upon prepayment, the entity has the right to occupy the building that will be used to provide the services which will contribute to the inflow of future economic benefits. By prepaying rent the entity gives up one asset, cash, and receives another, the right of occupancy. Therefore the bank column is decreased by R48 000 and the rent asset column is increased by R48 000.

4	Assets		=	Liabilities	+	Owner's equity
Bank		Fixed deposit investment				
(120 000)	+	120 000				

On 2 January, Simon transferred R120 000 from the business bank account to a fixed deposit. The fixed deposit is an asset from which interest income will be earned. The effect on the accounting equation is to increase one asset, the fixed deposit investment, by R120 000 and decrease another asset, bank, by R120 000.

5	Assets		=	Liabilities	+	Owner's equity
Bank		Furniture & fittings				
(240 000)	+	240 000				

On 2 January Smart Concepts purchased R240 000 of furniture and fittings for cash. The furniture and fittings column on the left side of the equation must be increased. These assets are now under the control of Smart Concepts. The other side of the transaction is to record the payment. The bank column, also on the left side of the equation, must be decreased by R240 000.

6	Assets				=	Liabilities	+	Owner's equity
Bank		Stationery supplies asset		Computer parts asset				
(17 000)	+	5 000	+	12 000				

On 5 January, Smart Concepts purchased stationery as well as computer parts for cash. The supplies and the parts are assets. The entity will use these assets in providing services which will contribute to the earning of income. The effect on the accounting equation is to increase the stationery supplies asset on the left side by R5 000, to increase the computer parts asset on the left side by R12 000, and to decrease the bank column also on the left side of the equation by R17 000.

7	Assets	=	Liabilities	+	Owner's equity
	No effect on the accounting equation				

On 7 January, Smart Concepts opened an account with Computer World, the supplier of its inventory. This event has no effect on the accounting equation since no financial transaction has taken place.

8	Assets	=	Liabilities	+	Owner's equity
	Inventory		Accounts payable		
	600 000	=	600 000		

On 10 January Smart Concepts purchased inventory of R600 000 on account. The purchase increases the inventory column on the left side of the equation. The computers are controlled by Smart Concepts and will generate future economic benefits when they are sold. The other side of the transaction is to increase the accounts payable column on the right side of the equation. This is an obligation which will result in outflow of resources when the amount is paid.

9	Assets	=	Liabilities	+	Owner's equity
	Bank				Internet expense
	(750)	=		+	(750) (E)

On 12 January, Smart Concepts paid a service provider R750 in respect of a data bundle for internet access. The payment represents an outflow of resources from the enterprise and will reduce the bank column on the left hand side of the accounting equation. Internet access is required in order to access emails and operate a website and is therefore a necessary expense incurred in order to earn income. The other side of the transaction decreases owners equity on the right side of the equation by recording R750 in the internet expense column.

10	Assets		=	Liabilities	+	Owner's equity	
	Accounts receivable	Inventory				Sales revenue	Cost of sales
	187 500		=			187 500 (I)	
		(150 000)	=				(150 000) (E)

On 25 January, Smart Concepts sold fifteen computers on account to a customer. The customer was billed R187 500, of which R125 000 was payable by 15 March and the balance by 15 April. Smart Concepts has a right to receive the amount of R187 500 in the future. Therefore, on the left side of the equation we increase accounts receivable by R187 500. The other side of the transaction is to increase owner's equity on the right side of the equation for the income earned by increasing the sales revenue column by R187 500. At the same time, we decrease owner's equity on the right side of the equation by recording R150 000 in the cost of sales column. In addition, the inventory column on the left side of the equation is decreased by R150 000 due to the outflow of resources embodied in the inventory now sold.

11	Assets	=	Liabilities	+	Owner's equity
	No effect on the accounting equation				

On 1 February, Smart Concepts employed a technician. This transaction has no effect on the accounting equation since there has been no economic impact.

12	Assets	=	Liabilities	+	Owner's equity
	Bank				Advertising expense
	(7 000)	=			(7 000) (E)

On 8 February Smart Concepts paid R7 000 for an advertisement in a newspaper. The payment represents an outflow of resources from the entity, and will reduce the bank column by R7 000 on the left side of the equation. The advertisement is used to gain new customers. Advertising is therefore an expense incurred in order to earn income. The other side of the transaction will decrease owner's equity on the right side of the equation by recording the R7 000 in the advertising expense column.

13	Assets		=	Liabilities	+ Owner's equity	
	Bank	Inventory	=		Sales revenue	Cost of sales
	375 000				375 000 (I)	
		(300 000)	=			(300 000) (E)

On 12 February, Smart Concepts sold thirty computers for cash. The R375 000 received is an inflow of cash. The bank column on the left side of the equation is increased by R375 000. The other side of the transaction is to increase owner's equity on the right side of the equation for the income earned by increasing the sales revenue column by R375 000. At the same time, we decrease owner's equity on the right side of the equation by increasing the cost of sales column by R300 000. In addition, the inventory column on the left side of the equation is decreased by R300 000 due to the outflow of resources embodied in the inventory now sold.

14	Assets	=	Liabilities	+	Owner's equity
	Bank		Service liability		
	48 000	=	48 000		

On 25 February Smart Concepts received R48 000 in respect of technical support contracts taken out by customers. The R48 000 received is an inflow of cash. The bank column on the left side of the equation is increased by R48 000. Smart Concepts has an obligation to perform services to the value of R48 000. This represents a liability and increases the service liability column on the right side of the equation by R48 000. No income can be recognised as the services have not yet been performed.

15	Assets	=	Liabilities	+	Owner's equity
	Bank				Salaries expense
	(8 000)	=			(8 000) (E)

On 28 February, the technician was paid R8 000 for the month. The payment represents an outflow of funds from the entity, and reduces the bank column by R8 000 on the left side of the equation. The assistant helps Smart Concepts to generate service revenue. Salaries are therefore an expense incurred in order to earn income. The other side of the transaction decreases owner's equity on the right side of the equation by recording the R8 000 in the salaries expense column.

16	Assets	=	Liabilities	+	Owner's equity
	Inventory		Accounts payable		
	750 000	=	750 000		

On 4 March Smart Concepts purchased inventory of R750 000 on account. The purchase increases the inventory column on the left side of the equation. The computers are controlled by Smart Concepts and will generate future economic benefits when they are sold. The other side of the transaction is to increase the accounts payable column on the right side of the equation. This is an obligation which will result in outflow of resources when the amount is paid.

17	Assets	=	Liabilities	+	Owner's equity
	Bank				Internet expense
	(750)			+	(750) (E)

This transaction, on 5 March, is the same as transaction 9 on 12 January.

18	Assets			=	Liabilities	+	Owner's equity
	Bank		Accounts receivable				
	125 000	+	(125 000)				

On 15 March a customer paid Smart Concepts an amount of R125 000. The R125 000 is an inflow of cash which will increase the bank column on the left side of the equation. The other side of the transaction reduces the accounts receivable column by R125 000.

19	Assets		=	Liabilities	+	Owner's equity
	Bank			Accounts payable		
	(600 000)		=	(600 000)		

On 25 March Smart Concepts paid Computer World an amount of R600 000. This transaction results in an outflow of cash which reduces the bank column on the left side of the equation by R600 000. The cash was used to settle a liability, and the other side of the transaction reduces the accounts payable column on the right side of the equation by R600 000.

20	Assets		=	Liabilities	+	Owner's equity	
	Bank	Inventory				Sales revenue	Cost of sales
	375 000		=			375 000 (I)	
		(300 000)	=				(300 000) (E)

On 29 March Smart Concepts sold thirty computers for cash. The effect on the accounting equation is the same as explained for transaction 13 on 12 February.

21	Assets		=	Liabilities	+	Owner's equity
	Bank					Salaries expense
	(8 000)		=			(8 000) (E)

This transaction, on 30 March, is the same as transaction 15 on 28 February.

22	Assets		=	Liabilities	+	Owner's equity
	Bank					Interest expense
	(18 000)		=			(18 000) (E)

On 30 March Smart Concepts paid the interest for the first quarter of R18 000. This transaction results in an outflow of cash which reduces the bank column on the left side of the equation by R18 000. Interest is an expense representing the cost of the borrowed funds. The other side of the transaction decreases owner's equity on the right side of the equation by recording R18 000 in the interest expense column.

23	Assets	=	Liabilities	+	Owner's equity
	Bank				Distribution
	(60 000)	=			(60 000) (D)

On 30 March Simon Smart withdrew R60 000 cash from the business for personal use. The R60 000 outflow of cash will reduce the bank column on the left side of the accounting equation. The distribution represents a decrease in the owner's claim against the assets of the business. The other side of the transaction decreases owner's equity on the right side of the equation by recording the R60 000 in the distribution column.

24	Assets	=	Liabilities	+	Owner's equity
			Service liability		Service revenue
			(6 000)	+	6 000 (I)

Smart Concepts' service records show that R6 000 of the cash received from customers in respect of technical support contracts (see transaction 14) has now been earned. The service liability column on the right side of the equation must be reduced, and the service revenue column, also on the right side of the equation, is increased by the amount earned of R6 000.

25	Assets	=	Liabilities	+	Owner's equity
	Interest asset				Interest revenue
	1 500	=			1 500 (I)

In transaction 4, R120 000 was transferred to a fixed deposit account earning interest at 5% per annum. On 31 March three months' interest of R1 500 has been earned. As a result, the interest revenue column on the right side of the equation is increased to reflect the income earned. The other side of the transaction is to increase the interest asset column on the left side of the equation.

26	Assets	=	Liabilities	+	Owner's equity
	Rent asset				Rent expense
	(36 000)	=			(36 000) (E)

On 31 March Smart Concepts accounted for the rent expense. At the beginning of the period four months' rent was paid in advance. This was recorded in the rent asset column since the entity had the right to occupy the building for four months. At the end of the period the entity has the right to occupy the building for one more month; therefore the three months need to be accounted for as being used. The rent asset column on the left side of the equation is decreased by R36 000, representing three months' rent. The other side of the transaction decreases owner's equity on the right side of the equation by recording R36 000 as rent expense for the period.

27	Assets	=	Liabilities	+	Owner's equity
			Telephone and electricity liability		Telephone and electricity expense
			4 000	+	(4 000) (E)

On 31 March, the telephone account for R1 500 and the electricity account for R2 500 were received. However, they have not yet been paid. Therefore the telephone and electricity liability column is increased by R4 000 to reflect the amount owing. The other side of the transaction decreases owner's equity on the right side of the equation by recording R4 000 in the telephone and electricity expense column.

28	Assets			=	Liabilities	+	Owner's equity
	Stationery supplies asset		Computer parts asset		Stationery supplies expense		Computer parts expense
	(3 000)	+	(8 500)	=	(3 000) (E)	+	(8 500) (E)

On 31 March, the stationery supplies on hand amounted to R2 000. This means that during the period R3 000 of supplies of stationery were used. The stationery supplies asset is decreased by R3 000 on the left side of the equation. The other side of the transaction decreases owner's equity on the right side of the equation by recording R3 000 in the stationery supplies expense column. Simon also determined that computer parts costing R8 500 had been used. The computer parts asset is decreased by R8 500 on the left side of the equation. The other side of the transaction decreases owner's equity on the right side of the equation by recording R8 500 in the computer parts expense column.

29	Assets	=	Liabilities	+	Owner's equity
	Furniture and fittings				Asset usage expense
	(12 000)	=			(12 000) (E)

The furniture and fittings need to be expensed over the periods when they are used to earn income. The total asset usage expense of R12 000 reduces the owner's equity column on the right hand side of the equation. The other side of the entry reduces the asset on the left side of the equation.

Solution: Analysing transactions and preparation of financial statements using the accounting equation

(All figures have been rounded to R000s)

	ASSETS								=	LIABILITIES			+	OWNER'S EQUITY			
No	Bank +	Rent asset +	Fixed deposit investment +	Accounts receivable +	Stationery supplies asset +	Computer parts asset +	Furniture and fittings +	Inventory +	Interest asset	Telephone and electricity liability –	Service liability +	Accounts payable +	Borrowings	S Smart capital +	Income –	Expenses –	Distributions
1	950													950			
2	600												600				
3	(48)	48															
4	(120)		120														
5	(240)						240										
6	(17)				5	12											
7																	
8								600				600					
9	(0,75)															(0,75)	
10				187,5				(150)							187,5	(150)	
11																	
12	(7)															(7)	
13	375							(300)							375	(300)	
14	48										48						
15	(8)															(8)	
16								750				750					
17	(0,75)															(0,75)	
18	125			(125)													
19	(600)											(600)					
20	375							(300)							375	(300)	
21	(8)															(8)	
22	(18)															(18)	
23	(60)																(60)
	1 345,5	48	120	62,5	5	12	240	600			48	750	600	950	937,5	(792,5)	(60)
24											(6)				6		
25									1,5						1,5		
26		(36)														(36)	
27										4						(4)	
28					(3)	(8,5)										(11,5)	
29							(12)									(12)	
	1 345,5 +	12 +	120 +	62,5 +	2 +	3,5 +	223 +	600 +	1,5	4 +	42 +	750 +	600	950 +	945 +	(856) +	(60)
	ASSETS = 2 370									**LIABILITIES = 1 396**				**OWNER'S EQUITY = 979**			

SMART CONCEPTS
INCOME STATEMENT
FOR THE THREE MONTHS ENDED 31 MARCH 20X5

	R
INCOME	945 000
Sales revenue	937 500
Service revenue	6 000
Interest revenue	1 500
EXPENSES	(856 000)
Cost of sales	750 000
Internet expense	1 500
Advertising	7 000
Salaries	16 000
Interest expense	18 000
Rent expense	36 000
Telephone & electricity expense	4 000
Stationery supplies expense	3 000
Computer parts expense	8 500
Asset usage expense	12 000
Profit for the period	89 000

SMART CONCEPTS
STATEMENT OF FINANCIAL POSITION
AT 31 MARCH 20X5

	R
ASSETS	2 375 000
Furniture and fittings	228 000
Fixed deposit investment	120 000
Inventory	600 000
Accounts receivable	62 500
Stationery supplies asset	2 000
Computer parts asset	3 500
Rent asset	12 000
Interest asset	1 500
Bank	1 345 500
	2 375 000
OWNERS EQUITY	979 000
LIABILITIES	1 396 000
Borrowings	600 000
Accounts payable	750 000
Service liability	42 000
Telephone and electricity liability	4 000
	2 375 000

SMART CONCEPTS
STATEMENT OF CHANGES IN EQUITY
FOR THE PERIOD ENDED 31 MARCH 20X5

	R
Balance at 1 January 20X5	-
Profit for the period	89 000
Distributions	(60 000)
Contribution to capital	950 000
Balance at 31 March 20X5	979 000

3.6 Conceptual proof of profit

Changes in an entity's equity between two reporting dates reflect the increase or decrease in its net assets or wealth during the period under review. Except for changes resulting from transactions with owners (capital contributions and distributions), the overall change in equity represents the profit or loss generated by the entity's activities during the period.[1]

Assuming no items of other comprehensive income, the *profit* can be calculated without details of the income and expenses, provided the following information is available:

- opening balance in owner's equity
- closing balance in owner's equity
- investment of capital by the owner, and
- distributions to the owner.

The movement in the owner's equity account is first calculated by subtracting the opening balance from the closing balance. The movement in the account is due to investments by the owner (which increase owner's equity), profit for the period (which also increases owner's equity) and distributions to the owner (which decrease owner's equity). Therefore profit can be calculated by reversing the effects of the investments and distributions; in other words, by subtracting the amount of the investments and adding back the amount of the distributions. This is illustrated in the following diagram:

Balance at end of year	Bal EOY
Balance at beginning of year	Bal BOY
	Movement
Add Distributions	+ D
Less Capital invested by owner	– C
Profit for the period	P

Diagram 3.5: Conceptual proof of profit

Example: Calculation of profit using the principles learnt from the accounting equation

A business entity had the following assets and liabilities at the beginning and at the end of the year:

	Assets	Liabilities
	R	R
Beginning of the year (BOY)	65 000	20 000
End of the year (EOY)	70 000	10 000

There are no items of other comprehensive income.

You are required to:

determine the profit or loss of the business entity during the year under each of the following unrelated assumptions:

1) There were no capital contributions by the owner and no distributions to the owner during the year.
2) There were no capital contributions by the owner but a distribution to the owner of R1 500 per month was made to cover personal living expenses.
3) There were no distributions to the owner but a capital contribution by the owner of R20 000 was made during the year.
4) A capital contribution by the owner of R10 000 was made during the year and a distribution to the owner of R1 500 per month was made to cover personal living expenses.

Solution: Calculation of profit using the principles learnt from the accounting equation

To calculate the profit for the period in the above example, the following information is required:

- opening balance in the owner's equity account
- closing balance in the owner's equity account
- any contributions by the owner, and
- any distributions to the owner.

Since we know the opening and closing balances for the assets and liabilities we must use the accounting equation to calculate the owner's equity balances at the respective dates.

After calculating the opening and closing balances on the owner's equity account, we need to work out the movement in the account for the year by subtracting the opening balance from the closing balance.

This movement represents contributions by the owner, plus profit, less distributions. Therefore, if we adjust for the investments and distributions, the balancing figure will be the profit for the period.

Owner's equity calculation

	Owner's equity R	=	Assets R	–	Liabilities R
BOY	?	=	65 000	–	20 000
	45 000	=	65 000	–	20 000
EOY	?	=	70 000	–	10 000
	60 000	=	70 000	–	10 000

Profit calculation

1)	R
Ending owner's equity	60 000
Opening owner's equity	(45 000)
Profit	15 000

In the first situation the there were no contributions from or distribution to the owner during the year. Therefore the movement in the owner's equity account represents the profit for the period.

2)	R
Ending owner's equity	60 000
Opening owner's equity	(45 000)
Movement	15 000
Distribution (R1 500 x 12)	18 000
Profit	33 000

In the second situation there was a distribution to the owner of R18 000 during the year. Therefore we reverse the effect of the distribution to calculate the profit for the period.

3)	R
Ending owner's equity	60 000
Opening owner's equity	(45 000)
Movement	15 000
Capital invested by owner	(20 000)
Loss	(5 000)

In the third situation there was a contribution of R20 000 by the owner during the year. Therefore we reverse the effect of the contribution to calculate the profit for the period.

4)

	R
Ending owner's equity	60 000
Opening owner's equity	(45 000)
Movement	15 000
Distribution	12 000
Capital invested by owner	(10 000)
Profit	17 000

In the fourth situation R12 000 was distributed to the owner during the year and an additional R10 000 contributed by the owner. Therefore we reverse the effect of the distribution and reverse the effect of the contribution to calculate the profit for the period.

3.7 Exam example

The records of Landmark Estates show the following assets and liabilities at 31 December 20X8 and 20X9.

	31 DECEMBER	
	20X8	**20X9**
	R	**R**
Bank	2 300	500
Accounts receivable	1 200	600
Office supplies (asset)	700	550
Vehicle	6 200	6 200
Office equipment	2 800	6 250
Land and buildings	–	165 000
Accounts payable	750	1 050
Loan: Citibank	–	112 500

During December 20X9 land and buildings costing R165 000 were purchased by the entity. The entity paid R52 500 in cash and borrowed the balance of the necessary funds from Citibank. G Landsman, the owner, had to contribute an additional R45 000 in the entity to enable it to pay the R52 500. The entity earned sufficient profits during 20X9 to enable Mr Landsman to withdraw R3 000 per month to pay personal living expenses.

You are required to:

calculate the profit earned by Landmark Estates during 20X9.

Solution: Exam example

	20X8	20X9
First calculate the owner's equity balance at the end of each year.		
	R	R
Assets	13 200	179 100
Bank	2 300	500
Accounts receivable	1 200	600
Office supplies	700	550
Vehicle	6 200	6 200
Office equipment	2 800	6 250
Land and buildings	–	165 000
Liabilities	750	113 550
Accounts payable	750	1 050
Loan: Citibank	–	112 500
Owner's equity at end of year	12 450	65 550

Profit calculation for 20X9	R
Owner's equity at 31/12/X9	65 550
Owner's equity at 31/12/X8	(12 450)
Movement	53 100
Add Distribution (3 000 x 12)	36 000
Less Contribution	(45 000)
Profit for 20X9	44 100

Summary of concepts and applications

1. Transactions are economic events that have an impact on the financial position of an entity. External transactions occur between the entity and another party, whereas internal transactions are internal adjustments made to the financial position of an entity in applying the accrual basis of accounting.

2. The accounting equation is a simple representation of the statement of financial position of a business entity and exists because owner's funds and borrowed funds represent the claims on the assets of the entity. The equation is 'Assets = liabilities + owner's equity'.

3. Transactions can be analysed using the accounting equation. This is achieved by separating the equation into a left side and right side and developing an accounting equation worksheet. Each transaction needs to be analysed to determine its effect on the accounting equation, which must always be in balance.
4. The accounting equation worksheet is constructed by creating account classifications. Each transaction is entered into the worksheet after determining the effect it has on the entity's financial position.
5. Transactions are analysed by entering each transaction as a line item on the accounting equation worksheet. The statement of financial position is prepared by extracting the balances from the asset, liability and owner's equity columns on the worksheet. The income statement is prepared by examining the income and expense columns within owner's equity.
6. Changes in owner's equity between two reporting dates reflect the increase or decrease in net assets or wealth during the period. The overall change in equity, apart from changes resulting from transactions with owners, represents the profit or loss generated by the entity's activities during the period.

Note

1. IAS 1, Presentation of Financial Statements, *The International Accounting Standards Board*, (2007), paragraph 109.

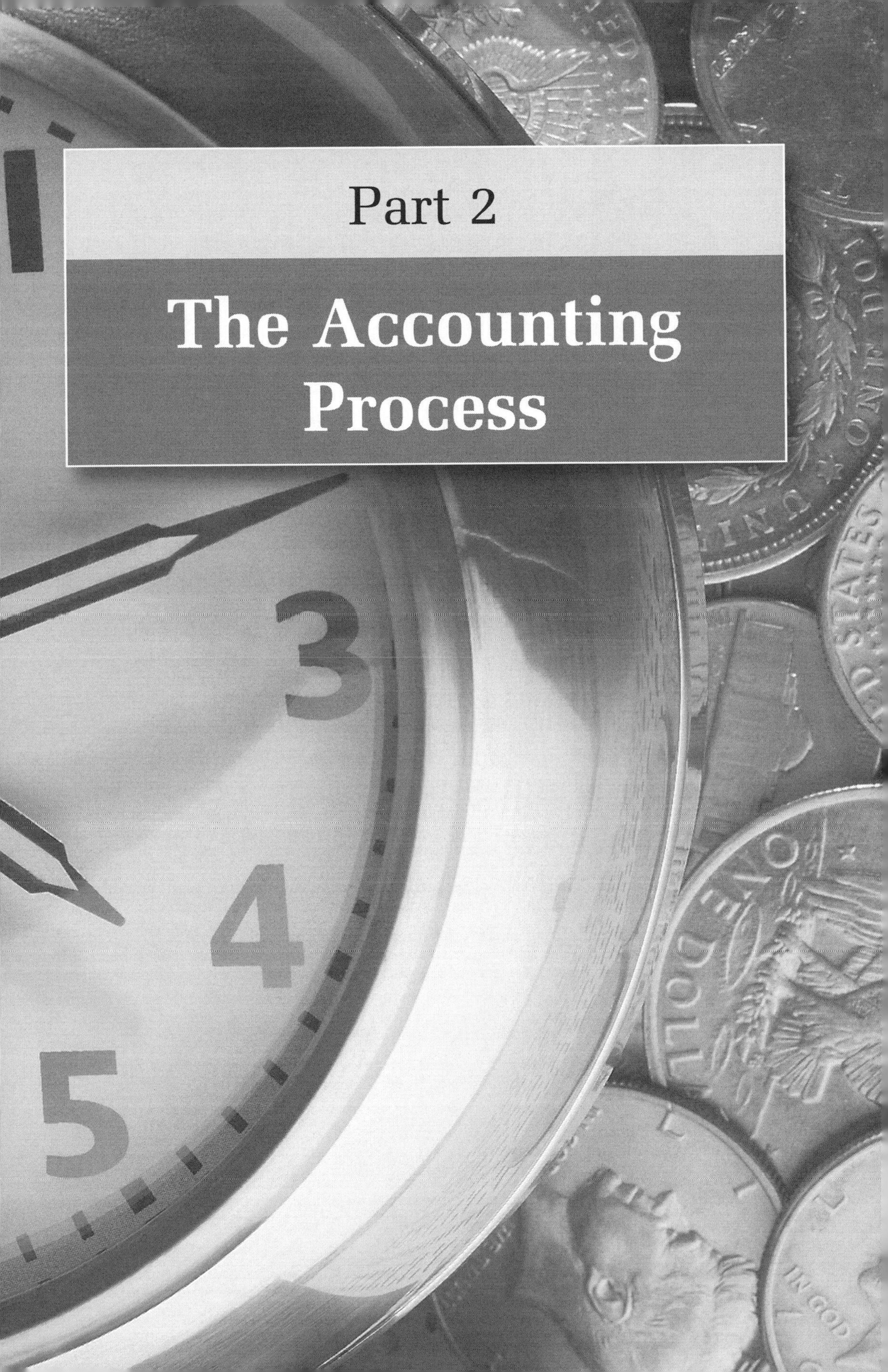

Part 2

The Accounting Process

4 Recording External Transactions

'The system of bookkeeping by double entry is one of consummate beauty.'
(Scott, 1820)

Outcomes

- Explain the accounting process.
- Describe the double-entry accounting system.
- Analyse transactions using the double-entry accounting system.
- Explain the purpose and structure of the general journal and prepare a general journal.
- Explain the purpose and structure of the general ledger and prepare a general ledger.
- Demonstrate the process of balancing the accounts and preparing a trial balance.

Chapter outline

BHP Billiton Limited
Income Statement for the year ended 31 June 2007

	($ millions)
Revenue	47 473
Cost of Sales	(17 981)
Gross profit	27 492
Expenses	(7 768)
Profit before tax	19 724
Tax	(5 716)
Profit for the period	14 008

With over $47 billion in revenue, BHP executes a huge number of transactions with its customers and suppliers every day. If it is a resource, BHP will produce it. From aluminium to zinc, BHP made 240 000 deliveries to more than 1 300 customers creating a mass of external transactions.

4.1 The accounting process

We mentioned in Chapter 1 that accounting is an information system that selects data, processes that data and produces information about an economic entity. In Chapter 2, the data was processed on a conceptual level to produce information in the form of a statement of comprehensive income, or a separate income statement and a statement of financial position.

In Chapter 3, you were introduced to the accounting equation and were shown how to process data using the accounting equation worksheet. This is one of the clearest methods of demonstrating the dual nature of recording transactions. In other words, for every left-hand entry there must be a right-hand entry of equal amount. The problem with this approach is that it is too cumbersome to use in practice as most business entities have many different assets, liabilities, income and expense items which lead to a very large number of columns in the accounting equation worksheet.

In this chapter we turn our attention to the processing of data using double-entry bookkeeping. It is stressed that the principles do not change - in fact you will see that double-entry bookkeeping is a direct outgrowth of the accounting equation. It is necessary before explaining the principles of double-entry bookkeeping to refer again to our definition of accounting and place it in the context of the accounting process. Refer to diagram 4.1, remembering that accounting is an information system that selects data, processes that data and produces information about an economic entity. Only **data** which has an economic impact on the entity is analysed as a transaction in order to determine the effect on the accounting equation. Data is **processed** through the accounting process by means of an activity known as bookkeeping. This involves recording the effects of the transactions in a *journal*, from there classifying it by transferring the recorded effects into accounts in a *ledger*, and then summarising the information in each account by preparing a *trial balance*. The final stage of the accounting process, the **producing of information** for users, involves adjusting the information in the ledger accounts to conform with the accrual basis of accounting, then preparing the annual financial statements, and finally closing the accounts for the year. These last steps of the accounting process are covered in Chapters 5 to 7. Chapter 5 deals with adjusting entries, Chapter 6 covers the preparation of financial statements and Chapter 7 completes the accounting process with closing entries.

4.2 Double-entry accounting

You learnt in Chapter 3 that every transaction affects and is recorded in two or more accounts. Also, in recording each transaction, the equality of the accounting equation must be maintained at all times. The left-hand side of the accounting equation represents the entity's assets and the right-hand side, the claims on the assets, or the entity's liabilities and owner's equity. Each asset, liability or owner's equity account can be split down the middle, with a left-hand side and a right-hand side.

In double-entry accounting, increases in assets are recorded on the left-hand side of asset accounts, for no reason other than that assets are typically shown on the left-hand side of the accounting equation. It follows, therefore, that increases in liabilities and owner's equity are recorded on the right-hand side of those accounts in order to maintain the equality of the accounting equation. In other words, if assets are increased with left-hand entries, the accounting equation will balance only if increases in liabilities and owner's equity are recorded on the opposite or right-hand side.

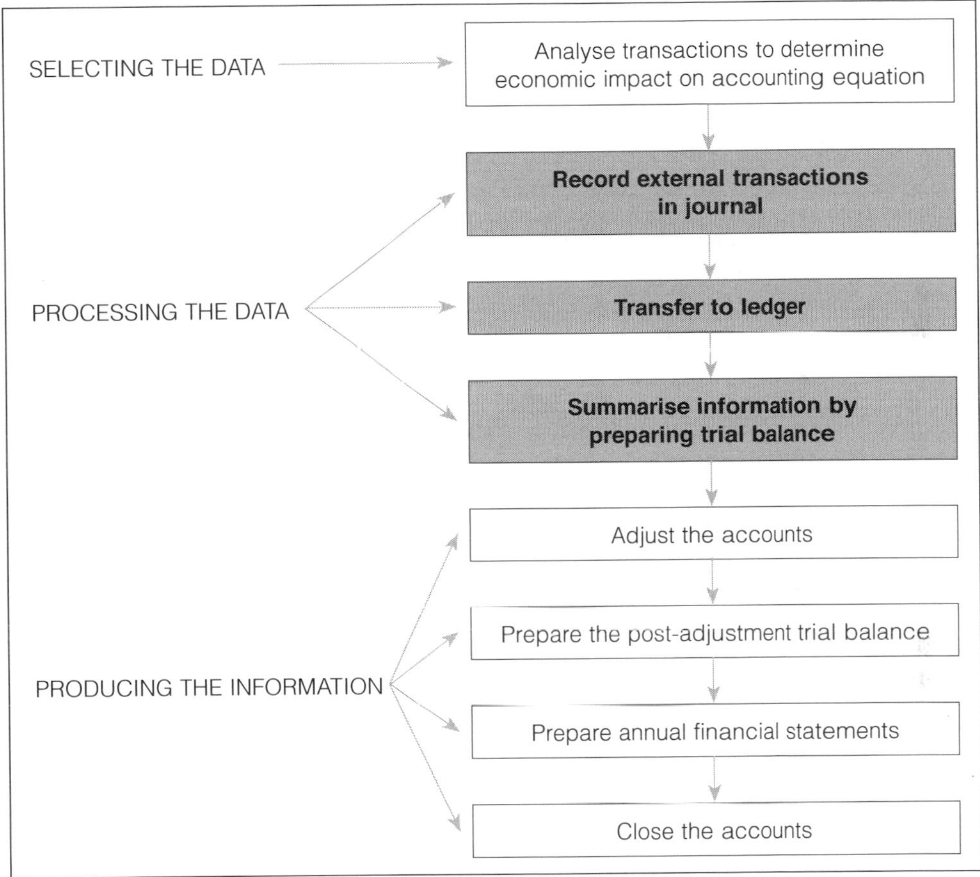

Diagram 4.1: The accounting process

Furthermore, the left-hand side of each account is called the ***debit*** side, abbreviated 'Dr' and the right-hand side of each account is called the ***credit*** side, abbreviated 'Cr'. There are no good or bad connotations attached to debit or credit *per se*, rather they are merely labels used to describe the left and right side of accounts. Remember that an account is simply a representation of a column in the accounting equation worksheet.

Diagram 4.2 summarises the principles of the double-entry system, which are then discussed in detail.

Left-hand side of accounting equation	=	**Right-hand side of accounting equation**		
Assets	=	**Claims on the assets**		
Assets	=	Liabilities	+	Owner's equity

Assets: *Left*	Assets: *Right*	Liabilities: *Left*	Liabilities: *Right*	Owner's equity: *Left*	Owner's equity: *Right*
+	–	–	+	–	+
Dr	*Cr*	*Dr*	*Cr*	*Dr*	*Cr*

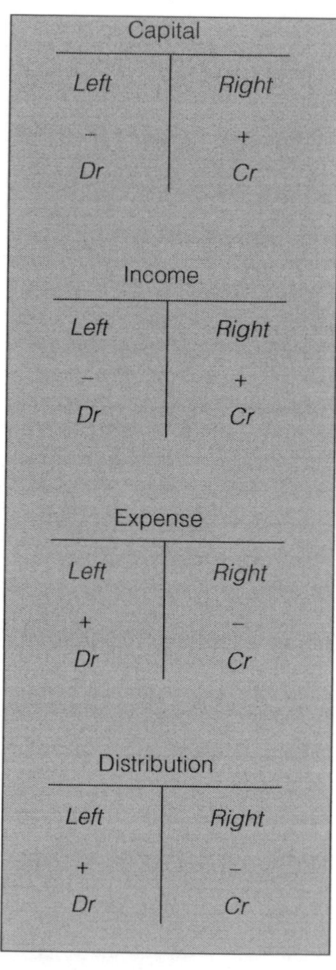

Diagram 4.2: Principles of the double-entry system

Looking at each element of the accounting equation in diagram 4.2, we can expand on the double-entry principles as follows:

- **Assets** are on the left-hand side of the equation, thus
  - increases in assets are recorded on the left side of the asset account as a debit.
  - decreases in assets are recorded on the right side of the asset account as a credit.
- **Liabilities** are on the right-hand side of the equation, thus
  - increases in liabilities are recorded on the right side of the liability account as a credit.
  - decreases in liabilities are recorded on the left side of the liability account as a debit.
- **Owner's equity**, although also on the right-hand side of the equation, requires more thought. As you should recall, there are only four types of transactions that affect owner's equity – investments by the owner, distributions to the owner, the earning of income and the incurral of expenses. Investments by the owner and distributions to the owner do not affect the income statement and therefore
  - increases in owner's equity as a result of investments by the owner are recorded on the right side of the owner's equity account as a credit.
  - decreases in owner's equity as a result of distributions to the owner are recorded on the left side of the distributions account as a debit.

The earning of income and the incurral of expenses do affect the income statement and also affect owner's equity.

- **Income** increases owner's equity, which is on the right side of the equation, thus
  - increases in income (which increase owner's equity) are recorded on the right side of the income account as a credit.
  - decreases in income (which decrease owner's equity) are recorded on the left side of the income account as a debit.
- **Expenses** decrease owner's equity, which again, it is emphasised, is on the right side of the equation, thus
  - increases in expenses (which decrease owner's equity) are recorded on the left side of the expense account as a debit.
  - decreases in expenses (which increase owner's equity) are recorded on the right side of the expense account as a credit.

You will notice that the principle which governs the recording of movements in income and expense items is based on the effect that the transaction has on owner's equity. As the earning of income increases owner's equity, increases in income are recorded on the right side of the income account as a credit because increases in owner's equity are recorded on the right side as a credit. Conversely, as the incurral of expenses decreases owner's equity, increases in expenses are recorded on the left side of expense accounts as a debit because decreases in owner's equity are recorded on the left side as a debit.

These are the principles of double-entry bookkeeping, the language of accounting.

You may find that you need to memorise them now, but soon you will be using this language fluently.

 **Pause and reflect...**

You know that assets represent future economic benefits and that expenses are outflows of economic benefits. Yet, assets increase with a debit entry and expenses also increase with a debit entry. Why is that so?

Response

Assets are on the left side of the accounting equation and therefore increases in assets are recorded on the left side of the asset account as a debit. Expenses decrease owner's equity, which you will recall, is on the right side of the equation. Thus increases in expenses (which decrease owners equity) are recorded on the left side of the expense account as a debit.

4.3 Example: Analysis of transactions using double-entry accounting

The following is a record of the *external* transactions of Smart Concepts for the period from 1 January 20X5 to 31 March 20X5. Note that only the external transactions are analysed here – the internal transactions are analysed at a later stage in the accounting process.

External transactions

1. On 2 January, Simon Smart started a business as a computer retailer. He drew R950 000 from a savings account and opened a bank account in the name of Smart Concepts into which he paid R950 000.
2. On 2 January, Smart Concepts negotiated a loan from Techno Bank for an amount of R600 000. The loan is repayable in four equal annual installments, beginning on 31 December 20X5. The interest rate is 12% per annum, payable quarterly in arrears.
3. On 2 January, Simon located premises from which to operate in Rosebank. The monthly rent for the premises is R12 000. Smart Concepts paid four months rent in advance.
4. On 2 January, Simon transferred R120 000 from the bank account into a fixed deposit account earning interest at 5% per annum.
5. On 2 January, Smart Concepts purchased furniture and fittings for R240 000. This was paid for from funds in the bank account. The expected useful life of the furniture and fittings is five years.
6. On 5 January, Smart Concepts purchased supplies of stationery for R5 000 as well as supplies of computer parts for R12 000. All the supplies were paid for in cash.
7. On 7 January, Smart Concepts opened an account with Computer World, the supplier of its inventory.
8. On 10 January, Smart Concepts purchased inventory of sixty computers from Computer World at a cost of R10 000 each. The total amount owing is to be paid by 25 March.
9. On 12 January, Smart Concepts paid a service provider R750 in respect of a data bundle for internet access.
10. On 25 January, Smart Concepts sold fifteen computers on account to a customer for R12 500 each. An amount of R125 000 is due by 15 March and the balance by 15 April.
11. On 1 February, Smart Concepts employed a computer technician at a salary of R8 000 per month.

12. On 8 February, Smart Concepts paid R7 000 for an advertisement in a newspaper, advertising the computers available for sale.
13. On 12 February, Smart Concepts sold thirty computers, to customers, for R12 500 each. The customers paid cash for the computers.
14. On 25 February, Smart Concepts received cash of R48 000 in respect of technical support contracts taken out by customers. The contracts are for a two year period.
15. On 28 February, Smart Concepts paid the computer technician his salary for February.
16. On 4 March, Smart Concepts purchased inventory of a further seventy five computers from Computer World at a cost of R10 000 each. The total amount owing is to be paid by 25 May.
17. On 5 March, Smart Concepts paid a service provider R750 in respect of a data bundle for internet access.
18. On 15 March, Smart Concepts received R125 000 from the customer in transaction 10.
19. On 25 March, Smart Concepts paid Computer World an amount of R600 000.
20. On 29 March, Smart Concepts sold thirty computers, to customers, for R12 500 each. The customers paid cash for the computers.
21. On 30 March, Smart Concepts paid the computer technician his salary for March.
22. On 30 March, Smart Concepts paid the interest on the loan from Techno Bank for the three month period.
23. On 30 March, Simon authorised a distribution to himself of R60 000 for personal use.

You are required to:

analyse the above transactions of Smart Concepts for the period from 1 January 20X5 to 31 March 20X5, using the accounting equation worksheet and applying the principles of double-entry accounting.

Solution: Analysis of transactions using double-entry accounting

By now you should be familiar with the activities of Simon Smart and his business entity, Smart Concepts. In Chapter 2 we processed the transactions and prepared financial statements using the concepts found in the conceptual framework. In Chapter 3 we again processed the transactions and prepared financial statements using the accounting equation. We are now going to begin processing the data by analysing the transactions using the principles of double-entry accounting. This will lead to another example further on in this chapter, where we will see the procedural activity of recording the transactions in a journal, posting of the transactions to a ledger and the preparation of a trial balance. As mentioned earlier in this chapter, these activities are normally referred to as bookkeeping.

1		**Assets**	**=**	**Liabilities**	**+**	**Owner's equity**	
Bank						S Smart capital	
+/L/Dr	*–/R/Cr*					*–/L/Dr*	*+/R/Cr*
950 000							950 000

On 2 January, the owner, Simon Smart, invested funds into the business entity. Bank is an asset on the left side of the accounting equation. To increase this asset requires a left or debit entry to the bank account. Funds contributed by the owner represent owner's equity on the right side of the accounting equation. To increase owner's equity requires a right or credit entry to the owner's capital account.

2	Assets			=	Liabilities		+	Owner's equity
Bank					**Borrowings**			
+/L/Dr	–/R/Cr				–/L/Dr	+/R/Cr		
600 000						600 000		

On 2 January, Smart Concepts negotiated a loan of R600 000 from Techno Bank. To increase the asset, bank, requires a left or debit entry to the bank account. The amount owing to Techno Bank. is a liability on the right side of the accounting equation. To increase this liability requires a right or credit entry to the borrowings account.

3	Assets			=	Liabilities	+	Owner's equity
Bank		**Rent asset**					
+/L/Dr	–/R/Cr	+/L/Dr	–/R/Cr				
	48 000	48 000					

On 2 January, the business entity paid four months' rent in advance. Rent paid in advance is an asset on the left side of the accounting equation. To increase this asset requires a left or debit entry to the rent asset account. Bank is also an asset on the left side of the accounting equation. To decrease the asset, bank, requires a right or credit entry to the bank account.

4	Assets			=	Liabilities	+	Owner's equity
Bank		**Fixed deposit investment**					
+/L/Dr	–/R/Cr	+/L/Dr	–/R/Cr				
	120 000	120 000					

On 2 January, Simon transferred R120 000 cash to a fixed deposit account. A fixed deposit is an asset on the left side of the accounting equation. To increase this asset requires a left or debit entry to the fixed deposit asset account. Bank is also an asset on the left side of the accounting equation. To decrease the asset, bank, requires a right or credit entry to the bank account.

5	Assets			=	Liabilities	+	Owner's equity
Bank		**Furniture and fittings**					
+/L/Dr	–/R/Cr	+/L/Dr	–/R/Cr				
	240 000	240 000					

On 2 January, Smart Concepts purchased R240 000 of furniture and fittings for cash. Furniture and fittings are an asset on the left side of the accounting equation. To increase this asset requires a left or debit entry to the furniture and fittings account. To decrease the asset, bank, requires a right or credit entry to the bank account.

6	**Assets**			=	**Liabilities**	+	**Owner's equity**
Bank		Stationery supplies asset					
+/L/Dr	–/R/Cr	+/L/Dr	–/R/Cr				
	17 000	5 000					
		Computer parts asset					
		+/L/Dr	–/R/Cr				
		12 000					

On 5 January, Smart Concepts purchased R5 000 of stationery supplies and R12 000 of computer parts for cash. Stationery supplies and computer parts supplies are assets on the left side of the accounting equation. To increase these assets requires a left or debit entry to the stationery supplies asset and computer parts asset accounts. To decrease the asset, bank, requires a right or credit entry to the bank account.

7	**Assets**			=	**Liabilities**		+	**Owner's equity**	
+/L/Dr	–/R/Cr	+/L/Dr	–/R/Cr		–/L/Dr	+/R/Cr		–/L/Dr	+/R/Cr

On 7 January, Smart Concepts opened an account with Computer World, the supplier of its inventory. This event has no effect on the accounting equation and therefore no entry is recorded.

8	**Assets**	=	**Liabilities**		+	**Owner's equity**
Inventory			Accounts payable			
+/L/Dr	–/R/Cr		–/L/Dr	+/R/Cr		
600 000				600 000		

On 10 January, the entiry purchased inventory of R600 000 on account. To increase the asset, inventory, requires a left or debit entry to the inventory account. The amount owing to the supplier is a liability on the right side of the accounting equation. To increase this liability requires a right or credit entry to the accounts payable account.

9		Assets		=	Liabilities		+	Owner's equity	
Bank								Internet expense	
+/L/Dr	–/R/Cr							+/L/Dr	–/R/Cr
	750							750	

On 12 January, a data bundle was purchased for internet access costing R750. Smart Concepts paid this in cash. Expenses decrease equity and therefore to increase an expense requires a left or debit entry to the internet expense account in the owner's equity column. Cash was paid for the data bundle. The payment is an increase in the asset, bank, on the left hand side of the accounting equation. To decrease this asset requires a right hand or credit entry to the bank account.

10		Assets		=	Liabilities		+	Owner's equity	
Accounts receivable								Sales revenue	
+/L/Dr	–/R/Cr							–/L/Dr	+/R/Cr
187 500									187 500
Inventory								Cost of sales	
+/L/Dr	–/R/Cr							+/L/Dr	–/R/Cr
	150 000							150 000	

On 25 January, Smart Concepts sold fifteen computers on account to a customer. To increase the asset, accounts receivable, requires a left or debit entry to the accounts receivable account. Income increases owner's equity and therefore to increase the income requires a right or credit entry to the sales revenue account in the owner's equity column. To decrease the asset, inventory, requires a right or credit entry to the inventory account. Cost of sales decreases owner's equity and therefore to increase the expense requires a left or debit entry to the cost of sales account in the owner's equity column.

11		Assets		=	Liabilities		+	Owner's equity	
+/L/Dr	–/R/Cr	+/L/Dr	–/R/Cr		–/L/Dr	+/R/Cr		–/L/Dr	+/R/Cr

On 1 February, Smart Concepts employed a technician. This transaction has no effect on the accounting equation since there has been no economic impact.

12	Assets	=	Liabilities	+	Owner's equity
Bank					Advertising expense
+/L/Dr	–/R/Cr			+/L/Dr	–/R/Cr
	7 000			7 000	

On 8 February, Smart Concepts paid R7 000 for an advertisement in a newspaper. To increase the advertising expense requires a left or debit entry to the advertising expense account in the owner's equity column. To decrease bank requires a right or credit entry to the bank account.

13	Assets	=	Liabilities	+	Owner's equity
Bank					Sales revenue
+/L/Dr	–/R/Cr			–/L/Dr	+/R/Cr
375 000					375 000
Inventory					Cost of sales
+/L/Dr	–/R/Cr			+/L/Dr	–/R/Cr
	300 000			300 000	

On 12 February, Smart Concepts sold thirty computers for cash. To increase the asset, bank, requires a left or debit entry to the bank account. Income increases owner's equity and therefore to increase the income requires a right or credit entry to the sales revenue account in the owner's equity column. To decrease the asset, inventory, requires a right or credit entry to the inventory account. Cost of sales decreases owner's equity and therefore to increase the expense requires a left or debit entry to the cost of sales account in the owner's equity column.

14	Assets	=	Liabilities		+	Owner's equity
Bank			Service liability			
+/L/Dr	–/R/Cr		–/L/Dr	+/R/Cr		
48 000				48 000		

On 25 February, Smart Concepts received R48 000 in respect of technical support contracts taken out by customers. The increase in bank requires a left or debit entry to the bank account. The obligation to provide the services is a liability and therefore a right or credit entry is required to the service liability account.

15	Assets		=	Liabilities		+	Owner's equity	
	Bank						Salaries expense	
	+/L/Dr	–/R/Cr					+/L/Dr	–/R/Cr
		8 000					8 000	

On 28 February, Smart Concepts paid the technician R8 000 for the month. To increase the salaries expense requires a left or debit entry to the salaries expense account in the owner's equity column. To decrease bank requires a right or credit entry to the bank account.

16	Assets		=	Liabilities		+	Owner's equity
	Inventory			Accounts payable			
	+/L/Dr	–/R/Cr		–/L/Dr	+/R/Cr		
	750 000				750 000		

On 4 March, Smart Concepts purchased inventory of R750 000 on account. To increase the asset, inventory, requires a left or debit entry to the inventory account. The obligation to pay the supplier is a liability and therefore a right or credit entry is required to the accounts payable account.

17	Assets		=	Liabilities		+	Owner's equity	
	Bank						Internet expense	
	+/L/Dr	–/R/Cr					+/L/Dr	–/R/Cr
		750					750	

This transaction on 5 March is the same as transaction 9 on 12 January.

18	Assets				=	Liabilities	+	Owner's equity
	Bank		Accounts receivable					
	+/L/Dr	–/R/Cr	+/L/Dr	–/R/Cr				
	125 000			125 000				

On 15 March, the customer paid Smart Concepts an amount of R125 000. The cash received is recorded with a left or debit entry to the bank account. Another asset, accounts receivable, decreases. This is recorded as a right or credit entry to the accounts receivable account.

19	**Assets**		=	**Liabilities**		+	**Owner's equity**	
	Bank			Accounts payable				
	+/L/Dr	*–/R/Cr*		*–/L/Dr*	*+/R/Cr*			
		600 000		600 000				

On 25 March, Smart Concepts paid an amount of R600 000 to Computer World. The decrease in the liability, which is on the right side of the equation, is recorded as a left or debit entry to the accounts payable account. The decrease in the asset, bank, is shown on the right or credit side of the bank account.

20	**Assets**		=	**Liabilities**	+	**Owner's equity**	
	Bank					Sales revenue	
	+/L/Dr	*–/R/Cr*				*–/L/Dr*	*+/R/Cr*
	375 000						375 000
	Inventory					Cost of sales	
	+/L/Dr	*–/R/Cr*				*+/L/Dr*	*–/R/Cr*
		300 000				300 000	

On 29 February, Smart Concepts sold thirty computers for cash. The effect on the accounting equation is the same as explained for transaction 13 on 12 February.

21	**Assets**		=	**Liabilities**	+	**Owner's equity**	
	Bank					Salaries expense	
	+/L/Dr	*–/R/Cr*				*+/L/Dr*	*–/R/Cr*
		8 000				8 000	

This transaction, on 21 March, is the same as transaction 15 on 28 February.

22	**Assets**		=	**Liabilities**	+	**Owner's equity**	
	Bank					Interest expense	
	+/L/Dr	*–/R/Cr*				*+/L/Dr*	*–/R/Cr*
		18 000				18 000	

On 30 March Smart Concepts paid interest of R18 000 for the first quarter. To increase the interest expense requires a left or debit entry to the interest expense account in the owner's equity column. To decrease bank requires a right or credit entry to the bank account.

23	Assets		=	Liabilities	+	Owner's equity	
	Bank					Distributions	
	+/L/Dr	–/R/Cr				+/L/Dr	–/R/Cr
		60 000				60 000	

On 30 March, Simon authorised a distribution to himself of R60 000 for personal use. Distributions to the owner decrease owner's equity and therefore a left or debit entry is required to the distributions account in the owner's equity column. The decrease in bank is recorded as a right or credit entry to the bank account.

4.4 The general journal

4.4.1 Use of the general journal

If you refer to diagram 4.1 earlier in this chapter, you will notice that, after a transaction has been analysed to determine its effect on the accounting equation, the processing begins by recording the effects of the transaction in a journal. We processed the transactions using underlying concepts in Chapter 2 and through the accounting equation worksheet in Chapter 3. In a double-entry bookkeeping system, before transactions are recorded in the ledger, they are first entered in a journal.

The journal that we are going to use here is referred to as a general journal. We will learn about other journals in Chapter 9. The journals are known collectively as books of original entry.

The general journal links the debit and credit of each transaction by providing, in one place, a complete record of each transaction, in chronological order. Each transaction is analysed and recorded in the general journal in a manner which identifies which accounts are affected and the amount by which each account is to be changed. In other words, the journal entry instructs the bookkeeper where to record the effects of each transaction in the accounts in the ledger – the next stage of the accounting process.

Double-entry principles are to be followed for each transaction:

- ❑ two or more accounts are affected
- ❑ total debits equal total credits
- ❑ equality of the accounting equation is maintained.

No transaction may be entered in the ledger unless it has first been entered in a journal. In a double-entry bookkeeping system, the journal does not replace the ledger.

Solution: Preparation of financial statements using double-entry accounting

(All figures have been rounded to R000s)

	ASSETS																=	LIABILITIES						OWNER'S EQUITY							
No	Bank		Rent asset		Fixed deposit investment		Accounts receivable		Stationery supplies asset		Computer parts asset		Furniture & fittings		Inventory		=	Service liability		Accounts payable		Borrowings		S Smart capital		Income		Expenses		Distribution	
	+ L Dr	- R Cr	+ L Dr	- R Cr	+ L Dr	- R Cr	+ L Dr	- R Cr	+ L Dr	- R Cr	+ L Dr	- R Cr	+ L Dr	- R Cr	+ L Dr	- R Cr		- L Dr	+ R Cr	- L Dr	+ R Cr	- L Dr	+ R Cr	- L Dr	+ R Cr	- L Dr	+ R Cr	+ L Dr	- R Cr	+ L Dr	- R Cr
1	950																=								950						
2	600																=						600								
3		48	48														=														
4		120			120												=														
5		240											240				=														
6		17							5		12						=														
7																															
8															600		=				600										
9		0,75															=											0,75			
10							187,5									150	=										187,5	150			
11																															
12		7															=											7			
13	375															300	=										375	300			
14	48																=		48												
15		8															=											8			
16															750		=				750										
17		0,75															=											0,75			
18	125							125									=														
19		600															=			600											
20	375															300	=										375	300			
21		8															=											8			
22		18															=											18			
23		60															=													60	
	1345,5		48		120		62,5		5		12		240		600				48		750		600		950		937,5	792,5		60	
	ASSETS = 2 433																=	LIABILITIES = 1 398						OWNER'S EQUITY = 1 035							

4.4.2 Format of the general journal

A typical format of the general journal is shown below. For each transaction it provides places for recording:

- the date
- the name of the accounts to be debited or credited
- a reference to the account in the ledger to which the transaction is to be transferred (the folio column)
- the amount
- an explanation of the transaction, known as the narration.

GENERAL JOURNAL OF (NAME OF ENTITY)

Date	Description	Fol	Dr	Cr
1 May 20X5	Name of account to be debited	GL1	21 400	
	Name of account to be credited	GL2		21 400
	Narration			

The details are entered in the journal as each transaction is analysed. You should be able to analyse the transaction in your mind by thinking about the underlying concepts and the accounting equation. Each journal entry represents one line in the accounting equation worksheet – the journal entry is simply a bookkeeping representation of the effects of a transaction on the elements of the equation.

You should note that when transactions are recorded in the general journal, no entry is made in the folio column. When the transactions are transferred to the ledger, the relevant ledger account number is then entered.

The general journal of Smart Concepts for the period from 1 January 20X5 to 31 March 20X5 is presented below. You should review each journal entry and make sure that you understand why each account is being debited or credited.

GENERAL JOURNAL OF SMART CONCEPTS (GJ 1)

Date	Description	Fol	Dr	Cr
20X5 January 02	Bank Simon Smart Capital *Investment by owner*	A1 OE1	950 000	 950 000
02	Bank Borrowings *Raising of loan from Techno Bank*	A1 L1	600 000	 600 000
02	Rent asset Bank *Payment of four months' rent in advance*	A2 A1	48 000	 48 000
02	Fixed deposit investment Bank *Transfered cash to fixed deposit*	A3 A1	120 000	 120 000
02	Furniture and fittings Bank *Purchase of furniture and fittings for cash*	A4 A1	240 000	 240 000
05	Stationery supplies asset Computer parts asset Bank *Purchase of stationery and computer parts for cash*	A5 A6 A1	5 000 12 000	 17 000
10	Inventory Accounts payable *Purchase of inventory on account*	A7 L2	600 000	 600 000
12	Internet expense Bank *Purchase of data bundle for cash*	E1 A1	750	 750
25	Accounts receivable Sales revenue *Sale of fifteen computers to customer on account*	A8 I1	187 500	 187 500
	Cost of sales Inventory *Recording the cost of inventory sold*	E2 A7	150 000	 150 000

GENERAL JOURNAL OF SMART CONCEPTS (GJ 2)

Date	Description	Fol	Dr	Cr
20X5 February				
08	Advertising expense	E3	7 000	
	Bank	A1		7 000
	Advertising paid for in cash			
12	Bank	A1	375 000	
	Sales revenue	I1		375 000
	Sale of thirty computers to customers for cash			
	Cost of sales	E2	300 000	
	Inventory	A7		300 000
	Recording the cost of inventory sold			
25	Bank	A1	48 000	
	Service liability	L3		48 000
	Receipts from clients for technical support contracts to be provided over the next two years			
28	Salaries expense	E4	8 000	
	Bank	A1		8 000
	Payment of salary expense			
March				
04	Inventory	A7	750 000	
	Accounts payable	L2		750 000
	Purchase of inventory on account			
05	Internet expense	E1	750	
	Bank	A1		750
	Purchase of data bundle for cash			
15	Bank	A1	125 000	
	Accounts receivable	A8		125 000
	Receipt from customer			
25	Accounts payable	L2	600 000	
	Bank	A1		600 000
	Payment to supplier			
29	Bank	A1	375 000	
	Sales revenue	I1		375 000
	Sale of thirty computers to customers for cash			
	Cost of sales	E2	300 000	
	Inventory	A7		300 000
	Recording the cost of inventory sold			
30	Salaries expense	E4	8 000	
	Bank	A1		8 000
	Payment of salaries			
30	Interest expense	E5	18 000	
	Bank	A1		18 000
	Payment of interest on borrowings			
30	Distributions	OE2	60 000	
	Bank	A1		60 000
	Distribution to owner			

4.5 The general ledger

4.5.1 Use of the general ledger

If you refer to diagram 4.1 again, you will see that, after the transaction has been recorded in a journal, the recorded effects are transferred to a ledger. This part of the accounting process is referred to as posting. Posting of journal entry information from the journal to the ledger may be done daily, weekly, monthly or at other intervals. Smart Concepts posts from the journal to the ledger quarterly.

The ledger that we are going to use here is known as the general ledger. Other ledgers will be introduced in Chapter 9. The ledger is known as a book of final entry.

The general ledger comprises a number of different accounts, which accumulate the effects of transactions recorded in the journal. Each account in the ledger is simply a formal representation of a column in the accounting equation worksheet. In the posting procedure, the amount in the debit column in the journal is posted to the debit of the named account in the general ledger. Similarly, the amount in the credit column in the journal is posted to the credit of the named account in the general ledger.

4.5.2 Format of the general ledger

The format of a typical general ledger account is shown below. The account has a debit side and a credit side, in other words a left side and a right side just as you found in the accounting equation worksheet. Given its shape, it is normally referred to as a ***T account***.

Dr		**ACCOUNT NAME (GL 1)**					**Cr**
Date	**Details**	**Fol**	**R**	**Date**	**Details**	**Fol**	**R**
10/02/X5	Name of account credited	GJ1	21 500	15/02/X5	Name of account debited	GJ 1	10 000

On each side it provides places for recording:

- the date
- the name of the other account affected in the transaction
- a reference to the page number in the journal where the transaction was recorded
- the amount.

Posting to the general ledger takes place by referring to the journal and transferring the recorded effects to each ledger account. The folio column is completed as each entry is posted from the journal. If the posting process is interrupted, the bookkeeper can look at the folio column in the journal to see which was the last entry posted.

The general ledger of Smart Concepts is shown below. All the entries have been posted from the journal.

Dr			BANK (GL A1)				Cr
Date	**Details**	**Fol**	**R**	**Date**	**Details**	**Fol**	**R**
02/01	Simon Smart capital	GJ1	950 000	02/01	Rent asset	GJ1	48 000
02/01	Borrowings	GJ1	600 000	02/01	Fixed deposit investment	GJ1	120 000
12/02	Sales revenue	GJ2	375 000	02/01	Furniture and fittings	GJ1	240 000
25/02	Service liability	GJ2	48 000	05/01	Stationery supplies asset	GJ1	5 000
15/03	Accounts receivable	GJ2	125 000	05/01	Computer parts asset	GJ1	12 000
				12/01	Internet expense	GJ1	750
29/03	Sales revenue	GJ2	375 000	08/02	Advertising expense	GJ2	7 000
				28/02	Salaries expense	GJ2	8 000
				05/03	Internet expense	GJ2	750
				25/03	Accounts payable	GJ2	600 000
				30/03	Salaries expense	GJ2	8 000
				30/03	Interest expense	GJ2	18 000
				30/03	Distributions	GJ2	60 000
				31/03	Balance	c/d	1 345 500
			2 473 000				2 473 000
01/04	Balance	b/d	1 345 500				

Dr			RENT ASSET (GL A2)				Cr
Date	**Details**	**Fol**	**R**	**Date**	**Details**	**Fol**	**R**
02/01	Bank	GJ1	48 000	31/03	Balance	c/d	48 000
			48 000				48 000
01/04	Balance	b/d	48 000				

Dr			FIXED DEPOSIT INVESTMENT (GL A3)				Cr
Date	**Details**	**Fol**	**R**	**Date**	**Details**	**Fol**	**R**
02/01	Bank	GJ1	120 000	31/03	Balance	c/d	120 000
			120 000				120 000
01/04	Balance	b/d	120 000				

Dr			FURNITURE AND FITTINGS (GL A4)				Cr
Date	**Details**	**Fol**	**R**	**Date**	**Details**	**Fol**	**R**
02/01	Bank	GJ1	240 000	31/03	Balance	c/d	240 000
			240 000				240 000
01/04	Balance	b/d	240 000				

Dr			STATIONERY SUPPLIES ASSET (GL A5)				Cr
Date	**Details**	**Fol**	**R**	**Date**	**Details**	**Fol**	**R**
05/01	Bank	GJ1	5 000	31/03	Balance	c/d	5 000
			5 000				5 000
01/04	Balance	b/d	5 000				

Dr			COMPUTER PARTS ASSET (GL A6)				Cr
Date	**Details**	**Fol**	**R**	**Date**	**Details**	**Fol**	**R**
05/01	Bank	GJ1	12 000	31/03	Balance	c/d	12 000
			12 000				12 000
01/04	Balance	b/d	12 000				

Dr			INVENTORY (GL A7)				Cr
Date	**Details**	**Fol**	**R**	**Date**	**Details**	**Fol**	**R**
10/01	Accounts payable	GJ1	600 000	25/01	Cost of sales	GJ1	150 000
04/03	Accounts payable	GJ2	750 000	12/02	Cost of sales	GJ2	300 000
				29/03	Cost of sales	GJ2	300 000
				31/03	Balance	c/d	600 000
			1 350 000				1 350 000
01/04	Balance	b/d	600 000				

Dr **ACCOUNTS RECEIVABLE (GL A8)** **Cr**

Date	Details	Fol	R	Date	Details	Fol	R
25/01	Sales revenue	GJ1	187 500	15/03	Bank	GJ2	125 000
				31/03	Balance	c/d	62 500
			187 500				187 500
01/04	Balance	b/d	62 500				

Dr **BORROWINGS (GL L1)** **Cr**

Date	Details	Fol	R	Date	Details	Fol	R
				02/01	Bank	GJ1	600 000
31/03	Balance	c/d	600 000				
			600 000				600 000
				01/04	Balance	b/d	600 000

Dr **ACCOUNTS PAYABLE (GL L2)** **Cr**

Date	Details	Fol	R	Date	Details	Fol	R
25/03	Bank	GJ2	600 000	10/01	Inventory	GJ1	600 000
31/03	Balance	c/d	750 000	04/03	Inventory	GJ2	750 000
			1 350 000				1 350 000
				01/04	Balance	b/d	750 000

Dr **SERVICE LIABILITY (GL L3)** **Cr**

Date	Details	Fol	R	Date	Details	Fol	R
				25/02	Bank	GJ2	48 000
31/03	Balance	c/d	48 000				
			48 000				48 000
				01/04	Balance	b/d	48 000

Dr **SIMON SMART CAPITAL (GL OE1)** **Cr**

Date	Details	Fol	R	Date	Details	Fol	R
				02/01	Bank	GJ1	950 000
31/03	Balance	c/d	950 000				
			950 000				950 000
				01/04	Balance	b/d	950 000

Dr **DISTRIBUTIONS (GL OE2)** **Cr**

Date	Details	Fol	R	Date	Details	Fol	R
30/03	Bank	GJ2	60 000	31/03	Balance	c/d	60 000
			60 000				60 000
31/03	Balance	b/d	60 000				

Dr **SALES REVENUE (GL I1)** **Cr**

Date	Details	Fol	R	Date	Details	Fol	R
				25/01	Accounts receivable	GJ1	187 500
				12/02	Bank	GJ2	375 000
31/03	Balance	c/d	937 500	29/03	Bank	GJ2	375 000
			937 500				937 500
				31/03	Balance	b/d	937 500

Dr **INTERNET EXPENSE (GL E1)** **Cr**

Date	Details	Fol	R	Date	Details	Fol	R
12/01	Bank	GJ1	750				
05/03	Bank	GJ2	750	31/03	Balance	c/d	1 500
			1 500				1 500
31/03	Balance	b/d	1 500				

Dr **COST OF SALES (GL E2)** **Cr**

Date	Details	Fol	R	Date	Details	Fol	R
25/01	Inventory	GJ1	150 000				
12/02	Inventory	GJ2	300 000				
29/03	Inventory	GJ2	300 000	31/03	Balance	c/d	750 000
			750 000				750 000
31/03	Balance	b/d	750 000				

Dr			ADVERTISING EXPENSE (GL E3)				Cr
Date	**Details**	**Fol**	**R**	**Date**	**Details**	**Fol**	**R**
08/02	Bank	GJ2	7 000	31/03	Balance	c/d	7 000
			7 000				7 000
31/03	Balance	b/d	7 000				

Dr			SALARIES EXPENSE (GL E4)				Cr
Date	**Details**	**Fol**	**R**	**Date**	**Details**	**Fol**	**R**
28/02	Bank	GJ2	8 000				
30/03	Bank	GJ2	8 000	31/03	Balance	c/d	16 000
			16 000				16 000
31/03	Balance	b/d	16 000				

Dr			INTEREST EXPENSE (GL E5)				Cr
Date	**Details**	**Fol**	**R**	**Date**	**Details**	**Fol**	**R**
30/03	Bank	GJ2	18 000	31/03	Balance	c/d	18 000
			18 000				18 000
31/03	Balance	b/d	18 000				

4.6 The trial balance

4.6.1 Balancing the accounts

The rules of double-entry bookkeeping have been used to journalise and post the transactions. Increases to each account have been entered on one side (debit for assets, withdrawals and expenses, credit for liabilities, capital and income) and decreases on the opposite side (credit for assets, withdrawals and expenses, debit for liabilities, capital and income). This makes it easy to determine the balance on each account. Regardless of whether the account is an asset, liability or owner's equity, the account balance is the difference between its increases and decreases, or its debit side and credit side. The balance on the account at the end of a period is the same as the equivalent accounting equation column.

When balancing each account in the general ledger, you should be aware of whether the balance in the account is *normally* a debit or credit. The normal balance results from the principles of double-entry bookkeeping.

Elements of the financial statements	Increases recorded as	Decreases recorded as	Normal balance
Asset	Dr	Cr	Dr
Liability	Cr	Dr	Cr
Owner's equity			
Capital	Cr	Dr	Cr
Withdrawals	Dr	Cr	Dr
Income	Cr	Dr	Cr
Expenses	Dr	Cr	Dr

Diagram 4.3: Normal balance of ledger accounts

4.6.2 Preparing the trial balance

The last stage in processing the data is to summarise the information in the general ledger by preparing a trial balance (see diagram 4.1). In double-entry bookkeeping, every transaction is recorded with equal debits and credits. This equality is tested by preparing a trial balance which lists the balance on each account. This procedure is equivalent to checking that the two sides of the bottom line of the accounting equation have equal totals.

To prepare a trial balance, you need to do the following:

- balance each account in the general ledger
- list all the accounts with their balances from the general ledger
- total the debit and credit column of the trial balance.

If the trial balance does not balance, an error has been made. However, the fact that the sum of the debit balances equals the sum of the credit balances is not proof that the bookkeeping procedures have been free from error. The composition of items in the general ledger can be incorrect if, for example, an item has been posted to say, the debit of an asset account instead of to the debit of an expense account.

The trial balance of Smart Concepts at the end of March is shown below:

SMART CONCEPTS
PRE-ADJUSTMENT TRIAL BALANCE AT 31 MARCH 20X5

Description	Folio	Dr	Cr
Bank	A1	1 345 500	
Rent asset	A2	48 000	
Fixed deposit investment	A3	120 000	
Furniture and fittings	A4	240 000	
Stationery supplies asset	A5	5 000	
Computer parts asset	A6	12 000	
Inventory	A7	600 000	
Accounts receivable	A8	62 500	

Borrowings	L1		600 000
Accounts payable	L2		750 000
Service liability	L3		48 000
Simon Smart Capital	OE1		950 000
Distributions	OE2	60 000	
Sales revenue	I1		937 500
Internet expense	E1	1 500	
Cost of sales	E2	750 000	
Advertising expense	E3	7 000	
Salaries expense	E4	16 000	
Interest expense	E5	18 000	
		3 285 500	3 285 500

Pause and reflect...

Errors can occur in the recording of transactions in the journal and posting to the ledger. Consider the following errors and the effect of each error on the balancing of the trial balance.

a) When the owner, Simon Smart, invested R950 000 in the business entity (Transaction 1), the capital account was debited with R950 000 and the bank account was credited with R950 000.
b) When Smart Concepts purchased furniture and fittings for R240 000 (Transaction 5), the furniture and fittings account was debited with R24 000 and the bank account was credited with R24 000.
c) When Smart Concepts paid an internet service provider an amount of R750 (Transaction 9), the internet expense account was debited with R750 and the bank account was also debited with R750.
d) When Smart Concepts paid Computer World an amount of R600 000 (Transaction 19), the accounts payable account was debited with R600 000 and the bank account was credited with R60 000.

Response

a) The incorrect account was debited (the capital account instead of the bank account) and the incorrect account was credited (the bank account instead of the capital account). However, the trial balance will balance as the debit of R950 000 equals the credit of R950 000 and the equality of the accounting equation is maintained.
b) The correct accounts were debited and credited but an incorrect amount was processed. However, the trial balance will balance as the debit of R24 000 equals the credit of R24 000 and the equality of the accounting equation is maintained.
c) The internet expense account was correctly debited with R750 but the bank account was also incorrectly debited with the same amount. The debit side of the trial balance will exceed the credit side of the trial balance by R1 500 and the trial balance will not balance.
d) The correct amount of R600 000 was debited to the accounts payable account but the incorrect amount of R60 000 was credited to the bank account. The debit side of the trial balance will exceed the credit side of the trial balance by R540 000 and the trial balance will not balance.

Summary of concepts and applications

1. Accounting is an information system that selects data, processes that data and produces information about an economic entity. Only data that has an economic impact on the entity is analysed as a transaction in order to determine the effect on the accounting equation. Data is processed through the accounting process by means of an activity known as book-keeping (recording the effects of transactions in a journal, transferring the recorded effects into accounts in a ledger and then preparing a trial balance). The final stage, the producing of information for users, involves adjusting the information in the ledger accounts to conform with the accrual basis of accounting, then preparing the annual financial statements, and finally closing the accounts for the year.
2. In double-entry accounting, increases in assets are recorded on the left-hand side of asset accounts, whereas increases in liabilities and owner's equity are recorded on the right-hand side of those accounts so as to maintain the equality of the accounting equation. The left-hand side of each account is called the debit side (Dr) and the right-hand side of each account is called the credit side (Cr)
3. Transactions are analysed using the principles of double-entry accounting by identifying which elements of the financial statements are affected by a transaction, establishing whether the item is increasing or decreasing, and thereby determining the debit or credit to be processed.
4. The general journal provides a complete record of each transaction. Each transaction is analysed and recorded in the general journal in a manner that identifies which accounts are affected and the amount by which each account is to be changed. Double-entry principles are to be followed for each transaction. Each journal entry represents one line in the accounting equation worksheet.
5. The general ledger comprises a number of different accounts, which accumulate the effects of transactions recorded in the journal. Each account in the ledger is a formal representation of a column in the accounting equation worksheet. In the posting procedure, the amount in the debit column in the journal is posted to the debit of the named account in the general ledger. Similarly, the amount in the credit column in the journal is posted to the credit of the named account in the general ledger.
6. In order to establish the balance on an account, whether the account is an asset, liability or owner's equity, one must determine the difference between its increases and decreases, or its debit side and credit side. The balance on an account at the end of a period is the same as the equivalent accounting equation column. The final stage in processing the data is to summarise the information in the general ledger by preparing a trial balance.

5 Recording Internal Transactions

'Annual income twenty pounds, annual expenditure nineteen and six, result happiness. Annual income twenty pounds, annual expenditure twenty pounds ought and six, result misery.'
(Micawber to Copperfield – Dickens, 1856)

Outcomes

- Explain the purpose of internal transactions.
- Interpret the classification of the adjustments made to items of income and expense.
- Prepare adjusting entries in respect of the internal transactions.
- Determine the accounting procedure whereby receipts and payments of cash are recorded into income and expense accounts.

Chapter outline

Famous Brands Limited
Notes to the financial statements for the year ended 29 February 2008

	(R Millions)
Trade and other payables	
Trade payables	38
Accruals	75
Advertising levy surplus	4
Other	7
	124

Policy

Accrued liabilities and deferred income represent miscellaneous contractual liabilities that relate to expenses that were incurred, but not paid for at the year-end and income received during the period, for which the Group had not supplied the goods or services at the end of the year.

With over 1 500 restaurants, including Steers, Debonairs and Wimpy, Famous Brands performs millions of transactions each year. In order to prepare the financial statements they need to process internal transactions to meet the accrual basis of accounting.

5.1 The need for adjustments

Diagram 5.1 illustrates the accounting process which you were introduced to in Chapter 4 of this book. You will recall that, after processing the data, the final stage of the accounting process is the producing of information for users. This involves adjusting the information in the ledger accounts to conform with the accrual basis of accounting, then preparing the annual financial statements and, finally, closing the accounts for the year. The current chapter examines adjusting entries, also referred to as internal transactions, Chapter 6 covers the preparation of financial statements and Chapter 7 completes the accounting process with closing entries.

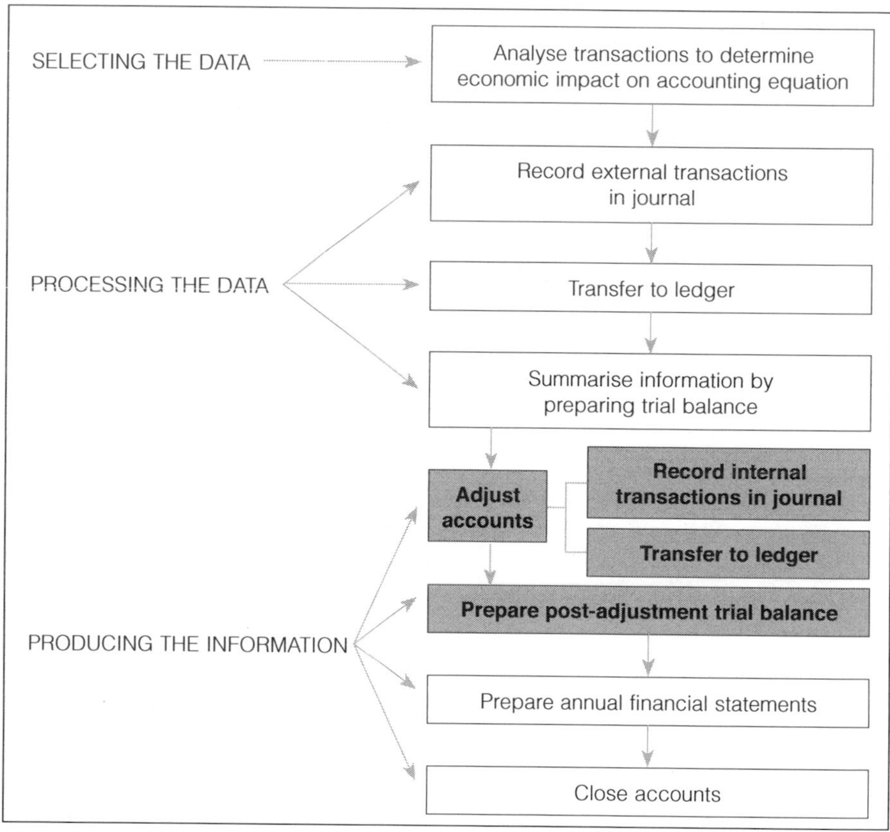

Diagram 5.1: The accounting process, highlighting the adjustments

5.1.1 The accrual basis of accounting and internal transactions

At the end of an accounting period, all the ***external*** transactions will have been processed through the accounting system, that is, recorded in a journal, posted to the ledger and a trial balance prepared. At this point, the ***internal*** transactions will not have been processed.

As the focus of the adjusting entries is on the measurement of performance, we will refer here to the *income statement* and the *profit for the period* and not to the statement of comprehensive income and total comprehensive income.

Remember that internal transactions are adjustments made to the financial position of an entity in order to comply with the accrual basis of accounting. The adjusting entries are therefore no more than internal adjustments to ensure that the income statement reports income which has been *earned* during the period, and expenses which have been *incurred* during the period. It is important to note that, if the cash received during the period equals the income earned, there will be no adjusting entries in respect of income, and, likewise, if the cash paid equals the expenses incurred, there will be no adjustments in respect of those expenses.

5.1.2 The accrual basis of accounting and the time-period concept

The activities of a business entity are identified as occurring during specific time periods, such as a week, a month, six months or a year. This is done so that timely information can be made available to management and to other users for decision-making purposes. A consequence of the time-period concept is that the natural trading cycles of a business are divided into reporting periods, and financial reports are prepared for each period. As mentioned above, the income statement measures profit for a reporting period as the difference between the income recognised as earned, and the expenses recognised as incurred, in that period. Adjusting entries, or internal transactions, need to be processed in each reporting period in order to comply with the accrual basis of accounting.

5.2 Classification of the adjustments

We processed both the external and internal transactions in Chapters 2 and 3. The internal transactions were not specifically identified as adjustments in those early chapters as the objective was to provide a conceptual introduction to accounting. We were concerned with analysing transactions, processing the transactions on a conceptual level and producing information in the form of an income statement and a statement of financial position. If you refer to diagram 5.1 at the beginning of this chapter, you will notice that the last step in processing the data is to summarise the information by preparing a trial balance. This was also demonstrated to you in Chapter 4. Once the external transactions have been processed and the trial balance prepared, the internal transactions or adjusting entries are processed.

The purpose of adjusting entries is to ensure that the income statement reports income which has been earned, and expenses which have been incurred during the period, irrespective of the receipt and payment of cash. Remember that, if the cash received during the period equals the income earned, there will be no adjusting entries in respect of income, and, likewise, if the cash paid equals the expenses incurred, there will be no adjustments in respect of those expenses. If the cash received *does not* equal the income, only two other scenarios exist – either the cash is received before the income is earned or the cash receipt is outstanding when the income has been earned. Similarly, if the cash paid *does not* equal the expenses, either the cash is paid before the expense is incurred or the cash payment is outstanding when the expense has been incurred.

We can therefore summarise the above paragraph and classify the adjustments as shown in diagram 5.2.

	External transactions during period	**Internal transaction / adjusting entry**
Income items	cash received equals income earned	no adjusting entry
	cash received in advance of earning of income (liability created representing obligation of entity)	increase the ***income*** on the income statement and decrease the ***liability*** on the statement of financial position
	cash receipt outstanding and income already earned	increase the ***income*** on the income statement and create an ***asset*** on the statement of financial position
Expense items	cash paid equals expense incurred	no adjusting entry
	cash paid in advance of incurral of expense (asset created representing resource controlled by entity)	increase the ***expense*** on the income statement and decrease the ***asset*** on the statement of financial position
	cash payment outstanding and ***expense*** already incurred	increase the ***expense*** on the income statement and create a ***liability*** on the statement of financial position

Diagram 5.2: Classification of the adjustments

5.2.1 Cash received in advance of earning income (unearned income)

When cash is received in advance of earning income, a liability is created at the time of receipt of the cash, representing the obligation of the entity to provide goods or services in the future. At the end of the period, an adjusting entry, or internal transaction, is needed to recognise that part of the liability earned during the period. This is known as the recognition of ***unearned income***.

Transaction 14 of the Smart Concepts example is the relevant external transaction.

Transaction *14* *25/02/X5* *On 25 February, Smart Concepts received cash of R48 000 in respect of technical support contracts taken out by customers. The support contracts are for a two year period.*

At the end of the period, part of the cash received will be earned, based on the service provided, and part will remain unearned. Transaction 24 is the relevant internal transaction.

Transaction *24* *31/03/X5* *On 31 March, Simon examined the records of the business and established that technical support in respect of contracts to the value of R6 000 had been provided to customers.*

These transactions can be analysed as follows:

Assets		=	**Liabilities**		+	**Owner's equity**	
Bank			Service liability			Service revenue	
+/L/Dr	*–/R/Cr*		*–/L/Dr*	*+/R/Cr*		*–/L/Dr*	*+/R/Cr*
14 48 000				48 000			
24			6 000				6 000
				42 000			6 000

Receiving the R48 000 in advance increased the cash of the entity and created the service liability. However, by the end of March, R6 000 of the liability had been discharged and the revenue earned. The service liability is decreased by R6 000 with a debit entry, and the equity item, service revenue, increased by the same amount with a credit entry. The service revenue account in the above worksheet shows a credit balance of R6 000 which will appear as revenue on the income statement for the period. The service liability account shows the balance of the obligation of R42 000 which will be shown as a liability on the statement of financial position.

5.2.2 Cash receipt outstanding and income already earned (accrued income)

Income needs to be recorded when earned, which may occur before the cash is received. If, at the end of the period, earned income is unrecorded because payment has not been received, an adjusting entry, or internal transaction, is needed to record the income earned during the period. This is known as the recording of ***accrued income***.

Transaction 4 of the Smart Concepts example records the transfer of R120 000 from the bank account to a fixed deposit account, earning interest at 5% per annum. At the end of the period, no cash has been received from the bank on the fixed deposit investment, but interest for three months has been earned. Transaction 25 is the relevant internal transaction.

Transaction *25* *31/03/X5* *On 31 March, Smart Concepts accounted for the interest on the fixed deposit earned for the period.*

This transaction can be analysed as follows:

Assets		=	**Liabilities**		+	**Owner's equity**	
Interest asset						Interest revenue	
+/L/Dr	*–/R/Cr*					*–/L/Dr*	*+/R/Cr*
25 1 500							1 500
1 500							1 500

At the end of the period, interest income of R1 500 has been earned (R120 000 x 5% x 3/12) and this income is recognised on the accrual basis income statement for the period. An asset account, interest asset, is increased by R1 500 with a debit entry representing the amount owed to Smart Concepts at the end of March, and the equity item, interest revenue, is increased by the same amount with a credit entry. The interest asset account in the above worksheet shows a debit balance of R1 500 which will appear as an asset on the statement of financial position at the end of March. The interest revenue account shows a credit balance of R1 500 which will appear as income on the income statement for the period.

5.2.3 Cash paid in advance of incurral of expenses (pre-paid expenses)

When cash is paid in advance of incurral of expenses, an asset is created at the time of payment of the cash representing the right of the entity to receive goods or services in the future. At the end of the period, an adjusting entry, or internal transaction, is needed to recognise that part of the asset that was used or expired during the period. This is known as the recognition of ***pre-paid expenses***.

Transaction 3 of the Smart Concepts example is the relevant external transaction.

Transaction *3* *2/01/X5* *On 2 January, Simon located premises to operate from in Rosebank. The monthly rent for the premises is R12 000. Smart Concepts paid four months' rent in advance on 2 January.*

As the period went by, part of the benefit of the rent asset expired and a portion of the rent asset became an expense. Transaction 26 is the relevant internal transaction.

Transaction *26* *31/03/X5* *On 31 March, Smart Concepts recognised the rent expense incurred for the period.*

	Assets				=	**Owner's equity**
	Bank		Rent asset		Rent expense	
	+/L/Dr	*–/R/Cr*	*+/L/Dr*	*–/R/Cr*	*+/L/Dr*	*–/R/Cr*
3		48 000	48 000			
26				36 000	36 000	
			12 000		36 000	

Paying the R48 000 rent in advance decreased the cash of the entity and created the rent asset. However, by the end of the period, R36 000 of the asset had expired and the expense incurred. The equity item, rent expense, is increased by R36 000 with a debit entry and the rent asset is decreased by the same amount with a credit entry. The rent expense account in the above worksheet shows a debit balance of R36 000 which will appear as an expense on the income statement for the period. The rent asset account also shows a debit balance of R12 000 representing the right of occupation for one month which will be shown as an asset on the statement of financial position.

5.2.4 Cash payment outstanding and expense already incurred (accrued expenses)

Expenses need to be recorded when incurred, which may be before the cash has been paid. If, at the end of a period, an incurred expense is unrecorded because payment has not been made, an adjusting entry, or internal transaction, is needed to record the expense incurred during the period. This is known as the recording of ***accrued expenses***.

Each month, Smart Concepts use the telephone as well as electricity to operate the business and earn income. At the end of the period no cash has been paid for these expenses, which have already been incurred. Transaction 27 is the relevant internal transaction.

Transaction *27 31/03/X5* *On 31 March, the telephone account for R1 500 and the electricity account for R2 500 had been received but not paid.*

This can be analysed as follows:

Assets	=	Liabilities	+	Owner's equity	
		Telephone & electricity liability		Telephone & electricity expense	
		–/L/Dr	*+/R/Cr*	*+/L/Dr*	*–/R/Cr*
23			4 000	4 000	
			4 000	4 000	

At the end of the period, telephone and electricity expenses totalling R4 000 have been incurred and these expenses should be recognised on the accrual basis income statement for the period. The equity item, telephone and electricity expense, is increased by R4 000 with a debit entry, and the liability account, telephone and electricity liability, is increased by the same amount with a credit entry. The telephone and electricity expense account in the above worksheet shows a debit balance of R4 000, which will appear as an expense on the income statement for the period. The telephone and electricity liability account shows a credit balance of R4 000, which will appear as a liability on the statement of financial position at the end of March.

5.2.5 Other period-end adjustments

The accrual basis of accounting requires assets purchased for use in the business to be recognised as an expense when used. This typically applies to non-current assets such as equipment and vehicles and also to current assets used in the business, such as consumable stores.

Recognition of current assets used

When cash is paid to acquire consumable stores such as office supplies or parts supplies, the items are treated as assets on purchase. The consumable stores are a resource controlled by the entity (they have been bought and are available for use), from a past event (the purchase transaction) and will contribute to an inflow of resources in the future (the consumable stores will be used to operate the business entity). At the end of the period, an adjusting or internal entry is needed to recognise that part of the asset used during the period.

Transaction 6 of the Smart Concepts example is the relevant external transaction.

Transaction *6* *05/01/X5* *On 5 January, Smart Concepts purchased supplies of stationery for R5 000 as well as supplies of computer parts for R12 000. All the supplies were paid for in cash.*

If no records are kept showing the amount used, it is necessary to count the remaining supplies on hand and then deduct the cost of the remaining supplies from the cost of the supplies purchased. Transaction 28 is the relevant internal transaction.

Transaction *28* *31/03/X5* *On 31 March, Simon counted stationery supplies on hand costing R2 000 and also determined from the records that computer parts costing R8 500 had been used.*

These transactions can be analysed as follows:

	Assets				=	**Owner's equity**	
	Stationery supplies asset		Bank			Stationery supplies expense	
	+/L/Dr	–/R/Cr	+/L/Dr	–/R/Cr		+/L/Dr	–/R/Cr
6	5 000			5 000			
28		3 000				3 000	
	2 000					3 000	
	Computer parts asset		Bank			Computer parts expense	
	+/L/Dr	–/R/Cr	+/L/Dr	–/R/Cr		+/L/Dr	–/R/Cr
6	12 000			12 000			
28		8 500				8 500	
	3 500					8 500	

Purchasing the stationery supplies for R5 000 increased the asset, stationery supplies, and also decreased the asset, bank, as the supplies were purchased for cash. At the end of March, supplies costing R2 000 remain on hand and therefore stationery supplies costing R3 000 were used during the period. The equity item, stationery supplies expense, is increased by R3 000 with a debit entry and the stationery supplies asset is decreased by a credit entry of the same amount. The stationery supplies asset account in the above worksheet shows a debit balance of R2 000 which will appear as an asset on the statement of financial position at the end of March. The stationery supplies expense account shows a debit balance of R3 000 which will be shown as an expense on the income statement for the period.

Purchasing the computer parts for R12 000 increased the asset, computer parts, and also decreased the asset, bank, as the parts were purchased for cash. At the end of March, Simon determined from the service records that computer parts costing R8 500 had been used and therefore parts costing R3 500 remain on hand. The equity item, computer parts expense, is increased by R8 500 with a debit entry and the computer parts asset is decreased by a credit entry of the same amount.

The computer parts asset account in the above worksheet shows a debit balance of R3 500, which will appear as an asset on the statement of financial position at the end of March. The computer parts expense account shows a debit balance of R8 500, which will be shown as an expense on the income statement for the period.

Recognition of non-current assets used

The use of non-current assets such as machines, vehicles, furniture or even professional libraries represents a consumption of benefits inherent in the assets. The cost of these assets must be charged as an expense during the periods over which the assets are expected to be available for use by an entity. This asset usage expense is known as depreciation. This is consistent with the accrual basis of accounting which recognises expenses when incurred (in this case, as the asset is used) and not when the cash is paid (on purchase or on repayment of a loan).

Non-current assets in the form of furniture and fittings were purchased by Smart Concepts. Transaction 5 of the Smart Concepts example is the relevant external transaction.

Transaction *5* *02/01/X5* *On 2 January, Smart Concepts purchased furniture and fittings for R240 000. This was paid for from funds in the bank account. The expected useful life of the furniture and fittings is five years.*

The portion of the cost of the asset used which is recognised as an expense is based on various factors, such as the estimated useful life of the asset.

Transaction 29 is the relevant internal transaction.

Transaction *29* *31/03/X5* *On 31 March, Smart Concepts accounted for the usage of the furniture and fittings for the period.*

These transactions can be analysed as follows:

	Assets				=	**Owner's equity**	
	Furniture and fittings		Bank			Depreciation expense	
	+/L/Dr	*–/R/Cr*	*+/L/Dr*	*–/R/Cr*		*+/L/Dr*	*–/R/Cr*
5	240 000			240 000			
29		12 000				12 000	
	228 000					12 000	

The furniture and fittings are expected to have a useful life of five years. The furniture and fittings have been used for three months and a usage expense needs to be charged to the income statement for that period. R12 000 of the furniture and fittings has been used (R240 000/5 years x 3/12). The equity item, depreciation expense, is increased by a total of R12 000 with a debit entry. The asset account, furniture and fittings, is reduced by R12 000 with a credit entry.

5.3 Example: Processing of internal transactions at the end of the accounting period

The previous section classified the internal transactions and explained the concept underlying each adjustment. Diagram 5.1 at the beginning of this chapter shows that adjusting the accounts is the first step in producing information. Much of the work of the accountant involves producing information, which begins by deciding what internal transactions are required.

The accountant is given the trial balance, often prepared by a bookkeeper. The trial balance, you will recall, is prepared after the transactions have been journalised and posted to the ledger. The following example takes the trial balance of Smart Concepts, prepared after the external transactions have all been processed (transactions 1–23), and shows how the internal transactions are entered in the journal and posted to the ledger.

SMART CONCEPTS
PRE-ADJUSTMENT TRIAL BALANCE AT 31 MARCH 20X5

Description	Folio	Dr	Cr
Bank	A1	1 345 500	
Rent asset	A2	48 000	
Fixed deposit investment	A3	120 000	
Furniture and fittings	A4	240 000	
Stationery supplies asset	A5	5 000	
Computer parts asset	A6	12 000	
Inventory	A7	600 000	
Accounts receivable	A8	62 500	
Borrowings	L1		600 000
Accounts payable	L2		750 000
Service liability	L3		48 000
Simon Smart Capital	OE1		950 000
Distributions	OE2	60 000	
Sales revenue	I1		937 500
Internet expense	E1	1 500	
Cost of sales	E2	750 000	
Advertising expense	E3	7 000	
Salaries expense	E4	16 000	
Interest expense	E5	18 000	
		3 285 500	3 285 500

As mentioned at the beginning of the chapter, once the external transactions have been processed and a trial balance prepared, the internal transactions, or adjusting entries, need to be taken into account before the financial statements are prepared. Transactions 24–29 are the internal transactions.

24. On 31 March, Simon examined the records of the business and established that technical support in respect of contracts to the value of R6 000 had been provided to customers.
25. On 31 March, Smart Concepts accounted for the interest on the fixed deposit earned for the period.

26. On 31 March, Smart Concepts recognised the rent expense incurred for the period.
27. On 31 March, the telephone account for R1 500 and the electricity account for R2 500 had been received but not paid.
28. On 31 March, Simon counted stationery supplies on hand costing R2 000 and also determined from the records that computer parts costing R8 500 had been used.
29. On 31 March, Smart Concepts accounted for the usage of the furniture and fittings for the period.

You are required to:

journalise the above adjustments, post to the relevant ledger accounts and prepare a post-adjustment trial balance.

Solution: Processing of internal transactions at the end of the accounting period

The conceptual explanation of each of the internal transactions was given in the previous section. It is important for you to be able to identify the adjustments required at the end of a period and classify them as described in the previous section. Detailed explanations of each adjustment will not be given here as the journalising and posting are mechanical procedures.

GENERAL JOURNAL OF SMART CONCEPTS (GJ 3)

Date	Description	Fol	Dr	Cr
20X5				
March				
31	Service liability	L3	6 000	
	Service revenue	I2		6 000
	Recognition of unearned income (24)			
31	Interest asset	A9	1 500	
	Interest revenue	I3		1 500
	Recording of accrued income (25)			
31	Rent expense	E6	36 000	
	Rent asset	A2		36 000
	Recognition of pre-paid expense (26)			
31	Telephone & electricity expense	E7	4 000	
	Telephone & electricity liability	L4		4 000
	Recording of accrued expenses (27)			
31	Stationery supplies expense	E8	3 000	
	Computer parts expense	E9	8 500	
	Stationery supplies asset	A5		3 000
	Computer parts asset	A6		8 500
	Current assets used (28)			
31	Depreciation expense	E10	12 000	
	Furniture & fittings	A4		12 000
	Non-current assets used (29)			

These transactions are then recorded in the ledger. The ledger accounts affected by each entry are shown, with the **adjustment highlighted**.

Recognition of unearned income

Dr — **SERVICE LIABILITY (GL L3)** — **Cr**

Date	Details	Fol	R	Date	Details	Fol	R
31/03	**Service revenue**	**GJ3**	**6 000**	25/02	Bank	GJ2	48 000
31/03	Balance	c/d	42 000				
			48 000				48 000
				01/04	Balance	b/d	42 000

Dr — **SERVICE REVENUE (GL I2)** — **Cr**

Date	Details	Fol	R	Date	Details	Fol	R
31/03	Balance	c/d	6 000	**31/03**	**Service liability**	**GJ3**	**6 000**
			6 000				6 000
				31/03	Balance	b/d	6 000

Recording of accrued income

Dr — **INTEREST ASSET (GL A9)** — **Cr**

Date	Details	Fol	R	Date	Details	Fol	R
31/03	**Interest revenue**	**GJ3**	**1 500**	31/03	Balance	c/d	1 500
			1 500				1 500
01/04	Balance	b/d	1 500				

Dr — **INTEREST REVENUE (GL I3)** — **Cr**

Date	Details	Fol	R	Date	Details	Fol	R
31/03	Balance	c/d	1 500	**31/03**	**Interest asset**	**GJ3**	**1 500**
			1 500				1 500
				31/03	Balance	b/d	1 500

Recognition of pre-paid expenses

Dr **RENT ASSET (GL A2)** **Cr**

Date	Details	Fol	R	Date	Details	Fol	R
02/01	Bank	GJ1	48 000	**31/03**	**Rent expense**	**GJ3**	**36 000**
				31/03	Balance	c/d	12 000
			48 000				48 000
01/04	Balance	b/d	12 000				

Dr **RENT EXPENSE (GL E6)** **Cr**

Date	Details	Fol	R	Date	Details	Fol	R
31/03	**Rent asset**	**GJ3**	**36 000**	31/03	Balance	c/d	36 000
			36 000				36 000
31/03	Balance	b/d	36 000				

Recording of accrued expenses

Dr **TELEPHONE AND ELECTRICITY LIABILITY (GL L4)** **Cr**

Date	Details	Fol	R	Date	Details	Fol	R
31/03	Balance	c/d	4 000	**31/03**	**Telephone and electricity expense**	**GJ3**	**4 000**
			4 000				4 000
				01/04	Balance	b/d	4 000

Dr **TELEPHONE AND ELECTRICITY EXPENSE (GL E7)** **Cr**

Date	Details	Fol	R	Date	Details	Fol	R
31/03	**Telephone and electricity liability**	**GJ3**	**4 000**	31/03	Balance	c/d	4 000
			4 000				4 000
31/03	Balance	b/d	4 000				

Recognition of current assets used

Dr **STATIONERY SUPPLIES ASSET (GL A5)** Cr

Date	Details	Fol	R	Date	Details	Fol	R
05/01	Bank	GJ1	5 000	**31/03**	**Stationery supplies expense**	**GJ3**	**3 000**
				31/03	Balance	c/d	2 000
			5 000				5 000
01/04	Balance	b/d	2 000				

Dr **STATIONERY SUPPLIES EXPENSE (GL E8)** Cr

Date	Details	Fol	R	Date	Details	Fol	R
31/03	**Stationery supplies asset**	**GJ3**	**3 000**	31/03	Balance	c/d	3 000
			3 000				3 000
31/03	Balance	b/d	3 000				

Dr **COMPUTER PARTS ASSET (GL A6)** Cr

Date	Details	Fol	R	Date	Details	Fol	R
05/01	Bank	GJ1	12 000	**31/03**	**Computer parts expense**	**GJ3**	**8 500**
				31/03	Balance	c/d	3 500
			12 000				12 000
01/04	Balance	b/d	3 500				

Dr **COMPUTER PARTS EXPENSE (GL E9)** Cr

Date	Details	Fol	R	Date	Details	Fol	R
31/03	**Computer parts asset**	**GJ3**	**8 500**	31/03	Balance	c/d	8 500
			8 500				8 500
31/03	Balance	b/d	8 500				

Recognition of non-current assets used

Dr			**FURNITURE AND FITTINGS (GL A4)**				Cr
Date	**Details**	**Fol**	**R**	**Date**	**Details**	**Fol**	**R**
02/01	Bank	GJ1	240 000	**31/03**	**Depreciation expense**	**GJ3**	**12 000**
				31/03	Balance	c/d	228 000
			240 000				240 000
01/04	Balance	b/d	228 000				

Dr			**DEPRECIATION EXPENSE (GL E10)**				Cr
Date	**Details**	**Fol**	**R**	**Date**	**Details**	**Fol**	**R**
31/03	**Furniture and fittings**	**GJ3**	**12 000**	31/03	Balance	c/d	12 000
			12 000				12 000
31/03	Balance	b/d	12 000				

After the internal transactions have been recorded and posted, a post-adjustment trial balance is extracted in order to assist in preparing the financial statements. Smart Concepts' post-adjustment trial balance is presented below.

SMART CONCEPTS
POST-ADJUSTMENT TRIAL BALANCE AT 31 MARCH 20X5

Description	**Folio**	**Dr**	**Cr**
Bank	A1	1 345 500	
Rent asset	A2	12 000	
Fixed deposit investment	A3	120 000	
Furniture and fittings	A4	228 000	
Stationery supplies asset	A5	2 000	
Computer parts asset	A6	3 500	
Inventory	A7	600 000	
Accounts receivable	A8	62 500	
Interest asset	A9	1 500	
Borrowings	L1		600 000
Accounts payable	L2		750 000
Service liability	L3		42 000
Telephone and electricity liability	L4		4 000

Simon Smart Capital	OE1		950 000
Distributions	OE2	60 000	
Sales revenue	I1		937 500
Service revenue	I2		6 000
Interest revenue	I3		1 500
Internet expense	E1	1 500	
Cost of sales	E2	750 000	
Advertising expense	E3	7 000	
Salaries expense	E4	16 000	
Interest expense	E5	18 000	
Rent expense	E6	36 000	
Telephone and electricity expense	E7	4 000	
Stationery supplies expense	E8	3 000	
Computer parts expense	E9	8 500	
Depreciation expense	E10	12 000	
		3 291 000	3 291 000

5.4 Recording receipts and payments into income and expense accounts

We have emphasised throughout this book that when cash is received in advance of earning income, a liability is created, representing the obligation to provide the service in the future. Similarly, when cash is paid in advance of incurral of expenses, an asset is created, representing the right to receive a service in the future. At the end of the period, adjustments are made to recognise the income earned and the expense incurred during the period. This procedure was described in the previous sections.

Some business entities may decide to record all cash receipts for services provided with credits to income accounts, and all cash paid for services acquired with debits to expense accounts. We will now address this procedure, and the corresponding adjusting entries.

5.4.1 Recording of receipts into income accounts

When cash is received in advance of earning income and it is known that the service will be provided in full by the end of the period, the credit may be recorded in an income account as opposed to a liability account. If the service is provided by the end of the period, no adjusting entry is required as the amount earned is correctly reflected in an income account.

On the other hand, the income account may also be credited on receipt of the cash even if the service is not to be provided in full by the end of the period. Then, if any amount of the income represented by the cash received remains unearned at the end of the period, an adjustment is made to transfer the amount unearned to a liability account.

To illustrate this, recall transaction 14 of Smart Concepts where R48 000 was received in respect of technical support contracts taken out by customers. At the end of the period (transaction 24), services to the value of R6 000 had been provided. Both methods (of recording the receipt in a liability account or an income account) are illustrated below, together with the relevant adjusting entry.

Transaction		**Receipt recorded as a liability**		**Receipt recorded as income**	
External		**Dr**	**Cr**	**Dr**	**Cr**
14	Bank	48 000			
	Service liability		48 000		
14	Bank			48 000	
	Service revenue				48 000
Internal					
24	Service liability	6 000			
	Service revenue		6 000		
24	Service revenue			42 000	
	Service liability				42 000

The required internal transaction, or adjusting entry, depends on how the external transaction or original entry was recorded. When the R48 000 cash received was recorded as a liability, the adjusting entry reduced the liability by the amount *earned* of R6 000, and transferred this amount to the income account, service revenue. The statement of financial position account, service liability, reported a balance of R42 000 representing the income *unearned* at the end of the period, and the income account, service revenue, showed R6 000 being the amount *earned* during the period. On the other hand, when the cash received was recorded as income, the adjusting entry reduced the income by the amount *unearned* of R42 000 and transferred this amount to the liability account, service liability. Again, the statement of financial position liability account reported a balance of R42 000 *unearned* at the end of the period, and the income statement income account a balance of R6 000 *earned* during the period.

5.4.2 Recording of payments into expense accounts

When cash is paid in advance of incurral of expenses and it is known that the service will be received in full by the end of the period, the debit may be recorded in an expense account as opposed to an asset account. If the service is received by the end of the period, no adjusting entry is required as the amount incurred is correctly reflected in an expense account.

On the other hand, the expense account may also be debited on payment of the cash even if the service is not to be received in full by the end of the period. Then, if any amount of the expense represented by the cash paid remains unexpired at the end of the period, an adjustment is made to transfer the amount unused to an asset account.

To illustrate this, recall transaction 3 of Smart Concepts where R48 000 was paid at the beginning of January in respect of rental from January to April. At the end of the period (transaction 26), rent of R36 000 had expired. Both methods (of recording the payment in an asset account or an expense account) are illustrated below, together with the relevant adjusting entry.

Transaction		Payment recorded as an asset		Payment recorded as an expense	
		Dr	**Cr**	**Dr**	**Cr**
External					
3	Rent asset	48 000			
	Bank		48 000		
3	Rent expense			48 000	
	Bank				48 000
Internal					
26	Rent expense	36 000			
	Rent asset		36 000		
26	Rent asset			12 000	
	Rent expense				12 000

The required internal transaction, or adjusting entry, depends on how the external transaction or original entry was recorded. When the R48 000 cash paid was recorded as an asset, the adjusting entry reduced the asset by the amount *expired* of R36 000, and transferred this amount to the expense account, rent expense. The statement of financial position account, rent asset, reported a balance of R12 000, representing the expense *prepaid* at the end of the period and the expense account, rent expense, showed R36 000, being the amount *incurred* during the period. On the other hand, when the cash paid was recorded as an expense, the adjusting entry reduced the expense by the *unexpired* amount of R12 000 and transferred this amount to the asset account, rent asset. Again, the statement of financial position asset account reported a balance of R12 000 *prepaid* at the end of the period, and the income statement expense account a balance of R36 000 *incurred* during the period.

5.5 Exam examples

5.5.1

The following information has been extracted from the pre- and post-adjustment trial balances of Buckingham Blues.

Transaction	Unadjusted		Adjusted	
	Dr	**Cr**	**Dr**	**Cr**
Rent asset	12 400		11 800	
Wages liability				2 800
Consumable stores	1 800		1 600	

The adjusting journal entries must have included these items:

(a) A R600 debit to rent expense, a R2 800 debit to wages expense, and a R200 debit to consumable stores expense.

(b) A R600 debit to rent expense, a R2 800 credit to wages liability, and a R200 debit to consumable stores.

(c) A R600 credit to rent asset, a R2 800 debit to wages liability, and a R200 credit to consumable stores.

(d) A R600 credit to rent expense, a R2 800 debit to wages expense, and a R200 debit to consumable stores expense.

(e) A R600 debit to rent asset, a R2 800 credit to wages liability, and a R200 credit to consumable stores.

5.5.2

Charles Polo School recorded R3 200 of accrued telephone charges with an adjusting entry on 28 February 20X5, the year-end of the entity. On 20 March 20X5, an amount of R16 000 was paid to Telkom. No other payments were made in respect of telephone charges during March 20X5. This information enables you to determine the following about the payment of R16 000:

(a) The entry on 20 March 20X5 included a R12 800 credit to bank.

(b) The telephone expense allocated to the 20X6 year is R16 000.

(c) The telephone expense allocated to the 20X6 year is R12 800.

(d) The telephone expense allocated to the 20X5 year is R12 800.

(e) On 1 March 20X5 an entry was passed to reverse the R3 200 accrual.

The following information relates to questions 5.5.3 and 5.5.4.

Pat Pillay owns properties in the municipalities of Sandton and Lenasia. Rates in Sandton are payable on 1 July each year for the current calendar year. In Lenasia, rates are payable quarterly in advance on 2 January, 1 April, 1 July and 1 October.

Pillay commenced business operations on 1 April 20X3 and on that date transferred the two properties into the business. The property in Sandton was valued at R100 000 and the one in Lenasia at R200 000.

The following transactions took place during the first year ending on 28 February 20X4:

- 1 April 20X3 Paid rates of R900 to the Lenasia municipality.
- 1 July 20X3 Paid rates of R900 to the Lenasia municipality and paid rates of R1 800 to the Sandton municipality (for the period from 1 April to 31 December).
- 1 October 20X3 Paid rates of R900 to the Lenasia municipality.
- 2 January 20X4 Paid rates of R900 to the Lenasia municipality.

5.5.3

The income statement of Pat Pillay for the period ended 28 February 20X4 will show rates expense as:

(a) R5 400
(b) R5 100
(c) R5 800
(d) R5 700
(e) R5 500

5.5.4

The statement of financial position of Pat Pillay at 28 February 20X4 will show a rates asset of:

(a) R300
(b) R400
(c) R700
(d) R100
(e) R900

Summary of concepts and applications

1. The purpose of internal transactions (or adjusting entries) is to ensure that the income statement reports income that has been earned and expenses that have been incurred during the period. Internal transactions need to be processed at the end of each reporting period in order to comply with the accrual basis of accounting.

2. If the cash received during the period equals the income earned, there will be no adjusting entries in respect of income, and likewise, if the cash paid equals the expenses incurred, there will be no adjustments in respect of those expenses. Adjusting entries are necessary when the receipt or payment of cash does not correspond with the earning of income or the incurral of expenses after the external transactions have been processed. The adjusting entries are processed by entering each transaction in the journal and posting to the ledger. There are two other period-end adjustments, namely, the recognition of current assets used.

3. Adjusting entries are processed in this chapter in respect of the internal transactions in the Smart Concepts example.

4. An alternative approach adopted is to record all cash receipts in respect of services provided with credits to income accounts and all cash paid for services acquired with debits to expense accounts. When cash is received in advance of earning income and the service is provided by the end of the period, no adjusting entry is required, as the amount earned is correctly reflected in an income account. However, if any amount of the income remains unearned at the end of the period, an adjustment is made to transfer the amount unearned to a liability account. When cash is paid in advance of incurral of expenses and the service is received by the end of the period, no adjusting entry is required, as the amount incurred is correctly reflected in an expense account. However, if any amount of the expense remains unexpired at the end of the period, an adjustment is made to transfer the amount unused to an asset account.

6 Preparation of the Financial Statements

'The system of bookkeeping enables a man at any time to know his exact worth, the nature of his assets and liabilities, the gains or losses in detail, and how they arise ...; he can compare his expenditures for similar objects during different periods, and he can analyse the results.'
(Battersby, 1878)

Outcomes

- Explain the role and purpose of financial statements in the accounting process.
- Recall the requirements of IAS 1 relating to the format of, and the information reflected in, financial statements.
- Explain the classification of assets and liabilities.
- Distinguish between the pre-adjustment and post-adjustment trial balances.
- Demonstrate the concept of recognition.
- Recall the format of, and the information reflected in the statement of comprehensive income, statement of financial position and statement of changes in equity.
- Determine an effective approach to answering exam questions related to the preparation of financial statements.

Chapter outline

6.1 Financial statements in the context of the accounting process
6.2 Structure and content of financial statements
6.3 Classification of assets and liabilities
6.4 The pre-adjustment and post-adjustment trial balances
6.5 Recognition of the elements of the financial statements
6.5.1 Recognition of assets
6.5.2 Recognition of liabilities
6.5.3 Recognition of income
6.5.4 Recognition of expenses
6.6 The financial statements
6.6.1 The statement of comprehensive income
6.6.2 The statement of financial position
6.6.3 The statement of changes in equity
6.7 Application of the general features
6.8 Exam technique
6.9 Exam example

Murray & Roberts Holdings Limited
Statement of financial position for the year ended 30 June 2007

	(R Millions)	
ASSETS		
Non-current assets		4 174
Property, plant and equipment	2 012	
Investment property	526	
Goodwill	206	
Intangible assets	74	
Investments	1 323	
Deferred tax	16	
Operating lease receivables	17	
Current assets		8 835
Inventories	814	
Trade and other receivables	5 189	
Cash and cash equivalents	2 832	
Total assets		13 009
EQUITY AND LIABILITIES		
Capital and reserves		3 814
Share capital and premium	1 037	
Non-distributable reserves	78	
Retained earnings	2 699	
Non-current liabilities		1 103
Long term loans	695	
Long term provisions	64	
Deferred tax	277	
Non-current payables	67	
Current liabilities		8 092
Trade and other payables	6 939	
Provisions for obligations	262	
Current tax payable	220	
Bank overdraft	671	
Total equity and liabilities		13 009

Murray and Roberts is a global construction company that focuses on infrastructure, such as the construction of power plants, stadiums and airports. Their engineers undertake groundbreaking projects while their accountants produce vital financial statements. The preparation of financial statements is crucial to meeting the objective of providing useful information to users.

6.1 Financial statements in the context of the accounting process

Diagram 6.1 illustrates the accounting process to which you have been introduced already. Up to now you have analysed transactions, recorded them in the accounting records, extracted a trial balance and adjusted the balances to conform with the accrual basis of accounting. The current chapter examines the preparation of financial statements from the adjusted accounting records.

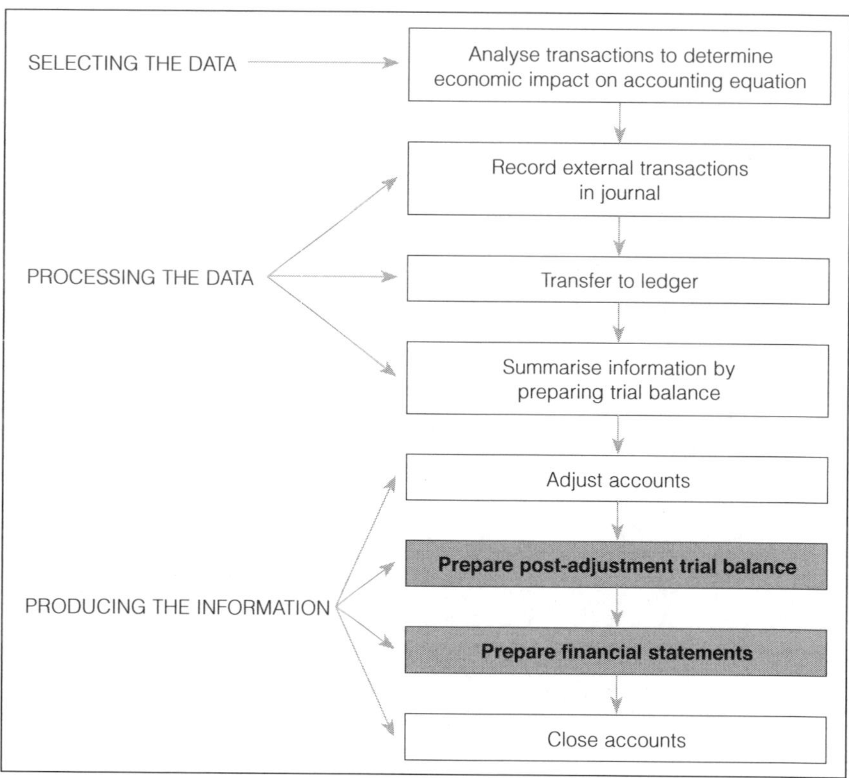

Diagram 6.1: The accounting process, highlighting the preparation of financial statements

6.2 Structure and content of financial statements

You were introduced to the components of the financial statements in Chapter 2 (the statement of financial position, statement of comprehensive income, statement of cash flows, statement of changes in equity, as well as accounting policies and explanatory notes).

IAS 1 requires each component to be clearly identified and also requires the following information to be displayed for a proper understanding of the financial statements:[1]

- the name of the entity and any change from the preceding statement of financial position date
- the statement of financial position date (referred to as the reporting date) and the period covered by the financial statements
- the presentation currency
- the level of rounding used in presenting amounts in the financial statements.

Judgement is required in determining the best way of presenting such information.

6.3 Classification of assets and liabilities

In earlier chapters you were introduced to the basic format of a statement of financial position and of an statement of comprehensive income. The statement of financial position has two sections, **assets** (the resources of the entity) and **equity and liabilities** (the sources of finance). The statement of financial position is derived directly from the accounting equation, assets = liabilities + owner's equity.

In order to understand the classification of assets and liabilities, it is necessary to review the operating cycle of an enterprise.

The operating cycle of an enterprise is the time between the acquisition of inventory and its ultimate realisation in cash. The operating cycle can be illustrated as follows:

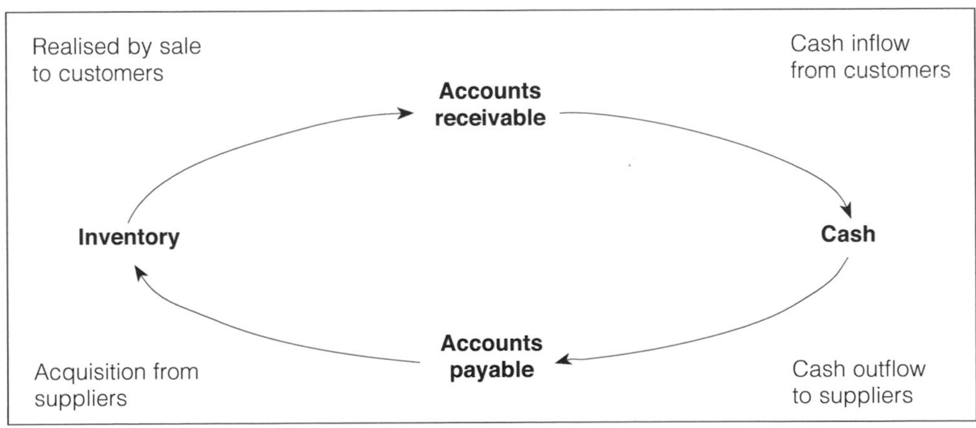

Diagram 6.2: The operating cycle

Inventory, accounts receivable and cash are typical assets which circulate in the operating cycle. Inventory is purchased from suppliers and then realised by sale to customers. When inventory is sold on credit to customers, accounts receivable are created which will ultimately result in a cash inflow when the customers settle their accounts. This completes the operating cycle. Cash is used to pay the suppliers for inventory purchased and the cycle begins again with the purchase of inventory.

When examining the financial statements of an enterprise you will notice that the assets are classified into two different types, ***non-current assets*** and ***current assets***.

According to IAS 1,[2] an entity shall classify an asset as current asset when:

- it expects to realise the asset, or intends to sell or consume it, in its normal operating cycle, **or**
- it holds the asset primarily for the purpose of being traded, **or**
- it expects to realise the asset within twelve months after the reporting period, **or**
- it is cash or a cash equivalent.

All other assets are classified as non-current assets.

The operating cycle of many entities is shorter than twelve months and the inventory and accounts receivable will normally be realised within that time. However, current assets include assets (such as inventory and accounts receivable) that are sold, consumed or realised as part of the normal operating cycle even when they are not expected to be realised within twelve months after reporting period.[3] In other words, inventory is classified as a current asset even if it is only expected to be realised beyond twelve months of the reporting date.

Examples of current assets include inventory, accounts receivable, supplies, bank and cash, prepaid expenses and accrued income. Examples of non-current assets include land, buildings, motor vehicles, plant and machinery, furniture and computer equipment.

Turning our attention to liabilities, the financial statements of an enterprise classify liabilities into two different types, ***non-current liabilities*** and ***current liabilities***.

According to IAS 1,[4] an entity shall classify a liability as current when:

- it expects to settle the liability in its normal operating cycle, **or**
- it holds the liability primarily for the purpose of trading, **or**
- the liability is due to be settled within twelve months after the end of the reporting period, **or**
- the entity does not have an unconditional right to defer settlement of the liability for at least twelve months after the the reporting period.

All other liabilities are non-current liabilities.

Current liabilities are therefore categorised in a similar way to current assets. Current liabilities such as accounts payable and accrued expenses are normally settled within twelve months of the reporting date. However, such items are classified as current liabilities even if they are due to be settled after more than twelve months from the reporting date.

Examples of current liabilities include accounts payable, unearned income and accrued expenses. Examples of non-current liabilties include loans and mortgage bonds.

The accounting equation can therefore be expanded as follows:

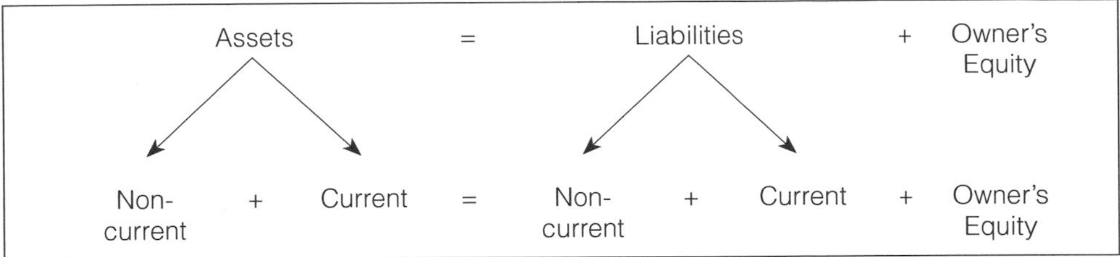

Diagram 6.3: The expanded accounting equation

Pause and reflect...

a) An entity that trades as an antique dealer buys inventory with a cost of R75 000 on 1 October 20X0. The inventory is not expected to be sold until early 20X2. The entity has a year end of 31 December. How will the inventory be classified on the statement of financial position at 31 December 20X0?

b) An entity raises a loan for R120 000 on 1 October 20X0. The loan is to be repaid in three equal annual instalments of R40 000 each on 30 September 20X1, 20X2 and 20X3. The entity has a year-end of 31 December. How will the loan be classified on the statement of financial position at 31 December 20X0?

Response

a) At 31 December 20X0, the inventory is expected to be realised beyond twelve months after the end of the reporting period. However, as inventory is being held primarily for the purposes of being traded, inventory of R75 000 is classified as a current asset.

b) At 31 December 20X0, R40 000 of the loan is due to be settled within twelve months after the end of the reporting period and R80 000 of the loan is due to be settled beyond twelve months after the end of the reporting period. Therefore, R40 000 will be classified as a current liability and R80 000 will be classified as a non-current liability.

6.4 The pre-adjustment and post-adjustment trial balances

The trial balance prepared in Chapter 4 is known as a pre-adjustment trial balance as it is prepared before the adjusting entries are processed. A post-adjustment trial balance is prepared after the adjusting entries are processed to assist in preparing the financial statements. The post-adjustment trial balance was prepared in Chapter 5.

The remainder of this chapter uses the Smart Concepts example to illustrate the preparation of financial statements. The accounting process is briefly reviewed to place the steps in context.

In Chapter 4 the external transactions, 1–23 below, were analysed and recorded in the accounting records:

External transactions

1. On 2 January, Simon Smart started a business as a computer retailer. He drew R950 000 from a savings account and opened a bank account in the name of Smart Concepts into which he paid R950 000.
2. On 2 January, Smart Concepts negotiated a loan from Techno Bank for an amount of R600 000. The loan is repayable in four equal annual installments, beginning on 31 December 20X5. The interest rate is 12% per annum, payable quarterly in arrears.
3. On 2 January, Simon located premises from which to operate in Rosebank. The monthly rent for the premises is R12 000. Smart Concepts paid four months rent in advance.
4. On 2 January, Simon transferred R120 000 from the bank account into a fixed deposit account earning interest at 5% per annum.
5. On 2 January, Smart Concepts purchased furniture and fittings for R240 000. This was paid for from funds in the bank account. The expected useful life of the furniture and fittings is five years.
6. On 5 January, Smart Concepts purchased supplies of stationery for R5 000 as well as supplies of computer parts for R12 000. All the supplies were paid for in cash.
7. On 7 January, Smart Concepts opened an account with Computer World, the supplier of its inventory.
8. On 10 January, Smart Concepts purchased inventory of sixty computers from Computer World at a cost of R10 000 each. The total amount owing is to be paid by 25 March.
9. On 12 January, Smart Concepts paid a service provider R750 in respect of a data bundle for internet access.
10. On 25 January, Smart Concepts sold fifteen computers on account to a customer for R12 500 each. An amount of R125 000 is due by 15 March and the balance by 15 April.
11. On 1 February, Smart Concepts employed a computer technician at a salary of R8 000 per month.
12. On 8 February, Smart Concepts paid R7 000 for an advertisement in a newspaper, advertising the computers available for sale.
13. On 12 February, Smart Concepts sold thirty computers, to customers, for R12 500 each. The customers paid cash for the computers.
14. On 25 February, Smart Concepts received cash of R48 000 in respect of technical support contracts taken out by customers. The contracts are for a two year period.
15. On 28 February, Smart Concepts paid the computer technician his salary for February.
16. On 4 March, Smart Concepts purchased inventory of a further seventy five computers from Computer World at a cost of R10 000 each. The total amount owing is to be paid by 25 May.
17. On 5 March, Smart Concepts paid a service provider R750 in respect of a data bundle for internet access.
18. On 15 March, Smart Concepts received R125 000 from the customer in transaction 10.
19. On 25 March, Smart Concepts paid Computer World an amount of R600 000.
20. On 29 March, Smart Concepts sold thirty computers, to customers, for R12 500 each. The customers paid cash for the computers.
21. On 30 March, Smart Concepts paid the computer technician his salary for March.
22. On 30 March, Smart Concepts paid the interest on the loan from Techno Bank for the three month period.
23. On 30 March, Simon authorised a distribution to himself of R60 000 for personal use.

This resulted in the pre-adjustment trial balance presented below:

SMART CONCEPTS
PRE-ADJUSTMENT TRIAL BALANCE AT 31 MARCH 20X5

Description	Folio	Dr	Cr
Bank	A1	1 345 500	
Rent asset	A2	48 000	
Fixed deposit investment	A3	120 000	
Furniture and fittings	A4	240 000	
Stationery supplies asset	A5	5 000	
Computer parts asset	A6	12 000	
Inventory	A7	600 000	
Accounts receivable	A8	62 500	
Borrowings	L1		600 000
Accounts payable	L2		750 000
Service liability	L3		48 000
Simon Smart Capital	OE1		950 000
Distributions	OE2	60 000	
Sales revenue	I1		937 500
Internet expense	E1	1 500	
Cost of sales	E2	750 000	
Advertising expense	E3	7 000	
Salaries expense	E4	16 000	
Interest expense	E5	18 000	
		3 285 500	3 285 500

In Chapter 5 you were introduced to the internal transactions. This resulted in internal adjustments made to the pre-adjustment balances. The adjustments had to be journalised and posted to the ledger. Transactions 24–29 below were the adjustments processed at the end of the period:

Internal transactions

24. On 31 March, Simon examined the records of the business and established that technical support in respect of contracts to the value of R6 000 had been provided to customers.
25. On 31 March, Smart Concepts accounted for the interest on the fixed deposit earned for the period.
26. On 31 March, Smart Concepts recognised the rent expense incurred for the period.
27. On 31 March, the telephone account for R1 500 and the electricity account for R2 500 had been received but not paid.
28. On 31 March, Simon counted stationery supplies on hand costing R2 000 and also determined from the records that computer parts costing R8 500 had been used.
29. On 31 March, Smart Concepts accounted for the usage of the furniture and fittings for the period.

After the internal transactions had been recorded and posted, a post-adjustment trial balance was extracted in order to assist in preparing the financial statements. Smart Concepts' post-adjustment trial balance is presented below.

SMART CONCEPTS
POST-ADJUSTMENT TRIAL BALANCE AT 31 MARCH 20X5

Description	Folio	Dr	Cr
Bank	A1	1 345 500	
Rent asset	A2	12 000	
Fixed deposit investment	A3	120 000	
Furniture and fittings	A4	228 000	
Stationery supplies asset	A5	2 000	
Computer parts asset	A6	3 500	
Inventory	A7	600 000	
Accounts receivable	A8	62 500	
Interest asset	A9	1 500	
Borrowings	L1		600 000
Accounts payable	L2		750 000
Service liability	L3		42 000
Telephone and electricity liability	L4		4 000
Simon Smart Capital	OE1		950 000
Distributions	OE2	60 000	
Sales revenue	I1		937 500
Service revenue	I2		6 000
Interest revenue	I3		1 500
Internet expense	E1	1 500	
Cost of sales	E2	750 000	
Advertising expense	E3	7 000	
Salaries expense	E4	16 000	
Interest expense	E5	18 000	
Rent expense	E6	36 000	
Telephone and electricity expense	E7	4 000	
Stationery supplies expense	E8	3 000	
Computer parts expense	E9	8 500	
Depreciation expense	E10	12 000	
		3 291 000	3 291 000

6.5 Recognition of the elements of the financial statements

According to the accounting framework,[5] recognition is the process of incorporating in the statement of financial position or statement of comprehensive income an item that meets the definition of an element and satisfies the recognition criteria. You were introduced to the *elements* of financial statements in Chapter 2 – assets, liabilities, income, expenses and equity. An item that meets the definition of an element should be *recognised* if:[6]

- ❑ it is probable that future economic benefits associated with the item will flow to or from the enterprise, **and**
- ❑ the item has a cost or value that can be measured reliably.

An assessment of the probability of future cash flows is made on the basis of the evidence available when the financial statements are prepared. This relates to the degree of uncertainty that the future economic benefits will flow to or from an enterprise.

For an item to be measured with reliability it must possess a cost or value that is free from material error or bias and is a truthful representation of the underlying economic events. This relates to the qualitative characteristic of reliability discussed in Chapter 1. In many cases, cost or value may need to be estimated. It is important to note that the use of estimates is an essential part of the preparation of financial statements and does not undermine their reliability. When, however, a reliable estimate cannot be made, the item is not recognised in the statement of financial position or statement of comprehensive income.

The recognition criteria for assets, liabilities, income and expenses are discussed below. There are no specific recognition criteria for equity, as equity is the residual interest in the assets of an enterprise after deducting all its liabilities.

6.5.1 Recognition of assets

An asset is recognised in the statement of financial position[7]

- when it is probable that the future economic benefits will flow to the enterprise, **and**
- the asset has a cost or value that can be measured reliably.

An asset is not recognised in the statement of financial position when expenditure has been incurred for which it is considered improbable that economic benefits will flow to the enterprise beyond the current period. In this situation, the transaction results in the recognition of an expense on the statement of comprehensive income.

Applying these principles to the Smart Concepts example, each asset on the statement of financial position must satisfy the definition of an asset and the recognition criteria for an asset in accordance with the accounting framework. This process is illustrated by the purchase of the furniture and fittings (transaction 5). Firstly, the item must meet the definition of an asset. Furniture and fittings are a resource controlled by the enterprise (Smart Concepts controls the furniture and fittings for their economic life), as a result of past events (Smart Concepts purchased the furniture and fittings) and from which future economic benefits are expected to flow to the enterprise (the furniture and fittings will facilitate the selling of computers). Therefore the furniture and fittings satisfy the definition of an asset. Secondly, the item must meet the recognition criteria for an asset. It is probable that future economic benefits will flow to the enterprise (Smart Concepts utilises the furniture and fittings to display the computers) and the asset has a cost or value that can be reliably measured (the furniture and fittings were purchased for R240 000). Thus the furniture and fittings satisfy the recognition criteria for assets and their recognition on the statement of financial position is appropriate.

6.5.2 Recognition of liabilities

A liability is recognised in the statement of financial position[8]
- when it is probable that an outflow of resources embodying economic benefits will result from the settlement of a present obligation, **and**
- the amount at which the settlement will take place can be measured reliably.

Applying these principles to the Smart Concepts example, each liability on the statement of financial position must satisfy the definition of a liability and the recognition criteria for a liability in accordance with the accounting framework. This process is illustrated by the purchase of inventory on credit from Computer World (transaction 8). Firstly, the item must meet the definition of a liability. The commitment to pay Computer World is a present obligation of the enterprise (Smart Concepts has undertaken to pay the supplier for the inventory received), arising from past events (Smart Concepts purchased the inventory on account from the supplier) and the settlement of which is expected to result in an outflow from the enterprise of resources embodying economic benefits (Smart Concepts will pay the supplier in cash for the inventory received). Therefore the commitment to pay Computer World satisfies the definition of a liability. Secondly, the item must meet the recognition criteria for a liability. It is probable that an outflow of resources embodying economic benefits will result from the settlement of a present obligation (Smart Concepts is obligated to pay the supplier in cash by 25 March) and the amount at which the settlement will take place can be measured reliably (Smart Concepts is obligated to pay the supplier R600 000). Thus the commitment to pay Computer World satisfies the recognition criteria for a liability and its recognition on the statement of financial position is appropriate.

6.5.3 Recognition of income

Income is recognised in the statement of comprehensive income[9]
- when an increase in future economic benefits related to an increase in an asset or a decrease in a liability has arisen
- that can be measured reliably.

Applying these principles to the Smart Concepts example, all income on the statement of comprehensive income must satisfy the definition of income and the recognition criteria for income in accordance with the Accounting Framework. This process is illustrated by the sale of computers to a customer on account (transaction 10). Firstly, the item must meet the definition of income. The credit sale is an increase in economic benefits during the accounting period in the form of inflows or enhancements of assets or decreases of liabilities that result in increases in equity, other than those relating to contributions from equity participants (Smart Concepts is entitled to receive payment from the customer in respect of the computers sold and creates an asset, accounts receivable). Therefore the sale of the computers to a customer on account satisfies the definition of income. Secondly, the item must meet the recognition criteria for income. Income is recognised when an increase in future economic benefits related to an increase in an asset or a decrease in a liability has arisen that can be measured reliably (Smart Concepts creates an asset, accounts receivable, of R187 500 in respect of the amount to be received from the customer). Thus the sale of the computers to a customer on account satisfies the recognition criteria for income and its recognition on the statement of comprehensive income is appropriate.

6.5.4 Recognition of expenses

Expenses are recognised in the statement of comprehensive income[10]
- when a decrease in future economic benefits related to a decrease in an asset or an increase in a liability has arisen
- that can be measured reliably.

Applying these principles to the Smart Concepts example, all expenses on the statement of comprehensive income must satisfy the definition of expenses and the recognition criteria for expenses in accordance with the accounting framework. This process is illustrated by the payment for the advertisement (transaction 12). Firstly, the item must meet the definition of an expense. The payment for the advertisement is a decrease in economic benefits during the accounting period in the form of outflows or depletions of assets or incurrences of liabilities that result in decreases in equity, other than those relating to distributions to equity participants (Smart Concepts has paid for the advertisement and reduced an asset, bank). Therefore the payment for the advertisement satisfies the definition of an expense. Secondly, the item must meet the recognition criteria for expenses. Expenses are recognised when a decrease in future economic benefits related to a decrease in an asset or an increase in a liability has arisen that can be measured reliably (Smart Concepts reduces an asset, bank, by R7 000 in respect of the amount paid for the advertisement). Thus the payment for the advertisement satisfies the recognition criteria for expenses and its recognition on the statement of comprehensive income is appropriate.

6.6 The financial statements

You learnt in Chapter 2 that the financial statements are a structured representation of the financial position and the financial performance of an entity. You also learnt that a complete set of financial statements includes a statement of comprehensive income, a statement of financial position, a statement of changes in equity, a statement of cash flows and notes. We will examine the statement of comprehensive income, statement of financial position and statement of changes in equity in this chapter.

6.6.1 The statement of comprehensive income

You will also recall from Chapter 2 that IAS1 requires an entity to present items of income and expense either in two separate statements

- ❑ The income statement (displaying components of profit or loss) and
- ❑ The statement of comprehensive income (displaying components of other comprehensive income),

or in a single statement, referred to as the statement of comprehensive income (displaying components of profit and loss as well as components of other comprehensive income).

Throughout the Smart Concepts example, we have used a separate income statement, both for the sake of clarity and because there are no transactions in the example giving rise to items of other comprehensive income. It is important now to revisit the concepts of *profit or loss and other comprehensive income* as well as the different presentation options of IAS 1.

The profit for the period includes items of income and expense that measure the performance of the entity for a period of time. The other comprehensive income includes items of income and expense that do not relate to the measurement of performance for the period.

The statement of comprehensive income is drafted from the post-adjustment trial balance using the income and expense elements of the financial statements. Remember that income earned represents a measure of accomplishment and expenses incurred represent a measure of effort.

You will recall from Chapter 1 that there are different types of business entities, such as a service entity and a retail entity. A service entity provides services to clients, whereas a retail entity buys goods from suppliers and then sells the goods to customers. Some entities, such as Smart Concepts, are involved in both retail and service activities. The format of the statement of comprehensive income needs to be adapted to take into account the nature of the entity's activities. The order of presentation and the descriptions used for line items are changed when necessary in order to achieve a fair presentation in each entity's particular circumstances.[11]

You also learnt in Chapter 2 that the elements of the financial statements in the accounting framework that relate to the statement of comprehensive income are income and expenses. It is important to relate the elements to the line items on the statement of comprehensive income in order to understand the format of the statement of comprehensive income. The following diagram links the elements of income and expense to alternative formats for a retail entity, a service entity and a combined retail and service entity.

Elements	Retail entity	Service entity	Combined retail and service entity
	Statement of comprehensive income		
	R	**R**	**R**
Income →	Sales	Fees	Sales
	less		*less*
Expense →	Cost of sales		Cost of sales
	Gross profit		**Gross profit**
			Other income
Income →			Fees
	less	*less*	*less*
Expenses →	Operating expenses	Operating expenses	Operating expenses
→	Finance costs	Finance costs	Finance costs
	Profit for the period	**Profit for the period**	**Profit for the period**
Income or expense →	**Other comprehensive income**	**Other comprehensive income**	**Other comprehensive income**
	Total comprehensive income	**Total comprehensive income**	**Total comprehensive income**

Diagram 6.4: Statement of comprehensive income formats

Note how the format of the statement of comprehensive income differs depending on the nature of the entity's activities. For a **retail entity**, the sales and cost of sales are grouped together, resulting in a sub-total known as the *gross profit*. This is the trading profit of the entity. The operating expenses and finance costs are then subtracted to give the profit for the period. Note that the finance costs are not an operating expense and are listed separately from the operating expenses. The statement of comprehensive income of a **service entity** shows the income, normally comprising fees, less the operating expenses and finance costs, resulting in the profit for the period. Looking at a **combined retail and service entity**, the 'trading' section is presented as for the retail entity. Other income, such as fees, is included after the gross profit before the subtraction of the operating expenses and finance costs.

The presentation option shown in diagram 6.4 is that of a single statement of comprehensive income. Looking at the combined retail and service entity, we could present a separate income statement and statement of comprehensive income as follows:

Elements		Combined retail and service entity
		Income statement
		R
Income	→	Sales
		less
Expense	→	Cost of sales
		Gross profit
		Other income
Income	→	Fees
		less
Expenses	→	Operating expenses
	→	Finance costs
		Profit for the period
		Statement of comprehensive income
		R
		Profit for the period
Income or expense	→	**Other comprehensive income**
		Total comprehensive income

Diagram 6.5: Format with separate income statement and statement of comprehensive income

As there are no items of other comprehensive income in the Smart Concepts example, and to be consistent with the presentation in previous chapters, the separate income statement of Smart Concepts is shown below.

SMART CONCEPTS
INCOME STATEMENT
FOR THE THREE MONTHS ENDED 31 MARCH 20X5

		R
Sales revenue		937 500
Cost of sales		(750 000)
		187 500
Gross profit		
Other income		7 500
Service revenue	6 000	
Interest revenue	1 500	
Operating expenses		(88 000)
Internet expense	1 500	
Advertising	7 000	
Salaries	16 000	
Rent expense	36 000	
Telephone and electricity expense	4 000	
Stationery supplies and computer parts expense	11 500	
Depreciation expense	12 000	
Finance cost		
Interest expense		(18 000)
Profit for the period		89 000

The income statement for Smart Concepts follows the suggested format for a combined retail and service entity. Smart Concepts' trading activities comprise the selling of computers, while the other income is earned through the technical support contracts. Note that there are two items of other income in this case, the service revenue and interest revenue.

Users of financial statements may find it useful to determine the ***profit from operations***, in addition to and distinct from the ***profit for the period***. To determine the profit from operations of Smart Concepts, we reverse the interest expense of R18 000 and the interest revenue of R1 500. The interest expense is a cost of financing the entity, as opposed to a cost of operations. Similarly, the interest revenue does not form part of the day-to-day operations of a computer dealer. The profit from operations is therefore R101 500, calculated as follows:

	R
Profit for the period	85 000
+ Interest expense	18 000
– Interest revenue	(1 500)
Profit from operations	101 000

6.6.2 The statement of financial position

The statement of financial position measures the financial position of an entity at a particular point in time. The objective of the statement of financial position is to assist users to understand the entity's

- resources, for predicting the ability of the entity to generate cash flows
- financial structure, for predicting future borrowing needs and to indicate how profits and cash flows may be allocated.

The statement of financial position is drafted from the post-adjustment trial balance using the asset, liability and equity elements of the financial statements – remember that assets are *resources* of the entity, liabilities are the *obligations* of the entity and equity represents the owner's interest in the entity.

The items on the statement of financial position are classified as explained in section 6.3 above. The format of the statement of financial position is not prescribed and should be changed to achieve fair presentation.

SMART CONCEPTS
STATEMENT OF FINANCIAL POSITION
AT 31 MARCH 20X5

	R
ASSETS	
Non-current assets	348 000
Furniture and fittings	228 000
Fixed deposit investment	120 000
Current assets	2 027 000
Inventory	600 000
Accounts receivable	62 500
Stationery supplies asset	2 000
Computer parts asset	3 500
Interest asset	1 500
Rent asset	12 000
Bank	1 345 500
	2 375 000
EQUITY AND LIABILITIES	
Capital	979 000
Non-current liabilities	
Long term borrowings	450 000
Current liabilities	946 000
Short term borrowings	150 000
Accounts payable	750 000
Service liability	42 000
Telephone and electricity liability	4 000
	2 375 000

Note the format of the statement of financial position. Both the assets and liabilities are categorised as either non-current or current. The distinction between non-current assets and current assets, as well as between non-current liabilities and current liabilities was discussed earlier in this chapter. You will note the separation of the borrowings into long-term and short-term components. This is because R150 000 of the total borrowing of R600 000 is repayable in less than 12 months. Thus the R150 000 represents a current liability. The service liability is also classified as current as it is considered to be part of the entity's normal operating cycle.

6.6.3 The statement of changes in equity

The statement of changes in equity reflects the increases or decreases in the net assets or wealth of an entity for a period of time.

SMART CONCEPTS
STATEMENT OF CHANGES IN EQUITY
FOR THE PERIOD ENDED 31 MARCH 20X5

	R
Balance at 1 January 20X5	–
Profit for the period	89 000
Distributions	(60 000)
Contribution to capital	950 000
Balance at 31 March 20X5	979 000

Pause and reflect...

Can you relate the definition of total comprehensive income to the four types of transactions that affect equity?

Response

Total comprehensive income is defined as the change in equity during a period resulting from transactions and other events, other than transactions with owners in their capacity as owners. As equity is affected only by four types of transactions (the earning of income, the incurral of expenses, contributions by owners and distributions to owners), by excluding transactions with owners in their capacity as owners (contributions and distributions), we are left with total comprehensive income (income and expenses).

6.7 Application of the general features

You will recall from Chapter 2 that IAS 1 discusses general features relevant to the measurement of financial statement items and the reporting of those items. Let us now see whether the general features have been observed in the preparation of the financial statements of Smart Concepts.

Fair presentation

IAS 1 suggests that the appropriate application of International Financial Reporting Standards should result in financial statements that achieve a fair presentation.

You should be able to appreciate at this point that the requirements of IAS 1 relating to the *components* of the financial statements as well as to the *structure and content* of the financial statements have been complied with in the preparation of the financial statements in the previous section. In later chapters in this book, you will learn about some of the other International Financial Reporting Standards, such as the standards relating to inventory (IAS 2) and property, plant and equipment (IAS 16), and you will realise that the appropriate requirements of those standards have also been complied with within the context of the Smart Concepts example.

Going concern

IAS 1 requires that financial statements should be prepared on a going concern basis unless management intends either to liquidate the enterprise or to cease trading, or has no realistic alternative but to do so. In addition, management should make an assessment of an entity's ability to continue as a going concern.

The information in the Smart Concepts example does not suggest that Smart Concepts will fail to continue as a going concern. Furthermore, one can assume that management has made an assessment of the entity's ability to continue as a going concern and is satisfied that Smart Concepts will remain a going concern. The financial statements have thus been prepared on a going concern basis.

Accrual basis of accounting

IAS 1 requires financial statements, except for information relating to cash flows, to be prepared using the accrual basis of accounting. You will recall that, according to the accrual basis, items are recognised as assets, liabilities, income and expenses when they satisfy the definitions and recognition criteria for those elements in the accounting framework.

The items reflected on the post-adjustment trial balance were analysed in the previous chapters to ensure their compliance with the definitions of the elements of financial statements. In addition, the recognition criteria applicable to the elements of financial statements, as discussed in section 6.5 above, were considered with reference to the items on the trial balance. In Chapter 5, the internal transactions were processed for the Smart Concepts example. You will recall that internal transactions are adjustments made to the financial position of an entity in order to comply with the accrual basis of accounting. Thus in generating the post-adjustment trial balance, from which the financial statements are prepared, the effect of the accrual basis of accounting has been considered.

Consistency of presentation and comparative information

IAS 1 requires the presentation and classification of items in the financial statements to be retained from one period to the next and the disclosure of comparative information in respect of the previous period for all amounts reported in the financial statements.

The period from 1 January 20X5 to 31 March 20X5 is the first period of trading for Smart Concepts and thus the information presented relates to the current period only.

Materiality and aggregation

IAS 1 requires each material class of similar items, as well as items of a dissimilar nature, to be presented separately.

Applying this consideration to the Smart Concepts example, it is clear that there are no items that satisfy the criteria for aggregation. It is submitted that the office supplies and parts supplies are sufficiently different in nature to be treated as separate classes. In addition, there are no items in the example that appear significantly immaterial.

Offsetting

IAS 1 does not permit the offsetting of assets and liabilities, as well as income and expenses unless required or permitted by a standard or an interpretation.

The offset of items in the Smart Concepts example is therefore disallowed, as there are no standards, pertaining to items in the example, that require offsetting.

6.8 Exam technique

A common exam question is one where you are given a pre-adjustment trial balance with additional information. You would usually be expected to draft the statement of comprehensive income and/or the statement of financial position and/or the statement of changes in equity for the entity. The pre-adjustment trial balance of Smart Concepts is reproduced below, together with the internal transactions presented as 'additional information'. The solution explains how to approach such a question in an exam and how to present your answer with appropriate workings.

SMART CONCEPTS
PRE-ADJUSTMENT TRIAL BALANCE AT 31 MARCH 20X5

Description	Folio	Dr	Cr
Bank	A1	1 345 500	
Rent asset	A2	48 000	
Fixed deposit investment	A3	120 000	
Furniture and fittings	A4	240 000	
Stationery supplies asset	A5	5 000	
Computer parts asset	A6	12 000	
Inventory	A7	600 000	
Accounts receivable	A8	62 500	
Borrowings	L1		600 000
Accounts payable	L2		750 000
Service liability	L3		48 000
Simon Smart Capital	OE1		950 000
Distributions	OE2	60 000	
Sales revenue	I1		937 500
Internet expense	E1	1 500	
Cost of sales	E2	750 000	
Advertising expense	E3	7 000	
Salaries expense	E4	16 000	
Interest expense	E5	18 000	
		3 285 500	3 285 500

Additional information

24. On 31 March, Simon examined the records of the business and established that technical support in respect of contracts to the value of R6 000 had been performed on customers' computers.
25. On 31 March, Smart Concepts accounted for the interest on the fixed deposit earned for the period.
26. On 31 March, Smart Concepts recognised the rent expense incurred for the period.
27. On 31 March, the telephone account for R1 500 and the electricity account for R2 500 had been received but not paid.
28. On 31 March, Simon counted stationery supplies on hand costing R2 000 and also determined from the service records that computer parts costing R8 500 had been used.
29. On 31 March, Smart Concepts accounted for the usage of the furniture and fittings for the period.

You are required to:

(a) prepare the income statement of Smart Concepts for the three-month period ended 31 March 20X5.
(b) prepare the statement of changes in equity of Smart Concepts for the three-month period ended 31 March 20X5.
(c) prepare the statement of financial position of Smart Concepts at 31 March 20X5.

Solution: Exam technique

In an exam you would not usually have enough time to journalise the adjustments, post to the ledger, and extract the post-adjustment trial balance before drafting the financial statements. In any event, all these steps would not be required of you. You will need to manually adjust the trial balance for the adjustments in the additional information.

Additional information point 24

On 31 March, Simon examined the records of the business and established that technical support to the value of R6 000 had been performed on customers' computers.

Income of R6 000 is now earned. Smart Concepts received cash of R48 000 in respect of technical support contracts taken out by customers. This was originally recorded as a debit to bank and a credit to service liability. Therefore the liability needs to be reduced and income increased, as R6 000 of the services have been provided:
- decrease service liability (Dr) R6 000
- increase service revenue (Cr) R6 000.

Additional information point 25

On 31 March, Smart Concepts accounted for the interest on the fixed deposit earned for the period.

5% of R120 000 for 3 months = R1 500 interest earned but not yet received:
- increase interest asset (Dr) R1 500
- increase interest revenue (Cr) R1 500.

Since these accounts were not on the preadjustment trial balance, you need to include them to be able to make the adjustment.

Additional information point 26

On 31 March, Smart Concepts recognised the rent expense incurred for the period.

This requires an adjustment to the prepaid rent. Before the adjustment is made, examine the trial balance to see how the payment was originally recorded. In this example it was recorded in the rent asset account. Therefore an adjustment is required for the portion used:
- increase rent expense (Dr) R36 000
- decrease rent asset (Cr) R36 000.

Additional information point 27

On 31 March, the telephone account for R1 500 and the electricity account for R2 500 had been received but not paid.

These are expenses incurred but not yet paid:
- increase telephone and electricity expense (Dr) R4 000
- increase telephone and electricity liability (Cr) R4 000.

Since these accounts were not on the preadjustment trial balance, you need to include them to be able to make the adjustment.

Additional information point 28

On 31 March, Simon counted stationery supplies on hand costing R2 000 and also determined from the records that computer parts costing R8 500 had been used.

R3 000 of the stationery supplies asset and R8 500 of the computer parts asset have been used and need to be expensed:

- increase stationery supplies expense (Dr) R3 000
- decrease stationery supplies asset (Cr) R3 000
- increase computer parts expense (Dr) R8 500
- decrease computer parts asset (Cr) R8 500.

Additional information point 29

On 31 March, Smart Concepts accounted for the usage of the furniture and fittings for the period.

Non-current assets are accounted for as being used (depreciated):

- increase depreciation expense (Dr) R12 000
- decrease furniture and fittings (Cr) R12 000.

The income statement, statement of financial position and statement of changes in equity are presented below:

SMART CONCEPTS
INCOME STATEMENT
FOR THE THREE MONTHS ENDED 31 MARCH 20X5

			R
Sales revenue	(From TB)		937 500
Cost of sales	(From TB)		(750 000)
Gross profit			187 500
Other income			7 500
Service revenue	(6 000 (24))	6 000	
Interest revenue	(120 000 x 0,05 x $^{3}/_{12}$ (25))	1 500	
Operating expenses			(88 000)
Internet expense	(From TB)	1 500	
Advertising	(From TB)	7 000	
Salaries	(From TB)	16 000	
Rent expense	(36 000 (26))	36 000	
Telephone and electricity expense	(1 500 + 2 500 (27))	4 000	
Stationery supplies and computer parts expense	(3 000 + 8 500 (28))	11 500	
Depreciation expense	(240 000 / 5 x $^{3}/_{12}$ (29))	12 000	
Finance cost			
Interest expense	(From TB)		(18 000)
Profit for the period			89 000

SMART CONCEPTS
STATEMENT OF FINANCIAL POSITION
AT 31 MARCH 20X5

		R
ASSETS		
Non-current assets		348 000
Furniture and fittings	(240 000 – 12 000 (29))	228 000
Fixed deposit investment	(From TB)	120 000
Current assets		2 027 000
Inventory	(From TB)	600 000
Accounts receivable	(From TB)	62 500
Stationery supplies asset	(2 000 (28))	2 000
Computer parts asset	(3 500 (28))	3 500
Interest asset	(1 500 (25))	1 500
Rent asset	(48 000 – 36 000 (26))	12 000
Bank	(From TB)	1 345 500
		2 375 000
EQUITY AND LIABILITIES		
Capital		979 000
Non-current liabilities		
Long term borrowings	(600 000 - 150 000)	450 000
Current liabilities		946 000
Short term borrowings	(600 000 – 450 000)	150 000
Accounts payable	(From TB)	750 000
Service liability	(48 000 – 6 000 (24))	42 000
Telephone and electricity liability	(4 000 (27))	4 000
		2 375 000

SMART CONCEPTS
STATEMENT OF CHANGES IN EQUITY
FOR THE PERIOD ENDED 31 MARCH 20X5

	R
Balance at 1 January 20X5	–
Profit for the period	89 000
Distributions	(60 000)
Contribution to capital	950 000
Balance at 31 March 20X5	979 000

6.9 Exam example

The Shark Tank is a retail store that sells a range of clothing and other items depicting the 'Sharks' emblem. The post-closing entry trial balances of The Shark Tank at 31 May 20X1 and 20X2 are shown below:

	20X1		20X2	
	Dr	**Cr**	**Dr**	**Cr**
Owner's equity		69 350		73 200
Bank	5 400		9 450	
Inventory	39 700		34 000	
Accounts receivable	18 500		22 600	
Insurance prepaid	750		900	
Shop fittings	87 000		96 000	
Loan		50 000		50 000
Accounts payable		28 300		36 250
Unearned rent income		1 500		1 800
Interest payable		2 200		1 700
	151 350	151 350	162 950	162 950

The summarised bank account taken from the general ledger of The Shark Tank for the year from 1 June 20X1 to 31 May 20X2 is as follows:

Dr — **BANK** — **Cr**

Date	Details		R	Date	Details		R
01/6/X1	Balance		5 400		Accounts payable		198 050
	Accounts receivable		339 900		Insurance prepaid		7 200
	Unearned rent income		14 400		Administrative expenses		75 000
					Shop fittings		40 000
					Interest expense		6 000
					Distributions		24 000
				31/5/X2	Balance		9 450
			359 700				359 700
01/6/X2	Balance		9 450				

The following information is relevant:

- All purchases of inventory and all sales are on credit.
- Shop fittings at a cost of R40 000 were purchased on 1 December 20X1. No shop fittings were sold during the year.
- The loan is repayable on 31 December 20X4.

You are required to:

(a) Prepare an income statement for The Shark Tank for the year ended 31 May 20X2.
(b) Prepare a statement of changes in equity for The Shark Tank for the year ended 31 May 20X2.
(c) Prepare a statement of financial position for The Shark Tank at 31 May 20X2.
(d) Justify your classification of the inventory and the loan on the statement of financial position.
(e) Describe the objective of financial reporting.

Solution: Exam example

(a) THE SHARK TANK
INCOME STATEMENT
FOR THE YEAR ENDED 31 MAY 20X2

			R
Revenue	(18 500 + ***344 000*** – 339 900 = 22 600)		344 000
Cost of sales			(211 700)
Opening inventory		39 700	
Purchases	(28 300 + ***206 000*** – 198 050 = 36 250)	206 000	
Closing inventory		(34 000)	
Gross profit			132 300
Other income			
Rent	(1 500 + 14 400 – 1 800)		14 100
Operating expenses			(113 050)
Insurance expense	(750 + 7 200 – 900)	7 050	
Administrative expense		75 000	
Depreciation expense	(87 000 + 40 000 – 96 000)	31 000	
Finance cost			
Interest expense	(6 000 – 2 200 + 1 700)		(5 500)
Profit for the period			27 850

(b) THE SHARK TANK
STATEMENT OF CHANGES IN EQUITY
FOR THE YEAR ENDED 31 MAY 20X2

	R
Balance at 1 June 20X1	69 350
Profit for the period	27 850
Distributions	(24 000)
Balance at 30 May 20X2	73 200

(c) THE SHARK TANK
STATEMENT OF FINANCIAL POSITION
AT 30 MAY 20X2

		R
ASSETS		
Non-current assets		
Shop fittings		96 000
Current assets		66 950
Inventory	34 000	
Accounts receivable	22 600	
Insurance prepaid	900	
Bank	9 450	
		162 950

EQUITY AND LIABILITIES	
Capital	73 200
Non-current liabilities	
Borrowings	50 000
Current liabilities	39 750
Accounts payable	36 250
Unearned rent	1 800
Interest payable	1 700
	162 950

(d) Classification on the statement of financial position

- According to IAS 1, inventory is classified as a current asset because
  - it is expected to be realised in or is intended for sale or consumption in the enterprise's normal operating cycle;
  - it is expected to be realised within 12 months of the reporting date;
  - it is held primarily for trading purposes.
- According to IAS 1, the loan (which is repayable two years and seven months from the reporting date) is classified as a non-current liability as it does not meet the definition of a current liability, which
  - is due to be settled within 12 months after the reporting date,
  - is expected to be settled in the entity's normal operating cycle.

(e) The objective of financial reporting is to provide information about the financial position, performance and cash flows of an enterprise that is useful to a wide range of users in making economic decisions.

Summary of concepts and applications

1. Financial statements are prepared from the post-adjustment trial balance.
2. IAS 1 requires each component of the financial statements to be clearly identified and also requires the following information to be displayed: the name of the entity, the statement of financial position date and the period covered by the financial statements, the presentation currency and the level of rounding used.
3. In order to appreciate the classification of assets and liabilities, it is necessary to understand the operating cycle of an enterprise. Assets are classified into two different types: non-current assets and current assets. Liabilities are also classified into two different types: non-current liabilities and current liabilities.
4. The pre-adjustment trial balance is prepared before the adjusting entries are processed, while the post-adjustment trial balance is prepared after the adjusting entries are processed. The post-adjustment trial balance assists in the preparation of financial statements.
5. The Accounting Framework explains that recognition is the process of incorporating in the statement of financial position or statement of comprehensive income an item that meets the definition of an element

and satisfies the recognition criteria. An item that meets the definition of an element should be recognised if it is probable that future economic benefits associated with the item will flow to or from the enterprise and the item has a cost or value that can be measured reliably.

6. The income statement measures the performance of an entity for a period of time and is drafted from the post-adjustment trial balance using the income and expense items. The statement of financial position measures the financial position of an entity at a particular point in time and is drafted from the post-adjustment trial balance using the asset, liability and equity items. The statement of changes in equity reflects the increases or decreases in the net assets or wealth of an entity for a period of time.
7. The general features need to be taken into account in the preparation of the financial statements.
8. It is important to know the format of the statement of comprehensive income, the statement of financial position and the statement of changes in equity to answer exam questions effectively. Each transaction in the question (often in the form of additional information) needs to be analysed and the balances adjusted, based on the information provided. You should deal with the complete double entry for each transaction, entering your answers on the statement of comprehensive income and/or the statement of financial position, as appropriate.

Notes

1. IAS 1, Presentation of Financial Statements, The International Accounting Standards Board, (2007), paragraph 51.
2. IAS 1 (2007), paragraph 66.
3. IAS 1 (2007), paragraph 68.
4. IAS 1 (2007), paragraph 69.
5. Framework for the Preparation and Presentation of Financial Statements, The International Accounting Standards Board, (2001), paragraph 82.
6. Framework for the Preparation and Presentation of Financial Statements (2001), paragraph 83.
7. Framework for the Preparation and Presentation of Financial Statements (2001), paragraph 89.
8. Framework for the Preparation and Presentation of Financial Statements (2001), paragraph 91.
9. Framework for the Preparation and Presentation of Financial Statements (2001), paragraph 92.
10. Framework for the Preparation and Presentation of Financial Statements (2001), paragraph 94.
11. IAS 1 (2007), paragraph IG 1.

Closing Entries

'By summing the debit and credit entries to this account, the profit or loss will be known … From the capital account … you may learn the entire value of your property.'
(Pacioli, 1494)

Outcomes

- Explain the role performed by closing entries in the accounting process.
- Describe the procedure to close the income and expense accounts, as well as the distributions account.
- Prepare closing entries.
- Prepare accounting entries in respect of accrued items in the following period.

Chapter outline

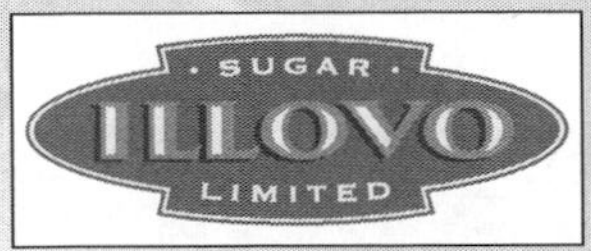

Illovo Sugar Limited
Statement of changes in equity for the year ended 31 March 2008

				(R Millions)
	Share capital	**Share premium**	**NDR**	**Retained Earnings**
Opening balance	2	296	504	1 011
Total comprehensive income	–	–	34	516
Dividends paid: ordinary	–	–	–	(194)
Proceeds from the issue of shares	1	53	–	–
Closing balance	3	349	538	1 333

Africa's largest sugar producer may only be known for its table sugar but its sugar-based products are used in many industrial processes, from the purification of oils to the production of resins. This statement of changes in equity is the culmination of their entire accounting process after all the necessary closing entries have been performed.

7.1 The need for closing entries

By now you should be familiar with the stages of the accounting process. Part 2 of this book, dealing with the accounting process, has covered the recording of transactions in Chapter 4, adjusting entries in Chapter 5, and has demonstrated how to prepare financial statements from the adjusted trial balance in Chapter 6. Chapter 7 completes the accounting process with the processing of closing entries.

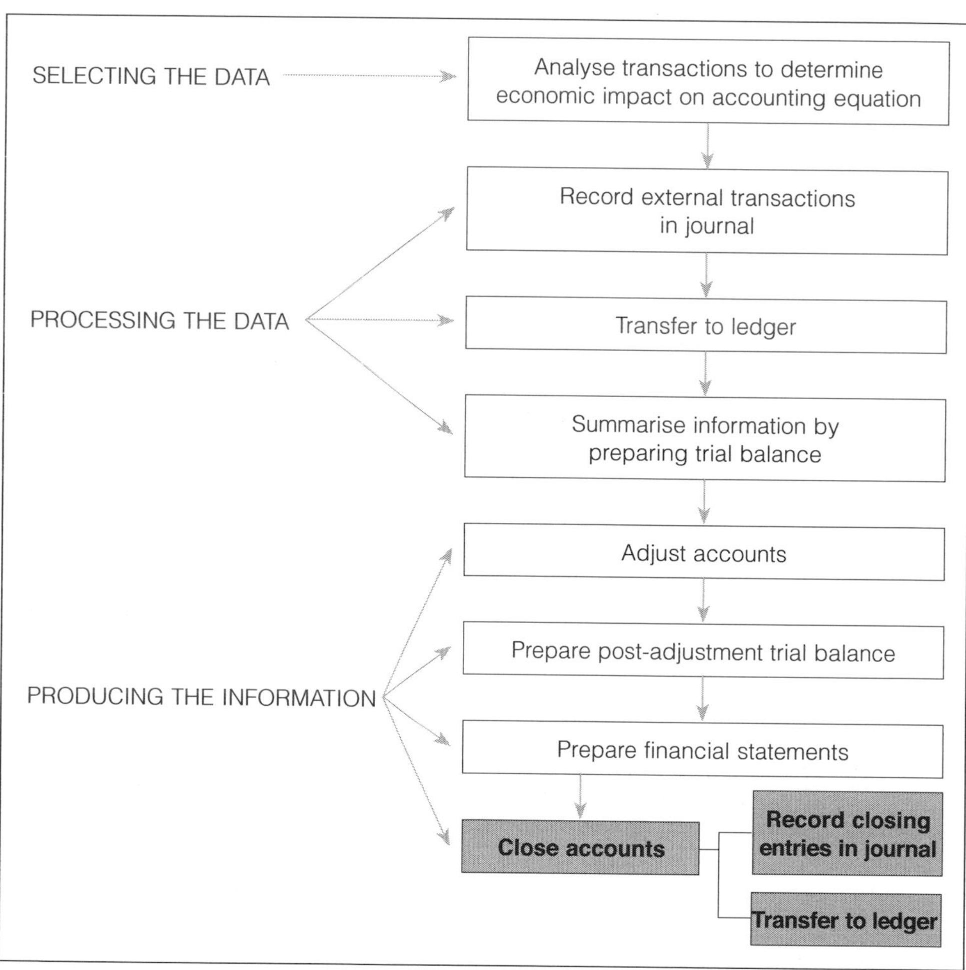

Diagram 7.1: The accounting process, highlighting closing entries

7.1.1 Updating the owner's equity

You will recall from Chapter 3 that owner's equity is affected by four types of transactions – contributions by the owner, distributions to the owner, the earning of income and the incurral of expenses.

During the accounting period, movements in income and expense items are recorded in separate accounts for each type of income and expense, and not directly to the owner's capital account. The same applies to distributions, which are also recorded in a separate distributions account. Only contributions by the owner are entered directly into the capital account.

The closing entries serve the purpose of transferring the end-of-period balances in the income and expense accounts, as well as the distributions account, to the capital account so that the balance on the capital account in the statement of financial position represents the correct amount of the owner's interest in the business.

7.1.2 Clearing the income, expense and distributions accounts

Processing of closing entries also clears the income, expense and distributions accounts so that the following accounting period can begin with zero balances in those accounts.

As you are aware, the income statement reports the profit of a period as being the difference between income earned and expenses incurred. The information for the income and expense items on the income statement is taken from the balances on each income and expense account in the trial balance. These accounts therefore need to be closed at the end of each period so that the following period can begin with zero balances.

The owner's equity section of the statement of financial position reports the opening capital balance, the profit for the period and the amount of the distributions to the owner. The distributions account therefore also needs to be cleared in preparation for the next period.

7.2 Procedure to close the accounts

The balances on the income and expense accounts are transferred to owner's equity through temporary accounts known as the ***trading account*** and the ***profit and loss*** account. This account accumulates the income and expenses of the period before transferring the profit (or loss) to the owner's capital account. As mentioned above, the balance on the distributions account is transferred directly to the owner's capital account.

The adjusted trial balance which was used to prepare the financial statements in Chapter 6 is shown below. The accounts which need to be closed off or cleared are highlighted. All other accounts are either the asset or liability accounts which are not closed off, or the owner's capital account to which the balances on the income, expense and distributions accounts are being transferred.

SMART CONCEPTS
POST-ADJUSTMENT TRIAL BALANCE AT 31 MARCH 20X5

Description	Folio	Dr	Cr
Bank	A1	1 345 500	
Rent asset	A2	12 000	
Fixed deposit investment	A3	120 000	
Furniture and fittings	A4	228 000	
Stationery supplies asset	A5	2 000	
Computer parts asset	A6	3 500	
Inventory	A7	600 000	
Accounts receivable	A8	62 500	
Interest asset	A9	1 500	
Borrowings	L1		600 000
Accounts payable	L2		750 000
Service liability	L3		42 000
Telephone and electricity liability	L4		4 000
Simon Smart capital	OE1		950 000
Distributions	**OE2**	**60 000**	
Sales revenue	**I1**		**937 500**
Service revenue	**I2**		**6 000**
Interest revenue	**I3**		**1 500**
Internet expense	**E1**	**1 500**	
Cost of sales	**E2**	**750 000**	
Advertising expense	**E3**	**7 000**	
Salaries expense	**E4**	**16 000**	
Interest expense	**E5**	**18 000**	
Rent expense	**E6**	**36 000**	
Telephone and electricity expense	**E7**	**4 000**	
Stationery supplies expense	**E8**	**3 000**	
Computer parts expense	**E9**	**8 500**	
Depreciation expense	**E10**	**12 000**	
		3 291 000	3 291 000

7.2.1 Closing the sales revenue and cost of sales accounts

The accounts relating to the trading activities of the enterprise, namely the sales revenue and cost of sales accounts, need to be closed off to the trading account.

Sales revenue

The income account relevant to the trading activities of an enterprise is the sales revenue account. The sales revenue account has a right-hand or credit balance. Therefore to clear the sales revenue account requires a left-hand or debit entry to the account (by an amount equal to the credit balance), with the credit side of the entry appearing in the trading account.

The only income account on Smart Concepts' trial balance that is relevant to the trading activities of the enterprise is the sales revenue account.

A = L +			**Owner's equity**	
	Sales revenue		Trading account	
	–/L/Dr	*+/R/Cr*	*–/L/Dr*	*+/R/Cr*
Bal		937 500		
c/e	937 500			937 500
				937 500

The sales revenue account is reduced by R937 500 with a left or debit entry. The sales revenue is transferred to the right or credit side of the trading account. The balance in the sales revenue account has been reduced to zero and the trading account temporarily shows a balance of R937 500, before the cost of sales account is cleared.

Cost of sales

The expense account relevant to the trading activities of an enterprise is the cost of sales account. The cost of sales account has a left-hand or debit balance. Therefore to clear the cost of sales account requires a right-hand or credit entry to the account (by an amount equal to the debit balance), with the debit side of the entry appearing in the trading account.

The only expense account on Smart Concepts' trial balance that is relevant to the trading activities of the enterprise is the cost of sales account.

A = L +			**Owner's equity**	
	Cost of sales		Trading account	
	+/L/Dr	*–/R/Cr*	*–/L/Dr*	*+/R/Cr*
Bal	750 000			937 500
c/e		750 000	750 000	
				187 500

The cost of sales account is reduced by R750 000 with a right or credit entry. The cost of sales amount is transferred to the left or debit side of the trading account. The balance in the cost of sales account has been reduced to zero and the trading account temporarily shows a balance of R187 500.

7.2.2 Closing the trading account

After the balances on the sales revenue and cost of sales accounts have been closed off or reduced to zero, the balance on the trading account represents the gross profit.

This gross profit is now transferred to the profit and loss account.

A = L +		Owner's equity		
	Trading account		Profit & loss	
	–/L/Dr	+/R/Cr	–/L/Dr	+/R/Cr
c/e		937 500		
c/e	750 000			
Bal		187 500		
c/e	187 500			187 500
Bal				187 500

The trading account is reduced by R187 500 with a left or debit entry. The gross profit of R187 500 is transferred to the right or credit side of the profit and loss account. The balance in the trading account has been reduced to zero and the balance in the profit and loss account increased by the gross profit.

7.2.3 Closing the other income and expense accounts

We have already closed off the income and expense accounts relating to the trading activities of the enterprise. You will recall that these accounts are the sales revenue account and the cost of sales account. The next step in the process is to close off the other income and expense accounts.

Income accounts

All income accounts have right-hand or credit balances. Therefore to clear an income account requires a left-hand or debit entry to the relevant income account (by an amount equal to the credit balance), with the credit side of the entry appearing in the profit and loss account.

The only remaining income accounts on Smart Concepts' trial balance are the service revenue account and the interest revenue account.

A = L +		Owner's equity				
	Service revenue		Interest revenue		Profit & loss	
	–/L/Dr	+/R/Cr	–/L/Dr	+/R/Cr	–/L/Dr	+/R/Cr
Bal		6 000		1 500		187 500
c/e	6 000		1 500			7 500
						195 000

The service revenue and interest revenue accounts are reduced by R6 000 and R1 500 respectively with left or debit entries. The total amount of R7 500 is transferred to the right or credit side of the profit and loss account. The balances in both income accounts have been reduced to zero and the profit and loss account temporarily shows a balance of R195 000, before the expense items are cleared.

Expense accounts

All expense accounts have left-hand or debit balances. Therefore to clear an expense account requires a right-hand or credit entry to the relevant expense account (by an amount equal to the debit balance), with the debit side of the entry appearing in the profit and loss account.

There are a number of remaining expense accounts on Smart Concepts' trial balance, namely petrol, advertising, salaries, interest, rent, telephone and electricity, office supplies, parts supplies and depreciation.

A = L +	**Owner's equity**																			
	Internet		Adver-tising		Salaries		Interest expense		Rent expense		Telephone & electricity		Stationery supplies expense		Computer parts expense		Depre-ciation		Profit & loss	
	Dr	Cr	Dr	Cr	Dr	Cr	Dr	Cr	Dr	Cr	Dr	Cr	Dr	Cr	Dr	Cr	Dr	Cr	Dr	Cr
Bal	1,5		7		16		18		36		4		3		8,5		12			195
c/e		1,5		7		16		18		36		4		3		8,5		12	106	
																				89

The amount in the above diagram have been rounded to R000s. All the expense accounts are reduced by the amount of the balance in the respective accounts with right or credit entries. The total expenses of R106 000 are transferred to the left or debit side of the profit and loss account. The balances in all the expense accounts have been reduced to zero and the profit and loss account temporarily shows a balance of R89 000, after the expense items are cleared.

7.2.4 Closing the profit and loss account

After the balances on the income and expense accounts have been closed off or reduced to zero, the balance on the profit and loss account represents the profit or loss for the period. Where income exceeds expenses, the profit and loss account will reflect a credit balance representing the profit for the period. Conversely, where expenses exceed income, the profit and loss account will show a debit balance representing the net loss for the period.

A = L +	**Owner's equity**			
	Profit & loss		Simon Smart capital	
	–/L/Dr	+/R/Cr	–/L/Dr	+/R/Cr
Bal				950 000
c/e		187 500		
c/e		7 500		
c/e	106 000			
Bal		89 000		
c/e	89 000			89 000
Bal				1 039 000

The profit and loss account is reduced by R89 000 with a left or debit entry. The profit for the period of R89 000 is transferred to the right or credit side of the owner's capital account. The balance in the profit and loss account has been reduced to zero and the balance in the owner's capital account increased by the profit for the period.

Recall that in Chapter 2 we described equity as the owner's interest in the business. When we processed the transactions for Simon Smart's business on a conceptual level, we added the profit for the period to the owner's equity, as it increases the owner's interest in the business. We have now reached the same point in the accounting process, with the profit being transferred from the profit and loss account to the owner's capital account.

7.2.5 Closing the distributions account

The distributions account has a left-hand or debit balance. Therefore to reduce this account to zero and to transfer the distributions for the period to the owner's capital account requires a right-hand or credit entry to the distributions account (by an amount equal to the debit balance), with the debit side of the entry posted to the owner's capital account.

A = L +	**Owner's equity**			
	Distributions		Simon Smart capital	
	+/L/Dr	–/R/Cr	–/L/Dr	+/R/Cr
Bal	60 000			1 039 000
c/e		60 000	60 000	
Bal				979 000

The distributions account is reduced by R60 000 with a right or credit entry. This amount is transferred to the left or debit side of the owner's capital account. The balance on the capital account is now R979 000, the amount that will appear on the statement of financial position.

Having closed off the distributions account, the balance on the capital account is now fully representative of the equity of the business. All the transactions affecting equity – contributions by the owner, earning of income, incurral of expenses and distributions to the owner – have now been incorporated in the capital account. It is important that you do not lose sight of these concepts when processing data through the journals and ledger.

Pause and reflect...

Think of transaction 10 where fifteen computers were sold to a customer on credit for a total of R187 500. Can you describe the flow of data relating to this transaction through the accounting process?

Response

Transaction 10 (a transaction affecting trading income) was analysed as an increase in an asset account, accounts receivable and an increase in an income account, sales, for an amount of R187 500. The transaction was then entered into the journal as a debit to accounts receivable and a credit to sales. The journal entry was posted to the ledger and the sales account in the ledger was credited with R187 500. The balance on the sales account in the ledger was transferred to the trading account as part of the closing entry process. The sales are incorporated into the computation of gross profit which is transferred to the profit and loss account as part of the closing entry process. All other income items and expense items are transferred to profit and loss as part of the closing entry process. The balance on the profit and loss account is transferred to the capital account as part of the closing entry process.

7.3 Example: Processing of closing entries at the end of the period

The previous section provided a conceptual explanation of the closing entries and their impact on equity. As with the adjusting entries, the closing entries need to be entered in the general journal and posted to the general ledger. This is the last step in the accounting process, and the last phase of the year-end procedures.

This example takes the trial balance of Smart Concepts, prepared *after* the adjusting entries have been processed, and shows the mechanics of entering the closing entries in the journal and posting to the ledger. The same trial balance that was used for the conceptual explanation above is reproduced here.

SMART CONCEPTS
POST-ADJUSTMENT TRIAL BALANCE AT 31 MARCH 20X5

Description	Folio	Dr	Cr
Bank	A1	1 345 500	
Rent asset	A2	12 000	
Fixed deposit investment	A3	120 000	
Furniture and fittings	A4	228 000	
Stationery supplies asset	A5	2 000	
Computer parts asset	A6	3 500	
Inventory	A7	600 000	
Accounts receivable	A8	62 500	
Interest asset	A9	1 500	
Borrowings	L1		600 000
Accounts payable	L2		750 000
Service liability	L3		42 000
Telephone and electricity liability	L4		4 000
Simon Smart capital	OE1		950 000
Distributions	**OE2**	**60 000**	
Sales revenue	**I1**		**937 500**

Service revenue	**I2**		**6 000**
Interest revenue	**I3**		**1 500**
Internet expense	**E1**	**1 500**	
Cost of sales	**E2**	**750 000**	
Advertising expense	**E3**	**7 000**	
Salaries expense	**E4**	**16 000**	
Interest expense	**E5**	**18 000**	
Rent expense	**E6**	**36 000**	
Telephone and electricity expense	**E7**	**4 000**	
Stationery supplies expense	**E8**	**3 000**	
Computer parts expense	**E9**	**8 500**	
Depreciation expense	**E10**	**12 000**	
		3 291 000	3 291 000

You are required to:
enter the closing entries in the general journal of Smart Concepts and post to the general ledger.

Solution: Processing of closing entries at the end of the period

When journalising the closing entries, you should bear in mind the objective, which is to transfer to the owner's capital account the effects of the income, expenses and withdrawals for the period.

As there are likely to be a number of income and expense items, the closing entries are usually made in the form of cumulative journal entries, as demonstrated below.

GENERAL JOURNAL OF SMART CONCEPTS (GJ 4)

Date	Description	Fol	Dr	Cr
20X5 March				
31	Sales revenue Trading *Closing entry for trading income item*	I1 T	937 500	 937 500
31	Trading Cost of sales *Closing entry for trading expense item*	T E2	750 000	 750 000
31	Trading Profit and loss *Transfer of gross profit to profit and loss*	T PL	187 500	 187 500
31	Service revenue Interest revenue Profit and loss *Closing entry for other income items*	I2 I3 PL	6 000 1 500	 7 500

31	Profit and loss	PL	106 000	
	Internet expense	E1		1 500
	Advertising	E3		7 000
	Salaries	E4		16 000
	Interest expense	E5		18 000
	Rent expense	E6		36 000
	Telephone and electricity expense	E7		4 000
	Stationery supplies expense	E8		3 000
	Computer parts expense	E9		8 500
	Depreciation expense	E10		12 000
	Closing entry for other expense items			
31	Profit and loss	PL	89 000	
	Simon Smart capital	OE1		89 000
	Transfer of profit to capital			
31	Simon Smart capital	OE1	60 000	
	Distributions	OE2		60 000
	Transfer of distributions to owner			

Dr **SALES REVENUE (GL I1)** **Cr**

Date	Details	Fol	R	Date	Details	Fol	R
31/03	Balance	c/d	937 500	25/01	Accounts receivable	GJ 1	187 500
				12/02	Bank	GJ 2	375 000
				29/03	Bank	GJ 2	375 000
			937 500				937 500
31/03	**Trading**	**GJ 4**	**937 500**	31/03	Balance	b/d	937 500

Dr **SERVICE REVENUE (GL I2)** **Cr**

Date	Details	Fol	R	Date	Details	Fol	R
31/03	Balance	c/d	6 000	31/03	Service liability	GJ 3	6 000
			6 000				6 000
31/03	**Profit & loss**	**GJ 4**	**6 000**	31/03	Balance	b/d	6 000

Dr **INTEREST REVENUE (GL I3)** **Cr**

Date	Details	Fol	R	Date	Details	Fol	R
31/03	Balance	c/d	1 500	31/03	Interest asset	GJ 3	1 500
			1 500				1 500
31/03	**Profit & loss**	**GJ 4**	**1 500**	31/03	Balance	b/d	1 500

Dr — INTERNET EXPENSE (GL E1) — Cr

Date	Details	Fol	R	Date	Details	Fol	R
12/01	Bank	GJ 1	750	31/03	Balance	c/d	1 500
05/03	Bank	GJ 2	750				
			1 500				1 500
31/03	Balance	b/d	1 500	**31/03**	**Profit & loss**	**GJ4**	**1 500**

Dr — COST OF SALES (GL E2) — Cr

Date	Details	Fol	R	Date	Details	Fol	R
25/02	Inventory	GJ 1	150 000	31/03	Balance	c/d	750 000
12/02	Inventory	GJ 2	300 000				
29/03	Inventory	GJ 2	300 000				
			750 000				750 000
31/03	Balance	b/d	750 000	**31/03**	**Trading**	**GJ 4**	**750 000**

Dr — ADVERTISING EXPENSE (GL E3) — Cr

Date	Details	Fol	R	Date	Details	Fol	R
08/02	Bank	GJ 2	7 000				
				31/03	Balance	c/d	7 000
			7 000				7 000
31/03	Balance	b/d	7 000	**31/03**	**Profit & loss**	**GJ 4**	**7 000**

Dr — SALARIES EXPENSE (GL E4) — Cr

Date	Details	Fol	R	Date	Details	Fol	R
28/02	Bank	GJ 2	8 000	31/03	Balance	c/d	16 000
30/03	Bank	GJ 2	8 000				
			16 000				16 000
31/03	Balance	b/d	16 000	**31/03**	**Profit & loss**	**GJ 4**	**16 000**

Dr INTEREST EXPENSE (GL E5) Cr

Date	Details	Fol	R	Date	Details	Fol	R
30/03	Bank	GJ 2	18 000	31/03	Balance	c/d	18 000
			18 000				18 000
31/03	Balance	b/d	18 000	**31/03**	**Profit & loss**	**GJ 4**	**18 000**

Dr RENT EXPENSE (GL E6) Cr

Date	Details	Fol	R	Date	Details	Fol	R
31/03	Rent asset	GJ 3	36 000	31/03	Balance	c/d	36 000
			36 000				36 000
31/03	Balance	b/d	36 000	**31/03**	**Profit & loss**	**GJ 4**	**36 000**

Dr TELEPHONE AND ELECTRICITY EXPENSE (GL E7) Cr

Date	Details	Fol	R	Date	Details	Fol	R
31/03	Telephone and electricity liability	GJ 3	4 000	31/03	Balance	c/d	4 000
			4 000				4 000
31/03	Balance	b/d	4 000	**31/03**	**Profit & loss**	**GJ 4**	**4 000**

Dr STATIONERY SUPPLIES EXPENSE (GL E8) Cr

Date	Details	Fol	R	Date	Details	Fol	R
31/03	Stationery supplies asset	GJ 3	3 000	31/03	Balance	c/d	3 000
			3 000				3 000
31/03	Balance	b/d	3 000	**31/03**	**Profit & loss**	**GJ 4**	**3 000**

Dr COMPUTER PARTS EXPENSE (GL E9) Cr

Date	Details	Fol	R	Date	Details	Fol	R
31/03	Computer parts asset	GJ 3	8 500	31/03	Balance	c/d	8 500
			8 500				8 500
31/03	Balance	b/d	8 500	**31/03**	**Profit & loss**	**GJ 4**	**8 500**

Dr			DEPRECIATION EXPENSE (GL E10)				Cr
Date	Details	Fol	R	Date	Details	Fol	R
31/03	Furniture and fittings	GJ 3	12 000	31/03	Balance	c/d	12 000
			12 000				12 000
31/03	Balance	b/d	12 000	**31/03**	**Profit & loss**	**GJ 4**	**12 000**

Dr			TRADING (GL T)				Cr
Date	Details	Fol	R	Date	Details	Fol	R
31/03	**Cost of sales**	**GJ 4**	**750 000**	**31/03**	**Sales revenue**	**GJ 4**	**937 500**
31/03	**Profit & loss**	**GJ 4**	**187 500**				
			937 500				937 500

Dr			PROFIT & LOSS (GL PL)				Cr
Date	Details	Fol	R	Date	Details	Fol	R
31/03	**Internet**	**GJ 4**	**1 500**	**31/03**	**Trading**	**GJ 4**	**187 500**
31/03	**Advertising**	**GJ 4**	**7 000**	**31/03**	**Service revenue**	**GJ 4**	**6 000**
31/03	**Salaries**	**GJ 4**	**16 000**	**31/03**	**Interest revenue**	**GJ 4**	**1 500**
31/03	**Interest expense**	**GJ 4**	**18 000**				
31/03	**Rent expense**	**GJ 4**	**36 000**				
31/03	**Telephone and electricity expense**	**GJ 4**	**4 000**				
31/03	**Stationery supplies expense**	**GJ 4**	**3 000**				
31/03	**Computer parts expense**	**GJ 4**	**8 500**				
31/03	**Depreciation**	**GJ 4**	**12 000**				
31/03	**Simon Smart capital**	**GJ 4**	**89 000**				
			195 000				195 000

Dr			DISTRIBUTIONS (GL OE2)				Cr
Date	Details	Fol	R	Date	Details	Fol	R
30/03	Bank	GJ 2	60 000	31/03	Balance	c/d	60 000
			60 000				60 000
31/03	Balance	b/d	60 000	**31/03**	**Simon Smart capital**	**GJ 4**	**60 000**

SIMON SMART CAPITAL (GL OE1)

Dr							Cr
Date	Details	Fol	R	Date	Details	Fol	R
				02/01	Bank	GJ 1	950 000
31/03	Balance	c/d	950 000				
			950 000				950 000
31/03	**Distributions**	**GJ 4**	**60 000**	31/03	Balance	b/d	950 000
31/03	Balance	c/d	979 000	**31/03**	**Profit & loss**	**GJ 4**	**89 000**
			1 039 000				1 039 000
				01/04	Balance	b/d	979 000

You will notice that all the income and expense accounts have zero balances, as does the distributions account. The only accounts with balances at this stage are the statement of financial position asset and liability accounts, and the owner's capital account. The accounting process for the current period is complete and a final post-closing entry trial balance can be drawn up to ensure that there were no bookkeeping errors in the processing of the closing entries.

SMART CONCEPTS
POST-CLOSING TRIAL BALANCE AT 31 MARCH 20X5

Description	Folio	Dr	Cr
Bank	A1	1 345 500	
Rent asset	A2	12 000	
Fixed deposit investment	A3	120 000	
Furniture and fittings	A4	228 000	
Stationery supplies asset	A5	2 000	
Computer parts asset	A6	3 500	
Inventory	A7	600 000	
Accounts receivable	A8	62 500	
Interest asset	A9	1 500	
Borrowings	L1		600 000
Accounts payable	L2		750 000
Service liability	L3		42 000
Telephone and electricity liability	L4		4 000
Simon Smart capital	OE1		979 000
Distributions	**OE2**	-	
Sales revenue	**I1**		-
Service revenue	**I2**		-
Interest revenue	**I3**		-
Internet expense	**E1**	-	
Cost of sales	**E2**	-	
Advertising expense	**E3**	-	
Salaries expense	**E4**	-	
Interest expense	**E5**	-	
Rent expense	**E6**	-	
Telephone and electricity expense	**E7**	-	
Stationery supplies expense	**E8**	-	
Computer parts supplies expense	**E9**	-	
Depreciation expense	**E10**	-	
		2 375 000	2 375 000

7.4 Treatment of accrued items in the following period

Having completed the accounting process for one period, it is appropriate to consider the impact, if any, that the internal transactions, or adjusting entries, at the end of one period will have on the recording of transactions in the following period.

You will recall from Chapter 5 that the adjusting entries are classified according to the relationship between cash received and income, and cash paid and expenses. If cash is received in advance of the earning of income, the adjusting entry transfers the amount earned to an income account, leaving the amount unearned in the liability account. This process will continue each period until the income has been earned and the liability reduced to zero. No special treatment is required in this situation at the beginning of the following period.

If cash is paid in advance of the incurral of expenses, the adjusting entry transfers the amount incurred to an expense account, leaving the amount prepaid in the asset account. This process will continue each period until the expense has been incurred and the asset reduced to zero. Again, no special treatment is required in this situation at the beginning of the following period.

7.4.1 Accrued income

However, where the cash receipt is outstanding at period-end and the income has already been earned, the adjusting entry creates an asset in respect of the accrued income and recognises the income that has been earned during the period. This income will be received in cash at some time during the following period and, when received, the relevant income account will be credited as with all other receipts of this nature. You should now realise that this will result in double-counting the income adjusted at the end of the previous period. It is for this reason that accrued income is reversed at the beginning of the new period. Consider the accrual of the interest revenue at the end of March in the Smart Concepts example.

		Dr	Cr
31/03/X5	Interest asset	1 500	
	Interest revenue		1 500

The income of R1 500 is correctly recognised as earned for the period ended 31 March 20X5. Assume that no reversing entry is processed, and that, on 30 June 20X5, the interest for the quarter ended 31 March of R1 500 as well as the interest for the quarter ended 30 June of R1 500 is received from the bank. The receipt of the interest will be recorded as follows:

		Dr	Cr
30/06/X5	Bank	3 000	
	Interest revenue		3 000

The result of these two entries is that the interest revenue for the period from 1 April to 30 June is R3 000. To avoid this situation arising, a reversing entry is recorded at the beginning of each new period, so that when the cash is received it does not result in the double-counting of the income. The reversing entry is recorded as follows:

		Dr	Cr
01/04/X5	Interest revenue	1 500	
	Interest asset		1 500

Taking into account the two entries shown above, the interest income for the three-month period ended 30 June 20X5 is R1 500 (R3 000 – R1 500).

The reversing entry could be avoided if the receipt of the accrued income is specifically identified, and the *asset* credited upon receipt of the accrual (and not the income). The net effect of these entries can be illustrated as follows:

		Dr	Cr
30/06/X5	Bank	3 000	
	Interest asset		1 500
	Interest revenue		1 500

7.4.2 Accrued expenses

Following the same logic, where the cash payment is outstanding at period-end and the expense has already been incurred, the adjusting entry creates a liability in respect of the accrued expense and recognises the expense that has been incurred during the period. This expense will be paid in cash at some time during the following period, and, when paid, the relevant expense account will be debited, as with all other expenses of this nature. Again you should realise that this will result in double-counting the expense adjusted at the end of the previous period. It is for this reason that accrued expenses are reversed at the beginning of the new period. Consider here the accrual of the telephone and electricity expense at the end of March in the Smart Concepts example:

		Dr	Cr
31/03/X5	Telephone and electricity expense	4 000	
	Telephone and electricity liability		4 000

The expense of R4 000 is correctly recognised as incurred for the quarter ended 31 March 20X5. Assume that no reversing entry is processed and that during the quarter ended 30 June 20X5 the amount of R4 000 is paid, as well as the amount for that period of, say, R3 000. The payment of the two amounts will be recorded as follows:

		Dr	Cr
10/04/X5	Telephone and electricity expense	4 000	
	Bank		4 000
30/06/X5	Telephone and electricity expense	3 000	
	Bank		3 000

The result of these two entries is that the telephone and electricity expense for the period from 1 April 20X5 to 30 June 20X5 is R7 000. To avoid this situation arising, a reversing entry is recorded at the beginning of each new period, so that when the cash is paid it does not result in the double-counting of the expense. The reversing entry is recorded as follows:

		Dr	Cr
01/04/X5	Telephone and electricity liability	4 000	
	Telephone and electricity expense		4 000

Taking into account the three entries shown above, the telephone and electricity expense for the three-month period ended 30 June 20X5 is R3 000 (R7 000 – R4 000).

As with the accrued income, the reversing entry could be avoided if the payment of the accrued expense is specifically identified and the *liability* debited upon payment of the accrual (and not the expense). The net effect of these entries can be illustrated as follows:

		Dr	Cr
10/04/X5	Telephone and electricity liability	4 000	
	Bank		3 000
30/06/X5	Telephone and electricity expense	3 000	
	Bank		3 000

7.5 Exam example

Rose Gardner is a retired lady. She decided at the beginning of last spring to enter the business of landscaping gardens. The business trades under the name of The Rose Garden and the financial year end of the business is 31 March.

On 1 October 20X8 Rose paid R24 000 into the business bank account. She then purchased gardening tools and equipment for the business at a total cost of R28 000. She paid cash for the tools and equipment, utilising part of the cash invested and borrowing R8 000, at an interest rate of 15% per annum, from a bank. It is estimated that the tools and equipment can be sold for R2 400 at the end of their useful life of two years.

Rose Gardner owns a 4X4 vehicle which she uses for the business. She does not wish to transfer the vehicle into the business but she does want the use of the vehicle to be recognised in the determination of the profit of the business. The value of the vehicle to the business is estimated at R2 000 per quarter.

In order to exercise control over the financial affairs of her business, Rose prepares a trial balance at the end of every quarter. Closing entries are processed at the end of the financial year when financial statements are prepared.

Details of transactions for the first six months of trading are as shown below. All amounts paid relate to the relevant period.

	01/10/X8 – 31/12/X8	**01/01/X9 – 31/03/X9**
	R	**R**
Fees on credit	49 600	46 400
Receipts from clients	46 400	48 400
Wages paid	4 400	4 800
Administration costs paid	400	800
Supplies purchased on credit	4 800	2 000
Repayment of loan	4 000	4 000
Payment of accounts payable	4 000	2 800
Distributions to owner	31 300	31 050

The following additional information is relevant:

- ❑ Upon enquiry, Rose visits the client's home and provides a free quote. Rose sends out accounts upon completion of the landscaping work.
- ❑ At 31 December 20X8, all the clients indicated that they would pay the outstanding amounts owed by them for services provided at the end of January 20X9.
- ❑ At 31 March 20X9, all outstanding amounts owed by clients for services rendered are not recoverable.
- ❑ At the end of March 20X9, thieves stole Rose's 4X4 with all the gardening tools and equipment. The insurance company agreed to pay proceeds of R130 000 for the vehicle and R17 200 for the tools and equipment. Both amounts were received early in May 20X9.
- ❑ Supplies on hand at 31 December 20X8 amounted to R2 000. There were no supplies on hand at 31 March 20X9.
- ❑ The loan is repayable in equal installments on 31 December 20X8 and 31 March 20X9. Interest on the loan is payable quarterly in arrears on 1 January and 1 April.

You are required to:

(a) prepare a post-adjustment trial balance of The Rose Garden at 31 December 20X8.
(b) record all the closing entries in the journal of The Rose Garden at 31 March 20X9.
(c) prepare a statement of changes in equity of The Rose Garden for the six months ended 31 March 20X9.
(d) prepare the statement of financial position of The Rose Garden at 31 March 20X9.

Solution: Exam example

(a)

ROSE GARDNER
TRIAL BALANCE AT 31 DECEMBER 20X8

		Dr	Cr
Bank	(24 000 + 8 000 – 28 000 + 46 400 – 4 400 – 400 – 4 000 – 4 000 – 31 300)	6 300	
Tools & equipment	(28 000 – 3 200)	24 800	
Accounts receivable	(49 600 – 46 400)	3 200	
Supplies asset		2 000	
Loan	(8 000 – 4 000)		4 000
Accounts payable	(4 800 – 4 000)		800
Interest liability	(8 000 X 0,15 X 3/12)		300
Fees			49 600
Wages expense		4 400	
Administrative expense		400	
Interest expense	(8 000 X 0,15 X 3/12)	300	
Supplies expense	(4 800 – 2 000)	2 800	
Depreciation expense	(28 000 – 2 400) X 3/24	3 200	
Vehicle usage		2 000	
Capital			24 000
Distributions	(31 300 – 2 000)	29 300	
		78 700	78 700

(b)

ROSE GARDNER
JOURNAL

Description		Dr	Cr
Fees	(49 600 + 46 400)	96 000	
Profit and loss			96 000
Profit and loss		33 650	
Wages expense	(4 400 + 4 800)		9 200
Administrative expenses	(400 + 800)		1 200
Supplies expense	[2 800 + (2 000 + 2 000 – 0)]		6 800
Depreciation expense	(3 200 + 3 200)		6 400
Bad debts expense	(3 200 + 46 400 – 48 400)		1 200
Loss on tools & equipment	(17 200 – 21 600*) *(28 000 – 3 200 – 3 200)		4 400
Interest expense	(300 + 150*) *[(8 000 – 4 000) X 0,15 X 3/12]		450
Motor vehicle usage expense	(2 000 + 2 000)		4 000
Profit and loss	(96 000 – 33 650)	62 350	
Owner's equity			62 350
Owner's equity		58 350	
Distributions	(29 300 + 31 050 – 2 000)		58 350

(c)

ROSE GARDNER
STATEMENT OF CHANGES IN EQUITY
FOR THE SIX MONTHS ENDED 31 MARCH 20X9

	R
Balance at 1 October 20X8	–
Profit for the period	62 350
Distributions	(58 350)
Contribution to capital	24 000
Balance at 31 March 20X9	28 000

(d)

ROSE GARDNER
STATEMENT OF FINANCIAL POSITION AT 31 MARCH 20X9

	R
ASSETS	
Current assets	
Insurance claim owing	17 200
Cash	10 950
	28 150
EQUITY AND LIABILITIES	
Capital	28 000
Current liabilities	
Interest liability	150
	28 150

Summary of concepts and applications

1. The recording of closing entries completes the accounting process. The processing of closing entries achieves two outcomes. Firstly, owner's equity is updated, and secondly, the income, expense and distributions accounts are cleared.
2. The balances on the income and expense accounts are transferred to owner's equity through temporary accounts known as the trading account and the profit and loss account. The balance on the distributions account is transferred directly to the owner's capital account.
3. The chapter uses the post-adjustment trial balance from the Smart Concepts example and demonstrates the mechanics of entering the closing entries in the journal and posting to the ledger.
4. In a subsequent period, no special accounting treatment is required for unearned income and for prepaid expenses. However, two possible treatments exist to account for accrued income and accrued expenses in a subsequent period.

Part 3

The Accounting Process Expanded

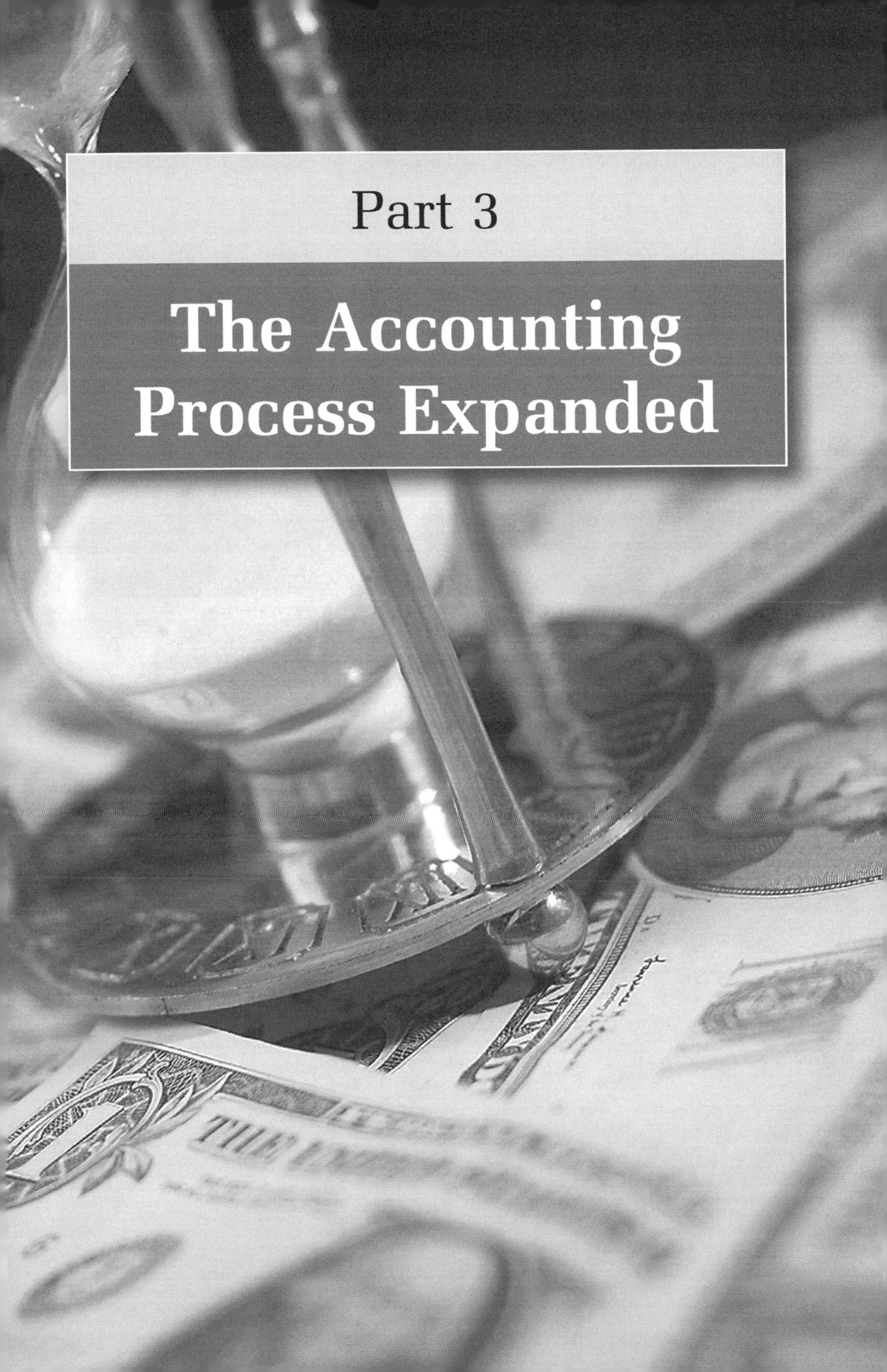

8 Recording Purchase and Sale Transactions

'[A perfect merchant] ought to be a good penman, a good arithmetician, and a good accountant, by that noble order of debtor and creditor, which is used only among merchants ...' (Mun, 1664)

Outcomes

- Compare service and retailing entities.
- Record purchase and sale transactions involving settlement discount, cash discount and trade discount.
- Record transactions using the periodic inventory system and compare it to the perpetual inventory system.

Chapter outline

The Spar Group Limited
Notes to the financial statements for the year ended 30 September 2007

	(R Millions)
Inventories	
Merchandise	607
Provision for obsolescence	(13)
Net merchandise	594

Policy

Inventories are valued at the lower of cost and net realisable value. Cost is determined on the weighted average basis using a perpetual accounting system. Obsolete, redundant and slow moving inventory is identified and written down to estimated economic or realisable values. Net realisable value represents the selling price less all estimated costs to be incurred in marketing, selling and distribution thereof.

When inventory is sold, the carrying amount is recognised to cost of sales. Any write-down of inventory to net realisable value and all losses of inventory or reversals of previous write-downs are recognised in cost of sales.

The Spar group acts as a wholesaler and distributor of food and household goods to Spar Retail grocery stores. It is all about inventory, the prime focus of this chapter.

8.1 The nature of business activities

You will recall from the Smart Concepts example in Parts 1 and 2 of this book that computers were purchased and sold and technical support contracts offered to customers. The purchase and sale of computers represent the retailing aspect of Smart Concepts' business, whereas the technical support contracts represent the service component of the business. It is appropriate at this stage to briefly review the nature of a service entity as distinguished from a retailer. A brief summary of the nature of these two entity forms, followed by a discussion of a combined entity, is provided below.

8.1.1 Service entity

In this type of business entity a service is performed for a commission or fee. Profit for the period is the difference between fees or commissions earned and the operating and financing expenses incurred. A service entity does not hold a stock of goods for resale.

8.1.2 Retailing entity

As mentioned above, a retailing entity is involved in the purchase and sale of goods. Profit from this type of entity comprises revenue earned from sales, after deducting the cost of the goods sold as well as the operating and financing expenses. The entity will hold a stock of goods for resale, known as the **inventory** or **stock** of the business.

8.1.3 Combining a retailing and service entity

Smart Concepts is an example of a business entity that combines retailing and service activities. The retailing activity generates an income item, sales revenue, and an expense item, cost of sales. You have learnt in previous chapters that the trading results of an entity are represented by the gross profit, calculated as the difference between sales and cost of sales. The service activity generates an income item, service revenue. The service revenue is added to the gross profit followed by the deduction of the operating and financing expenses to calculate the profit or loss for the period.

8.2 Transactions resulting in adjustments to amounts recorded in sales and purchases of inventory

One of the main issues relating to the purchase and sale of goods is the measurement of the cost of the inventory to the purchasing entity and the revenue from sales to the selling entity.

According to *IAS 18, Revenue*, revenue should be measured at the fair value of the consideration received or receivable and this is usually determined by agreement between the entity and the buyer of the goods.

Fair value is defined as the amount for which an asset could be exchanged, or a liability settled, between knowledgeable, willing parties in an arm's length transaction.

Determining fair value in most transactions does not usually present a problem. However, where goods are bought or sold and discounts are involved, the measurement of fair value is not as straightforward. The discounts could take one of the following forms:

- A settlement discount, where goods are bought or sold on credit and a discount is offered for early settlement
- A cash discount at the point of purchase or sale
- A trade discount, normally associated with purchases and sales between a retailer and supplier in a particular industry.

These issues will be examined in detail in the example that follows in section 8.4.

8.3 Perpetual and periodic inventory systems

Recording transactions in a retailing entity can be done through different systems. Traditionally there have been two systems available: the perpetual inventory system and the periodic inventory system.

When a **perpetual** inventory system is used, the inventory records are referred to at the time of each sale to determine the cost of the goods sold. The cost of goods sold is recorded each time a sale is made and an up-to-date record of the physical goods on hand is kept. You will now realise that a perpetual inventory system has been used in the Smart Concepts example described in the previous chapters. Prior to the introduction of computerised inventory systems, a perpetual inventory system was applicable to enterprises that sold low volumes of goods at relatively high prices, such as car dealers, jewellery stores and antique shops. These enterprises would have operated this system successfully because relatively few transactions would have been processed.

When a **periodic** inventory system is used, an enterprise does not constantly maintain records of the quantity and cost of goods physically on hand or sold. It is only at the end of the period, when the inventory is counted, that the cost of goods sold can be determined. This procedure is explained in detail in section 8.6 of this chapter. Prior to the introduction of computerised inventory systems, a periodic inventory system was applicable to enterprises that sold high volumes of goods at relatively low prices, such as supermarkets, department stores and pharmacies. These enterprises would have operated this system because it was not practical or feasible to determine the cost of each item sold at the time of sale.

Although it is essential to count the inventory on hand at the end of a period when using a periodic inventory system, it is also important to do so when using a perpetual inventory system, so as to verify the accuracy of the perpetual records.

With the advent of affordable computerised inventory systems, the number of enterprises using a perpetual inventory system has increased significantly. Therefore, computerised inventory systems have removed the aforementioned association of perpetual systems with enterprises selling low volumes of high-priced goods and periodic systems with enterprises selling high volumes of low-priced goods. Consequently, perpetual inventory systems are now more accessible to retailing enterprises. However, the periodic inventory system is nevertheless relevant, and will be examined in detail in this chapter, as it is still used by many retailers.

 **Pause and reflect...**

Have you thought about how a perpetual inventory system works when you buy goods from a retail store such as a supermarket?

Response

When you arrive at the check-out counters, you pass the goods that you have selected to the check-out assistant. The assistant scans the bar codes of the items that you are buying. The optical scanner reads the bar code which contains a lot of information relating to the relevant item. Upon scanning the bar code, the accounting system performs the following operations:

- Records the sale, by debiting cash and crediting sales revenue
- Records the cost of sales, by debiting cost of sales and, at the same time, updates the perpetual inventory records relating to the goods sold, by crediting inventory.

You will recall that a retailer operates by purchasing goods from suppliers and selling the goods to customers at a marked-up price. The goods that are bought and sold are referred to as inventory. The inventory can be purchased for cash or on credit. We shall now examine the recording of purchase and sale transactions with particular emphasis on the measurement of revenue from sales and purchases of inventory as well as on the differences between a perpetual and periodic inventory system.

8.4 Example: Recording of purchase and sale transactions

On 1 April 20X5, Simon Smart opened a new business entity to complement Smart Concepts. This entity is called Sharp Moves and sells accessories such as printers, modems and USB storage devices. The activities of Sharp Moves will be used to illustrate the recognition and measurement of transactions giving rise to revenue from sales and purchases of inventory, as well as to compare the perpetual and periodic inventory systems.

Listed below are the transactions of Sharp Moves for the month of April 20X5.

#	Date	Transaction	R
		Opening inventory and purchases	
-	01/04/X5	Opening inventory consists of 4 items at a cost of R60 each.	240
1	04/04/X5	Purchased 15 items at R60 each on account from Computer World. Computer World does not offer settlement discounts.	900
2	08/04/X5	Purchased 20 items at R62,50 each on account from Plug & Play Limited. Plug & Play Limited allows a 4% settlement discount if payment is received within 15 days.	1 250 (50) 1 200
3a	23/04/X5	Paid Plug & Play Limited the amount owing to them *within the settlement period*, taking advantage of the settlement discount.	1 200
3b	24/04/X5	Paid Plug & Play Limited the amount owing to them *after the settlement period.*	1 250
4	25/04/X5	Purchased 20 items at R75 each for cash. Received a 20% discount for paying cash.	1 200
5	30/04/X5	Purchased 100 items on account from Digital World. The normal selling price from Digital World is R75 an item. Smart Moves is a good customer and Digital World grants a trade discount of 20%.	6 000
		Sales	
6	06/04/X5	Sold 2 items at R100 each for cash. No discount was offered to the customers.	200
7	09/04/X5	Sold 15 items at R100 each on account to a customer. Smart Moves allows a 5% settlement discount if payment is received within 15 days.	1 500 (75) 1 425
8a	24/04/X5	Received from the customer in transaction 7 the amount owing by them *within the settlement period*, taking advantage of the settlement discount.	1 425
8b	25/04/X5	Received from the customer in transaction 7 the amount owing by them *after the settlement period.*	1 500
9	27/04/X5	Sold 20 items at R100 each for cash. The customers were offered a cash discount of 5% for paying cash.	1 900
10	30/04/X5	Sold 75 items on account to Sandton Computers. The normal selling price is R100 each. Sandton Computers is a good customer and is allowed a 20% trade discount on all purchases.	6 000
		Operating expenses	
11	30/04/X5	Administration expenses amounted to R1 200. Marketing and selling expenses amounted to R1 400.	

8.4.1 The recording of goods purchased

In the following paragraphs we are going to describe how Smart Moves records transactions relating to the purchase of inventory, assuming a **perpetual inventory system** is used. In particular, we will focus on the purchase of inventory where discounts are concerned.

The perpetual inventory system takes its name from the fact that the inventory account (sometimes referred to as the trading stock account) is perpetually up to date, that is, at any point in time the cost of inventory on hand is known. As you already know, the inventory account is updated after each purchase and sale of inventory, the cost of the goods sold being recorded at the time of sale. The balance on the inventory account must be verified against physical inventory figures.

8.4.1.1 Credit purchases and potential settlement discount

A retail entity does not usually purchase its inventory for cash. It is normal practice for the entity to open an account with its suppliers. The buying department is responsible for selecting suppliers to supply the entity with inventory and will negotiate the best prices and payment terms with the suppliers.

When the credit period offered by a supplier is longer than normal credit terms, the supplier may offer a settlement discount to encourage early payment of the account. Settlement discounts are indicated on the invoice as part of the terms of payment.

The purchase of inventory is recognised at fair value at the transaction date.

Think back to the definition of fair value earlier in this chapter and relate it to the concept of a settlement discount. The settlement discount offered by a supplier serves as an incentive for the purchasing entity to pay early. The total amount payable includes a potential interest expense. In other words, the amount payable to the supplier (100%) includes a financing component (say, 4%) which is only recognised if the payment to the supplier is not made within the specified period. The purchase of inventory is therefore recognised at the fair value at the transaction date, being 96% of the amount payable.

Let us now start analysing the transactions of Smart Moves relating to the purchase of inventory.

Transaction: *1* *04/04/X5* *Purchased 15 items at R60 each on account from Computer World. Computer World does not offer settlement discounts.*

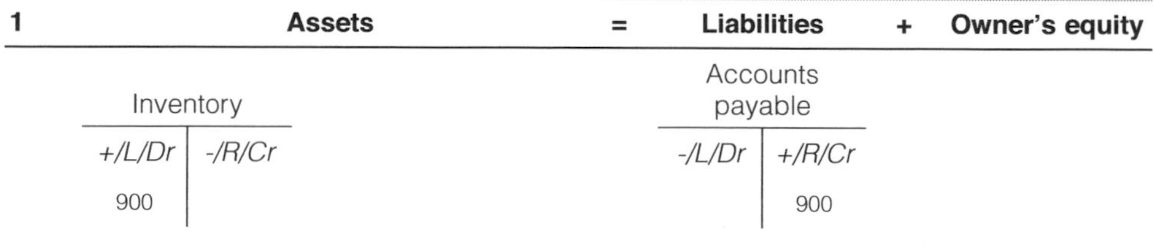

1	Assets	=	Liabilities	+	Owner's equity
	Inventory		Accounts payable		
	+/L/Dr | -/R/Cr		-/L/Dr | +/R/Cr		
	900 |		| 900		

This transaction for the purchase of inventory is similar to the ones that you analysed in the Smart Concepts example. You should be able to explain the increase in inventory with a left entry and the increase in accounts payable with a right entry.

Look closely at transaction 2. Do you see how it differs from transaction1? In transaction 2, the supplier allows a settlement discount and this is going to affect how the purchase of inventory is recorded.

Transaction: *2*	*08/04/X5*	*Purchased 20 items at R62,50 each on account from Plug & Play Limited. Plug & Play Limited allows a 4% settlement discount if payment is received within 15 days.*

2	**Assets**		**=**	**Liabilities**				**+ Owner's equity**
	Inventory			Deferred finance expense		Accounts payable		
	+/L/Dr	*-/R/Cr*		*+/L/Dr*	*-/R/Cr*	*-/L/Dr*	*+/R/Cr*	
	1 200			50			1 250	

The inventory purchased is recorded as an asset at its fair value of R1 200 and therefore the inventory account is increased on the left side of the equation. The inventory was purchased on credit from Plug & Play Limited. The accounts payable account on the right side of the equation is increased by the full amount of the obligation owing to Plug & Play Limited. The potential settlement discount is recorded as a negative liability, as a deferred finance expense.

As you have seen above, the potential settlement discount offered by the supplier was recorded as a deferred finance expense at the date of purchase.

Pause and reflect...

Assume that Smart Moves prepares a statement of financial position immediately after the above transaction, how would the amount owing to Plug & Play be reported?

Response

It will be reported as a current liability, accounts payable, at an amount of R1 200 (1 250 – 50).

Two scenarios now exist:

a) If the supplier is paid within the settlement period, the purchasing entity would not have obtained finance from the supplier and the deferred finance expense is reversed on settlement of the amount owing (Transaction 3a below).

b) On the other hand, if the supplier is not paid within the settlement period, the substance of the transaction is that the purchasing entity obtained finance from the supplier (Transaction 3b below).

Transaction: *3a*	*23/04/X5*	*Paid Plug & Play Limited amount owing to them within the settlement discount period, taking advantage of the 4% settlement discount.*

3a	Assets		=	Liabilities				+ Owner's equity
	Bank			Deferred finance expense		Accounts payable		
	+/L/Dr	-/R/Cr		+/L/Dr	-/R/Cr	-/L/Dr	+/R/Cr	
		1 200			50	1 250		

The invoiced amount owing to Plug & Play Limited was R1 250. Therefore the accounts payable account is reduced by R1 250 to reflect that the obligation has been settled. The amount of cash paid to settle the account was R1 200 as Smart Moves took advantage of the 4% settlement discount offered by Plug & Play Limited. The bank account is reduced by this amount on the left side of the equation. As the amount was paid within the settlement period, there is no finance expense and the deferred finance expense is reversed.

Transaction: *3b* *24/04/X5* *Paid Plug & Play Limited amount owing to them after the settlement period.*

3b	Assets		=	Liabilities				+ Owner's equity	
	Bank			Deferred finance expense		Accounts payable		Interest expense	
	+/L/Dr	-/R/Cr		+/L/Dr	-/R/Cr	-/L/Dr	+/R/Cr		
		1 250				1 250			
					50			50	

The amount owing to Plug & Play Limited was R1 250. Therefore the accounts payable account is reduced by R1 250 to reflect that the obligation has been settled. The amount of cash paid to settle the account was R1 250 as Smart Moves did not take advantage of 4% settlement discount offered by Plug & Play Limited. The bank account is reduced by this amount on the left side of the equation. As the amount was paid after the settlement period, the substance of the transaction is that Smart Moves obtained finance from Plug & Play Limited. The difference of R50 represents the financing component. Therefore the deferred finance expense is reversed and an interest expense is recognised (as a reduction in equity) on the right side of the equation.

8.4.1.2 Cash purchases and cash discount

Purchase transactions are measured after taking into account the amount of point of sale discounts. Cash discounts are point of sale discounts and the purchase is recognised at the net amount payable at the transaction date. The cash purchase price of the inventory purchased is the amount that the purchaser is prepared to pay in cash for the inventory. In other words, the inventory is purchased at its fair value and the inventory is recognised at that amount.

Transaction: *4* *25/04/X5* *Purchased 20 items at R75 each for cash. Received a 20% discount for paying cash.*

4	Assets				=	Liabilities	+	Owner's equity
	Bank		Inventory					
	+/L/Dr	-/R/Cr	+/L/Dr	-/R/Cr				
		1 200	1 200					

The inventory purchased had a list price of R1 500. As the supplier has allowed a 20% cash discount, the consideration paid amounts to R1 200. The inventory account is increased on the left side of the equation at the fair value of R1 200, to reflect the increase in the asset. The bank account must be reduced by R1 200 to record the payment.

8.4.1.3 Trade discount

IAS 2, Inventory, requires that trade discounts are deducted when determining the cost of goods purchased. Trade discounts are thus treated in the same way as cash discounts.

Transaction: *5* *30/04/X5* *Purchased 100 items on account from Digital World. The normal selling price from Digital World is R75 an item. Smart Moves is a good customer and Digital World grants a trade discount of 20%.*

5	Assets		=	Liabilities		+	Owner's equity
	Inventory			Accounts payable			
	+/L/Dr	-/R/Cr		-/L/Dr	+/R/Cr		
	6 000				6 000		

The invoice price of the goods purchased is R6 000 after deducting the trade discount. Inventory is increased by this amount to reflect the increase in the asset. Since the goods purchased have not been paid for, accounts payable on the right side of the equation is increased to reflect the increase in the liability.

Before moving on to the recording of goods sold and cost of sales, it is appropriate at this point to review the journal entries that have been processed in relation to the goods purchased. The following is the journal of Smart Moves for the month of April 20X5, showing all of the above transactions:

GENERAL JOURNAL OF SMART MOVES

#	Date	Description	Fol	Dr	Cr
1	04/04/X5	Inventory		900	
		Accounts payable			900
		Purchase of 15 items at R60 each on account			
2	08/04/X5	Inventory		1 200	
		Deferred finance expense		50	
		Accounts payable			1 250
		Purchase of 20 items at R62,50 each on account subject to a 4% settlement discount.			
3a	23/04/X5	Accounts payable		1 250	
		Bank			1 200
		Deferred finance expense			50
		Cash paid to Plug & Play Limited within the settlement period			
or					
3b	24/04/X5	Accounts payable		1 250	
		Bank			1 250
		Interest expense		50	
		Deferred finance expense			50
		Settled account with Plug & Play Limited after the settlement period.			
4	25/04/X5	Inventory		1 200	
		Bank			1 200
		Purchase of 20 items at R75 each for cash less 20% cash discount			
5	30/04/X5	Inventory		6 000	
		Accounts payable			6 000
		Purchase of 100 items at R75 each on account less a 20% trade discount			

8.4.2 The recording of goods sold and cost of sales

You know that a retail entity earns revenue by selling goods and that these sales can be either cash sales or credit sales. In the following paragraphs we are going to describe how Smart Moves records transactions relating to revenue from sales, assuming a **perpetual inventory system** is used. In particular, we will focus on revenue from sales where discounts are concerned. The recording of revenue from sales is identical for both the perpetual and periodic systems.

As you learnt in the Smart Concepts example in parts 1 and 2 of this book, *both* the revenue and the expense aspects of the transaction must be recorded at the time of sale when using the perpetual system.

The cost of goods sold in a retailing entity is reported on the statement of comprehensive income as a trading expense as opposed to an operating expense. It is typically referred to as cost of sales and is recorded differently depending on whether a perpetual or periodic system is being used.

8.4.2.1 Credit sales and potential settlement discount

Before a sale is made, the customer needs to open an account. The entity will investigate the creditworthiness of the customer before they will allow goods to be sold on credit.

Once the account has been approved the customer is given specific credit terms. This means that the customer can purchase goods from the entity up to a predetermined level and the payment must be made before a certain date.

The sale of inventory is recognised at fair value at transaction date.

Again, think back to the definition of fair value earlier in this chapter and relate it to the concept of a settlement discount. The settlement discount offered by a seller serves as an incentive for the customer to pay early. The total amount receivable includes a potential interest income. In other words, the amount receivable from the customer (100%) includes a financing component (say, 5%) which is only recognised if the receipt from the customer is not forthcoming within the specified period. The sale of inventory is therefore recognised at the fair value at the transaction date, being 95% of the amount receivable.

We can now turn our attention to analysing the transactions of Smart Moves relating to revenue from sales

Transaction: *6* *06/04/X5* *Sold 2 items at R100 each for cash. No discount was offered to the customers.*

6	**Assets**		**=**	**Liabilities**	**+**	**Owner's equity**	
	Cash					Sales revenue	
	+/L/Dr	*-/R/Cr*				*-/L/Dr*	*+/R/Cr*
	200						200

This sales revenue transaction is similar to the ones that you analysed in the Smart Concepts example. You should be able to explain the increase in cash with a left entry and the increase in sales revenue with a right entry.

The expense part of the transaction is to record the cost of sales.

Assets			=	Liabilities	+	Owner's equity	
Inventory						Cost of sales expense	
+/L/Dr	-/R/Cr					+/L/Dr	-/R/Cr
	120					120	

Again, this cost of sales transaction is similar to the ones that you analysed in the Smart Concepts example. You should be able to explain the increase in cost of sales expense with a left entry and a decrease in inventory with a right entry.

As with the purchase of inventory transactions, look closely at transaction 7 and see how it differs from transaction 6. In transaction 7, Smart Moves allows a settlement discount and this is going to affect how the sales revenue transaction is recorded

Transaction: *7* *09/04/X5* *Sold 15 items at R100 each on account to a customer. Smart Moves allows a 5% settlement discount if payment is received within 15 days.*

7 Assets				=	Liabilities	+	Owner's equity	
Accounts receivable		Deferred finance income					Sales revenue	
+/L/Dr	-/R/Cr	-/L/Dr	+/R/Cr				-/L/Dr	+/R/Cr
1 500			75					1 425

Once the sale has taken place, the customer owes R1 500 to Smart Moves. The amount owed is an asset and the accounts receivable account on the left side of the equation is increased by the full amount of the amount receivable from the customer. The revenue from sales is recorded at its fair value of R1 425 and therefore the sales revenue account is increased on the right side of the equation. The potential settlement discount is recorded as a negative asset, as a deferred finance income.

The expense part of the transaction is to record the cost of sales. Note that the measurement of the cost of sales is not affected by the measurement of the sales revenue transaction.

Assets			=	Liabilities	+	Owner's equity	
Inventory						Cost of sales expense	
+/L/Dr	-/R/Cr					+/L/Dr	-/R/Cr
	900					900	

As you now know, when inventory is sold it must be removed as an asset and treated as a cost of sales expense. The cost of the 15 items sold is R900 (15 X R60).

Pause and reflect...

Assume that Smart Moves prepares a statement of financial position immediately after the above transaction, how would the amount owing from the customer be reported?

Response

It will be reported as a current asset, accounts receivable, at an amount of R1 425 (1 500 – 75).

Again, two scenarios now exist:

a) If the customer pays within the settlement period, the selling entity would not have granted finance to the customer and the deferred finance income is reversed on receipt of the amount owing (Transaction 8a below).

b) On the other hand, if the customer does not pay within the settlement period, the substance of the transaction is that the selling entity granted finance to the customer (Transaction 8b below).

Transaction: *8a* *24/04/X5* *Received from the customer in transaction 7 the amount owing by them within the settlement period, taking advantage of the 5% settlement discount.*

8a	**Assets**					**= Liabilities**	**+ Owner's equity**
Cash		Accounts receivable		Deferred finance income			
+/L/Dr	-/R/Cr	+/L/Dr	-/R/Cr	-/L/Dr	+/R/Cr		
1 425			1 500	75			

The invoiced amount receivable from the customer was R1 500. Therefore the accounts receivable account is reduced by R1 500 to reflect that the amount has been received. The amount of cash received to settle the account was R1 425 as the customer took advantage of the 5% settlement discount offered by Smart Moves. The cash account is increased by this amount on the left side of the equation. As the amount was received within the settlement period, there is no finance income and the deferred finance income is reversed.

Transaction: *8b* *25/04/X5* *Received from the customer in transaction 7 the amount owing by them after the settlement period.*

8b	**Assets**					**= Liabilities**	**+ Owner's equity**	
Cash		Accounts receivable		Deferred finance income			Interest income	
+/L/Dr	-/R/Cr	+/L/Dr	-/R/Cr	-/L/Dr	+/R/Cr		-/L/Dr	+/R/Cr
1 500			1 500					
				75				75

The amount receivable from the customer was R1 500. Therefore the accounts receivable account is reduced by R1 500 to reflect that the amount has been received. The amount of cash received to settle the account was R1 500 as the customer did not take advantage of the 5% settlement discount offered by Smart Moves. The cash account is increased by this amount on the left side of the equation. As the amount was received after the settlement period, the substance of the transaction is that Smart Moves granted finance to the customer. The difference of R75 represents the financing component. Therefore the deferred finance income is reversed and an interest income is recognised (as an increase in equity) on the right side of the equation.

8.4.2.2 Cash sales and cash discount

Sale transactions are measured after taking into account the amount of point of sale discounts.

Cash discounts are point of sale discounts and the sale is recognised at the net amount receivable at the transaction date.

The cash selling price of the inventory sold is the amount that the customer is prepared to pay in cash for the inventory. In other words, the inventory is sold at its fair value and the sales revenue is recognised at that amount.

Transaction: *9* *27/04/X5* *Sold 20 items at R100 each for cash. The customers were offered a cash discount of 5% for paying cash.*

9	Assets		=	Liabilities	+	Owner's equity	
	Cash					Sales revenue	
	+/L/Dr	*-/R/Cr*				*-/L/Dr*	*+/R/Cr*
	1 900						1 900

The inventory sold had a list price of R2 000. As Smart Moves has allowed a 5% cash discount, the consideration received amounts to R1 900. The cash account is increased on the left side of the equation to reflect the receipt. The sales revenue account is increased on the right side at the fair value of R1 900, to record the amount earned.

The expense part of the transaction is to record the cost of sales.

Assets		=	Liabilities	+	Owner's equity	
Inventory					Cost of sales expense	
+/L/Dr	*-/R/Cr*				*+/L/Dr*	*-/R/Cr*
	1 200				1 200	

As you now know, when inventory is sold it must be removed as an asset and treated as a cost of sales expense. The cost of the 20 items sold is R1 200 (20 x R60)

8.4.2.3 Trade discount

IAS 18, Revenue, requires that revenue transactions be measured after taking into account any trade discounts. Trade discounts are thus treated in the same way as cash discounts.

Transaction: *10* *30/04/X5* *Sold 75 items on account to Sandton Computers. The normal selling price is R100 each. Sandton Computers is a good customer and is allowed a 20% trade discount on all purchases.*

10	**Assets**		**=**	**Liabilities**	**+**	**Owner's equity**	
	Accounts receivable					Sales revenue	
	+/L/Dr	*-/R/Cr*				*-/L/Dr*	*+/R/Cr*
	6 000						6 000

The invoice price of the goods sold is R6 000 after deducting the trade discount. Since the goods sold have not been paid for, accounts receivable on the right side of the equation is increased to reflect the increase in the asset. Sales revenue is increased by this amount to reflect the increase in equity.

The expense part of the transaction is to record the cost of sales.

	Assets		**=**	**Liabilities**	**+**	**Owner's equity**	
	Inventory					Cost of sales expense	
	+/L/Dr	*-/R/Cr*				*+/L/Dr*	*-/R/Cr*
		4 500				4 500	

Again, when inventory is sold it must be removed as an asset and treated as a cost of sales expense. The cost of the 75 items sold is R4 500 (75 X R60)

8.4.3 Journal entries

Before moving onto the recording of goods sold and cost of sales, it is appropriate at this point to review the journal entries that have been processed in relation to the goods sold and cost of sales. The following is an extract from the journal of Smart Moves for the month of April 20X5, showing all of the revenue and cost of sales transactions:

GENERAL JOURNAL OF SMART MOVES

#	Date	Description	Fol	Dr	Cr
6	06/04/X5	Cash		200	
		Sales revenue			200
		Sold 2 items at R100 each for cash.			
	06/04/X5	Cost of sales		120	
		Inventory			120
		Cost of goods sold			
7	09/04/X5	Accounts receivable		1 500	
		Sales			1 425
		Deferred finance income			75
		Sold 15 items at R100 each on account subject to a 5% settlement discount.			
	09/04/X5	Cost of sales		900	
		Inventory			900
		Cost of goods sold			
8a	24/04/X5	Bank		1425	
		Deferred finance income		75	
		Accounts receivable			1 500
		Cash received from the customer within the settlement period.			
	or				
8b	25/04/X5	Bank		1 500	
		Accounts receivable			1 500
		Deferred finance income		75	
		Interest income			75
		Cash received from the customer after the settlement period			
9	27/04/X5	Cash		1 900	
		Sales			1 900
		Sold 20 items at R100 each less a 5% cash discount.			
	27/04/X5	Cost of sales		1 200	
		Inventory			1 200
		Cost of goods sold			

10	30/04/X5	Accounts receivable		6 000	
		Sales			6 000
		Sold 20 items at R100 each on account less a 20% trade discount.			
	30/04/X5	Cost of sales		4 500	
		Inventory			4 500
		Cost of goods sold			

8.4.3 Ledger accounts

Following on from the journal entries, the relevant ledger accounts reflecting all of the transactions are shown below. The ledger accounts shown here are abridged ledger accounts, without date and folio columns. Remember that the transactions have been recorded in this section using a perpetual system.

INVENTORY

Details	R	Details	R
Balance	240	Cost of sales	120
Accounts payable	900	Cost of sales	900
Accounts payable	1 200	Cost of sales	1 200
Bank	1 200	Cost of sales	4 500
Accounts payable	6 000	Balance	2 820
	9 540		9 540
Balance	2 820		

COST OF SALES

Details	R	Details	R
Inventory	120	Balance	6 720
Inventory	900		
Inventory	1 200		
Inventory	4 500		
	6 720		6 720
Balance	6 720		

SALES REVENUE

Details	R	Details	R
Balance	9 525	Bank	200
		Accounts receivable	1 425
		Bank	1 900
		Accounts receivable	6 000
	9 525		9 525
		Balance	9 525

8.4.5 Summary of goods purchased and sold

It is useful at this stage to reflect on all the transactions that have been processed. This will assist you in understanding the presentation of the income statement in the section that follows.

#	Details	Qty	Inventory		Sales	
			Cost	Total	SP	Total
			R	R	R	R
0	Opening inventory	4	60	240		
		155		9 300		
1	Purchases	15	60	900		
2	Purchases	20	60	1 200		
4	Purchases	20	60	1 200		
5	Purchases	100	60	6 000		
	Goods available for sale / Cost of goods available for sale	159		9 540		
	Goods sold / Cost of sales	(112)		(6 720)		
6	Sales	(2)	60	(120)	100	200
7	Sales	(15)	60	(900)	95	1 425
9	Sales	(20)	60	(1 200)	95	1 900
10	Sales	(75)	60	(4 500)	80	6 000
	Closing inventory / Sales	47	60	2 820		9 525

Pause and reflect...

a) Do you understand the difference between the 'cost of goods available for sale' and the 'cost of sales'?
b) Can you see a relationship between the opening inventory, the goods purchased, the goods sold and the closing inventory?

Response

a) The 'cost of goods available for sale' is the cost of the opening inventory + the cost of the goods purchased during the period. In other words, it is the cost of the goods that the entity had *available for sale* to customers during the period. The 'cost of sales', on the other hand, is the cost of the goods *actually sold* during the period.
b) Opening inventory + goods purchased – goods sold = closing inventory.
Looking at quantity, 4 + 154 – 112 = 47.
In Rands, R240 + R9 300 – R6 720 = R2 820.
This relationship becomes very important in understanding the periodic inventory system.

8.4.6 Income statement presentation

In addition to the above transactions, Smart Moves had incurred administration expenses during the period of R1 200 and marketing and selling expenses of R1 400.

Two income statements are presented below. The first income statement includes the effects of transactions 3a and 8a (where the payment to the supplier and the receipt from the customer occurred within the settlement period). The second income statement includes the effects of transactions 3b and 8b (where the payment to the supplier and the receipt from the customer occurred after the settlement period and thus an interest expense and an interest income, respectively were recorded).

Income statement with no financing transactions (3a and 8a)

SMART MOVES
INCOME STATEMENT
FOR THE MONTH ENDED 30 APRIL 20X5

		R
Sales revenue		9 525
Cost of sales		(6 720)
Opening inventory		240
Purchases	(900 + 1 200 + 1 200 + 6 000)	9 300
Cost of goods available for sale		9 540
Closing inventory	(47 x R60)	(2 820)
Gross profit		2 805
Operating expenses		(2 600)
Administration expenses		1 200
Marketing and selling expenses		1 400
Profit for the period		205

Income statement with financing transactions (3b and 8b)

SMART MOVES
INCOME STATEMENT
FOR THE MONTH ENDED 30 APRIL 20X5

		R
Sales revenue		9 525
Cost of sales		(6 720)
Opening inventory		240
Purchases	(900 + 1 200 + 1 200 + 6 000)	9 300
Cost of goods available for sale		9 540
Closing inventory	(47 x R60)	(2 820)
Gross profit		2 805

Other income	
Interest income	75
Operating expenses	(2 600)
Administration expenses	1 200
Marketing and selling expenses	1 400
Finance costs	
Interest expense	(50)
Profit for the period	230

8.4.7 Closing entries

The closing entry process was explained in Chapter 7. For completeness, and to compare to the closing entries for the periodic inventory system, this section describes the closing entry process for a perpetual inventory system.

The relevant accounts here are the inventory account, the cost of sales account and the sales account. We learnt earlier in this chapter that the cost of sales is recorded each time that a sale is made. The sales and the cost of sales will both be transferred to the trading account, and the gross profit will be determined from the trading account.

The trial balance of Sharp Moves (using the perpetual system) at the end of April 20X5 is shown below.

SHARP MOVES
TRIAL BALANCE AT 30 APRIL 20X5

Description	Dr	Cr
Cash	1 125	
Inventory	2 820	
Accounts receivable	6 000	
Accounts payable		6 900
Owner's equity		2 840
Cost of sales	6 720	
Administration expenses	1 200	
Marketing and selling expenses	1 400	
Sales revenue		9 525
	19 265	19 265

Cost of sales

The cost of sales account, as an expense, will have a debit balance representing the cost of goods sold during the period. To reduce this account to zero, the balance must be transferred by a right hand or credit entry to the cost of sales account with the debit entered in the trading account.

Sales

The sales account is closed off to the trading account.

Inventory

As the inventory account in the perpetual system is updated each time goods are bought or sold, the balance of R2 820 in the inventory account on the trial balance is the amount that will appear as an asset on the statement of financial position. As you have seen in Chapter 7, there is thus no need to include the inventory account in the closing entry process when using the perpetual system.

The effect of the closing entries in the perpetual system can be demonstrated as follows. Again, only those accounts affecting trading activities have been included.

	Assets	=			Owners equity			
	Inventory		Sales		COS		Trading	
	+/L/Dr	*-/R/Cr*	*-/L/Dr*	*+/R/Cr*	*+/L/Dr*	*-/R/Cr*	*-/L/Dr*	*+/R/Cr*
Bal	2 820			9 525	6 720			
c/e 1						6 720	6 720	
c/e 2			9 525					9 525
	2 820							2 805

Closing entry 1 transfers the cost of sales to the trading account, while closing entry 2 transfers the sales to the trading account. The balance on the trading account then reflects the gross profit for the period of R2 805.

You should know from Chapter 7 that the trading account is then closed off by transferring the gross profit to the profit and loss account, followed by the closing off of the income and expense accounts, also to the profit and loss account. The profit and loss account is then closed off by transferring the profit or loss for the period to the capital account.

The completed ledger accounts, incorporating the closing entries are shown below:

INVENTORY

Details	R	Details	R
Balance	240	Cost of sales	120
Accounts payable	900	Cost of sales	900
Accounts payable	1 200	Cost of sales	1 200
Bank	1 200	Cost of sales	4 500
Accounts payable	6 000	Balance	2 820
	9 540		9 540
Balance	2 820		

COST OF SALES

Details	R	Details	R
Inventory	120	Balance	6 720
Inventory	900		
Inventory	1 200		
Inventory	4 500		
	6 720		6 720
Balance	6 720	**Trading**	**6 720**

TRADING

Details	R	Details	R
Cost of sales	**6 720**	**Sales revenue**	**9 525**
Profit and loss	**2 805**		
	9 525		9 525

SALES REVENUE

Details	R	Details	R
Balance	9 525	Bank	200
		Accounts receivable	1 425
		Bank	1 900
		Accounts receivable	6 000
	9 525		9 525
Trading	**9 525**	Balance	9 525

8.5 Recording of inventory transactions using a periodic system

The previous sections have described the recording of inventory transactions using a perpetual inventory system. In this section, we will examine the principles relating to a **periodic** inventory system. The recognition and measurement principles that you learnt for the perpetual system do not change. It is only the procedure to record the purchases of inventory and to record cost of sales that differs.

More specifically,

- a ***purchases account*** is used to accumulate the cost of goods purchased for resale (as opposed to an inventory account in the perpetual system), and
- the cost of goods sold is **not** recorded at the time of sale (whereas the cost of goods sold is recorded at the time of sale in a perpetual system).

8.5.1 The purchases account

The purchases account is neither an asset account nor an expense account, but a temporary account which records and accumulates the cost of goods purchased during the period.

When inventory is purchased, the purchases account is debited and the bank account or the accounts payable account is credited (depending if the purchase was for cash or on credit). However, any additional costs incurred, such as freight, duty or transport are recorded in separate accounts (and not in the purchases account).

At the end of the period, those goods which are sold become part of the cost of sales expense and those which are still on hand will form part of the closing inventory, an asset on the statement of financial position.

8.5.2 Cost of sales

At the time the sale is made, only the revenue aspect of the transaction is recorded. Similarly, if sales are returned, only the revenue returned aspect is recorded. The cost of goods sold is not recorded at the time of sale. At the end of the accounting period the cost of all goods sold during that period is determined. The following information is needed to compute the cost of goods sold:

- ❑ the cost of inventory on hand at the beginning of the period
- ❑ the cost of inventory purchased during the period
- ❑ the cost of inventory on hand at the end of the period (determined by performing a physical count).

Pause and reflect...

How would Sharp Moves determine the cost of its closing inventory?

Response

Employees at Sharp Moves would physically count the number of items of inventory on hand at the end of the period. Based on the quantity of opening inventory as well as the quantities of goods bought and sold during the current period, a total of 47 units is counted at the end of the period (4 + 154 – 112). Each item cost R60 and therefore the cost of the closing inventory is R2 820.

Note that the cost of sales as computed here is the same as the balance on the cost of sales account when using the perpetual inventory system.

SHARP MOVES
COST OF SALES CALCULATION

Opening inventory		240
Add Purchases	(transaction 1, 2, 4 & 5)	9 300
Cost of goods available for sale		9 540
Less Closing inventory	(47 x R60)	(2 820)
Cost of sales		6 720

It is important at this stage to compare what we have learnt about cost of goods sold and closing inventory using the perpetual inventory system to that using the periodic inventory system.

In a **perpetual inventory system**

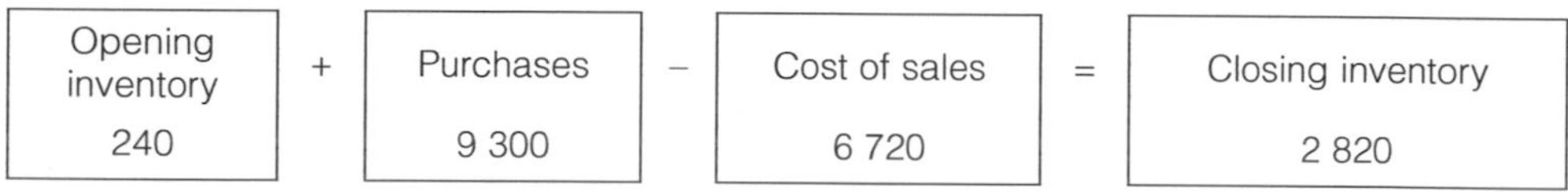

The cost of sales of R6 720 is the balance in the cost of sales account after processing the cost of sales transactions during the period. The balance of R2 820 in the inventory account needs to be *verified* by a physical inventory count.

In a **periodic inventory system**

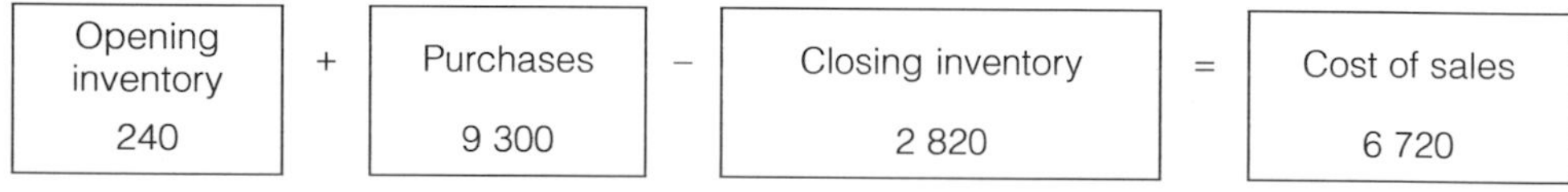

The closing inventory of R2 820 is *computed* by a physical count and then used to *determine* the cost of sales of R6 720. The closing inventory is recorded in the accounting records through the closing entry process.

8.5.3 Ledger accounts

As mentioned above, all the accounting entries to record inventory transactions are the same using either the perpetual or periodic system, except for the recording of purchases and the determination of cost of sales. Using the same information in the Sharp Moves example from section 8.4, the ledger accounts using a periodic system are shown below.

INVENTORY

Details	R	Details	R
Balance	240	Cost of sales	240
Cost of sales	2 820	Balance	2 820
	3 060		3 060
Balance	2 820		

PURCHASES

Details	R	Details	R
Accounts payable	900	Balance	9 300
Accounts payable	1 200		
Bank	1 200		
Accounts payable	6 000		
	9 300		9 300
Balance	9 300		

SALES REVENUE

Details	R	Details	R
Balance	9 525	Bank	200
		Accounts receivable	1 425
		Bank	1 900
		Accounts receivable	6 000
	9 525		9 525

COST OF SALES

Details	R	Details	R
Inventory	240	Inventory	2 820
Purchases	9 300	Balance	6 720
	9 540		9 540
Balance	6 720		

8.5.4 Income statement presentation

The presentation of the income statement is the same using a perpetual system or a periodic system. Please refer back to the income statements shown in section 8.4.4.

8.5.5 Closing entries

The closing entry process was explained in Chapter 7. This section describes the process for a periodic inventory system.

The relevant accounts here are the inventory account, the purchases account, accounts recording additional costs and the sales account. Cost of sales is arrived at by subtracting the closing inventory from the sum of the opening inventory and the purchases. In addition, the gross profit is calculated by subtracting the cost of sales from the sales. It is this information that will be reflected in the trading account.

The trial balance of Smart Moves (using the periodic system) at the end of April 20X5 is shown below. It is important to note that the inventory of R240 on the trial balance is the opening inventory, in other words, the balance at the beginning of the period. In the periodic system the inventory account is used to record the inventory on hand at the end of a period and then remains unchanged until the end of the following period when the new ending inventory is recorded. Therefore, by examining the trial balance at 30 April 20X5, we can immediately establish that the closing entries have not been processed as the inventory account shows the balance at the beginning of the period.

SMART MOVES
TRIAL BALANCE AT 30 April 20X5

Description	Dr	Cr
Cash	1 125	
Inventory (01/04/X5)	240	
Accounts receivable	6 000	
Accounts payable		6 900
Owner's equity		2 840
Purchases	9 300	
Administration expenses	1 200	
Marketing and selling expenses	1 400	
Sales		9 525
	19 265	19 265

Opening inventory

The inventory account will have a left hand or debit balance representing the *opening inventory* at the beginning of the period. This balance must be transferred out of the inventory account so that the *closing inventory* can be entered into the account. This is achieved by a right hand or credit entry to the account (by an amount equal to the balance of the opening inventory) with the debit side of the entry appearing in the trading account.

Purchases and other costs

The purchases account, as well as the accounts used to record other costs of purchase in the periodic system, will have a debit balance at the end of the period. To reduce these accounts to zero requires right hand or credit entries to the purchases and related accounts (by amounts equal to the debit balances) with the debit side of the entries appearing in the trading account.

Closing inventory

The inventory account, which has a zero balance after the transfer of the opening inventory must be re-established with the amount of the closing inventory which will appear as an asset on the balance sheet. To increase a left hand account requires a left or debit entry to the inventory account (by an amount of the closing inventory) with the credit side of the entry appearing in the trading account.

Sales

The sales account has a credit balance at the end of the period, representing the revenue earned from goods sold during the period. To reduce a right hand account requires a left or debit entry to the sales account (by an amount equal to the credit balance) with the credit side of the entry also appearing in the trading account.

The effect of the above closing entries can be shown as follows. Only those accounts affecting the trading activities of the entity have been included.

	Assets						**Owners equity**			
	Inventory		Purchases		Cost of sales		Sales		Trading a/c	
	+/L/Dr	-/R/Cr	+/L/Dr	-/R/Cr	+/L/Dr	-/R/Cr	-/L/Dr	+/R/Cr	-/LDr	+/R/Cr
Bal	240		9 300					9 525		
c/e 1		240			240					
c/e 2				9 300	9 300					
c/e 3	2 820					2 820				
Bal	2 820				6 720			9 525		
c/e 4						6 720			6 720	
c/e 5							9 525			9 525
Bal	2 820									2 805

The effect of closing entries 1 and 2 is to transfer the cost of the opening inventory as well as the cost of purchases to the cost of sales account. This amounts to R9 540 and represents the *cost of goods available for sale* during the period. Closing entry 3 records the closing inventory as a debit in the inventory account and as a credit in the cost of sales account. The debit in the inventory account establishes the asset for the statement of financial position and the credit to the cost of sales account reduces the cost of goods available for sale by R2 820 to arrive at the *cost of sales* for the period of R6 720. Closing entry 4 closes off the cost of sales for the period by placing a credit to the cost of sales account of R6 720 and a debit of the same amount to the trading account. Closing entry 5 closes off the sales for the period by placing a debit to the sales account of R9 525 and a credit of the same amount to the trading account. This leaves the trading account with a credit balance of R2 805 representing the *gross profit* for the period.

The remainder of the closing entry process is the same as you learnt in Chapter 7 and as you saw with the perpetual inventory system in section 8.4.7.

The completed ledger accounts, incorporating the closing entries, are shown below:

INVENTORY

Details	R	Details	R
Balance	240	**Cost of sales**	**240**
Cost of sales	**2 820**	Balance	2 820
	3 060		3 060
Balance	2 820		

PURCHASES

Details	R	Details	R
Accounts payable	900	**Cost of sales**	**9 300**
Accounts payable	1 200		
Bank	1 200		
Accounts payable	6 000		
	9 300		9 300
	9 300		

SALES REVENUE

Details	R	Details	R
Trading	**9 525**	Bank	200
		Accounts receivable	1 425
		Bank	1 900
		Accounts receivable	6 000
	9 525		9 525

TRADING

Details	R	Details	R
Cost of sales	**6 720**	**Sales revenue**	**9 525**
Profit and loss	**2 805**		
	9 525		9 525

COST OF SALES

Details	R	Details	R
Inventory (Opening)	**240**	**Inventory (Closing)**	**2 820**
Purchases	**9 300**	**Balance**	**6 720**
	9 540		9 540

Pause and reflect...

What do you notice about the entries in the cost of sales ledger account?

Response

The entries in the cost of sales ledger account represent the components of the cost of sales computation – the opening inventory and the purchases on the debit side and the closing inventory on the credit side.

8.6 Other aspects relating to perpetual and periodic inventory systems

The focus of this chapter has been on the recording of purchase and sale transactions involving adjustments to inventory and revenue where discounts are offered as well as to compare the perpetual and periodic inventory systems.

Two aspects relating to inventory systems that were not included in the example are the determination of the cost of inventory purchased and the recording of returns.

The cost of inventory includes all costs of purchase incurred in bringing the inventories to their present location and condition.

Thus the cost of purchase of inventory comprises:

- the invoice price
- import duties and other taxes
- transport
- handling and other costs.

Pause and reflect...

Sharp Moves purchases 100 items at an invoice price of R50 each. Import duties of R700 are incurred and paid to the South African Revenue Service and R300 is paid to transport the goods from the harbour to Sharp Moves' premises. What is the cost per item to be used to record the inventory and subsequent cost of sales in the accounting records of Sharp Moves?

Response

	R
100 items X R50	5 000
Import duties	700
Transport	300
	6 000

The cost incurred to bring the inventory to its present location and condition amounts to R6 000. Therefore the cost per item is R60 (R6 000 / 100 items).

The following table incorporates the accounting entries relating to other costs as well as returns with the entries learnt throughout the chapter.

Transaction	Perpetual	Periodic
Purchase of goods on credit	Dr Inventory Cr Accounts payable	Dr Purchases Cr Accounts payable
Other costs paid in cash (for example, transport)	Dr Inventory Cr Bank	Dr Transport Cr Bank
Return of goods purchased on credit	Dr Accounts payable Cr Inventory	Dr Accounts payable Cr Purchases or Purchases returns
Sale of goods on credit	Dr Accounts receivable Cr Sales *and*	Dr Accounts receivable Cr Sales
Recording cost of goods sold	Dr Cost of sales Cr Inventory	Computed at end of period
Return of goods sold on credit	Dr Sales Cr Accounts receivabe *and*	
Recording of cost of goods returned	Dr Inventory Cr Cost of sales	Incorporate in computation at end of period

Diagram 8.1 Accounting entries using perpetual and periodic inventory systems

8.7 Exam example

The following list of balances was extracted from the ledger of Mr Neil Downe, trading as The Duvet Shop, at 28 February 20X8:

THE DUVET SHOP
LIST OF BALANCES AT 28 FEBRUARY 20X8

	R
Accrued expenses (28/02/X7)	1 145
Advertising	900
Bank charges	139
Bank overdraft	772
Capital (28/02/X7)	15 339
Commission expense	1 400
Accounts payable	2 322
Accounts receivable	3 311
Distributions	2 500
Insurance expense	269
Interest income – Mr Knox Dover	500

Loan to Mr Knox Dover	8 000
Motor vehicles – at carrying amount (28/02/X7)	4 200
Motor vehicle expenses	1 127
Prepaid expenses (28/02/X7)	437
Purchases	23 225
Railage inwards	412
Rent expense	1 775
Returns inwards	1 720
Returns outwards	617
Salaries	3 135
Sales	40 020
Stationery	1 280
Inventory (28/02/X7)	6 885

In addition, the following relevant information is available:

1. The accrued expenses account at 28/2/X7 is made up as follows:

Commission	800
Railage inwards	45
Rent	300
	R1 145

All the above amounts have been paid (the payments were recorded in the expense accounts).

2. The advertising account includes a current payment of R495 in respect of a contract for the period 01/08/X7 – 30/04/X8.
3. The commission is paid to The Duvet Shop's sales manager, Mr Roll Dupp. This is calculated at 5% of the net sales for the year and is paid during the next financial year. During February 20X8, an advance was made to Mr Roll Dupp in respect of some of the commission for the year owing to him. This advance was debited to the commission expense account.
4. Insurance owing at 28/02/X8, but not yet provided for, amounted to R69.
5. The loan to Mr Knox Dover was made on 1 March 20X7. The capital amount outstanding bears interest at 10% per annum, payable in arrears on 1 September and 1 March each year. On 01/12/X7, an amount of R2 000 was repaid by him.
6. Motor vehicle expenses owing at 28/02/X8, but not yet provided for, amounted to R73. The motor vehicle is to be depreciated at the rate of 20% per annum on the carrying amount.
7. The prepaid expenses account at 28/02/X7 is made up as follows:

Advertising	233
Insurance	69
Salaries	135
	R437

8. Rent was increased from R100 per month to R125 per month. The rent expense account includes a payment of R375 on 01/02/X8 in respect of the quarter ended 31/03/X8.
9. Stationery inventory is maintained on the perpetual system. Stationery amounting to R170, purchased just before year end, had not been recorded. Stationery on hand at 28/02/X8 amounted to R300.
10. Inventory is maintained on the periodic system. Inventory on hand at 28/02/X8 amounted to R4 515.
11. The owner's wife, Mrs Eileen Downe, took a summer duvet for use on their bed at home

during the particularly hot month of February. No entry has been made for this duvet, which was marked for sale at R140. The Duvet Shop marks up all its goods at 25% on cost.

You are required to:

(a) enter in the general journal any adjusting entries considered necessary at 28/02/X8.
(b) prepare an income statement and a statement of changes in equity for the year ended 28/02/X8 and the statement of financial position at 28/02/X8.

Solution: Exam example

(a) GENERAL JOURNAL OF THE DUVET SHOP

Date	Description	Dr	Cr
20X8 Feb28			
	Accrued expenses	1 145	
	Commission		800
	Railage inwards		45
	Rent		300
	Accrued expenses at 28/02/X7 reversed		
28	Prepaid expenses	110	
	Advertising		110
	Amount paid in advance at 28/02/X8 (R495 x 2/9)		
28	Commission expense	1 315	
	Accrued expenses		1 315
	Balance of amount accrued at 28/02/X8 (R40 020 – R1 720) x 5% = R1 915, less advance of R600 (R1 400 – R800)		
28	Insurance	69	
	Accrued expenses		69
	Amount accrued at 28/02/X8		
28	Interest owing – Mr Knox Dover	450	
	Interest income		450
	Accrual of interest receivable ((R10 000 x 10% x 9/12 = R750) + (R8 000 x 10% x 3/12 = R200) less already received of R500)		
28	Motor vehicle expenses	73	
	Accrued expenses		73
	Amount accrued at 28/02/X8		
28	Depreciation expenses	840	
	Accumulated depreciation		840
	Depreciation provided for the year ended 28/02/X8 (R4 200 x 20%)		

Date	Description	Dr	Cr
28	Advertising Insurance Salaries Pre-paid expenses *Pre-paid expenses at 28/02/X7 expensed in 20X8*	233 69 135	 437
28	Pre-paid expenses Rent expense *Amount pre-paid at 28/02/X8 (R375 x 1/3)*	125	 125
28	Stationery Accounts payable *Recording of further stationery purchased*	170	 170
28	Cost of stationery used Stationery *Record stationery used (R1 280 + R170 – R300)*	1 150	 1 150
28	Drawings Purchases *Duvet taken from stock for personal use (Cost 100% + markup 25% = selling price 125% . . . to relate cost to selling price (given) requires 100/125 x R140)*	112	 112

(b) THE DUVET SHOP
INCOME STATEMENT
FOR THE YEAR ENDED 28 FEBRUARY 20X8

			R
Revenue from sales	(40 020 – 1 720)		38 300
Cost of sales			(25 233)
Opening inventory		6 885	
Purchases	(23 225 – 617 – 112)	22 496	
Railage inwards	(412 – 45)	367	
Cost of goods available for sale		29 748	
Closing inventory		(4 515)	
Gross profit			13 067
Other income			
Interest income			950
Operating expenses			(11 294)
Advertising	(900 – 110 + 233)	1 023	
Bank charges		139	
Commission	(1 400 – 800 + 1 315)	1 915	
Insurance	(269 + 69 + 69)	407	
Motor vehicle depreciation		840	
Motor vehicle expense		1 200	
Rent		1 350	
Salaries		3 270	
Stationery used		1 150	
Profit for the period			2 723

THE DUVET SHOP
STATEMENT OF FINANCIAL POSITION
AT 28 FEBRUARY 20X8

ASSETS	**R**
Non-current assets	
Motor vehicles	3 360
Current assets	16 811
Inventory	4 515
Stationery	300
Loan to Mr K Dover	8 000
Interest owing – Mr K Dover	450
Accounts receivable	3 311
Prepaid expenses	235
	20 171
EQUITIES AND LIABILITIES	
Capital and reserves	15 450
Current liabilities	4 721
Accounts payable	2 492
Accrued expenses	1 457
Bank overdraft	772
	20 171

THE DUVET SHOP
STATEMENT OF CHANGES IN EQUITY
FOR THE YEAR ENDED 28 FEBRUARY 20X8

	Capital R
Balance at 28/02/X7	15 339
Profit for the period	2 723
Distributions	(2 612)
Balance at 28/02/X8	15 450

Summary of concepts and applications

1. A service entity performs a service for a commission or fee, while a retailing entity is involved in the purchase and sale of goods. A business entity can combine service and retailing activities.
2. Sale and purchase transactions are recorded at fair value.
3. A retailing entity may employ either a perpetual or a periodic inventory system. When a perpetual inventory system is used, the cost of goods sold is recorded each time a sale is made, and an up-to-date record of the physical goods on hand is kept. When a periodic inventory system is used, an enterprise does not constantly maintain records of the quantity and cost of goods physically on hand or sold. It is only at the end of the period, when the inventory is counted, that the cost of goods sold can be determined.
4. Through the detailed example, the chapter demonstrates, using the perpetual inventory system, the recording of transactions in respect of goods purchased as well as goods sold. In addition, the resulting ledger accounts are presented, and on the income statement presentation is explained. The example is concluded with an illustration of the closing entries.
5. Using the periodic system, a purchases account is used to accumulate the cost of goods purchased. In addition, the cost of sales is not recorded at the time of the sale.
6. The chapter provides a summary of the relevant accounting entries processed under the perpetual and periodic inventory systems.

Notes

1. IAS 2, Inventories, *The International Accounting Standards Board*, (2004), paragraph 10.
2. IAS 2, paragraph 11.

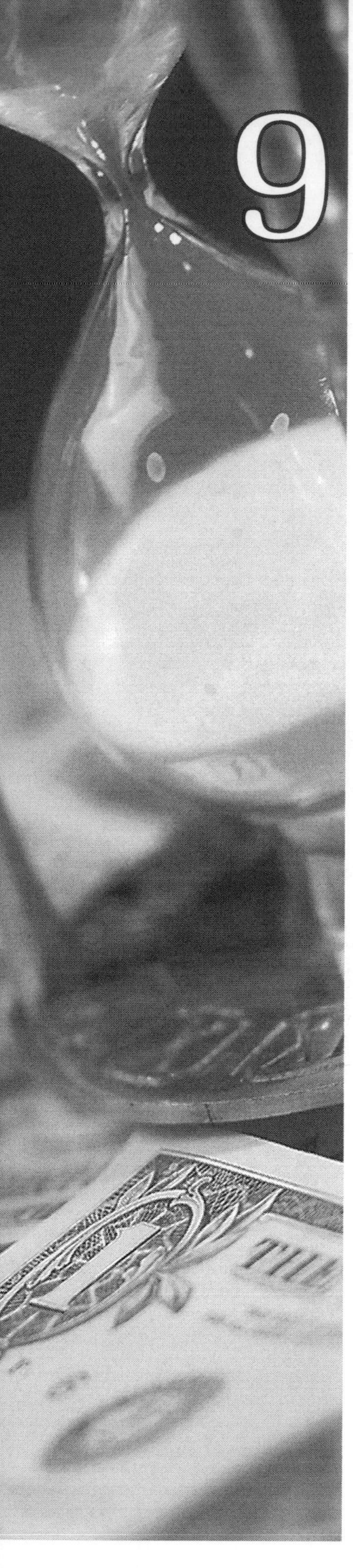

The Analysis Journals

'What is poetry to one, may be bookkeeping to another.' (Scott, 1816)

Outcomes

- Describe the function of the analysis journals.
- Explain the relationship between subsidiary ledgers and the control accounts.
- Prepare the sales, purchases, cash receipts and cash payments journals.
- Prepare the procedures for using the sales returns, purchases returns and petty cash journals.
- Describe the interaction of computerised accounting systems with the analysis journals.

Chapter outline

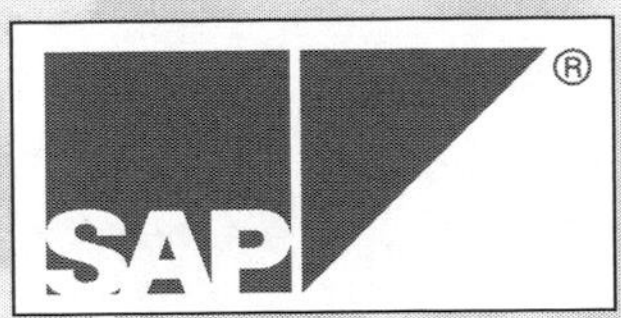

SAP AG
Income Statement for the year ended 31 December 2007

	(€ Millions)
Revenue	10 242
Cost of software	(1 310)
Cost of services used	(2 091)
Research and development	(1 458)
Other expenses	(2 543)
Profit before tax	2 840
Tax	(921)
Profit for the period	1 919

SAP is the largest Enterprise Application software vendor and third largest independent software company in the world with over 76 000 customers across 120 countries. SAP software enables companies to run their entire operations on integrated bases in real time. The software covers areas from accounting, HR, CRM, logistics to after sales services for 25 different industry verticals.

9.1 The use of analysis journals

When the accounting process was introduced in Chapter 4 the general journal was used as the book of prime entry to record the transactions of a business. This resulted in the posting of many debits and credits to the general ledger. There is, however, a more efficient way to process the financial data of a business enterprise. This chapter will introduce accounting systems that reduce the time and effort involved in recording the transactions and the subsequent postings to the general ledger.

For both practical and pedagogical reasons, this chapter describes the workings of a manual accounting system. The principles and procedures of a computerised accounting system are similar and you will quickly and easily follow the workings of the particular computerised system that you may encounter in practice.

The accounting systems referred to are the analysis journals. The analysis journals assist the bookkeeper in reducing the amount of postings to the general ledger.

The accounting process does not change as a result of introducing the analysis journals (see diagram 9.1). Rather, the recording of the transactions in the journals and the posting to the general ledger are refined, to speed up the processing of data phase in the accounting process.

Analysis journals are created for each major group of transactions typically entered into by a business enterprise. The primary analysis journals are used to record the effects of the following transaction groups:

- the sale of goods and the rendering of services on credit
- the purchase of goods and the acquisition of services on credit
- the receipt of cash
- the payment of cash.

The secondary analysis journals are used to record the effects of the following transaction groups:

- the return of goods sold and adjustments in relation to services rendered
- the return of goods purchased and adjustments in relation to services acquired
- petty cash funds.

The above transactions occur frequently and 'common elements' are debited or credited to the general ledger in each case. It is therefore more efficient to use an analysis journal, with cumulative postings taking place at the end of the period. The general journal is retained for recording all other transactions that do not fall into a typical group.

With the introduction of the analysis journals, we need to distinguish between cash and bank transactions. Cash is regarded as notes, coins and unbanked cheques received by a business from cash sales or from account payments by customers. These amounts are then deposited in the business bank account, and only when deposited are the amounts recorded in the bank account in the accounting records.

9.2 Subsidiary ledgers and control accounts

In addition to the analysis journals, this chapter will introduce you to the use of subsidiary ledgers. Efficient business operations require up-to-date information on amounts due from individual customers and amounts due to each supplier.

The general ledger accounts for accounts receivable and accounts payable provide details on the total amount owing by customers and owing to suppliers. The general ledger could be expanded to include accounts for each customer and supplier. However, this would make the general ledger voluminous and unwieldy.

Separate and distinct ledgers, referred to as subsidiary ledgers, are created to provide data relating to each customer and supplier. A subsidiary ledger is not part of the general ledger (see diagram 9.1). It represents only the details of one general ledger account. The general ledger account is a summary, or aggregation, of the accounts in the relevant subsidiary ledger. The aggregated accounts in the general ledger are known as the accounts receivable control and the accounts payable control.

The posting to the control accounts in the general ledger constitutes part of the double-entry accounting system, and the control accounts will therefore appear on the general ledger trial balance.

The postings to the individual customer and supplier accounts in the subsidiary ledgers can be regarded as an analysis of the entries posted to the accounts receivable and accounts payable control accounts. These postings do not form part of the double-entry system and therefore do not form part of the general ledger trial balance.

9.3 Procedures for using the primary analysis journals

Simon Smart decided in late 20X5 to diversify his business interests further and expand into the growing home entertainment market. On 2 January 20X6, Simon opened a new business, Bright Life, selling mobile music products, console games and lifestyle software. In the following sections we are going to analyse how Bright Life records its transactions using analysis journals.

9.3.1 Sales journal

The transactions that are recorded in the sales journal are sales made to customers *on credit*. *Cash* sales are recorded in the cash receipts journal which is discussed in 9.3.3 below.

Consider a credit customer such as a retail store that places orders with the sales department of a manufacturing entity. The order is an instruction to supply the customer with specific goods. This instruction is passed on to the stores department to select the items to be delivered to the customer. The storeman produces a delivery note to accompany the goods. The delivery note is a document detailing the goods to

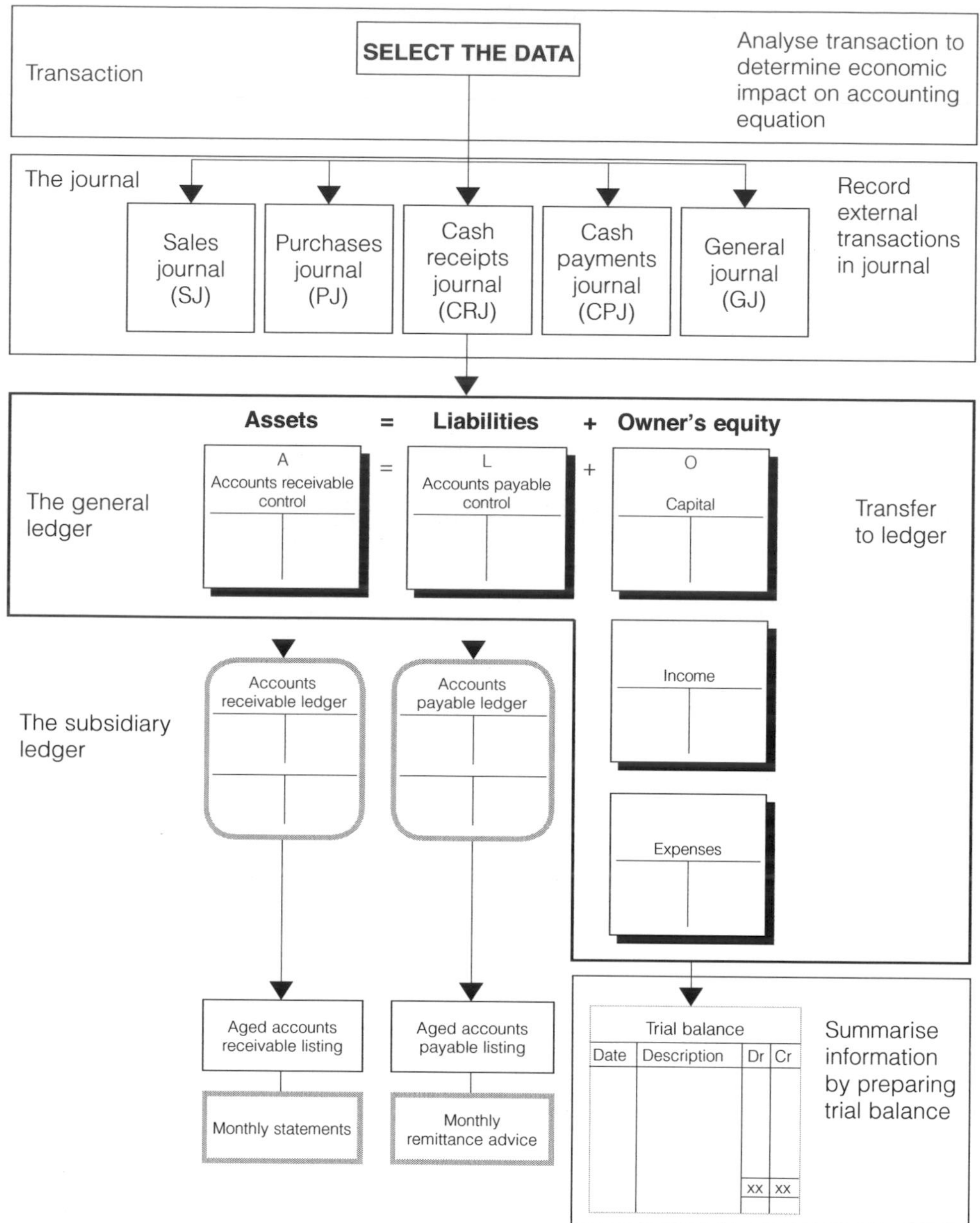

Diagram 9.1: The expanded accounting process to trial balance

be delivered, the date of delivery and the customer to whom they are delivered. When the customer receives the goods, the delivery note is signed as acknowledgement of receipt of the goods. It is at this point that the sales transaction has taken place and the revenue has been earned. The delivery note is then passed on to the accounts department which produces a sales invoice and records the sale in the accounting records. The invoice has all the information from the delivery note as well as the prices charged for the goods supplied.

The sales journal can also be referred to as a columnar journal. (See diagrams 9.2 and 9.3 for illustrations of typical sales journals.) There are columns in the journal to record the invoice number, date, name of the customer, folio-posting reference and amount of the sales transaction. In a perpetual inventory system there is an additional column to record the cost of sales. The credit sales are recorded in the sales journal on a daily basis from the information on the sales invoice. Each invoice is entered on a separate line.

At the end of each day, the individual sales invoices are posted to the debit side of the individual customers' accounts in the accounts receivable subsidiary ledger. This is to keep the individual customer accounts up to date in case of queries, and to ensure that customers do not exceed their credit limits. Once the amount has been posted, the customer's account number is filled in under the folio-posting reference column in the sales journal as evidence of the individual posting.

In posting to the subsidiary ledger the normal double-entry principles do not apply. In other words, there is no corresponding credit entry. This is because the purpose of a subsidiary ledger is to give a detailed breakdown of the control account in the general ledger. The general ledger is where the complete double entry is posted.

You will notice that the subsidiary ledger has the same format as a general ledger account, that is, columns for the date, details, folio and amount. However, the detail column will not record the other side of the entry; instead it will record the document number on which the transaction was recorded. The folio reference will still be used to indicate the page in the journal where the transaction was first recorded, but, since there are many journals, the initials of the specific journal will be used together with the page number. For example, a sales journal page 2 will have the reference SJ2.

At the end of the month the sales journal is totalled. The total sales are then posted to the general ledger as a debit to the accounts receivable control account and a credit to the sales account. The time saved in posting to the general ledger can now be appreciated, as only one entry is posted as compared to the many entries that would have to be posted if the general journal was used. As evidence of the posting to the general ledger, the account numbers are filled in below the amount column in the sales journal to indicate where the debit and credit were posted in the general ledger. At the end of the month the balance in the accounts receivable control account should equal the total of the balances in the accounts receivable subsidiary ledger.

Summary of the procedure for using the sales journal:

- Enter each invoice (representing a credit sale of merchandise) as a line item in the sales journal.
- Post the amount of each invoice to the debit side of each individual customer's account in the accounts receivable subsidiary ledger.
- At the end of the month, post the total of these transactions to the general ledger.

	Perpetual inventory system	Periodic inventory system
General ledger	Dr Accounts receivable control Cr Sales ***and*** Dr Cost of sales Cr Inventory	Dr Accounts receivable control Cr Sales
Accounts receivable subsidiary ledger	Dr Individual customers' accounts	Dr Individual customers' accounts

The recording process will be illustrated through the use of the sales transactions of Bright Life. The perpetual system is illustrated first, followed by the periodic system.

For the month of January 20X6, Bright Life made the following credit sales to customers:

1 01/01/X6 Sold goods on credit to F. Jones for R1 000 (Invoice 23). Cost R500.
2 08/01/X6 Sold goods on credit to S. Pillay for R500 (Invoice 24). Cost R250.
3 19/01/X6 Sold goods on credit to M. Ndlovu for R2 000 (Invoice 25). Cost R1 000.
4 30/01/X6 Sold goods on credit to F. Jones for R1 500 (Invoice 26). Cost R750.

Bright Life does not allow settlement discount to its customers

Perpetual System

Sales journal – January 20X6 ***SJ2***

Invoice	Date	Customer	Fol	Sales	Cost of sales
23	01/01/X6	F. Jones	ARL15	1 000	500
24	08/01/X6	S. Pillay	ARL25	500	250
25	19/01/X6	M. Ndlovu	ARL35	2 000	1 000
26	30/01/X6	F. Jones	ARL15	1 500	750
				5 000	2 500
				Dr GL: AR Control Cr GL: Sales	Dr GL: COS Cr GL: Inventory

Accounts receivable *subsidiary ledger*

Individual customer accounts

(The individual sales are posted to the subsidiary ledger accounts on a daily basis)

General ledger

Financial statement accounts

General ledger posting

Dr Accounts receivable control (255)

Cr Sales (580)

&

Dr Cost of sales (660)

Cr Inventory (325)

(The total sales and cost of sales are posted at the end of the month to the general ledger)

F. Jones (ARL15)

Date	Details	Fol	R	Date	Details	Fol	R
01/01	23	SJ2	1 000				
30/01	26	SJ2	1 500				

S. Pillay (ARL25)

Date	Details	Fol	R	Date	Details	Fol	R
08/01	24	SJ2	500				

M. Ndlovu (ARL35)

Date	Details	Fol	R	Date	Details	Fol	R
19/01	25	SJ2	2 000				

Accounts receivable control (255)

Date	Details	Fol	R	Date	Details	Fol	R
31/01	Sales	SJ2	5 000				

Sales (580)

Date	Details	Fol	R	Date	Details	Fol	R
				31/01	Accounts receivable	SJ2	5 000

Inventory (325)

Date	Details	Fol	R	Date	Details	Fol	R
				31/01	Cost of sales	SJ2	2 500

Cost of sales (660)

Date	Details	Fol	R	Date	Details	Fol	R
31/01	Inventory	SJ2	2 500				

Diagram 9.2: Perpetual inventory system

In diagram 9.2 we have demonstrated how to record the credit sales in a suitable sales journal assuming that Bright Life was using a perpetual inventory system. In addition, the individual credit sales have been posted to the individual customers' accounts in the accounts receivable subsidiary ledger and the month-end postings have been made to the general ledger accounts.

Periodic system

Sales journal – January 20X6 ***SJ2***

Invoice	Date	Customer	Fol	Sales
23	01/01/X6	F. Jones	DL15	1 000
24	08/01/X6	S. Pillay	DL25	500
25	19/01/X6	M. Ndlovu	DL35	2 000
26	30/01/X6	F. Jones	DL15	1 500
			5 000	
				Debit GL: AR Control Credit GL: Sales

Accounts receivable subsidiary ledger

Individual customer accounts

(The individual sales are posted to the subsidiary ledger accounts on a daily basis)

General ledger

Financial statement accounts

General ledger posting

Dr Accounts receivable control (255)

Cr Sales (580)

(The total sales are posted at the end of the month to the general ledger)

F. Jones (ARL15)

Date	Details	Fol	R	Date	Details	Fol	R
01/01	23	SJ2	1 000				
30/01	26	SJ2	1 500				

S. Pillay (ARL25)

Date	Details	Fol	R	Date	Details	Fol	R
08/01	24	SJ2	500				

M. Ndlovu (ARL35)

Date	Details	Fol	R	Date	Details	Fol	R
19/01	25	SJ2	2 000				

Accounts receivable control (255)

Date	Details	Fol	R	Date	Details	Fol	R
31/01	Sales	SJ2	5 000				

Sales (580)

Date	Details	Fol	R	Date	Details	Fol	R
				31/01	Accounts receivable	SJ2	5 000

Diagram 9.3: Periodic inventory system

In diagram 9.3 we have demonstrated how to record the credit sales in a suitable sales journal, assuming that Bright Life was using a periodic inventory system. In addition, the individual credit sales have been posted to the individual customers' accounts in the accounts receivable subsidiary ledger and the month-end postings have been made to the general ledger accounts.

Pause and reflect...

Have you thought how one decides what columns are needed in the sales journal?

Response

You just need to think of the underlying accounting entry. For the perpetual system, there are two entries. Firstly, there is a debit to accounts receivable control and credit to sales. Secondly, there is a debit to cost of sales and a credit to inventory. We therefore need a column for the sales (the debit to accounts receivable is for the same amount) and a column for the cost of sales (the credit to inventory is for the same amount).

9.3.2 Purchases journal

The transactions that are recorded in the purchases journal are purchases made *on credit* from suppliers. *Cash* purchases are recorded in the cash payments journal, which is discussed in section 9.3.4 below.

An enterprise does not only buy goods for resale on credit. In addition, non-current assets and other supplies and services are purchased on credit. The buying department is responsible for placing orders with a supplier. The order details the goods required, the price negotiated for the goods and the delivery address. The supplier then sends the goods ordered to the entity. The storeman is responsible for agreeing the goods received to the authorised order before signing the supplier's delivery note as acceptance of the goods. Once the storeman is satisfied he makes out a goods received note (GRN) for the items received. The GRN is an internal document evidencing the receipt of goods from a supplier. The GRN is matched to the order and sent to the accounts department. In the accounts department these documents are filed in an outstanding GRN file until the supplier's invoice arrives. Once the supplier's invoice arrives all three documents are matched and recorded in the accounting records. The supplier's invoice gives the details and the price of the goods purchased.

The purchases journal is a multicolumn journal. (See diagrams 9.4 and 9.5 for illustrations of typical purchases journals.) The journal has columns to record the supplier's invoice number, the invoice date, the name of the supplier, folio-posting reference and amount of the purchase transaction. Additional columns are required to analyse details of the purchases. For example, in diagram 9.4 (a perpetual inventory system) there are columns for inventory, stationery and sundries. In diagram 9.5 (a periodic inventory system) there are columns for purchases, stationery and sundries. The additional columns will vary from organisation to organisation, depending on the items that are purchased on credit. Items which are not regular purchases are entered into the sundries column. The credit purchases are recorded in the purchases journal on a daily basis from the information on the supplier's invoice. Each invoice is entered on a separate line.

At the end of each day the individual suppliers' invoices are posted to the credit side of the individual suppliers' accounts in the accounts payable subsidiary ledger. This is to keep the individual suppliers' accounts up to date in case of queries, and to ensure that suppliers' credit limits are not exceeded. The information in the subsidiary ledger is used as a basis for determining payments that need to be made to the suppliers in order to take advantage of discounts offered. Once the amount has been posted, the supplier's account number is filled in under the folio-posting reference column in the purchases journal as evidence of the individual posting.

At the end of the month the purchases journal is totalled. The total of each column is posted to the general ledger as a debit to the individual accounts, as indicated by the additional columns (for example, purchases or stationery), and a credit to the accounts payable control account for the accounts payable amount column. The additional column for sundry items is not posted in total. It must be analysed and posted to the individual accounts as indicated in the details column. Remember, the reason for a sundries column is to record transactions on credit which do not occur regularly. For regular credit purchases, a separate column will be allocated in the purchases journal. As evidence of the posting to the general ledger, the account numbers are filled in below the amount column in the purchases journal to indicate where the debit or credit was posted in the general ledger. For the sundry items there is a separate general ledger folio-posting reference column to confirm that the item has been posted to the general ledger. Note that the total debits posted must equal the total credits posted. At the end of the month the balance in the accounts payable control account should equal the balances in the accounts payable subsidiary ledger.

Summary of the procedure for using the purchases journal:

- Enter each invoice received from the supplier as a separate line item.
- The total amount owing will be entered into the accounts payable column. The items charged on the invoice must be analysed and allocated to the appropriate column, for example, purchases.
- Post the total of each invoice to the credit side of each individual supplier's account in the accounts payable subsidiary ledger.
- At the end of the month, post totals (except for the sundry items) to the general ledger. Sundry items must be posted to the debit side of the appropriate general ledger accounts.

	Perpetual inventory system	**Periodic inventory system**
General ledger	Dr Inventory Dr Stationery Dr Other individual accounts in the general ledger with the items recorded in the sundries column Cr Accounts payable control	Dr Purchases Dr Stationery Dr Other individual accounts in the general ledger with the items recorded in the sundries column Cr Accounts payable control
Accounts payable subsidiary ledger	Cr Individual suppliers' accounts	Cr Individual suppliers' accounts

The recording process will be illustrated through the use of the purchases transactions of Bright Life. The perpetual system is illustrated first followed by the periodic system.

For the month of January 20X6, Bright Life made the following credit purchases from suppliers:

5	01/01/X6	Purchased goods for resale from Games for Africa for R1 000 (Invoice 242).
6	02/01/X6	Purchased stationery from Paper Limited for R220 (Invoice 128).
7	07/01/X6	Purchased goods for resale from Master's Music for R1 200 (Invoice 891).
8	14/01/X6	Purchased a computer for the accountant from Computer World for R8 000 (Invoice 315).
9	21/01/X6	Purchased refreshments from Mr Thirsty for R50 (Invoice 99).
10	24/01/X6	Purchased goods for resale from Games for Africa for R1 500 (Invoice 281).

Perpetual system

Purchases journal — January 20X6 **PJ4**

Inv	Date	Details	Fol	Accounts payable	Inventory	Stationery	Sundry		
							Detail	Fol	Amount
242	01/01	Games for Africa	APL1	1 000	1 000				
128	02/01	Paper Limited	APL2	220		220			
891	07/01	Masters Music	APL3	1 200	1 200				
315	14/01	Computer World	APL4	8 000			Computer	GL75	8 000

99	21/01	Mr Thirsty	APL5	50			Refreshments	GL45	50
281	24/01	Games for Africa	APL1	1 500	1 500				
				11 970	3 700	220			8 050
				Credit GL: AP Control	Debit GL: Inventory	Debit GL: Stationery	Debit individual accounts detailed		

Accounts payable subsidiary ledger

Individual customer accounts

(The individual purchases are posted to the subsidiary ledger accounts on a daily basis)

Games for Africa (APL)

Date	Details	Fol	R	Date	Details	Fol	R
				01/01	242	PJ4	1 000
				24/01	281	PJ4	1 500

Paper Limited (APL)

Date	Details	Fol	R	Date	Details	Fol	R
				02/01	128	PJ4	220

Master's Music (APL)

Date	Details	Fol	R	Date	Details	Fol	R
				07/01	891	PJ4	1 200

Computer World (APL)

Date	Details	Fol	R	Date	Details	Fol	R
				14/01	315	PJ4	8 000

Mr Thirsty (APL)

Date	Details	Fol	R	Date	Details	Fol	R
				21/01	99	PJ4	50

General ledger

Financial statement accounts

(The totals are posted at the end of the month to the general ledger as indicated below each column in the purchases journal)

Accounts payable control (GL90)

Date	Details	Fol	R	Date	Details	Fol	R
				31/01	Purchases	PJ4	11 970

Inventory (GL325)

Date	Details	Fol	R	Date	Details	Fol	R
31/01	Accounts payable	PJ4	3 700				

Stationery (GL50)

Date	Details	Fol	R	Date	Details	Fol	R
31/01	Accounts payable	PJ4	220				

Computer equipment (GL75)

Date	Details	Fol	R	Date	Details	Fol	R
31/01	Accounts payable	PJ4	8 000				

Refreshments (GL45)

Date	Details	Fol	R	Date	Details	Fol	R
31/01	Accounts payable	PJ4	50				

Diagram 9.4: Perpetual inventory system

In diagram 9.4 we have demonstrated how to record the credit purchases in a suitable purchases journal, assuming that Bright Life was using a perpetual inventory system. In addition, the individual credit purchases have been posted to the individual suppliers' accounts in the accounts payable subsidiary ledger and the month-end postings have been made to the general ledger accounts.

Periodic system

Purchases journal — January 20X6 **PJ4**

Inv	Date	Details	Fol	Accounts payable	Purchases	Stationery	Sundry		
							Detail	Fol	Amount
242	01/01	Games for Africa	APL1	1 000	1 000				
128	02/01	Paper Limited	APL2	220		220			
891	07/01	Masters Music	APL3	1 200	1 200				
315	14/01	Computer World	APL4	8 000			Computer	GL75	8 000
99	21/01	Mr Thirsty	APL5	50			Refreshments	GL45	50
281	24/01	Games for Africa	APL1	1 500	1 500				
				11 970	3 700	220			8 050
				Cr GL: AP Control	Dr GL: Inventory	Dr GL: Stationery	Dr individual accounts detailed		

Accounts payable *subsidiary ledger*

Individual customer accounts

(The individual purchases are posted to the subsidiary ledger accounts on a daily basis)

General ledger

Financial statement accounts

(The totals are posted at the end of the month to the general ledger as indicated below each column in the purchases journal)

Games for Africa (APL)

Date	Details	Fol	R	Date	Details	Fol	R
				01/01	242	PJ4	1 000
				24/01	281	PJ4	1 500

Paper Limited (APL)

Date	Details	Fol	R	Date	Details	Fol	R
				02/01	128	PJ4	220

Master's Music (APL)

Date	Details	Fol	R	Date	Details	Fol	R
				07/01	891	PJ4	1 200

Computer World (APL)

Date	Details	Fol	R	Date	Details	Fol	R
				14/01	315	PJ4	8 000

Mr Thirsty (APL)

Date	Details	Fol	R	Date	Details	Fol	R
				21/01	99	PJ4	50

Accounts payable control (GL90)

Date	Details	Fol	R	Date	Details	Fol	R
				31/01	Purchases	PJ4	11 970

Purchases (GL60)

Date	Details	Fol	R	Date	Details	Fol	R
31/01	Accounts payable	PJ4	3 700				

Stationery (GL50)

Date	Details	Fol	R	Date	Details	Fol	R
31/01	Accounts payable	PJ4	220				

Computer equipment (GL75)

Date	Details	Fol	R	Date	Details	Fol	R
31/01	Accounts payable	PJ4	8 000				

Refreshments (GL45)

Date	Details	Fol	R	Date	Details	Fol	R
31/01	Accounts payable	PJ4	50				

Diagram 9.5: Periodic inventory system

In diagram 9.5 we demonstrated how to record the credit purchases in a suitable purchases journal, assuming that Bright Life was using a periodic inventory system. In addition, the individual credit purchases have been posted to the individual suppliers' accounts in the accounts payable subsidiary ledger and the month-end postings have been made to the general ledger accounts.

Pause and reflect...

Have you thought how one decides what columns are needed in the purchases journal?

Response

Again you just need to think of the underlying accounting entry. It is different from the sales journal situation in that a number of separate accounts are debited with a single credit to the accounts payable control account. For the perpetual system, there are debits to each major category purchased, such as inventory, supplies and furniture and then a credit to the accounts payable control with the total. We therefore need columns for each of the categories of items purchased and a column for accounts payable control.

9.3.3 Cash receipts journal

The transactions that are recorded in the cash receipts journal are cash sales, receipts from customers in settlement of amounts owing and sundry receipts (such as cash from the sale of a non-current asset, interest received from the bank or cash introduced by the owner at the start of a business). When cash is received from a cash sale it is usually entered using a cash register. At the end of the day the sales as recorded by the cash register are totalled up and agreed to the cash in the register. If cash is received from a customer in settlement of amounts owing or from another source, such as cash from the sale of a non-current asset, a cash receipt is issued. The cash receipt will detail the amount of cash received, from whom it was received and the reason for the cash received, for example, customer paying an account. Cheques received from customers are entered into a cheque register on a daily basis. The cheque register will list the cheques received, detailing the amounts received and from whom they were received. At the end of each day the total cash sales, individual cash receipts, and cheques received are recorded in the accounting records.

For an enterprise to maintain proper control over its receipts the money is banked intact daily. This means that all money received in one day is deposited into the bank account the following day. Cash should not be used to pay expenses.

The cash receipts journal is a multicolumn journal. (See diagrams 9.6.1 and 9.7.1 for illustrations of typical cash receipts journals.) The journal has columns to record the document number, date, account name, folio-posting reference and amount for the specific receipts to be credited (such as sales, accounts receivable and sundry receipts) and debited (for example, bank). The credit columns will vary from organisation to organisation, depending on the reasons for cash being received. For items which are regular receipts, a separate column is allocated so as to accumulate these receipts – non-regular receipts are entered into the sundries column. The debit columns are for analysis and bank – the analysis column analyses the total receipts before they are deposited. Once they are deposited, the total of the deposit slip is entered into the bank column. This is important in order to trace deposits to the bank statement received from the bank. In a perpetual inventory system there is an additional column to record the cost of sales for the cash sales transactions. Cash receipts are recorded in the cash receipts journal on a daily basis from the information on the cash receipts, total till readings or the cheque register. Each receipt is entered on a separate line, except for cash sales which are entered as a daily total.

At the end of each day the individual customer receipts are posted to the credit side of the individual customers' accounts in the accounts receivable subsidiary ledger. This is to keep the individual customers' accounts up to date in case of queries. Once the amount has been posted, the supplier's account number is filled in under the folio-posting reference column in the cash receipts journal as evidence of the individual posting.

At the end of the month the amount columns of the cash receipts journal are totalled. The total of each column is posted to the general ledger as a debit to bank, and a credit to the individual accounts for which the cash was received, for example, sales and accounts receivable control. The column for sundry items is not posted in total. It must be analysed and posted to the individual accounts as indicated in the details column. As evidence of the posting to the general ledger, the account numbers are filled in below the amount column in the cash receipts journal to where the debit or credit was made. For sundry items, the posting reference for the general ledger is entered into the folio-posting reference column. Note that the total debits posted must equal the total credits posted. At the end of the month the balance in the accounts receivable control account should equal the balances in the accounts receivable subsidiary ledger. If a perpetual inventory system is in operation, an additional entry will have to be posted to the general ledger to account for the cost of sales. The cost of sales column will be posted as a debit to the cost of sales account and a credit to the inventory account.

Summary of the procedure for using the cash receipts journal:

- ❑ Enter each cash amount received as a line item.
- ❑ Where cash is received from a credit customer, the cash received is entered into the analysis column (and subsequently into the bank column when deposited and in the accounts receivable control column.)
- ❑ The analysis column is used to record all cash received until it is banked. If a perpetual system is being used, the cost price of the goods sold for cash will be entered in the cost of sales column. The cost of sales column is not part of the double entry to record cash received.
- ❑ Post the amounts received from individual customers to the credit side of each individual customer's account in the accounts receivable subsidiary ledger.
- ❑ At the end of the month, post totals, except for the sundry items, to the general ledger. Sundry items must be posted to the credit side of the appropriate general ledger accounts.

	Perpetual inventory system	Periodic inventory system
General ledger	Dr Bank Cr Accounts receivable control Cr Sales Cr Other individual accounts in the general ledger with the items recorded in the sundry column **and** Dr Cost of sales Cr Inventory	Dr Bank Cr Accounts receivable control Cr Sales Cr Other individual accounts in the general ledger with the items recorded in the sundry column
Accounts receivable subsidiary ledger	Cr Individual customers' accounts	Cr Individual customers' accounts

The recording process will be illustrated through the use of the cash receipts transactions of Bright Life. The perpetual system is illustrated first, followed by the periodic system.

For the month of January 20X6, Bright Life received the following cash receipts:

11 01/01/X6 The owner, Mr S Smart, invested R20 000 into the business (deposit slip 1).
12 15/01/X6 Sold goods for cash R200 (cost price R100, cash sale slip 18).
13 15/01/X6 Received R1 000 from F. Jones (receipt 90).
14 25/01/X6 Sold goods for cash for R800 and allowed a 10% cash discount (cost price R400, cash sale slip 19).
15 25/01/X6 Received interest of R20 from the bank (receipt 91).
16 28/01/X6 Received payment from S. Pillay for amount due (receipt 92).

Perpetual system

Cash receipts journal — January 20X6 **CRJ7**

Doc	Date	Account name	Fol	Sales	Accounts receivable control	Sundries	Cost of sales	Analysis	Bank
DS01	01/01	Capital - S Smart	GL10			20 000		20 000	20 000
CSS18	15/01	Sales		200			100	200	
Rec90	15/01	F. Jones	ARL15		1 000			1 000	1 200
CSS19	25/01	Sales		720			400	720	
Rec91	25/01	Interest received	GL70					20	740
Rec92	28/01	S. Pillay	ARL25		500	20		500	500
				920	**1 500**	**20 020**	**500**		**22 440**
				Cr GL: Sales	Cr GL: AR Control	Cr individual accounts	Dr GL: COS Cr GL: Inventory		Dr GL: Bank

Diagram 9.6.1: Perpetual inventory system (cash receipts journal)

In diagram 9.6.1 we have demonstrated how to record the cash receipts in a suitable cash receipts journal, assuming that Bright Life was using a perpetual inventory system.

Accounts receivable *subsidiary ledger*

Individual customer accounts

(The individual receipts from customers are posted to the subsidiary ledger accounts on a daily basis)

F. Jones (ARL15)

Date	Details	Fol	R	Date	Details	Fol	R
01/01	23	SJ2	1 000	15/01	Rec90	CRJ7	1 000
30/01	26	SJ2	1 500	31/01	Bal	c/d	1 500
			2 500				2 500
01/02	Bal	b/d	1 500				

S. Pillay (ARL25)

Date	Details	Fol	R	Date	Details	Fol	R
08/01	24	SJ2	500	28/01	Rec92	CRJ7	500
				31/01	Bal	c/d	0
			500				500
01/02	Bal	b/d	0				

M. Ndlovu (ARL35)

Date	Details	Fol	R	Date	Details	Fol	R
19/01	25	SJ2	2 000				
				31/01	Bal	c/d	2 000
			2 000				2 000
01/02	Bal	b/d	2 000				

Bank (GL150)

Date	Details	Fol	R	Date	Details	Fol	R
31/01	Deposits	CRJ7	22 440				

General ledger

Financial statement accounts

(The totals are posted at the end of the month to the general ledger as indicated below each column in the receipts journal)

Accounts receivable control (GL255)

Date	Details	Fol	R	Date	Details	Fol	R
31/01	Sales	SJ2	5 000	31/01	Bank	CRJ7	1 500
				31/01	Bal	c/d	3 500
			5 000				5 000
01/02	Bal	b/d	3 500				

Sales (GL580)

Date	Details	Fol	R	Date	Details	Fol	R
				31/01	Accounts receivable	SJ2	5 000
31/01	Bal	c/d	5 970	31/01	Bank	CRJ7	970
			5 970				5 970
				01/02	Bal	b/d	5 970

Inventory (GL325)

Date	Details	Fol	R	Date	Details	Fol	R
31/01	Accounts payable	PJ4	3 700	31/01	Cost of sales	SJ2	2 500
				31/01	Cost of sales	CRJ7	500
				31/01	Bal	c/d	700
			3 700				3 700
01/02	Bal	b/d	700				

Cost of sales (GL660)

Date	Details	Fol	R	Date	Details	Fol	R
31/01	Inventory	SJ2	2 500				
31/01	Inventory	CRJ7	500	31/01	Bal	c/d	3 000
			3 000				3 000
01/02	Bal	b/d	3 000				

Capital – S Smart (GL10)

Date	Details	Fol	R	Date	Details	Fol	R
				01/01	Bank	CRJ7	20 000

Interest received (GL70)

Date	Details	Fol	R	Date	Details	Fol	R
				25/01	Bank	CRJ7	20

Diagram 9.6.2: Perpetual inventory system (subsidiary ledger and general ledger postings)

In diagram 9.6.2 the individual receipts from customers have been posted to the individual customers' accounts in the accounts receivable subsidiary ledger. In addition, the month-end postings have been made to the general ledger accounts.

Periodic system

Cash receipts journal — January 20X6 **CRJ7**

Doc	Date	Account name	Fol	Sales	Accounts receivable control	Sundries	Analysis	Bank
DS01	01/01	Capital - S Smart	GL10			20 000	20 000	20 000
CSS18	15/01	Sales		200			200	
Rec90	15/01	F. Jones	ARL15		1 000		1 000	1 200
CSS19	25/01	Sales		720			720	
Rec91	25/01	Interest received	GL70			20	20	740
Rec92	28/01	S. Pillay	ARL25		500		500	500
				920	**1 500**	**20 020**		**22 440**
				Cr GL: Sales	Cr GL: AR Control	Credit individual accounts		Dr GL: Bank

Diagram 9.7.1: Periodic inventory system (cash receipts journal)

In diagram 9.7.1 we have demonstrated how to record the cash receipts in a suitable cash receipts journal, assuming that Bright Life was using a periodic inventory system.

Accounts receivable subsidiary ledger

Individual customer accounts

(The individual receipts from customers are posted to the subsidiary ledger accounts on a daily basis)

F. Jones (ARL15)

Date	Details	Fol	R	Date	Details	Fol	R
01/01	23	SJ2	1 000	15/01	Rec90	CRJ7	1 000
30/01	26	SJ2	1 500	31/01	Bal	c/d	1 500
			2 500				2 500
01/02	Bal	b/d	1 500				

S. Pillay (ARL25)

Date	Details	Fol	R	Date	Details	Fol	R
08/01	24	SJ2	500	28/01	Rec92	CRJ7	500
				31/01	Bal	c/d	0
			500				500
01/02	Bal	b/d	0				

General ledger

Financial statement accounts

(The totals are posted at the end of the month to the general ledger as indicated below each column in the cash receipts journal)

Accounts receivable control (GL255)

Date	Details	Fol	R	Date	Details	Fol	R
31/01	Sales	SJ2	5 000	31/01	Bank	CRJ7	1 500
				31/01	Bal	c/d	3 500
			5 000				5 000
01/02	Bal	b/d	3 500				

Sales (GL580)

Date	Details	Fol	R	Date	Details	Fol	R
				31/01	Accounts receivable	SJ2	5 000
31/01	Bal	c/d	5 920	31/01	Bank	CRJ7	920
							5 920
				01/02	Bal	b/d	5 920

M. Ndlovu (ARL35)

Date	Details	Fol	R	Date	Details	Fol	R
19/01	25	SJ2	2 000				
				31/01	Bal	c/d	2 000
			2 000				2 000
01/02	Bal	b/d	2 000				

Capital – S Smart (GL10)

Date	Details	Fol	R	Date	Details	Fol	R
				01/01	Bank	CRJ7	20 000
31/01	Bal	c/d	20 000				
			20 000				20 000
				01/02	Bal	b/d	20 000

Interest received (GL70)

Date	Details	Fol	R	Date	Details	Fol	R
				25/01	Bank	CRJ7	20

Bank (GL150)

Date	Details	Fol	R	Date	Details	Fol	R
31/01	Deposits	CRJ7	22 440				

Diagram 9.7.2: Periodic inventory system (subsidiary ledger and general ledger postings)

In diagram 9.7.2 the individual receipts from customers have been posted to the individual customers' accounts in the accounts receivable subsidiary ledger. In addition, the month-end postings have been made to the general ledger accounts.

Pause and reflect...

There is a sales column in both the sales journal and the cash receipts journal. Can you identify the types of sales transactions that are recorded in each journal?

Response

The sales journal records sales on credit whereas the cash receipts journal records cash sales.

9.3.4 Cash payments journal

The transactions that are recorded in the cash payments journal are payments made out of the bank account for purchases, settlement of balances on suppliers' accounts, salaries, wages and sundry payments. Payments are only made once all documentation is received. The accounts payable clerk in the accounts department then makes out a cheque requisition. This is passed on to the accountant who is an authorised cheque signatory, to review together with the supporting documents and prepare the cheque. The payment is then recorded in the accounting records.

For an enterprise to maintain proper control over its disbursements, all payments should be made by way of cheques. This is because a cheque has to be signed by an authorised person before payment can be made.

The cash payments journal is a multicolumn journal. (See diagram 9.8.1 and 9.9.1 for illustrations of typical cash receipts journals.) The journal has columns to record the document number, date, account name, folio-posting reference, and amount for the specific payments to be debited (such as inventory for a perpetual inventory system, purchases for a periodic inventory system, accounts payable control, salaries and sundry receipts) and credited (for example bank). The debit columns will vary from organisation to organisation, depending on the reason for the payments. A separate column is allocated for items which are regular payments, so as to accumulate these payments. Non-regular payments are entered into the sundries column. Payments are recorded in the cash payments journal on a daily basis from the information on the cheque counterfoils. Each payment is entered on a separate line.

At the end of each day the individual suppliers' payments are posted to the debit side of the individual suppliers' accounts in the accounts payable subsidiary ledger. This is to keep the individual suppliers' accounts up to date in case of queries. Once the amount has been posted, the supplier's account number is filled in under the folio-posting reference column in the cash payments journal as evidence of the individual posting.

At the end of the month the amount columns of the cash payments journal are totalled. The total of each column is posted to the general ledger as a debit to the individual account for which the payment was made (for example, purchases, accounts payable control and salaries) and a credit to bank. The column for sundry items is not posted in total. It must be analysed and posted to the individual accounts as indicated in the details column. As evidence of the posting to the general ledger, the account numbers are filled in below the amount column in the cash payments journal to where the debit or credit was made. For sundry items, the posting reference for the general ledger is entered into the folio-posting reference column. Note that the total debits posted must equal the total credits posted. At the end of the month the balance in the accounts payable control account should equal the balances in the accounts payable subsidiary ledger.

Summary of the procedure for using the cash payments journal:

- Enter each cheque drawn, or reduction in bank balance, as a line item.
- Post amounts paid to each individual supplier to the debit side of each individual supplier's account in the subsidiary accounts payable ledger.
- At the end of the month, post totals, except for the sundry items, to the general ledger. Sundry items must be posted to the debit side of the appropriate general ledger accounts.

	Perpetual inventory system	**Periodic inventory system**
General ledger	Dr Inventory Dr Accounts payable control Dr Salaries Dr Other individual accounts in the general ledger with the items recorded in the sundry column Cr Bank	Dr Purchases Dr Accounts payable control Dr Salaries Dr Other individual accounts in the general ledger with the items recorded in the sundry column Cr Bank
Accounts payable subsidiary ledger	Dr Individual suppliers' accounts	Dr Individual suppliers' accounts

The recording process will be illustrated through the use of the cash payments transactions of Bright Life. The perpetual inventory system is illustrated first, followed by the periodic system.

For the month of January 20X6, Bright Life made the following payments:

17 01/01/X6 Purchased R200 of goods for resale and paid by cheque (cheque 141).
18 15/01/X6 Paid Games for Africa R1 000 (cheque 142).
19 18/01/X6 Purchased R500 worth of goods for resale and paid by cheque. Received a 10% cash discount (cheque 143).
20 27/01/X6 Paid Computer World the amount outstanding (cheque 144).
21 30/01/X6 Paid salaries for the month, R2 000 (cheque 145).
22 30/01/X6 Paid the January rent R1 500 (cheque 146).

Perpetual system

Cash payments journal — January 20X6 **CPJ7**

Doc	Date	Details	Fol	Inventory	Salaries	Accounts payable	Sundries	Bank
CHQ141	01/01	Inventory	APL1	200				200
CHQ142	15/01	Games for Africa				1 000		1 000
CHQ143	18/01	Inventory	APL4	450				450
CHQ144	27/01	Computer World				8 000		8 000
CHQ145	30/01	Salaries			2 000			2 000
CHQ146	30/01	Rent	GL95				1 500	1 500
				650	**2 000**	**9 000**	**1 500**	**13 150**
				Dr GL: Inventory	Dr GL: Salaries	Dr GL: APControl	Dr Individual accounts	Cr GL: Bank

Diagram 9.8.1: Perpetual inventory system (cash payments journal)

In diagram 9.8.1 we have demonstrated how to record the cash payments in a suitable cash payments journal, assuming that Bright Life was using a perpetual inventory system.

Accounts payable subsidiary ledger

Individual supplier accounts

(The individual payments made to suppliers are posted to the subsidiary ledger accounts on a daily basis)

General ledger

Financial statement accounts

(The totals are posted at the end of the month to the general ledger as indicated below each column in the cash payments journal)

Games for Africa (APL)

Date	Details	Fol	R	Date	Details	Fol	R
15/01	142	CPJ7	1 000	01/01	242	PJ4	1 000
31/01	Bal	c/d	1 500	24/01	281	PJ4	1 500
			2 500				2 500
				01/02	Bal	b/d	1 500

Accounts payable control (GL90)

Date	Details	Fol	R	Date	Details	Fol	R
31/01	Bank	CPJ7	9 000	31/01	Purchases	PJ4	11 970
31/01	Bal	c/d	2 970				
			11 970				11 970
				01/02	Bal	b/d	2 970

Paper Limited (APL)

Date	Details	Fol	R	Date	Details	Fol	R
				02/01	128	PJ4	220
31/01	Bal	c/d	220				
			220				220
				01/02	Bal	b/d	220

Inventory (GL325)

Date	Details	Fol	R	Date	Details	Fol	R
31/01	Accounts payable	PJ4	3 700	31/01	Cost of sales	SJ2	2 500
31/01	Bank	CPJ7	650	31/01	Cost of sales	CRJ7	500
				31/01	Bal	c/d	1 350
			4 350				4 350
01/02	Bal	b/d	1 350				

Master's Music (APL)

Date	Details	Fol	R	Date	Details	Fol	R
				07/01	891	PJ4	1 200
31/01	Bal	c/d	1 200				
			1 200				1 200
				01/02	Bal	b/d	1 200

Salaries (GL55)

Date	Details	Fol	R	Date	Details	Fol	R
31/01	Bank	CPJ7	2 000				
				31/01	Bal	c/d	2 000
			2 000				2 000
01/02	Bal	b/d	2 000				

Computer World (APL)

Date	Details	Fol	R	Date	Details	Fol	R
27/01	144	CPJ7	8 000	14/01	315	PJ4	8 000
31/01	Bal	c/d	0				
			8 000				8 000
				01/02	Bal	b/d	0

Rent (GL95)

Date	Details	Fol	R	Date	Details	Fol	R
30/01	Bank	CPJ7	1 500				
				31/01	Bal	c/d	1 500
			1 500				1 500
01/02	Bal	b/d	1 500				

Mr Thirsty (APL)

Date	Details	Fol	R	Date	Details	Fol	R
				21/01	99	PJ4	50
31/01	Bal	c/d	50				
			50				50
				01/02	Bal	b/d	50

Bank (GL150)

Date	Details	Fol	R	Date	Details	Fol	R
31/01	Deposits	CRJ7	22 440	31/01	Payments	CPJ7	13 150
				31/01	Bal	c/d	9 290
			22 440				22 440
01/02	Bal	b/d	9 290				

Diagram 9.8.2: Perpetual inventory system (subsidiary ledger and general ledger postings)

In diagram 9.8.2 the individual payments to suppliers have been posted to the individual suppliers' accounts in the accounts payable subsidiary ledger. In addition, the month-end postings have been made to the general ledger accounts.

Periodic system

Cash payments journal — January 20X6 **CPJ7**

Doc	Date	Details	Fol	Purchases	Salaries	Accounts payable	Sundries	Bank
CHQ141	01/01	Purhases		200				200
CHQ142	15/01	Games for Africa	APL1			1 000		1 000
CHQ143	18/01	Purchases		450				450
CHQ144	27/01	Computer World	APL4			8 000		8 000
CHQ145	30/01	Salaries			2 000			2 000
CHQ146	30/01	Rent	GL95				1 500	1 500
				650	**2 000**	**9 000**	**1 500**	**13 150**
				Dr GL: Purchases	Dr GL: Salaries	Dr GL: APControl	Dr Individual accounts	Cr GL: Bank

Diagram 9.9.1: Periodic inventory system (cash payments journal)

In diagram 9.9.1 we have demonstrated how to record the cash payments in a suitable cash payments journal, assuming that Bright Life was using a periodic inventory system.

Accounts payable subsidiary ledger

Individual supplier accounts

(The individual payments made to suppliers are posted to the subsidiary ledger accounts on a daily basis)

Games for Africa (APL)

Date	Details	Fol	R	Date	Details	Fol	R
15/01	142	CPJ7	1 000	01/01	242	PJ4	1 000
31/01	Bal	c/d	1 500	24/01	281	PJ4	1 500
			2 500				2 500
				01/02	Bal	b/d	1 500

Paper Limited (APL)

Date	Details	Fol	R	Date	Details	Fol	R
				02/01	128	PJ4	220
31/01	Bal	c/d	220				
			220				220
				01/02	Bal	b/d	220

Master's Music (APL)

Date	Details	Fol	R	Date	Details	Fol	R
				07/01	891	PJ4	1 200
31/01	Bal	c/d	1 200				
			1 200				1 200
				01/02	Bal	b/d	1 200

General ledger

Financial statement accounts

(The totals are posted at the end of the month to the general ledger as indicated below each column in the cash payments journal)

Accounts payable control (GL90)

Date	Details	Fol	R	Date	Details	Fol	R
31/01	Bank	CPJ7	9 000	31/01	Purchases	PJ4	11 970
31/01	Bal	c/d	2 970				
			11 970				11 970
				01/02	Bal	b/d	2 970

Purchases (GL60)

Date	Details	Fol	R	Date	Details	Fol	R
31/01	Accounts payable	PJ4	3 700				
31/01	Bank	CPJ7	650	31/01	Bal	c/d	4 350
			4 350				4 350
01/02	Bal	b/d	4 350				

Salaries (GL55)

Date	Details	Fol	R	Date	Details	Fol	R
31/01	Bank	CPJ7	2 000				
				31/01	Bal	c/d	2 000
			2 000				2 000
01/02	Bal	b/d	2 000				

Computer World (APL)							
Date	Details	Fol	R	Date	Details	Fol	R
27/01	144	CPJ7	8 000	14/01	315	PJ4	8 000
31/01	Bal	c/d	0				
			8 000				8 000
				01/02	Bal	b/d	0

Rent (GL95)							
Date	Details	Fol	R	Date	Details	Fol	R
30/01	Bank	CPJ7	1 500				
				31/01	Bal	c/d	1 500
			1 500				1 500
01/02	Bal	b/d	1 500				

Mr Thirsty (APL)							
Date	Details	Fol	R	Date	Details	Fol	R
				21/01	99	PJ4	50
31/01	Bal	c/d	50				
			50				50
				01/02	Bal	b/d	50

Bank (GL150)							
Date	Details	Fol	R	Date	Details	Fol	R
31/01	Deposits	CRJ7	22 440	31/01	Payments	CPJ7	13 150
				31/01	Bal	c/d	9 209
			22 440				22 440
01/02	Bal	b/d	9 290				

Diagram 9.9.2: Periodic inventory system (subsidiary ledger and general ledger postings)

In diagram 9.9.2 the individual payments to suppliers have been posted to the individual suppliers' accounts in the accounts payable subsidiary ledger. In addition, the month-end postings have been made to the general ledger accounts.

Pause and reflect...

Look carefully at the cash payments journal (either the perpetual inventory system or the periodic inventory system). Explain why,

a) On 1 January, when inventory was purchased, there is no entry in the folio column?
b) On 15 January, when Bright Life paid Games for Africa, the folio column records an entry to the accounts payable ledger?
c) On 30 January, when the rent is paid, the folio column records an entry to the general ledger?

Response

a) When the inventory was purchased, the underlying accounting entry is a debit to inventory / purchases and a credit to bank. No subsidiary ledger is involved and the posting to the general ledger accounts takes place in total at the end of the period.
b) When Bright Life paid Games for Africa, both the accounts payable control account in the general ledger *as well as* the Games for Africa account in the accounts payable ledger need to be reduced or debited. The folio reference to APL 1 results in a posting to the debit of the Games for Africa account in the accounts payable ledger while the posting to the accounts payable account in the general ledger takes place in total at period end with the posting reference beneath the column total (Dr AP Control).
c) When the rent is paid, a folio reference to the rent account in the general ledger is needed as there is no separate column for rent in this cash payment journal. Rent is entered into the sundries column and thus the posting to the debit of the rent account in the general ledger is done on a transaction by transaction basis and not in total.

9.4 Procedures for using the secondary analysis journals

9.4.1 Sales returns journal

This is used to record goods returned from customers, or allowances granted in respect of items such as overcharges and trade discounts not deducted. A credit note is issued as evidence that the amount is authorised and to be recorded. The format of the sales return journal is very similar to the sales journal. However, when we post to the accounts receivable subsidiary ledger and the general ledger, the reverse entry is posted.

Procedure for using the sales returns journal:

- ❑ Enter each credit note (representing a reduction in the amount owing by a customer) as a line item.
- ❑ Post the amount of each credit note to the credit side of each individual customer's account in the accounts receivable subsidiary ledger.
- ❑ At the end of the month, post the total of these transactions to the general ledger.

	Perpetual inventory system	**Periodic inventory system**
General ledger	Dr Sales returns Cr Accounts receivable control ***and*** Dr Inventory Cr Cost of sales	Dr Sales returns Cr Accounts receivable control
Accounts receivable subsidiary ledger	Cr Individual customers' accounts	Cr Individual customers' accounts

9.4.2 Purchases returns journal

This is used to record goods returned to suppliers or allowances granted in respect of items such as overcharges or trade discounts not granted. The supplier will issue a credit note as evidence of the reduction. The format of the purchases returns journal is the same as the purchases journal. However, when we post to the accounts payable subsidiary ledger and the general ledger, the reverse entry is posted.

Procedure for using the purchases returns journal:

- ❑ Enter each credit note received from a supplier as a separate line item.
- ❑ The total amount of the credit note will be entered in the control column. The reduction granted on the credit note must be analysed and allocated to the appropriate column.
- ❑ Post the total amount of each credit note to the debit side of each individual supplier's account in the accounts payable subsidiary ledger.

- At the end of the month, post totals, except for the sundry items, to the general ledger.

	Perpetual inventory system	Periodic inventory system
General ledger	Dr Accounts payable control Cr Inventory Cr Stationery Cr Other individual accounts in the general ledger with the items recorded in the sundry column	Dr Accounts payable control Cr Purchases returns Cr Stationery Cr Other individual accounts in the general ledger with the items recorded in the sundy column
Accounts payable subsidiary ledger	Dr Individual suppliers' accounts	Dr Individual suppliers' accounts

9.4.3 Petty cash journal

This is used to record all payments made in cash. The payments are usually of a small amount. A petty cash voucher is made out and is attached to the receipt from the supplier, as evidence of the amount paid. The format is the same as the cash payments journal, except that the bank column is changed to petty cash.

Procedure for using the petty cash journal:

- Same as for cash payments journal, except record from the petty cash voucher.

	Perpetual inventory system	Periodic inventory system
General ledger	Dr Inventory Dr Stationery Dr Wages Dr Other individual accounts in the general ledger with the items recorded in the sundry column Cr Discount received Cr Petty cash	Dr Purchases Dr Stationery Dr Wages Dr Other individual accounts in the general ledger with the items recorded in the sundry column Cr Discount received Cr Petty cash

9.5 Computerised accounting systems

In today's business world, the traditional accounting systems have been replaced by computerised accounting systems.

The computer has been introduced as a tool to assist management to fulfil their responsibilities. The computer performs all the tedious tasks of posting the journal to the general ledger and subsidiary ledgers. The posting process is mechanical and is a task which the computer is capable of doing much faster than any human being. However, the principles of basic bookkeeping have not changed as a result of the introduction of the computer.

Computer accounting packages group similar transactions together for input into the system. A typical computerised accounting system will have a section for entering credit sales, credit purchases, cash receipts, cash payments, petty cash payments and other transactions. Therefore, it is structured in a similar way to the traditional manual system which uses analysis journals.

9.6 Exam examples

9.6.1

Bryan Bagel decided that his school accounting knowledge was sufficient to see him through the first block of Accounting 1 at university. He decided to take on a bookkeeping job instead of attending Accounting 1 lectures and tutorials. The trial balance he prepared did not balance, and you (who attended all your lectures) found the following errors:

- The total of the sales column in the sales journal, amounting to R10 250, was posted as R10 520 to the correct accounts in the general ledger. In addition, one transaction for R700 was not posted to the customer's account in the accounts receivable ledger.
- The total of the discount column in the cash payments journal, amounting to R370, was posted to the incorrect side of the discount account in the general ledger. All other postings from the cash payments journal were correct.
- The bank column in the cash payments journal was undercast by R120 and posted to the general ledger at the incorrect amount.

In the trial balance prepared by Bryan Bagel:

(a) total credits exceeded total debits by R250
(b) total credits exceeded total debits by R700
(c) total credits exceeded total debits by R620
(d) **total debits exceeded total credits by R860**
(e) total debits exceeded total credits by R490

9.6.2

Mr P Andy operates a business enterprise trading as Andrew of York. He uses analysis journals to record the transactions of the business. No discounts are offered on credit sales.

The following transactions were made during March 20X5:

March 3	Sold goods on credit to K Stark for R600.
March 12	Sold goods for cash to Ms Beatrice for R250.
March 25	Received in cash the full amount owed by K Stark.
March 30	Sold goods on credit to Ms Eugenie for R375.

In posting the transactions from the special journals to the ledger accounts:

(a) nothing would be posted to the accounts receivable subsidiary ledger account of K Stark because payment in full was received in the same month as the sale
(b) an amount of R250 would be posted to the accounts receivable subsidiary ledger account of Ms Beatrice
(c) **an amount of R975 would be posted from the sales journal to the credit of the sales account in the general ledger**
(d) an amount of R600 would be posted from the cash receipts journal to the credit of the sales account in the general ledger

(e) an amount of R1 225 would be posted from the sales journal to the debit of the accounts receivable control account in the general ledger.

Summary of concepts and applications

1. The analysis journals reduce the time and effort involved in recording transactions and the subsequent postings to the general ledger. These accounting systems accelerate the processing of data phase in the accounting process. Primary analysis journals and secondary analysis journals are used to record the effects of specific transaction groups. The common elements of these repetitive transactions are debited or credited to the general ledger through cumulative postings that take place at the end of the period. The general journal is retained for recording all other transactions that do not fall into a typical group.
2. Accounts receivable and accounts payable subsidiary ledgers are created to provide data relating to each customer and supplier. The accounts receivable and the accounts payable control accounts in the general ledger account are an aggregation of the entries in the subsidiary ledgers.
3. Credit sales are recorded in the **sales journal**. Credit purchases are recorded in the **purchases journal**. Cash sales and cash purchases are not recorded in the sales or purchases journals. Cash receipts from customers as well as cash sales are recorded in the **cash payments journal**. Cash payments to suppliers as well as cash purchases are recorded in the **cash payments journal**.
4. Goods returned from customers or allowances granted in respect of items such as overcharges and trade discounts not deducted are recorded in the **sales returns journal**. Goods returned to suppliers or allowances granted in respect of items such as overcharges or trade discounts not granted are recorded in the **purchases returns journal**. All payments made in cash are recorded in the **petty cash journal**.
5. Traditional accounting systems have been replaced by computerised accounting systems. Although these systems are able to perform the posting process, the underlying principles of basic bookkeeping have not changed.

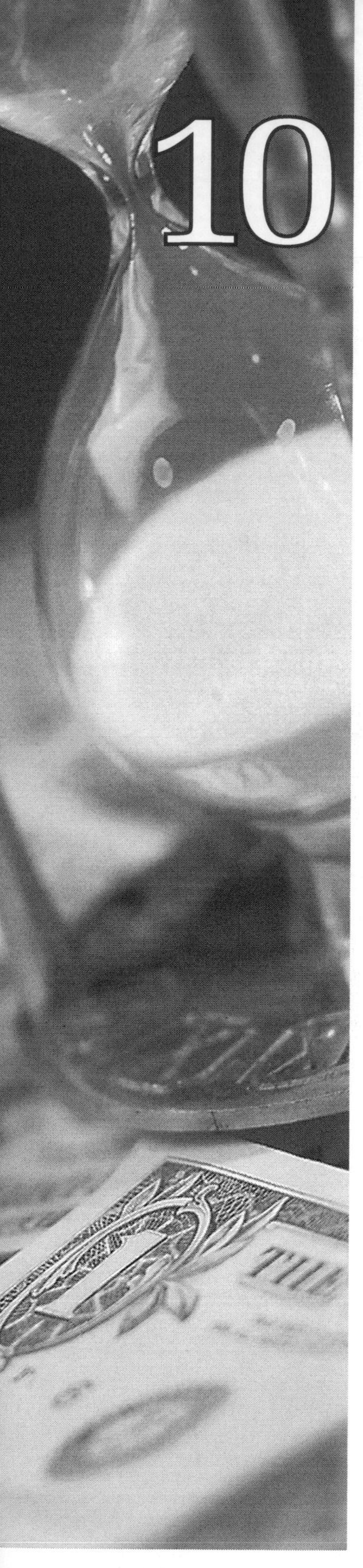

10 Value-Added Tax

'But in this world nothing can be said to be certain, except death and taxes.'
(Benjamin Franklin, 1789)

Outcomes

- Explain the working of the of value-added tax (VAT) system.
- Compute input VAT and output VAT.
- Record VAT in the analysis journals.
- Calculate VAT payable to, or due from, SARS.

Chapter outline

10.1 Introduction to value-added tax
10.2 How the value-added tax system works
10.2.1 Input VAT and output VAT
10.2.2 Input VAT which may not be claimed as an input credit
10.3 Example: Accounting for value-added tax
10.4 Preparation of the value-added tax return
10.5 Exam example

Exxaro Resources Limited
Notes to the financial statements for the year ended 31 December 2007

	(R Millions)
Revenue	
Sale of goods	10 197
Services rendered	636
	10 793

Policy

Revenue, which excludes value added tax, represents the gross value of goods invoiced. Export revenues are recorded according to the relevant sales terms, when the risks and rewards of ownership are transferred.

Revenue from the sale of goods is recognised when significant risks and rewards of ownership of the goods are transferred to the buyer.

Revenue arising from services and royalties is recognised on the accrual basis in accordance with the substance of the relevant agreements.

The coal and minerals producer has R10 billion worth of sales and for each rand of those sales value-added tax (VAT) must be collected and handed over to the South African Revenue Service.

10.1 Introduction to value-added tax

Value-added tax, which is usually referred to as VAT, is a transaction tax which was introduced in South Africa in 1991. A transaction tax is a tax which is levied on certain transactions. The rate at which VAT is levied changes from time to time, with the standard rate currently being 14%.

When a business entity, which is a registered vendor, sells goods or provides services which attract VAT (referred to as a taxable supply), the selling price (or consideration) must include VAT. If a registered vendor sells goods with a list price of R570, the VAT portion of the consideration is calculated as follows, using a VAT rate of 14%:

	R
Consideration	570
VAT (14/114 x R570)	70
Selling price excluding VAT	500

The selling price excluding VAT is therefore R500, the VAT component is R70 and the list price or consideration is R570.

Registration as a vendor for VAT purposes is compulsory if the total value of taxable supplies made by a business entity exceeds R1 000 000 for a twelve-month period. If the value of taxable supplies made is less than R1 000 000, registration is voluntary.

The VAT which the registered vendor *collects* from the transactions entered into with customers must be paid over to the South African Revenue Service at the end of the VAT period when the VAT return is submitted. The amount due to be paid to the South African Revenue Service in respect of VAT *collected* is reduced by the amount of the VAT which has been *paid to suppliers* (except for the VAT paid on certain items which may not be claimed as an input credit, as described in 10.2.2 below). To enable the registered vendor to prepare the VAT return, the VAT collected from customers and the VAT paid to suppliers must be correctly accounted for.

In this chapter, we shall examine the main principles of the VAT system in South Africa. We shall use the example of Simon Smart's business, Sharp Moves, to illustrate these principles. You will remember from Chapter 8 that Sharp Moves sold accessories such as printers, modems and USB storage devices. We shall then examine the accounting treatment for VAT.

10.2 How the value-added tax system works

10.2.1 Input VAT and output VAT

When goods or services which are taxable supplies, as defined in the Value-Added Tax Act of 1991, are acquired from a registered vendor, the consideration payable will include VAT. The VAT which is paid to a supplier is **input VAT** or **input tax** in the hands of the acquirer of the goods or service.

Assume that Sharp Moves purchases inventory from a supplier that is a registered vendor, for an amount of R684. The consideration paid for the inventory, R684, will include VAT, which is calculated as follows:

	R
Consideration paid for inventory purchased	684
VAT (14/114 x R684)	84
Purchase price excluding VAT	600

When Sharp Moves prepares its VAT return at the end of the VAT period, it may claim the input VAT of R84 as a deduction, (referred to as an ***input credit***) when calculating the net amount of VAT due to, or from the South African Revenue Service.

When a registered vendor sells goods or services which are taxable supplies, as defined in the Value-Added Tax Act of 1991, the consideration charged to the customer will include VAT. The VAT collected from a customer is called **output VAT** or **output tax** in the hands of the supplier of the goods or service.

Therefore, assuming Sharp Moves sells goods to its customers for R51,30, the consideration of R51,30 includes output VAT, which is calculated as follows:

	R
Consideration received for accessories sold	51,30
Output VAT (14/114 x R51,30)	6,30
Selling price excluding VAT	45,00

When Sharp Moves prepares its VAT return at the end of the VAT period, it must reflect the output VAT of R6,30 as an amount due to the South African Revenue Service.

It is important to note that not all supplies of goods and services are taxable supplies which attract VAT at the ***standard rate*** of 14%.

Certain supplies are ***zero-rated*** and attract VAT at a rate of 0%. Examples of zero-rated supplies are exports and the supply of certain foodstuffs. A registered vendor who makes zero-rated supplies may still deduct the input VAT paid, when preparing the VAT return.

Certain other supplies are ***exempt*** supplies and attract no VAT. Examples include long-term residential rentals, the supply of childcare services by a crèche and the supply of tuition and boarding fees by a school or university. A vendor who makes exempt supplies may not deduct the input VAT paid on goods or services used in making the exempt supply, when preparing the VAT return.

 **Pause and reflect...**

What is the implication to the entity of supplying goods and services which are zero-rated as opposed to exempt?

Response

VAT will not be collected on both zero-rated supplies and exempt supplies. However, input VAT paid may be deducted on zero-rated supplies but input VAT paid may not be deducted on exempt supplies.

10.2.2 Input VAT which may not be claimed as an input credit

No input credit may be claimed for the input VAT paid on the following:

- entertainment
- club subscriptions
- motor cars (defined as vehicles used on public roads, having three or more wheels and constructed wholly or mainly for the carriage of passengers).

The VAT paid on any of these items is therefore not recoverable and should be included in the cost of the item. This aspect will be covered in detail in Chapter 11, Property, Plant and Equipment. As the VAT is not recoverable, it should not be shown as input VAT.

A business entity that is not a registered vendor for VAT purposes does not submit VAT returns and may therefore not claim any input credits for input VAT paid on the acquisition of goods or services. VAT paid by such a business is therefore part of the cost of the acquisition of the goods or services.

10.3 Example: Accounting for value-added tax

As we have seen, a business entity that is a registered vendor must be able to identify its input and output VAT in order to prepare the VAT return at the end of each VAT period. VAT is therefore normally shown separately in the books of original entry.

If no input credit may be claimed for the VAT paid for a supply of goods or services, the VAT must not be shown separately, but must be included as part of the cost of the expense or asset.

The following is a summary of the transactions in the sales journal, purchases journal and cash journals of Sharp Moves for March 20X6. A perpetual inventory system is used.

Sharp Moves Sales journal – March 20X6 **PJ6**

Doc	Date	Customer	Fol	Total	Sales	Output VAT	Cost of Sales
123	01/03/X6	Sandton Car Rentals		14 250	12 500	1 750	6 250
124	12/03/X6	City Motors		7 125	6 250	875	3 125
125	28/03/X6	Accessory Connection		7 125	6 250	875	3 125
				28 500	25 000	3 500	12 500

Sharp Moves Purchases journal – March 20X6 **PJ6**

Doc	Date	Customer	Fol	Accounts payable	Inventory	VAT	Sundry		
							Detail	Fol	Amount
427	02/03	Deckers Limted		17 100	15 000	2 100			
510	15/03	Print Wholesalers		6 840	6 000	840			
9874	25/03	Key Technologies		10 260	9 000	1 260			
				34 200	30 000	4 200			

Sharp Moves Cash payments journal – March 20X6 **CPJ7**

Doc	Date	Details	Fol	Rent	Enter-tainment	Sundries	VAT	Bank
CHQ111	01/03	G Props		1 500			210	1 710
CHQ112	15/03	Steers			70			70
CHQ113	28/03	S Smart				3 000		3 000
				1 500	70	3 000	210	4 780

Sharp Moves Cash receipts journal – March 20X6 **CRJ5**

Doc	Date	Details	Fol	Sales	VAT	Accounts receivable	Cost of Sales	Analysis	Bank
254	02/03	Cash Sale		4 000	560		2 000	4 560	4 560
255	08/03	Cash Sale		12 000	1 680		6 000	13 680	13 680
256	20/03	Cash Sale		800	112		400	912	912
257	27/03	Cash Sale		3 200	448		1 600	3 648	3 648
				20 000	2 800		10 000		22 800

You are required to:

show the postings that arise from the journals and show the VAT accounts in the general ledger.

Solution: Accounting for value-added tax

The following postings will arise from the information in the journals for the month of March 20X6:

Sales journal	Dr	Cr
Accounts receivable	28 500	
Sales		25 000
Output VAT control		3 500
and		
Cost of sales	12 500	
Inventory		12 500

Purchases journal	Dr	Cr
Inventory	30 000	
Input VAT control	4 200	
Accounts payable		34 200

Cash payments journal	Dr	Cr
Rent	1 500	
Entertainment	70	
Drawings	3 000	
Input VAT control	210	
Bank		4 780

Cash receipts journal	Dr	Cr
Cash	22 800	
Sales		20 000
Output VAT control		2 800
and		
Cost of sales	10 000	
Inventory		10 000

At the end of *each month*, the totals of the output VAT columns in the books of original entry are posted to the output VAT control account in the general ledger and the totals of the input VAT control account are posted to the input VAT control account in the general ledger.

At the end of *each VAT period*, the output VAT and input VAT control accounts are closed off by the transfer of their balances to the VAT recoverable or payable account. The balance on the VAT recoverable or payable account reflects the amount recoverable from, or payable to, the South African Revenue Service.

At the end of the VAT period, 1 March 20X6 to 31 March 20X6, Sharp Moves's VAT control accounts will reflect the following:

Dr — INPUT VAT CONTROL ACCOUNT (GL7) — Cr

Date	Details	Fol	R	Date	Details	Fol	R
20X6							
31/03	Accounts payable	PJ 9	4 200				
31/03	Bank	CPJ 7	210				
			4 410				

Dr — OUTPUT VAT CONTROL ACCOUNT (GL8) — Cr

Date	Details	Fol	R	Date	Details	Fol	R
				20X6			
				31/03	Accounts receivable	SJ 6	3 500
				31/03	Bank	CRJ 5	2 800
							6 300

The balance on the output VAT control account is a liability as it is an amount owing to the South African Revenue Service. The balance on the input VAT control account is an asset as it is an amount owing by the South African Revenue Service.

To transfer the balances on the output VAT and input VAT control accounts to the VAT recoverable or payable account, the following journal entry will be processed:

GENERAL JOURNAL OF SHARP MOVES

Date	Description	Fol	Dr	Cr
31/03/X6	Output VAT control	GL 8	6 300	
	Input VAT control	GL 7		4 410
	VAT recoverable/payable account	GL 9		1 890
	Transfer of end of period balances			

The cheque made out in favour of the South African Revenue Service in settlement of the amount owing of R1 890 will be posted to the VAT recoverable or payable account, which will then reflect a nil balance.

Dr — VAT RECOVERABLE OR PAYABLE ACCOUNT (GL9) — Cr

Date	Details	Fol	R	Date	Details	Fol	R
20X6				20X6			
10/04	Bank	CPJ	1 890	31/03	VAT payable	GJ	1 890
			1 890				1 890

10.4 Preparation of the value-added tax return

Every vendor who is registered for VAT must submit a VAT return to the South African Revenue Service at the end of the tax period. Depending on the level of annual taxable supplies made by the vendor, the tax period may be either a one- or two-month period.

On the VAT return, the registered vendor will offset the input tax paid to suppliers against the output tax collected from customers. If the output tax exceeds the input tax, the net amount must be paid to the South African Revenue Service by the 25th day of the month following the end of the VAT period.

As Sharp Moves has collected R6 300 of output VAT and has paid R4 410 input VAT during the tax period, the payment it must make to the South African Revenue Service is calculated as follows:

	R
Output VAT	6 300
Input VAT	4 410
Amount payable to South African Revenue Service	1 890

If the input tax exceeds the output tax for a particular tax period, the South African Revenue Service will make a refund of the net amount to the registered vendor.

Assume that Sharp Moves collected only R3 000 output VAT during the tax period in the previous example. The refund due from the South African Revenue Service is calculated as follows:

	R
Output VAT	3 000
Input VAT	4 410
Refund due from South African Revenue Service	1 410

It is important to realise that any input tax which can be claimed as an input credit is not a cost to the registered vendor as it is recovered from the South African Revenue Service.

10.5 Exam example

Andrew's Batting Academy is a registered vendor for VAT purposes and buys and sells bats, protective pads and cricket clothing. The total of the accounts payable column in the purchases journal amounted to R2 280, and the total of the accounts receivable column in the sales journal amounted to R6 840. The rate of VAT is 14%. The amount of VAT payable to, or recoverable from, the South African Revenue Service is:

(a) R638,40 payable
(b) R560,00 recoverable
(c) R0
(d) R638,40 recoverable
(e) **R560,00 payable**

Summary of concepts and applications

1. VAT is a transaction tax that is levied on certain transactions at a standard rate (currently 14%). Registration as a VAT vendor is compulsory if the total value of taxable supplies made by a business entity exceeds R1 000 000 for a 12-month period. Selling prices charged by registered vendors must include VAT.

2. The VAT paid to a supplier of goods or services is input VAT in the hands of the purchaser and may be claimed as a deduction by the purchaser when calculating the net amount of VAT due to or from the South African Revenue Service. The VAT collected from a customer in respect of goods sold or services rendered is output VAT in the hands of the seller and is payable by the seller to the South African Revenue Service. In addition, certain supplies are zero-rated and attract VAT at a rate of 0% (vendors making such supplies may deduct input VAT paid), while other supplies are exempt and attract no VAT (vendors making such supplies may not deduct the input VAT paid).

3. The chapter uses information from the sales, purchases, cash receipts and cash payments journals of Sharp Moves to demonstrate the VAT accounting implications of the transactions.

4. All VAT vendors must submit a VAT return to the South African Revenue Service at the end of the tax period. On the VAT return, the input VAT paid to suppliers will be offset against the output VAT collected from customers. The net amount will result in either a payment to or a refund from the South African Revenue Service.

Part 4

Recognition and Measurement of the Elements of the Financial Statements

11 Property, Plant and Equipment

'The question of depreciation is one upon which so many articles have been written, and so many opinions expressed, that there would not appear to be much more which could profitably be said on the subject.'
(Armstrong, 1903)

Outcomes

- Explain the recognition criteria for property, plant and equipment.
- Measure property, plant and equipment at recognition.
- Calculate depreciation.
- Record the reassessment of the useful life and residual value of property, plant and equipment.
- Record the disposal of property, plant and equipment.
- Measure property, plant and equipment after recognition and process the accounting entries for a revaluation and an impairment.

Chapter outline

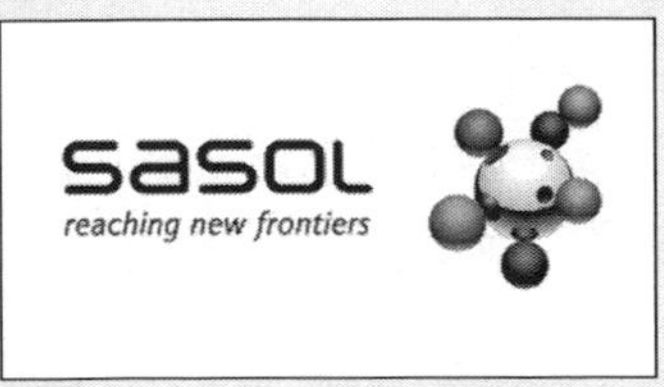

Sasol Limited
Notes to the financial statements for the year ended 30 June 2007

	(R Millions)
Property, Plant and Equipment	
Land	716
Buildings	4 571
Petrol stations and convenience stores	944
Plant, equipment and vehicles	83 263
Mineral assets	9 665
Closing balance	99 159

Sasol has transformed itself into a truly global petro-chemical company, operating in 20 countries and exporting to over 100 countries. As a result of this global expansion, Sasol has accumulated almost R100 billion in Property, Plant and Equipment.

11.1 Recognition of property, plant and equipment

An asset is defined in the accounting framework as a resource controlled by the enterprise as a result of past events and from which future economic benefits are expected to flow to the enterprise.[1]

Property, plant and equipment often represent a major portion of the total assets of an enterprise and therefore are significant in the presentation of an enterprise's financial position. In addition, the determination of whether an expenditure represents an asset or an expense can have a significant effect on an enterprise's financial position and results of operations.

The applicable accounting standard is IAS 16, entitled 'Property, Plant and Equipment'.

IAS 16 defines property, plant and equipment as tangible assets that:

- are held by an enterprise for use in the production or supply of goods or services, for rental to others, or for administration purposes, and
- are expected to be used during more than one period.[2]

IAS 16 requires that an item of property, plant and equipment should be recognised as an asset if, and only if:

- it is probable that **future economic benefits** associated with the item will flow to the entity, and
- the cost of the item can be **measured** reliably.[3]

In determining whether or not an item satisfies the criteria for recognition as an asset, an enterprise needs to assess whether it controls the risks and rewards associated with the item, and the degree of certainty attaching to the flow of **future economic benefits**. The two are related, as existence of sufficient certainty that the future economic benefits will flow to the enterprise necessitates an assurance that the enterprise will receive the rewards attaching to the asset and will undertake the associated risks. This assurance is usually only available when the risks and rewards have passed to the enterprise.

The reliable **measurement** of the cost is usually satisfied because of the exchange transaction relating to the purchase of the asset.

Under this recognition principle, an entity is required to evaluate all costs associated with property, plant and equipment at the time they are incurred. These costs include costs incurred ***initially*** to acquire an item of property, plant and equipment and costs incurred ***subsequently*** to add to it, replace part of it or service it.[4] In other words, when costs are incurred in relation to property, plant and equipment, management is required to apply the recognition principle in order to decide whether the costs incurred should be recognised as an asset or an expense. If the recognition principle of IAS 16 is met (probable that future benefits associated with the item will flow to the entity and the cost of the item can be measured reliably), the costs incurred are recognised as an asset.

Parts of some items of property, plant and equipment may require replacement at regular intervals, such as the replacement of the lining of a furnace or the replacement of the seats and galley of an aircraft. These costs are recognised as an asset if the recognition principles are met.

Costs of day-to-day servicing are recognised as an expense as incurred. These costs are primarily the costs of labour, consumables and small parts and are often referred to as 'repairs and maintenance' on the income statement.

Pause and reflect...

Smart Concepts purchased a delivery vehicle on 1 June 20X5. The vehicle cost R220 000. On 1 July 20X5, a satellite navigation system was installed at a cost of R12 000. The vehicle was serviced late in December 20X5 at a cost of R1 200. Which costs are to be recognised as an asset and which costs are to be recognised as an expense?

Response

The cost of R220 000 incurred initially to acquire the motor vehicle is recognised as an asset as it meets the recognition criteria for an asset. It is probable that future economic benefits will flow to the entity (the vehicle is used to deliver goods to customers) and the cost can be measured reliably (the amount of R220 000 is known). The cost of R12 000 incurred subsequently to install the satellite navigation system is also recognised as an asset. Future economic benefits will flow to the entity (the ability of the business entity to deliver the goods to its customers is enhanced) and the cost can be measured reliably (the amount of R12 000 is known). The cost of R1 200 incurred for the servicing of the vehicle is recognised as an expense when incurred.

11.2 Measurement at recognition

IAS 16 states that an item of property, plant and equipment that qualifies for recognition as an asset should be measured at its cost.[5]

11.2.1 Elements of cost

The ***cost*** of an item of property, plant and equipment comprises its purchase price, including import duties and non-refundable purchase taxes, and any costs directly attributable to bringing the asset to the location and condition necessary for it to be *capable of operating in the manner intended by management*.

Any trade discounts are deducted in arriving at the purchase price.[6] Examples of directly attributable costs include the cost of site preparation, delivery and handling costs, installation and assembly costs, net costs of testing whether the asset is functioning properly and professional fees such as those of architects and engineers.[7]

Only non-refundable purchase taxes are included in the cost of property, plant and equipment. If the enterprise is a registered vendor for VAT, the input VAT will be recovered and will therefore not form part of the cost. However, if the enterprise is not a registered VAT vendor the VAT paid would not be recoverable and would form part of the cost of the asset.

The elements of the cost of an item of property, plant and equipment are shown diagramatically below.

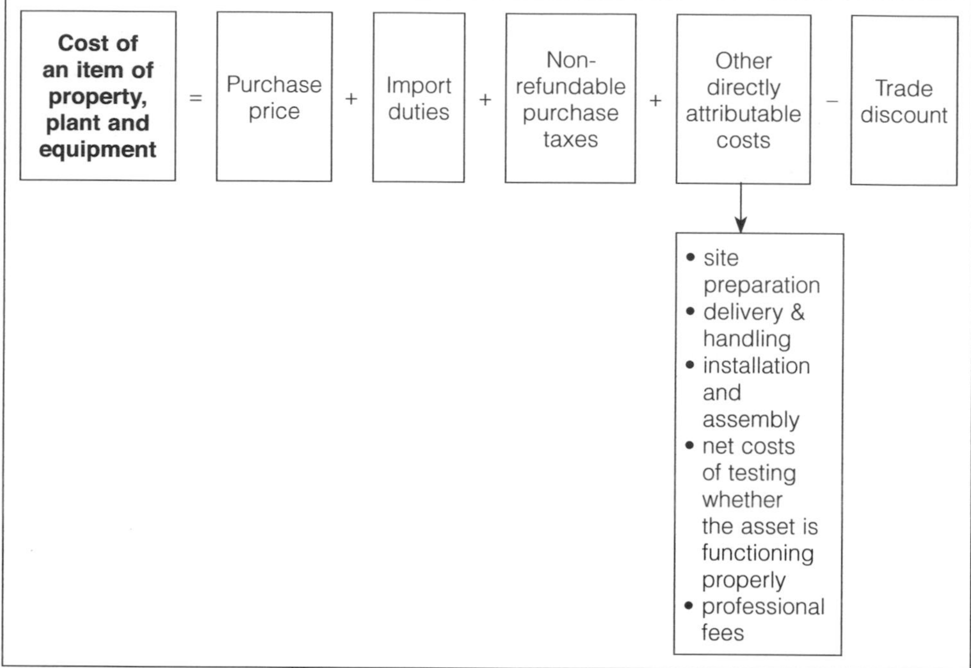

Diagram 11.1: Elements of cost of an item of property, plant and equipment

Recognition of costs in the carrying amount of an item of property, plant and equipment ceases when the item is in the location and condition necessary for it to be capable of operating in the manner intended by management.[8] Thus, costs incurred for an item of property, plant and equipment, while it is capable of operating in the manner intended by management but not yet brought into use, are not included in the carrying amount of the item. These costs are expensed in the statement of comprehensive income. Similarly, initial operating losses are also expensed in the statement of comprehensive income.

Example 1: Elements of cost

Smart Concepts purchased equipment for the repair of computers at an invoice price of R45 600 (inclusive of VAT at 14%). Transport costs of R1 254 (inclusive of VAT at 14%) were paid. Installation fees amounted to R1 000 (exclusive of VAT as the consultants are not registered for VAT purposes).

You are required to:

compute the cost of the equipment

(a) if Smart Concepts is a registered vendor for VAT purposes

(b) if Smart Concepts is not a registered vendor for VAT purposes.

Solution 1: Elements of cost

(a) If Smart Concepts is a registered vendor for VAT purposes

		R
Invoice price	(45 600 x 100/114)	40 000
Transport costs	(1 254 x 100/114)	1 100
Installation fees		1 000
		42 100

(b) If Smart Concepts is not a registered vendor for VAT purposes

	R
Invoice price	45 600
Transport costs	1 254
Installation fees	1 000
	47 854

Example 2: Elements of cost

Computer World purchased a new item of equipment for the assembly of computer screens on 1 July 20X5. The equipment cost an amount of R729 600 (inclusive of VAT at 14%). The cost of testing the plant amounted to R72 500. Five screens that were produced during the testing phase were sold to schools for R5 000 each. Commission of R2 500 was paid to the sales agent. The testing phase was complete by 31 July 20X5 and the equipment was in a condition capable of operating in the manner intended by management on that date. The equipment operated at less than full capacity during August 20X5 and further modifications were made at a cost of R4 000. Initial operating losses during August and September 20X5 amounted to R14 000. Computer World is a registered vendor for VAT purposes.

You are required to:

identify the elements of the cost of the equipment.

Solution 2: Elements of cost

		R
Cost/invoice price	(729 600 X 100/114)	640 000
Costs of testing		72 500
Net proceeds from sale of test products	(25 000 – 2 500)	(22 500)
Further modifications		–
Initial operating losses		–
		690 000

The invoice price is recorded net of VAT, as Computer World is a registered vendor for VAT purposes. The cost of testing whether an asset is functioning properly is a *directly attributable* cost required to be included in the cost of the item of equipment. The net proceeds from selling any items produced while bringing the asset to the location and condition necessary for it to be capable of operating in the manner intended by management are deducted from the costs of testing the asset. Thus the cost of testing the equipment of R72 500 is included in the cost, reduced by the net proceeds from the sale of the test products of R22 500. The cost of the further modifications and the initial operating losses were incurred after the equipment was in a condition capable of operating in the manner intended by management. Therefore, the cost of the further modifications of R4 000 and the initial operating losses of R14 000 are recognised as expenses when incurred and are not included in the carrying amount of the equipment.

You have seen that the point at which an item of property, plant and equipment is in the *location and condition necessary for it to be capable of operating in the manner intended by management* is important for determining when costs are to be included in the carrying amount of the asset or expensed in the income statement.

11.2.2 Measurement of cost

The cost of an item of property, plant and equipment is the ***cash price equivalent*** at the recognition date.

If payment is deferred beyond normal credit terms, the difference between the cash price equivalent and the total payments is recognised as interest expense over the period of credit.[9]

Interest expense	=	Total payments	–	Cash price equivalent of an item of property, plant and equipment

Diagram 11.2: Finance costs for an item of property, plant and equipment

Example: Measurement of cost

Smart Concepts purchased a photocopy machine for the office at an invoice price of R112 000 on 1 April 20X5. Delivery and installation costs of R8 000 were paid to the supplier. Smart Concepts is to finance the photocopy machine by raising a loan of R120 000 from Investors Bank at 15% interest per annum. The loan is to be repaid in 12 monthly instalments of R10 831, starting at the end of April 20X5. The entity has a 31 December year end.

You are required to:

(a) Show the relevant journal entries for the month of April 20X5.
(b) Show the relevant journal entries for the month of December 20X5.
(c) Show extracts from the income statement for the period ended 31 December 20X5 and from the statement of financial position at that date, relating to the borrowing.

Solution: Measurement of cost

The *total payments* over the credit term amount to R129 972 (R10 831 x 12). The *cost* of the asset to be recorded at recognition date is its *cash price equivalent* of R120 000, which includes the invoice price of R112 000, as well as the delivery and installation costs of R8 000. The total finance cost to be recorded as *interest expense* is R9 972, calculated as total payments of R129 972 less the cash price equivalent of R120 000.

It is necessary to complete an amortisation table in order to calculate the amount of interest expense to recognise each period, as well as the amount by which the liability is to be reduced. It is important to understand that the balance of the liability at each date represents the present value of future cash flows relating to the loan. In other words, the balance of R110 669 at the end of April 20X5 is the present value of the eleven payments of R10 831 from the end of May 20X5 to the end of March 20X6, discounted at the rate of 1,25% per month (15%/12).

The amortisation table appears below.

	Balance at beginning of period	Payment	Interest expense	Reduction in liability	Balance at end of period
20X5					
April	120 000	10 831	1 500	9 331	110 669
May	110 669	10 831	1 383	9 448	101 221
June	101 221	10 831	1 265	9 566	91 656
July	91 656	10 831	1 146	9 685	81 970
August	81 970	10 831	1 025	9 806	72 164
September	72 164	10 831	902	9 929	62 235
October	62 235	10 831	778	10 053	52 182
November	52 182	10 831	652	10 179	42 003
December	42 003	10 831	525	10 306	31 697
			9 176		
20X6					
January	31 697	10 831	396	10 435	21 262
February	21 262	10 831	266	10 565	10 697
March	10 697	10 831	134	10 697	0
		129 972	9 972	120 000	

You will notice that each instalment of R10 831 represents partly the interest expense for the period and partly a reduction in the liability. Looking at the month of April, the balance at the beginning of the month (the date that the loan was raised) was R120 000. At the end of April, the first payment of R10 831 is made. The payment of R10 831 comprises the interest expense for the month of R1 500 (R120 000 x 15% x 1/12) and the reduction in the liability of R9 331 (R10 831 – R1 500). The balance at the end of April/beginning of May is then R110 669 (R120 000 – R9 331). The same procedure is then followed for May where the payment at the end of the month of R10 831 results in an interest expense of R1 383 (R110 669 x 15% x 1/12) and a reduction in the liability of R9 448 (R10 831 – R1 383), resulting in a balance at the end of the month of R101 221 (R110 669 – R9 448).

You will also notice that, as the balance in the liability decreases, the amount of the interest expense also decreases.

(a) Journal entries for April 20X5

GENERAL JOURNAL OF SMART CONCEPTS			
Date	**Description**	**Dr**	**Cr**
01/04/X5	Bank Borrowings *Loan raised to purchase photocopy machine*	120 000	 120 000
01/04/X5	Photocopy machine Bank *Recognition of cost of asset*	120 000	 120 000
30/04/X5	Interest expense Borrowings Bank *Payment of instalment for April 20X5 and allocation of payment between interest and liability*	1 500 9 331	 10 831

(b) Journal entries for December 20X5

GENERAL JOURNAL OF SMART CONCEPTS			
Date	**Description**	**Dr**	**Cr**
31/12/X5	Interest expense Borrowings Bank *Payment of instalment for December 20X5 and allocation of payment between interest and liability*	525 10 306	 10 831

(c) Income statement and statement of financial position extracts

SMART CONCEPTS
INCOME STATEMENT FOR THE PERIOD ENDED 31 DECEMBER 20X5

	R
Finance costs	
Interest expense	9 176

SMART CONCEPTS
STATEMENT OF FINANCIAL POSITION AT 31 DECEMBER 20X5

	R
Current liabilities	
Short-term borrowings	31 697

The interest expense of R9 176 comprises the total of the finance costs for the months of April to December of 20X5.

You will recall from Chapter 6 that a liability is classified as current when the amount is due to be settled within twelve months of statement of financial position date. In this example, the balance at 31 December 20X5 of R31 697 will be settled by the end of March 20X6 and is thus shown as a current liability. The following calculation proves that the balance of R31 697 is the present value of the future cash flows:

Date of cash flow	Amount of cash flow	PV at (15%/12)
	R	R
31/01/X6	10 831	10 697
28/02/X6	10 831	10 565
31/03/X6	10 831	10 435
		31 697

11.3 Depreciation expense

The use of an item of property, plant and equipment represents a consumption of the benefits inherent in the asset. This expense is known as depreciation. The accounting terminology relating to the acquisition and use of items of property, plant and equipment has specific meanings which need to be understood before we can continue with our discussion of depreciation.

These terms are defined in IAS 16 as follows.[10]:

- ***Depreciation*** is the systematic allocation of the depreciable amount of an asset over its useful life.
- ***Depreciable amount*** is the cost of an asset, less its residual value.
- ***Useful life*** is either
  - the period of time an asset is expected to be available for use by the entity, or
  - the number of production or similar units expected to be obtained from the asset by the entity.
- ***Residual value*** is the estimated amount that the entity would currently obtain from the disposal of the asset (net of costs of disposal) if the asset were already of the age and in the condition expected at the end of its useful life.
- ***Carrying amount*** is the amount at which the asset is recognised after deducting any accumulated depreciation.

Let us consider the photocopy machine purchased by Smart Concepts on 1 April 20X5. Delivery and installation took place during April 20X5 and the machine was available for use from 1 May 20X5. Use of the new machine only began on 1 June 20X5, as Smart Concepts had rented another photocopy machine until the end of May 20X5. The amount initially recognised as the ***cost*** of the machine is R120 000. For the moment, let us assume that the ***estimated useful life*** is four years, which is the period of time that the machine is expected to be available for use. It has a ***residual value*** of R15 000, which is the estimated amount that the entity would obtain on 1 April 20X5 if the machine were already four years old.

11.3.1 Depreciable amount, depreciation period, useful life and carrying amount

Depreciable amount

IAS 16 requires the depreciable amount of an asset to be allocated on a systematic basis over its useful life.[11]

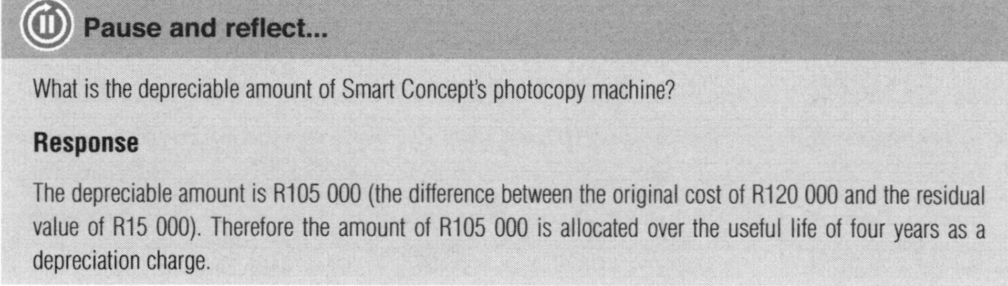

Pause and reflect...

What is the depreciable amount of Smart Concept's photocopy machine?

Response

The depreciable amount is R105 000 (the difference between the original cost of R120 000 and the residual value of R15 000). Therefore the amount of R105 000 is allocated over the useful life of four years as a depreciation charge.

We will learn about different methods of depreciation in the section that follows, but for the purposes of our discussion at present, let us assume that the *straight-line* method of depreciation is used. This means that the depreciable amount of R105 000 will be charged as depreciation by R26 250 (R105 000/4 years) each year, apportioned as discussed in the section below.

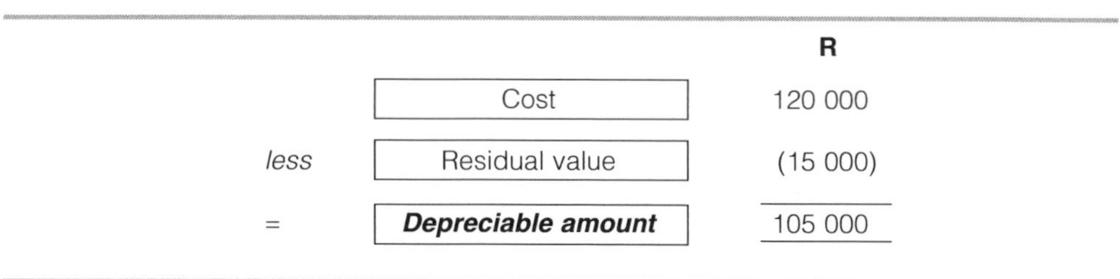

Diagram 11.3: Depreciable amount

Depreciation period

Depreciation of an asset begins when it is *available for use*, which is when it is in the location and condition necessary for it to be *capable of operating in the manner intended by management*. Depreciation of an asset ceases when the asset is derecognised, for example, when it is sold.[12] Accounting for the disposal of property, plant and equipment is covered in section 11.5, below. It is important to note that depreciation does not cease when an asset is idle. This is done so that the financial statements reflect the consumption of the asset's service potential that occurs while the asset is held and is available for use.[13]

Pause and reflect...

a) On what date will depreciation of Smart Concept's photocopy machine begin?
b) What is the depreciation expense for the year ended 31 December 20X5?

Response

a) Depreciation will begin on 1 May 20X5, the date from which it is available for use. Note that depreciation is charged during the month of May 20X5 even though the asset is idle.
b) The depreciation expense for the year ending 31 December 20X5 amounts to R17 500 (R105 000/4 years x 8/12).

Useful life

The future economic benefits embodied in an item of property, plant and equipment are consumed by an entity principally through the use of the asset. However, other factors, such as technical or commercial obsolescence and wear and tear while an asset remains idle, often result in the reduction of the economic benefits that might have been obtained from the asset. All of the following factors therefore need to be considered in determining the useful life of an asset:

- the expected usage of the asset by the enterprise
- the expected physical wear and tear, which depends on operational factors such as the number of shifts for which the asset is to be used and the repair and maintenance programme
- technical or commercial obsolescence arising from changes or improvements in technology, or from a change in the market demand for the product or service output of the asset.[14]

As mentioned above, we are assuming an estimated useful life of four years for the purposes of the discussion at present.

Carrying amount

We have seen that depreciation expense for the year ending 31 December 20X5 amounts to R17 500. The R17 500 represents the *accumulated depreciation*, in other words, that part of the depreciable amount of R105 000 that has been charged as depreciation. Remember that the carrying amount is the amount at which the asset is recognised after deducting any accumulated depreciation

Pause and reflect...

What is the carrying amount of Smart Concept's photocopy machine at 31 December 20X5?

Response

The carrying amount at 31 December is R102 500, comprising the cost of R120 000 less the accumulated depreciation of R17 500.

As the economic benefits embodied in an asset are consumed by the enterprise, the carrying amount of the asset is reduced to reflect this consumption by charging an expense for depreciation.

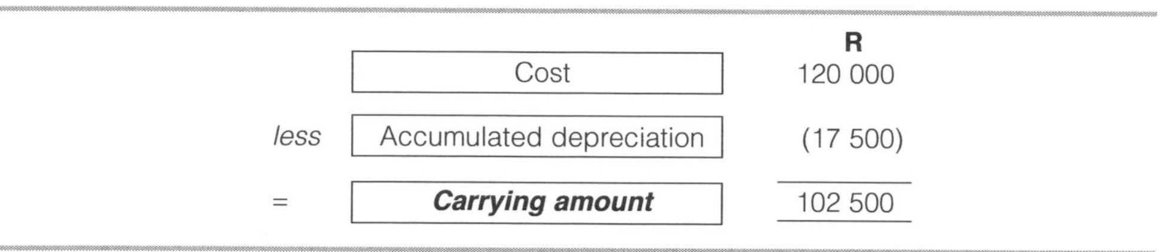

		R
	Cost	120 000
less	Accumulated depreciation	(17 500)
=	***Carrying amount***	102 500

Diagram 11.4: Carrying amount

To sum up, we have seen that the purpose of the depreciation expense is one of cost allocation. Depreciation is that part of the cost of the asset which has been or is being charged to the income statement, and the carrying amount in the statement of financial position is that part of the original cost that has not yet been charged against revenue. In other words, the carrying amount represents future benefits yet to be consumed as depreciation.

11.3.2 Methods of depreciation

A variety of depreciation methods can be used to allocate, on a systematic basis, the depreciable amount of an asset over its useful life. The depreciation method should reflect the pattern in which the future economic benefits are expected to be consumed by the entity.[15] These methods include the ***straight-line*** method, the ***diminishing balance*** method and the ***units of production*** method. Each method will be examined in detail. Straight-line depreciation results in a constant charge over the useful life of the asset. The diminishing balance method results in a decreasing charge over the useful life of the asset. The units of production method results in a charge based on the expected use or output.

Straight-line method

The straight-line method results in a constant charge over the useful life of the asset. This method is appropriate if the asset's usefulness is considered to be equal in each accounting period. The depreciation charge is calculated as:

$$\text{Depreciation expense} = \frac{\text{Cost} - \text{residual value}}{\text{Useful life}}$$

Note that the residual value is subtracted from the cost so that the *depreciable amount* is allocated over the useful life. Referring to the asset mentioned above with a cost of R120 000 and a residual value of R15 000, the depreciation expense each period will be R26 250, assuming a useful life of four years ([R120 000 – 15 000]/4). As discussed above, the charge is opportioned for a part period, resulting in a depreciation charge of R17 500 for the first year.

Diminishing balance method

The diminishing balance method results in a decreasing charge over the useful life of the asset. This method applies a fixed percentage to the carrying amount of the asset at the beginning of each period. The carrying amount at the beginning of the first period is the cost, as no depreciation has yet been charged. The depreciation charge is simply:

$$\text{Depreciation expense} = \text{Carrying amount} \times \%\ \text{rate}$$

Note that the depreciation rate is applied to the cost (and thereafter the carrying amount) and not to the depreciable amount, as with the straight-line method. The effect of the residual value is taken into account in the determination of the fixed percentage, according to the following formula:

$$\%\ \text{rate} = (1 - \sqrt[n]{\tfrac{r}{c}})$$

In this formula, n = the useful life of the asset in years, r = the residual value of the asset and c = the cost of the asset. Applying the formula to the machine that we are working with results in a depreciation rate of 40, 539% ($1 - \sqrt[4]{\tfrac{15\,000}{120\,000}}$). This has been rounded down to 40,5% for ease of calculation. Applying a depreciation rate of 40,5%, the depreciation expense is R32 400 (R120 000 x 40,5% x 8/12) for the first year. This results in a carrying amount at the end of the first year of R87 600 (R120 000 – R32 400). The depreciation charge for the second year is R35 478 (R87 600 x 40,5%). This charge is higher than the charge in the first year because of the apportionment for the part period. The decreasing pattern is evident from the diagram in 11.3.3 below.

Units of production method

Where the potentially available benefits from the asset can be expressed in terms of a maximum potential output, the depreciable amount can be allocated to each period based on the output produced. Output can be measured in a variety of ways, such as units, kilograms or kilometres. The depreciation charge is calculated as:

$$\text{Depreciation expense} = \text{Depreciable amount} \times \frac{\text{Output in period}}{\text{Total estimated output}}$$

Assume that the photocopy machine in our example has an estimated total output of 5 000 000 copies over its useful life. If 800 000 copies were made in the first year, the depreciation charge for that year is R16 800 (R105 000 x [800 000/5 000 000]). Assume that the units of output are 1 400 000 in 20X6, 1 250 000 in 20X7, 1 300 000 in 20X8 and 250 000 in 20X9.

 **Pause and reflect...**

What predominant factor influences the choice of depreciation method?

Response

The entity selects the method that most closely reflects the expected pattern of consumption of the future economic benefits embodied in the asset.

11.3.3 Comparison of the depreciation methods

The diagram below completes and compares the depreciation calculation relating to the photocopy machine purchased by Smart Concepts, using the depreciation methods refered to in 11.3.2. Note that the carrying amount of the asset at the end of its useful life is equal to the originally estimated residual value of R15 000. The difference on the diminishing balance method is due to rounding.

			Straight line	Diminishing balance	Units of production
01/05/X5	Cost		120 000	120 000	120 000
20X5	Depreciation	*(x 8/12)	*(17 500)	*(32 400)	(16 800)
31/12/X5	Carrying amount		102 500	87 600	103 200
20X6	Depreciation		(26 250)	(35 478)	(29 400)
31/12/X6	Carrying amount		76 250	52 122	73 800
20X7	Depreciation		(26 250)	(21 109)	(26 250)
31/12/X7	Carrying amount		50 000	31 013	47 550
20X8	Depreciation		(26 250)	(12 560)	(27 300)
31/12/X8	Carrying amount		23 750	18 453	20 250
20X9	Depreciation	*(x 4/12)	*(8 750)	*(2 491)	(5 250)
30/04/X9	Carrying amount		15 000	15 962	15 000

Diagram 11.3: Comparison of depreciation methods

 **Pause and reflect...**

You will notice that depreciation on the photocopy machine is recognised from 1 May 20X5 to 31 December 20X5 even though the asset is idle for the month of May. What is the implication of the idle month for the depreciation calculation using the units of production method?

Response

Depreciation calculated using the units of production method is a function of output and not a function of time. In the idle month no units are produced, and thus the asset's service potential is not decreased. Therefore, no depreciation is recorded for the idle month when using the units of production method.

11.3.4 Accounting entries

When the concept of depreciation was first introduced in Part Two of this book, the accounting entry was described as a debit to depreciation expense and a credit to the asset. The depreciation expense decreases equity on the right side of the accounting equation which gives rise to the debit to depreciation expense. The charging of depreciation, as you are now aware, is an allocation of the cost of the asset over its useful life and therefore the asset account on the left side of the accounting equation is reduced by a right or credit entry.

However, for presentation purposes, the original cost of the asset and the related accumulated depreciation are normally shown separately on the statement of financial position. For this reason, a separate column in the accounting equation worksheet, and hence a separate account in the ledger, is used for the accumulated depreciation. The accounting entry for recording depreciation expense then becomes:

Dr Depreciation expense
Cr Accumulated depreciation

The accumulated depreciation column appears on the right side of the accounting equation as a provision. To increase the accumulated depreciation therefore requires a right or credit entry. The accounting equation is therefore expanded to accommodate the accumulated depreciation and appears as follows:

Assets			=	Provisions	+	Liabilities	+	Owner's equity
Non-current assets	+	Current assets	=	***Accumulated depreciation***				

To illustrate the accounting entries for depreciation, refer again to our example of the photocopy machine which was recorded at a total cost of R120 000 at the beginning of April 20X5. For the purposes of this illustration, we will work with the straight-line method. The entries for all the methods are naturally the same; only the amounts differ.

	Assets		= **Provisions**		+ **Owner's equity**	
	Machinery		Accumulated depreciation		Depreciation expense	
	+/L/Dr	–/R/Cr	–/L/Dr	+/R/Cr	+/L/Dr	–/R/Cr
Bal	120 000					
20X5				17 500	17 500	
31/12/X5	120 000			17 500	17 500	
c/e						17 500
20X6				26 250	26 250	
31/12/X6	120 000			43 750	26 250	
c/e						26 250

The cost of the machine is shown as an asset of R120 000. For the year ending 31 December 20X5, depreciation of R17 500 is charged. The equity account, depreciation expense, is increased with a left or debit entry of R17 500 and the provision, accumulated depreciation, is increased by the same amount with a right or credit entry. At the end of December 20X5, the depreciation expense of R17 500 is closed off to the profit and loss account as part of the normal year-end procedures. The machinery account shows a debit balance of R120 000 which is reported as an asset on the statement of financial position. The accumulated depreciation account reflects a credit balance of R17 500 which is set off against the cost of R120 000 to report a carrying amount of R102 500 on the statement of financial position. The same procedure is repeated for the year ended 31 December 20X6.

11.3.5 Depreciation of components

Each part of an item of property, plant and equipment with a cost that is significant in relation to the total cost of the item is required to be depreciated separately.[16] Examples of this include an aircraft, where the airframe, engines and interior are identified as significant parts, or an item of industrial plant where the mechanised components and the casing are significant parts.

Separate but significant parts of an item of property, plant and equipment may have the same useful life and depreciation method. Such parts are grouped together for depreciation purposes. For example, the significant parts of a forklift may be identified as the engine, the tyres, the lifting mechanism and the fork. If the lifting mechanism and the fork are considered to have the same useful life and depreciation method, they may be grouped together as a component.

Once the significant parts have been identified, the remainder of the non-significant parts are grouped together as a depreciable component. Using the example of the forklift, the remainder of the cost (after identifying the engine, the tyres and the combination of the lifting mechanism and fork), is grouped together as a component.

For this purpose, it is also important to understand that land and buildings are separable assets even when acquired together. Land is generally not depreciated, whereas buildings are depreciable assets.[17]

Example: Component depreciation

On 1 July 20X6, Computer World purchased new business premises for R10 000 000. The following components were identified:

Component	R	Useful life and depreciation method
Building structure	6 500 000	Useful life of 40 years, depreciated using the straight line method.
Other fittings (such as partitions and air conditioning system)	1 600 000	Useful life of 8 years, depreciated using the straight line method.
Windows	1 000 000	Useful life of 10 years, depreciated using the straight line method.
Lifts	900 000	Useful life of 10 years, depreciated using the diminishing balance method.

You are required to:

Calculate the depreciation and carrying amount of the business premises for the year ended 31 December 20X7

Solution: Component depreciation

Component	Cost		Depreciation	Carrying amount
Building structure	6 500 000	(6 500 000 x 1/40)	162 500	6 337 500
Other fittings	1 600 000	(1 600 000 x 1/8)	200 000	1 400 000
Windows	1 000 000	(1 000 000 x 1/10)	100 000	900 000
Lifts	900 000	(900 000 – 45 000) x 10%	85 500	814 500
Total	10 000 000		548 000	9 452 500

The total cost of the business premises is R10 000 000. The building structure, other fittings, windows and lifts are identified as separate components as each has a cost that is significant in relation to the total cost of the item. Each component is depreciated separately over its useful life using the specified depreciation method. Although the windows and lifts both have a useful life of ten years, they are not grouped together as an individual component as the depreciation methods are different. Note that the depreciation for the lifts is calculated based on the carrying amount of the asset at 1 January 20X7 which is reduced by the depreciation of R45 000 for the six months to 31 December 20X6.

11.4 Reassessment of useful life and residual value

The useful life and residual value of an item of property, plant and equipment need to be reviewed annually and, if expectations are *significantly* different from original estimates, the depreciation charge for the *current* and *future* periods should be adjusted.

The useful life may be extended by subsequent expenditure on the asset which improves the condition of the asset beyond its originally assessed standard of performance. On the other hand, technological changes may reduce the useful life of the asset. This is particularly the case with high-technology assets like computers.

We will refer again to Smart Concepts and the photocopy machine purchased for R120 000 on 1 April 20X5 and that was available for use from 1 May 20X5. The straight-line depreciation method will be used for the purposes of this illustration. At the end of December 20X7, the carrying amount of the asset is R50 000 (R120 000 – R17 500 – R26 250 – R26 250), and the remaining useful life is one year and four months (01/01/X8 – 30/04/X9). Assume that, at the end of 20X8, the useful life and residual value were reviewed. It was considered that the photocopy machine would be used for an additional two years, thus extending the remaining useful life to three years and four months, and that the residual value is R12 000. The revised depreciation charge for the current year and future years is calculated as follows:

$$\text{Revised depreciation charge} = \frac{\text{Carrying amount} - \text{residual value}}{\text{Remaining useful life}}$$

The depreciation expense for the years from 20X8 to 20Y1 is as follows:

31/12/X7	Carrying amount		50 000
20X8	Depreciation	[(50 000 – 12 000) / 40 months x 12 months]	(11 400)
31/12/X8	Carrying amount		38 600
20X9	Depreciation	[(50 000 – 12 000) / 40 months x 12 months]	(11 400)
31/12/X9	Carrying amount		27 200
20Y0	Depreciation	[(50 000 – 12 000) / 40 months x 12 months]	(11 400)
31/12/Y0	Carrying amount		15 800
20Y1	Depreciation	[(50 000 – 12 000) / 40 months x 4 months]	(3 800)
30/04/Y1	Carrying amount		12 000

Diagram 11.4: Revised depreciation charge

Pause and reflect...

In the above example, the useful life and residual value were reviewed at year end, that is, on 31 December 20X8. Would the measurement of the depreciation expense for the year ended 31 December 20X8 and future years change if the estimate of the useful life and residual value were reviewed on 30 June 20X8?

Response

If the estimate of useful life and/or residual value changes, the depreciation charge for the current and future periods is adjusted. It does not matter whether the review takes place on 30 June 20X8 or 31 December 20X8 – the depreciation expense for the year ending 31 December 20X8 is adjusted.

11.5 Disposals

The cost of an item of property, plant and equipment and the related accumulated depreciation must be eliminated from the statement of financial position on disposal of the asset. This is referred to as the ***derecognition*** of the asset. ***Profits*** or ***losses*** on disposal are determined as the difference between the proceeds on disposal and the carrying amount of the asset and are recognised as an income or expense on the income statement.

	Proceeds on disposal
less	Carrying amount
=	Profit or loss

There are four steps to follow when derecognising an item of property, plant and equipment:

- The cost is eliminated as an asset from the accounting records.
- The accumulated depreciation is eliminated as a provision from the accounting records.
- The proceeds on disposal are recorded.
- The profit or loss on disposal is recorded.

This procedure will be demonstrated in the examples that follow.

Example: Disposal for cash

At 1 January 20X6 the equipment account of Computer World reflected a balance of R100 000, and on that date the accumulated depreciation account reflected a balance of R40 000. Equipment is depreciated at 20% per annum on the diminishing balance basis. On 30 June 20X6, the equipment was sold for R50 000 cash. The financial year ends on 31 December 20X6.

You are required to:

account for the disposal of the equipment.

Solution: Disposal for cash

	Assets				= Provisions		+ Owner's equity			
	Cash		Equipment		Accumulated depreciation		Disposal		Loss on disposal	
	+/L/Dr	–/R/Cr	+/L/Dr	–/R/Cr	–/L/Dr	+/R/Cr	+/L/Dr	–/R/Cr	+/L/Dr	–/R/Cr
01/01			100			40				
Depreciation						6				
30/06						46				
1				100			100			
2					46			46		
3	50							50		
4								4	4	
Balance									4	

The balance on the accumulated depreciation of R40 000 must be updated by R6 000 to reflect the accumulated depreciation at the date of disposal. Entry 1 reverses the cost of the equipment sold from the assets, entry 2 reverses the accumulated depreciation from the provisions and entry 3 records the proceeds in the cash account. The loss on disposal of R4 000 is the balancing figure in the disposal account, which is transferred to the loss on disposal account. (Figures in the worksheet are stated in R000s.)

Example: Disposal with a trade-in

At 1 January 20X6 the machinery account of Computer World reflected a balance of R200 000. At that date the accumulated depreciation account had a credit balance of R38 000. Machinery is depreciated at 10% per annum on the reducing balance method. On 30 June 20X6 new machinery costing R500 000, was purchased for cash from S.A. Manufacturers. On that date, the existing machinery was traded in for R150 000.

You are required to:

account for the disposal of the machinery.

Solution: Disposal with a trade-in

	Assets				**=**	**Provisions**	**+**	**Owner's equity**		
	Cash		Machinery		Accumulated depreciation		Disposal		Loss on disposal	
	+/L/Dr	*–/R/Cr*	*+/L/Dr*	*–/R/Cr*	*–/L/Dr*	*+/R/Cr*	*+/L/Dr*	*–/R/Cr*	*+/L/Dr*	*–/R/Cr*
01/01			200,0			38,0				
Depreciation						8,1				
30/06			200,0			46,1				
1				200,0			200,0			
2					46,1			46,1		
3a			150,0					150,0		
3b		350,0	350,0							
4								3,9	3,9	
Balance			500,0						3,9	

As in the previous example, the balance on the accumulated depreciation needs to be updated to the date of disposal. R8 100 is the depreciation for six months based on the carrying amount of R162 000 at 1 January 20X6. Entries 1 and 2 follow the same principle as in the previous example, reversing the cost and accumulated depreciation to the disposal account. New machinery costing R500 000 is purchased and old plant is traded in for an amount of R150 000. Therefore, entry 3a debits the machinery account with R150 000 (the trade-in value) and credits the disposal account with the same amount. Entry 3b records the payment of the additional R350 000 to the supplier of the machinery. The loss on disposal of R3 900 is the balancing figure in the disposal account, which is transferred to the loss on disposal account. (Figures in the worksheet are stated in R000s.)

11.6 Measurement after recognition

You will recall from section 11.2 of this chapter that property, plant and equipment that qualifies for recognition as an asset is measured at its ***cost***. IAS 16 provides two possible treatments for the measurement of property, plant and equipment after recognition, the *cost model* or the *revaluation model*.[18]

11.6.1 Cost model

In applying the cost model, an item of property, plant and equipment is carried at its cost less any accumulated depreciation.[19]

The discussion in this chapter thus far, relating to the recognition and measurement of property, plant and equipment, has been on the cost model.

11.6.2 Revaluation model

In applying the revaluation model, an item of property, plant and equipment is carried at a ***revalued amount***, which is its ***fair value*** at the date of revaluation less any ***subsequent accumulated depreciation***.[20]

The fair value is the amount for which an asset could be exchanged between knowledgeable, willing parties in an arm's length transaction.[21]

The fair value of land and buildings is usually their market value, normally determined by appraisal undertaken by professionally qualified valuers. The fair value of items of plant and equipment is also their market value determined by appraisal.

When an item of property, plant and equipment is revalued, any accumulated depreciation at date of revaluation should be eliminated against the cost of the asset and the asset account restated to the revalued amount of the asset.

According to IAS 16, a revaluation increase is ***credited directly to equity*** in a ***re-valuation surplus*** account.

When preparing the financial statements of a sole proprietor, the balance on the revaluation surplus account is transferred to the owner's capital account. In Part 5 of this book, dealing with the different forms of entity, you will learn how to record a revaluation surplus in the accounting records of a partnership, close corporation and company.

You will recall that in Parts 1 and 2 of this book you were introduced to the concept of a revaluation. This was done in order to illustrate the presentation of the statement of comprehensive income. To review briefly, IAS 1 requires total comprehensive income to comprise the profit for the period and other comprehensive income. The revaluation surplus is identified in IAS 1 as a component of other comprehensive income. As such, the revaluation surplus is reported on the statement of comprehensive income under the heading of other comprehensive income.

The following example extends your knowledge of revaluations by considering the revaluation of a depreciable asset.

Example: Revaluation of property, plant and equipment

At 31 December 20X6, Computer World has an item of plant with a cost of R100 000 and accumulated depreciation of R60 000. The plant is depreciated at 10% per annum on the straight-line basis. The plant is revalued to R70 000, and the remaining useful life of the plant is unchanged. The profit for the period is R120 000.

You are required to:

(a) account for the revaluation of the plant.
(b) prepare an extract from the statement of comprehensive income for the year ended 31 December 20X6.
(c) calculate the depreciation in the first year after revaluation.

Solution: Revaluation of property, plant and equipment

(a)	Assets		=	Provisions		+	Owner's equity	
	Plant			Accumulated depreciation			Revaluation surplus	
	+/L/Dr	–/R/Cr		–/L/Dr	+/R/Cr		–/L/Dr	+/R/Cr
Bal	100 000				60 000			
1		60 000		60 000				
	40 000							
2	30 000							30 000
Bal	70 000							30 000

Entry 1 eliminates, or reverses, the balance of accumulated depreciation against the cost of the plant. The plant account then reflects the carrying amount. Entry 2 increases the carrying amount of the plant to its revalued amount of R70 000, with the surplus on revaluation being placed to the credit of a revaluation account.

(b)

SMART CONCEPTS
EXTRACT FROM STATEMENT OF COMPREHENSIVE INCOME
FOR THE YEAR ENDED 31 DECEMBER 20X6

	R
Profit for the period	120 000
Other comprehensive income:	
Revaluation of plant	30 000
Total comprehensive income	150 000

(c) As the useful life of the plant is unchanged, the revalued amount of R70 000 will be written off over four years at R17 500 per year (R70 000/4 yrs). The additional depreciation to be provided each year over the plant's remaining life of four years amounts to R7 500 (R17 500 – R10 000). This represents the depreciation on the revaluation of R30 000 over the remaining four years (R7 500 x 4 yrs = R30 000).

11.6.3 Impairment of assets

IAS 16 needs to be read together with IAS 36 entitled 'Impairment of Assets', which provides guidance on the recognition and measurement of revaluation decreases, or impairments. The objective of IAS 36 is to ensure that an enterprise's assets are not overstated. If the ***carrying amount*** of an asset exceeds its ***recoverable amount***, the carrying amount will probably not be recovered in the future either through use or sale. The asset is described as impaired and IAS 36 requires the enterprise to recognise an impairment loss.

The recoverable amount is defined in IAS 36 as the higher of an asset's ***fair value less costs to sell*** and its ***value in use***.[22]

Fair value less costs to sell is defined in IAS 36 as the amount obtainable from the sale of an asset in an arm's length transaction between knowledgeable, willing parties, less the costs of disposal.[23]

The best evidence of an asset's net selling price is a price in a sale agreement. If there is no sale agreement but the asset is traded in an active market, the net selling price would be equal to its market price. On the other hand, if there is no sale agreement or active market for an asset, the net selling price is based on the best information available to reflect the amount the enterprise could obtain for the disposal of the asset in an arm's length transaction.

It is important to remember that costs of disposal are deducted in arriving at ***net*** selling price. Examples of such costs are legal costs and costs of removing the asset.

Value in use is defined in IAS 36 as the present value of estimated cash flows expected from the continuing use of the asset and from its disposal at the end of its useful life.[24]

The calculation of value in use involves predictions about future cash flows as well as an estimation of an appropriate discount rate.

An entity should assess at each statement of financial position date whether or not there are indications that items of property, plant and equipment may be impaired. Such indicators include external factors such as:

- a large decline in the asset's market value
- changes in the technological, market economic or legal environment in which the enterprise operates

and internal factors such as:

- obsolescence or physical damage
- evidence that the economic performance of the asset is, or will be, worse than expected.[25]

If such indications exist, calculations should be made of the recoverable amount, which you will recall is the higher of an asset's fair value less costs to sell and value in use. If the carrying amount exceeds the recoverable amount, the asset is impaired and the carrying amount needs to be written down to the recoverable amount. If the recoverable amount exceeds the carrying amount, the requirements of IAS 36 do not apply.

The accounting treatment of an impaired asset will be dependent upon the measurement basis used, that is, the cost model or the revaluation model.

- Following the cost model, the asset is carried at ***cost*** less ***accumulated depreciation*** and ***accumulated impairment*** losses.

- Following the revaluation model, the asset is carried at a ***revalued amount*** less ***subsequent accumulated depreciation*** and ***subsequent accumulated impairment*** losses.

Example: Impairment of property, plant and equipment

Computer World has an item of plant with a cost of R100 000 and accumulated depreciation of R60 000. The plant is depreciated at 10% per annum on the straight-line basis. There are indications at 31 December 20X6, the end of the financial year, that the asset may be impaired. The selling price in an active market is R34 000 and costs of disposal are estimated at R4 000. The estimated cash flows, as well as the present value of R1 at 10%, are shown below.

Year ending	Cash flow	Years	PV of R1 at 10%
31/12/X7	15 000	1	0,909
31/12/X8	12 000	2	0,826
31/12/X9	8 000	3	0,751

You are required to:

(a) calculate the recoverable amount of the plant.
(b) account for the impairment of the plant.

Solution: Impairment of property, plant and equipment

(a) Calculation of recoverable amount

		R
Carrying amount		40 000
Recoverable amount – higher of		(30 000)
❑ Fair value less costs to sell	30 000	
❑ Value in use	29 555	
Impairment loss		10 000

(b) Accounting for the impairment of the plant

	Assets		=	Provisions		+	Owner's equity	
	Plant			Accumulated depreciation/ impairment			Impairment loss expense	
	+/L/Dr	–/R/Cr		–/L/Dr	+/R/Cr		+/L/Dr	–/R/Cr
Bal	100 000				60 000			
Impairment					10 000		10 000	
Bal	100 000				70 000		10 000	

The impairment is accounted for by recognising an expense of R10 000 and increasing the accumulated depreciation/impairment by the same amount. The impairment loss expense is closed off to the profit and loss account and reported on the income statement as an expense.

Workings

Date of cash flow	Amount of cash flow R	PV of R1 at 10% R
31/12/X7	15 000	13 635
31/12/X8	12 000	9 912
31/12/X9	8 000	6 008
		29 555

11.7 Exam examples

11.7.1 Exam example 1

The following account balances appeared in the accounting records of Sparks Spare Parts on 1 October 20X4:

	R
Land and building, cost	350 000
Motor vehicles, cost	106 000
Computer equipment, cost	36 000
Accumulated depreciation – buildings	7 600
Accumulated depreciation – motor vehicles	52 310
Accumulated depreciation – computer equipment	16 000

The accounting policies for depreciation are as follows:

1. Land with a cost price of R160 000 is not depreciated.
2. Buildings are depreciated at 2% per annum using the straight-line method.
3. Motor vehicles and related components are depreciated at 30% per annum using the diminishing balance method.
4. Computer equipment is depreciated on a straight-line basis and is expected to have a useful life of three years with a zero residual value.

On 30 June 20X5 Sparks Spare Parts traded in a delivery van for R23 000 on a used newer model. The second van cost R65 000 and the difference on the purchase price was paid by cheque. The original van was purchased on 30 November 20X2 for R50 000.

An account for R3 515 was received from Fix-it Garage on 2 August 20X5 in respect of work done on the second delivery van. The account comprised the following amounts:

	R
40 000 km service	415
New tyres	3 100
	3 515

The old tyres had a zero carrying amount and were scrapped.

Due to an increase in sales demand, another sales assistant was hired and a new computer was purchased for R6 800 cash on 1 September 20X5. Installation and transport costs of R400 were due to Computer World.

No other purchases or sales took place.

All transactions (including cash transactions) are journalised and all calculations are made to the nearest rand.

You are required to:

(a) journalise the above transactions for the year ended 30 September 20X5. The journal entries for depreciation at year end need not be shown.

(b) prepare an extract from the statement of financial position of Sparks Spare Parts in respect of non-current assets at 30 September 20X5.

Solution: Exam example 1

(a) Journal of Sparks Spare Parts for the year ended 30 September 20X5

Date	Description	Dr	Cr
20X5			
June 30	Depreciation – motor vehicles	5 906	
	Accumulated depreciation – motor vehicles		5 906
	Depreciation on vehicle traded in		
	Asset disposal	50 000	
	Motor vehicles		50 000
	Cost of van traded in		
	Accumulated depreciation – motor vehicles	29 656	
	Asset disposal		29 656
	Accumulated depreciation on van traded in		
	Motor vehicles	65 000	
	Bank		42 000
	Asset disposal		23 000
	New van purchased & old van traded in		
	Asset disposal	2 656	
	Profit on sale of non-current assets		2 656
	Profit on van traded in		
Aug 2	Motor vehicles	3 100	
	Motor vehicle repairs expenses	415	
	Accounts payable		3 515
	Motor vehicle repairs expensed		
Sept 1	Computer equipment	7 200	
	Bank		6 800
	Accounts payable		400
	Purchase of new computer		

(b)

SPARKS SPARE PARTS
STATEMENT OF FINANCIAL POSITION AS AT 30 SEPTEMBER 20X5

Non-current assets	**Cost**	**Accumulated depreciation**	**Carrying amount**
	R	**R**	**R**
Land & buildings	350 000	11 400	338 600
Motor vehicles	124 100	41 822	82 278
Computer equipment	43 200	28 200	15 000
	517 300	81 422	435 878

Workings

Van traded in

Accumulated depreciation – van traded in

1/12/X2 – 30/9/X3	(50 000 X 30% X 10/12)	= 12 500
1/10/X3 – 30/9/X4	(*37 500 X 30%) *(50 000 – 12 500)	= 11 250
1/10/X4 – 30/6/X5	(**26 250 X 30% X 9/12)	
	**(50 000 – 12 500 –11 250)	= 5 906
		29 656

Cost	50 000
Accumulated depreciation	(29 656)
Carrying amount	20 344
Proceeds	23 000
Profit on trade-in	2 656

Motor vehicles

			Cost	**Accumulated depreciation**
Balance 1/10/X4			106 000	52 310
Van traded in	- depreciation to date of trade in			5 906
	- removal of cost & accumulated depreciation		(50 000)	(29 656)
Depreciation on remaining MV	cost (106 000 – 50 000)	56 000		
	accumulated depreciation (52 310 – 23 750)	(28 560)		
		27 440		
	Carrying amount 1/10/X4 (27 440 x 30%)			8 232
Van purchased	- cost		65 000	
	- depreciation to end of year (65 000 x 30% x 3/12)			4 875
Expenditure on Van purchased	- cost		3 100	
	- depreciation to end of year (3 100 x 30% x 2/12)			155
			124 100	41 822

Computer equipment

		Cost	Accumulated depreciation
Balance 1/10/X4		36 000	16 000
Depreciation	(36 000/3)		12 000
New computer purchased		7 200	
Depreciation on new computer	(7 200/3 x 1/12)		200
		43 200	28 200

Land & buildings

Land & buildings		350 000
Less: cost of land		(160 000)
Cost of building		190 000
Depreciation	(190 000 x 2%)	3 800

11.7.2 Exam example 2

Ringo's Book Store is owned and managed by Ringo who is supported by his able-bodied assistant, Dylane. The following is a post-closing trial balance of Ringo's Book Store at 31 May 20X1.

RINGO'S BOOK STORE
POST-CLOSING TRIAL BALANCE AT 31 MAY 20X1

	Dr	Cr
Furniture and equipment	160 000	
Accumulated depreciation: furniture and equipment		24 000
Motor vehicles	40 000	
Accumulated depreciation: motor vehicles		16 000
Accounts receivable	75 200	
Accounts payable		58 400
Inventory	56 300	
Bank	10 500	
Capital		243 600
	342 000	342 000

The following additional information is relevant:

Furniture & equipment

- A computerised cash till, purchased on 1 September 20X0 and included in the furniture & equipment on the above trial balance, was sold for cash on 30 November 20X1. The selling price was R34 000. The cash till was originally purchased at an invoice price of R37 500 and installation costs amounted to R2 500.

- ❑ The remaining furniture and equipment was revalued by R13 400 on 31 May 20X2.
- ❑ Furniture & equipment is depreciated at 20% per annum on the diminishing balance method.

Motor vehicles

- ❑ The motor vehicles comprise two Mini panel vans used to deliver books to customers. Both Minis were purchased on 1 June 19X7 at a total cost of R40 000. The residual value was estimated to be zero.
- ❑ On 1 June 20X1, the engines of both Minis were overhauled at a total cost of R12 000. The estimated useful life was considered to be extended by two years, and the residual value was re-estimated to be R6 000.
- ❑ On 31 May 20X2, Dylane informed Ringo that there were indications that the Minis were impaired. Dylane's calculations reveal that the Minis could be disposed of to a willing buyer for R25 000. The present value of future expected cash flows from the use of the Minis over the remainder of their useful life amounts to R24 200 and the present value of the estimated residual value amounts to R2 800.
- ❑ The motor vehicles are depreciated at 10% per annum on the straight-line basis.

Current assets and current liabilities

- ❑ For the year from 1 June 20X1 to 31 May 20X2, sales to customers on credit amounted to R340 000. Cash received from customers amounted to R322 900 and settlement discount allowed totalled R10 200. There were no cash sales.
- ❑ For the year from 1 June 20X1 to 31 May 20X2, purchases from suppliers on credit amounted to R209 700. Cash paid to suppliers amounted R195 400 and settlement discount received totalled R8 100. A perpetual inventory system is used.
- ❑ Operating expenses incurred during the year from 1 June 20X1 to 31 May 20X2 amounted to R157 800. At 31 May 20X2, prepayments totalled R11 200 and accrued expenses totalled R8 600. There was no unearned income or accrued income at 31 May 20X2.
- ❑ The inventory count at 31 May 20X2 revealed inventory with a cost of R62 000 on hand.

Details of cash transactions

- ❑ A summary of the bank account in the general ledger is provided.
- ❑ All the information shown in the account is correct.

Dr BANK Cr

Date	Description	R	Date	Description		R
01/06/X1	Balance	10 500	01/06/X1	?		12 000
31/11/X1	Disposal	34 000		Accounts payable		195 400
	Accounts receivable	322 900		Operating expenses		?
31/05/X2	Balance	?				
		?				?
			01/6/X2	Balance		?

You are required to:

(a) Prepare all the journal entries relating to the furniture and equipment for the year ended 31 May 20X2. You should include the entries relating to depreciation expense, the sale of the cash till and the revaluation of the remaining equipment.
(b) Prepare a schedule showing all movements in the carrying amount of the motor vehicles. You should begin from the date of purchase on 1 June 19X7 to the end of the current year on 31 May 20X2.
(c) Prepare the statement of financial position of Ringo's Book Store at 31 May 20X2.
(d) Discuss whether it is necessary to reduce the carrying amount of the equipment in the current year by accounting for depreciation expense when the carrying amount is increased by the revaluation.
(e) Explain why it is necessary to account for the impairment of the motor vehicles when the carrying amount exceeds the recoverable amount.

Solution: Exam example 2

(a) Journal entries relating to furniture and equipment

Date	Description	Dr	Cr
	Depreciation expense	3 400	
	Accumulated depreciation:		
	Furniture and equipment		3 400
	Depreciation on item sold		
	[(40 000 – 6 000) x 0,20 x 6/12]		
	Accumulated depreciation (6 000 + 3 400)	9 400	
	Furniture and equipment		40 000
	Bank	34 000	
	Disposal		3 400
	Disposal of cash till		
	Depreciation expense	20 400	
	Accumulated depreciation:		
	Furniture and equipment		20 400
	Depreciation on remaining items		
	[(120 000 – 18 000) x 0,20]		
	Accumulated depreciation:		
	Furniture and equipment	38 400	
	Furniture and equipment		38 400
	Reversal of accumulated depreciation on revaluation		
	Furniture and equipment	13 400	
	Revaluation		13 400
	Revaluation of furniture and equipment		

Workings

Furniture and equipment sold			
01/09/X0	Cost		40 000
01/09/X0 – 31/05/X1	Depreciation	(40 000 X 0,20 X 9/12)	(6 000)
			34 000
01/06/X1 – 30/11/X1	Depreciation	(34 000 X 0,20 X 6/12)	(3 400)
			30 600
	Selling price		34 000
	Profit		3 400

Furniture and equipment		Cost/ Valuation	Accumulated depreciation	Revaluation
01/06/X1	Balance	160 000	(24 000)	
01/06/X1 – 30/11/X1	Depreciation on item sold		(3 400)	
30/11/X1	Removal of cost and accumulated depreciation	(40 000)	9 400	
		120 000	(18 000)	
01/06/X1 – 31/05/X2	Depreciation on remaining F&E [(120 000 – 18 000) x 0,20]		(20 400)	
		120 000	(38 400)	
31/05/X2	Revaluation	(38 400)	38 400	
		13 400		13 400
		95 000	–	

(b) Motor vehicles schedule

				Life
01/06/X7*	Cost		40 000	10
01/06/X7* – 31/05/X1	Depreciation	(40 000 X 0,10 X 4 yrs)	(16 000)	(4)
			24 000	6
01/06/X1	Improvement		12 000	2
			36 000	8
01/06/X1 – 31/05/X2	Depreciation	(36 000 – 6 000)/8 yrs	(3 750)	
			32 250	
31/05/X2	Impairment		(5 250)	
		(Recoverable amount = Greater of (24 200 + 2 800) or 25 000	27 000	

* X7 = 19X7

(c) RINGO'S BOOK STORE
STATEMENT OF FINANCIAL POSITION
AT 31 MAY 20X2

ASSETS		
Non-current assets		
Furniture and equipment		95 000
– At revaluation		95 000
– Accumulated depreciation		–
Motor vehicles		27 000
– At cost	(40 000 + 12 000)	52 000
– Accumulated depreciation/impairment	(16 000 + 3 750 + 5 250)	(25 000)
Current assets		155 300
Accounts receivable	(75 200 + 340 000 – 322 900 – 10 200)	82 100
Inventory		62 000
Prepayments		11 200
		277 300
EQUITY AND LIABILITIES		
Capital and reserves		203 700
Capital		190 300
Revaluation reserve		13 400
Current liabilities		73 600
Accounts payable	(58 400 + 209 700 – 195 400 – 8 100)	64 600
Accrued expenses		8 600
Bank	(10 500 + 34 000 – 12 000 + 322 900 – 195 400 – *160 400) * (157 800 + 11 200 – 8 600) (All other movements in bank given)	400
		277 300

(d) An asset is an embodiment of future economic benefits. As the economic benefits embodied in an asset are consumed by an enterprise, the carrying amount of the asset is reduced to reflect this consumption by charging an expense for depreciation. The depreciation charge is made even if the asset is revalued.

(e) The objective of IAS 36 is to ensure that an enterprise's assets are not overstated. If the carrying amount of the motor vehicle exceeds the recoverable amount, the carrying amount will probably not be recovered in the future either through use or sale. An impairment loss is required to be recognised.

Summary of concepts and applications

1. IAS 16, 'Property, Plant and Equipment', defines property, plant and equipment as tangible assets held for use in the production or supply of goods or services, for rental to others or for administrative purposes, and which are expected to be used during more than one period. The standard allows recognition of property, plant and equipment only if the inflow of future economic benefits is probable and the cost of the item can be measured reliably.
2. IAS 16 indicates that an item of property, plant and equipment that qualifies for recognition as an asset should be measured at its cost. The cost of an item of property, plant and equipment comprises its purchase price, including import duties and non-refundable purchase taxes, and any costs directly attributable to bringing the asset to the location and condition necessary for it to be capable of operating in the manner intended by management. The cost of an item of property, plant and equipment is the cash price equivalent at the recognition date.
3. Depreciation is an expense arising through the consumption of the benefits inherent in an asset. The terms relevant to the calculation of depreciation, namely depreciable amount, depreciation period, useful life and carrying amount, are defined, explained and illustrated through an example. There are three principal methods of depreciation: the straight-line method, the diminishing balance method and the units of production method. The chapter discusses the methods and demonstrates their effects through an example. A comparison among the methods of depreciation is also provided. The accounting entry for the recognition of the depreciation expense requires a debit to depreciation expense and a credit to accumulated depreciation (a separate account in the ledger). Each part of an item of property, plant and equipment with a cost that is significant in relation to the total cost of the item is required to be depreciated separately.
4. The useful life and residual value of an item of property, plant and equipment needs to be reviewed periodically, and, if expectations are significantly different from original estimates, the depreciation charge for the current and future periods should be adjusted.
5. The procedure for the derecognition of an item of property, plant and equipment is as follows: the cost is eliminated as an asset from the accounting records while the accumulated depreciation is eliminated as a provision from the accounting records, the proceeds on disposal are recorded and, finally, the profit or loss on disposal is recorded.
6. There are two possible treatments for the measurement of property, plant and equipment after recognition, namely the cost model or the revaluation model. The cost model requires an item of property, plant and equipment to be carried at its cost less any accumulated depreciation, while the revaluation

model requires an item of property, plant and equipment to be carried at a revalued amount, which is its fair value at the date of revaluation, less any subsequent accumulated depreciation. When using the revaluation model, the revaluation increase is credited directly to equity in a revaluation surplus account. IAS 36, 'Impairment of Assets', provides guidance on the recognition and measurement of impairments. An asset is impaired if its carrying amount exceeds its recoverable amount (the higher of the asset's fair value less costs to sell and its value in use) and an impairment loss must be recognised. The accounting treatment of an impaired asset will be dependent upon the measurement basis used – that is, the cost model or the revaluation model.

Notes

1. Framework for the Preparation and Presentation of Financial Statements. The *International Accounting Standards Board*, (2001), paragraph 49(a).
2. IAS 16, Property, Plant and Equipment, *The International Accounting Standards Board*, (2007), paragraph 2.
3. IAS 16, paragraph 7.
4. IAS 16, paragraph 10.
5. IAS 16, paragraph 15.
6. IAS 16, paragraph 16.
7. IAS 16, paragraph 17.
8. IAS 16, paragraph 20.
9. IAS 16, paragraph 23.
10. IAS 16, paragraph 6.
11. IAS 16, paragraph 50.
12. IAS 16, paragraph 55.
13. IAS 16, paragraph BC 31.
14. IAS 16, paragraph 56.
15. IAS 16, paragraph 60.
16. IAS 16, paragraph 43.
17. IAS 16, paragraph 58.
18. IAS 16, paragraph 29.
19. IAS 16, paragraph 30.
20. IAS 16, paragraph 31.
21. IAS 16, paragraph 6.
22. IAS 36, paragraph 6.
23. IAS 36, paragraph 6.
24. IAS 36, paragraph 6.
25. IAS 36, paragraph 12.

12

Inventory and Cost of Sales

'[On taking inventory] – Debit Mechini ginger ... credit capital for so many packages weighing so many pounds, in my store or at my house, which according to current prices I value so many ducats per hundred ...'
(Pacioli, 1494)

Outcomes

- Explain recognition and measurement principles relating to inventory.
- Compute the relationship between cost, gross profit and selling price.
- Determine the cost of inventory, and account for goods in transit, goods on consignment and inventory shortages.
- Use the inventory cost formulae.
- Measure and record inventories.
- Calculate inventory errors.
- Estimate the value of closing inventory.

Chapter outline

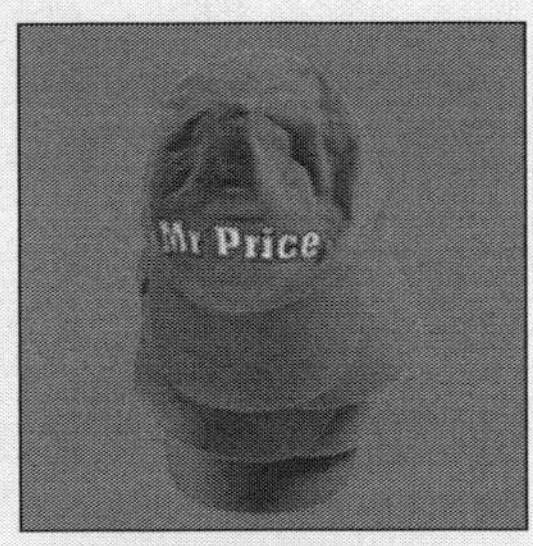

Mr Price Group Limited
Income statement for the year ended 31 March 2008

	(R Millions)
Revenue	7 350
Cost of Sales	(4 364)
Gross Profit	2 986

Notes to the financial statements for the year ended 31 March 2008

	(R Millions)
Merchandise purchased for resale	902
Consumable stores	7
	909

Mr Price has over R7 billion in revenues and sells thousands of items each and every day through its 896 stores in Southern Africa. Effective inventory control is vital in a business such as this.

12.1 Recognition and measurement of inventory

Inventory often comprises a substantial part of the assets of a business entity, particularly a merchandising entity. It is usually sold within one year, or operating cycle, and is therefore classified as a current asset. The recognition and measurement of inventory affects both the statement of comprehensive income and the statement of financial position. The cost of inventory available for sale is allocated between the cost of sales expense (which is included on the statement of comprehensive income of the current period) and the inventory asset (which is carried forward to be included on the statement of comprehensive income of a future period). Diagram 12.1 illustrates this point.

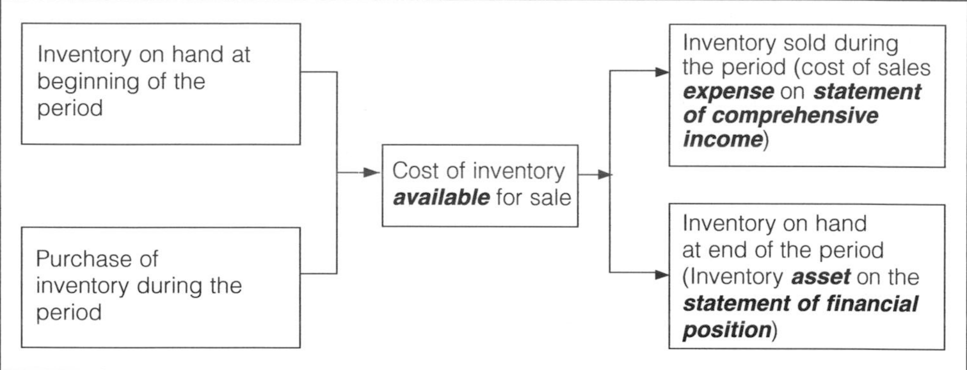

Diagram 12.1: Effect of inventory on income statement and statement of financial position

You are now familiar with the definition of an asset in the accounting framework – a resource controlled by the enterprise as a result of past events and from which future economic benefits are expected to flow to the enterprise.[1]

The cost of inventory is recorded initially as an asset (using the perpetual system), or in a temporary purchases account (using the periodic system), and subsequently transferred to the income statement as the inventory is used up. The inventory amount on the statement of financial position thus represents that portion of the inventory purchased in the past which has not yet been expensed – it is carried forward as an asset which will provide future economic benefits to the enterprise.

The applicable accounting standard is IAS 2, entitled 'Inventories'.

IAS 2 defines inventories as assets:
- held *for sale* in the ordinary course of business.
- held in the form of materials or supplies to be consumed within the business operation.[2]

You will notice that the definition refers to inventory as an asset. As such, the definition of an asset must also be satisfied. To be an asset, the risks and rewards of ownership must have been transferred from the seller to the buyer. For most retail sales, the transfer of the risks and rewards of ownership coincides with the passing of possession or transfer of legal title to the buyer.

Applying the definition, inventory is a resource controlled by the enterprise (risks and rewards of ownership have passed), as a result of a past event (the purchase transaction), from which future economic benefits are expected to flow to the enterprise (sale of the inventory to customers).

Pause and reflect...

What are the risks and rewards of ownership that we have been referring to?

Response

The risks relate to the risk of loss of inventory through obsolescence or damage. The rewards relate to the profit and cash flows that will result from selling the inventory.

It is very important to distinguish between goods held for sale and consumable goods, commonly known as consumable stores. Although both are included in the definition of inventory, it is only the cost of the goods held for sale that is included in the determination of the gross profit from *trading* activities. The cost of consumable stores is taken into account in calculating net profit from operations. This is illustrated in diagram 12.2 below.

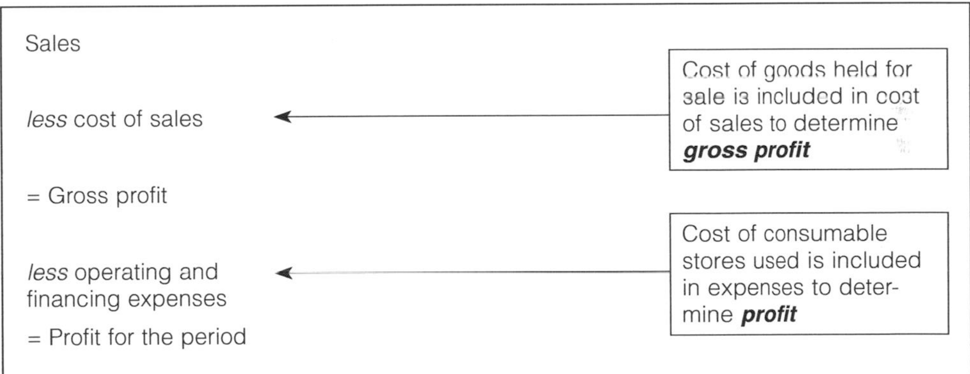

Diagram 12.2: Cost of goods held for sale and consumable stores

Inventory should be measured at the lower of its ***cost*** and ***net realisable value***.[3]

The accounting issues relating to the measurement of cost and net realisable value are discussed in the sections that follow.

12.2 Relationship between cost, gross profit and selling price

The relationship between the cost of inventory, the mark-up applied to achieve the gross profit, and the selling price is crucial in a number of issues relating to accounting for inventory. In establishing the relationship, it is important to distinguish between the mark-up on cost and the gross profit percentage (GP %).

Assume that a business applies a ***mark-up on cost*** of 25% to all of its goods. The following relationships can be established:

Cost	100	*mark-up on cost* = GP/C = 25% (25/100)
Gross profit	25	
Selling price	125	*expected GP %* = GP/SP = 20% (25/125)

On the other hand, assume that the ***expected GP %*** is 25%. The relationship between cost, gross profit and selling price is different and is established as follows:

Cost	75	*mark-up on cost* = GP/C = 33.33% (25/75)
Gross profit	25	
Selling price	100	*expected GP %* = GP/SP = 25% (25/100)

In some situations (which you will encounter later in this chapter), you will need to calculate the expected GP % from a known mark-up on cost. In other situations, you may need to establish the mark-up applied to cost from a known GP %.

Pause and reflect...

a) An enterprise applies a constant markup on cost of 25% to all of its goods. The sales amount to R500. What would you expect the cost of sales to be?

b) An enterprise marks up all of its goods to achieve an expected GP% of 25%. The sales amount to R500. What would you expect the cost of sales to be?

Response

a) The relationship between cost, gross profit and selling price is as follows:

	%	R	
Cost	100	400	(500 x 100/125)
Gross profit	25	100	((500 x 25/125) or (400 x 25/100))
Selling price	125	500	

The cost of sales is therefore R400.

b) The relationship between cost, gross profit and selling price is as follows:

	%	R	
Cost	75	375	(500 x 75/100)
Gross profit	25	125	((500 x 25/100) or (375 x 25/75))
Selling price	100	500	

The cost of sales is therefore R375.

12.3 Establishing the cost of inventory

According to IAS 2, the cost of inventory of a merchandising entity comprises all ***costs of purchase*** and ***other costs*** incurred in bringing the inventory to its present location and condition.[4]

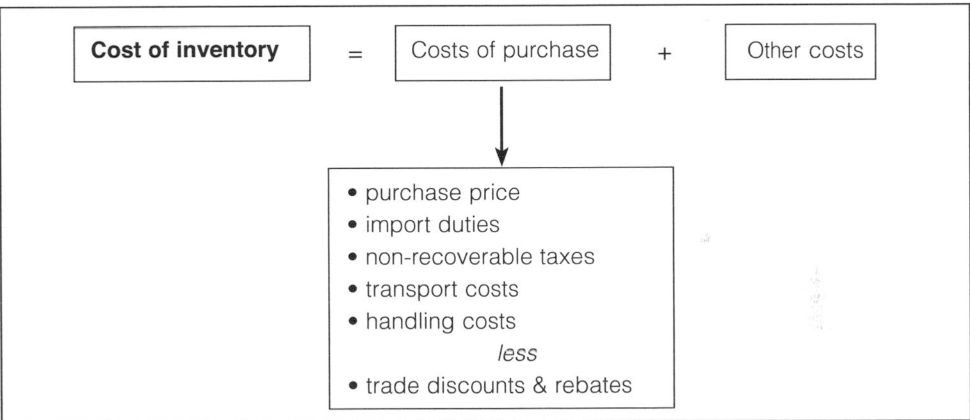

Diagram 12.3: Cost of inventory

The **costs of purchase** of inventory comprise the purchase price, import duties and other taxes (other than those which are recoverable, such as VAT), transport and handling costs directly attributable to the acquisition of goods for resale. Trade discounts and rebates are deducted in determining the costs of purchase.[5]

Other costs are included in the cost of inventory only to the extent that they are incurred in bringing the inventories to their present location and condition[6] – for example the cost of customising an item for a customer. The cost of storing maturing inventory such as wine might also be included.

Most items present no problem in counting and determining the cost. There are, however, a few issues which require special attention. These include goods in transit at the end of the period, goods on consignment, and inventory shortages.

12.3.1 Goods in transit

Goods in transit, as the name implies, are goods which have not physically arrived at the premises of the reporting entity. There are two problems which need to be addressed: firstly, whether **ownership** of the goods has passed from the supplier to the buyer (the reporting entity) and, secondly, whether the buyer has **processed the purchase of the goods** through the accounting system.

Deciding whether **ownership** of the goods has passed from the seller to the buyer is crucial in deciding whether the goods are to appear as inventory on the statement of financial position of the reporting entity. If ownership *has not* passed, then the goods in question remain the property of the seller and do not affect the financial statements of the buyer at all. If ownership *has* passed (and the goods have not been delivered), then the goods in question are regarded as 'in transit' and have to be accounted for accordingly. Naturally, if the goods have been delivered, they will be included in the physical count of closing inventory to the extent that they remain unsold, and the problem of being 'in transit' falls away.

In deciding whether ownership has passed from the seller to the buyer, it is necessary, as discussed in 12.1 above, to consider whether the risks and rewards of ownership have passed. When the inventory is imported, it is necessary to look at the terms of the agreement. The following are some of the agreements that may be encountered in such situations:

FOB (free on board) foreign airport/harbour

- ❑ Ownership passes as soon as goods are loaded onto aircraft/ship.
- ❑ Costs incurred to airport/harbour are paid by supplier.
- ❑ Costs of shipping, rail/road transport as well as freight and insurance paid by buyer.

FOR (free on rail) destination station

- ❑ Ownership passes when goods reach the destination station.
- ❑ Costs incurred to destination station, including unloading, agent fees, custom's duty and railage paid by supplier.
- ❑ Costs of road transport to buyer's premises paid by buyer.

Diagram 12.4: Terminology relating to the purchase and sale of inventory

Once it is confirmed that ownership has passed and the goods are not delivered, it is necessary to establish whether the **purchase of the goods has been processed** through the accounting records. This is significant because both the assets and the liabilities on the statement of financial position are affected by this transaction. As the *risks* and *rewards* of ownership have passed, the goods in transit are a resource, controlled by the entity, from which future economic benefits are expected to flow, and therefore need to be recorded as an asset. For the same reason, the amount owing to the supplier is an obligation of the entity which will result in an outflow of economic benefits in the future and must be recorded as a liability.

The procedure to account for the goods in transit will depend upon whether the purchase has been processed through the accounting records.

No entry processed for the goods in transit

If it is established that no entry has been processed for the goods in transit and the financial statements are being prepared, an adjusting entry is required to state the asset (goods in transit) and the liability (accounts payable) at the correct amount.

The adjusting entry is the same for both the ***periodic*** and ***perpetual*** systems, as the adjustment affects two *statement of financial position* items only. The income statement is not affected.

Assume that inventory costing R70 000 was in transit at the end of the financial year and that no entry has been processed to record this purchase. The adjustment to the assets and liabilities can be shown as follows:

	Assets		=	**Liabilities**		+	**Owner's equity**
	Goods in transit			Accounts payable			
	+/L/Dr	–/R/Cr		–/L/Dr	+/R/Cr		
Adjusting entry	70 000				70 000		

Entry processed for the goods in transit

If it is established that an entry has been processed to record the purchase of the goods in transit, the adjusting entry must take into account the original entry, which will be different depending on whether the periodic or perpetual system has been used.

Periodic system

Assume again that inventory costing R70 000 was in transit at the end of the financial year and that the correct entry, as shown below, has been processed to record this purchase. The purchases account, and hence cost of sales and gross profit, has been affected by the original entry. However, the cost of the goods in transit is not included in the closing inventory figure, thus:

- ❑ the cost of sales is overstated.
- ❑ the gross profit and profit for the period are understated.

An adjusting entry is required to debit goods in transit to ensure that the assets are reported at the correct amount. The credit to purchases corrects the cost of sales and gross profit. The liability is correctly stated and therefore the accounts payable account is not affected by the adjustment.

	Assets				=	**Liabilities**		+	**Owner's equity**
	Purchases		Goods in transit			Accounts payable			
	+/L/Dr	–/R/Cr	+/L/Dr	–/R/Cr		–/L/Dr	+/R/Cr		
Original entry	70 000						70 000		
Adjusting entry		70 000	70 000						

Perpetual system

Once again assume that inventory costing R70 000 was in transit at the end of the financial year and that the correct entry, as shown below, has been processed to record this purchase. As the purchase of goods using the perpetual system is debited to the inventory account and not the purchases account, the cost of sales and the gross profit are not affected by the original entry. Recall that the cost of sales in a perpetual system is recorded as sales are made and is unaffected by the count of closing inventory. In addition, cost of the goods in transit is included in the closing inventory figure by virtue of the entry mentioned above. In summary:

- the cost of sales is correctly stated.
- the gross profit and profit for the period are correctly stated.

The adjusting entry simply reclassifies the goods in transit from the inventory account to a goods in transit account. No entry is needed to correct the income statement. The liability is correctly stated and therefore the accounts payable account is not affected by the adjustment.

	Assets				**=**	**Liabilities**	**+**	**Owner's equity**
	Inventory		Goods in transit		Accounts payable			
	+/L/Dr	*–/R/Cr*	*+/L/Dr*	*–/R/Cr*	*–/L/Dr*	*+/R/Cr*		
Original entry	70 000					70 000		
Adjusting entry		70 000	70 000					

Summary of entries to account for goods in transit

	Periodic	**Perpetual**
No entry processed for the goods in transit	Dr Goods in transit Cr Accounts payable	Dr Goods in transit Cr Accounts payable
Entry processed for the goods in transit	Dr Goods in transit Cr Purchases/Cost of sales	Dr Goods in transit Cr Inventory

Example: Goods in transit

Sharp Moves had an opening inventory at the beginning of 20X7 costing R90 000. Purchases of R330 000 were made during a three-month period to the end of March 20X7. The closing inventory was valued at R100 000, and there were goods in transit at period-end costing R70 000. Sales for the period amounted to R400 000. Sharp Moves marks up its goods at 25% above cost.

You are required to:

(a) show the computation of the gross profit and the entries in the cost of sales and the trading account if the periodic system is used:
  (i) assuming no entry has been made for the goods in transit in the accounting records of Sharp Moves.
  (ii) assuming an entry has been made to record the purchase of the goods in transit in the accounting records of Sharp Moves.

(b) show the inventory account if the perpetual system is used.

Solution: Goods in transit

(a) Periodic inventory system

Periodic	No entry made for goods in transit		Entry for the purchase of goods in transit already made	
Revenue from sales		400 000		400 000
Cost of sales		(320 000)		(320 000)
Opening inventory	90 000		90 000	
Purchases	330 000		400 000	
Cost of goods available for sale	420 000		490 000	
Closing inventory	(100 000)		(100 000)	
Goods in transit (GIT)	–		(70 000)	
Gross profit (GP)		80 000		80 000
Gross profit %	20%		20%	
Mark-up %	25%		25%	

(i) No entry made for goods in transit

Cost of sales

Details	R	Details	R
O/Inventory	90 000	C/Inventory	400 000
Purchases	330 000	Trading	320 000
	420 000		420 000

(ii) Entry for the purchase of the goods in transit already made

Cost of sales

Details	R	Details	R
O/Inventory	90 000	C/Inventory	100 000
Purchases	400 000	Goods in transit	70 000
		Trading	320 000
	490 000		490 000

Trading

Details	R	Details	R
Cost of sales	320 000	Sales	400 000
Profit & loss	80 000		
	400 000		400 000

Trading

Details	R	Details	R
Cost of sales	320 000	Sales	400 000
Profit & loss	80 000		
	400 000		400 000

In (i) above, where no entry has been made in respect of the goods in transit, the cost of sales account is not affected by the adjustment. The goods in transit are correctly excluded from the purchases of R330 000 and the closing inventory of R100 000. In situation (ii), where the goods in transit have already been recorded as a purchase, the purchases of R400 000 include the goods in transit of R70 000. The adjusting entry, as described above, debits goods in transit and credits purchases. In this example, the credit has been placed to the cost of sales account. You should appreciate that it makes no difference whether the purchases account is credited (and is closed off to the cost of sales account) or whether the adjustment is credited directly to the cost of sales account. In both cases, the overstatement of cost of sales and the understatement of gross profit, caused by the goods in transit, is corrected.

(b) Perpetual inventory system

Inventory

Details	R	Details	R
Balance b/d	90 000	Cost of sales	320 000
Accounts payable	330 000	Goods in transit	70 000
Accounts payable	70 000	Balance c/d	100 000
	490 000		490 000
Balance b/d	100 000		

Goods in transit

Details	R	Details	R
Inventory	70 000		
		Balance c/d	70 000
	70 000		70 000
Balance b/d	70 000		

The cost of sales of R320 000 is determined independently of the count of the closing inventory. The gross profit is therefore unaffected by the goods in transit. The liability is correctly shown by the accounts payable of R70 000 and, therefore, the only entry required is to transfer the goods in transit of R70 000 from the inventory account to the goods in transit account.

12.3.2 Goods on consignment

Goods on consignment are goods delivered by the entity owning these goods (known as the consignor) to another entity (known as the consignee), who will sell these goods on behalf of the owner. The goods are not sold to the consignee and the risks and rewards of ownership of the goods remain with the consignor.

Goods on consignment held by the consignee at the end of the period must be included as inventory on the consignor's statement of financial position. Although future economic benefits will flow to the consignee when the goods are sold, the goods do not comprise a resource controlled by the consignee and are therefore correctly excluded from the consignee's statement of financial position.

Example: Goods on consignment

Sharp Moves delivered ten printers on consignment to Peoples Printers during October 20X6. The printers cost R2 000 each and Peoples Printers sell the printers at a mark-up on cost of 25%. Sharp Moves has agreed to pay Peoples Printers a commission of 15% of the selling price of the printers. At 31 December 20X6, Peoples Printers had sold six of the printers. A perpetual inventory system is used.

You are required to:

(a) prepare the relevant journal entries in the accounting records of Sharp Moves relating to the goods on consignment

(b) prepare the relevant journal entries in the accounting records of Peoples Printers relating to the goods on consignment.

Solution: Goods on consignment

(a)

GENERAL JOURNAL OF SHARP MOVES

Date	Description	Dr	Cr
31/12/X6	Cash (15 000 – 2 250)	12 750	
	Commission expense (15 000 x 0,15)	2 250	
	Sales (2 500 x 6)		15 000
	Cost of sales (2 000 x 6)	12 000	
	Inventory (2 000 x 6)		12 000

When the goods on consignment are delivered to Peoples Printers, there is no entry in the accounting records of either Sharp Moves or Peoples Printers. When the goods are sold by the consignee (in this case, Peoples Printers), the consignor (Sharp Moves) records the full selling price as sales revenue, and the corresponding cost of sales as an expense, as well as the expense relating to the commission.

(b)

GENERAL JOURNAL OF PEOPLES PRINTERS

Date	Description	Dr	Cr
31/12/X6	Cash	2 250	
	Commission income		2 250

There is no purchase or sale transaction to record in the accounting records of the consignee. The risks and rewards of ownership of the goods on consignment remained with the consignor until sold by the consignee, at which point the consignor recorded the sales revenue and the corresponding cost of sales. The consignee records the commission earned as income.

12.3.3 Inventory shortages

The detection and prevention of inventory shortages is a key area of management responsibility concerning the trading activities of a business. The inventory system used (periodic or perpetual) will influence management's ability to exercise the necessary levels of control. Whichever inventory system is used, physical inventory needs to be counted at regular intervals. A gross profit percentage is computed for the periodic system, whereas for the perpetual system the cost of the inventory counted is compared to the balance in the inventory account. The procedure to establish and account for inventory shortages using either the periodic or perpetual system is described below.

Periodic system

It is much more difficult to establish inventory shortages when using a periodic system than it is when using a perpetual system. As no entry is made to record the cost of inventory sold on a day-to-day basis, there is no inventory value in the accounting records to compare to the physical count. The only technique available to an owner or manager in this situation is to compare the ***actual gross profit percentage*** (determined by incorporating the cost of closing inventory counted into the cost of sales computation) with the ***expected gross profit percentage***.

Assume that a business enterprise marks up its goods at 100% above cost. The following relationships then exist between cost, gross profit and selling price:

Cost	100	*mark-up on cost* = GP/C = 100% (100/100)
Gross profit	100	
Selling price	200	*expected GP %* = GP/SP = 50% (100/200)

At the end of a period, the actual gross profit percentage is calculated and compared to the expected gross profit percentage. If the actual gross profit percentage is less than the expected gross profit percentage, management needs to investigate the difference and identify the reasons. Shortages may arise from theft, evaporation or inventory lost through fire or flood damage.

Assume further that sales are R400 000 and that cost of sales is computed at R205 000 (taking into account the cost of opening inventory of R50 000, purchases of R250 000 and closing inventory of R95 000). Cost of sales is therefore R205 000, gross profit is R195 000 and the actual GP % is 48,75% (R195 000/R400 000). This is lower than the expected GP % of 50%.

The difference between the actual GP % and expected GP % is 1,25% and this difference needs to be investigated. If it is known that goods costing R2 000 were lost through flood damage, this accounts for 0,5% of the difference (R2 000/R400 000). The remaining difference of 0,75% is therefore an unknown shortage, presumably theft. The total difference can be summarised as follows:

Expected GP %	50,00%
Actual GP %	48,75%
Difference	1,25%
Known shortage – flood (R2 000/R400 000)	0,50%
Unknown shortage – theft (R3 000/R400 000)	0,75%
	1,25%

Note that, using the periodic system, the cost of the inventory shortage is included in the cost of sales by virtue of the fact that the cost of the inventory lost is included in either the opening inventory or purchases and not in the closing inventory.

A = L +			**Owner's equity**			
	Cost of sales		Trading		Profit and loss	
	+/L/Dr	*–/R/Cr*	*–/L/Dr*	*+/R/Cr*	*–/L/Dr*	*+/R/Cr*
Sales				400 000		
Opening inventory	50 000					
Purchases	250 000					
Closing inventory		95 000				
Closing entry 1		205 000	205 000			
Closing entry 2			195 000			195 000
Closing entry 3 (to owner's equity)					195 000	

Perpetual system

When a perpetual system is used, the cost of the inventory according to the physical count is compared to the balance in the inventory account in the general ledger. This is because the inventory account reflects the cost of all goods purchased and sold. The inventory account is adjusted to reflect the amount of the physical count by recording the difference as an inventory shortage.

Assume that the inventory account reflects a balance of R100 000 at the end of a period, whereas the physical count of inventory shows R95 000 to be on hand. In addition, assume sales of R400 000 and a mark-up on cost of 100%, as in the example above.

The adjusting entry to take into account the known inventory shortage debits the cost of sales account and credits the inventory account. At a mark-up of 100% above cost, sales of R400 000 result in a cost of sales of R200 000 (R400 000 x 100/200) gross profit of R200 000 (R400 000 x 100/200). The adjusting entry debits the cost of sales with the inventory shortage of R5 000 and credits the inventory account to reduce the balance on the inventory account from R100 000 to R95 000, the cost of the physical count of inventory.

The difference between the original balance in the inventory account and the physical count of inventory amounts to R5 000 and this difference also needs to be investigated. If we again assume that goods costing R2 000 were lost through flood damage, the remaining R3 000 presumably results from theft. The same numerical reconciliation can be done as was illustrated with the periodic system.

	Assets		=		Owner's equity			
	Inventory		Cost of sales		Trading		Profit and loss	
	+/L/Dr	–/R/Cr	+/L/Dr	–/R/Cr	–/L/Dr	+/R/Cr	–/L/Dr	+/R/Cr
Balance	100 000		200 000			400 000		
Adjusting entry		5 000	5 000					
Closing entry 1				205 000	205 000			
Closing entry 2					195 000			195 000
Closing entry 3 (to owner's equity)							195 000	
Balance	95 000							

Summary of entries to account for inventory shortages

	Periodic	Perpetual
Recording the shortage	Included in cost of sales because of reduced closing inventory	Dr Cost of sales Cr Inventory

Example: Inventory shortages

Assume that Sharp Moves has an opening inventory of 10 projectors at the beginning of July 20X7. During the three-month period to the end of September 20X7, 50 projectors were purchased and 40 were sold. Projectors cost R5 000 each and are sold for R10 000 each. Other expenses total R75 000. Sharp Moves marks up its goods at 100% above cost.

You are required to:

(a) show the computation of the gross profit and the entries in the cost of sales account, trading account and profit and loss account if the periodic system is being used:
   (i) assuming 20 projectors were counted at the end of the period.
   (ii) assuming 19 projectors were counted at the end of the period.

(b) show the entries in the inventory account, cost of sales account, trading account and profit and loss account if the perpetual system is being used:
   (i) assuming 20 projectors were counted at the end of the period.
   (ii) assuming 19 projectors were counted at the end of the period.

Solution: Inventory shortages

(a) Periodic inventory system

Periodic	20 units on hand (no inventory shortage)			19 units on hand (inventory shortage)		
Revenue from sales	40 x R10 000		400 000	40 x R10 000		400 000
Cost of sales			(200 000)			(205 000)
Opening inventory	10 x R5 000	50 000		10 x R5 000	50 000	
Purchases	50 x R5 000	250 000		50 x R5 000	250 000	
Cost of goods available for sale	60 x R5 000	300 000		60 x R5 000	300 000	
Closing inventory	20 x R 5 000	(100 000)		19 x R 5 000	(95 000)	
Gross profit			200 000			195 000
Other expenses			(75 000)			(75 000)
Profit for the period			125 000			120 000
Mark-up %	100%			100%		
Gross profit %	50%			48,75%		

(i) No inventory shortage

Cost of Sales

Details	R	Details	R
O/Inventory	50 000	C/Inventory	100 000
Purchases	250 000	Trading	200 000
	300 000		300 000

Trading

Details	R	Details	R
Cost of sales	200 000	Sales	400 000
Profit and loss	200 000		
	400 000		400 000

(ii) Inventory shortage

Cost of Sales

Details	R	Details	R
O/Inventory	50 000	C/Inventory	95 000
Purchases	250 000	Trading	205 000
	300 000		300 000

Trading

Details	R	Details	R
Cost of sales	205 000	Sales	400 000
Profit and loss	195 000		
	400 000		400 000

Profit and loss

Details	R	Details	R
Expenses	75 000	Trading	200 000
Capital	125 000		
	200 000		200 000

Profit and loss

Details	R	Details	R
Expenses	75 000	Trading	195 000
Capital	120 000		
	195 000		195 000

In situation (i), where there is no inventory shortage, the gross profit of R200 000 results in an actual GP % of 50% (R200 000/R400 000), which is equal to the expected GP % based on a mark-up on cost of 100%. In situation (ii), where there is a shortage of R5 000 (1 x R5 000), the actual GP % is 48.75% (R195 000/R400 000). The difference between the expected GP % of 50% and the actual GP % of 48,75 (R195 000/R400 000) is attributable to an inventory shortage. The amount of the shortage is R5 000 (R400 000 x 1,25%).

Note also that the profit for the period of R120 000 in situation (ii) is R5 000 lower than the profit for the period of R125 000 in situation (i), reflecting the impact of the shortage.

(b) Perpetual inventory system

(i) No inventory shortage

Inventory

Details	R	Details	R
Balance b/d	50 000	Cost of sales	200 000
Accounts payable	250 000		
		Balance c/d	100 000
	300 000		300 000

Cost of sales

Details	R	Details	R
Inventory	200 000	Trading	200 000
	200 000		200 000

Trading

Details	R	Details	R
Cost of sales	200 000	Sales	400 000
Profit and loss	200 000		
	400 000		400 000

(ii) Inventory shortage

Inventory

Details	R	Details	R
Balance b/d	50 000	Cost of sales	200 000
Accounts payable	250 000	Cost of sales	5 000
		Balance c/d	95 000
	300 000		300 000

Cost of sales

Details	R	Details	R
Inventory	200 000	Trading	205 000
Inventory	5 000		
	205 000		205 000

Trading

Details	R	Details	R
Cost of sales	205 000	Sales	400 000
Profit and loss	195 000		
	400 000		400 000

Profit and loss			
Details	**R**	**Details**	**R**
Expenses	75 000	Trading	200 000
Capital	125 000		
	200 000		200 000

Profit and loss			
Details	**R**	**Details**	**R**
Expenses	75 000	Trading	195 000
Capital	120 000		
	195 000		195 000

As you are aware, the cost of sales in a perpetual system is recorded each time a sale is made. In situation (i), the recorded cost of sales of R200 000 (40 x R5 000) results in a gross profit of R200 000 and an actual GP% of 50%, which is equal to the expected GP%. In situation (ii), the recorded cost of sales is again R200 000, representing 40 items sold at a cost of R5 000 each. However, the cost of sales needs to be increased, and the inventory decreased, to account for the inventory shortage. As with the periodic system, this results in an actual GP% of 48,75% compared to the expected GP% of 50%.

The profit for the period in situation (ii) is R5 000 less than the profit in situation (i), as was the case with the periodic system. Note that the entry to credit inventory is not required in the periodic system, as the closing inventory is brought into the system at its reduced value of R95 000.

12.4 Cost formulae

Several different methods for determining the cost of sales and the cost of inventories on hand are used in practice. Each method may lead to widely differing results being reported. These methods are:

- Specific identification
- FIFO (first in, first out)
- Weighted average cost

It must be stressed that all these formulae are ***cost flow assumptions***, used to allocate the cost of goods available for sale between the income statement and statement of financial position. They do not necessarily represent the actual physical movement of goods.

12.4.1 Specific identification

IAS 2 indicates that, where items of inventory are *dissimilar* and *not interchangeable*, inventories should be measured by specific identification of costs.[7] If practical, this is the best approach to adopt because no assumptions have to be made about the flow of costs in order to allocate either to cost of sales or closing inventory.

This method is only feasible when the inventory items are uniquely identifiable and of sufficient value to justify keeping such detailed records. For businesses such as a jewellery shop, a motor car dealer or an antique shop, the individual inventory items are normally specifically identifiable and of high enough value to maintain the necessary records.

Assume that a jewellery shop holds, among other items, 110 diamond rings at the beginning of the current year. Of the 110 rings, 30 rings were purchased two years ago at R2 000 each and a further 80 rings were acquired during the previous year at R5 500 each. During the current year, 40 rings were purchased at R10 000 each.

A total of 100 diamond rings were sold during the current year at R12 000 each. Applying the specific identification method, it is determined that, of the 100 rings sold, 26 were from the batch purchased two years previously, 50 were from those acquired during the previous year and 24 were of those purchased during the current year. We can then compute cost of sales and gross profit as follows:

Opening inventory	[(30 X R2 000 + (80 X R5 500)]	500 000
Purchases	(40 x R10 000)	400 000
Cost of goods available for sale		900 000
Closing inventory	[(4 x R2 000) + (30 x R5 500) + (16 x R10 000)]	(333 000)
Cost of sales	[(26 x R2 000) + (50 x R5 500) + (24 x R10 000)]	567 000
Revenue from sales	(100 x R12 000)	1 200 000
Gross profit		633 000

However, specific identification of costs is inappropriate when there are large numbers of inventory items which are *similar* or *interchangeable*. It is therefore necessary to apply a consistent policy to the allocation of costs, namely FIFO or weighted average cost.

12.4.2 FIFO

The FIFO method is based on the *cost flow assumption* that the first units acquired are the first units sold. Often this assumption is justified by normal business practice, because many businesses attempt to maintain an orderly flow of goods so that they do not have old merchandise on hand.

When using FIFO:

- cost of sales is represented by the cost of the ***earliest*** purchases
- closing inventory is represented by the cost of the ***latest*** purchases.

In times of rising prices, this does not achieve a matching of current costs with current revenue in the income statement. Outdated costs from the beginning of the period are matched against current revenue, resulting in an artificially high profit.

12.4.3 Weighted average

The weighted average method is based on the *cost flow assumption* of the weighted average of the cost of similar items at the beginning of the period, and the cost of similar items purchased during the period. We can calculate a weighted average cost per item as follows:

$$\text{Weighted average cost per item} = \frac{\text{Cost of inventory on hand at the beginning of the period + cost of inventory purchased during the period}}{\text{Total number of units available for sale}}$$

Diagram 12.5: Calculation of weighted average cost per item

In times of rising prices:

- cost of sales is reported at an amount above the FIFO amount.
- closing inventory is reported at an amount below the FIFO amount.

Example: Cost formulae

Bright Life's inventory records reveal the following information for the three-month period from July 20X5 to September 20X5:

	Date	Quantity	R
Opening inventory	01/07/X5	150	11
Purchases	15/07/X5	150	12
Sales	10/08/X5	200	20
Purchases	08/09/X5	150	13
Sales	20/09/X5	90	20

You are required to:

(a) compute the cost of sales and closing inventory, assuming that a periodic inventory system is used:
  (i) and inventory is valued on the FIFO basis
  (ii) and inventory is valued on the weighted average basis.

(b) compute the cost of sales and closing inventory, assuming that a perpetual inventory system is used:
  (i) and inventory is valued on the FIFO basis
  (ii) and inventory is valued on the weighted average basis.

Solution: Cost formulae

(a) Periodic	(i) FIFO			(ii) Weighted average		
	Qty	R	Total	Qty	R	Total
Opening inventory	150	11,00	1 650	150	11,00	1 650
Purchases	150	12,00	1 800	150	12,00	1 800
Purchases	150	13,00	1 950	150	13,00	1 950
Cost of goods available for sale	450		5 400	450		5 400
Closing inventory (1)	160		2 070	160		1 920
Cost of sales (2)	290		3 330	290		3 480
Working (1)	150	13,00	1 950	Average price		
	10	12,00	120	5 400/450 = 12,00		
	160		2 070	160	12,00	1 920
Working (2)	150	11,00	1 650	Average price		
	140	12,00	1 680	5 400/450 = 12,00		
	290		3 330	290	12,00	3 480

(b) Perpetual	(i) FIFO			(ii) Weighted average		
	Qty	R	Total	Qty	R	Total
01/07 Opening inventory	150	11,00	1 650	150	11,00	1 650
15/07 Purchases	150	12,00	1 800	150	12,00	1 800
15/07 Balance	300		3 450	300	11,50	3 450
10/08 Sales (1)	(200)		(2 250)	(200)	11,50	(2 300)
10/08 Balance (2)	100		1 200	100	11,50	1 150
08/09 Purchases	150	13,00	1 950	150	13,00	1 950
20/09 Sales (3)	(90)		(1 080)	(90)	12,40	(1 116)
Closing inventory (4)	160		2 070	160	12,40	1 984
Working (1)	150	11,00	1 650	3 450/300 = 11,50		
	50	12,00	600			
	200		2 250	200	11,50	2 300
Working (2)	100	12,00	1 200	100	11,50	1 150
Working (3)	90	12,00	1 080	100	11,50	1 150
				150	13,00	1 950
	90		1 080	250	12,40	3 100
Working (4)	10	12,00	120			
	150	13,00	1 950			
	160		2 070	160	12,40	1 984

12.5 Lower of cost and net realisable value

IAS 2 requires inventory to be measured at the ***lower*** of cost and net realisable value.[8]

Cost, as described earlier in this chapter, comprises all costs of purchase and other costs incurred in bringing the inventory to its present location and condition. It is then computed based on one of the cost formulae, namely specific identification, FIFO or weighted average.

Net realisable value is the estimated selling price in the ordinary course of business, less the estimated costs of completion and the estimated costs to make the sale.[9]

When estimates of net realisable value are made, they are based on the most reliable evidence available at the time as to the amount the inventories are expected to realise. The costs of completion include any additional costs (over and above the original acquisition costs) in getting the goods into a saleable condition. Costs to make the sale include any additional selling expenses over and above normal selling expenses.

	Estimated selling price in ordinary course of business
less	Costs of completion
less	Costs to make the sale
=	Net realisable value

Diagram 12.6: Computation of net realisable value

The cost of inventories may exceed the net realisable value if those inventories are damaged, if they have become wholly or partially obsolete, or if selling prices have declined. This situation may also arise if the estimated costs of completion or the estimated costs to be incurred to make the sale have increased.

If the net realisable value of the closing inventory is lower than cost, then an expense must be recognised and the cost of the inventory must be written down, representing the expected reduction in future economic benefits. Remember that inventory is an asset, and that an asset is defined as a resource controlled by the enterprise, as a result of past events and from which future economic benefits are expected to flow to the enterprise. The writing down of inventories below cost to net realisable value is consistent with the view that assets should not be carried in excess of amounts expected to be realised from their sale or use.

 **Pause and reflect...**

You have learnt that if the net realisable value of closing inventory is lower than cost, the inventory is written down and an expense is recognised. What would happen if the net realisable value of the closing inventory is higher than the cost?

Response

IAS 2 requires inventory to be valued at the lower of cost and net realisable value. Therefore, if the net realisable value of closing inventory is higher than cost, no adjustment is required. It would make no sense to write up inventory and recognise income as the inventory has not yet been realised.

12.5.1 Accounting for the write-down of inventory

When preparing the financial statements, management needs to assess the net realisable value of individual items of inventory or, if more appropriate, of groups of items. If the net realisable value exceeds cost, the closing entries are processed as usual, based on either the periodic or perpetual system. These entries, which are described in detail in Chapter 8, are summarised below for ease of reference.

Periodic	Perpetual
Transfer of opening inventory and purchases	
Dr Cost of sales	
Cr Inventory	
Dr Cost of sales	
Cr Purchases	
Closing inventory entered into accounting system	
Dr Inventory	
Cr Cost of sales	
Transfer of cost of sales	***Transfer of cost of sales***
Dr Trading	Dr Trading
Cr Cost of sales	Cr Cost of sales
Transfer of sales	***Transfer of sales***
Dr Sales	Dr Sales
Cr Trading	Cr Trading

Diagram 12.7: Summary of closing entries for trading activities

 IAS 2 requires the amount of any write-down of inventory to net realisable value to be recognised as a cost of sales expense in the period of the write-down.[10]

Periodic system

If the net realisable value is lower than the cost, the closing inventory is entered into the accounting system at the reduced value. A lower closing inventory will lead to a higher cost of sales and a lower gross profit and profit for the period. The reduction in the gross profit, and therefore the GP %, will need to be taken into account in the reconciliation of the expected GP % to the actual GP %.

Perpetual system

As the inventory account in the perpetual system is updated each time goods are purchased or sold, the balance on the account represents the cost of inventory on hand at the end of the period. No specific entry is required to introduce the closing inventory into the accounting system, as with the periodic system. An adjusting entry will be required to reduce the balance in the inventory account from cost to net realisable value and to create an expense for the write-down, representing that part of the cost that will not be recovered in the future. The entry therefore debits cost of sales, and credits the inventory account. The higher cost of sales will result in a lower gross profit and GP % and, as with the periodic system, will need to be taken into account in the reconciliation of the expected GP % to the actual GP %.

Summary of entries on write-down of inventory

	Periodic	**Perpetual**
Recording the write-down	Included in cost of sales because of reduced closing inventory	Dr Cost of sales Cr Inventory

Example: Lower of cost and net realisable value (NRV)

The following details relate to Bright Life for the 20X6 year:

	Quantity	**R per item**	**Total**
Opening inventory	1 000	20	20 000
Purchases	2 500	20	50 000
Cost of sales	1 500	20	30 000
Sales	1 500	50	75 000
Closing inventory	2 000	20	40 000
Operating expenses	–	–	20 000

You are required to:

show the relevant ledger accounts

(a) using a periodic inventory system, and assuming:

  (i) that the NRV of the closing inventory is R120 000

  (ii) that the NRV of the closing inventory is R30 000.

(b) using a perpetual inventory system, and assuming:
   (i) that the NRV of the closing inventory is R120 000
   (ii) that the NRV of the closing inventory is R30 000.

Solution: Lower of cost and NRV

(a) (i) Periodic inventory system (NRV R120 000)

Inventory

Details	R	Details	R
Balance b/d	20 000	Cost of sales	20 000
Cost of sales	40 000	Balance c/d	40 000
	60 000		60 000
Balance b/d	40 000		

Purchases

Details	R	Details	R
Bank/Accounts payable	50 000	Cost of sales	50 000
	50 000		50 000

Cost of sales

Details	R	Details	R
Opening inventory	20 000	Closing inventory	40 000
Purchases	50 000	Trading	30 000
	70 000		70 000

Trading

Details	R	Details	R
Cost of sales	30 000	Sales	75 000
Profit and loss	45 000		
	75 000		75 000

Operating expenses

Details	R	Details	R
Balance b/d	20 000	Profit and loss	20 000
	20 000		20 000

Profit and loss

Details	R	Details	R
Operating expenses	20 000	Trading	45 000
Capital	25 000		
	45 000		45 000

(a) (ii) Periodic inventory system (NRV R30 000)

Inventory

Details	R	Details	R
Balance b/d	20 000	Cost of sales	20 000
Cost of sales	30 000	Balance c/d	30 000
	50 000		50 000
Balance b/d	30 000		

Purchases

Details	R	Details	R
Bank/Accounts payable	50 000	Cost of sales	50 000
	50 000		50 000

Cost of sales

Details	R	Details	R
Opening inventory	20 000	Closing inventory	30 000
Purchases	50 000	Trading	40 000
	70 000		70 000

Trading

Details	R	Details	R
Cost of sales	40 000	Sales	75 000
Profit & loss	35 000		
	75 000		75 000

Operating expenses

Details	R	Details	R
Balance b/d	20 000	Profit & loss	20 000
	20 000		20 000

Profit and loss

Details	R	Details	R
Operating expenses	20 000	Trading	35 000
Capital	15 000		
	35 000		35 000

Part (a) of the question examines a periodic system.

In situation (i), where the NRV of the closing inventory is higher than the cost (R120 000 compared to R40 000), the closing entries relating to the trading activities are processed as normal and the NRV of R120 000 is ignored. The gross profit is R45 000 and the profit for the period is R25 000. The actual GP % is 60% (R45 000/R75 000), which is equal to the expected GP % of 60%.

In situation (ii), the NRV of the closing inventory is lower than the cost (R30 000 compared to R40 000). The closing inventory is entered into the accounting records at the lower of cost and NRV, in this case at R30 000. This causes the cost of sales to increase to R40 000, the gross profit to decrease to R35 000, and the profit for the period to decrease to R15 000. The actual GP % is 46,67% (R35 000/ R75 000), which is less than the expected GP % of 60% As you are aware, any difference between the expected GP % and the actual GP % needs to be investigated and reconciled. In this situation, the difference can be entirely attributed to the inventory write-down of R10 000 (R75 000 x 13,33%), confirming that there are no unknown shortages.

In summary,

Expected GP %	60,00%
Actual GP %	46,67%
Difference	13,33%
Inventory write-down (R10 000/R75 000)	13,33%
Unknown shortage	–
	13,33%

(b) (i) Perpetual inventory system (NRV R120 000)

Inventory				Trading			
Description	**R**	**Description**	**R**	**Description**	**R**	**Description**	**R**
Balance b/d Bank/Accounts payable	20 000 50 000	Cost of sales Balance c/d	30 000 40 000	Cost of sales Profit and loss	30 000 45 000	Sales	75 000
	70 000		70 000		75 000		75 000
Balance b/d	40 000						

Cost of sales				Profit and loss			
Description	**R**	**Description**	**R**	**Description**	**R**	**Description**	**R**
Inventory	30 000	Trading	30 000	Operating expenses Capital	20 000 25 000	Trading	45 000
	30 000		30 000		45 000		45 000

(b) (ii) Perpetual inventory system (NRV R30 000)

Inventory				Trading			
Description	**R**	**Description**	**R**	**Description**	**R**	**Description**	**R**
Balance b/d Bank/Accounts payable	20 000 50 000	Cost of sales Cost of sales Balance c/d	30 000 10 000 30 000	Cost of sales Profit and loss	40 000 35 000	Sales	75 000
	70 000		70 000		75 000		75 000
Balance b/d	40 000						

Cost of sales				Profit and loss			
Description	**R**	**Description**	**R**	**Description**	**R**	**Description**	**R**
Inventory Inventory	30 000 10 000	Trading	40 000	Operating expenses Capital	20 000 15 000	Trading	35 000
	40 000		40 000		35 000		35 000

Part (b) of the question looks at a perpetual system.

As with the periodic system, in situation (i) where the NRV of the closing inventory is higher than the cost, the NRV of R120 000 is ignored. As you should expect, the actual GP% is 60%, which is equal to the expected GP% of 60%.

In situation (ii), where the NRV of the closing inventory is lower than the cost, an adjusting entry is required to increase the cost of sales and to decrease the inventory to account for the write-down. As with the periodic system, this causes the actual GP% to be less than the expected GP%. The reconciliation in this case is identical to part (a) (ii).

12.6 Inventory errors

In determining the effect of inventory errors on the financial statements, it is important to understand the relationship between closing inventory and cost of sales, and the ultimate impact on gross profit.

In a **periodic** system, cost of sales is computed by adding opening inventory and purchases and subtracting closing inventory. Any overstatement in closing inventory will result in an understatement of cost of sales and overstatement of gross profit. Conversely, an understatement in closing inventory will result in an overstatement of cost of sales and understatement of gross profit.

Turning to a **perpetual** system, the balance in the inventory account is made up of the opening balance and the purchases during the period, reduced by the cost of sales. Here, an understatement of cost of sales will lead to an overstatement of closing inventory. Similarly, an overstatement of cost of sales will result in an understatement of closing inventory.

Pause and reflect...

Using your understanding of how cost of sales is computed in a periodic system, show the effect of the following errors on the cost of sales and gross profit:

a) An overstatement of opening inventory
b) An overstatement of closing inventory

Response

	Correct	a) Overstatement of opening inventory by R1	b) Overstatement of closing inventory by R1
Opening inventory	10	11	10
+ Purchases	8	8	8
- Closing Inventory	(6)	(6)	(7)
= Cost of sales	12	13	11
Sales	15	15	15
Gross Profit	3	2	4

You can see that in (a), the cost of sales is overstated by R1 and the gross profit is understated by R1. In (b), the cost of sales is understated by R1 and the gross profit is overstated by R1.

12.7 Estimating inventory

A business enterprise that does not use the perpetual system may in certain circumstances need to estimate the value of closing inventory. It is important to understand the circumstances leading to the estimation of inventory. The valuation of closing inventory may need to be estimated in relation to the following two different points in time:

- the closing inventory *at some point in time* in the *current* period where, for example, a fire destroys the inventory or a burglary results in the theft of inventory and inventory needs to be estimated so that an insurance claim can be submitted.
- the closing inventory *at the end* of a *previous* period, where inventory was not counted at the end of that period and financial statements need to be prepared.

The principle is the same in both cases. The value of inventory is estimated by applying the historical, or estimated, relationship between cost, gross profit and selling price to the sales for the current period. This is done to estimate the cost of sales for the current period.

If it is the closing inventory at some point in the current period that needs to be estimated (because of an insurance claim, for example), then the *estimated cost of sales* is compared to the cost of goods available for sale to determine the inventory destroyed. If any inventory was salvaged, this must obviously be taken into account in calculating the insurance claim.

If, on the other hand, the inventory was not counted at the end of the previous period, the closing inventory at a chosen date in the current period is counted. The cost of sales and cost of goods available for sale from the beginning of the period to the current date can then be computed. The closing inventory at the end of the previous period is then calculated as the opening inventory of the current period.

Typical periodic inventory computation of cost of sales and gross profit	Insurance claim	Inventory not counted at the end of previous period
Opening inventory	Opening inventory	***Opening inventory (?)***
+ Purchases	+ Purchases	-+ Purchases
= Cost of goods available for sale	= Cost of goods available for sale	= Cost of goods available for sale
– Closing inventory	– Inventory salvaged	– Closing inventory
	– ***Inventory destroyed (?)***	
= Cost of sales	= Cost of sales	= Cost of sales
Revenue from sales	Revenue from sales	Revenue from sales
= Gross profit	= Gross profit	= Gross profit

Diagram 12.8: Estimating inventory

Example: Estimating closing inventory

Hadit Traders' premises were destroyed by fire towards the end of the year. The following information was extracted from salvaged records:

	R
Opening inventory	30 000
Purchases (to date of fire)	60 000
Revenue from sales (to date of fire)	100 000

Inventory costing R5 000 was saved. Hadit Traders has constantly achieved a 25% gross profit percentage in recent years.

You are required to:

estimate the cost of inventory destroyed in the fire.

Solution: Estimating closing inventory

		R
Opening inventory	(Known)	30 000
add Purchases	(Known)	60 000
Cost of goods available for sale		90 000
less Inventory salvaged	(Known)	(5 000)
less Inventory destroyed	?	***(10 000)***
Cost of sales	(R100 000 x 75/100)	75 000
Revenue from sales	(Known)	100 000
Gross profit		25 000

To calculate the amount of the insurance claim, the inventory on hand at the date of the fire needs to be estimated. It is known that a GP % of 25% has been achieved in recent years. This translates into a relationship between cost, GP and selling price as follows:

Cost	75%
GP	25%
SP	100%

As the actual GP % is 25%, the selling price is set at 100%, resulting in the cost being 75%.

Given that sales to the date of the fire are R100 000, the cost of sales for the period is calculated at R75 000 (R100 000 x 75/100). The cost of goods available for sale is determined as R90 000, which means that the inventory on hand at the date of the fire was R15 000. Since inventory costing R10 000 was salvaged, the cost of the inventory destroyed is estimated at R5 000.

12.8 Exam example

R Rocky owns a store known as Keppel Island Traders. Keppel Island Traders uses a consistent mark-up of 50% on the cost price of goods to calculate their selling price.

On 31 May 20X9 the shop was destroyed by fire. The salvaged inventory was sold at cost price for R1 000.

From a survey of Keppel Island Traders' records and other information supplied to you, you ascertain the following:

Balances at 31 May 20X9	**R**
Accounts receivable control	21 800
Non-current assets at carrying amount	33 000
Purchases	45 700
Railage inwards	3 900
Railage outwards	2 300
Expenses	8 500
Sales	78 750
Inventory at 1 January 20X9	18 250

(1) During March 20X9, a shop assistant misappropriated R750 from cash sale takings. He had failed to complete a cash sale docket at the time of sale. This fraud was discovered when the customer returned the goods to have a minor fault repaired. At the same time, the assistant had stolen goods costing R1 200. This amount includes the railage in respect of the goods stolen. To disguise the inventory shortage, the assistant had invoiced these goods to a fictitious customer for R1 800. No adjustments have been made to correct the above, and nothing can be recovered in respect of any of these items.

(2) During two weeks in April 20X9, a 'cut-price sale' was held. The normal selling price of goods was reduced by 10%. Sales during this period amounted to R8 100.

(3) Goods costing R300 were donated to a local welfare organisation on 16 April 20X9. No entry was made in respect of this transaction.

(4) On 31 May 20X9, goods invoiced by a supplier for R4 500, which was included in purchases, were at the local railway station awaiting collection. Railage of R200 on these goods was not recorded in Keppel Island Traders' books.

(5) On 31 May 20X9, goods were sold and invoiced to a customer for R3 000. The customer arranged for these goods to be collected on 3 June 20X9.

You are required to:

(a) prepare the journal entries to correct the falsification described in 1 above

(b) prepare a statement showing the cost price of *all* the goods destroyed by the fire.

Solution: Exam example

(a)

Date	Description	Dr	Cr
31/05/X4	Cash shortage expense	750	
	Sales		750
	Shortage iro cash stolen		
	Sales	1 800	
	Accounts receivable		1 800
	Reversal of fictitious invoice		

(b)

Opening inventory			18 250
+ Purchases		45 700	
+ Railage inwards	(3 900 + 200)	4 100	49 800
– Donation		(300)	
– Goods in transit	(4 500 + 200)	(4 700)	(5 000)
= Cost of goods available for sale			63 050
Theoretical closing inventory	(63 050 – 52 400)		10 650
Inventory salvaged			(1 000)
Inventory shortage			(1 200)
Inventory destroyed			***(8 450)***
Cost of sales – normal SP	[(70 650^{W1} – 1 800 + 750) x 100/150^{W2}]	46 400	
– reduced SP	(8 100^{W1} x 100/135^{W2})	6 000	52 400

		R
Cost of inventory destroyed		8 450
Customer's goods on premises	(3 000 x 100/150)	2 000
Total cost of all goods destroyed		10 450

Working 1: Allocation of sales		**Working 2: Calculation of relationship between cost, GP and selling price**	
Total sales	78 750	Cost	100
		Mark-up	50
Sales during 'normal' period	70 650	Normal selling price	150
		Mark-down	(15)
Sales during 'mark-down' period	8 100	Reduced selling price	135

Summary of concepts and applications

1. Inventories are defined as assets held for sale in the ordinary course of business or held in the form of materials or supplies to be consumed within the business operation. The recognition and measurement of inventory affects both the income statement and the statement of financial position.
2. In computing the relationship between cost, gross profit and selling price, it is important to distinguish between the mark-up on cost and the gross profit percentage.
3. The cost of inventory comprises all costs of purchase and other costs incurred in bringing the inventory to its present location and condition. Goods

in transit are goods which have not physically arrived at the premises of the reporting entity. The accounting treatment applicable to goods in transit depends on whether ownership of the goods has passed to the buyer and whether the buyer has processed the purchase of the goods through the accounting system. Goods on consignment are goods delivered by the entity owning these goods to another entity who will sell these goods on behalf of the owner. Management's ability to exercise the necessary levels of control over the detection and prevention of inventory shortages will be influenced by the use of the perpetual inventory system (the cost of the inventory counted is compared to the balance in the inventory account) or the periodic inventory system (allowing for the calculation of a gross profit percentage).

4. Three methods for determining the cost of sales and the cost of inventories on hand are used, namely specific identification, FIFO and weighted average cost.
5. IAS 2 requires inventory to be measured at the lower of cost and net realisable value. If the net realisable value of closing inventory is lower than cost, then an expense must be recognised and the cost of the inventory must be written down.
6. In determining the effect of inventory errors on the financial statements, the relationship between closing inventory and cost of sales as well as the ultimate impact on gross profit must be understood.
7. A business operating on the periodic inventory system may need to estimate the value of closing inventory in relation to two different points in time, namely at some point in the current period or at the end of a previous period.

Notes

1. Framework for the Preparation and Presentation of Financial Statements, *International Accounting Standards Board*, (2001), paragraph 49(a).
2. IAS2, Inventories, *International Accounting Standards Board*, (2004), paragraph 6.
3. IAS 2, paragraph 9.
4. IAS 2, paragraph 10.
5. IAS 2, paragraph 11.
6. IAS 2, paragraph 15.
7. IAS 2, paragraph 23.
8. IAS 2, paragraph 9.
9. IAS 2, paragraph 6.
10. IAS 2, paragraph 34, read with paragraph 38.

13 Accounts Receivable and Bad Debts

'Observe that the accounts always balance – and thus be made to prove anything; if you throw 100 pounds into the sea, the sea becomes your debtor for that amount, it would appear in the balance sheet accordingly, and you appear as neither richer nor poorer for that transaction.'
(Cayley, 1894)

Outcomes

- Describe accounts receivable.
- Explain and record a bad debts expense and an allowance for doubtful debts.
- Record the recovery of debts previously written off.

Chapter outline

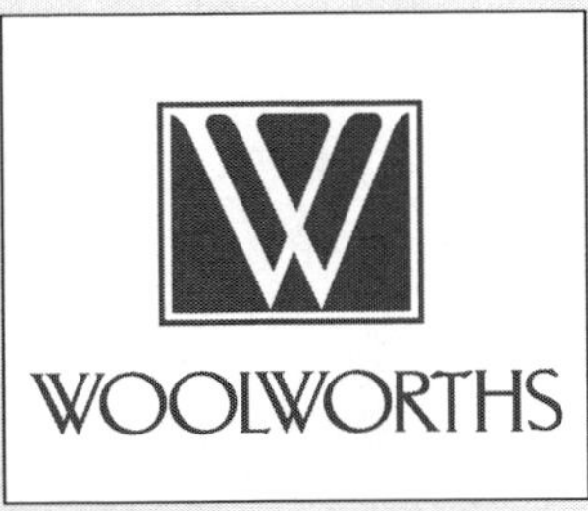

Woolworths Holding Limited
Notes to the financial statements for the year ended 30 June 2007

	(R Millions)
Receivables	
Woolworths card debtors	3 742
Provision for doubtful debts	(182)
Credit card receivables	978
Provision for doubtful debts	(73)
Loans to customers	1 129
Allowance for doubtful debts	(58)
Closing balance	5 536

Store cards are a favourite with retailers and Woolworths is no different. It allows them to increase their sales by selling on credit to their customers. However, not all those customers will be able to repay those accounts, and the company needs to create an allowance for doubtful debts.

13.1 Accounts receivable

The sale of goods and services on credit forms an integral part of economic activity and many business entities have a large number of customers who buy on credit. When goods are sold on credit, the earning of revenue and the receipt of cash will not correspond. The accrual concept requires the revenue to be recognised in the period when the goods are sold and not when the cash is received. You learnt in earlier chapters how to account for the sale of goods on credit and the subsequent receipt of cash.

You also learnt in Chapter 9, The Analysis Journals, how to maintain an accounts receivable subsidiary ledger along with the accounts receivable control account in the general ledger. Remember that the equality of the accounting equation is maintained in the general ledger. The balances on the accounts receivable subsidiary ledger are not included on the trial balance, as the subsidiary ledger serves only as a supplementary record of detailed information concerning each customer.

The accounts receivable are an asset. They represent a resource controlled by the enterprise (the right to collect an amount from a customer), from a past event (the credit sale), from which future economic benefits are expected to flow (the receipt of cash from the customers).

 **Pause and reflect...**

On 25 January 20X5 Smart Concepts sold computers to the value of R187 500 to a customer. An amount of R125 000 was due by 15 March and the balance by 15 April. How can the asset definition be applied to determine the value of accounts receivable recognised by Smart Concepts at 31 March 20X5?

Response

At 31 March, the value of accounts receivable was R62 500. This amount represents a resource controlled by Smart Concepts as the business has the right to receive the amount outstanding, it results from a past event being the sale of the computers on 25 January and it will result in the inflow of economic benefits when the entity receives the cash of R62 500 from the customer.

The accounts receivable are also regarded as a financial instrument, and more specifically, a financial asset.

The accounting standard on the recognition and measurement of financial instruments, IAS 39, defines a financial instrument as any contract that gives rise to both a financial asset of one enterprise and a financial liability of another enterprise.[1] The definition of a financial asset includes a contractual right to receive cash or another financial asset from another enterprise.[2]

Accounts receivable are therefore classified as a financial asset because of the contractual right arising from the sale agreement to collect cash from the customers.

It is important to note here that prepaid expenses are not a financial asset, as the future benefit is the right to receive services and not the right to receive cash or another financial asset.

13.2 Bad debts

When a business entity sells goods on credit, it takes the risk that some customers will not pay the amounts owing by them. At the end of the accounting period, an assessment must be made of the future economic benefits that will flow to the enterprise from the accounts receivable, in other words, the amount of cash that will be received from customers. The accounting implications of this are discussed in the following sections.

13.2.1 Creating an allowance for doubtful debts

Accounts receivable are recognised as an asset if it is probable that the future economic benefits will flow to the entity (that is, cash will be collected) and the value of the accounts receivable can be measured reliably.

If some degree of non-payment is considered probable, an estimate must be made at the end of the period of the amount which is unlikely to be received from customers. You will recall from Chapter 6, when discussing the recognition of assets, that the use of estimates is an essential aspect of the preparation of financial statements and does not undermine their reliability. This estimate is known as the ***allowance for doubtful debts***.

An estimate of the future cash flows expected from the accounts receivable is necessary in order to determine the amount of the allowance for doubtful debts. The estimate of future cash flows is determined using statistical provisioning models based on historical experience modified for recent changes in economic circumstances.

A useful tool in examining payment history is a debtors' age analysis. This analysis is used by entities to highlight the days for which the debts of each customer are outstanding. In addition, a debtors' age analysis assists entities in making decisions on whether to continue supplying existing customers. A debtors' age analysis for Bright Life at 31 March 20X6 is presented below.

BRIGHT LIFE
DEBTORS' AGE ANALYSIS AT 31 MARCH 20X6

Customer name	Total	Current	30-60 days	60-90 days	More than 90 days
	R	R	R	R	R
Mr W	4 000	0	2 750	0	1 250
Ms X	2 000	1 200	800	0	0
Ms Y	1 650	700	450	500	0
Mr Z	5 000	5 000	0	0	0
	12 650	6 900	4 000	500	1 250

 **Pause and reflect...**

If you are told that the results of Bright Life's statistical provisioning model indicate that amounts outstanding for more than 90 days are unlikely to be recovered, what is the amount of the allowance to be recognised?

Response

In estimating the future cash flows expected from its accounts receivable, Bright Life could consider the results of the statistical provisioning models. On this basis, an allowance of R1 250 is recognised, relating to amounts outstanding for more than 90 days.

Accounting for the allowance for doubtful debts is not affected by the manner in which the amount was estimated.

Accounts receivable is not credited because it is not yet certain which customers will not pay their accounts, nor are the amounts which will not be paid known with certainty. The amount of the estimate is therefore credited to an allowance.

The allowance is regarded as an adjustment to the carrying amount of the asset, accounts receivable. Remember that an asset is a resource controlled by the entity, as a result of past events and from which future economic benefits are expected to flow to the enterprise. In the case of accounts receivable, the resource controlled by the entity is the right to collect the amount owing from the customer, the past event is the sale of the goods or the provision of services on credit and the future economic benefits is the cash to be received from the customers. If the future economic benefits expected to be received by the enterprise are less than the balance on accounts receivable because some customers may not settle their accounts, the carrying amount of the asset must be reduced to reflect this.

Example: Creating an allowance for doubtful debts

The balance in the accounts receivable control account of Bright Life totalled R12 500 at 31/03/X6, the end of its first financial year. The cash flow from accounts receivable expected in the future amounts to R11 250.

Solution: Creating an allowance for doubtful debts

GENERAL JOURNAL OF BRIGHT LIFE

Date	Description	Fol	Dr	Cr
31/03/X6	Bad debts expense		1 250	
	Allowance for doubful debts			1 250
	Allowance for doubtful debts created			

The expected future cash flows amount to only R11 250, requiring the carrying amount of the accounts receivable to be reduced by R1 250. The debit to bad debts expense causes the expense to appear on the income statement of the year when the sales were made. The account credited, the allowance for doubtful debts, is known as a contra account and is used because at the time the allowance is made, it is not known which customers will not pay. Therefore, it is not possible to credit the accounts of specific customers in the accounts receivable subsidiary ledger, and because of this, the accounts receivable control account also cannot be credited. Instead, the credit is placed to the allowance for doubtful debts.

An extract from the statement of financial position at the end of the period is shown below. It shows that although R12 500 is legally owed to Bright Life at the end of the period, the future economic benefits likely to be received amount to R11 250. You will recall from Chapter 2 that offsetting of items in the statement of comprehensive income and statement of financial position is not permitted. The measurement of the asset, accounts receivable, net of the allowance for doubtful debts, is not regarded as offsetting.

BRIGHT LIFE
(EXTRACT FROM) STATEMENT OF FINANCIAL POSITION AT 31/03/X6

		R
Current assets		
Accounts receivable	12 500	
Allowance for doubtful debts	(1 250)	11 250

13.2.2 Writing off bad debts

If a customer defaults on an amount owing, this will result in a decrease in the future economic benefits that will flow to the enterprise. The asset, accounts receivable, must be reduced to reflect this decrease and a corresponding ***bad debts*** expense is recognised. The accounting entry is to debit the bad debts expense and credit the accounts receivable control account in the general ledger as well as the specific customer's account in the accounts receivable subsidiary ledger. This is because the accounts of specific customers have now been identified as uncollectable.

 **Pause and reflect...**

Looking at Bright Life's debtors age analysis, if you are told that Mr Z's business has been liquidated and that the amount outstanding of R5 000 will not be recovered, what is the appropriate accounting treatment?

Response

Accounts receivable is reduced by R5 000 to reflect the decrease in the future economic benefits that will flow to Bright Life from Mr Z and a corresponding bad debts expense of R5 000 is recognised. In addition, Mr Z's account in the accounts receivable subsidiary ledger is reduced by R5 000.

The decision to write off the balance owing by a customer as a bad debt is usually only taken after every possible means of collection has been attempted. It is likely that this will not happen in the same period as the original sale was made. However, the creation of the allowance for doubtful debts, with a corresponding increase in the bad debts expense, is an estimation of the expense incurred for the period in accordance with the accrual basis of accounting. As discussed previously, the use of reasonable estimates is an essential part of the preparation of financial statements and does not undermine their reliability. Before looking at an example, we need to discuss the principles relating to an increase or decrease in the allowance for doubtful debts.

13.2.3 Adjusting the allowance for doubtful debts

At the end of each period a current estimate needs to be made regarding the allowance required for doubtful debts. The factors taken into account are the same as those considered when creating the allowance – that is, estimating future cash flows.

If an increase in the allowance is required, the allowance for doubtful debts account is credited, whereas to decrease the allowance, the allowance for doubtful debts account is debited. In both cases the other account affected is the bad debts expense account. This principle is also addressed in the following example.

Example: Writing off bad debts and adjusting the allowance for doubtful debts

An extract of the trial balance of Bright Life at 31/03/X7, its next financial year end, is presented below.

BRIGHT LIFE
(EXTRACT FROM) TRIAL BALANCE AT 31/03/X7

	Dr	Cr
Bad debts expense	350	
Accounts receivable	15 500	
Allowance for doubtful debts (01/04/X6)		1 250

Additional information

- The bad debts expense of R350 arose from the write-off of the account of a customer who purchased the goods in December 20X5.
- An amount owing by Ms Y of R500 is considered to be irrecoverable.
- The cash flow from accounts receivable expected in the future amounts to R13 550.

You are required to:

(a) complete the necessary journal entries
(b) post to the relevant ledger accounts
(c) show how the bad debts expense will be presented in the income statement and how the accounts receivable will be presented in the statement of financial position.

Solution: Writing off bad debts and adjusting the allowance for doubtful debts

(a) GENERAL JOURNAL OF BRIGHT LIFE

Date	Description	Fol	Dr	Cr
31/03/X7	Bad debts expense		500	
	Accounts receivable control			500
	Ms Y			500
	Ms Y's account written off as irrecoverable			
31/03/X7	Bad debts expense		200	
	Allowance for doubtful debts			200
	Increase in allowance for doubtful debts			

The balance on the bad debts expense account of R350 at 31/03/X7 represents the amount expensed in respect of bad debts for the period from 01/04/X6 to 31/03/X7. Note that the expense is recognised in the year ending 31/03/X7 even though the income from the sale was recognised in the year ending 31/03/X6. This is an inevitable consequence of the accounting estimation process, and, as mentioned previously, does not undermine reliability. Remember that the accrual basis of accounting is complied with by the creation or adjustment to the allowance for doubtful debts each year.

The computation to adjust the allowance for doubtful debts is computed after taking into account any additional bad debts at the end of the period, such as Ms Y's account. The computation of the adjustment is as follows:

Balance on accounts receivable (15 500 - 500)	15 000
Expected future cash flow	13 550
Allowance required at end of period	1 450
Balance in the allowance for doubtful debts account	(1 250)
Increase in the allowance	200

(b) GENERAL LEDGER OF BRIGHT LIFE

Accounts receivable control

Details	R	Details	R
Balance b/d	15 500	Bad debts expense	500
		Balance c/d	15 000
	15 500		15 500
Balance b/d	15 000		

Allowance for doubful debts

Details	R	Details	R
		Balance b/d	1 250
Balance c/d	1 450	Bad debts expense	200
	1 450		1 450
		Balance b/d	1 450

Bad debts expense

Details	R	Details	R
Balance b/d	350	Profit and loss	1 050
Accounts receivable	500		
Allowance for doubtful debts	200		
	1 050		1 050

(c) BRIGHT LIFE
(EXTRACT FROM) INCOME STATEMENT
FOR THE YEAR ENDED 31/03/X7

	R
Operating expenses	
Bad debts (350 + 500 + 200)	1 050

BRIGHT LIFE
(EXTRACT FROM) STATEMENT OF FINANCIAL POSITION
AT 31/03/X7

		R
Current assets		
Accounts receivable	15 000	
Allowance for doubtful debts	(1 450)	13 550

13.3 Bad debts recovered

When a customer's account is written off, that person's credit rating is jeopardised. Subsequently, and often long after the account has been written off, the defaulting customer may choose to pay all or part of the amount that was owing. This helps to restore the credit rating.

Example: Bad debts recovered

During the next financial year, Ms Y's position changed and at the end of October 20X7 she advised Bright Life that she could afford to pay R400 of the R500 originally owed by her.

You are required to:

record the recovery of the bad debt in the general journal.

GENERAL JOURNAL OF BRIGHT LIFE

Date	Description	Fol	Dr	Cr
31/10/X7	Cash		400	
	Bad debts recovered			400
	Amount recovered from Ms Y			

The cash received from the customer is recorded as a debit to cash and a credit to an income statement account, bad debts recovered.

The bad debts recovered appears as income on the statement of comprehensive income. It should not be set off against the bad debts expense as this would distort the amount charged as a write-off during the current period.

Note that, financial reporting requires many ***estimates***, and the accounting for bad debts is an estimation process.

13.4 Exam example

Justin Thyme, trading as 'The Clock Shop', reports the following statement of financial position for the years ending 31 December 20X6 and 31 December 20X7:

	31/12/X7 **R**	**31/12/X6** **R**
ASSETS		
Non-current assets		
Furniture and fittings	52 000	50 000
Cost	66 000	60 000
Accumulated depreciation	(14 000)	(10 000)
Current assets	74 000	59 200
Inventory	32 000	30 000
Accounts receivable	30 000	19 200
Bank	12 000	10 000
	126 000	109 200
EQUITY AND LIABILITIES		
Capital and reserves	104 000	94 200
Current liabilities		
Accounts payable	22 000	15 000
	126 000	109 200

The following information is available:

- Cash collected from customers during the year ended 31/12/X7, R145 000. All sales are on credit.
- Accounts receivable is reported net of the allowance for doubtful debts in the statement of financial position:
  - The allowance for doubtful debts amounts to R4 800 at 31/12/X6 and to R7 500 at 31/12/X7.
  - Bad debts of R1 500 were written off accounts receivable during the year.
  - Cash payments to suppliers of goods for resale, R95 000.

- Included in accounts payable are the following amounts owing to suppliers for purchase of goods for resale:
  - at 31/12/X6, R12 000
  - at 31/12/X7, R20 000.
- Purchases of furniture and fittings (in cash), R6 000.
- Cash distributions to owner, R5 000.

You are required to:

compute for the year ended 31 December 20X7:
(a) sales revenue
(b) cost of sales
(c) depreciation expense
(d) profit for the period.

Solution: Exam example

(a) **Accounts receivable**

Date	Details	R	Date	Details	R
20X7			20X7		
Jan 1	Balance b/d	24 000		Cash (collections)	145 000
				Bad debts expense (write-off)	1 500
	Sales	***160 000***	Dec 31	Balance c/d	37 500
		184 000			184 000
20X8					
Jan 1	Balance b/d	37 500			

Allowance for doubtful debts (not required as part of answer)

Date	Details	R	Date	Details	R
20X7			20X7		
Dec 31	Balance c/d	7 500	Jan 1	Balance	4 800
				Bad debts expense (increase in allowance)	2 700
		7 500			7 500
			20X8		
			Jan 1	Balance b/d	7 500

(b) Need to first calculate the purchases for the year.

Accounts payable

Date	Details	R	Date	Details	R
20X7			20X7		
Dec 31	Cash (payment)	95 000	Jan 1	Balance b/d	12 000
				Purchases	***103 000***
	Balance c/d	20 000			
		115 000			115 000
			20X8		
			Jan 1	Balance b/d	20 000

Then, opening inventory + purchases – closing inventory = cost of sales

R30 000 + R103 000 – R32 000 = R101 000

(c) Ending accumulated depreciation	14 000
Beginning accumulated depreciation	(10 000)
= depreciation expense	R4 000

(d) Closing owner's equity	104 000
Opening owner's equity	(94 200)
	9 800
+ Distributions	5 000
= Profit for the period	R14 800

Summary of concepts and applications

1. The asset, accounts receivable, arises as a result of the sale of goods or the provision of services on credit. Accounts receivable satisfy the definition of an asset (the right to collect an amount from a customer, due to the credit sale, resulting in the receipt of cash from the customers) and, in addition, are classified as financial assets (the contractual right arising from the sale agreement to collect cash from customers).

2. At the end of the accounting period, an assessment must be made of the future economic benefits that will flow to the enterprise from the accounts receivable because some customers may not pay the amounts owed by them. If some degree of non-payment is considered probable, an estimate – the allowance for doubtful debts – must be made at the end of the period of the amount which is unlikely to be received. When a customer defaults on an amount owing, the asset, accounts receivable, is reduced to reflect this decrease and a corresponding bad debts expense is recognised. At the end of each period, a current estimate needs to be made regarding the allowance required for doubtful debts. If an increase in the allowance is required, the allowance for doubtful debts account is credited, whereas

to decrease the allowance, the allowance for doubtful debts account is debited. In both cases, the other account affected is the bad debts expense account.

3. After an entity has written off a customer's account, the defaulting customer may choose to pay all or part of the amount that was owing.

Notes

1. IAS 39, Financial Instruments: Recognition and Measurement, *International Accounting Standards Board* (2004), paragraph .09.
2. IAS 39, paragraph .09.

14 Cash and Bank

'[Cash] hath directly neither profit nor loss upon it; yet ... it is a most important account, and in some sorts of business possesseth the whole traffic; as bankers for instance, who daily fill whole pages with cash in and out.'
(North, 1714)

Outcomes

- Describe the components of cash, and list the relevant internal controls.
- Distinguish between the accounting records of the reporting entity and the bank.
- Prepare a bank reconciliation.

Chapter outline

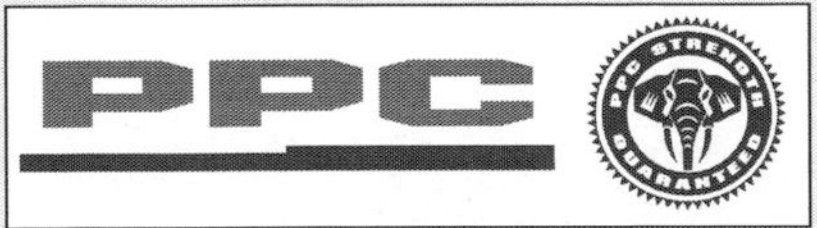

Pretoria Portland Cement Company Limited
Notes to the financial statements for the year ended 30 September 2007

	(R millions)
Cash and cash equivalents	
Cash on hand and on deposit	1 301
Cash and cash equivalents:	
South African Rand	1 242
Foreign currency	59
	1 301

There are restrictions on the ability to utilise R31 million relating to the PPC Environmental Trust.

Cement is the cornerstone of construction, which makes PPC vital in the development of Southern Africa. As a result of PPC's positioning within the market and the rapid economic growth occurring in many developing nations, PPC has created a large cash holding through its exposure to such circumstances.

14.1 Cash and its internal control

The asset, cash, includes currency and coins, amounts on deposit in banking accounts and deposits in savings accounts. To prevent misappropriation of its cash resources, a business needs to ensure that an adequate internal control system is installed. To maintain control over cash:

- custody must be separated from recordkeeping for cash
- all cash receipts should be deposited intact into the bank on a daily basis
- all payments should be made by cheque (except for minor payments)
- minor payments should be made from a petty cash float, which is maintained on an imprest system
- a bank reconciliation statement needs to be prepared to prove the accuracy of the records of both the reporting entity and the bank.

14.2 The records of the reporting entity and of the bank

When working with cash and bank transactions, it is important to have an understanding of the relationship between the entries in the reporting entity's records and those in the bank's records.

In the records of the reporting entity, *increases* in the bank balance brought about by deposits of cash into the bank are recorded with a *debit* to the bank account. This, as you are aware, is because the balance in the bank is an asset and assets increase with debit entries. Conversely, *decreases* in the bank balance caused by cheques written out are recorded with a *credit* to the bank account, as assets decrease with credit entries.

From the bank's perspective, *deposits* of cash into the bank by the reporting entity are recorded with a *credit* to the account of the entity. This is because the amount deposited represents a liability of the bank, as the bank has an obligation to provide the cash when it is requested by the entity. Therefore, *cheques* written out by the entity are recorded with a *debit* to the entity's account, as liabilities decrease with debit entries.

You will remember from Chapter 9, *The Analysis Journals*, that the **reporting entity** records cash and bank transactions in a cash receipts and cash payments journal reflecting:

- amounts deposited into the bank (entered from a deposit slip)
- cheques written out (entered from a cheque counterfoil)
- direct charges or deposits by the bank (entered from debit or credit notes received from the bank).

The **bank** records the deposits and cheque payments by referring to:

- ❑ the total on the deposit slips used by the entity to deposit cash into the bank.
- ❑ cheques presented for payment by the payees.

In addition, the bank itself may initiate:

- ❑ a credit to the entity's account (that is, an increase) with direct deposits and interest earned.
- ❑ a debit to the entity's account (that is, a decrease) with bank charges, interest charged, debit orders and other miscellaneous debits.

These principles are summarised in the diagram below.

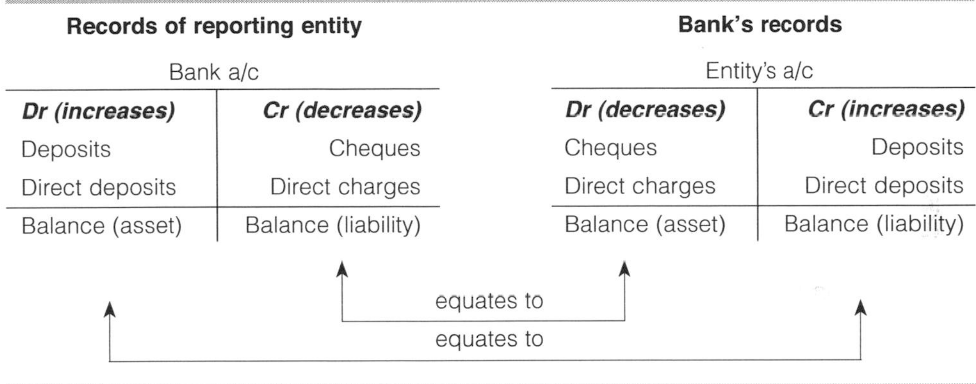

Diagram 14.1: Summary of entries in records of reporting entity and bank

A *favourable* balance in the reporting entity's bank account is an asset and thus has a debit balance. This corresponds to a credit balance on the entity's account in the bank's records, representing a liability from the bank's point of view. On the other hand, an *overdraft* in the reporting entity's bank account is a liability with a credit balance. This equates to a debit balance on the entity's account in the bank's records, an asset from the bank's perspective.

Pause and reflect...

A bank manager explains to an account holder that the payment of the latest cheque resulted in a debit to the customer's account, yet the account remains in credit. What does this mean?

Response

The customer's account in the bank's records represents a liability from the bank's point of view. Thus, when a customer issues a cheque and the funds are paid from his bank account, this represents a decrease, and therefore a debit, to the liability from the bank's point of view. The fact that the account remains in credit means that there are funds in the bank account.

14.3 The bank reconciliation

Bank reconciliations are necessary because of timing differences between the date that receipt and payment transactions are recorded in the entity's records, and the date that these transactions are responded to by the bank. Further differences arise because of bank-initiated entries and because of errors.

The differences between the bank balance in the entity's records and the balance per the bank statement can be identified as follows:

- Deposits made and recorded by the entity which have not yet been acknowledged by the bank (that is, not yet *credited* to the entity's account).
- Cheques made out and recorded by the entity which have not yet been presented to the bank (that is, not yet *debited* to the entity's account).
- Bank-initiated entries:
  - direct charges (*debits*) by the bank
  - direct deposits (*credits*) to the entity's account at the bank.

Errors:

- in the entity's records
- in the bank's records.

14.3.1 The purpose of the bank reconciliation

If you understand the objective or purpose of reconciling the bank account balance in the reporting entity's records with the balance according to the bank statement, you should have no difficulty in following the bank reconciliation procedure. The purpose of the reconciliation is:

- *not to* make the bank account balance equal the bank statement balance
- *to* explain and set out the reasons for the bank account balance and bank statement balance not being equal.[1]

14.3.2 Procedure to prepare a bank reconciliation

The first step towards preparing a bank reconciliation is to compare the entries in the cash journals with those on the bank statement. The second step is to update the bank account in the general ledger of the reporting entity by recording bank-initiated transactions (identified on the bank statement). The bank reconciliation statement is then prepared as the third step. This procedure is explained below and then illustrated with examples.

Compare the cash journals to the bank statement

- Compare each deposit in the bank column of the cash receipts journal to the deposits listed on the bank statement.
- Compare each cheque payment in the bank column of the cash payments journal to the cheques listed on the bank statement.
- Identify any bank-initiated charges or deposits on the bank statement.
- Identify any errors in the entity's records or on the bank statement.

Amend the bank account in the general ledger of the reporting entity

Before preparing the bank reconciliation statement, the entity's records must be updated. This is done by recording the bank-initiated charges or deposits identified in the first step, and by correcting errors made in the entity's records.

Bank-initiated charges include commission on cheques, fees, and interest on overdraft, as well as debits for unpaid cheques. Direct deposits arise when customers deposit their payments directly into the business bank account, often by way of electronic payment. Errors in the entity's records, for example, deposits or cheques incorrectly entered, must also be corrected.

These items are journalised in the cash receipts or payments journal if the closing entries have not been processed. If the closing entries have been prepared and posted to the general ledger, the most convenient and practical way to journalise these amendments is to use the general journal.

It is very important to understand and appreciate which of the differences are accounted for by amending the records of the reporting entity and which are listed on the bank reconciliation statement. The principle is straightforward. The bank-initiated transactions, *already recorded by the bank* and identified on the bank statement, are *journalised in the entity's records*, along with errors made by the entity. The cheques and deposits, *already entered in the cash journals*, are *listed as reconciling items* on the bank reconciliation statement, along with the bank's errors. This is summarised below.

Differences	Treatment
• Direct charges or deposits • Errors made by entity	• Adjusted in entity's records (before preparation of the bank reconciliation statement)
• Cheques not yet presented • Deposits not yet acknowledged • Errors made by bank	• Listed on the bank reconciliation statement

Diagram 14.2: Summary of differences

Pause and reflect...

Another person's cheque is erroneously processed by the bank as a debit to the entity's account.

a) Explain whether or not a journal entry is required in the accounting records of the entity to correct this error.

b) Explain whether or not the error is listed on the bank reconciliation, and if so, whether it is added to or subtracted from the balance per the general ledger bank account.

Response

a) No journal entry is required in the accounting records of the entity. As the error is made by the bank, it is the bank's records that are in error, not those of the entity. A journal entry in the records of the entity is not required to correct this.

b) If the bank reconciliation begins with the balance per the general ledger bank account, the error must be subtracted to reconcile to the incorrect, lower balance appearing on the bank statement.

Example: Mechanics of a bank reconciliation

The following are the relevant extracts of the cash journals, bank account and bank statement of Bright Life for March 20X6. The information recorded in the books of Bright Life has been recorded correctly.

Cash receipts journal — March 20X6 **CRJ 2**

Doc	Date	Account name	Fol	Sales	Accounts receivable control	Sundries		Deferred finance income	Analysis	Bank
DS 01	01/03	Capital	GL100			25 000			25 000	25 000
CS 01	05/03	Cash sales		5 600					5 600	5 600
REC 01	10/03	Barons	DL09		4 000			200	3 800	
CS 02	10/03	Cash sales		2 000					2 000	5 800
REC 02	29/03	Linus	DL74		6 000				6 000	
CSS 03	29/03	Cash sales		1 000					1 000	7 000
CSS 04	31/03	Cash sales		2 250					2 250	2 250
				10 850	10 000	25 000		250	–	45 650
				Cr GL: Sales	Cr GL: AR Control	Cr individual accounts		Dr GL: DFI		Dr GL: Bank

Cash payments journal — March 20X6 **CPJ 5**

Doc	Date	Details	Fol	Purchases	Salaries	Accounts payable control	Sundries	Deferred finance expense	Bank
0001	01/03	Rent	GL80				2 500		2 500
0002	02/03	Cash purchases		4 500					4 500
0003	09/03	Cash purchases		1 800					1 800
0004	18/03	Swift supplies	CL63			20 000		1 000	19 000
0005	25/03	Salaries			6 000				6 000
0006	29/03	Telephone	GL85				500		500
0007	31/03	Drawings	GL99				5 000		5 000
				6 300	6 000	20 000	8 000	1 000	39 300
				Dr GL: Purchases	Dr GL: Salaries	Dr GL: AP Control	Dr individual accounts	Cr GL: DFE	Cr GL: Bank

Dr **Bank (GL150)** **Cr**

Date	Details	Fol	R	Date	Details	Fol	R
20X6				20X6			
31/03	Deposits	CRJ 2	45 650	31/03	Payments	CPJ 5	39 300
				31/03	Balance c/d		6 350
			45 650				45 650
01/04	Balance b/d		6 350				

BB Limited	The Brall Bank of South Africa Reg. No. 56 00574/12 ✉ P O Box 15520 ☎ 402-6308 Sandton 2028

CURRENT ACCOUNT STATEMENT 31 March 20X6	Bright Life P O Box 8745 Woodmead 2054

Date	Doc #	Details	Dr	Cr	Balance
01/03	DEP	Deposit		25 000	25 000
06/03	DEP	Deposit		5 600	30 600
07/03	0001	Cheque	2 500		28 100
07/03	0002	Cheque	4 500		23 600
11/03	DEP	Deposit		5 800	29 400
13/03	0003	Cheque	1 800		27 600
20/03	0004	Cheque	19 000		8 600
25/03	EFT	Electronic transfer – Ometer		1 500	10 100
25/03	DO	Debit order – Insurance	600		9 500
26/03	0005	Cheque	6 000		3 500
30/03	DEP	Deposit		7 000	10 500
31/03	INT	Interest on credit balance		150	10 650
31/03	BC	Bank charges	200		10 450
31/03		***Month end balance***			***10 450***

You are required to:

(a) compare the cash journals of Bright Life for March 20X6 with the bank statement for March 20X6 and identify the differences between them

(b) prepare the journal entries to record the bank-initiated transactions in the accounting records of Bright Life, and then post the journal entries to the bank account in the general ledger

(c) complete the bank reconciliation statement at 31 March 20X6.

Suggested solution: Mechanics of a bank reconciliation

As mentioned above, the first step in preparing a bank reconciliation is to compare the entries in the cash journals with those on the bank statement. The relevant columns have been reproduced below for explanation purposes and ease of reference.

(a)

CRJ Bank		Bank Statement Cr		CPJ Bank		Bank statement Dr	
25 000	✔	25 000	✔		✗		
5 600	✔	5 600	✔	4 500	✗		
				1 800	✗	2 000	✗
5 800	✔			19 000	✗	4 500	✗
		5 800	✔	6 000	✗		
7 000	✔			500	*o/s chq*	1 800	✗
2 250	*o/s dep*			5 000	*o/s chq*	19 000	✗
45 650		1 500	*Direct credit*	39 300			
Debit GL 150				*Credit GL 150*		600	*Direct debit*
						6 000	✗
		7 000	✔				
		150	*Direct credit*				
						200	*Direct debit*

A ✔ symbol is used here to identify common entries in the cash receipts journal and the credit column on the bank statement. The amount of R2 250 appearing in the cash receipts journal and not on the bank statement is noted as an *outstanding deposit.* Amounts of R1 500 and R150 appearing on the bank statement and not in the cash receipts journal are noted as *direct credits.*

A ✗ symbol is used to compare the cash payments journal with the debit column on the bank statement. The amounts of R500 and R5 000 appearing in the cash payments journal and not on the bank statement are noted as *outstanding cheques.* Amounts of R600 and R200 appearing on the bank statement and not in the cash payments journal are noted as *direct debits.*

To ensure that all the differences have been identified, the following analysis can be done before the journal entries are processed in the entity's records and before the bank reconciliation statement is prepared.

Date	Description	Entity's records	Bank's records
31/03/X6	Balance	6 350	10 450
25/03/X6	Electronic transfer – Ometer	1 500	
25/03/X6	Debit order – insurance	(600)	
31/03/X6	Interest income	150	
31/03/X6	Bank charges	(200)	
31/03/X6	Outstanding deposit		2 250
31/03/X6	Outstanding cheques		
	– 0006		(500)
	– 0007		(5 000)
	Reconciled balance	7 200	7 200

The second step is to enter the direct debits and credits identified in the first step into the journal of Bright Life and to post the entries to the general ledger. Only the bank account in the general ledger is shown here.

(b)

GENERAL JOURNAL OF BRIGHT LIFE

Date	Description	Fol	Dr	Cr
25/03/X6	Bank		1 500	
	Accounts receivable control			1 500
	Ometer			1 500
	Electronic payment received from Ometer			
31/03/X6	Bank		150	
	Interest income			150
	Interest earned on credit balance			
25/03/X6	Insurance expense		600	
	Bank			600
	Insurance debit order			
31/03/X6	Bank charges		200	
	Bank			200
	March bank charges			

Dr — Bank (GL 150) — Cr

Date	Details	Fol	R	Date	Details	Fol	R
20X6				20X6			
31/03	Balance	b/d	6 350	25/03	Insurance (debit order)	GJ	600
25/03	Accounts receivable (EFT)	GJ	1 500	31/03	Bank charges	GJ	200
31/03	Interest income	GJ	150	31/03	Balance	c/d	7 200
			8 000				8 000
01/04	Balance	b/d	7 200				

The third and last step is to prepare the bank reconciliation statement. It is normally prepared by starting with the ***adjusted*** balance as per the bank account in the entity's general ledger, and reconciling to the balance on the bank statement. It may also be prepared by reconciling from the balance on the bank statement to the ***adjusted*** balance in the general ledger. Both presentation formats are shown below.

In order to understand the bank reconciliation statement, remember the purpose is *not to* make the bank account balance equal the bank statement balance. Rather, it *is* to explain and set out the reasons for the bank account balance and bank statement balance not being equal.

(c)

BRIGHT LIFE
BANK RECONCILIATION STATEMENT AS AT 31/03/X6

		R	R
Balance per bank account			7 200
add	Outstanding cheques		5 500
	0006	500	
	0007	5 000	
less	Outstanding deposits		(2 250)
	31/03	2 250	
Balance per bank statement			10 450

The balance per the bank account of R7 200 is the balance after the bank-initiated debits and credits have been journalised and posted to the general ledger. The outstanding cheques of R5 500 are added because the bank has not yet paid these cheques. Conversely, the outstanding deposit is subtracted as the bank has not yet processed the deposit.

Alternatively, the bank reconciliation statement may be prepared by reconciling from the balance on the bank statement to the adjusted balance in the general ledger.

BRIGHT LIFE
BANK RECONCILIATION STATEMENT AS AT 31/03/X6

		R	R
Balance per bank statement			10 450
less	Outstanding cheques		(5 500)
	0006	500	
	0007	5 000	
add	Outstanding deposits		2 250
	31/03	2 250	
Balance per bank account			7 200

When reconciling from the bank statement balance to the entity's records, the outstanding cheques are subtracted, as the entity has already recorded the cheques as payments. Conversely, the outstanding deposits are added because the entity has recorded the deposits as receipts.

Example: Mechanics of a bank reconciliation – subsequent month and an overdraft situation

The bank reconciliation performed in the previous example was for the first month of operations of Bright Life. There are certain additional considerations to take into account when preparing a bank reconciliation in subsequent months. The following are the relevant extracts of the cash journals, bank account and bank statement of Bright Life for April 20X6. The information recorded in the books of Bright Life has been recorded correctly.

Cash receipts journal – April 20X6 **CRJ 3**

Doc	Date	Account name	Fol	Sales	Accounts receivable control	Sundries		Deferred finance income	Analysis	Bank
REC 03	04/04	Barons	DL 09		6 000			300	5 700	5 700
CSS 05	10/04	Cash sales		9 000					9 000	
CSS 06	10/04	Cash sales		3 000					3 000	12 000
REC 04	15/04	Promo Trade	DL 26		1 000				1 000	1 000
CSS 07	25/04	Cash sales		6 300					6 300	
REC 05	25/04	Linus	DL 74		8 000				8 000	14 300
CSS 08	30/04	Cash sales		500					500	500
				18 800	15 000			300		33 500
				Cr GL: Sales	Cr GL: AR Control	Cr: individual accounts		Dr GL: DFI		Dr GL: Bank

Cash payments journal – April 20X6 **CPJ 6**

Doc	Date	Details	Fol	Purchases	Salaries	Accounts payable control	Sundries	Deferred finance expense	Bank
0008	01/04	Rent	GL 80				2 500		2 500
0009	04/04	Cash purchases		9 000					9 000
0010	11/04	Lights and water	GL 83				1 800		1 800
0011	14/04	Repairs	GL 87				900		900
0012	22/04	Swift Supplies	CL 63			28 000		700	27 300
0013	25/04	Salaries			6 000				6 000
0014	29/04	Telephone	GL 85				700		700
				9 000	6 000	28 000	5 900	700	48 200
				Dr GL: Purchases	Dr GL: Salaries	Dr GL: AP Control	Debit individual accounts	Cr GL: DFE	Cr GL: Bank

Dr				Bank (GL 150)			Cr
Date	Details	Fol	R	Date	Details	Fol	R
20X6				20X6			
01/04	Balance	b/d	7 200	30/04	Payments	CPJ 6	48 200
30/04	Deposits	CRJ 3	33 500				
30/04	Balance	c/d	7 500				
			48 200				48 200
				01/05	Balance	b/d	7 500

BB
Limited

The Brall Bank of South Africa
Reg. No. 56 00574/12
✉ P O Box 15520 ☎ 402-6308
Sandton
2028

CURRENT ACCOUNT STATEMENT
30 April 20X6

Bright Life
P O Box 8745
Woodmead
2054

Date	Doc #	Details	Dr	Cr	Balance
01/04		***Balance brought forward***			***10 450***
01/04	DEP	Deposit		2 250	12 700
03/04	0006	Cheque	500		12 200
04/04	0008	Cheque	2 500		9 700
04/04	DEP	Deposit		5 700	15 400
11/04	DEP	Deposit		12 000	27 400
12/04	0009	Cheque	9 000		18 400
13/04	0010	Cheque	1 800		16 600
15/04	DEP	Deposit		1 000	17 600
15/04	0011	Cheque	900		16 700
16/04	RD	Cheque – refer to drawer	1 000		15 700
25/04	DO	Debit order – Insurance	600		15 100
25/04	0012	Cheque	27 300		– 12 200
27/04	DEP	Deposit		13 400	1 200
27/04	0013	Cheque	6 000		– 4 800
30/04	INT	Interest on credit balance		50	– 4 750
30/04	INT	Interest charged	10		– 4 760
30/04	BC	Bank charges	250		– 5 010
30/04		***Month-end balance***			***– 5 010***

You are required to:

(a) compare the cash journals of Bright Life for April 20X6 with the bank statement for April 20X6 and identify the differences between them
(b) prepare the journal entries to record the bank-initiated transactions in the accounting records of Bright Life, and to post the journal entries to the bank account in the general ledger
(c) complete the bank reconciliation statement at 31 April 20X6.

Solution: Mechanics of a bank reconciliation – subsequent month and an overdraft situation

To avoid repetition, only those aspects which were not addressed in the first example are explained here. Again, the relevant columns from the cash journals and bank statement have been reproduced below for explanation purposes and ease of reference.

(a)

CRJ Bank		Bank Statement Cr		CPJ Bank		Bank statement Dr	
5 700	✔	2 250	*	2 500	✗	500	*
				9 000	✗	2 500	✗
12 000	✔			1 800	✗		
1 000	✔	5 700	✔	900	✗		
		12 000	✔	27 300	✗	9 000	✗
14 300	✔			6 000	✗	1 800	✗
500	*o/s dep*			700	*o/s chq*		
33 500		1 000	✔	48 200		900	✗
Debit GL 150				*Credit GL 150*		1 000	*Direct debit*
						600	*Direct debit*
						27 300	✗
		13 400	*(Bank error)*			6 000	✗
		50	*Direct credit*			10	*Direct debit*
						250	*Direct debit*

The two entries marked with a * appear on the April bank statement but not in the cash journals for April. The question that needs to be asked is how a deposit and a cheque payment can appear on the bank statement without being recorded in the cash journals. There are two possibilities. Either an error has been made by the reporting entity or by the bank, or the deposit and cheque payment were recorded in the cash journals in a previous month. In this case, the cheque of R500 and the deposit for R2 250 were recorded in the cash journals in March and were both listed as 'outstanding' on the March bank reconciliation statement. As they have both been processed by the bank during April, they are no longer outstanding. However, if a reconciling item in one month is not processed by the bank in the following month, that item will again appear on future bank reconciliation statements until it is processed by the bank.

As was done for the previous example, the following analysis is prepared as proof that all the differences have been taken into account.

Date	Description	Entity's records	Bank's records
30/04/X6	Balance	(7 500)	(5 010)
16/04/X6	RD cheque	(1 000)	
25/04/X6	Debit order – Insurance	(600)	
27/04/X6	Bank error on deposit		900
30/04/X6	Interest income	50	
30/04/X6	Interest expense	(10)	
30/04/X6	Bank charges	(250)	
30/04/X6	Outstanding deposit		500
30/04/X6	Outstanding cheques		
	– 0007		(5 000)
	– 0014		(700)
	Reconciled balance	(9 310)	(9 310)

(b)

GENERAL JOURNAL OF BRIGHT LIFE				
Date	**Description**	**Fol**	**Dr**	**Cr**
16/04/X6	Promo Trade		1 000	
	Accounts receivable control		1 000	
	Bank			1 000
	Promo Trade cheque payment returned			
25/04/X6	Insurance		600	
	Bank			600
	Insurance debit order			
30/04/X6	Interest expense		10	
	Bank			10
	Interest charged on debit balance			
30/04/X6	Bank charges		250	
	Bank			250
	April bank charges			
30/04/X6	Bank		50	
	Interest income			50
	Interest earned on credit balance			

Dr			Bank (GL 150)				Cr
Date	**Details**	**Fol**	**R**	**Date**	**Details**	**Fol**	**R**
20X6				20X6			
30/04	Interest income	GJ	50	30/04	Balance	b/d	7 500
				16/04	Accounts receivable control	GJ	1 000
				25/04	Insurance	GJ	600
				30/04	Interest expense	GJ	10
30/04	Balance	c/d	9 310	30/04	Bank charges	GJ	250
			9 360				9 360
				01/05	Balance	b/d	9 310

(c)

BRIGHT LIFE
BANK RECONCILIATION STATEMENT AS AT 30/04/X6

		R	R
Balance per bank account			(9 310)
add	Outstanding cheques		5 700
	0007	5 000	
	0014	700	
less	Outstanding deposits		(500)
	30/04	500	
less	Bank error		(900)
	27/04 deposit (14 300—13 400)	900	
Balance per bank statement			(5 010)

The bank error arose when Brall Bank credited the account of Bright Life with an amount of R13 400, when the amount actually deposited was R14 300. In other words, the bank has understated Bright Life's account by R900. If you think back to the purpose of the bank reconciliation statement, you will recall that it is not to make the balance in the entity's records equal the balance on the bank statement, but to set out the reasons why they are not equal. Therefore, as the bank statement balance is understated, the error of R900 must be subtracted when reconciling from the balance per the bank account in Bright Life's general ledger to the balance according to the statement from Brall Bank.

You will notice that the balance of R9 310 in Bright Life's bank account is a credit balance, representing an overdraft. On the bank reconciliation statement, this is shown in brackets as a negative number.

Example: Bank reconciliation in successive months

The following information was obtained from the bank statements and cash journals of Bright Life for the two months ended 30 September and 31 October 20X6.

The cash journals are correct.

Cheques drawn in September		1 600
Cheques paid by the bank in September	1 460	
Cheques paid by the bank in October	80	
Cheques not yet presented for payment	60	
Cheques drawn in October		2 330
Cheques paid by the bank in October	2 160	
Cheques not yet presented for payment	170	
Deposits made in September		2 080
Deposits credited by the bank in September	1 960	
Deposits credited by the bank in October	120	
Deposits made in October		2 150
Deposits credited by the bank in October	2 000	
Deposits credited by the bank in November	150	
Bank charges		60
Bank charges debited by the bank in September	15	
Bank charges debited by the bank in October	45	

Another person's cheque for R65 was paid by the bank and debited to Bright Life's account in error in September, but reversed in the bank's records in October. The balance in the bank as per the bank statement at 30 September was R200.

You are required to:

(a) prepare the bank reconciliation statement at 30 September 20X6
(b) draw up the bank account in the ledger of Bright Life for the month of October 20X6
(c) prepare the bank reconciliation statement at 31 October 20X6.

Solution: Bank reconciliation in successive months

(a)

BRIGHT LIFE
BANK RECONCILIATION STATEMENT AT 30/09/X6

		R	R
Balance per bank statement			200
add	Bank error		65
	Cheque incorrectly debited	65	
less	Cheques not yet presented		(140)
	(80 + 60)	140	

		R	R
add	Deposits not yet credited		120
	September deposit credited by bank in October	120	
	Balance per bank account		245

(b)

Dr **Bank** **Cr**

Date	Details	Fol	R	Date	Details	Fol	R
20X6				20X6			
01/10	Balance	b/d	245	31/10	Payments	CPJ	2 330
31/10	Deposits	CRJ	2 150	31/10	Bank charges	GJ	45
				31/10	Balance	c/d	20
			2 395				2 395
01/11	Balance	b/d	20				

(c)

BRIGHT LIFE
BANK RECONCILIATION STATEMENT AT 31/10/X6

		R	R
Balance per bank account			20
add	Cheques not yet presented		230
	September	60	
	October	170	
less	Deposits not yet credited		(150)
	October deposit credited by bank in November	150	
Balance per bank statement			100

14.4 Exam example

The following is a correct list of the differences between the bank account in the ledger and the bank statement of Mishy's Sweet Shop on 30 April 20X1.

	R
Deposit not credited by the bank	3 750
Outstanding cheques	
106	210
128	128
133	328

Cheque no 8322, drawn by Mishy on his personal bank account for R2 861, was debited by the bank to the business bank account in error.

A month later, on 31 May 20X1, the bookkeeper identified the following factors which he considered relevant:

1. Of the outstanding cheques at 30 April 20X1, cheques no 128 and 133 appeared on the May bank statement.
2. The error made by the bank involving Mishy's personal cheque had not yet been corrected.
3. The following cheques issued in May had not been presented for payment:
   210 R400
   234 R1 536
4. No entries appeared in the May cash journals to record the following which *did* appear on the May bank statement:
   (a) A stop order for an insurance premium of R500 paid by the bank on 15 May 20X1.
   (b) A cheque for R651 from Jones in repayment of a loan which was returned by the bank marked 'R/D'.
   (c) Interest on overdraft R50.
   (d) Service fees R54.
5. A deposit of R8 261 on 28 May 20X1 (of amounts received from debtors), correctly reflected on the bank statement, had been entered in the cash receipts journal as R8 621.
6. There were no outstanding deposits at 31 May 20X1.
7. The opening balance on the bank account in the ledger at 1 May 20X1 was R2 500 credit.
8. The bank statement for May 20X1 reflected a closing debit balance of R3 280.

You are required to:

(a) prepare a bank reconciliation statement at 31 May 20X1
(b) complete the bank account in the ledger in as much detail as is possible, based on the information given.

Solution: Exam example

Workings – Bank balance before adjustment

31 May	Balance per bank statement – overdraft		(3 280)
	April cheques not presented	(210)	
	Error by bank	2 861	
	Cheques not presented (400 + 1 536)	(1 936)	
	Stop orders not entered	500	
	R/D Cheque – Jones	651	
	Charges not entered (54 + 50)	104	
	Deposit error (8 621 – 8 261)	360	2 330
31 May	Balance per ledger		950

(a)

MISHY'S SWEET SHOP
BANK RECONCILIATION STATEMENT AT 31 MAY 20X1

		R	R
Balance per bank statement			(3 280)
less	Cheques not yet presented		(2 146)
	106	210	
	210	400	
	234	1 536	
add	Error by bank		2 861
Balance per bank account			(2 565)

(b)

Dr			Bank (GL 150)				Cr
Date	**Details**	**Fol**	**R**	**Date**	**Details**	**Fol**	**R**
				20X1			
				31 May	Balance	b/d	950
					Accounts receivable	GJ	360
					Interest	GJ	50
					Bank charges	GJ	54
					Loan: Jones	GJ	651
31 May	Balance	c/d	2 565		Insurance	GJ	500
			2 565				2 565
				01 June	Balance	b/d	2 565

Summary of concepts and applications

1. Cash includes currency and coins, amounts on deposit in banking accounts and deposits in savings accounts. Various internal controls are employed to prevent the misappropriation of cash.
2. Cash and bank transactions are recorded in the general ledger bank account in the records of the reporting entity and are reflected on the bank statement, which is a representation of the reporting entity's account in the records of the bank.
3. The purpose of the bank reconciliation is to explain and set out the reasons for the bank account balance and bank statement balance not being equal. The procedure to prepare the bank reconciliation statement involves comparing the cash journals to the bank statement, adjusting the bank account in the general ledger of the reporting entity and, finally, the actual preparation of the statement.

Note

1. Weil, S. *Accounting Skills: A Guide to the Mastery of Elementary Accounting*, Cape Town: Juta, 1989. p. 73.

15 Non-current and Current Liabilities

'The liabilities of a business consist of all sums due to outside creditors as distinguished from the sums due to partners or shareholders.'
(Lisle, 1899)

Outcomes

- Define a liability and a financial liability.
- Classify liabilities.
- Demonstrate how to account for non-current liabilities.
- Prepare a suppliers' reconciliation statement.

Chapter outline

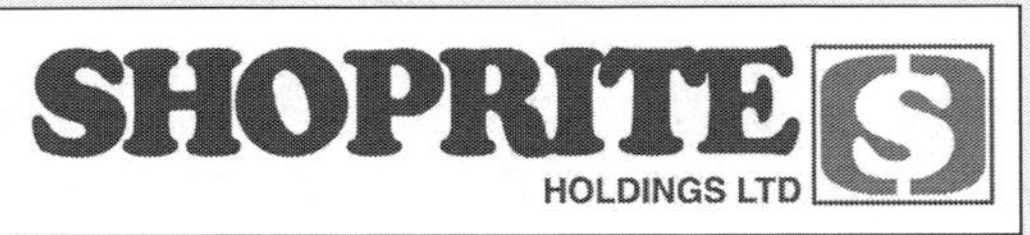

Shoprite Holdings Limited
Notes to the financial statements for the year ended 30 June 2007

	(R millions)
LIABILITIES	
Non-current liabilities	724
Long term borrowings	2
Deferred tax	9
Provisions	264
Operating lease accrual	449
Current liabilities	7 465
Trade and other payables	7 153
Current tax payable	216
Provisions	70
Bank overdraft	24
Shareholders for dividends	2
	8 189

The key to Shoprite's business model is that they purchase goods from suppliers with payment terms of 60 to 90 days, yet they receive cash from their customers on the day of the sale. This allows them to earn interest on the money before they pay their suppliers. On the other hand, it creates a R7 billion trade payable!

15.1 Definition of liabilities

The accounting framework defines a **liability** as:

- a present obligation of the enterprise
- arising from past events
- the settlement of which is expected to result in an outflow from the enterprise of resources embodying economic benefits.[1]

A fundamental characteristic of a liability is that the entity has a *present obligation*. Obligations may be legally enforceable or may arise from normal business practice or custom. An example of a legally enforceable obligation is amounts payable for goods and services received. However, if an enterprise decides to rectify defects in its products after the warranty period has expired, there is no legally enforceable obligation although the amounts that are expected to be expended in respect of goods already sold are liabilities.

Liabilities result from *past transactions or events*. For example, the purchase of goods gives rise to amounts payable, and the receipt of a loan gives rise to an obligation to repay the loan.

The settlement of an obligation involves the entity giving up resources embodying *economic benefits* in order to satisfy the claim of the other party. Settlement of a present obligation may occur in a number of ways.[2] These include:

- payment of cash
- transfer of other assets
- provision of services
- replacement of that obligation with another obligation
- conversion of the obligation to equity.

An obligation may also be extinguished by other means, such as suppliers waiving or forfeiting their rights.

Certain liabilities fall into the definition of a financial instrument.

A **financial instrument** is any contract that gives rise to both a financial asset of one entity (or individual) and a financial liability or equity instrument of another entity (or individual).[3]

A **financial liability** includes any liability that is a contractual obligation to deliver cash or another financial asset to another entity (or individual).[4]

You were introduced to the definition of a financial asset in Chapter 13. A financial asset includes cash or a contractual right to receive cash or another financial asset from another entity (or individual).

Pause and reflect...

On 5 January 20X5, Smart Concepts purchases stationery of R5 000 from its supplier. If the stationery is purchased on credit and the supplier agrees to accept a laptop computer valued at R5 000 in settlement of the amount owing,

a) Does Smart Concepts recognise a liability?
b) If yes, is the liability a financial liability?

Response

a) Smart Concepts recognises a liability as it has an obligation to settle the amount owing to the supplier as a result of the purchase of the stationery on 5 January 20X5. The laptop is an asset of the business, therefore, giving it to the supplier represents an outflow of economic benefits.
b) The liability is not a financial liability as Smart Concepts does not have an obligation to deliver cash or another financial asset.

There must be a contractual relationship between parties for a financial instrument to exist. Thus, liabilities which are not contractual in nature, such as amounts owing to the Receiver of Revenue that are created as a result of statutory requirements, are not financial liabilities.

Note also that liabilities for payments received in advance are not financial liabilities as the obligation is to provide goods or services, and not cash or another financial asset.

The importance of identifying a financial liability relates to risk and the measurement of its fair value.

15.2 Classification of liabilities

The statement of financial position is prepared to provide useful information to the users about the financial position of an enterprise. Part of the information in the statement of financial position is to inform the users of the obligations of the enterprise. However, as some obligations are payable over long periods and some over short periods, the information is more useful to the user if the statement of financial position classifies the liabilities.

The distinction between non-current and current liabilities was addressed in Chapter 6.

According to IAS 1,[5] an entity shall classify a liabilty as current when:

- it expects to settle the liability in its normal operating cycle; or
- it holds the liability primarily for the purposes of trading; or
- the liability is due to be settled within twelve months after the reporting period; or
- the entity does not have an unconditional right to defer settlement of the liability for at least twelve months after the reporting period.

An entity shall classify all other liabilities as non-current.

 **Pause and reflect...**

Discuss the classification of accounts payable that are not expected to be settled within twelve months of the financial reporting date.

Response

Accounts payable not expected to be realised within twelve months of the financial reporting date should be classified as a current liability. This is because the raising of this liability and its subsequent payment is part of the entity's operating cycle.

15.3 Non-current liabilities

Non-current liabilities include items such as long-term loans and mortgage bonds. There are three issues to examine when considering non-current liabilities:

- the cost of financing
- the terms of repayment
- the security offered to the lending institution.

We will examine each issue in turn.

15.3.1 Cost of financing

The cost of financing is the price paid to the lending institution for the use of the funds. The cost of financing is known as interest. The interest charged is payable to the lending institution at intervals determined by the terms agreed upon by the two parties. Interest charges are not dependent on an enterprise making a profit. Interest is an *expense* of the enterprise.

Nominal interest rate

The nominal interest rate is the rate at which interest will be paid on the ***nominal value***, or ***face value*** of the financial instrument.

Consider the situation where Smart Concepts establishes an overdraft facility of R300 000 with its bank on 1 January 20X7. Interest on the overdraft accrues at 12% per annum payable monthly in arrears. On 2 January 20X7, Smart Concepts utilised R100 000 of the overdraft facility. On 1 February 20X7, a further R150 000 was drawn against the overdraft. No further amounts were drawn or repaid during March 20X7. The interest expense for the three months ended 31 March 20X7 will be recorded as follows:

Assets		=	Liabilities	+	Owner's equity	
Bank					Interest expense	
+/L/Dr	–/R/Cr				+/L/Dr	–/R/Cr
	6 000				6 000	

GENERAL JOURNAL OF SMART CONCEPTS				
Date	**Description**	**Fol**	**Dr**	**Cr**
31/03/X7	Interest expense Bank *Interest expense for the period*		6 000	 6 000

The interest expense for the three months ended 31 March 20X7 is calculated by applying the nominal interest rate of 12% to the amount of the overdraft utilised during the period. Therefore, the interest expense is calculated as 12% of R100 000 for the period from 1 January 20X7 to 31 January 20X7 and 12% of R250 000 in respect of the period from 1 February 20X7 to 31 March 20X7, which amounts to R6 000 (R100 000 x 0,12 X 1/12 + R250 000 x 0,12 x 2/12). The interest expense will be increased by debiting the interest expense account. The other side of the entry is to decrease the asset, bank, by crediting the bank account.

Effective interest rate

The effective interest rate is the rate that, when used in a present value calculation, exactly discounts the expected future cash flows to equate to the initial carrying amount of the liability. The effective interest rate is sometimes referred to as the level yield to maturity and is the internal rate of return of the financial liability for the period of the contract.

Consider the example where Smart Concepts obtains a loan from a bank on 1 January 20X7. The nominal value of the loan is R1 000 000, the nominal interest rate is 15% per annum and the loan matures in five years. The costs to establish the loan facility were R20 000 and the net proceeds received by Smart Concepts amounted to R980 000.

The first step in calculating the interest expense for each year is to set up a schedule of cash flows for the period of the loan contract.

01/01/X7	31/12/X7	31/12/X8	31/12/X9	31/12/Y0	31/12/Y1
980 000	(150 000)	(150 000)	(150 000)	(150 000)	(1 150 000)

Secondly, it is necessary to calculate the effective interest rate, or the internal rate of return. The rate that equates the initial cash inflow of R980 000 with cash outflows of R150 000 per year for four years and a final cash outflow of R1 150 000 is 15,6052%.

The third step is to calculate the effective interest expense for each year. The effect of this is to allocate the cost of the loan over the period of the loan contract. This is done as shown in the following table:

Date	Effective interest (a)	Nominal interest (b)	(a) – (b)	Balance
01/01/X7				980 000
31/12/X7	152 931	150 000	2 931	982 931
31/12/X8	153 388	150 000	3 388	986 319
31/12/X9	153 917	150 000	3 917	990 236
31/12/Y0	154 529	150 000	4 529	994 765
31/12/Y1	155 235	150 000	5 235	1 000 000

The journal entries to record the raising of the loan, the interest expense each year and the repayment of the loan are shown below. Note that the loan is initially recorded on 1 January 20X7 at R980 000, the amount of the net proceeds received. The amount of R980 000 is, in fact, the present value at 1 January 20X7 of the future cash flows associated with the loan, discounted at the effective interest rate. This is proved in the following table:

Date	Cash flow	PV factor (at 15,6052%)	PV (R)
31/12/X7	(150 000)	0,86501	129 752
31/12/X8	(150 000)	0,74824	112 236
31/12/X9	(150 000)	0,64724	97 086
31/12/Y0	(150 000)	0,55987	83 981
31/12/Y1	(1 150 000)	0,48430	556 945
			980 000

The interest expense recorded each year is the effective interest expense as calculated in the above table. The last entry on 31 December 20Y1 records the repayment of the nominal value of the loan.

Date	Description	Fol	Dr	Cr
01/01/X7	Bank		980 000	
	Long-term loan			980 000
31/12/X7	Interest expense		152 931	
	Bank			150 000
	Long-term loan			2 931
31/12/X8	Interest expense		153 388	
	Bank			150 000
	Long-term loan			3 388
31/12/X9	Interest expense		153 917	
	Bank			150 000
	Long-term loan			3 917

31/12/Y0	Interest expense Bank Long-term loan		154 529	 150 000 4 529
31/12/Y1	Interest expense Bank Long-term loan		155 235	 150 000 5 235
	Long-term loan Bank		1 000 000	 1 000 000

An extract from Smart Concepts' financial statements for the 20X7 financial year is presented below.

SMART CONCEPTS
INCOME STATEMENT FOR THE YEAR ENDED 31 DECEMBER 20X7

Finance cost	**R**
Interest expense	152 931

SMART CONCEPTS
STATEMENT OF FINANCIAL POSITION AT 31 DECEMBER 20X7

Non-current liabilities	**R**
Long-term borrowings	982 931

15.3.2 Terms of repayment

At the time of a loan being advanced to an enterprise, it is usual for a date, in the future, to be decided on for its repayment. Remember, the repayment date must be more than a year after the statement of financial position date for the loan to be classified as long term. It is possible for a loan to be repaid over a period of time rather than at one point. This results in a series of payments being made. Each time a repayment is made, the balance on which interest is calculated is reduced. When a portion of the loan is paid, we refer to it as a capital reduction in the balance outstanding.

15.3.3 Security

When a long-term loan is granted to an enterprise, the lending institution may require some guarantee that their interest and capital will be paid to them. The lending institution can ask for security on the loan as guarantee of the payments being made. Security on a loan is the cession of rights or the pledge of an asset in favour of a lender.

In the event of the enterprise failing to make its interest payments or capital repayments, the lending institution has the right to take possession of the ceded or pledged assets and dispose of them. The proceeds that the lending institution receives will be used to settle the obligation and any additional monies will be given back to the enterprise. If the asset taken by the lending institution does not cover the loan, or if the loan was never secured, the lending institution could take action against the enterprise to recover its money.

15.4 Current liabilities

Current liabilities include items such as accounts payable, the short-term portion of long-term loans, bank overdrafts, accrued expenses and unearned income. Current liabilities such as accounts payable and accrued expenses are normally settled within twelve months of the financial reporting date. However, such items are classified as current liabilities even if they are due to be settled after more than twelve months from the financial reporting date, as they form part of the working capital used in the normal operating cycle of the business.

The most common and recurring current liabilities are the accounts an enterprise has with its suppliers. Transactions are entered into on a daily basis with payments being made to the supplier at regular intervals. Since the volume of transactions is numerous, it is usual for the accounts to be checked against the suppliers' statements for correctness before payments are made. We will be looking at the purpose of, and procedures for, preparing a supplier's reconciliation in the following sections.

15.4.1 Suppliers' reconciliation statements

Each month suppliers send statements to their customers, indicating transactions for the month and the balance owing at the end of the month. Before the customer pays the account, the statement should be checked for correctness. There may be timing differences and errors. If such discrepancies arise, a reconciliation statement should be prepared. The details of the differences will be indicated on a ***remittance advice***, to be sent with the cheque to the supplier.

The purpose of a supplier's reconciliation statement is, therefore, to reconcile the amount owing to the supplier, as reflected in the supplier's account in the accounts payable subsidiary ledger, with the amount owing to the supplier, as reflected on the supplier's statement.

The supplier's reconciliation statement then becomes the remittance advice which accompanies the customer's cheque and informs the supplier how the firm arrived at the amount of the cheque.

15.4.2 Reconciliation procedure

The preparation of a supplier's reconciliation statement involves two distinct steps.

- Identification of errors and omissions in the accounting records of the reporting entity, from the information in the supplier's statements, that require adjustments by means of journal entries.

- Identification of errors and omissions on the supplier's statement. These discrepancies result in a difference between the amount claimed by the supplier on the statement, and the remittance to be made to the supplier. The business communicates the reasons for this difference to the supplier on a remittance advice which accompanies the payment to the supplier. A remittance advice begins with the balance on the supplier's statement. If this figure is not given, the balance on the supplier's statement must first be calculated. Discount claimed from a supplier is also shown on the remittance advice.

Example: Supplier's reconciliation statement and remittance advice

Bright Life receives the following statement from Suppliers Limited, a wholesaler of home entertainment products, at the end of May 20X6:

Suppliers Limited
P O Box 25874 ☎ 728-5394
Edenglen
2028

STATEMENT MAY 20X6

Date	Doc #	Description	Dr	Cr
			R	R
01/05	B/F	Balance	10 314	
01/05	C245	Credit note		114
08/05	S478	Invoice	2 708	
09/05	C314	Credit note		633
18/05	P871	Payment		10 200
23/05	S574	Invoice	930	
24/05	C455	Credit note		50
28/05	S622	Invoice	11 833	
30/05	S789	Invoice	20 000	
31/05	C/F	Balance		24 788
			45 785	45 785

The Suppliers Limited ledger account in the accounts payable subsidiary ledger of Bright Life is as follows:

Dr **Suppliers Limited (GL 150)** **Cr**

Date	Details	Fol	R	Date	Details	Fol	R
09/05	Inventory (Credit note C314)		683	01/05	Balance	b/d	10 200
18/05	Bank		10 200	05/05	Inventory (Invoice S478)		2 780
31/05	Balance	c/d	38 920	23/05	Inventory (Invoice S574)		390
				24/05	Inventory (Invoice C455)		50
				28/05	Inventory (Invoice S622)		11 383
				30/05	Inventory (Invoice S789)		25 000
			49 803				49 803
				01/06	Balance	b/d	38 920

On comparing the supplier's statement with the account in his records, Simon discovers the following:

1. Goods returned (credit note C455) to the value of R50 were entered in the accounting records as an invoice.
2. Goods purchased (invoice S574) for R930 were entered in the accounting records as R390.
3. Invoice S789 was subject to a trade discount of 20%, which Bright Life did not take into account.
4. In all other respects the records of Bright Life are correct. Any further discrepancies are due to mistakes made by Suppliers Limited.
5. Credit note C245 relates to goods purchased in April.

You are required to:

(a) prepare a remittance advice to send with a cheque to Suppliers Limited on 10 June in full settlement of the amount outstanding at the end of May.

(b) prepare the journal entries to correct the errors in the accounting records of Bright Life (assume a perpetual inventory system is used).

(c) prepare Suppliers Limited's ledger account, starting with the balance of R38 920 as given, and post the journal entries as per (b) above.

Solution: Supplier's reconciliation statement and remittance advice

SUPPLIER'S RECONCILIATION

Doc #	Description	The reporting entity (Bright Life)	The supplier (Suppliers Limited)
Bal 31/05/X6	Closing balance	38 920	24 788
Invoice S478	Error on statement (2 780 – 2 708)		72
Credit note C314	Error on statement (683 – 633)		(50)
Invoice S574	Error on entry (930 – 390)	540	
Credit note C455	Credit note entered as an Invoice (50 x 2)	(100)	
Invoice S622	Error on statement (11 383 – 11 833)		(450)
Invoice S789	Trade discount	(5 000)	
Statement balance 31/05/X6	Error on statement due to casting (R24 788 should be R34 788)		10 000
	Reconciled balance	34 360	34 360

To be able to answer the question, you may find it useful to reconcile the account. This is shown above by starting with the balance on Suppliers Limited's account in the accounting records of Bright Life in one column and the balance per Suppliers Limited's statement in another column. Any difference identified is then either a difference requiring adjustment in the records of Bright Life and therefore entered into the reporting entity's column, or it is an error in the records of Suppliers Limited and therefore entered into the supplier's column.

The errors in the reporting entity's column are then journalised in order to correct the balance in its accounting records. The journal entries need to be posted to the general ledger, to correct the accounts payable control account, and to the accounts payable subsidiary ledger, to correct the individual supplier's account.

The supplier needs to be notified of the errors in its account. These errors are the ones in the supplier's column of the supplier's reconciliation. To notify the supplier, the reporting entity prepares a remittance advice which starts with the supplier's balance in the statement, and adds and subtracts the errors from the balance to calculate the correct balance. If a discount is granted, this is deducted from the corrected balance before arriving at the amount to be paid to the supplier.

(a)

BRIGHT LIFE
REMITTANCE ADVICE FOR ACCOUNT SUPPLIER'S LIMITED
MAY 20X6

		R	R
Balance owing per your statement			24 788
Add:	Error on invoice S478 (2 780 – 2 708)	72	
	Casting error on statement	10 000	10 072
Less:	Error on credit note C314 (683 – 633)	50	
	Error on invoice S622 (11 833 – 11 383)	450	(500)
Our cheque enclosed			34 360

(b)

GENERAL JOURNAL OF BRIGHT LIFE

Date	Description	Fol	Dr	Cr
31/05	Suppliers Limited Accounts payable control Inventory *Correction on credit note C455 entered as an invoice*		100 100	 100
31/05	Inventory Accounts payable control Suppliers Limited *Correction on invoice S574 from Suppliers Limited*		540	 540 540
31/05	Suppliers Limited Accounts payable control Inventory *Correction on invoice S789 as subject to trade discount*		5 000 5 000	 5 000

(c)

Dr SUPPLIERS LIMITED Cr

Date	Details	Fol	R	Date	Details	Fol	R
20X6				20X6			
31/05	Inventory		100	31/05	Balance	b/d	38 920
31/05	Inventory		5 000	31/05	Inventory		540
31/05	Balance	c/d	34 360				
			39 460				39 460
				01/06	Balance	b/d	34 360

15.5 Exam example: Remittance advice

Leebros Stores received a statement dated 31 May 20X0 from Epol Suppliers. Epol Suppliers allows Leebros Stores a 10% trade discount on all transactions.

The statement received from Epol reflected a debit balance of R19 031. The balance reflected in Leebros Stores' ledger at 31 May 20X0 was R13 940.

When the account in the ledger was compared with Epol Suppliers' statement, the following discrepancies were noted. All invoices referred to below are stated net of trade discount, unless otherwise specified:

(1) The credit side of the statement had been undercast by R1 570.
(2) Invoice no 2767 for a gross amount of R450 had been entered in the purchases journal as R504.
(3) Credit note no 223 for R125 was correctly recorded in the accounts payable subsidiary ledger, but was entered as an invoice on the statement.
(4) Invoice no 2863 for R432 was recorded in the purchases journal correctly, but entered in the accounts payable subsidiary ledger as if it were a credit note.
(5) Invoice no 2811 for a gross amount of R760 was entered on the statement as R648.
(6) Invoice no 2770 for R882 was incorrectly posted to Husky Traders, another of Leebros Stores' suppliers.
(7) Invoice no 2796 for R900 was debited twice on the statement.
(8) During May, Epol Suppliers purchased goods from Leebros Stores for R300. It was agreed that this amount should be deducted from the amount Leebros Stores owes Epol Suppliers. Epol Suppliers agreed that Leebros Stores would still be able to claim a cash discount on this amount. Leebros Stores entered this set-off in their accounting records, but Epol Suppliers' statement did not reflect this transaction.
(9) The statement reflects invoice no 2902 for R460. Leebros Stores' goods-received note indicates that the goods were received on 31 May 20X0. The invoice was received only on 2 June 20X0.

You are required to:

(a) prepare the remittance advice to accompany the cheque from Leebros Stores to Epol Suppliers (to reach them before 30 June 20X0). All details of discount calculations must appear on the remittance advice.
(b) prepare the necessary journal entries to correct any mistakes in Leebros Stores' accounting records. Control accounts are maintained.

Solution: Remittance advice

EPOL SUPPLIERS' RECONCILIATION WORKINGS

Doc #	Description	The reporting entity (Leebros Stores)	The Supplier (Epol Suppliers)
31/05/X0	Closing balance	13 940	19 031
1	Credit side of statement undercast		(1 570)
2	Error on entry of invoice 2767 (504 – 405)	(99)	
3	Credit note 223 entered as an invoice		(250)
4	Invoice 2863 recorded as a credit note	864	

5	Error on statement invoice 2811 (684 – 648)		36
6	Invoice 2770 posted to wrong account	882	
7	Invoice 2796 on statement twice		(900)
8	Goods purchased from Leebros set off		(300)
9	Invoice 2902 not recorded in accounting records	460	
31/05/X0	Reconciled balance	16 047	16 047

(a)

LEEBROS STORES
REMITTANCE ADVICE FOR ACCOUNT EPOL SUPPLIERS
MAY 20X0

Balance owing per your statement			19 031
add:	Error on invoice 2811 (684 – 648)	36	36
less:	Credit side of statement undercast	1 570	
	Credit note 223 entered as an invoice	250	
	Invoice 2796 on statement twice	900	
	Goods purchased from Leebros set off	300	(3 020)
Our cheque enclosed			16 047

(b)

LEEBROS STORES
GENERAL JOURNAL

Date	Description	Fol	Dr	Cr
31/05/X0	Epol Suppliers		99	
	Accounts payable control		99	
	Purchases/Inventory			99
	Invoice 2767 incorrectly entered			
	(450 gross x 0.90 = 405 net) (504 – 405 = 99)			
31/05/X0	Epol suppliers			864
	Invoice 2863 posted as a credit note in the subsidiary ledger			
31/05/X0	Husky Traders		882	
	Epol Suppliers			882
	Invoice 2770 posted to the wrong account in the subsidiary ledger			
31/05/X0	Purchases/Inventory		460	
	Accounts payable control			460
	Epol Suppliers			460
	Invoice 2902 omitted			

Summary of concepts and applications

1. A liability, as discussed in Chapter 2, is created when an enterprise has a present obligation, arising from past events that lead to the giving up of resources in settlement of the obligation. A financial liability includes any liability that is a contractual obligation to deliver cash or another financial asset to another party.
2. Liabilities, as discussed in Chapter 6, can be classified into non-current and current liabilities. This distinction enhances the usefulness of the information presented by an enterprise in respect of its obligations.
3. Non-current liabilities may include long-term loans and mortgage bonds. There are three issues relevant to non-current liabilities, namely, the cost of financing or the interest expense, the terms of repayment and the security offered to the lending institution. In considering the cost of financing, the chapter distinguishes, and illustrates the difference, between interest calculated using a nominal and an effective interest rate.
4. Current liabilities may include accounts payable, the short-term portion of long-term loans, bank overdrafts, accrued expenses and unearned income. A supplier's reconciliation statement reconciles the amount owing to a supplier per the accounts payable subsidiary ledger with the amount owing to the supplier per the supplier's statement. The reconciliation procedure requires the identification of errors and omissions in the accounting records of the reporting entity (adjusted through journal entries) and the identification of errors and omissions on the supplier's statement (explained to the supplier on a remittance advice when payment is made).

Notes

1. Framework for the Preparation and Presentation of Financial Statements, *International Accounting Standards Board*, (2001), paragraph 49(b).
2. Framework for the Preparation and Presentation of Financial Statements, paragraph 62.
3. IAS 32, Financial Instruments: Presentation, *International Accounting Standards Board*, (2007), paragraph 11.
4. IAS 32, paragraph 11.
5. IAS 1, Presentation of Financial Statements, *International Accounting Standards Board*, (2008), paragraph 69.

16 Owner's Equity

'... Then gather together the whole sum of your ready money, debts and goods, and therefrom subtract the total sum of your creditors, and the remainder is the net rest, substance or capital of the owner to be put in a traffic, etc.'
(North, 1714)

Outcomes

- Describe a business entity's sources of finance.
- Evaluate owner's equity as a form of finance.
- Compare equity in the various entity forms.

Chapter outline

Standard Bank Group Limited
Statement of changes in equity for the year ended 31 December 2007

					(R millions)
	Ordinary share capital	**Preference share capital**	**Share premium**	**NDR**	**Retained Earnings**
Opening balance	100	5 503	2 339	307	41 809
Total comprehensive income	-	-	-	28	13 651
Share repurchase	(10)	-	-	-	-
Issue of preference shares		328	-	-	-
Dividends paid: ordinary	-	-	-	-	(4 873)
preference	-	-	-	-	(450)
Closing balance	90	5 175	2 339	335	50 137

Being South Africa's largest bank, Standard Bank has a huge amount of equity, over R140 billion in fact! This is the net asset value of the business, being the assets less the liabilities.

16.1 Sources of finance

We learnt in Chapter 3 that a business entity is financed from two sources – funds provided by the owner and funds provided by lenders. Funds provided by the owner are known as owner's equity and funds provided by lenders are known as liabilities.

A business entity will raise finance in order to purchase assets. In general, non-current assets which are used for a long period of time should be financed by a long-term source of finance such as owner's equity or non-current liabilities. On the other hand, current assets that will be used by the entity over a short period of time ought to be financed by a short-term source of finance, for example, accounts payable or a bank overdraft.

This chapter focuses on owner's equity, specifically from the perspective of a sole proprietorship, and includes an introduction to the concept of equity of a partnership, close corporation and company. Liabilities were addressed in Chapter 15.

16.2 Owner's equity as a form of finance

Equity is the residual interest in the assets of the enterprise after deducting all its liabilities.[1] It includes both the funds invested in the business entity by the owner and the profit of the entity which has not been distributed to the owner. If you think back to the closing entry process in Chapter 7, you will remember that the profit is transferred to the owner's capital account, after the income and expense items have been closed off to the profit and loss account. In addition, the distributions for the period are also closed off to the owner's capital account. Owner's equity is often referred to as the net worth of a business, or the residual interest in the assets after deducting liabilities.

When examining equity as a form of finance, it is appropriate to consider:

- the cost of the financing
- the repayment terms
- the security offered

16.2.1 The cost of the financing

The cost to a sole proprietorship of funds provided by the owner does not have a fixed cost as exists for a long-term liability. The returns to the owner are represented by the entity's profit for the period, which is unlikely to equal the cash distributed to the owner. The amount distributed in cash depends on availability of cash resources and the extent to which cash is needed to finance future operations. As you are already aware, the distributions do not appear as an expense on the income statement.

The sole proprietor who invests funds in a business takes the risk that the return on ownership interest will fluctuate from year to year. It is certainly more volatile than the return on a long-term loan where the interest rate is fixed. However, by bearing the higher risk, the sole proprietor also has the chance to achieve a higher return than the fixed return on a long-term loan.

 **Pause and reflect...**

An owner of a business would like to recognise an expense in respect of a distribution. By applying the definition of an expense in IAS 1, consider whether or not this is appropriate.

Response

Although the payment will result in an outflow of assets in the form of cash paid and will decrease equity, the definition of an expense in IAS 1 specifically excludes distributions to equity participants. Consequently, it is incorrect to recognise an expense in respect of the distribution.

16.2.2 The repayment terms

The capital of the sole proprietor is not usually repaid until the activities of the business cease. There are few, if any, restrictions on the distribution to owners of amounts included in equity. It is important to bear in mind, however, that the owner and the business are the same legal entity and that the liabilities of the business cannot be avoided by simply withdrawing all the capital.

16.2.3 The security offered

As mentioned above, the individual who invests funds in the sole proprietorship is the ultimate risk-bearer. On the cessation of business activities, liability holders have a preferential claim over the owner for the repayment of the amounts owing to them.

16.3 Equity in the different entity forms

The four forms of business entity found in South Africa are the sole proprietor, the partnership, the close corporation and the company. Parts 1 to 4 of this book are concerned with the activities of a sole proprietor. The processing of data and producing year-end information is examined from the perspective of a sole proprietor, as are the chapters dealing with the recognition and measurement of financial statement items. In Part 5 of this book, covering Chapters 17 to 20, we will explore the differences in accounting for the other entry forms. In these chapters you will see that the major differences lie in the accounting for, and composition of, equity and in the allocation of profits to the owners. Most other items on the financial statements remain the same.

There is an accounting and legal relationship between the owner (or owners) and the business entity in each of the entity forms. This impacts upon the allocation of profit as well as the composition of equity. The accounting and legal relationship was described in Chapter 1 and is summarised in the following paragraph.

The sole trader and partnership can be referred to as ***unincorporated*** entities, while the close corporation and company can be referred to as ***incorporated*** entities. The owner of the sole trader and the partners of the partnership are *separate* *accounting entities* apart from the business enterprise, but from a legal viewpoint they are the *same legal entity*. The members of the close corporation and the shareholders of the company are both *separate accounting and legal entities* apart from the business. The close corporation and the company are incorporated as separate legal entities in terms of statute.

Part 5 of this book, entitled Entity Forms, deals with the accounting for partnerships, close corporations and companies. Each chapter examines the specific accounting requirements of the different entity forms. Particular attention is given to the allocation of profit to the owners as well as the composition of equity. As an introduction, these aspects are addressed briefly in the remainder of this chapter.

16.3.1 Allocation of profit to the owners

Sole proprietorship

All the profits belong to the sole proprietor. The profit from the profit and loss account is allocated directly to equity, that is, to the capital account of the sole proprietor.

Partnership

The profit needs to be adjusted for unequal capital and labour contributions by the partners. The profit from the profit and loss account is transferred to an appropriation account where appropriations of profit are made to the partners' equity depending on the resources invested and services performed by each partner. The remaining profit is then also allocated to equity according to an agreed profit-sharing ratio.

Close corporation

The profit earned belongs to the business entity, and only accrues to the owners (known as members) when formally declared in the form of a distribution. The profit is transferred from the profit and loss account to an undrawn profit account where appropriations are made for taxation and distributions to members.

Company

The profit earned also belongs to the business entity, and only accrues to the owners (known as shareholders) when formally declared in the form of a dividend. The profit is transferred from the profit and loss account to an accumulated profit account where appropriations are made for taxation and dividends to shareholders.

16.3.2 Composition of owner's equity

The composition of owner's equity of a partnership, close corporation and company is examined in detail in the following chapters. The following table provides a summary:

Sole proprietorship	**Partnership**	**Close corporation**	**Company**
Capital account	Capital accounts	Members' contribution	Share capital
	Current accounts	Undrawn profit (distributable)	Accumulated profit (distributable)
	Reserves	Revaluation reserve (non-distributable)	Revaluation reserve (non-distributable)

Diagram 16.1: Equity in different entity forms

Summary of concepts and applications

1. A business entity is financed from funds provided by the owners and/or funds provided by lenders.
2. Owner's equity is the net worth of the business or the residual interest in the assets after deducting liabilities. When examining equity as a form of finance, one should consider the cost of the financing, the repayment terms and the security offered.
3. There are four forms of business entity in South Africa, namely the sole proprietor, the partnership, the close corporation and the company. There is an accounting and legal relationship between the owners and the business entity in each of the entity forms. The allocation of profits to the owners, as well as the composition of owner's equity, is different in each of the entity forms.

Note

1. Framework for the Preparation and Presentation of Financial Statements. *International Accounting Standards Board*, (2001), paragraph 49 (c).

Part 5

Entity Forms

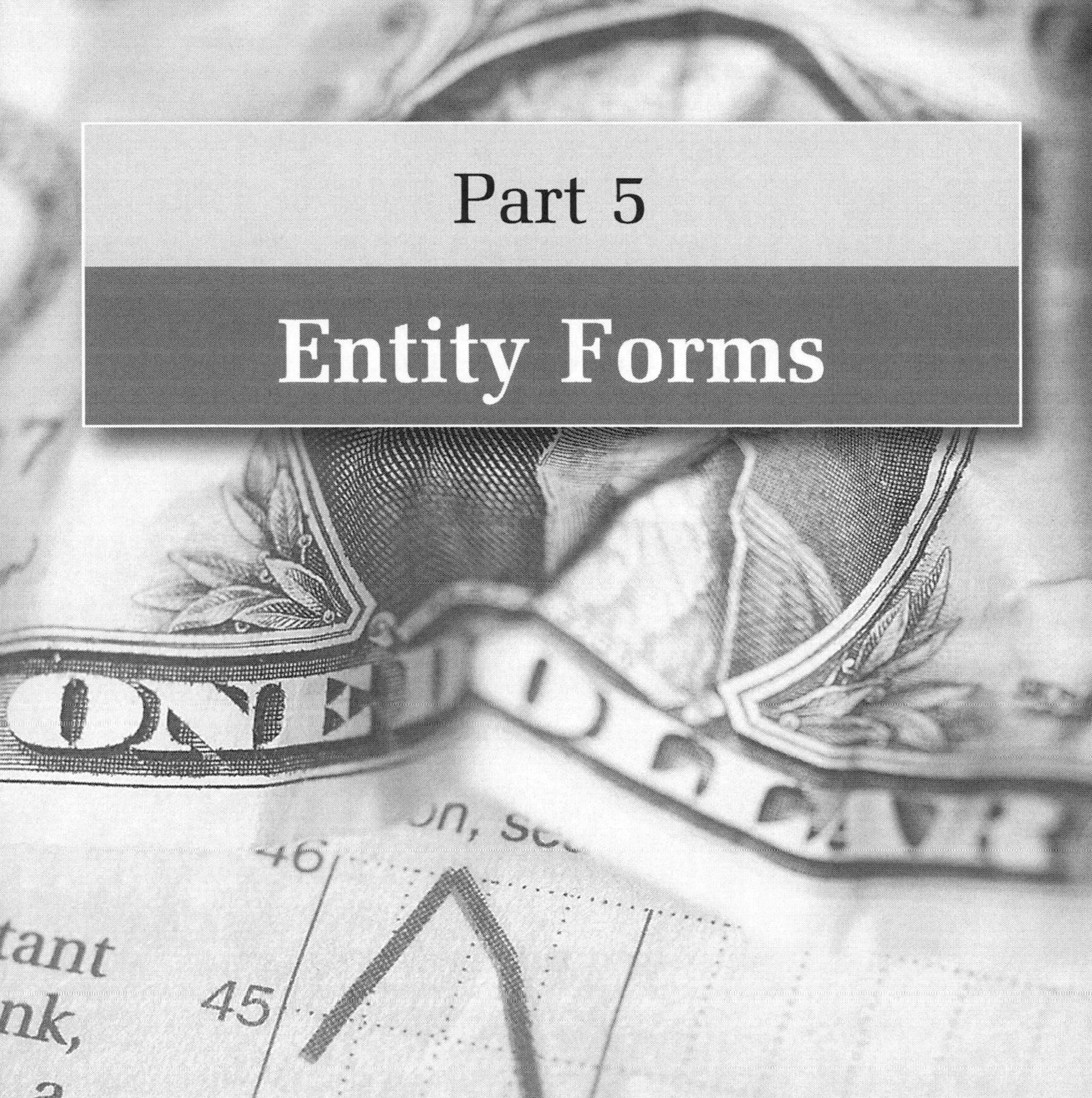

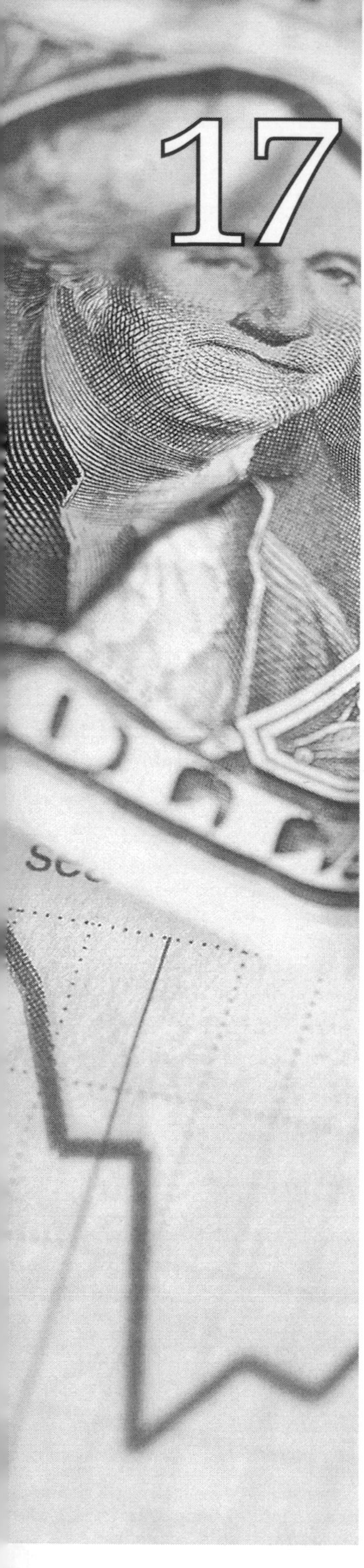

17 Accounting for Partnerships

'That the said partners shall keep, or cause to be kept, proper accounts in writing. That each of the said partners shall, in the said accounts, make true, plain and perfect entries of all the monies, goods, effects, credits, and other things received, purchased, sold, or contracted for ...' (Pulling, 1850)

Outcomes

- Understand the characteristics of a partnership.
- Understand the sources of finance, the distinction between capital contributions and profits retained and equity of a partnership.
- Describe the formation process of a partnership.
- Produce financial information for a partnership.
- Admit a new partner to an existing partnership.
- Dissolve a partnership.

Chapter outline

PRICEWATERHOUSECOOPERS

Aggregated revenues of PricewaterhouseCoopers firms by region

	(USD millions)
Asia	2 601
Australasia and Pacific Islands	1 366
Central and Eastern Europe	861
Western Europe	12 619
Middle East and Africa	715
North America and the Caribbean	9 332
South and Central America	691
Total gross revenues	**28 185**

Revenues are expressed in US dollars at average exchange rates. Gross revenues are inclusive of expenses billed to clients. Fiscal year ends 30 June.

PWC is structured as a network of member firms, connected through membership in PricewaterhouseCoopers International Limited. For many years, accounting and auditing practices in South Africa operated as partnerships and some still do. PWC is registered as a company, PricewaterhouseCoopers Inc, an authorised financial services provider.

17.1 Characteristics of a partnership

The partnership form of business entity is used for comparatively small businesses that wish to take advantage of the combined financial capital, managerial talent and experience of two or more persons. This form of entity is often found amongst the professions, such as doctors, dentists, and some firms of lawyers and accountants.

A partnership is a legal relationship which arises as a result of an agreement between two or more persons but not exceeding twenty. (The membership of organised professions which are designated by the Minister of Trade and Industries may, however, exceed twenty.) Each partner contributes cash and/or other assets to a legal undertaking with the objective of making a profit to the advantage of all concerned.

No legislation exists in South Africa to control partnerships. The principles of common law are therefore applicable. A partnership is not a legal entity and it has no legal standing apart from the members who constitute it. The individual partners are the joint owners of the assets and are jointly and severally liable for the liabilities of the partnership. In other words, each partner is potentially liable for all of the obligations of the enterprise and not only for his own share.

Participation in profits is not in itself conclusive evidence of the existence of a partnership. The relationship rests upon mutual intention. The true test is whether a business is being carried on, and whether every partner is empowered to act as an agent of the other. This is because a partnership entails the mutual agency of the individual partners – each partner, while himself a principal, is also an agent for the other partners within the scope of the business carried on and the other partners are bound by his acts.

No formalities are required in establishing a partnership. For example there need be no written agreement. It is, however, common practice and also desirable that the agreement be in writing. The agreement can be written, oral or implied, that is, by conduct.

A partnership may also operate in the form of a joint venture. A joint venture is a contractual arrangement whereby two or more parties undertake an economic activity that is subject to joint control. In order for a partnership to be regarded as a joint venture, the relationship between the partners must be formalised in a *contract* confirming the agreed sharing of control. *Joint control* in a partnership exists only when the strategic financial and operating decisions require the unanimous consent of the partners. For example, two partners may enter into a contract to control jointly a property. In this case, each of the partners receives the agreed share of the rent income and bears the agreed share of the expenses. The agreed extent of each partner's share in the joint venture is stated in the contract and is not necessarily 50%.

We mentioned in Chapter 16 that an important aspect of your understanding of partnerships and other entity forms is the distribution of profits to the owners and the composition of owner's equity in each entity form. These and other issues will be addressed in the sections that follow.

17.2 Sources of finance for a partnership

A partnership, like any other business entity, can be financed from two sources, investors' funds and borrowed funds.

Investors' funds come in the form of contributions by the partners to the **equity** of the partnership. The contributions may consist of cash or other assets.

Borrowed funds may come from a variety of sources, such as a financial institution or a private individual. The amount borrowed is a **liability** of the partnership and will appear on the statement of financial position of the partnership. Remember, however, that the partners are jointly and severally liable for debts of the partnership.

In addtion to the capital contribution of a partner to a partnership, a partner may also make a loan to the business. As the partner and partnership are separate accounting entities, the amount borrowed from a partner is a liability of the partnership and is not part of the capital contribution.

17.2.1 Distinction between capital contribution and profits retained

The **capital contribution**, whether of a sole proprietor or a partner in a partnership, represents the long-term or relatively permanent contribution by the owner to the business. As the business trades, profits accrue to the owner and increase the owner's equity. Periodically, the owner withdraws cash from the business which decreases owner's equity. The cumulative excess of profit over distributions represents the **profits retained** in the business enterprise.

When accounting for a sole proprietor, all profits belong to the sole owner and there is no need to distinguish between capital contributed by the owner and accumulated profit. In a partnership, there are multiple owners and it is therefore necessary to record the equity of each partner separately. In order to distinguish between the capital contribution and accumulated profit, a ***capital*** and ***current*** account is opened for each partner.

The **capital** account reflects the fixed amount of capital contributed by each partner. This is normally provided for in the partnership agreement. The **current** account is used to record the allocation of profit to, and distributions to partners. The balance on the current account represents the difference between profits allocated to a partner and distributions to that partner. (Distributions to partners in a partnership are often referred to as drawings.) This balance is therefore the accumulated profit, or the amount that the partnership owes to the partner (if the account has a credit balance). Conversely, if the balance on the current account is in debit, caused by distributions greater than share of profit, it represents the amount that the partner owes to the partnership.

17.2.2 Equity of a partnership

As we examine each entity form, it is important for you to appreciate and understand the composition of equity in the different entity forms. In a sole proprietorship, equity comprises the capital account of the owner. All transactions between the business entity and the owner take place through the capital account.

In a partnership, equity comprises both the capital and current accounts of the partners. The combined balance on these accounts represents the interest of each partner in the assets of the entity. A further component of the equity of a partnership is that of *reserves*. A reserve is essentially profits set aside which are not available for distribution. Reserves will be discussed in detail later in this chapter.

17.3 Formation of a partnership

As mentioned above, partners contribute cash or other assets to the capital of the partnership. If non-cash assets are introduced into the partnership, a value must be placed on these assets. All the partners must agree that the value placed on the non-cash assets is fair and reasonable. We will discuss here the formation of a partnership where two or more individuals decide to launch a business venture together. The formation of a partnership by combining two *existing* sole proprietorships will be addressed in Chapter 20, Entity Combinations and Conversions.

Example: Formation of a partnership

Towards the end of 20X6, Simon Smart reviewed the business entities that he had formed during the past two years – his principle business operation, Smart Concepts, was performing well, as were Bright Life and Sharp Moves. He realised that he did not have the time to devote to another business entity on his own. He therefore approached Gary Good with the idea of forming a partnership to begin a new business entity.

On 1 January 20X7, Simon Smart and Gary Good formed a partnership trading under the name of Intense Sports. The business is a retailer of endurance running and cycling equipment. Simon contributed R280 000 in cash, and Gary contributed land and buildings worth R250 000 and machinery which the partners agreed to be worth R75 000.

You are required to:

journalise the above transaction and prepare the statement of financial position at that date.

Solution: Formation of a partnership

Assets		**=**	**Owner's equity**			
Cash			**Capital – Simon**		**Capital – Gary**	
+/L/Dr	*–/R/Cr*		*–/L/Dr*	*+/R/Cr*	*–/L/Dr*	*+/R/Cr*
280 000				280 000		
L & B						
+/L/Dr	*–/R/Cr*					
250 000						250 000
Machinery						
+/L/Dr	*–/R/Cr*					
75 000						75 000
				280 000		325 000

On 1 January 20X7, the partners, Simon and Gary, invested cash and other assets into the business. The effect of this transaction is shown in the accounting equation above.

GENERAL JOURNAL OF INTENSE SPORTS PARTNERSHIP

Date	Description	Fol	Dr	Cr
01/01/X7	Bank		280 000	
	Capital – Simon			280 000
	Capital contribution			
01/01/X7	Land and buildings		250 000	
	Machinery		75 000	
	Capital – Gary			325 000
	Capital contribution			

INTENSE SPORTS PARTNERSHIP
STATEMENT OF FINANCIAL POSITION
AT 1 JANUARY 20X7

	R
ASSETS	
Non-current assets	325 000
Land and buildings	250 000
Machinery	75 000
Current assets	
Bank	280 000
	605 000
EQUITY AND LIABILITIES	
Capital and reserves	
Capital accounts	605 000
Simon	280 000
Gary	325 000
Current liabilities	–
	605 000

17.4 Producing information for a partnership

You know from Chapter 1 that accounting is an information system that selects data, processes that data and produces information about an economic entity. The *selection* and *processing* of data uses the same concepts in all entity forms. In this section we will review the accounting system, concentrating on those aspects of *producing information* that are unique to a partnership.

17.4.1 Determination of profit

The profit of a partnership is determined in the same way as that of a sole proprietorship. The profit is computed according to the accrual basis of accounting, taking into account the principles expounded in the conceptual framework. The procedural aspects of recording transactions in a journal, posting to a ledger and extracting a trial balance are performed as for a sole proprietorship. The internal transactions or adjusting entries are also identical in nature.

17.4.2 Appropriation of profit

The appropriation of profit in a sole proprietorship is a simple task that requires a closing entry to transfer the profit from the profit and loss account to the owner's capital account. In a partnership, however, the procedure is complicated by the fact that there is more than one owner. When resources invested and services performed by each partner are not equal, the appropriation of profits between the partners must be structured to achieve an equitable distribution. After the adjusting entries have been processed and before the financial statements are prepared, the *appropriating* entries must be processed. An extract of the accounting process diagram referred to in Parts 1 and 2 of the book is shown below, modified to take into account the appropriating entries.

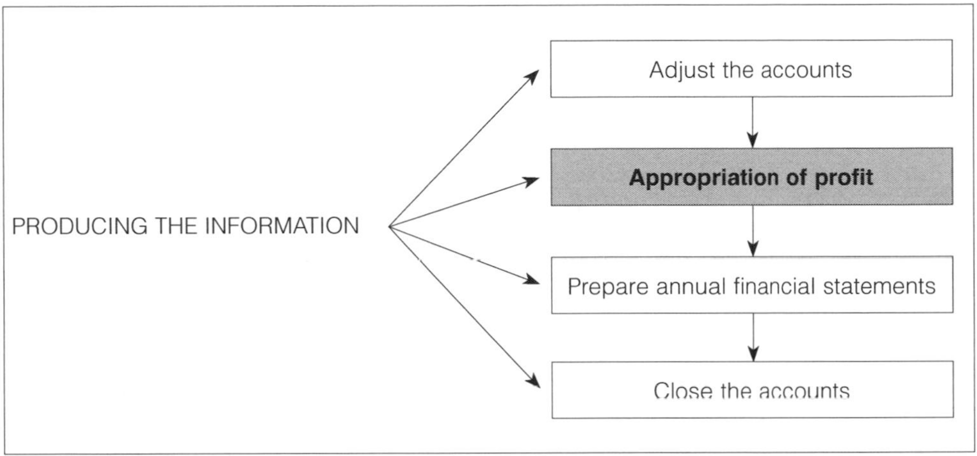

Diagram 17.1: Extract of accounting process highlighting the appropriating entries.

The objective of the appropriation of profit is to reward each partner for the services and resources provided to the firm. This is achieved by allocating salaries and interest on capital to the partners to compensate for unequal service and capital contributions.

The conceptual and legal arguments surrounding the accounting treatment of partners' salaries and interest on capital need to be considered. You are familiar with the **entity concept** which treats the partners and the partnership as separate accounting entities. Applying the entity concept, interest on capital and partners' salaries would be treated as expenses in the determination of profit on the income statement. The capital invested is regarded as finance from a separate accounting entity and the related interest is treated like interest on any liability. Likewise, the salary paid to a partner, as a separate entity, is treated in the same way as a salary paid to another employee of the partnership.

However, from a **legal** perspective, the partners and the partnership are treated as the same legal entity. This stems from English law which does not recognise the partnership as an entity distinct from the partners. Thus a partner may not be the debtor or creditor of the partnership or be employed by it because a partner cannot enter into a contractual relationship with himself.[4]

The implications of this, from an accounting perspective, are that all transactions with partners are treated as ***appropriations of profit*** and not as ***expenses in the determination of profit***. This includes interest on capital, partners' salaries as well as interest on partners' loans. We submit that the legal perspective should take preference over the entity concept in the treatment of interest on capital and partners' salaries.

It could be argued that, by treating interest on capital and partners' salaries as appropriations of profit, the profit of the partnership will be overstated compared to that of an equivalent close corporation or company where management salaries and interest on member or shareholder loans are recognised as expenses on the income statement.

However, the practical consideration of the level of the partners' salaries and interest on capital must also be taken into account. In a small partnership, the partners' salaries and the interest on capital or loans may not be market related and recognising these items as expenses could distort the profit.

Interest paid on loans to outside parties and salaries paid to employees of the partnership must be treated as expenses in the determination of profit.

Example: Producing information for a partnership

The activities of Intense Sports for its first year of trading will be used to illustrate the appropriation of profits, financial statement preparation, and closing entries of a partnership. The partnership agreement provides that:

- interest on capital is calculated at 10% per annum on the balances at the beginning of each year;
- Simon will be entitled to a salary of R132 000 per annum and Gary to a salary of R80 000 per annum, to be credited to their respective current accounts;
- interest on drawings is calculated at 10% per annum on the balances at the end of each year;
- profit (or losses) will be shared in the ratio 3:2 between Simon and Gary.

The following additional information is available for the year ended 31 December 20X7.

INTENSE SPORTS PARTNERSHIP
TRIAL BALANCE
AT 31 DECEMBER 20X7

Description	Folio	Dr	Cr
Capital – Simon			280 000
Capital – Gary			325 000
Drawings – Simon		24 000	
Drawings – Gary		30 000	
Long-term borrowings			80 000
Land and buildings		570 000	
Machinery		100 000	
Accumulated depreciation machinery			20 000
Inventory		70 000	
Accounts receivable		154 000	
Bank		362 000	
Accounts payable			141 000
Sales			1 980 000
Cost of sales		990 000	
Administration expenses		72 000	
Marketing expenses		51 000	
Telephone expenses		18 000	
Salaries – employees		340 000	
Light and water expense		25 000	
Depreciation expense		20 000	
		2 826 000	2 826 000

- Mega Bank advanced a long-term loan of R80 000 on 2 January 20X7 at an interest rate of 15% per annum
- The partners have decided to transfer R60 000 to a reserve at the end of the year.

Interest on capital

Following the legal perspective discussed above, interest on capital is not a charge against income. In other words, it does not appear as an *expense* on the income statement. It is an appropriation of profit, governed by the provisions of the partnership agreement. The objective is to compensate partners for unequal capital investments. The interest rate may be fixed in the partnership agreement or based on current rates.

The accounting entry to record interest on capital is:

	Dr	Cr
Interest on capital	60 500	
Current a/c: Simon		28 000
Current a/c: Gary		32 500

Partners' salaries

Again, following the legal perspective, partners' salaries are also not a charge against income but rather an allocation of profit governed by the provisions of the partnership agreement. The partners are *owners* of the partnership and not *employees*. The objective is to reward partners for the time, effort and expertise that they devote to the entity.

The entry to record partners' salaries is:

	Dr	Cr
Partners' salaries	212 000	
Current a/c: Simon		132 000
Current a/c: Gary		80 500

It is important to note that the above entry is an *appropriation of profit* and not a *cash payment* to the partners. This appropriation or allocation of partners' salaries takes place at the end of the period, which could be a month, three months, six months or a year. Amounts drawn in cash by the partners during the period are charged to their respective drawings accounts. This will be discussed in detail below.

Interest on drawings

In the same way that interest on capital and partners' salaries are appropriations of profit credited to a partner as a reward for resources and services provided, interest on drawings is charged against a partner to compensate other partners for unequal drawings.

It is important to understand the circumstances under which interest is charged on drawings. You learnt above that the current account is credited with appropriations of profit allocated to partners. When a partner then draws cash from the partnership, the debit to the drawings account represents a withdrawal of amounts owing to him. As long as the credit balance on a partner's current account exceeds the debit balance on his drawings account, no interest is charged on drawings as the partner is merely taking cash amounts owing to him. In fact, interest is only charged on drawings when the debit balance on the partner's drawing exceeds the credit balance on his current account, that is, if the partner takes an advance against expected future profits.

According to the trial balance, Simon and Gary withdrew R24 000 and R30 000 respectively. The entry to record the cash paid to them is:

	Dr	Cr
Drawings a/c: Simon	24 000	
Drawings a/c: Gary	30 000	
Bank		54 000

As this is the first period of trading, all of the amounts withdrawn during the year represent an advance against future profits. The entry to record interest on drawings is:

	Dr	Cr
Current a/c: Simon	2 400	
Current a/c: Gary	3 000	
Interest on drawings		5 400

17.4.3 Interest on loans

As mentioned earlier in this chapter, interest on loans to outside parties is treated as an expense on the income statement.

The interest on the loan from the bank is therefore regarded as an expense in the determination of profit, and *not as an appropriation* of profit. In our example, Wheels Bank has advanced an amount of R80 000 to the partnership at an interest rate of 15% per annum.

The entry to record interest on the loan is:

	Dr	Cr
Interest expense	12 000	
Interest accrued		12 000

17.4.4 Transfers to reserves

The profits earned by the business entity and allocated to the partners by means of the appropriating entries, *and* a share of the remaining profit are available for distribution to the partners in cash. If the partners wish to reduce the amount available for distribution in cash and retain profits in the business for expansion, they may decide to set aside profits in a reserve. The reserve forms part of the equity of the partnership.

The entry to record the transfer to a reserve is:

	Dr	Cr
Appropriation	60 000	
Reserve		60 000

The appropriation account is used to accumulate the effects of the appropriations of profit in the same way that the profit and loss account accumulates the income and expenses for a period. It is discussed in detail in the following section.

It is important to note that there is no movement in cash in the transfer to a reserve. The transfer to a reserve is the transfer of *profits,* which then reduces the amount available to the partners to withdraw in *cash*.

Pause and reflect...

Consider the implications of the partners' decision to transfer R60 000 to a reserve.

a) Does the transfer to the reserve reduce the partnership equity?
b) Can you think of a situation when it would be an advantage for the partnership to have this reserve?
c) Is the reserve a cash resource of the partnership?

Response

a) The reserve forms part of the partnership's equity, therefore, the transfer does not reduce equity. The reserve is simply another component within equity.
b) The reserve represents resources that may not be apportioned to the partners. Therefore, should the partnership encounter financial difficulties, the reserve will be intact and available for the partnership's benefit.
c) The reserve itself is definitely not a cash resource of the partnership. It is not an asset, but rather equity. Remember from Chapter 3 that equity and liabilities represent claims on the resources of the entity. The reserve simply ensures that underlying assets of an equivalent amount are not distributed to the partners. These assets would be available for distribution were it not for the transfer to the reserve.

17.4.5 Preparation of the financial statements

Once the appropriating entries have been completed, the financial statements of the partnership can be prepared. The income statement is presented in the same format as for a sole proprietor.

The only difference to the statement of financial position is the owner's equity section, which discloses the capital and current accounts for *each* partner.

The statement of changes in equity is expanded to include columns for the capital and current accounts of each partner, reserves and a column to accommodate the appropriation of profit.

INTENSE SPORTS PARTNERSHIP
INCOME STATEMENT
FOR THE YEAR ENDED 31 DECEMBER 20X7

	R
Revenue from sales	1 980 000
Cost of sales	(990 000)
Gross profit	990 000
Operating expenses	(526 000)
Administration	72 000
Marketing	51 000
Telephone	18 000
Salaries	340 000
Lights and water	25 000
Depreciation	20 000
Finance cost	
Interest on loan	(12 000)
Profit for the period	452 000

INTENSE SPORTS PARTNERSHIP
STATEMENT OF CHANGES IN EQUITY
FOR THE YEAR ENDED 31 DECEMBER 20X7

	Capital		Current		Reserve	Appro-priation	Total
	Simon	Gary	Simon	Gary			
	R	R	R	R	R	R	R
Balance at 1 January							
Profit for the period						452 000	452 000
Salaries			132 000	80 000		(212 000)	
Interest on capital			28 000	32 500		(60 500)	
Interest on drawings			(2 400)	(3 000)		5 400	
Transfer to reserve					60 000	(60 000)	
						124 900	
Share of remaining profit			74 940	49 960		(124 900)	
Distributions			(24 000)	(30 000)			(54 000)
Contribution to capital	280 000	325 000					605 000
Balance at 31 December	280 000	325 000	208 540	129 460	60 000	0	1 003 000

Note that the appropriation column shows a balance of profit of R124 900 after the appropriations and the reserve transfer have been taken into account. This is shared between the partners in their agreed profit-sharing ratio and transferred to their current accounts by means of a closing entry, described in section 17.4.6 below.

INTENSE SPORTS PARTNERSHIP
STATEMENT OF FINANCIAL POSITION
AT 31 DECEMBER 20X7

	Cost	Accumulated depreciation	Carrying amount	R
ASSETS				
Non-current assets				650 000
Land and buildings	570 000	–	570 000	
Machinery	100 000	20 000	80 000	
Current assets				586 000
Inventory				70 000
Accounts receivable				154 000
Bank				362 000
				1 236 000
EQUITY AND LIABILITIES				
Capital and reserves				1 003 000
Capital accounts				605 000
Simon			280 000	
Gary			325 000	
Current accounts				338 000
Simon			208 540	
Gary			129 460	
Reserve				60 000
Non current liabilities				
Borrowing – Mega Bank				80 000
Current liabilities				
Accounts payable				141 000
Interest accrued				12 000
				1 236 000

17.4.6 Closing entries for a partnership

The closing entries to transfer the trading activities to the trading account and the operating activities to the profit and loss account are identical for a sole proprietor and a partnership. When accounting for a sole proprietor, the profit from the profit and loss account is transferred to the owner's capital account. In a partnership situation, however, the profit from the profit and loss account is transferred to the ***appropriation account***, where the appropriations of profit (as discussed above) are also transferred.

The closing entry to transfer the profit from the profit and loss account to the appropriation account is:

	Dr	Cr
Profit & loss	452 000	
Appropriation		452 000

Further closing entries for a partnership are required to transfer the balances on the interest on capital, partners' salaries, and interest on drawings accounts to the appropriation account. These entries are as follows:

	Dr	Cr
Appropriation	272 500	
Interest on capital		60 500
Partners' salaries		212 000
Interest on drawings	5 400	
Appropriation		5 400

The objective of the appropriation has now been achieved. The partners have been fairly rewarded for resources invested and services rendered to the partnership. In addition, the partners have compensated each other for unequal distributions. The balance in the appropriation account represents the remaining profit available to share between the partners in the agreed profit-sharing ratio.

Since the essence of a partnership is mutual agreement, it is desirable for the partners to agree, before entering into partnership, to the conditions upon which the business is to be carried on, and to their respective rights and powers. Where the agreement is silent with regard to a particular aspect, common law requirements are applied. For example, where the profit-sharing ratio has not been agreed upon, partners share profits and losses in proportion to their capital contributions to the partnership. Where such contributions cannot be determined, it is assumed that partners share equally in the profits. It is important to remember that the partnership agreement must be studied before the financial statements for the partnership are prepared.[5]

In our example the balance of R124 900 in the appropriation account is the amount available for allocation to the partners in their profit-sharing ratio. Note that we have used the word allocation and not distribution, as the amount is credited to the partners' current accounts and not actually paid to the partners. The share allocated to each partner is transferred to the partners' current accounts with the following closing entry:

	Dr	Cr
Appropriation	124 900	
Current a/c: Simon		74 940
Current a/c: Gary		49 960

The final closing entry that is required is to transfer the drawings account of each partner to their respective current accounts:

	Dr	Cr
Current a/c: Simon	24 000	
Current a/c: Gary	30 000	
Drawings a/c: Simon		24 000
Drawings a/c: Gary		30 000

The relevant ledger accounts of Intense Sports after the closing entries have been taken into account appear as follows:

Trading

Details	R	Details	R
Cost of sales	990 000	Sales	1 980 000
Profit & loss	990 000		
	1 980 000		1 980 000

Profit and loss

Details	R	Details	R
Administration	72 000	Trading	990 000
Marketing	51 000		
Telephone	18 000		
Salaries	340 000		
Lights and water	25 000		
Depreciation	20 000		
Interest	12 000		
Appropriation	452 000		
	990 000		990 000

Interest on loan

Details	R	Details	R
Interest accrued	12 000	Profit & loss	12 000
	12 000		12 000

Interest on drawings

Details	R	Details	R
Appropriation	5 400	Current – Simon	2 400
		Current – Gary	3 000
	5 400		5 400

Interest on capital

Details	R	Details	R
Current – Simon	28 000	Appropriation	60 500
Current – Gary	32 500		
	60 500		60 500

Partners' salaries

Details	R	Details	R
Current – Simon	132 000	Appropriation	212 000
Current – Gary	80 000		
	212 000		212 000

Appropriation

Details	R	Details	R
Interest on on capital	60 500	Profit & loss	452 000
Partners' salaries	212 000	Interest on drawings	5 400
Reserve	60 000		
Current – Simon	74 940		
Current – Gary	49 960		
	457 400		457 400

Current a/c – Simon

Details	R	Details	R
Interest on drawings	2 400	Interest on capital	28 000
Drawings	24 000	Salary	132 000
		Appropriation	74 940
Balance c/d	208 540		
	234 940		234 940
		Balance b/d	208 540

Current a/c – Gary

Details	R	Details	R
Interest on drawings	3 000	Interest on capital	32 500
Drawings	30 000	Salary	80 000
		Appropriation	49 960
Balance c/d	129 460		
	162 460		162 460
		Balance b/d	129 460

Drawings – Simon

Details	R	Details	R
Cash	24 000	Current – Simon	24 000
	24 000		24 000

Drawings – Gary

Details	R	Details	R
Cash	30 000	Current – Gary	30 000
	30 000		30 000

17.4.7 Provisions in partnership agreement

The preceding sections have described in detail that part of the accounting process related to producing information for a partnership. Remember, it is important when preparing the financial statements of a partnership to take into account the provisions of the partnership agreement. General provisions which relate to financial statements and which are normally contained in partnership agreements are summarised below.

- Whether each partner should contribute a fixed amount of capital or otherwise.
- Whether the capitals are to remain fixed, with drawings and profits being adjusted on current accounts, or whether they are to be adjusted on the capital accounts.
- The division of profits and losses between the partners, including capital profits and losses.
- Whether interest on capital or on drawings, or both, is to be allowed or charged before arriving at the profits divisible in the agreed proportions and, if so, at what rate.
- Whether partners are to be allowed remuneration for their services before arriving at divisible profit and, if so, the amounts thereof.
- Whether current accounts (if any) are to bear interest and, if so, at what rate.
- Whether partners' drawings are to be limited in amount.
- That proper financial statements shall be prepared at least once a year and signed by all the partners.
- That such financial statements when duly signed shall be binding on the partners, but shall be capable of being re-opened within a specific period on an error being discovered.

17.5 Admission of a partner

We will examine here the issues which relate to the admission of a partner to a partnership. In terms of common law, a change in the members of the partnership ends the existing partnership and a new partnership comes into existence. A change in composition of a partnership results in a change in the profit-sharing ratio. In addition, it is necessary to ensure that the equity of the existing partners is fairly stated. This involves revaluing the assets and liabilities of the partnership. Once the assets and liabilities have been revalued and the equity adjusted, a value for goodwill (if any) needs to be determined. The capital contribution of the new partner is recorded and lastly the reserve (if any) must be redistributed among the partners.

The procedure to follow an admission of a partner is summarised as follows:

- Adjustment to the profit-sharing ratio.
- Revaluation of the assets of the partnership.
- Accounting for goodwill.
- Recording the new partner's contribution.
- Redistribution of the reserve.

Each step will be discussed in detail, continuing with the Intense Sports example.

Example: Admission of a partner

On 1 January 20X8 Simon and Gary agree to admit Mark Main into the partnership on the following terms:

- The following values are placed on the assets and liabilities:
  - Land and buildings R700 000
  - Machinery R 90 000
  - Inventory R 65 000
  - Accounts receivable R144 000

All other assets and liabilities are considered to be fairly valued.

- Mark contributed R440 000 to the partnership for a 1/3 share of the business which the remaining partners are to relinquish so that each partner will have a third of the future profits.

You are required to:

prepare the statement of financial position of Intense Sports at 1 January 20X8, immediately after the admission of Mark.

17.5.1 Adjustment to the profit-sharing ratio

The profit-sharing ratio is an important aspect of a partnership agreement because it determines how the profit remaining after appropriations is shared among the partners. On change in partnership composition, the existing partners must agree on the basis of relinquishing profit share and all the partners must agree on the profit share to be allocated to the new partner. Three possible agreements could be reached.

(a) The share that the new partner will acquire is relinquished by the *existing* partners according to their *existing* ratio. As a result, future profits accruing to the partnership will be shared between the original partners in their original profit-sharing ratio.
(b) The share that the new partner will acquire is relinquished by the *existing* partners *equally*. As a result, future profits accruing to the partnership will be shared between the original partners in a *different* profit-sharing ratio.
(c) The share that the new partner will acquire is relinquished by the *existing* partners according to a ratio *agreed* between them.

Simon and Gary are sharing profits and losses in the ratio of 3:2. For illustration purposes, we will consider all three possible agreements and then continue the example with the agreement as decided.

(a) If Simon and Gary relinquish the 1/3 share of profits given to Mark according to their **existing ratio**, Simon will relinquish 3/15 (3/5 x 1/3) and Gary will relinquish 2/15 (2/5 x 1/3). The new profit-sharing ratio of 6 : 4 : 5 is calculated as follows:

Simon	3/5	–	3/15	=	6/15
Gary	2/5	–	2/15	=	4/15
	1				10/15
Mark	(1/3)				5/15
	2/3				1

Note that, according to this agreement, Simon has given up 3/15 (his share has decreased from 9/15 to 6/15), Gary has given up 2/15 (from 6/15 to 4/15) and Mark has gained 5/15 (3/15 from Simon and 2/15 from Gary).

(b) If Simon and Gary relinquish the 1/3 share of profits given to Mark **equally**, both Simon and Gary will relinquish 1/6 (1/2 x 1/3). The new profit-sharing ratio of 13 : 7 : 10 is calculated as follows:

Simon	3/5	–	1/6	=	13/30
Gary	2/5	–	1/6	=	7/30
	1				20/30
Mark	(1/3)				10/30
	2/3				1

Note that, according to this agreement, Simon has given up 5/30 (his share has decreased from 18/30 to 13/30), and Gary has also given up 5/30 (from 12/30 to 7/30) while Mark has gained 10/30 (5/30 from Simon and 5/30 from Gary).

(c) If Simon and Gary **agree** to relinquish profits according to an agreement (in this case, each partner will have 1/3 of future profits) Simon and Gary will relinquish 4/15 and 1/15 respectively of the 1/3 share of profits given to Mark. The new profit sharing ratio of 5 : 5 : 5 or 1/3 : 1/3 : 1/3 is calculated as follows:

Simon	3/5	–	4/15	=	5/15
Gary	2/5	–	1/15	=	5/15
	1				10/15
Mark	(1/3)				5/15
	2/3				1

This is the new profit-sharing ratio that the partners in our example agreed upon and it will be used when recording the change in partnership composition in the accounting records. Note that, according to this agreement, Simon has given up 4/15 (his share has decreased from 9/15 to 5/15), Gary has given up 1/15 (from 6/15 to 5/15) while Mark has gained 5/15 (4/15 from Simon and 1/15 from Gary). This analysis of the profit share relinquished by the existing partners and taken over by the new partner is important as it impacts on your understanding of the treatment of goodwill and reserves on the admission of a partner.

 **Pause and reflect...**

In admitting a new partner, the existing partners can relinquish the new partner's share of the partnership's profits according to their existing ratio, equally or in terms of a specific agreement. What is the effect of the method selected on the profit-sharing relationship between the existing partners after the new partner has been admitted, compared to the profit-sharing relationship before the new partner was admitted?

Response

When relinquishing profits according to the existing ratio, the relationship between the existing partners is the same after, as it was before, the admission of the new partner. (Before, Simon 3/5 and Gary 2/5; After, Simon 6/10 and Gary 4/10.)

When the new partner's share of profits is relinquished equally, the relationship between the existing partners changes after admission. (Before, Simon 3/5 and Gary 2/5; After, Simon 13/20 and Gary 7/20.)

When the profit is relinquished in terms of a specific arrangement, the relationship between the existing partners may or may not be the same after as it was before the admission of the new partner. In this example, it is not the same. (Before, Simon 3/5 and Gary 2/5; After, Simon 5/10 and Gary 5/10.)

17.5.2 Revaluation of assets

As a new partnership comes into existence on the admission of another partner, it is important to determine the fair value of the partnership equity at the date of admission of the new partner. The underlying assets and liabilities need to be valued to determine the consideration to be paid by the incoming partner, and to recognise any change in the share of equity of the existing partners.

A ***revaluation account*** is used to record movements in the values of assets and liablities, as agreed by the partners. The balance on the revaluation account is referred to as a gain or loss on revaluation and is allocated to the existing partners in the existing profit-sharing ratio. This is because the existing partners must benefit or lose from changes in the value of equity while they controlled the business. The consequence of the revaluation procedure is that the new firm begins with its assets recorded at their agreed values and the partners' equity is adjusted to reflect the interest of the partners in the assets of the business.

It is important to consider how the change in equity resulting from the revaluation is reported in the financial statements. You will recall from Chapter 2 that IAS 1 requires the statement of changes in equity to present changes in equity separated into *owner* changes in equity and *non-owner* changes in equity. Owner changes in equity are changes in equity arising from transactions with owners in their capacity as owners. This incorporates contributions to capital by owners and distributions to owners. Non-owner changes in equity are changes in equity arising from income and expense transactions.

The revaluation process on admission of a partner does not generate components of income or expense to be included in comprehensive income, as a non-owner change in equity. Rather, the gain or loss on revaluation represents an owner change in equity. As such, it will not appear on the statement of comprehensive income but will appear on the statement of changes in equity as an adjustment to the partners' capital accounts on the admission of a new partner.

An extract of the statement of changes in equity is presented later in this chapter.

Accounting entries

The accounting entries to record the revaluation of non-current assets were described in Chapter 11, *Property, Plant and Equipment*. We will review these entries and also consider the revaluation of current assets.

The partners value the land and buildings at R700 000 – an increase of R130 000 over the cost as reported on the statement of financial position. As the land and buildings are not depreciated, the entry to record the revaluation is:

	Dr	Cr
Land and buildings	130 000	
Revaluation		130 000

The machinery is valued at R90 000, compared to its *carrying amount* of R80 000. The machinery is a depreciable asset and therefore the balance in the accumulated depreciation account must be reversed. The effect is to record the asset at valuation, with only the depreciation subsequent to the valuation recorded as accumulated depreciation. There are a number of bookkeeping entries which could be processed, all of which achieve the same result. We suggest the following entries:

	Dr	Cr
Accumulated depreciation	20 000	
Machinery		20 000
Machinery	10 000	
Revaluation		10 000

The effect of these two entries on the machinery account is to record the machinery at the valuation amount of R90 000 (R100 000 – R20 000 + R10 000). The increase of R10 000 (R90 000 – R80 000) is credited to the revaluation account.

Turning to the current assets, the inventory is valued at R65 000 – a decrease of R5 000 compared to the cost on the balance sheet. The accounts receivable are valued at R144 000, in other words, R10 000 is considered to be uncollectable.

	Dr	Cr
Revaluation	5 000	
Inventory		5 000
Revaluation	10 000	
Allowance for doubtful debts		10 000

The entry to adjust the value of the inventory credits the inventory account to reduce the balance. The entry to adjust the accounts receivable credits the allowance for doubtful debts. This is in line with the treatment of inventory write-downs and allowance for doubtful debts described in earlier chapters.

The balance on the revaluation account after processing all the changes in asset values, as agreed by the partners (except goodwill) is R125 000. (The recognition of goodwill will be dealt with separately in the next section.) This balance is the surplus on revaluation and represents an increase in the net assets of the partnership. As any change in the net assets changes the interest of the owners in the business, the surplus on revaluation must be allocated to the capital accounts of the existing partners in the existing ratio. The accounting entry is as follows:

	Dr	**Cr**
Revaluation	125 000	
Capital – Simon		75 000
Capital – Gary		50 000

It is important to notice and understand that the surplus on revaluation is transferred to the capital accounts and not the current accounts. This is because the surplus on revaluation is an ***unrealised*** surplus. In other words, the surplus has not been realised in cash. It is therefore not available for distribution to the partners and cannot be credited to the current accounts.

The revaluation account is shown below:

Revaluation

Details	R	Details	R
Inventory	5 000	Land & buildings	130 000
Allowance for doubtful debts	10 000	Machinery	10 000
Capital – Simon	75 000		
Capital – Gary	50 000		
	140 000		140 000

17.5.3 Identification of goodwill

Nature of goodwill

The revaluation of the partnership's tangible assets results in the net assets being stated at their fair value. However, the value of the business as a whole could be greater than the sum of the individual net assets. The excess of the value of a business as a whole (as indicated by the purchase consideration) over the fair value of its identifiable net assets is known as goodwill.

Goodwill is an intangible asset. Goodwill represents anticipated future economic benefits from assets that are not capable of being individually identified and separately recognised.[6] Goodwill arises through factors such as sound management, a well-trained workforce and loyal customers.

Accounting practice has distinguished between ***internally generated goodwill*** and ***purchased goodwill***. IAS 38, entitled Intangible Assets, states that internally generated goodwill (also known as inherent goodwill) is not recognised as an asset because it is not an identifiable resource controlled by the entity and its cost cannot be measured reliably.[7] This is because internally generated goodwill could be valued differently by different parties and could fluctuate in value as various factors which affect the business change on a daily basis. On the other hand, the value of purchased goodwill is based on an arm's length transaction between the seller and purchaser of a business or part of a business.

Goodwill arising on acquisition represents a payment made by the acquirer in anticipation of future economic benefits.[8] With the passage of time, goodwill diminishes, reflecting that its service potential is decreasing. However, in some cases, the value of goodwill may appear not to decrease over time. This is because the potential for economic benefits that was purchased initially is being replaced by internally generated goodwill.

There is thus no difference in nature between internally generated goodwill and purchased goodwill – a successful business continually creates internally generated goodwill which is only recognised (as purchased goodwill) on a change in composition of ownership.

Turning our attention again to partnerships, the additional amount paid by the incoming partner, which cannot be attributed to any asset, is regarded as internally generated goodwill developed by the effort of the existing partners. It must be taken into account so that the equity of the existing partners correctly reflects their share of the business at the date of admission of the new partner.

We will now apply the concepts discussed in the above paragraphs to Intense Sports, as shown in the following calculation. Remember that Mark is being admitted to the partnership on 1 January 20X8.

		Mark 1/3 share	**Total for partnership**
Purchase consideration	(Total = 440 000 X 3)	440 000	1 320 000
Fair value of identifiable net assets	(Mark 1/3 share = 1 128 000 x 1/3)	376 000	1 128 000
Owners' equity per statement of financial position at 31/12/X7			1 003 000
Revaluation of identifiable net assets			125 000
Goodwill	(Total = 64 000 x 3)	64 000	192 000

It is important to note that the purchase consideration paid by Mark of R440 000 for a 1/3 share of the partnership results in an implied purchase consideration for the partnership as a whole of R1 320 000. The fair value of the identifiable net assets of R1 128 000 (total for partnership) is calculated by taking the owners equity per the statement of financial position at 31 December 20X7 of R1 003 000 and adding the gain on revaluation of the identifiable net assets of R125 000. The amount to recognise as goodwill is the total goodwill for the partnership of R192 000.

The recognition of goodwill is also an owner change in equity and as such, will appear on the statement of changes in equity as an adjustment to the partners' capital accounts on the admission of a new partner.

The R192 000 is internally generated goodwill which, when raised as an asset in the accounting records of the new partnership, will represent purchased goodwill. The accounting entries for goodwill will be described in the following section.

Accounting for goodwill

If there is a value for purchased goodwill on the statement of financial position, arising from a previous change in partnership composition, then it is only necessary to account for the *difference* between the total goodwill as currently valued and the latest statement of financial position value. Applying this principle to our example:

	R
Total goodwill as currently valued	192 000
Goodwill on statement of financial position	–
Goodwill to be recognised	192 000

Pause and reflect...

Refer to the goodwill calculation on Mark's admission to the partnership. How would the calculation of the goodwill be affected if there was existing goodwill of R100 000 included on the statement of financial position at 31 December 20X7 and therefore included in the fair value of the net assets of R1 128 000?

Response

The goodwill calculation is modified to take into account the existing goodwill.

		Total for partnership
Purchase consideration	(440 000 X 3)	1 320 000
		1 028 000
Fair value of identifiable net assets		1 128 000
Existing goodwill		(100 000)
Goodwill		292 000
Existing goodwill		(100 000)
Goodwill to be recognised		192 000

IFRS 3, entitled Business Combinations, states that purchased goodwill should be recognised as an asset on the statement of financial position and carried at cost less accumulated impairment losses.[9] The amount of goodwill raised as an asset must be allocated to the existing partners in the existing profit-sharing ratio. The accounting entry is:

	Dr	Cr
Goodwill	192 000	
Capital – Simon		115 200
Capital – Gary		76 800

According to IFRS 3, an impairment test should be performed on the amount of goodwill annually, or more frequently if events or changes in circumstances indicate that it might be impaired. Such an impairment test should be performed in accordance with the impairment principles outlined in Chapter 11.[10] Any impairment loss relating to goodwill should be recognised as an expense. Therefore, an impairment test will be performed at least annually on the goodwill of R192 000 raised in our example. The goodwill account, after initial recognition, is shown below.

Goodwill

Details	R	Details	R
Capital – Simon	115 200	Balance c/d	192 000
Capital – Gary	76 800		
	192 000		192 000
Balance b/d	192 000		

17.5.4 Contribution to capital

The new partner's contribution to the equity of the partnership needs to be recorded. The total amount paid by Mark amounts to R440 000. The accounting entry is:

	Dr	Cr
Cash	440 000	
Capital – Mark		440 000

Before examining the capital accounts, one further item that needs to be taken into account is the reserve.

17.5.5 Redistribution of the reserve

A reserve, as you are now aware, is part of equity and, in the case of a partnership, represents profits that have not been allocated to the partners' current accounts. This is to restrict the cash withdrawn from the entity. As the new partner is entitled to a share of the partnership equity, Mark is entitled to a 1/3 share of the reserve of R60 000. However, the underlying profits in the reserve of R60 000 were earned while Simon and Gary were in partnership and before Mark was admitted. An accounting entry is therefore required to redistribute the reserve so that the equity of the existing partners is adjusted to reflect their share of those profits. The entry is:

	Dr	Cr
Capital – Mark (60 000 x 5/15)	20 000	
Capital – Simon (60 000 x 4/15)		16 000
Capital – Gary (60 000 x 1/15)		4 000

If you recall the change in the profit-share calculation, you will realise that the R20 000 debit to the capital of the incoming partner, Mark, is 5/15 of the R60 000 reserve. In other words, Mark is being charged with the share of the reserve to which he has become entitled. Simon and Gary, in turn, are being compensated for their share of the reserve given up, R16 000 to Simon (R60 000 x 4/15) and R4 000 to Gary (R60 000 x 1/15).

There is an alternative approach to the bookkeeping, which achieves the same result. The reserve is allocated to the capital accounts of the existing partners in the existing profit-sharing ratio. As the reserve is to retain its nature, it is immediately re-established, and the capital accounts of the new partners debited in the new profit sharing ratio.

The entries required are:

	Dr	Cr
Reserve	60 000	
Capital – Simon (60 000 x 3/5)		36 000
Capital – Gary (60 000 x 2/5)		24 000
Capital – Simon (60 000 x 1/3)	20 000	
Capital – Gary (60 000 x 1/3)	20 000	
Capital – Mark (60 000 x 1/3)	20 000	
Reserve		60 000

If we analyse the effect of these entries on the capital accounts of Simon, Gary and Mark, we see the following:

	Reserve	Simon	Gary	Mark
Allocate reserve	60 000 Dr	36 000 Cr	24 000 Cr	–
Reinstate reserve	60 000 Cr	20 000 Dr	20 000 Dr	20 000 Dr
Net effect	–	16 000 Cr	4 000 Cr	20 000 Dr

You will notice that the net effect of these two entries is a debit to the capital account of Mark of R20 000 and a credit to the capital accounts of Simon and Gary of R16 000 and R4 000 respectively. Thus the same result is achieved as in the one entry shown above which adjusted the balance on the partners' capital accounts.

Having examined in detail all the aspects relating to the admission of a partner to a partnership, we can now prepare the statements of financial position at 1 January 20X8 (immediately after the admission of Mark). An extract from the statement of changes in equity for the current period as well as the capital accounts of the partners are shown as well for illustrative purposes.

Solution: Admission of a partner

INTENSE SPORTS PARTNERSHIP
STATEMENT OF FINANCIAL POSITION
AT 1 JANUARY 20X8

	Cost	Accumulated depreciation/ impairment losses	Carrying amount	R
ASSETS				
Non-current assets				982 000
Land and buildings	700 000	–	700 000	
Machinery	90 000	–	90 000	
Goodwill	192 000	–	192 000	
Current assets				999 000
Inventory				65 000
Accounts receivable	(154 000 – 10 000)			144 000
Bank	(350 000 + 440 000)			790 000
				1 981 000
EQUITY AND LIABILITIES				
Capital and reserves				1 760 000
Capital accounts			1 362 000	
Simon			486 200	
Gary			455 800	
Mark			420 000	
Current accounts			338 000	
Simon			208 540	
Gary			129 460	
Mark			–	
Reserve			60 000	
Non current liabilities				
15% Loan Simon				80 000
Current liabilities				
Accounts payable				141 000
				1 981 000

INTENSE SPORTS PARTNERSHIP
EXTRACT FROM STATEMENT OF CHANGES IN EQUITY
FOR THE YEAR ENDED 31 DECEMBER 20X8

		Capital		**Reserve**	**Total**
	Simon	**Gary**	**Mark**		
	R	**R**	**R**	**R**	**R**
Balance at 01/01/X8	280 000	325 000	–	60 000	665 000
Contribution to capital			440 000		440 000
Revaluation on admission of partner	75 000	50 000	–		125 000
Recognition of goodwill	115 200	76 800	–		192 000
Redistribution of reserve	16 000	4 000	(20 000)	–	–
Preliminary balance	486 200	455 800	420 000	60 000	1 422 000

The line items shown in the above extract from the statement of changes in equity are all *owner* changes in equity. When the complete statement of changes in equity is prepared for the year ended 31 December 20X8, a line item for the total comprehensive income will be included as the *non-owner* change in equity. As this is only an extract, columns for the partners' current accounts as well as the appropriation column are not shown.

Capital – Simon

Details	R	Details	R
		Balance b/d	280 000
		Revaluation	75 000
		Goodwill	115 200
		Capital – Mark (Reserve)	16 000
Balance c/d	486 200		
	486 200		486 200
		Balance b/d	486 200

Capital – Gary

Details	R	Details	R
		Balance b/d	325 000
		Revaluation	50 000
		Goodwill	76 800
		Capital – Mark (Reserve)	4 000
Balance c/d	455 800		
	455 800		455 800
		Balance b/d	455 800

Capital – Mark

Details	R	Details	R
Capital – Simon/Gary (Reserve)	20 000	Bank	440 000
Balance c/d	420 000		
	440 000		440 000
		Balance c/d	420 000

Reserve

Details	R	Details	R
		Balance b/d	60 000
Balance c/d	60 000		
	60 000		60 000
		Balance b/d	60 000

17.6 Partnership dissolution

The dissolution of a partnership can take two forms.

- Retirement or death of a partner where the interests of a retired/deceased partner are taken over by either:
  - a new partner
  - the remaining partners.
- Liquidation of a partnership where the activities are terminated.

17.6.1 Retirement or death of a partner

A partner who retires from a partnership or the estate of a deceased partner is entitled to the settlement of his/her interest in the partnership. The interest of a partner is determined by the partner's share of the equity of the partnership. A partner's share of equity will include:

- the balance on the partner's capital account;
- the balance on the partner's current account;
- the partner's share of any reserves on the statement of financial position;
- the partner's share of any gains or losses on revaluation of assets at date of retirement or death;
- the partner's share of any movement in the value of goodwill, as agreed between the partners;
- a charge against the retiring partner for any assets taken over;
- the partner's share of any costs incurred in the change in partnership composition.

The adjustments are typically made through a ***revaluation account***, as was the case on the admission of a partner. You may, however, come across situations where the revaluations are allocated directly to the partners' capital accounts, either on retirement or on admission. The principles involved are similar to the admission of a partner, as will be seen from the next phase of the activities of Intense Sports.

Pause and reflect...

Does the decision to allocate movements in the carrying amounts of assets and liabilities to the revaluation account as opposed to the partners' capital accounts affect the value of the existing partners' share of the partnership on the retirement of a partner?

Response

As discussed, the balance on the revaluation account is allocated to the partners' capital accounts in the existing profit-sharing ratio. Therefore, the decision to record movements in the carrying amounts of assets and liabilities to the revaluation account or to the capital accounts does not affect the value of the existing partners' share of the partnership on the retirement of a partner.

Example: Retirement of a partner

Gary decided to retire at 31 December 20X8. Simon and Mark continued the partnership, sharing profits and losses equally.

On 2 January 20X8, the entity purchased three identical motor vehicles at a cost of R100 000 each. Each motor vehicle has an estimated useful life of four years and an estimated residual value of R20 000. The straight-line basis of depreciation is used.

The partners of Intense Sports performed an impairment test on the goodwill at 31 December 20X8. They estimated that the goodwill had a recoverable amount of R172 800. An impairment loss of R19 200 will therefore be expensed during the year ended 31 December 20X8.

The balance sheet of Intense Sports at 31 December 20X8, *before the retirement of Gary*, is as shown below:

INTENSE SPORTS PARTNERSHIP
STATEMENT OF FINANCIAL POSITION
AT 31 DECEMBER 20X8

	Cost	Accumulated depreciation/ impairment losses	Carrying amount	R
ASSETS				
Non-current assets				1 184 800
Land and buildings	700 000	–	700 000	
Motor vehicles	300 000	60 000	240 000	
Machinery	90 000	18 000	72 000	
Goodwill	192 000	19 200	172 800	
Current assets				962 000
Inventory				87 000
Accounts receivable	(175 000 – 10 000)			165 000
Pre-paid expenses				20 000
Bank				690 000
				2 146 800
EQUITY AND LIABILITIES				
Capital and reserves				1 921 800
Capital accounts			1 362 000	
Simon			486 200	
Gary			455 800	
Mark			420 000	
Current Accounts			499 800	
Simon			253 600	
Gary			173 600	
Mark			72 600	
Reserve			60 000	

Non current liabilities	
15% Loan Simon	80 000
Current liabilities	
Accounts payable	145 000
	2 146 800

The carrying amounts of the assets and liabilities at 31 December 20X8 were reviewed by an independent consultant and the following fair values were agreed upon at that date:

- Land and buildings R897 200
- Machinery R 80 000
- Inventory R 83 000
- Accounts receivable R160 000

An amount of R3 000 is owing for the consultant's fees in connection with the revaluation.

As already stated, goodwill has an estimated recoverable amount of R172 800.

Simon and Mark wish to maintain a reserve of R60 000 on the statement of financial position. It was agreed that Gary would take over (at carrying amount) one of the three motor vehicles and the balance would be paid to him in cash.

You are required to:

(a) draw up the revaluation account
(b) draw up the capital accounts in columnar format
(c) prepare the statement of financial position for Simon and Mark after Gary's retirement.

Solution: Retirement of a partner

As mentioned above, a partner who retires from a partnership is entitled to the settlement of his interest in the partnership. The accounting procedures on retirement of a partner are therefore directed towards establishing the retiring partner's share of the true equity of the partnership as well as the share belonging to the remaining partners. The discussion that follows will consider each of the components of equity and the adjustments required to equity as described in the introductory paragraphs to this section.

The starting point is with the **balances on the capital accounts** of the partners. The **balance on the current account** of the *retiring* partner is transferred to the capital account.

The **reserve**, as mentioned previously, forms part of the equity of the partnership and needs to be redistributed on the change in partnership composition. This will ensure that the retiring partner, Gary, is allocated his share of the reserve. Simon, Gary and Mark were sharing profits 1/3 : 1/3 : 1/3 and the remaining partners (Simon and Mark) agreed to share profits equally. The change in profit share can be shown as follows:

Simon	1/3	+	1/6	=	3/6
Gary	1/3	–	1/3	=	–
Mark	1/3	+	1/6	=	3/6
	1				1

As you can see from the calculation above, Gary is relinquishing 1/3 (or 2/6) of profits, which is being taken over 1/6 each by Simon and Mark. The reserve on the balance sheet at 31 December 20X8, the date of Gary's retirement, amounts to R60 000. An amount of R20 000 (R60 000 x 1/3) must be credited to Gary's capital account with R10 000 (R60 000 x 1/6) debited to the capital accounts of Simon and Mark respectively. The accounting entry arising from this is as follows:

	Dr	Cr
Capital – Simon (60 000 x 1/6)	10 000	
Capital – Mark (60 000 x 1/6)	10 000	
Capital – Gary (60 000 x 2/6)		20 000

This entry is posted to the capital accounts shown in the solution. Another bookkeeping procedure which achieves the same effect is to allocate the reserve to the existing partners in their existing ratio and then to re-allocate the same amount between the remaining partners in the new profit-sharing ratio. This is shown below for illustrative purposes and is not included in the ledger accounts in the solution.

	Dr	Cr
Reserve	60 000	
Capital – Simon (60 000 x 1/3)		20 000
Capital – Gary (60 000 x 1/3)		20 000
Capital – Mark (60 000 x 1/3)		20 000
Capital – Simon (60 000 x 1/2)	30 000	
Capital – Mark (60 000 x 1/2)	30 000	
Reserve		60 000

The next step is to account for the **revaluation of the assets** at the date of Gary's retirement. The revaluation of the assets will not be described in detail as the principles were explained in the section on partnership admission. The following is an example of the accounting entries that could be processed to take account of the changes in asset values. Note that the revaluation account shown in the solution has been drawn up on the assumption that each adjustment is debited or credited individually to the account.

	Dr	Cr
Accumulated depreciation	18 000	
Machinery		18 000
Land and buildings	197 200	
Machinery	8 000	
Inventory		4 000
Allowance for doubtful debts		5 000
Fees accrued		3 000
Revaluation		193 200

The only new concept that needs to be explained is the treatment of a **depreciable asset which is not revalued** on change in partnership composition. The motor vehicles are considered to be worth their carrying amount of R240 000. As the new partnership constitutes a new entity, the cost of the motor vehicles to the new partnership is taken as the carrying amount of the motor vehicles to the existing partnership. An entry is therefore required to adjust the existing cost and accumulated depreciation in the accounting records in order to record the carrying amount of R240 000 as the cost to the new partnership. The entry is as follows:

	Dr	**Cr**
Accumulated depreciation	60 000	
Motor vehicles		60 000

There is no impact on the equity of the partnership and therefore the capital accounts are unaffected.

The value of **goodwill** must also be taken into account on the retirement of a partner. The partners must agree on a value for goodwill in order to correctly reflect the equity of the partnership. As goodwill is an asset and the new partnership constitutes a new entity, the existing cost and accumulated impairment losses must be removed from the accounting records.

If the value placed on goodwill is different from the carrying amount, the carrying amount must be increased or decreased and the movement allocated to the partners' capital accounts.

Remember that, in our example, the carrying amount of goodwill on the statement of financial position is R172 800 (cost of R192 000 and accumulated impairment losses of R19 200). As the cost of the goodwill to the new partnership is taken as the carrying amount of the goodwill to the existing partnership, an accounting entry is needed. The entry is as follows:

	Dr	**Cr**
Accumulated impairment	19 200	
Goodwill		19 200

The carrying amount of any **assets taken over** by a retiring partner needs to be charged against his capital account. In this case, Gary is taking over one of the motor vehicles at a carrying amount of R80 000. The accounting entry to record this transaction is:

	Dr	**Cr**
Capital – Gary	80 000	
Motor vehicle		80 000

The partners' current accounts reflect their share of profits or losses up to the date of the balance sheet prepared for the change in partnership composition. Any further **costs** incurred need to be taken into account in arriving at the share of equity due to the retiring partner. In this case, provision needs to be made for professional fees in connection with the revaluation. A provision is similar in nature to an accrual, except that the amount of an accrual is known whereas a provision is an amount that cannot be determined with substantial accuracy. Costs relating to the retirement of a partner are normally taken into account through the revaluation account. The accounting entry is:

	Dr	Cr
Revaluation	3 000	
Fees accrued		3 000

If the costs involved are paid, then the credit would be posted to the bank account. Now the balance on the retiring partner's capital account represents the share of the equity owing to the retiring partner. The amount owing to Gary is R633 800 and is paid to him from the funds in the bank account.

(a)

Revaluation

Details	R	Details	R
Inventory	4 000	Land & buildings	197 200
Allowance for doubtful debts	5 000	Machinery	8 000
Fees accrued	3 000		
Capital – Simon	64 400		
Capital – Gary	64 400		
Capital – Mark	64 400		
	205 200		205 200

(b)

Capital

Details	Simon	Gary	Mark	Details	Simon	Gary	Mark
Capital – Gary	10 000		10 000	Balance b/d	486 200	455 800	420 000
				Current – Gary		173 600	
Motor vehicle		80 000		Capital – Simon/ Mark		20 000	
Bank		***633 800***		Revaluation	64 400	64 400	64 400
Balance c/d	540 600	–	474 400				
	550 600	713 800	484 400		550 600	713 800	484 400
				Balance b/d	540 600	–	474 400

(c) Below is the statement of financial position of the partnership *after the retirement of Gary*:

INTENSE SPORTS PARTNERSHIP
STATEMENT OF FINANCIAL POSITION
AT 31 DECEMBER 20X8

		Cost	Accumulated depreciation/ impairment losses	Carrying amount	R
ASSETS					
Non-current assets					1 310 000
Land and buildings		897 200	–	897 200	
Motor vehicles	(240 000 – 80 000)	160 000	–	160 000	
Machinery		80 000	–	80 000	
Goodwill		172 800	–	172 800	
Current assets					319 200
Inventory	(87 000 – 4 000)				83 000
Accounts receivable	(175 000 – 15 000)				160 000
Pre-paid expenses					20 000
Bank	(690 000 – 633 800)				56 200
					1 629 200
EQUITY AND LIABILITIES					
Capital and reserves					1 401 200
Capital accounts				1 015 000	
Simon				540 600	
Mark				474 400	
Current accounts				326 200	
Simon				253 600	
Mark				72 600	
Reserve				60 000	
Non-current liabilities					
15% Loan Simon					80 000
Current liabilities					148 000
Accounts payable					145 000
Fees accrued					3 000
					1 629 200

17.6.2 Liquidation of the partnership

The liquidation of a business means the cessation of its activities. The assets of the business are sold and the liabilities settled. Once the liquidation procedure is complete, the only items remaining on the statement of financial position are the cash in the bank and the owners' equity. The balance on each partner's capital account represents the amount to be paid to each partner on liquidation.

The objective of the liquidation procedure is therefore to realise the maximum possible cash from the assets, to settle the liabilities and to ensure that the partners are paid out their share of the equity of the partnership. The procedure is summarised below.

- Transfer the current account balances to the partners' capital accounts.
- Transfer the balance on reserves (if any) to the partners' capital accounts in the profit-sharing ratio.
- Transfer assets at carrying amount to a ***realisation*** account.
- Record the proceeds on realisation, as well as other profits or losses on liquidation in the realisation account. It is possible for a partner to take over assets for his own account, at a value agreed between the partners, instead of selling the asset. This will result in the partner's capital account being debited, and the realisation account being credited with the agreed value of the asset taken over.
- Settle liabilities and record the profit or loss on settlement in the realisation account.
- Pay expenses.
- Determine the profit or loss on realisation and transfer to the partners' capital accounts.
- The remaining cash is paid to the partners to settle the balances on their capital accounts. It may happen that a partner's interest is not sufficient to cover the loss on realisation, and he will thus have a shortfall on his capital account, shown by a debit balance. The other partners have a claim against that partner for the amount of the shortfall. If the partner can make good the shortfall, he is required to pay the amount into the partnership. Any further remaining cash is distributed to the partners in accordance with the credit balances on their capital accounts.

Pause and reflect...

In accounting for the admission of a partner to, or the retirement of a partner from a partnership, a revaluation account was used. Why is a realisation account used on the liquidation of a partnership?

Response

A revaluation account is used to record *unrealised* movements in the values of the specific assets and liabilities that have been revalued on the admission or retirement of a partner. You will recall that such movements are not realised in cash as there has not been a transaction involving a disposal or settlement. On liquidation, however, all partnership assets are *realised*, and liabilities settled, in cash. Therefore, a realisation account is used to record the cash realisation of the partnership's equity.

Example: Liquidation of the partnership

Another year later, on 31 December 20X9, Simon and Mark decided to dissolve the partnership. The statement of financial position at that date is presented below:

INTENSE SPORTS PARTNERSHIP
STATEMENT OF FINANCIAL POSITION
AT 31 DECEMBER 20X9

				R
ASSETS				
Non-current assets				1 250 000
	Cost	**Accumulated depreciation/ impairment losses**	**Carrying amount**	
Land and buildings	897 200	–	897 200	
Motor vehicles	160 000	40 000	120 000	
Machinery	80 000	20 000	60 000	
Goodwill	172 800	–	172 800	
Current assets				199 400
Inventory				74 000
Accounts receivable	(124 000 – 10 000)			114 000
Bank				11 400
				1 449 400
EQUITY AND LIABILITIES				
Capital and reserves				1 261 400
Capital accounts			1 015 000	
Simon			540 600	
Mark			474 400	
Current accounts			186 400	
Simon			151 800	
Mark			34 600	
Reserve			60 000	
Non current liabilities				
15% Loan Simon				80 000
Current liabilities				
Accounts payable				108 000
				1 449 400

The following additional information is available:
- ❑ The land and buildings were sold for R850 000
- ❑ The machinery was sold for R58 000

- The inventory was sold for R64 000
- Accounts receivable collected was R104 000
- Suppliers were paid R100 000 in full settlement
- Each partner agreed to take over one of the two remaining motor vehicles at carrying amount.

You are required to:

complete the following ledger accounts in the accounting records of Intense Sports: Realisation, Bank, Loan – Simon, Accounts payable, Capital – Simon, Capital – Mark.

Solution: Liquidation of partnership

Realisation

Details	R	Details	R
Land & buildings	897 200	Acc: Dep-MV	40 000
Motor vehicles	160 000	Accumulated depreciation–Machinery	20 000
Machinery	80 000		
Goodwill	172 800	Prov for doubtful debts	10 000
Inventory	74 000		
Accounts receivable	124 000	Bank (L & B)	850 000
		Bank (Machinery)	58 000
		Bank (Inventory)	64 000
		Bank (Accounts receivable)	104 000
		Accounts payable	8 000
		Capital – Simon (MV)	60 000
		Capital – Mark (MV)	60 000
		Balance	234 000
	1 508 000		1 508 000
Balance	234 000	Capital Simon (1/2)	117 000
		Capital Mark (1/2)	117 000

Bank

Details	R	Details	R
Balance b/d	11 400	Accounts payable	100 000
Realisation	850 000	Balance c/d	987 400
Realisation	58 000		
Realisation	64 000		
Realisation	104 000		
	1 087 400		1 087 400
Balance b/d	987 400	Capital – Simon	625 400
		Capital – Mark	362 000
	987 400		987 400

Loan – Simon

Details	R	Details	R
Capital – Simon	80 000	Balance b/d	80 000
	80 000		80 000

Accounts payable

Details	R	Details	R
Bank	100 000	Balance b/d	108 000
Realisation	8 000		
	108 000		108 000

Capital – Simon

Details	R	Details	R
Realisation (MV)	60 000	Balance b/d	540 600
Realisation	117 400	Current – Simon	151 800
Bank	***625 400***	Reserve	30 000
		Loan – Simon	80 000
	802 400		802 400

Capital – Mark

Details	R	Details	R
Realisation (MV)	60 000	Balance b/d	474 400
Realisation	117 400	Current – Mark	34 600
Bank	***362 000***	Reserve	30 000
	539 000		539 000

The realisation account is used to determine the profit or loss on realisation of the net assets of the business. The amount of the profit or loss is the difference between

- the proceeds on realisation of the assets and income earned as part of the liquidation, and
- the carrying amount of assets and expenses incurred as part of the liquidation.

Note that the realisation account shows a loss on realisation of R234 000. This is divided equally between the partners, and an amount of R117 000 is debited to the capital accounts of both Simon and Gary

As mentioned in the introduction to this section, when the liquidation procedure is complete, the only items on the statement of financial position are the cash in the bank and the owners' equity. In this case the bank account has a balance of R987 400, and the capital accounts of Simon and Mark have balances of R625 400 and R362 000 respectively. The final transaction is for the remaining cash of R987 400 to be paid to the partners to settle the balances on their capital accounts.

Pause and reflect...

The balance on the goodwill account of R172 800 was transferred to the realisation account together with the other assets. You will notice that no proceeds were recorded in the realisation account in relation to the goodwill. What is the reason for this?

Response

As goodwill represents anticipated future economic benefits, there can be no value placed on goodwill of an entity in liquidation.

Pause and reflect...

In this example, the accounts payable balance of R108 000 was settled for R100 000 and the profit of R8 000 recorded in the realisation account. Can you think of any alternative accounting procedure to record the settlement of the accounts payable?

Response

The accounts payable balance of R108 000 could be transferred to the realisation account, and the settlement for R100 000 then recorded in the realisation account. The net result of this procedure would be a profit on settlement of R8 000 in the realisation account.

17.7 Exam example

Boet and Jules have been trading as sole proprietors for a number of years in similar fields. They decided to combine their businesses from 1 January 20X1, at which date the net asset value per the accounting records of Boet's business was R14 000 and Jules's business was R21 000.

The two partners agreed to the following with respect to their new partnership:

- The partners are to share profits and losses in the ratio of 2 : 3.
- It was considered that the net asset value of Boet's business was understated by R1 000 and that of Jules's business was overstated by R3 000.
- Prior to the amalgamation of the firms, no allowance for doubtful debts was recorded. The fair value of the account receivable is R1 000 lower than the carrying amount.
- Boet is to get a bonus of 10% of net sales and Jules is to get a commission of 12% of gross profit. The balance of the profits is to be shared between the partners in their agreed ratio.
- The business is to use the perpetual inventory method of accounting for trading stock.

The summarised trading results of the partnership for the half year to 30 June 20X1 were as follows:

	R
Cost of sales	13 500
General expenses	12 200
Returns inward	2 400
Returns outward	900
Sales	38 400

On 1 July 20X1, it was decided to admit Freyja to the partnership. At a meeting of the three partners it was agreed:

- that Freyja was to introduce cash of R19 720;
- that Freyja was to get a 40% share of the profits while Boet and Jules would share between themselves as they did prior to the admission of Freyja;
- that Boet and Jules would no longer be entitled to any bonus or commission.

On 30 September 20X1, after the partnership of Boet, Jules and Freyja had been in existence for three months, Jules was run over by a bus. Boet and Freyja then decided to share profits and losses in the ratio of 3 : 5.

Upon drawing up a profit and loss account for the period 1 July 20X1 to 30 September 20X1, profit of R2 500 was transferred to the appropriation account.

On 30 September 20X1, the recoverable amount of goodwill was estimated to be R6 650. This has not been taken into account in the determination of the profit.

During the three months between 1 July and 30 September, Boet and Jules had withdrawn R3 000 each and Freyja had withdrawn R600.

You are required to:

prepare the partners' capital accounts in columnar form to record the formation of the partnership, the admission of Freyja, and the change caused by the death of Jules.

Solution: Exam example

	Total	**Boet**	**Jules**	**Freyja**
Net assets introduced	35 000	14 000	21 000	–
Asset adjustment written in	(2 000)	1 000	(3 000)	–
Provision for doubtful debts	(1 000)	(400)	(600)	–
Starting capitals	32 000	14 600	17 400	–
Bonus/commission	6 300	3 600	2 700	–
Share of profit (1/1/X1 – 30/6/X1)	4 000	1 600	2 400	–
Balance before Freyja's admission	42 300	19 800	22 500	–
Cash	19 720	–	–	19 720
Goodwill write-up	7 000	2 800	4 200	–
	69 020	22 600	26 700	19 720
Share of profit (1/7/X1 – 30/9/X1)	2 500	600	900	1 000
Goodwill impairment	(350)	(84)	(126)	(140)
	71 170	23 116	27 474	20 580
Withdrawals	(6 600)	(3 000)	(3 000)	(600)
	64 570	20 116	24 474	19 980
Amount due to Jules's estate	(24 474)	–	(24 474)	–
	40 096	20 116	–	19 980

Workings

Profit for first half year

Sales	(38 400 – 2 400)	36 000
Cost of sales		(13 500)
Gross profit		22 500
General expenses		(12 200)
Profit		10 300
		(6 300)
Bonus	(10% of 36 000)	3 600
Commission	(12% of 22 500)	2 700
Balance of profits		4 000
Boet		(1 600)
Jules		(2 400)

New profit sharing ratios

Boet	2/5	x	3/5	=	6/25
Jules	3/5	x	3/5	=	9/25
	1				
Freyja	(2/5)			=	10/25
Balance	3/5				
or					
Boet gives up	2/5	x	2/5	=	4/25
Jules gives up	3/5	x	2/5	=	6/25
Boet	10/25	–	4/25	=	6/25
Jules	15/25	–	6/25	=	9/25

Goodwill on admission of Freyja

	R
Purchase consideration (19 720/0,40)	49 300
Owners' equity at 30/06/X1	42 300
Total goodwill	7 000

Goodwill on winding up Jules's estate

	R
Value on admission of Freyja	7 000
Fair value	6 650
Impairment	350

Summary of concepts and applications

1. A partnership is a legal relationship which arises as a result of an agreement between two or more persons but not exceeding twenty. South African partnerships are not governed by legislation, are not legal entities and are not subject to formalities on establishment.
2. Partnerships can be financed from investors' funds and/or borrowed funds. Cash or other assets represent the relatively permanent contribution by the partners to the business, while profits retained represent the cumulative excess of profit over withdrawals. Capital and current accounts are opened for each partner so as to distinguish between capital contributions and accumulated profits. Equity comprises both the capital and current accounts of the partners.
3. In order to form a partnership, the partners may contribute cash or other assets to the capital of the partnership.
4. A partnership's profit is determined in the same way as that of a sole proprietorship. The appropriation of the partnership's profit rewards each partner for the resources and services provided to the firm. In addition, interest on capital and partners' salaries are treated as an appropriation of profit.
5. The profit-sharing ratio may change on the admission of a new partner to an existing partnership. The procedure followed ensures that the equity of the existing partners is fairly stated.
6. Dissolution of a partnership may occur as a result of the death or retirement of a partner or because of the liquidation of a partnership. A partner who retires from a partnership, or the estate of a deceased partner, is entitled to the settlement of his or her interest (the partner's share of the equity of the partnership) in the partnership. On liquidation of a partnership, the assets of the business are sold and the liabilities settled. The balance on each partner's capital account represents the amount to be paid to each partner on liquidation

Notes

1. IAS 31, Interests in Joint Ventures, *International Accounting Standards Board*, (2005), paragraph 3.
2. IAS 31, paragraph 3.
3. IAS 31, paragraph 20.
4. Henning, J. J. and Delport, H. J. *Partnership*, Butterworths: Durban, (1984).
5. Kolitz, D. L. and Rabin, C. E. *Financial Accounting, An Introduction for South African Students*, Boston: Irwin, (1993), pp. 11–15.
6. IFRS 3, Business Combinations, *International Accounting Standards Board*, (2008), Appendix A.
7. IAS 38, Intangible Assets, *International Accounting Standards Board*, (2004), paragraph 48.
8. IFRS 3, (2008), paragraph 52.
9. IFRS 3, paragraph 54.
10. IFRS 3, paragraph 55.

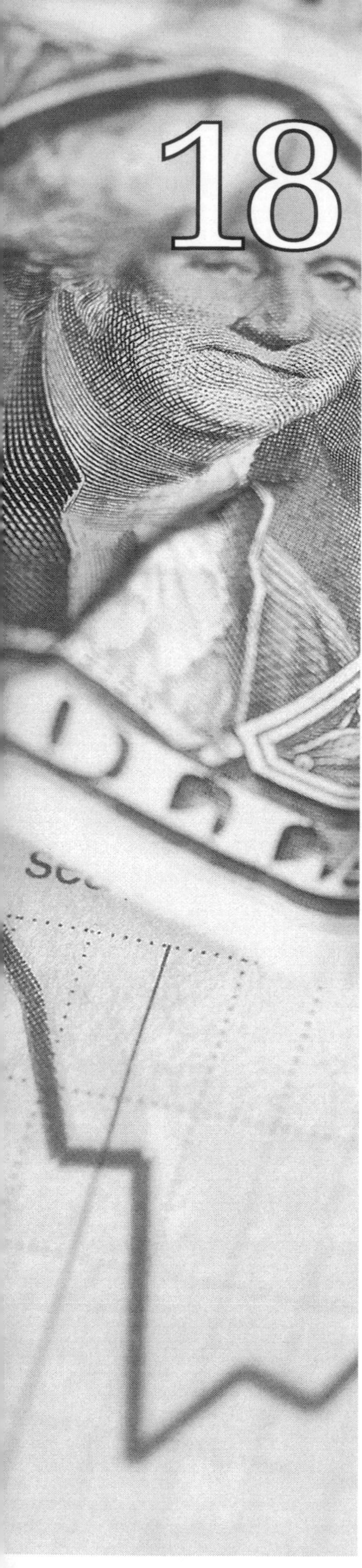

Accounting for Companies

'The science of accounting ... arises primarily out of the need that accounting parties should from time to time render to those to whom they are responsible an account of their stewardship ...'
(Dicksee, 1905)

Outcomes

- Recall the specific characteristics of a company.
- Describe the sources of finance available to a company, the identification of profits retained and the composition of a company's equity.
- Describe the formation process.
- Prepare financial information for a company.
- Prepare accounting entries relating to share issues.
- Prepare accounting entries relating to debenture issues.

Chapter outline

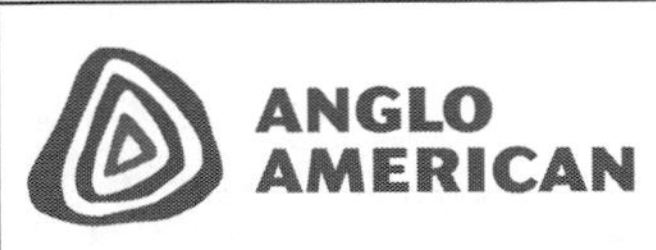

Anglo American plc
Key Financial Statistics

Market capitalisation	R700 billion
Annual revenue	R215 billion
Annual profit	R32 billion
Number of employees	116 000
Number of shares	1.3 billion

Large companies are the ultimate business entity. Anglo American is the largest company listed on the Johannesburg Stock Exchange (JSE). It is also listed in London and New York. This chapter introduces the company as a business entity.

18.1 Introduction

In South Africa, all matters relating to companies are regulated by the Companies Act, No 61 of 1973, as amended (referred to in this chapter as the 'Companies Act'). The Companies Act, 1973 is undergoing a comprehensive transformation that is expected to result in a new Act being introduced in 2010. At the time of writing this text, the latest draft of the new legislation is in the form of the Companies Bill, 61 of 2008 (referred to in this chapter as the 'Companies Bill'). Where relevant, this chapter refers to the requirements of both the Companies Act and the Companies Bill. However, further changes are expected before the new Act is implemented.

There are detailed transitional provisions in the Companies Bill so companies already in existence and formed under the existing Companies Act will continue to exist as if they were incorporated under the new Act. This means that most of the requirements and provisions of the existing Companies Act will continue to be relevant for many years to come.

18.2 Characteristics of a company

A company is a legal entity distinct from its owners, who are known as the ***shareholders***. The shareholders, as a group, own the company through ownership of its shares. A share simply represents ownership of part of the equity of the company.

The Companies Act recognises that the owners and management may be separate and distinct groups of persons. The Act provides for shareholders to appoint a board of directors to manage the company. The directors are appointed at a general meeting of shareholders. The company acts through its board of directors who report periodically to the shareholders. The financial statements comprise one part of the annual report to shareholders.

As mentioned above, the shareholders and the company are separate legal entities. This has two important consequences. Firstly, there is ***limitation of liability***. The lenders can recover from the company only, not from its shareholders. As a trade-off for the benefit of limited liability and to protect lenders, legislation provides that once capital has been paid to the company, it cannot be refunded to shareholders unless certain formalities are complied with which may require the confirmation of the court before implementation. Note that the buying and selling of a company's shares on the stock exchange does not constitute the repayment of capital. Secondly, and related to the above, the company has an ***indefinite life*** and a shareholder may transfer his shares in the company to another party without affecting its existence or continuation.

The Companies Act requires every company to appoint an auditor to report on the company's annual financial statements. The role of the auditor is to express an opinion on the fair presentation of the financial information and whether or not it has been prepared in accordance with the requirements of company law and accounting standards. However the Companies Bill requires an auditor to be appointed only for public companies and state-owned enterprises. The requirement to appoint an auditor is a costly burden to smaller companies and the new Act proposes to ease this burden.

As a separate legal entity, the company is a taxpayer and pays tax at a flat rate of 28% on its taxable profits.

There are two types of companies that can be formed in terms of the Companies Act – a ***company having a share capital*** and a ***company not having a share capital***. A company having a share capital is the type of company used by business entities who choose to incorporate through a company. A company not having a share capital is formed for the purpose of non-business entities such as charitable, cultural or educational institutions.

A company having a share capital can be either a private company or a public company. A private company must have the words '(Proprietary) Limited' behind its name, and a public company must have the word 'Limited' behind its name.

Both private companies and public companies have the characteristics described in the previous paragraphs. There are, however, some important differences between a private company and a public company. We will consider some of these differences now.

18.2.1 Private company

A private company can have **between 1 and 50 shareholders**. On the one hand, this means that an entrepreneur trading as a sole proprietor could form a private company and conduct his business operations using a company as the form of business entity. On the other hand, the maximum of 50 shareholders limits the availability of investors' funds and ultimately limits the growth potential of the company.

The **free transfer of shares is restricted**. This means that the transfer of ownership of shares in a private company need to be approved by either the directors or the other shareholders. Although this constrains existing shareholders in terms of their ability to sell their shareholding, it does enable shareholders to maintain control over the ownership of the company.

There is a **prohibition from inviting the public to subscribe for shares** in a private company. In other words, a private company that wishes to increase its equity by issuing shares will not be able to offer shares to the general public. Offers of shares in a private company are normally made to potential investors who are known to the directors and who have expressed an interest in investing in the company.

18.2.2 Public company

A public company must have a minimum of 7 shareholders. There is no limit to the maximum number of shareholders. As such, a public company has the potential for large growth as it has access to unlimited investors' funds, particularly if it is listed on a stock exchange.

The shares in a public company are **freely transferable** and a public company is

able to offer shares to the general public. The offer of shares to the public is made through the means of a prospectus. A prospectus is a document advertising the sale of the shares and is normally sent to all existing shareholders as well as appearing in newspapers.

The Companies Bill proposes two types of companies to be formed, namely a ***profit company*** and a ***non-profit company***. A profit company is a company incorporated for financial gain for its shareholders whereas a non-profit company is a company incorporated for public benefit.

The Bill sets out four categories of profit companies, namely:

- Private companies, which are comparable to companies of the same status under the Companies Act, 1973.
- Personal liability companies, which provide an avenue for professional services firms, such as chartered accountants to incorporate.
- Public companies, which are comparable companies of the same status under the Companies Act, 1973.
- State-owned enterprises, which were often incorporated or registered under the Companies Act, 1973, but were not recognised in that Act as requiring separate legislative treatment in respect to certain matters to avoid conflict or overlap with other legislation specifically applicable to them, and not to companies in general.

18.3 Listing of a public company

A public company can be **listed** on a stock exchange, which in South Africa is known as the JSE Securities Exchange. When a company's shares are listed on the JSE Securities Exchange, the company is referred to as a listed public company. Not all public companies are listed, these companies being referred to as unlisted public companies.

When applying for a listing on the JSE Securities Exchange, a company will qualify for one of two possible listings: the Main Board or the Alternative Exchange (known as AltX).

There are a number of specific requirements that have to be met before a public company can apply for a listing on the main board.[1] These include equity of at least R25 million; at least 25 million shares in issue; a satisfactory profit history for the preceding three years, the last of which reported an audited profit before taxation of at least R8 million and a minimum of 20% of the equity shares held by the public.

The Alternative Exchange is for smaller, recently established companies that want a public listing but do not have the capital or profit history to apply to the main board. The requirements for an AltX listing[2] include equity of R2 million; a profit forecast and a minimum of 10% of the equity shares held by the public.

Directors considering listing need to seriously consider all the implications, both financial and other, that are associated with a listing. The following factors require careful consideration[3]:

- A clear vision and plan is needed. Directors of a listed company are selling both the company and their vision of what it can be. The presentation of that vision in a clear, thoughtful manner will greatly enhance the potential investor's decision-making process. A comprehensive business plan is required, supported by market information that identifies the market the company is in, its future potential and the competition.
- A strong board of executive and non-executive directors. Investors will want to know the composition of the board of directors and what strengths they bring to the company. Executive directors need to be capable of implementing the company vision and plans while non-executive directors need to represent a varied business background, who also understand the industry in which the company operates.
- Good tangible asset backing. The company's tangible assets need to support earnings growth. If the company's statement of financial position has a number of intangible assets such as goodwill, these may need to be discounted when the company is valued for sale in a public market.
- Suitable accounting and information systems. Listed companies are required to report on a timely basis and this requires appropriate accounting and information systems.
- Proven product. The company needs a product that has a proven market and can form the basis of future plans for the company.
- Financial costs. Substantial costs are involved in a listing. This includes expenses such as legal, accounting and auditing fees, printing costs as well as listing costs that range between 1,5% and 4% of the total issue value. Underwriting fees vary between 5% and 15% of the issue value. In addition, there will also be ongoing costs including a JSE fee of approximately R22 000 per annum and designated advisor or sponsoring broker fees (depending on whether the listing is on JSE main board or AltX) fees that range between R5 000 and R15 000 a month.
- Hidden costs. Extensive management time is involved in preparing for a listing. This can result in lost opportunities in other areas while management focus is on the listing. The cost of lost opportunities is hard to quantify.
- Loss of privacy. Listing a company results in a loss of the privacy that a private company enjoys. The financial statements are public information and disclose potentially sensitive information such as salaries paid to directors.
- Potential loss of control. The initial issue may not include more than 50% of the shares of the company. However, subsequent offers of shares to the public may affect the ability of the founding owners to maintain a controlling interest.

18.4 Sources of finance for a company

Like a sole proprietorship, a partnership and a close corporation, a company can be financed from two sources, investors' funds and borrowed funds.

Cash invested by shareholders in a company is known as the ***share capital***. A company may borrow funds by taking out ***loans*** or by issuing ***debentures.***

Finance obtained by a company by taking out a loan is no different from a loan taken out by any other form of business entity. We will therefore focus our attention in the following paragraphs on the issue of share capital and debentures, as these financial instruments are unique to companies. You should recall from Chapter 15 that a financial instrument is any contract that gives rise to both a financial asset of one enterprise (or individual) and a financial liability or equity instrument of another enterprise (or individual).

18.4.1 Share capital

There are different classes of shares, such as ordinary and preference shares. The Companies Act also make provision for different types of ordinary or preference shares known as par value and no par value shares. The concept of par value shares, although it will continue for existing companies, will no longer apply when the Companies Bill becomes effective as an Act.

Share capital is an ***equity instrument***, which is any contract that evidences a residual interest in the assets of an enterprise after deducting its liabilities.[4]

Classes of shares

Ordinary shares are the main risk-bearing shares of the company. If the company succeeds, the ordinary shareholders benefit through growth in the value of their investment as the share price increases, and also from ***dividends*** received. Dividends are profits authorised for payment to shareholders. It is important to appreciate that shareholders have no legal right to the profit of the company until the directors have authorised the distribution of the profit in the form of a dividend. If the company fails, and the share price drops, the ordinary shareholders bear all the losses of the company, limited however, to the amount of their initial investment.

Preference shares are shares which receive a dividend prior to dividends paid to ordinary shareholders. The amount of the dividend and the rights attaching to the shares are set out in terms of their issue. Whether the shareholders have preference on winding-up of the company depends upon the terms of issue.

The dividend is normally expressed as a percentage of the par value of the shares. For example, a 6% preference share of R2 will entitle the holder to an annual dividend of 12c per share if profits are available for distribution.

Dividends on preference shares are either cumulative or non-cumulative. If the preference dividend is cumulative and profits are insufficient to pay part or all of the dividend, such shortfall is carried forward until such time as sufficient profits are available to pay arrears and current preference dividends. This right does not apply when the preference dividend is non-cumulative.

Preference shares may also have a further right to participate pro rata with the ordinary shares above a specified preference rate. These shares are known as participating preference shares.

As an exception to the general rule regarding non-repayment of share capital, a company may issue redeemable preference shares, which will be repaid to shareholders according to the terms of the issue.

It is important to note that redeemable preference shares are classified on the balance sheet of the issuing company as a liability. The focus is on the substance of a financial instrument, rather than its legal form. In substance, a redeemable preference share is a financial liability as there is a contractual obligation of the issuing company to deliver cash to the holder of the instrument.[5] It follows that dividends on redeemable preference shares classified as liabilities should be included with interest expense on the income statement and not with dividends on the statement of changes in equity.

The terms of issue of preference shares normally provide that preference shareholders will be entitled to vote at general and other meetings only if the preference dividend is in arrears or if their rights are invoked. This factor should never be overlooked because in such circumstances the votes of preference shareholders could materially alter the voting strength of ordinary shareholders and could be decisive in the passing of resolutions.

Types of shares

Par value shares are those shares stated in the constitution of the company to be of a specified *nominal value per share*. The par value thus represents the minimum amount which must be paid to the company in respect of each share issued. For example, a company may issue 500 000 shares of R2 par value in order to raise one million rand. Once the share is issued and it is traded on the stock exchange, the par value ceases to be an indication of what the share is actually worth.

Par value shares may be issued at a ***premium*** but never, except in terms of section 81 of the Companies Act, at a discount. A premium is an excess issue price over the par value of the share, and is described in detail in section 18.5.2 which deals with share issues. Dividends on par value shares are usually stated as a *specified number of cents per share* but are sometimes calculated as a *percentage of the par value.*

No-par value shares do not have a specified nominal value per share. They may be issued at any price considered appropriate by the directors at the date of issue. Dividends on no-par value shares must therefore be expressed as a *specified number of cents per share.*

Recall, as mentioned above, that only no-par value shares are permitted to be issued in terms of the Companies Bill.

18.4.2 Debentures

A debenture is a financial liability. It is a type of loan that enables the company to borrow funds from members of the public or other entities as the total loan is divided up into smaller units. It exists in the form of a document issued by a company evidencing its indebtedness to those from whom it has borrowed money. Such a loan is usually secured by a mortgage over the company's property or by a general notarial bond over other assets. A company wishing to borrow, for example, R5 000 000, could issue 50 000 debentures of R100 each. A debenture bears a fixed rate of interest and its terms of repayment are specified.

A company may issue debentures in terms of section 116 of the Companies Act, provided it is permitted to do so in terms of its constitution. A trust deed is drawn up between the company and trustee on behalf of debenture holders. Section 128 of the Companies Act requires that the company keep a register of all debenture-holders, listing the number of debentures issued and outstanding, and the names and addresses of the debenture-holders.

Debentures are negotiable documents and may be sold to a third party. Debentures may be issued and redeemed either at par, at a premium or at a discount.

The accounting for the issue of debentures will be described in detail further on in this chapter.

18.4.3 Identification of profits retained

The share capital is usually the dominant source of financing for a company. As the business trades, profits are earned. However, like the members of a close corporation, the shareholders of a company do not have an automatic claim to the profits.

As a separate legal entity, a company pays tax on its profits and, again like a close corporation, it is only the after-tax profits which are available for distribution to shareholders. It is the duty of the directors to decide how much of the after-tax profit to ***declare*** to shareholders as a ***dividend***. Amounts not allocated to shareholders as a dividend, in other words the profits retained, are referred to as ***reserves***. The reserves therefore form part of the equity of a company and the directors need to decide to what extent the reserves are to be regarded as ***distributable*** or ***non-distributable***.

Distributable reserves

Distributable reserves are retained profits which, at the discretion of the directors, may be declared as a dividend to shareholders. They are, however, retained to finance future growth of the company. All of the distributable reserves of a company are known as the retained earnings.

When the directors declare a dividend to shareholders, a ***dividends payable*** account is used to record the liability to shareholders. As management and owners of a public company are, to a large extent, different persons, the payment of a dividend to shareholders must be initiated and carried out by the company as opposed to the shareholders withdrawing the amounts owing to them.

Any dividend declared and not paid to shareholders at the end of the financial year is reported as a liability on the statement of financial position. However, if a dividend is declared after the end of the reporting period, the amount should not be recognised as a liability at the reporting period date.[6] Diagram 18.1 shows the difference between profits retained and profits authorised for distribution.

Non-distributable reserves

A non-distributable reserve is one which is not available to be declared as a dividend to shareholders. Other than those originating by statute, non-distributable reserves can be created in two ways.

You are familiar with the *unrealised surplus* on **revaluation of a non-current asset**. The asset account is debited and the revaluation surplus account is credited with the upward movement in the value of the asset. This revaluation surplus is categorised as a non-distributable reserve on the statement of financial position of a company.

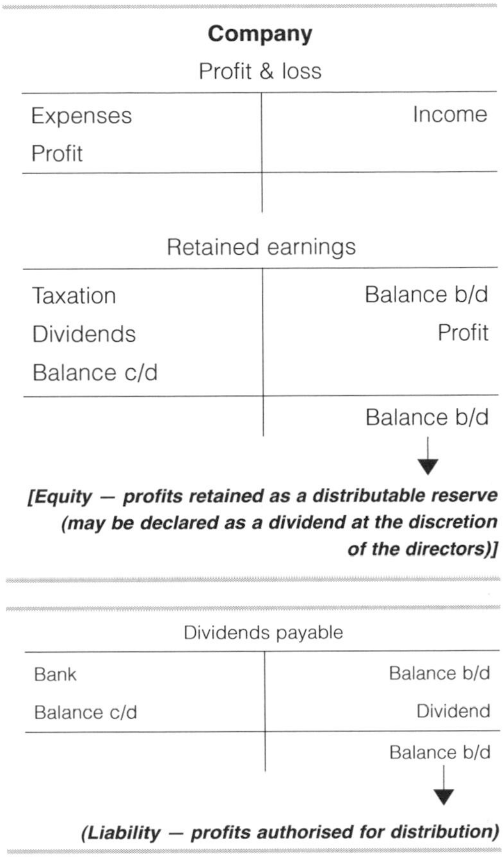

Company

Profit & loss

Expenses	Income
Profit	

Retained earnings

Taxation	Balance b/d
Dividends	Profit
Balance c/d	
	Balance b/d

[Equity — profits retained as a distributable reserve (may be declared as a dividend at the discretion of the directors)]

Dividends payable

Bank	Balance b/d
Balance c/d	Dividend
	Balance b/d

(Liability — profits authorised for distribution)

Diagram 18.1: Difference between profits retained and profits authorised for distribution

You are also familiar with the *realised surplus* on **disposal of a non-current asset**. The gain on disposal is accounted for by debiting the disposal account and crediting the gain on disposal account. The gain on disposal account is, in turn, transferred to the profit and loss account by a closing entry and therefore appears as an income item on the income statement. As an income item, the gain will be included in the profit for the period and will ultimately be included in the retained earnings as a distributable reserve.

The issue that then arises is whether to leave the gain in distributable reserves or to transfer the gain to a non-distributable reserve. If the gain remains in distributable reserves, it may be declared as a dividend to shareholders at the discretion of the directors. If the gain is transferred to a non-distributable reserve, it may not be declared as a dividend to shareholders.

In deciding whether to make the transfer or not, the directors need to consider the solvency and liquidity of the company. The Companies Bill provides guidance in assessing the solvency and liquidity of a company. A company satisfies the solvency and liquidity requirements if the fair value of its assets exceed its liabilities and it

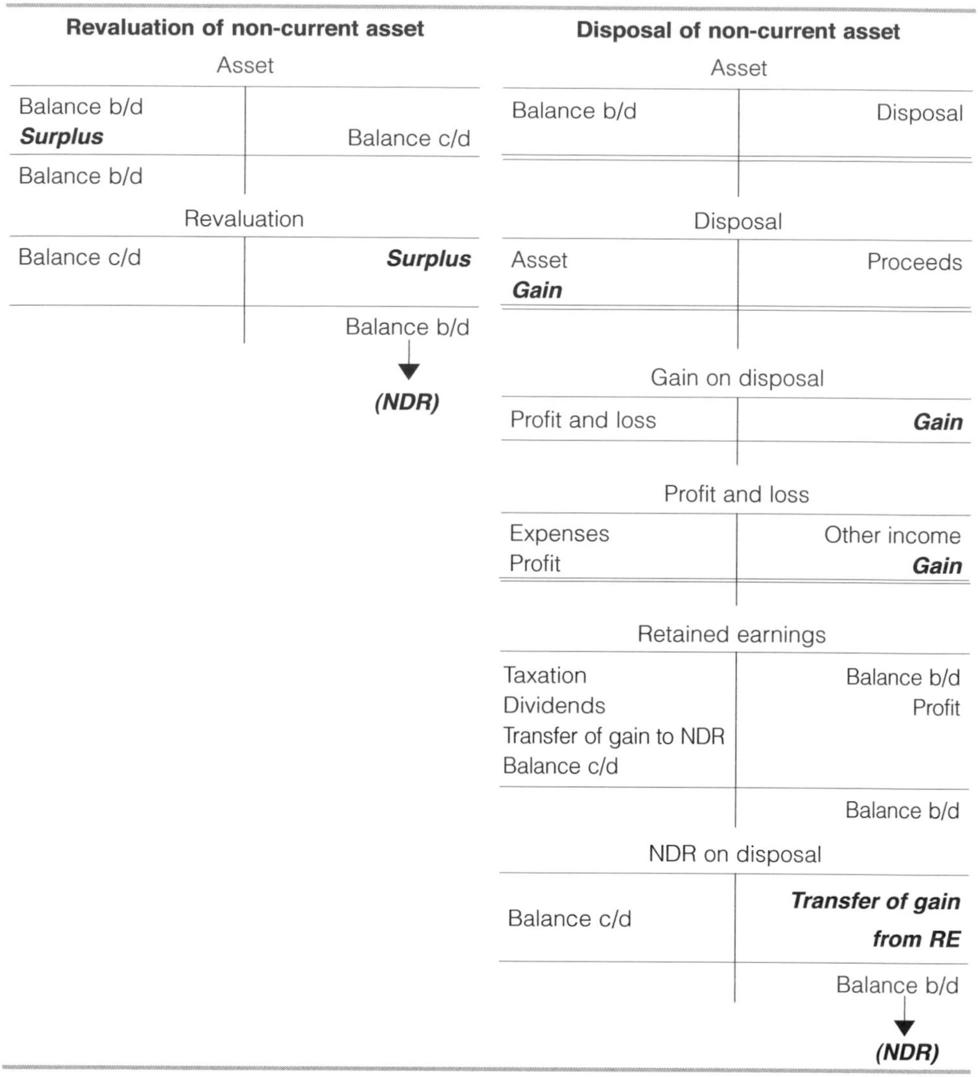

Revaluation of non-current asset

Asset

Balance b/d	
Surplus	Balance c/d
Balance b/d	

Revaluation

Balance c/d	***Surplus***
	Balance b/d

↓ ***(NDR)***

Disposal of non-current asset

Asset

Balance b/d	Disposal

Disposal

Asset	Proceeds
Gain	

Gain on disposal

Profit and loss	***Gain***

Profit and loss

Expenses	Other income
Profit	***Gain***

Retained earnings

Taxation	Balance b/d
Dividends	Profit
Transfer of gain to NDR	
Balance c/d	
	Balance b/d

NDR on disposal

Balance c/d	***Transfer of gain from RE***
	Balance b/d

↓ ***(NDR)***

Diagram 18.2: NDR arising from unrealised and realised surplus

appears that the company will be able to pay its debts as they become due in the ordinary course of business for a period of twelve months.

If there is doubt about the solvency and liquidity test, the directors may, to be prudent, transfer the gain on disposal to a non-distributable reserve. Note that the gain on disposal is first reported as an income item in the determination of profit or loss and subsequently transferred to a non-distributable reserve as an appropriation of profit.

It is important to compare the accounting entries on the creation of a non-distributable reserve when a non-current asset is *revalued* with the entries that are processed if it is decided to make such a transfer when a non-current asset is *sold*. When a non-current asset is revalued, and the surplus is therefore unrealised, the unrealised surplus is not recorded as *income* in the determination of profit or loss. Rather, it is recorded as *other comprehensive income* in the determination of the total comprehensive income. On disposal of a non-current asset, however, the realised surplus is reported on the comprehensive income statement as an *income* item, and as mentioned above, a transfer is made to the non-distributable reserve if the directors feel it appropriate to do so. This principle is illustrated in diagram 18.2 on page 456.

Remember that, as the non-distributable reserve is part of equity, all movements in the non-distributable reserve need to be reported on the statement of changes in equity.

Pause and reflect...

Examine the two scenarios below and consider how each scenario will be reported on the statement of changes in equity.

a) A company has a profit for the period of R1 200 000 and has revalued land by an amount of R100 000.

b) A company has a profit for the period of R1 300 000, including a profit on sale of land of R100 000, which the directors wish to transfer to a non-distributable reserve.

Response

a)

EXTRACT FROM STATEMENT OF CHANGES IN EQUITY

	Revaluation surplus (Non-distributable Reserve)	Retained earnings (Distributable Reserve)	Total
	R	R	R
Total comprehensive income	100 000	1 200 000	1 300 000

b)

EXTRACT FROM STATEMENT OF CHANGES IN EQUITY

	Non-distributable reserve	Retained earnings (Distributable Reserve)	Total
	R	R	R
Total comprehensive income	–	1 300 000	1 300 000
Transfer to NDR	100 000	(100 000)	

18.4.4 Equity of a company

The components of the equity of a company were discussed in the previous sections. In summary, the equity comprises the share capital and the reserves of the company, both distributable and non-distributable.

18.5 Formation of a company

The Companies Act provides for two documents to regulate the activities of a company. They are:

- The ***Memorandum of Association*** (the constitution of the company), which sets out its objectives, the powers of the company, its name and main business activity and details of share capital.
- The ***Articles of Association***, which are the set of rules of the company. The Articles of Association define the rights of members and specify the powers and duties of directors. The articles include, among many others, regulations governing:
  - the issue and transfer of shares
  - procedures at directors' and shareholders' meetings
  - voting rights
  - borrowing powers of the company.

The Companies Bill requires all companies to have one document entitled ***The Memorandum of Incorporation***. This is the sole governing document of the company. The Bill imposes certain specific requirements on the content of a Memorandum of Incorporation, as necessary to protect the interests of shareholders in the company, and provides a number of default rules, which companies may accept or alter as they wish to meet their needs and serve their interests. In addition, the Bill allows for companies to add to the required or default provision to address matters not addressed in the Bill itself. However, a company cannot fundamentally 'contract out' of the proposed Companies Act.

On initial formation of a company, the first issue of shares is made to the founders of the company. This is a legal requirement in order for the company to be formed and incorporated. The founders of the company are referred to as the subscribers to the memorandum. This applies to all types of companies. When the required documents are lodged with the Registrar of Companies and are in order, he will impress his seal on one copy and endorse thereon the date of registration. The company is then incorporated.

You will recall from Chapter 17 that Simon Smart and Gary Good formed Intense Sports, a partnership retailing endurance running and cycling equipment. The examples in this chapter examine the activities of Simon and Gary, assuming they choose to operate their business as a company, Intense Sports Limited.

Example: Formation of a company

On 2 January 20X7, Simon Smart and Gary Good form Intense Sports Ltd with a capital of R30 000 divided into shares of R1 each. The subscribers to the memorandum (Simon and Gary) subscribe for 5 000 shares at par and pay for them in full.

You are required to:

(a) journalise the above transactions
(b) prepare the statements of financial position immediately after formation.

Solution: Formation of a company

Assets				=	Liabilities	+	Owner's equity	
Subscribers to the memorandum		Cash					Share capital	
+/L/Dr	–/R/Cr	+/L/Dr	–/R/Cr				–/L/Dr	+/R/Cr
5 000								5 000
	5 000	5 000						

The amount owing by the subscribers to the memorandum is recorded as an asset. This represents the amount owing by the subscribers for shares issued to them. The share capital is credited with the issue price of the shares allotted to them.

GENERAL JOURNAL OF INTENSE SPORTS LIMITED

Date	Description	Fol	Dr	Cr
02/01/X7	Subscribers to the memorandum		5 000	
	Share capital			5 000
	5 000 shares allotted to subscribers to the memorandum			
	Cash		5 000	
	Subscribers to the memorandum			5 000
	Cash received for the 5 000 shares			

INTENSE SPORTS LTD
STATEMENT OF FINANCIAL POSITION
AT 2 JANUARY 20X7

	R
ASSETS	
Current assets	
Bank	5 000
EQUITY	
Capital and reserves	
Share capital	5 000

18.6 Producing information for a company

Remember that the objective of financial reporting is to provide information that is useful to a wide range of users in making economic decisions. The financial statements also show the results of the stewardship of management; in other words, the accountability of the board of directors for the resources entrusted to them. Shareholders access the stewardship of management in order to decide, for example, whether to hold or sell their investment in the enterprise and whether to re-appoint or replace the management.

18.6.1 Determination of the profit for the period

The profit for the period of a company is determined in the same way as that of a sole proprietorship, partnership or close corporation.

18.6.2 Appropriation of profit

There are three aspects that need to be taken into account in the appropriation of the profit of a company. These are the **taxation** charge against the profits, any **transfer to non-distributable reserves** that may be required and the **dividends** to shareholders.

Example: Producing information for a company

Assume that Simon Smart and Gary Good formed Intense Sports Ltd on 2 January 20X7. The following information is available for Intense Sports Ltd for the year ended 31 December 20X8:

INTENSE SPORTS LTD
TRIAL BALANCE AT 31 DECEMBER 20X8

Description	Folio	Dr	Cr
Ordinary share capital			100 000
Preference share capital (6%)			100 000
Retained earnings			105 000
Loan from bank – 15%			240 000
Debentures (12%)			100 000
Land and buildings		510 000	
Furniture and fittings		100 000	
Accumulated depreciation: furniture and fittings			40 000
Inventory		70 000	
Accounts receivable		154 000	
Bank		360 000	
Accounts payable			161 000

SARS		54 000	
Sales			1 860 000
Cost of sales		930 000	
Administration expenses		72 000	
Marketing expenses		63 000	
Directors' salaries		180 000	
Telephone expenses		18 000	
Employees' salaries		334 000	
Light and water expenses		25 000	
Depreciation		20 000	
Disposal of fixed assets			210 000
Preference dividends		6 000	
Ordinary dividends		20 000	
		2 916 000	2 916 000

- The preference shares are non-redeemable.
- The debentures were issued on 2 January 20X8 at par
- Intense Sports Ltd borrowed R240 000 from the bank on 2 November 20X8 at an interest rate of 15% pa.
- The directors' salaries for the year are R200 000.
- Land and buildings which originally cost R150 000 were sold for R210 000. The directors wish to transfer the gain on sale to a non-distributable reserve.
- The current taxation for the year is R72 000.
- An interim dividend of R20 000 was declared at the end of June 20X8 and paid during July 20X8. The final dividend declared by the directors on 24 December 20X8 is R50 000.

Taxation

Owing to its legal status as a separate legal entity apart from its shareholders, a company is subject to normal income tax at a rate of 28% on its taxable income. A company is also required to make provisional payments during the financial year. A provisional payment is an advanced payment of the taxation obligation and is based on an estimate of the total obligation for the year. A company makes two provisional payments, the first payment half way through the year and the second payment at the end of the year.

At the end of the year, a taxation calculation is performed to determine the amount of the current tax charge for the year. The amount owing could be higher or lower than the total provisional payments, resulting in either a debit or credit balance on the Receiver of Revenue account.

The entry to record the provisional tax payment is as follows:

	Dr	**Cr**
Receiver of Revenue	54 000	
Bank		54 000

The entry to record the current tax charge for the year is:

	Dr	Cr
Taxation expense	67 200	
Receiver of Revenue		67 200

The Receiver of Revenue account reflects a credit balance of R13 200, representing the amount owing to the Receiver of Revenue at the end of the year.

Dividends to shareholders

Shareholders, both ordinary and preference, do not have an automatic claim to the retained profit of the company. A liability to shareholders is only established when the directors declare a dividend. Remember, that before the directors declare a divident, the solvency and liquidity requirements must be considered.

Dividends to shareholders are an appropriation of profits and are not recorded as an expense on the income statement. Rather, dividends are recorded in the statement of changes in equity. Remember that the definition of an expense in the accounting framework specifically excludes distributions to equity participants, namely the shareholders.

Most companies declare dividends to their shareholders twice during the year. An ***interim*** dividend is declared halfway through the financial year and a ***final*** dividend is declared at the end of the year. If the final dividend is declared before the reporting period date but only paid after the reporting period date, the liability for the dividend is reported on the statement of financial position as a current liability. On the other hand, and as mentioned in 18.4.3 above, if the final dividend is only declared after the reporting period date, the amount is not recognised as a liability at the end of the reporting period.

Preference dividends

Preference shareholders must be allocated their dividend before the ordinary shareholders are entitled to share in the profits. In our example, Intense Sports Ltd has issued preference shares with a fixed dividend rate of 6%. The accounting entries to record the declaration and payment of the preference dividends are:

	Dr	Cr
Preference dividends	6 000	
Dividend payable		6 000
Declaration of preference dividend		
Dividend payable	6 000	
Bank		6 000
Payment of preference dividend		

Ordinary dividends

The trial balance shows an ordinary dividend account with a debit balance of R20 000. This represents the *interim* dividend, which was processed as follows:

	Dr	**Cr**
Ordinary dividends	20 000	
Dividend payable		20 000
Declaration of interim dividend		
Dividend payable	20 000	
Bank		20 000
Payment of interim dividend		

Note that a company does not have a separate liability account for each shareholder, compared to a partnership where there is a current account for each partner and a close corporation where there is a short-term loan account for each member. There are two reasons for this. Firstly, it is impractical because of the large number of shareholders. Secondly, it is not necessary because a company *initiates the payment* of dividends to shareholders, whereas partners in a partnership and members in a close corporation *withdraw* cash as they need it.

The entry to process the declaration of the *final* dividend is the same as for the interim dividend. The entry is:

	Dr	**Cr**
Ordinary dividends	50 000	
Dividend payable		50 000
Declaration of final dividend		

The statement of changes in equity will show ordinary dividends of R70 000, comprising the interim dividend of R20 000 declared and paid and the final dividend (declared but not paid) of R50 000. The statement of financial position will reflect a dividend liability of R50 000, representing the obligation of the company to the shareholders for the final dividend.

Capitalisation issue

Many listed companies offer their shareholders a choice of receiving a cash dividend, as described above, or of receiving further shares in the company in place of a cash dividend. This is referred to as a capitalisation issue.

The capitalisation issue is a well-accepted option for shareholders in successful companies as it, in effect, allows the shareholders to reinvest their dividends in the company.

Accounting practice and the Companies Act allow for a number of possible options in providing for a capitalisation issue. One option is to provide for the capitalisation issue from retained earnings as follows:

Dr	Retained earnings
Cr	Share capital

You should realise that the same effect is achieved by processing two separate entries:

Dr	Dividends
Cr	Share capital
and	
Dr	Retained earnings
Cr	Dividendsl

The dividend account (for cash dividends or a capitalisation issue processed in this manner) is closed off to the retained earnings account, as will be shown in section 18.6.3 below.

Another option, provided for in terms of section 76 of the Companies Act, is to provide for the capitalisation issue from the share premium account. This is described in detail in section 18.7.2.

You should note that there is no cash payment to shareholders with a capitalisation issue.

Transfer to non-distributable reserve

A portion of the land and buildings which cost R150 000 was sold for R210 000. The gain on sale is reported on the income statement as an income item. As the directors wish to transfer the gain to a non-distributable reserve, the following entry must be processed:

	Dr	**Cr**
Retained earnings	60 000	
Non-distributable reserve		60 000
Transfer of gain on sale of		
Land & buildings to NDR		

Solution: Producing information for a company

INTENSE SPORTS LIMITED
INCOME STATEMENT
FOR THE YEAR ENDED 31 DECEMBER 20X8

		R	R
Revenue from sales			1 860 000
Cost of sales			(930 000)
Gross profit			930 000
Other income			
Profit on disposal of land and buildings			60 000
Operating expenses			(732 000)
Administration		72 000	
Marketing		63 000	
Directors' salaries		200 000	
Telephone		18 000	
Employees' salaries		334 000	
Lights and water		25 000	
Depreciation		20 000	
Finance cost			
Interest	[(100 000 x 0,12) + (240 000 x 0,15 x 2/12)]		(18 000)
Profit before tax			240 000
Income tax expense			(67 200)
Profit for the period			172 800

INTENSE SPORTS LIMITED
STATEMENT OF CHANGES IN EQUITY
FOR THE YEAR ENDED 31 DECEMBER 20X8

	Share capital Ordinary	**Share capital Preference**	**Non-distributable reserve**	**Retained earnings**	**Total**
	R	**R**	**R**	**R**	**R**
Balance at 01/01/X8	100 000	100 000	–	105 000	305 000
Profit for the period				172 800	172 800
Transfer to NDR			60 000	(60 000)	
Dividends					
preference				(6 000)	(6 000)
ordinary				(70 000)	(70 000)
Balance at 31/12/X8	100 000	100 000	60 000	141 800	401 800

INTENSE SPORTS LIMITED
STATEMENT OF FINANCIAL POSITION
AT 31 DECEMBER 20X8

	Cost	Accumulated depreciation	Carrying amount	R
ASSETS				
Non-current assets				420 000
Land and buildings	360 000	–	360 000	
Furniture and fittings	100 000	40 000	60 000	
Current assets				584 000
Inventory				70 000
Accounts receivable				154 000
Bank				360 000
				1 004 000
EQUITY AND LIABILITIES				
Capital and reserves				401 800
Ordinary share capital				100 000
Preference share capital				100 000
Non-distributable reserve				60 000
Distributable reserve – Retained earnings				141 800
Non-current liabilities				340 000
Loan from bank				240 000
12% Debentures				100 000
Current liabilities				262 200
Accounts payable				161 000
Directors' salaries payable				20 000
Dividends payable				50 000
Interest payable				18 000
Receiver of Revenue (67 200 - 54 000)				13 200
				1 004 000

18.6.3 Closing entries for a company

The closing entries to transfer the trading activities to the trading account, as well as the operating and financing activities to the profit and loss account, are identical for all entity forms. When accounting for a partnership, the profit from the profit and loss account is transferred to the appropriation account. In a close corporation, the profit from the profit and loss account is transferred to the undrawn profit account, where the taxation charge and the distributions are also transferred. In a company, the profit is transferred to the ***retained earnings*** account.

The closing entry to transfer the profit from the profit and loss account to the retained earnings account is:

	Dr	Cr
Profit & loss	240 000	
Retained earnings		240 000

Further closing entries for a company are required to transfer the balances on the taxation expense and dividend accounts to the retained earnings account. These entries are as follows:

	Dr	Cr
Retained earnings	67 200	
Taxation expense		67 200
Retained earnings	76 000	
Preference dividend		6 000
Ordinary dividend		70 000

18.7 Share issues

It is important to understand the process that is involved when issuing shares before examining the relevant accounting entries. A description of the process is as follows:

- A public company may apply for a listing on one of the boards of the JSE once the criteria for listing have been complied with (as set out in section 18.3, above). There are three methods of obtaining a listing[7]:
  - An introduction. This is suitable where the company does not need to raise capital and has a sufficiently wide public spread of shareholdings. It is the quickest and cheapest means of listing, as there is no offer to the public and minimal formalities are required.
  - A private placing. This has proved to be the most common method of obtaining a listing. In this instance, shares in the company are placed or offered to prospective shareholders through private negotiation. Usually this will be done through a sponsor or a merchant bank.
  - A public offer. A public offer may be an offer for subscription or an offer for sale. In an offer for subscription, members of the public are invited to subscribe for unissued shares and the proceeds accrue to the company, while in an offer for sale, existing shareholders invite subscribers to purchase their shares and therefore the proceeds accrue to the shareholders.
- If the public offer is for a subscription, there are further factors to consider and steps to follow:
  - Appointment of an underwriter. Although it is not a requirement that an offer be underwritten, the appointment of an underwriter has a number

of advantages. The company is assured of raising the desired amount of capital and creates a good impression if a prominent institution is prepared to underwrite the offer.

- A prospectus is issued and the public has a certain period of time within which to submit their applications and payment.
- The company then allots shares to the applicants. If the offer is oversubscribed, the company will have to decide on a basis of allocation. The company also earns interest on the payments received until the date of refund. This interest may be used to offset the costs of the offer.

- The shareholding is recorded electronically by Strate[8]. Strate is the authorised central securities depository for the electronic settlement of all financial instruments in South Africa. These electronic records take the place of the register of shareholders kept by Transfer Secretaries on behalf of companies. Investors receive regular statements detailing their electronic holdings and, as these statements are not negotiable instruments, investors need not fear the loss or duplication of such statements. These statements take the place of share certificates. This is in direct contrast to the paper settlement environment where risks of lost, forged or stolen documents existed.

Pause and reflect...

How is the equity of a company affected when a company issues shares as opposed to a shareholder selling shares?

Response

When a company issues shares, cash is received by the company and the share capital of the company is increased. On the other hand, when a shareholder sells shares, the transaction is between two shareholders and the equity of the company remains unchanged.

The examples that follow examine the different share issue transactions that could occur, relating to Intense Sports Ltd.

18.7.1 Recording an issue of par value shares

The same procedure is followed on the issue of both ordinary and preference shares. The proceeds on issue of par value shares at par are recorded in a share capital account. The examples that follow deal with the issue of ordinary shares.

Example: Recording an issue of par value shares at par

On 2 January 20X7, Simon Smart and Gary Good form Intense Sports Ltd with an authorised capital of R30 000 divided into ordinary shares of R1 each. The subscribers to the memorandum (Simon and Gary) subscribe for 5 000 shares at par and pay for them in full.

On 5 January 20X9, after two years of successful trading, the company lists on the AltX by means of a public offer 25 000 shares. Applications for 40 000 shares are received. On 1 March 20X9, 25 000 shares are allotted.

You are required to:

(a) journalise the above transactions
(b) prepare the equity section of the statement of financial position at 1 March 20X9.

Solution: Recording an issue of par value shares at par

GENERAL JOURNAL OF INTENSE SPORTS LIMITED

Date	Description	Fol	Dr	Cr
02/01/X7	Subscribers to the memorandum		5 000	
	Share capital			5 000
	5 000 shares allotted to subscribers to the memorandum			
	Bank		5 000	
	Subscribers to the memorandum			5 000
	Cash received for the 5 000 shares			
05/01/X9	Bank		40 000	
	Application account			40 000
	Amount received on application for 40 000 shares			
01/03/X9	Application account		25 000	
	Share capital			25 000
	25 000 shares allotted as per directors' resolution			
	Application account		15 000	
	Cash			15 000
	Cash refunded to unsuccessful applicants			

INTENSE SPORTS LIMITED
(EXTRACT FROM) STATEMENT OF FINANCIAL POSITION AT 1 MARCH 20X9

	R
EQUITY	
Capital and reserves	
Share capital (5 000 + 25 000)	30 000

18.7.2 Recording an issue of par value shares at a premium

A share premium arises when the issue price of par value shares exceeds their par value. The proceeds on issue are recorded in both the share capital account and a ***share premium account***. The *nominal value* of the shares issued is recorded in the share capital account, and the *premium* is recorded in the share premium account. For example, if 100 000 shares of R1 par value are issued at R1,10, then an amount of R100 000 (100 000 x R1,00) is credited to the share capital account and R10 000 (100 000 x 0,10) is credited to the share premium account.

The share premium account is part of the equity of a company and, as part of the permanent capital, may not be distributed as a dividend to shareholders.

In terms of section 76 of the Companies Act, 1973, the share premium may be used by the company for the following purposes:

- Issuing un-issued shares of the company to the members as fully paid capitalisation shares.
- Writing off:
  - the preliminary expenses of the company
  - the expenses of, or the commission paid on, the creation or issue of ***any*** shares of the company.
- Providing for the premium payable on redemption of any redeemable preference shares of the company.

Each of these items is discussed below.

Capitalisation issue

The concept of a capitalisation issue was addressed in section 18.6.2. When using the share premium account to provide for a capitalisation issue, the accounting entry required is as follows:

Dr	Share premium
Cr	Share capital

Preliminary expenses

The preliminary expenses relate to establishing a company or raising capital. The benefit of these expenses extends over the life of the company. When paid, the preliminary expense account is debited and bank is credited. The preliminary expenses can then be dealt with in one of two ways.

- ❑ They can be set off against the share premium account, as provided for in section 76 of the Companies Act.
- ❑ They can be set off against the retained earnings account.

Note that both of these options do not charge the preliminary expenses as an expense on the income statement. This is not permitted by accounting standards because of the conflict with the accrual basis of accounting.

Share-issue expenses

Share-issue expenses include all amounts paid relating to the issue of shares by a company, such as the fees of a sponsoring broker, accounting and legal fees, advertising and marketing fees, and underwriting commission (explained in section 18.7.4). The amount of the share issue expenses can be significant.

The share-issue expenses can be dealt with in the same manner as the preliminary expenses, that is, setting off against the share premium account or setting off against the retained earnings account.

Premium on redemption of preference shares

If preference shares are redeemed at an amount above par value, the premium *payable* may be provided from the share premium account. The accounting and legal principles relating to the redemption of preference shares are beyond the scope of this text.

Example: Recording an issue of par value shares at a premium

On 2 January 20X7, Simon Smart and Gary Good form Intense Sports Ltd with an authorised share capital of R200 000 divided into 100 000 ordinary shares of R2 each. The company issued 50 000 shares at par to the founders.

On 01 June 20X9, the company met the requirements for listing on the AltX. The directors issued the remaining shares by means of a private placing at a premium of 50c per share. All the shares were allotted on 30 June 20X9. Share-issue expenses of R5 000 were incurred and paid. The directors wish to write off the share-issue expenses with the minimum impact on distributable reserves.

You are required to:

(a) journalise the transactions that take place on 30 June 20X9.
(b) prepare the equity section of the statement of financial position at 30 June 20X9.

Solution: Recording an issue of par value shares at a premium

GENERAL JOURNAL OF INTENSE SPORTS LIMITED

Date	Description	Fol	Dr	Cr
30/06/X9	Bank		125 000	
	Share application account			125 000
	Application received for 50 000 shares			
	Share application account		125 000	
	Share capital			100 000
	Share premium			25 000
	50 000 shares allotted			
30/06/X9	Share issue expenses		5 000	
	Bank			5 000
	Share issue expenses paid			
30/06/X9	Share premium		5 000	
	Share issue expenses			5 000
	Share issue expenses written off to the share premium account			

INTENSE SPORTS LIMITED
(EXTRACT FROM) STATEMENT OF FINANCIAL POSITION AT 30 JUNE 20X9

EQUITY		**R**
Capital and reserves		220 000
Share capital	(100 000 + 100 000)	200 000
Share premium	(25 000 – 5 000)	20 000

18.7.3 Recording an issue of no-par value shares

Shares having no par value can be issued at any price. The only condition imposed by the Companies Act is that, if shares are issued to the public and the issue price is lower than a price arrived at by dividing the existing share capital by the number of shares existing at that date, a special resolution is necessary to authorise the issue. The procedure on issue of no-par value shares is identical to the issue of par value shares. The whole of the proceeds of an issue of shares having no par value is credited to an account called the ***stated capital account***.

In terms of section 77 of the Companies Act, 1973, the stated capital account may be applied by the company in writing off:

- the preliminary expenses of the company
- the expenses of, or the commission paid on, the creation or issue of any ***such*** shares.

We have already explained the principles surrounding preliminary expenses and share issue expenses.

Example: Recording an issue of no-par value shares

On 2 January 20X7, Simon Smart and Gary Good form Intense Sports Ltd with an authorised capital of 200 000 ordinary shares of no par value. 100 000 shares were issued to the founders (Simon and Gary) at a price of R2 per share.

On 1 June 20X9, the company invites subscriptions by means of a public offer for 100 000 shares at a price of R4 per share. Applications, which close on 15 July 20X9, are received for 400 000 shares. Expenses of the issue amount to R10 000 and are to be written off with the minimum impact on distributable reserves.

You are required to:

(a) journalise transactions that take place during June and July 20X9.
(b) prepare the equity section of the statement of financial position of Intense Sports Ltd at 31 July 20X9.

Solution: Recording an issue of no-par value shares

GENERAL JOURNAL OF INTENSE SPORTS LIMITED

Date	Description	Fol	Dr	Cr
15/07/X9	Bank Share application account *Application received for 400 000 shares*		1 600 000	 1 600 000
	Share application account Stated capital *100 000 shares allotted at R4 per share in terms of directors' resolution dated ...*		400 000	 400 000
	Application account Bank *Refund to unsuccessful applicants*		1 200 000	 1 200 000
	Share-issue expenses Bank *Share-issue expenses paid*		10 000	 10 000
	Stated capital Share-issue expenses *Share issue expenses written off*		10 000	 10 000

INTENSE SPORTS LIMITED
(EXTRACT FROM) STATEMENT OF FINANCIAL POSITION
AT 31 JULY 20X9

EQUITY	**R**
Capital and reserves	
Stated capital (200 000 + 400 000 – 10 000)	590 000

We have now addressed the procedure on issue of par value shares at a premium as well as the issue of no-par value shares. Section 76 of the Companies Act governs the expenses permitted to be written off against the share premium account, and section 77 controls the write-off of expenses against the stated capital account. The two sections have their similarities, but also some important differences. The provisions of sections 76 and 77 are compared and summarised below.

Share premium account (created on issue of par value shares at a premium) may be used for the following purposes:

- capitalisation issues
- preliminary expenses
- share-issue expenses relating to the issue of par value ***or*** no-par value shares
- premium on redemption of preference shares

Stated capital account (created on issue of no-par value shares) may be used for the following purposes:

- preliminary expenses
- share-issue expenses ***only*** of no-par value shares

Diagram 18.3: Comparison between share premium account and stated capital accounts

18.7.4 Underwriting an issue of shares

A company may, if it wishes, have the offer of its shares underwritten by a merchant bank or some other financial institution. The underwriter is paid a commission for underwriting the issue and, in return, undertakes to subscribe for any shares not taken up by the public. The underwriting institution is taking a risk as it may have to purchase a large number of shares if the offer is under-subscribed. The commission is usually calculated on the issue price.

Example: Underwriting, share issue and preliminary expenses

On 2 January 20X7, Simon Smart and Gary Good form Intense Sports Ltd with an authorised capital of 102 000 ordinary shares of R1 each. The founders (Simon and Gary) subscribe for 2 000 shares at par and pay for them in full.

On 1 June 20X9, the company applies for a listing on the AltX and the remaining shares are offered to the public at a premium of 25 cents. The issue is underwritten by Underwriters Limited for 1% underwriting commission. 80 000 shares are applied for by the public and R1,25 is received with each application. Preliminary expenses amounting to R3 000 and share-issue expenses of R2 000 are paid. The above transactions are finalised on 30 June 20X9. The preliminary and share-issue expenses are to be written off against the share premium account.

You are required to:

(a) journalise all of the above transactions
(b) prepare the statement of financial position at 30 June 20X9.

Solution: Underwriting, share issue and preliminary expenses

GENERAL JOURNAL OF INTENSE SPORTS LIMITED

Date	Description	Fol	Dr	Cr
02/01/X7	Subscribers to the memorandum		2 000	
	Share capital			2 000
	2 000 shares allotted to the subscribers of the memorandum			
	Bank		2 000	
	Subscribers to the memorandum			2 000
	Cash received from the subscribers to the memorandum			
30/06/X9	Bank		100 000	
	Application account			100 000
	Cash received in respect of application for 80 000 shares			
	Application account		100 000	
	Share capital			80 000
	Share premium			20 000
	80 000 shares allotted as per directors' resolution dated …			

		Dr	Cr
	Underwriting commission Underwriters Limited *1% underwriting commission on R125 000 due in terms of agreement dated …*	1 250	1 250
	Underwriters Limited Share capital Share premium *20 000 shares allotted to Underwriters Limited in terms of agreement dated … and directors' resolution dated …*	25 000	20 000 5 000
	Bank Underwriters Limited *Balance due*	23 750	23 750
	Share-issue expenses Preliminary expenses Bank *Share-issue and preliminary expenses paid*	2 000 3 000	5 000
	Share premium Underwriter's commission Share-issue expenses Preliminary expenses *Share-issue and preliminary expenses written off*	6 250	1 250 2 000 3 000

INTENSE SPORTS LIMITED
(EXTRACT FROM) STATEMENT OF FINANCIAL POSITION AT 30 JUNE 20X7

		R
ASSETS		
Current assets		
Bank		120 750
		120 750
EQUITY		
Capital and reserves		120 750
Share capital	(2 000 + 80 000 + 20 000)	102 000
Share premium	(20 000 + 5 000 – 6 250)	18 750
		120 750

18.7.5 Conversion of shares

Conversion of par value shares into no-par value shares

- Section 78 of the Companies Act, 1973, states that, where a company converts all its ordinary or preference shares having a par value, or both such ordinary and such preference shares, into shares of no par value, there shall be transferred to the *stated capital* account of the company:

- the whole of the *ordinary or preference share capital* as the case may be, and
- the whole of the *share premium* account or that part thereof contributed to it by the shares so converted.

Example: Conversion of par value shares to no-par value shares

On 2 January 20X7, Simon Smart and Gary Good form Intense Sports Ltd with an authorised and issued share capital consisting of:

100 000 ordinary shares of R1 each	R100 000
50 000 10% preference shares of R1 each	R50 000

A share premium of R50 000 arose on the issue of the ordinary shares. On 1 July 20X7 the company decided to convert the ordinary shares into shares of no par value.

You are required to:

prepare the journal entry necessary to record the conversion.

Solution: Conversion of par value shares to no-par value shares

GENERAL JOURNAL OF INTENSE SPORTS LIMITED				
Date	**Description**	**Fol**	**Dr**	**Cr**
01/07/X7	Ordinary share capital		100 000	
	Share premium		50 000	
	Ordinary stated capital			150 000
	Conversion of 100 000 ordinary shares of R1 each into ordinary shares of no par value in terms of special resolution dated …			

Conversion of no-par value shares into par value shares

In terms of section 78 of the Companies Act, 1973, where a company converts all its ordinary or preference shares of no-par value, or both such ordinary and such preference shares, into shares having a par value, there shall be transferred to the *share capital* account of the company the whole of the *stated capital* account or that part thereof contributed to it by the shares so converted.

The par value of the newly created shares cannot be greater than the average value of the no-par value shares. If, however, the par value of the new shares is less than the average value of the no-par value shares, the excess must be transferred to a *non-distributable reserve.* This is similar in principle to the issue of par value shares at a premium. The share premium account is legally a non-distributable reserve.[9]

Example: Conversion of no-par value shares to par value shares

Assume that, on 2 January 20X7, Simon Smart and Gary Good form Intense Sports Ltd with an authorised and issued share capital consisting of:

100 000 ordinary shares of no par value – stated capital account	R154 663
50 000 10% preference shares of R1 each	R50 000

On 1 July 20X7 the company decided to convert the ordinary shares of no par value into ordinary shares having a par value of R1,50 each.

You are required to:

prepare the journal entry necessary to record the above transactions.

Solution: Conversion of no-par value shares to par value shares

GENERAL JOURNAL OF INTENSE SPORTS LIMITED

Date	Description	Fol	Dr	Cr
01/07/X7	Stated capital account		154 663	
	Ordinary share capital			150 000
	Non-distributable reserve			4 663
	Conversion of 100 000 ordinary shares of no par value into par value shares of R1,50 each and transfer of resultant surplus to non-distributable reserve in terms of special resolution dated ...			

The par value of R1,50 is less than the average value of the no-par value shares of R1, 54 663 (R154 663/100 000). The share capital is credited with the par value of the shares issued (100 000 x R1,50), and a non-distributable reserve is credited with the excess of R4 663 (100 000 x R0,04663)..

18.8 Debenture issues

The debenture trust deed specifies the par value of the debentures as well as the ***nominal rate*** of interest payable on the debentures. As with other financial liabilities, the nominal rate determines the amount of interest *paid* each year and is calculated by multiplying the par value of the debentures by the nominal rate.

The ***market rate*** of interest, on the other hand, is the rate determined by the supply and demand for funds on the money market.

Related to the nominal and market rates is the ***effective rate*** of interest. If a company issues debentures at par value, the effective rate will be equal to the nominal rate. However, the effective rate can be increased or decreased by issuing the debentures at a discount or premium, respectively. The discount on issue is a 'loss' to the company and is accounted for as additional interest expense over the life of the debentures. This causes the effective rate to be greater than the nominal rate. Conversely, the premium on issue is a 'profit' to the company and is accounted for as a reduction in the interest expense over the life of the debentures. This causes the effective rate to be lower than the nominal rate.

It is common for debentures to be issued at a discount when the nominal rate offered is less than the current or projected market rate. This is because investors are willing to pay only an amount lower than par value because of the lower nominal rate offered. By issuing the debentures at a discount, the effective rate (and hence the cost to the company or return to the investor) is increased above the nominal rate. On the other hand, it is common for debentures to be issued at a premium when the nominal rate offered is greater than the current or projected market rate. This is because investors are willing to pay an amount greater than par value because of the higher interest rate offered. By issuing the debentures at a premium, the effective rate is decreased below the nominal rate.

These relationships can be summarised as follows:

Debenture issued at	Circumstance	Relationship between effective rate and nominal rate
Par value	Nominal rate = market rate	Effective rate = nominal rate
A discount	Nominal rate < market rate	Effective rate > nominal rate
A premium	Nominal rate > market rate	Effective rate < nominal rate

Diagram 18.4: Issue of debentures at par, discount or premium

18.8.1 Issue of debentures at par

As mentioned above, debentures are issued at par when the nominal rate is equal to the market rate.

Example: Issue of debentures at par

Assume that, on 2 January 20X7, Simon Smart and Gary Good form Intense Sports Ltd. After trading for a few years, the company offers 10 000 10% debentures of R100 each to the public *at par*, payable in full on application. Applications are received for 12 000 debentures. The debentures are secured over land and buildings with a carrying amount of R1 500 000. The debentures are issued on 2 January 20Y0 and are repayable on 31 December 20Y4.

You are required to:

(a) journalise the above transactions for the year ended 31 December 20Y0.
(b) show how the interest expense is reported on the income statement for the year ended 31 December 20Y0
(c) show how the debentures are reported on the statement of financial position at 31 December 20Y0.

Solution: Issue of debentures at par

(a)

GENERAL JOURNAL OF INTENSE SPORTS LIMITED

Date	Description	Fol	Dr	Cr
02/01/Y0	Bank Debenture application account *Amount received on application for 12 000 debentures*		1 200 000	 1 200 000
	Debenture application account Debenture liability *10 000 debentures allotted per directors' resolution dated …*		1 000 000	 1 000 000
	Debenture application account Bank *Cash refunded to unsuccessful applicants*		200 000	 200 000
31/12/Y0	Interest expense Bank *Interest paid for the year*		100 000	 100 000

(b)

INTENSE SPORTS LIMITED
(EXTRACT FROM) INCOME STATEMENT FOR THE YEAR ENDED 31 DECEMBER 20Y0

	R
Finance cost	
Interest	100 000

(c)

INTENSE SPORTS LIMITED
(EXTRACT FROM) STATEMENT OF FINANCIAL POSITION AT 31 DECEMBER 20Y0

	R
EQUITY AND LIABILITIES	
Capital and reserves	**?**
Non-current liability	
10% debentures	1 000 000

The interest paid is based on the nominal value of the debentures and the amount paid is therefore R100 000 (R1 000 000 x 0,10). The debenture liability is reported at par value, irrespective of the issue price.

18.8.2 Issue of debentures at a discount

When the nominal rate of interest offered on a debenture issue is lower than the market rate, the debentures can be issued to the public at a discount below par value. As mentioned previously, this will result in the effective interest rate being greater than the nominal interest rate.

Example: Issue of debentures at a discount

Assume that, on 2 January 20X7, Simon Smart and Gary Good form Intense Sports Ltd. After trading for a few years, the company offers 10 000 10% debentures of R100 each to the public *at a discount* of 4%, payable in full on application. All the debentures are applied for, and allotted on 2 January 20Y0. The debentures are repayable on 31 December 20Y4.

You are required to:

(a) Journalise the transaction relating to the debentures for the year ended 31 December 20Y0.
(b) Show how the interest expense is reported on the income statement for the year ended 31 December 20Y0
(c) Show how the debentures are reported on the statement of financial position at 31 December 20Y0.

Solution: Issue of debentures at a discount

Firstly, it is necessary to set up a schedule of cash flows relating to the debentures in order to calculate the effective interest rate.

02/01/Y0	31/12/Y0	31/12/Y1	31/12/Y2	31/12/Y3	31/12/Y4
960 000	(100 000)	(100 000)	(100 000)	(100 000)	(1 100 000)

The internal rate of return that equates the initial cash inflow of R960 000 with cash outflows of R100 000 per year for four years and a final cash outflow of R1 100 000 is 11,0845%. This is the effective interest rate.

Secondly, an amortisation table is prepared to calculate the interest expense as well as the carrying amount of the liability on the statement of financial position.

Date	Effective interest	Nominal interest	Discount	Discount balance	PV
02/01/Y0				40 000	960 000
31/12/Y0	106 411	100 000	6 411	33 589	966 411
31/12/Y1	107 122	100 000	7 122	26 467	973 533
31/12/Y2	107 912	100 000	7 912	18 555	981 445
31/12/Y3	108 789	100 000	8 789	9 766	990 234
31/12/Y4	*109 766	100 000	9 766	–	1 000 000

* Rounded

(a)

GENERAL JOURNAL OF INTENSE SPORTS LIMITED

Date	Description	Fol	Dr	Cr
02/01/Y0	Bank		960 000	
	Debenture discount		40 000	
	Debenture liability			1 000 000
	Receipt of cash for debentures			
31/12/Y0	Interest expense		106 411	
	Debenture discount			6 411
	Bank			100 000
	Interest paid			

(b)

INTENSE SPORTS LIMITED
(EXTRACT FROM) INCOME STATEMENT FOR THE YEAR ENDED 31 DECEMBER 20Y0

	R
Finance costs	
Interest on debentures	106 411

The interest expense reported on the income statement is the effective interest for the year. This comprises the nominal interest paid of R100 000 plus the amortisation of the discount of R6 411.

(c)

INTENSE SPORTS LIMITED
(EXTRACT FROM) STATEMENT OF FINANCIAL POSITION AT 31 DECEMBER 20Y0

	R
Non-current liabilities	
10% Debentures	966 411

The carrying amount of the debentures on the statement of financial position at 31 December 20Y0 is R966 411 (R960 000 + R6 411). This amount equates to the present value of future cash flows associated with the debentures. This can be proved as follows:

Date of cash flow	Amount of cash flow	PV at 11,0845%
	R	R
31/12/Y1	100 000	90 021
31/12/Y2	100 000	81 038
31/12/Y3	100 000	72 951
31/12/Y4	1 100 000	722 401
		966 411

The carrying amount can also be proved by taking the par value of the debentures and subtracting the *unamortised* discount (R1 000 000 – R33 589).

18.8.3 Issue of debentures at a premium

When the nominal rate of interest offered on a debenture issue is higher than the market rate, the debentures can be issued to the public at a premium above par value. As mentioned previously, this will result in the effective interest rate being lower than the nominal interest rate.

Example: Issue of debentures at a premium

Assume that, on 2 January 20X7, Simon Smart and Gary Good form Intense Sports Ltd. After trading for a few years, the company offers 10 000 10% debentures of R100 each to the public *at a premium* of 3%, payable in full on application. All the debentures are applied for, and allotted on 2 January 20Y0. The debentures are repayable on 31 December 20Y4.

You are required to:

(a) Journalise the transactions relating to the debentures for the year ended 31 December 20Y0.

(b) Show how the interest expense is reported on the income statement for the year ended 31 December 20Y0.

(c) Show how the debentures are reported on the statement of financial position at 31 December 20Y0.

Solution: Issue of debentures at a premium

Again, it is necessary to set up a schedule of cash flows relating to the debentures in order to calculate the effective interest rate.

02/01/Y0	31/12/Y0	31/12/Y1	31/12/Y2	31/12/Y3	31/12/Y4
1 030 000	(100 000)	(100 000)	(100 000)	(100 000)	(1 100 000)

The internal rate of return that equates the initial cash inflow of R1 030 000 with cash outflows of R100 000 per year for four years and a final cash outflow of R1 100 000 is 9,2242%. This is the effective interest rate.

As shown previously, an amortisation table is prepared to calculate the interest expense as well as the carrying amount of the liability on the statement of financial position.

Date	Effective interest	Nominal interest	Premium	Premium balance	PV
02/01/Y0				30 000	1 030 000
31/12/Y0	95 010	100 000	4 990	25 010	1 025 010
31/12/Y1	94 549	100 000	5 451	19 559	1 019 559
31/12/Y2	94 097	100 000	5 953	13 606	1 013 606
31/12/Y3	93 498	100 000	6 502	7 104	1 007 104
31/12/Y4	*92 896	100 000	7 104	–	1 000 000

* Rounded

(a)

GENERAL JOURNAL OF INTENSE SPORT LIMITED

Date	Description	Fol	Dr	Cr
02/01/Y0	Bank		1 030 000	
	Debenture premium			30 000
	Debenture liability			1 000 000
	Receipt of cash for debentures			
31/12/Y0	Interest expense		95 010	
	Debenture premium		4 990	
	Bank			100 000
	Interest paid			

(b)

INTENSE SPORTS LIMITED
(EXTRACT FROM) INCOME STATEMENT FOR THE YEAR ENDED 31 DECEMBER 20Y0

	R
Finance costs	
Interest on debentures	95 010

The interest expense reported on the income statement is the effective interest for the year. This comprises the nominal interest paid of R100 000 less the amortisation of the premium of R4 990.

(c)

INTENSE SPORTS LIMITED
(EXTRACT FROM) STATEMENT OF FINANCIAL POSITION AT 31 DECEMBER 20Y0

	R
Non-current liabilities	
10% Debentures	1 025 010

The carrying amount of the debentures on the statement of financial position at 31 December 20Y0 is R1 025 010 (R1 030 000 – R4 990). This amount equates to the present value of future cash flows associated with the debentures. This can be proved as follows:.

Date of cash flow	Amount of cash flow	PV at 9,2242%
	R	R
31/12/Y1	100 000	91 555
31/12/Y2	100 000	83 823
31/12/Y3	100 000	76 743
31/12/Y4	1 100 000	772 889
		1 025 010

The carrying amount can also be proved by taking the par value of the debentures and adding theunamortised premium (R1 000 000 + R25 010).

18.9 Exam example

Skimbleshanks Limited is a company listed on the JSE Securities Exchange and is involved in distributing components for the railways. The trial balance of the company at 30 September 20X2 appears as follows:

SKIMBLESHANKS LIMITED
TRIAL BALANCE AT 30 SEPTEMBER 20X2

Description	Dr	Cr
Land and buildings	3 250 000	
Plant and equipment	1 100 000	
Accumulated depreciation – plant & equipment		120 000
Inventory	810 000	
Trade accounts receivable	536 000	
Bank	512 724	
Trade accounts payable		425 000
SARS	90 000	
Ordinary share capital		2 000 000
Share premium		600 000
Retained earnings		942 000
Ordinary dividend	90 000	
12% Debentures		1 500 000
Debenture discount	75 000	
15% Redeemable preference shares		250 000
Gross profit		1 801 724
Administration expenses	550 000	
Distribution expenses	385 000	
Other operating expenses	240 000	
	7 638 724	7 638 724

The following information is relevant for the preparation of the financial statements:

1. The land and buildings were valued on 25 September 20X2 by an independent valuer at an amount of R3 400 000.
2. The plant and equipment is depreciated on the sum of units method. The total estimated output of the plant and equipment is 20 million units. During the current period, a total of 1 750 000 units were produced. All of the plant and equipment was purchased on the same date during the previous financial year.
3. The ordinary share capital at 30 September 20X2 consists of 2 000 000 shares of R1 par value. On 1 July 20X2, 1 000 000 ordinary shares were issued to the public at an issue price of R1,60 each. Share issue expenses of R40 000 were incurred and paid and are included in the 'other operating expenses' on the trial balance.
4. The preference share capital at 30 September 20X2 consists of 100 000 15% redeemable

preference shares of no par value. The shares were placed privately at a large financial institution on 1 April 20X2 for an amount of R2.50 each and are subject to compulsory redemption by the company after a period of three years. Share issue expenses of R15 000 were incurred and paid and are included in the 'other operating expenses' on the trial balance.

5. On 1 October 20X1 the company issued 10 000 debentures of R150 par value at a discount of 5%. The debentures are to be redeemed on 30 September 20X6 at par. The interest rate is 12% per annum and is payable annually in arrears on 1 October each year. Debenture issue expenses of R12 000 were incurred and paid and are included in the 'other operating expenses' on the trial balance.

   The debenture discount is to be amortised over the life of the debentures using the effective interest rate method. The effective interest rate is 13,43675% and the accountant has correctly prepared the following amortisation schedule:

	Par value	**Effective interest**	**Actual interest**	**Debenture discount**	**PV**
01/10/X1	1 500 000			75 000	1 425 000
30/09/X2		191 474	180 000	(11 474)	1 436 474
30/09/X3		193 015	180 000	(13 015)	1 449 489
30/09/X4		194 764	180 000	(14 764)	1 464 253
30/09/X5		196 748	180 000	(16 748)	1 481 001
30/09/X6		198 999	180 000	(18 999)	1 500 000

6. Current normal tax must still be accounted for at the correctly calculated amount of R110 320.
7. An extract from the minutes of a directors' meeting on 30 September 20X2 appears as follows:
   (i) Resolved to revalue the land and buildings to reflect the valuation of the independent valuer.
   (ii) Resolved to write off the maximum amount of the ordinary and preference share issue expenses permissible in terms of sections 76 and 77 of the Companies Act. This is to be done in such a way as to maximise the write-off against the share premium account.
   (iii) Declared the preference dividend to all shareholders registered on 30 September 20X2, to be paid on 15 October 20X2.
   (iv) Declaration of ordinary dividend
   - 8 cents per share cash dividend to all shareholders registered on 30 September 20X2, to be paid on 15 October 20X2.
   - 4 cents per share capitalisation issue to all shareholders registered on 30 September 20X2, which is to have the minimum impact on retained earnings.

You are required to

(a) prepare the statement comprehensive income of Skimbleshanks Limited for the year ended 30 September 20X2.
(b) prepare the statement of changes in equity of Skimbleshanks Limited for the year ended 30 September 20X2.
(c) prepare the *assets* and *liabilities* sections *only* of the statement of financial position of Skimbleshanks Limited at 30 September 20X2.

Solution to exam example

(a)

SKIMBLESHANKS LIMITED
STATEMENT OF COMPREHENSIVE INCOME
FOR THE YEAR ENDED 30 SEPTEMBER 20X2

			R
Gross profit			1 801 724
Administrative expenses			(550 000)
Distribution expenses			(385 000)
Other operating expenses	(240 000 – 40 000 – 15 000)		(185 000)
Depreciation expense	(1 750 000 / 20 000 000)		(96 250)
Finance costs			(210 224)
Debenture interest expense		191 474	
Preference dividend	(250 000 x 0,15 x 6/12)	18 750	
Profit before tax			375 250
Taxation			(110 320)
Profit for the period			264 930
Other comprehensive income			
Revaluation			150 000
Total comprehensive income			414 930

(b)

SKIMBLESHANKS LIMITED
STATEMENT OF CHANGES IN EQUITY
FOR THE YEAR ENDED 30 SEPTEMBER 20X2

		Ordinary share capital	Share premium	NDR	Distributable reserve	Total
		R	R	R	R	R
Balance at 01/10/X1		1 000 000			942 000	1 942 000
Issue of ordinary shares		1 000 000	600 000			1 600 000
Share issue expenses	(40 000 + 15 000)		(55 000)			(55 000)
Total comprehensive income				150 000	264 930	414 930
Ordinary dividend	(90 000 + *160 000) *(2 000 000 x 0,08)				(250 000)	(250 000)
Capitalisation issue	(2 000 000 x 0,04)	80 000	(80 000)			
Balance at 30/09/X2		2 080 000	465 000	150 000	956 930	3 651 930

(c)

SKIMBLESHANKS LIMITED
STATEMENT OF FINANCIAL POSITION
AT 30 SEPTEMBER 20X2

		R	R
ASSETS			
Non-current assets			4 283 750
Land and buildings	(3 250 000 + 150 000)		3 400 000
Plant and equipment			883 750
– At cost		1 100 000	
– Accumulated depreciation	(120 000 + 96 250)	(216 250)	
Current assets			1 858 724
Inventory			810 000
Accounts receivable			536 000
Bank			512 724
			6 142 474
EQUITY AND LIABILITIES			
Share capital and reserves			3 651 930
Ordinary share capital			2 080 000
Share premium			465 000
Non-distributable reserve			150 000
Distributable reserve			956 930
Non-current liabilities			1 686 474
12% Debentures			1 436 474
– Par value		1 500 000	
– Debenture discount	(75 000 – 11 474)	(63 526)	
15% Redeemable preference shares			250 000
Current liabilities			804 070
Trade accounts payable			425 000
SARS	(90 000 – 110 320)		20 320
Debenture interest accrued	(1 500 000 x 0,12)		180 000
Preference dividend owing	(250 000 x 0,15 x 6/12)		18 750
Ordinary dividend owing	(2 000 000 x 0,08)		160 000
			6 142 474

(The full statement of financial position is shown here for completeness)

Summary of concepts and applications

1. The Companies Act, 1973 is undergoing a comprehensive transformation that is expected to result in a new Act being introduced in 2010.
2. The chapter discusses the role of the shareholders in a company, the benefit of the limitation of liability, a company's indefinite life, and the different types of company that may be formed, as well as the distinction between private and public companies.
3. A company can be listed on a stock exchange if specific requirements are met.
4. A company can be financed from two sources, namely investors' funds and borrowed funds. The chapter discusses the equity instrument, share capital, and outlines the different classes of shares (ordinary and preference shares), as well as the different types of shares (par value and no-par value shares). The concept of using debentures as a source of finance and their principal features are introduced. Reserves in a company comprise the amounts not allocated to shareholders as a dividend – the profits retained.
5. The Companies Act requires all companies to register both a Memorandum of Association and Articles of Association. The Companies Bill requires only one document, the Memorandum of Incorporation.
6. The profit of a company is determined in the same way as the other entity forms described in previous chapters. The appropriation of profit involves the consideration of the taxation charge and dividends to shareholders. A company's closing entries to the trading and profit and loss accounts are identical to those of the other entity forms. A company's profit is transferred to the retained earnings account.
7. A company may issue par value shares at par (the proceeds on issue are recorded in a share capital account) or at a premium (the proceeds on issue are recorded in both a share capital account and a share premium account). If par value shares are issued at a premium, the resulting share premium account may be utilised by the company in terms of the provisions of the Companies Act. In addition, a company may issue shares of no-par value (the proceeds on issue are recorded in a stated capital account). In certain circumstances, a company may have the offer of its shares underwritten. The Companies Bill only allows the issue of no-par value shares.
8. In considering debentures, one must understand the relationship between the nominal, effective and market rates of interest. Debentures may be issued at par (when the nominal rate is equal to the market rate), a discount (when the nominal rate is lower than the market rate) or a premium (when the nominal rate is higher than the market rate).

Notes

1. http://www.jse.co.za/docs/listings/guidelines.pdf.
2. http://www.jse.co.za/docs/listings/guidelines.pdf.
3. Consider going public? *The Bottom Line*, Grant Thornton, (2008).
4. IAS 32, Financial Instruments: Disclosure and Presentation, *International Accounting Standards Board*, (2007), paragraph 11.
5. IAS 32, paragraphs 20, 21 and 22.
6. IAS 10, Events after the Reporting Period Date, *The International Accounting Standards Board*, (2007), paragraph 12.
7. http://www.jse.co.za/docs/listings/guidelines.pdf.
8. http://www.strate.co.za/strate.
9. Cilliers, H. S. and Rossouw, S. *Corporate Financial Reporting*, Durban: Butterworths (1994), pp. 3–6.

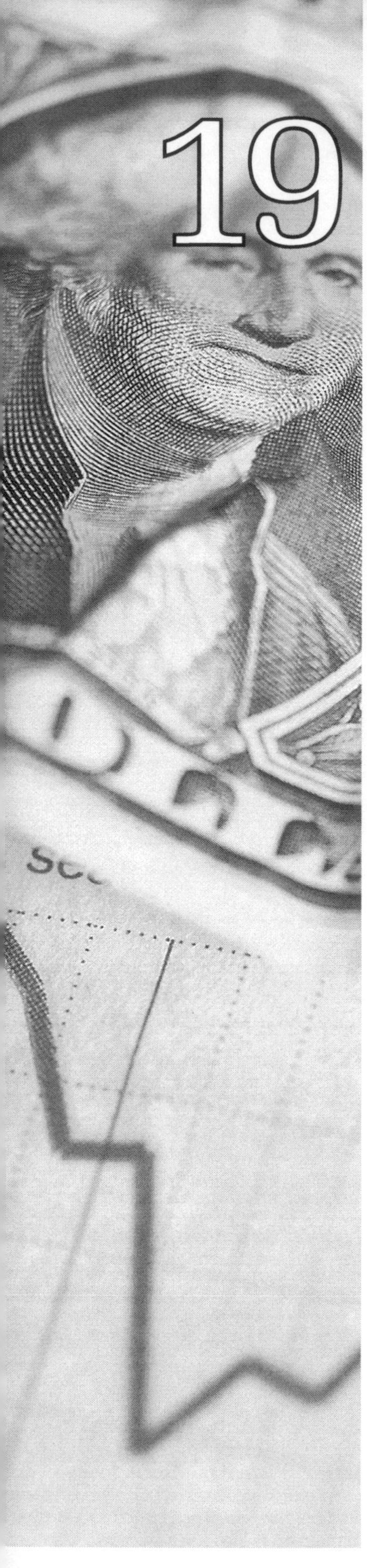

19 Accounting for Close Corporations

'If any general rule can be laid down in the present state of authority, it is that a corporation will be looked upon as a legal entity as a general rule and until sufficient reason to the contrary appears; but when the notion of legal entity is used to defeat public convenience, justify wrong, protect funds or defend crime, the law will regard the corporation as an association of persons.'
(Judge Sanborn, US v Milwaukee Refrigerator Corporation, 1905)

Outcomes

- Recall the characteristics of a close corporation.
- Describe the sources of finance, the distinction between members' contributions and profits retained and the equity of a close corporation.
- Describe the formation process of a close corporation.
- Produce financial information for a close corporation.

Chapter outline

Minister's Forward

"The promotion of entrepreneurship and small business remains an important priority of the government of South Africa. Our commitment is to ensure that small businesses progressively increase their contribution growth and performance of the South African economy in critical areas such as job creation, equity and access to markets. Since 1994, with the advent of a new democratic era, government has taken measures to ensure that small business development becomes a key policy focus."

The government has strongly illustrated the importance of small businesses in driving the economy. Once the new Companies Act takes effect, no further close corporations will be formed. Existing close corporations will be encouraged to convert to a company, the intention being that all close corporations will eventually be phased out. This will ensure that South Africa has a consistent and harmonious regime of business incorporation and regulation.

19.1 Introduction

The Companies Bill, 2008 provides for the co-existence of the new Companies Act and the Close Corporations Act, 1984 with amendments to the latter to harmonise the laws as far as practicable. The Department of Trade and Industry believes that the regime in the new Companies Act for forming and maintaining small companies, which has drawn on the characteristics of the Close Corporations Act, is sufficiently streamlined and simplified as to render it unnecessary to allow for the formation of new close corporations.

However, it is recognised that existing close corporations should be free to retain their current status until such time as their members may determine that it is in their interest to convert to a company. Therefore, the Companies Bill provides for the indefinite continued existence of the Close Corporations Act, but the avenue is closed for incorporation of new close corporations, or for the conversion of companies into close corporations, as of the effective date of the new Act. Provision is made for the conversion of close corporations into companies.

The sections and paragraphs that follow describe the provisions of the Close Corporations Act, 1984.

19.2 Characteristics of a close corporation

In 1984 an additional form of business ownership was introduced into South African law when the Close Corporations Act No 69 of 1984 was passed by parliament. This means of conducting a business was included to provide a less complex and more easily administered legal entity than a company.

A close corporation enables a smaller undertaking to acquire corporate status with a legal personality distinct from its owners, who are known as the ***members*** of the close corporation. A close corporation may not have more than ten members, all of whom must be natural persons.

No distinction is envisaged between owners and management of a close corporation. As most close corporations are smaller businesses, the owners and management will normally be the same group of persons.

The fact that the members and the close corporation are separate legal entities has two important consequences. Firstly, the members have ***limited liability***. This means that they cannot lose more than the amount of their investment, unless they transgress certain provisions of the Act, including carrying on business recklessly, with gross negligence or for any fraudulent purpose. In such circumstances, the members may be held jointly and severally liable for the debts of the close corporation. Secondly, the close corporation has ***perpetual succession*** and continues to exist as a juristic person despite changes in its membership.

There are a number of advantages and disadvantages of a close corporation. The advantages mainly relate to the relative ease of administering this type of corporate entity. The **advantages** can be summarised as follows:[1]

- There is no formal decision-making structure. A close corporation is not required to hold any meetings, and although members may request meetings, decisions can be taken informally on the basis of consultation between members. Actions requiring written agreement by all members can be dealt with by a written resolution signed by all members without the need of a formal meeting.
- There is no separate board of directors, and management is the responsibility of members.
- All statutory information is contained in a single document, the founding statement or amended founding statement, which has to be lodged with the Registrar.
- Financial statements are not required to be audited.
- A member or employee of a close corporation may be appointed its accounting officer provided he is qualified to be so appointed and all members agree in writing.
- No transfer duty is payable on transfer of members' interests.
- A close corporation may acquire the interest of a member and may also give financial assistance to a person who wants to acquire an interest. This is permissible only with the written consent of all members and if the corporation meets the solvency and liquidity requirements of the Act.

Any person or persons who wish to form a close corporation should bear in mind the following potential **disadvantages**:

- A member can be personally liable to the close corporation for a breach of his fiduciary duty, or for loss through failure to act with the skill and care that can reasonably be expected from a person of his skill and experience.
- Every member is an agent for the close corporation, can act on its behalf and can participate in its management. Where the power of a member to bind the corporation is restricted by an association agreement, or he is otherwise disqualified from so doing, his actions will still bind the corporation in respect of transactions with a third party unless that third party ought reasonably to have knowledge of such restriction or disqualifications.
- The restriction on the number and nature of members could be an inhibiting factor in expansion of a successful business. For instance:
  - a close corporation cannot become a subsidiary of a company or another close corporation. Consequently, it is not possible to include a close corporation in a group structure other than as the top holding enterprise.
  - a close corporation cannot be sold to a company. It would first have to be converted to a company before it could be sold as a going concern. This could complicate the disposal of a successful business.
  - members with interests in close corporations will be unable to re-arrange their holdings by transferring them to *inter-vivos* trusts or to companies, nor can other investors participate in the enterprise other than as individuals.
- Unless the association agreement provides otherwise, certain fundamental decisions regarding the close corporation can be taken by a member/members holding an interest of at least 75%.
- Normal tax at the rate applicable to companies, currently 28%, applies irrespective of the size of the enterprise or its profits. This may not compare favourably with

personal tax rates applicable in a sole trader or partnership situation, especially at lower levels of profit.

- Where a member borrows money to invest in a close corporation, the interest he pays will not be deductible for tax purposes because the distribution he receives from the corporation is not taxable.

19.3 Sources of finance for a close corporation

Like a sole proprietor and a partnership, a close corporation can be financed from two sources, investors' funds and borrowed funds.

Cash or other assets invested by a member in a close corporation are known as the ***member's contribution***. Once a contribution has been made by a member to the close corporation, the legal ownership of that asset vests in the corporation. Members' contributions on the statement of financial position are therefore not apportioned to individual members but are shown in aggregate.

Each member of a close corporation has an ***interest*** in the corporation, expressed as a percentage. It is important for you to note that there is *no requirement* for a member's percentage interest to be in proportion to his share of total members' contributions. It is the members' interest, and not their contributions, which determines the proportion in which the after-tax profit is to be shared.

A member may also loan funds to the close corporation. ***Loans from members*** are a liability of the business and are recorded separately from the member's contribution. A close corporation may also borrow funds from outside sources.

19.3.1 Members' contributions and profits retained

The members' contribution in a close corporation is the long-term investment by the owners in the business, similar to the capital contribution of a sole proprietor or a partner in a partnership. As the business trades, profits are earned, but, unlike the sole proprietor or partnership where the owners have the right to withdraw the profits, the members of a close corporation do not have an automatic claim to the profits.

As a separate legal entity, the close corporation pays tax on its profits and it is only the after-tax profit which is available for distribution to members. Amounts authorised for payment to members are known as ***distributions*** and the profits retained are known as the ***undrawn profit.*** In a close corporation, therefore, the cumulative excess of profit over taxation and distributions to members represents the profits retained in the business, or the undrawn profit.

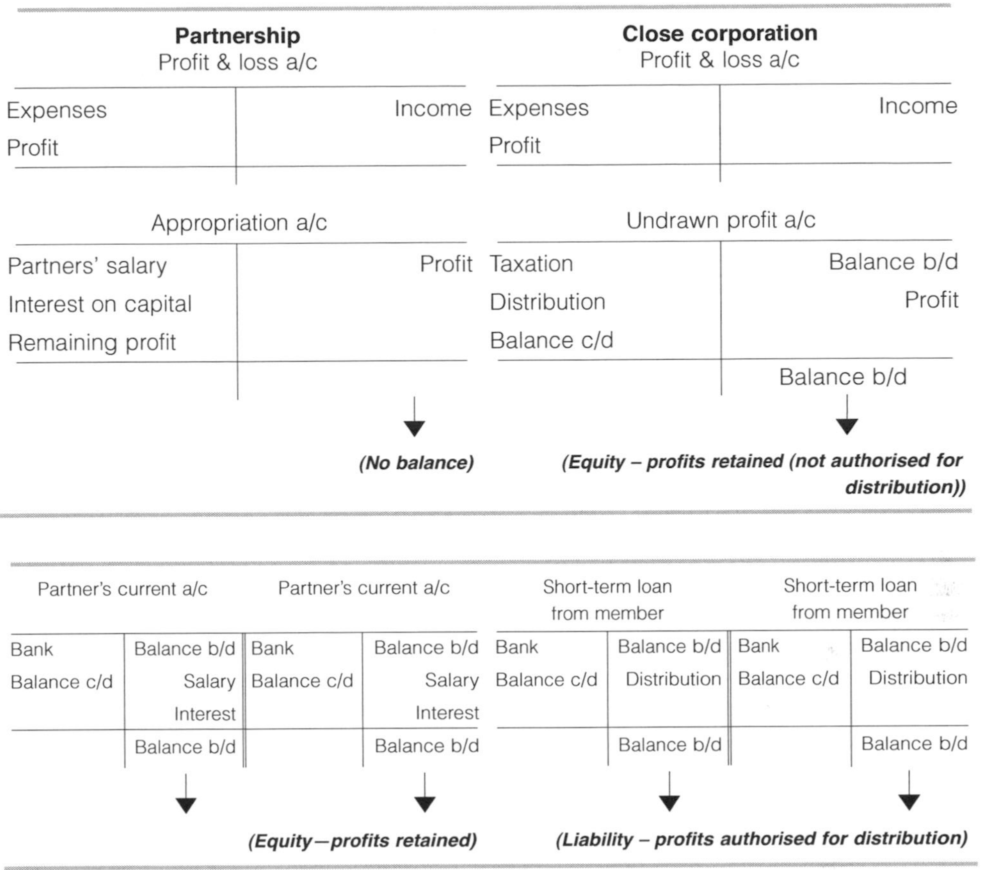

Diagram 19.1: Difference between profits retained in a partnership and a close corporation

Members of a close corporation do not have an automatic claim to the undrawn profit and are only entitled to it after it has been authorised for distribution. Once the distribution has been authorised, it is available for members to withdraw in cash. A ***short-term loan from members' account*** is used to record the distributions to members. As the close corporation and the members are separate legal entities, the short-term loan from members' account is a *liability* of the corporation and not part of equity. This is a very important difference between a close corporation as an *incorporated* entity and a partnership as an *unincorporated* entity, where the partners' current accounts are part of equity. This is illustrated in diagram 19.1.

19.3.2 Equity of a close corporation

The equity of a close corporation comprises the members' contributions, the undrawn profit and any revaluation surplus that the corporation may have. The revaluation surplus arises on the revaluation of the non-current assets of a close corporation and remains a reserve of the corporation until formally distributed.

As the close corporation is a juristic person, the members' contributions, undrawn profit and revaluation surplus belong to the corporation and not to the members. The equity, also known as ***members' funds***, is therefore not allocated to each member on the balance sheet, but is shown in aggregate.

19.4 Formation of a close corporation

Incorporation requires only a ***founding statement***, which is a document that sets out details relating to the close corporation and its members. Details relating to the corporation include its name, address, main business activity and financial year-end. Information about the members includes their names, identity numbers, addresses, contributions to the corporation and percentage interests.

A founding member acquires an interest in the corporation after making an initial contribution. After incorporation, a new member may acquire an interest in one of two ways.

- ❑ By purchasing an interest from an existing member or a deceased estate.
- ❑ By making a contribution to the corporation, in which case the new member's interest is determined by agreement with the existing members.

You will recall from Chapter 17 that Simon Smart and Gary Good formed Intense Sports, a partnership retailing endurance running and cycling equipment. The examples in this chapter examine the activities of Simon and Gary assuming that they chose to operate this business enterprise through a close corporation, namely, Intense Sports CC.

Example: Formation of a close corporation

On 2 January 20X7, Simon Smart and Gary Good formed a close corporation trading under the name of Intense Sports CC. Simon contributed R280 000 in cash while Gary contributed land and buildings worth R250 000 and machinery which the members agreed to be worth R75 000.

It was agreed that:

- ❑ the members' contributions from Simon and Gary would be R100 and R200 respectively. The additional funds invested would be regarded as a loan from the members.
- ❑ the members each have a 50% interest in the close corporation.

You are required to:

journalise the above transactions and prepare the statement of financial position immediately after the formation of the close corporation.

Solution: Formation of a close corporation

Assets		=	Liabilities		+	Owner's equity		
Bank			**Member's loan Simon**			**Member's contribution Simon**		**Member's contribution Gary**	
+/L/Dr	*–/R/Cr*		*–/L/Dr*	*+/R/Cr*		*–/L/Dr*	*+/R/Cr*	*–/L/Dr*	*+/R/Cr*
280 000				279 900			100		
Land and buildings			**Member's loan Gary**						
+/L/Dr	*–/R/Cr*		*–/L/Dr*	*+/R/Cr*					
250 000				324 800					200
Machinery									
+/L/Dr	*–/R/Cr*								
75 000									
							100		200

Only a nominal amount of the total investment by the members has been allocated to members' contributions. This is a practical consideration and is often done for tax purposes and to avoid the legal requirements of the Close Corporation Act relating to the reduction of members' contributions.

GENERAL JOURNAL OF INTENSE SPORTS CC

Date	Description	Fol	Dr	Cr
02/01/X7	Bank		280 000	
	Member's contribution – Simon			100
	Long-term loan from member – Simon			279 900
	Capital contribution			
02/01/X7	Land and buildings		250 000	
	Machinery		75 000	
	Member's contribution – Gary			200
	Long-term loan from member – Gary			324 800
	Capital contribution			

INTENSE SPORTS CC
STATEMENT OF FINANCIAL POSITION
AT 2 JANUARY 20X7

	R
ASSETS	
Non-current assets	325 000
Land and buildings	250 000
Machinery	75 000
Current assets	
Bank	280 000
	605 000
EQUITY AND LIABILITIES	
Capital and reserves	
Members' funds	
Members' contribution	300
Non-current liabilities-	
Loans from members	604 700
Current liabilities	–
	605 000

19.5 Producing information for a close corporation

Since owners and management in a close corporation are presumed to be the same group of persons, the financial statements of a corporation should, as a primary objective, fully meet the needs of members, both as owners and as concerned management.[2] This will impact upon the content and format of the financial statements, as you will see in the sections that follow.

Before turning our attention to the disclosure requirements of the Act, those aspects relating to the determination of profit and the appropriation of profit that are specific to close corporations need to be addressed.

19.5.1 Determination of profit

The profit of a close corporation is determined in the same way as that of a sole proprietor and a partnership. As the members and the corporation are separate legal entities, interest or loans paid to members and members' salaries are treated as expenses in the determination of profit.

19.5.2 Appropriation of profit

There are two aspects that need to be dealt with in the appropriation of the profit of a close corporation. These are the **taxation** charge against the profits of the corporation and the **distribution** to members. The appropriations take place through an undrawn profit account. The profit from the profit and loss account is transferred to the undrawn profit account, and the taxation and distribution to members is charged against this account. The book-keeping procedure relating to the appropriation of profit will be described in more detail below, under the heading of *closing entries*.

 **Pause and reflect...**

A close corporation requires additional funding to expand. The members do not have available cash to invest. What are the available options and are there any tax implications?

Response

The additional funding could either be provided through member borrowings or through loans taken out by the close corporation. The ability of the members or the close corporation to borrow would be assessed by the lender. As the close corporation is a legal entity, the interest on the borrowings would be allowed as a tax deduction. This deduction would not be available to members in respect of their personal borrowings.

Example: Appropriation of members' profits and taxation

The Intense Sport CC founding statement agreement provides that:

- Simon will be entitled to a salary of R120 000 per annum and Gary to a salary of R80 000 per annum.
- Simon and Gary each have a 50% interest in the close corporation.

The following additional information is available for the year ended 31 December 20X7:

INTENSE SPORTS CC
TRIAL BALANCE AT 31 DECEMBER 20X7

Description	Folio	Dr	Cr
Member's contribution – Simon			100
Member's contribution – Gary			200
Long-term loan from member – Simon			279 900
Long-term loan from member – Gary			324 800
Loan from bank – 15%			80 000
Land and buildings		530 000	
Machinery		100 000	
Accumulated depreciation machinery			20 000
Inventory		70 000	
Accounts receivable		154 000	
Bank		159 000	

Accounts payable		141 000
Receiver of Revenue	45 000	
Sales		1 860 000
Cost of sales	930 000	
Administration expenses	72 000	
Marketing expenses	63 000	
Members' salaries	180 000	
Telephone expenses	18 000	
Employees' salaries	340 000	
Light and water expenses	25 000	
Depreciation	20 000	
	2 706 000	2 706 000

- On 2 January 20X7, Intense Sports CC borrowed R80 000 from the bank at an interest rate of 15% pa.
- The land and buildings are revalued to a fair value of R590 000 on 31 December 20X7.
- Simon has drawn R100 000 of his salary while Gary has drawn the full R80 000 salary allowed to him.
- Simon and Gary decided to distribute R100 000 of the year's profits.

Taxation

Owing to its legal status as a separate legal entity apart from its members, a close corporation is subject to normal income tax at a rate of 28% on its taxable income. A close corporation is also required to make provisional payments during the financial year. The entry to record a provisional tax payment is as follows:

	Dr	Cr
Receiver of Revenue	45 000	
Bank		45 000

At this stage, the Receiver of Revenue account has a debit balance, reflecting the advance payment of income tax for the year. A debit balance on the Receiver of Revenue account is also referred to as a tax asset.

At the end of the year, a tax computation is performed and the tax charge for the year is established. The entry to record the tax charge is:

	Dr	Cr
Taxation expense	50 400	
Receiver of Revenue		50 400

The Receiver of Revenue account then reflects a credit balance of R5 400, representing the amount owing to the Receiver of Revenue at the end of the year. The R5 400 credit balance is the excess of the tax charge for the year over the provisional payment(s). It is often referred to as a tax liability.

Distributions to members

Remember, a member does not have an automatic claim to the undrawn profit of a close corporation, owing to its legal status as a separate legal entity apart from its members. A formal decision must be taken by the members to authorise a distribution. The distribution can only be authorised if the following conditions are satisfied after the payment is made:[3]

- the corporation's assets, fairly valued, exceed its liabilities
- the corporation will be able to pay its debts as they become due in the ordinary course of business.

The practical application of these requirements could lead to difficulties, especially relating to the time lapse between a distribution and when a corporation may not be able to pay its debts.[4]

The entry to record a distribution to members is:

	Dr	Cr
Distribution	100 000	
Short-term loan from member – Simon		50 000
Short-term loan from member – Gary		50 000

We suggest that a *short-term loan from member* account is used to record the amounts owing to the members of the close corporation, in respect of distributions, interest or salaries. These are amounts that members are likely to draw in cash in the short term, as opposed to long-term loans from members which are part of the more permanent financing of the business.

19.5.3 Revaluation surplus

You are familiar with the concept of asset revaluations from previous chapters. The gain on revaluation is reported in a separate ***revaluation surplus*** account. This is because the revaluation surplus, as part of equity, is not distributable to the members unless properly authorised. In any event it would not be prudent to make available for distribution an *unrealised* surplus. The accounting entry is shown below for completeness:

	Dr	Cr
Land and buildings	60 000	
Revaluation surplus		60 000

19.5.4 Preparation of the financial statements

When producing information for an incorporated entity, the requirements of the relevant act need to be considered. The Close Corporations Act requires that the financial statements consist of:[5]

- a balance sheet
- an income statement
- a report of the accounting officer.

It is submitted that a statement of changes in equity, as required by IAS1, should also be prepared. Further, this chapter refers to a statement of financial position rather than a balance sheet, and a statement of comprehensive income is prepared where there are items of other comprehensive income.

A further requirement of the Close Corporations Act is for the financial statements to disclose separately the aggregate amounts at the end of the year, and the movements during the year, of each of the following:[6]

- members' contributions
- undrawn income
- revaluation surplus
- loans from and to members.

This requirement of the act is best achieved by preparing a ***members' net investment statement.***[7]

Although not required by the Close Corporations Act, a ***transactions with members statement*** is normally included with the financial statements.[8] Financial statements are prepared for the benefit of members and should assist them in managing and controlling the business of the corporation. A transactions with members statement highlights transactions with individual members which have been included in arriving at the profit for the period.

The statement of comprehensive income, statement of changes in equity, statement of financial position, the members' net investment statement and transactions with members statement are shown on the pages that follow.

INTENSE SPORTS CC
STATEMENT OF COMPREHENSIVE INCOME
FOR THE YEAR ENDED 31 DECEMBER 20X7

		R
Revenue from sales		1 860 000
Cost of sales		(930 000)
Gross profit		930 000
Operating expenses		(738 000)
Administration		72 000
Marketing		63 000
Members' salaries	(180 000 + 20 000)	200 000
Telephone		18 000
Employees' salaries		340 000
Lights and water		25 000
Depreciation		20 000
Finance cost		
Interest	(80 000 x 0.15)	(12 000)
Profit before tax		180 000
Income tax expense		(50 400)
Profit for the period		129 600
Other comprehensive income		
Revaluation of land and buildings		60 000
Total comprehensive income		189 600

INTENSE SPORTS CC
STATEMENT OF CHANGES IN EQUITY
FOR THE YEAR ENDED 31 DECEMBER 20X7

	Members contribution	**Revaluation surplus**	**Undrawn profit**	**Total**
	R	**R**	**R**	**R**
Balance at 2 January 20X7	–	–	–	–
Total comprehensive income		60 000	129 600	189 600
Distributions			(100 000)	(100 000)
Increase in members' contribution	300			300
Balance at 31 December 20X7	300	60 000	29 600	89 900

INTENSE SPORTS CC
STATEMENT OF FINANCIAL POSITION
AT 31 DECEMBER 20X7

		Cost	Accumulated depreciation	Carrying amount	R
ASSETS					
Non-current assets					670 000
Land and buildings	(530 000 + 60 000)	590 000	-	590 000	
Machinery		100 000	20 000	80 000	
Current assets					383 000
Inventory					70 000
Accounts receivable					154 000
Bank					159 000
					1 053 000
EQUITY AND LIABILITIES					
Capital and reserves					89 900
Members' contribution					300
Revaluation surplus					60 000
Undrawn profit					29 600
Non-current liabilities					684 700
Long-term loan					80 000
Long-term loans from members	(279 900 + 324 800)				604 700
Current liabilities					278 400
Accounts payable					141 000
Short-term loans from members	(70 000 + 50 000)				120 000
Interest payable					12 000
Receiver of Revenue	(50 400 – 45 000)				5 400
					1 053 000

INTENSE SPORTS CC
MEMBERS NET INVESTMENT STATEMENT
AT 31 DECEMBER 20X7

		R
Members interest at beginning of year		0
Movements during the year:		
Contributions introduced		300
Revaluations		60 000
Profit for the year		129 600
Distributions		(100 000)
Long-term loans from members	(279 900 + 324 800)	604 700
Short-term loans from members	(200 000 + 100 000 – 180 000)	120 000
Members' interest at end of year		814 600
Represented by:		
Members contribution		300
Revaluation surplus		60 000
Undrawn profit		29 600
Long-term loans from members	(279 900 + 324 800)	604 700
Short-term loans from members	(70 000 + 50 000)	120 000
		814 600

INTENSE SPORTS CC
TRANSACTIONS WITH MEMBERS STATEMENT
FOR THE YEAR ENDED 31 DECEMBER 20X1

	Simon	Gary	Total
Members' salaries	120 000	80 000	200 000

Remember that the financial statements of a close corporation are prepared for the benefit of members. The members' net investment statement shows both the equity interest and debt interest of the members in the close corporation. It therefore provides additional information to that provided in the statement of changes in equity. Note that the short-term loans from members have also been included in the members' net investment statement as they are part of the interest of the members in the close corporation.

19.5.5 Closing entries for a close corporation

The closing entries to transfer the trading activities to the trading account and the operating activities to the profit and loss account are identical for all entity forms. When accounting for a partnership, the profit from the profit and loss account is transferred to the appropriation account. In a close corporation situation, however, the profit from the profit and loss account is transferred to the ***undrawn profit account***, where the taxation charge and the distributions are also transferred.

The closing entry to transfer the profit from the profit and loss account to the undrawn profit account is:

	Dr	Cr
Profit & loss	180 000	
Undrawn profit		180 000

Further closing entries for a close corporation are required to transfer the balances on the taxation expense account and the distributions account to the undrawn profit account. These entries are as follows:

	Dr	Cr
Undrawn profit	50 400	
Taxation expense		50 400
Undrawn profit	100 000	
Distributions		100 000

The relevant ledger accounts of Intense Sports CC after the closing entries have been taken into account appear as follows:

Trading

Details	R	Details	R
Cost of sales	930 000	Sales	1 860 000
Profit & loss	930 000		
	1 860 000		1 860 000

Profit and loss

Details	R	Details	R
Administration	72 000	Trading	930 000
Marketing	63 000		
Members' salaries	200 000		
Telephone	18 000		
Salaries	340 000		
Light & water	25 000		
Depreciation	20 000		
Interest	12 000		
Undrawn profit	180 000		
	930 000		930 000

Undrawn profit

Details	R	Details	R
Taxation	50 400	Profit and loss	180 000
Distributions	100 000		
Balance c/d	29 600		
	180 000		180 000
		Balance b/d	29 600

Taxation

Details	R	Details	R
Receiver of Revenue	50 400	Undrawn profit	50 400
	50 400		50 400

Receiver of Revenue

Details	R	Details	R
Balance b/d	45 000	Taxation	50 400
Balance c/d	5 400		
	50 400		50 400
		Balance b/d	5 400

Members' salaries

Details	R	Details	R
Balance b/d	180 000	Profit and loss	200 000
Short-term member's loan – Simon	20 000		
	200 000		200 000

Distributions

Details	R	Details	R
Short-term member's loan – Simon	50 000	Undrawn profit	100 000
Short-term member's loan – Gary	50 000		
	100 000		100 000

Interest expense

Details	R	Details	R
Interest liability	12 000	Profit and loss	12 000
	12 000		12 000

Interest liability

Details	R	Details	R
Balance c/d	12 000	Interest expense	12 000
	12 000		12 000
		Balance b/d	12 000

Long-term loan from member – Simon

Details	R	Details	R
Balance c/d	279 900	Balance b/d	279 900
	279 900		279 900
		Balance b/d	279 900

Long-term loan from member – Gary

Details	R	Details	R
Balance c/d	324 800	Balance b/d	324 800
	324 800		324 800
		Balance b/d	324 800

Short-term loan from member – Simon

Details	R	Details	R
Bank	100 000	Members' salaries	100 000
Balance c/d	70 000	Distributions	50 000
		Members' salaries	20 000
	170 000		170 000
		Balance b/d	70 000

Short-term loan from member – Gary

Details	R	Details	R
Bank	80 000	Members' salaries	80 000
Balance c/d	50 000	Distributions	50 000
	130 000		130 000
		Balance b/d	50 000

Revaluation

Details	R	Details	R
Balance c/d	60 000	Land & buildings	60 000
	60 000		60 000
		Balance b/d	60 000

Land and buildings

Details	R	Details	R
Balance b/d	530 800	Balance c/d	590 000
Revaluation	60 000		
	590 000		590 000
Balance b/d	590 000		

19.6 Exam example

Mr Mordecai Moribund commenced trading on 1 June 20X6 by forming a close corporation, Kit Bagge CC, to sell sports goods. He invested R200 000 in the corporation as the member's contribution.

He employed a general manager, Ms Ester, who is to receive a commission of 10 per cent of profit before tax (after all commissions), and a sales manager, Mr Haman, who is to receive a commission of 5 per cent on net sales.

The following is the trial balance as at 30 September 20X6:

KITT BAGGE CC
TRIAL BALANCE AT 30 SEPTEMBER 20X6

Description	Dr	Cr
Advertising	950	
Bad debts	800	
Bank	27 200	
Member's contribution		200 000
Carriage outwards	2 000	
Commission (sales manager, Mr Haman)	7 000	
Accounts payable		73 000
Customs duty	12 600	
Accounts receivable	80 800	
Short-term loan to member	53 020	
Furniture – purchased 1 June 20X6	21 000	
General expenses	3 000	
Land and buildings	100 000	
Purchases	153 350	
Rates	1 500	
Returns inwards	9 000	
Rent of warehouse	800	
Salaries and wages	7 980	
Sales		214 000
Stationery	6 000	
	487 000	487 000

The following information is available:

- On formation of the business, Mordecai Moribund paid (from his own personal cash resources) the following items, all of which have been entered in the accounting records of the business:
  - Land and building R100 000
  - Rates thereon for the year ended 31 May 20X7 1 500
- During the first few months of trading, Mordecai Moribund withdrew varying amounts of cash from the business, which were properly recorded and debited to the short-term

member's loan account. Mordecai used some of the amounts drawn to pay for the following items on behalf of the business. None of these items have been entered in the records of the business:

- advertising R1 200
- rent of warehouse, at the rate of R4 800 per annum 800
- fire insurance – annual premium (paid on 1 June 20X6) 300

- The customs duty reflected in the trial balance is made up as follows:
  - on goods for re-sale R11 700
  - on stationery received from overseas for business use 900
- Goods for resale costing R4 000 had been cleared through customs on 20 September 20X6, but were not received until after the end of the period. The purchase has already been entered into the accounting records.
- Further bad debts totalling R4 370 must be written off.
- Furniture costing R3 000 had been purchased on credit on 30 September but no entry was made in the accounting records.
- Depreciation of furniture must be provided for at the rate of 10% per annum on cost.
- Two-thirds of the stationery purchased during the period had not been used by 30 September 20X6.
- Inventory on hand at 30 September 20X6 had cost R49 000, but it is estimated that it could only be sold for R40 000. A periodic inventory system is being used.
- Current tax must still be accounted for at a rate of 28%.

You are required to:

(a) prepare an income statement for Kit Bagge CC for the period to 30 September 20X6 and a statement of financial position for the close corporation at that date.

(b) prepare a statement of changes in equity for Kit Bagge CC for the period to 30 September 20X6.

(c) prepare a member's net investment statement to support the financial statements.

Suggested solution: Exam example

(a)

KITT BAGGE CC
INCOME STATEMENT
FOR THE PERIOD ENDED 30 SEPTEMBER 20X6

			R
Revenue from sales	(214 000 – 9 000)		205 000
Cost of sales			(121 050)
Opening inventory			0
Purchases			153 350
Customs duty			11 700
Goods in transit			(4 000)
			161 050
Closing inventory			(40 000)
Gross profit			83 950
Operating expenses			(35 750)
Advertising	(950 + 1 200)		2 150
Bad debts	(800 + 4 370)		5 170
Carriage outwards			2 000
Commission – sales manager	(205 000 x 5%)		10 250
Customs duty (on stationery)	(900 x 1/3)		300
General expenses			3 000
Stationery expense	(6 000 x 1/3)		2 000
Rates	(1 500 x 4/12)		500
Rent of warehouse	(800 + 800)		1 600
Salaries and wages			7 980
Fire insurance premium	(300 x 4/12)		100
Depreciation on furniture	(21 000 x 10% x 4/12)		700
			48 200
Commission – general manager	(4 820/1,1)		(4 382)
Profit before tax			43 818
Taxation			(12 269)
Profit for the period			31 549

KIT BAGGE CC
STATEMENT OF FINANCIAL POSITION
AT 30 SEPTEMBER 20X6

		R
ASSETS		
Non-current assets		174 020
Land and buildings		100 000
Furniture		23 300
– at cost		24 000
– accumulated depreciation		(700)
Members' loan account	(53 020 - 1 200 - 800 - 300)	50 720
Current assets		153 430
Inventory	(at lower of cost or NRV)	40 000
Goods in transit		4 000
Stationery on hand	(6 000 + 900) x 2/3	4 600
Bank		27 200
Accounts receivable	(80 800 - 4 370)	76 430
Rates pre-paid	(1 500 x 8/12)	1 000
Fire insurance pre-paid	(300 x 8/12)	200
		327 450
EQUITY AND LIABILITIES		
Members' funds		231 549
Members' contribution		200 000
Undrawn profit		31 549
Current liabilities		95 901
Accounts payable		76 000
Commissions owing:		
Sales manager	(10 250 - 7 000)	3 250
General manager		4 382
Receiver of Revenue		12 269
		327 450

(b)

KITT BAGGE CC
STATEMENT OF CHANGES IN EQUITY
FOR THE PERIOD ENDED 30 SEPTEMBER 20X6

	Members' contribution	**Undrawn profit**	**Total**
	R	**R**	**R**
Balance at 1 June 20X6	–	–	–
Profit for the period		31 549	31 549
Distributions		–	–
Increase in members' contribution	200 000		200 000
Balance at 30 September 20X6	200 000	31 549	231 549

(c)

KITT BAGGE CC
MEMBERS' NET INVESTMENT STATEMENT

	R
Members' interest at 01/06/X6	0
Movements during the year	180 829
Contributions introduced	200 000
Profit for the period	31 549
Increase in loans to members	(53 020)
Amounts paid on behalf of CC	2 300
Members' interest at 30/09/X6	180 829
Represented by	
Members' contribution	200 000
Undrawn profit	31 549
Loans to members	(50 720)
	180 829

Summary of concepts and applications

1. A close corporation enables smaller undertakings to acquire corporate status with a legal personality distinct from its members. The members have limited liability and the entity benefits from perpetual succession. The Companies Bill provides for the indefinite continued existence of the Close Corporations Act, but the avenue is closed for the incorporation of new close corporations.

2. Close corporations can be financed from investors' funds and/or borrowed funds. Cash or other assets invested by a member in the entity are known as the member's contribution. Each member has an interest in the entity, which determines the proportion in which the after-tax profit is to be shared. Loans from members are recorded separately from the member's contribution as they are liabilities of the business. The cumulative excess of profit over taxation and distributions to members represents the profits retained in the business, or the undrawn profit. The equity of a close corporation comprises the members' contributions, the undrawn profit and any revaluation surplus.
3. The formation of a close corporation requires the creation of a founding statement, and founding members acquire interests after making their initial contributions.
4. The profit of a close corporation is determined in the same way as the other entity forms described in previous chapters. The appropriation of profit involves the consideration of two issues, namely the taxation charge and distributions to members. The gain recorded by a close corporation on the revaluation of an asset is recorded in a revaluation surplus account. The chapter discusses the specific characteristics of the financial information prepared for close corporations. A close corporation's closing entries to the trading and profit and loss accounts are identical to those of the other entity forms described in previous chapters. A close corporation's profit is transferred to the undrawn profit account.

Notes

1. Close Corporations: An Introduction and Guide to Some of the More Important Aspects of the Close Corporations Act, No. 69 of 1984 (as amended), *The South African Institute of Chartered Accountants*, (1991), paragraph 8.
2. Close Corporations: An Introduction and Guide to Some of the More Important Aspects of the Close Corporations Act (1991), paragraph 61.
3. Close Corporations Act (1984), section 51.
4. Geach, W. D. and Schoeman T., *Guide to The Close Corporations Act and Regulations*, Cape Town: Juta, (1995).
5. Close Corporations Act (1984, as amended), section 58(2)(a).
6. Close Corporations Act (1984), section 58(2)(c).
7. Close Corporations: An Introduction and Guide to Some of the More Important Aspects of the Close Corporations Act (1991), paragraph 83.
8. Close Corporations: An Introduction and Guide to Some of the More Important Aspects of the Close Corporations Act (1991), paragraph 83.

20 Entity Combinations and Conversions

'When a combination is deemed to be a purchase the assets purchased should be recorded on the books of the acquiring company at cost, measured in money or the fair value of the property acquired, whichever is most clearly evident.'
(A/A, 1950)

Outcomes

- Identify a business combination.
- Process the accounting entries relevant to a business combination or conversion.
- Perform the conversion process of incorporated entities.

Chapter outline

Edcon Holdings (Proprietary) Limited
Statement of comprehensive income for the year ended 29 March 2008

	(R millions)
Revenue	18 244
Cost of sales	(11 407)
Gross profit	6 837
Operating expenses	(5 819)
Profit before interest and tax	1 018
Finance costs	(3 100)
Profit before tax	(2 082)
Tax	522
Profit for the period	(1 560)

In 2007 Edcon, which is the holding company of such names as Edgars and Jet, was acquired by a private equity firm for R25 billion and taken off the Johannesburg Stock Exchange. This represented one of South Africa's largest ever private equity deals. Mergers and acquisitions such as this can result in conversions, combinations or changes in an entity, as dealt within this chapter.

20.1 Identifying a business combination

Entity combinations involve the bringing together of separate, existing entities into a new entity. The relevant accounting standard is IFRS 3, Business Combinations. Most of the standard is beyond the scope of this text; however, the standard is useful in identifying a business combination and understanding the terminology that is used.

A business combination is a transaction or event in which an ***acquirer*** obtains ***control*** of one or more businesses from an ***acquiree***. [1]

A business is defined as an integrated set of activities and assets that is capable of being conducted and managed for the purpose of providing a return directly to investors or other owners. All business combinations involve the identification of an acquirer and an acquiree.

The acquirer is the entity that obtains control of the acquiree. The acquiree is the business or businesses that the acquirer obtains control of in a business combination.[2]

Control is the power to govern the financial and operating policies of an entity so as to obtain benefits from its activities.[3]

A business combination may be structured in a number of ways, for legal, taxation or other reasons. To structure a business combination involves making decisions relating to the nature of the combination, how the purchase consideration is to be settled and the legal form of the entities involved.

20.1.1 Nature of the combination

A **business combination** may involve the purchase by an entity of the net assets of another entity or it may involve the purchase of the equity of the other entity.

When the acquirer purchases the net assets of the acquiree, this is sometimes referred to as a **takeover**. Note that the acquirer may purchase all or some of the assets of the acquiree and may assume all or some of the liabilities of the acquiree.

Where shares or equity are purchased, this gives rise to a parent-subsidiary relationship in the form of a group where the acquirer is the parent and the acquiree a subsidiary. This results in the requirement for consolidated financial statements, which is beyond the scope of this text.

Where two or more entities combine to form a new business entity, this is often referred to as a **merger**.

20.1.2 Settlement of purchase consideration

The purchase consideration may be settled by means of equity or cash, or a combination of both. The transaction may be between the owners of the combining entities or between one entity and the owners of the other entity.

20.1.3 Legal form of entities

The business combination may involve the establishment of a new entity to take over the combining entities (which are then dissolved), or the transfer of the assets and liabilities of one entity to another entity (and the first entity is then dissolved).

A **conversion** refers to the situation where a business entity changes its form of ownership. An unincorporated entity can convert into an incorporated entity, such as a partnership converting into a company, or the conversion may be from a close corporation to a company, both incorporated entities. A new entity is formed by the owners of the original entity, and the new entity acquires the assets and liabilities of the original entity at an agreed purchase consideration. The newly formed entity is unlikely to have any cash resources in addition to the original entity, and it is therefore common for the purchase consideration to be settled by the allocation of an ownership interest in the new entity.

20.2 Accounting issues

There are two important accounting issues to consider in relation to entity combinations and conversions.

- Which accounting records to use. That is, to open a new set of accounting records for the newly formed entity or to continue to use the same accounting records used by one of the entities involved in the combination or conversion.
- The treatment of any excess of the purchase consideration over the net asset value of an entity subject to a combination or conversion.

These issues are addressed in the following paragraphs.

20.2.1 The accounting records

It is common to open a new set of accounting records for the new entity. However, the same set of accounting records used by one of the entities involved may be used, with adjustments to equity. The procedure to follow for each option is described below.

New set of accounting records used

When a new set of accounting records is opened, there are entries to be recorded in both the existing accounting records and in the new records. Entries are required in the existing accounting records to close those records, and, in the new accounting records, entries are required to enter the assets, liabilities and equity of the new entity.

Closing the existing accounting records

It is not possible to provide a set of rules as the procedure will differ depending on the entity forms involved and the circumstances of the combination or conversion. The following guidelines may, however, be applied and adapted to most situations:

- The assets and liabilities are transferred at carrying amount into a realisation account.
- The purchase consideration is recorded in the realisation account by debiting the new entity (with the amount of the purchase consideration) and crediting the realisation account.
- The settlement of the purchase consideration is recorded by debiting the assets given in settlement and crediting the new entity.
- Expenses incurred are paid and recorded in the realisation account.
- The profit or loss on realisation is determined and transferred to equity.
  - For a sole proprietor and partnership, the profit or loss can be transferred directly to the capital account.
  - For a close corporation or company, the profit or loss must be transferred to the profit and loss account from where it will be included in the profits retained and equity.
- The balance in equity is distributed to the owners.

Opening the new accounting records:

Again, only guidelines which must be adapted to specific situations can be given:

- The assets and liabilities of the aquiree are recorded at ***fair value*** (including the purchase consideration owing to the owners of the aquiree as a liability).
- The purchase consideration is settled by debiting the aquiree and crediting bank (if settled in cash) or crediting equity (if settled by giving the owners of the aquiree an interest in the new entity).
- The above two steps are often combined into one, by recording the assets and liabilities of the aquiree and crediting the difference to the equity of the new entity.
- Pay any expenses on formation of the new entity.

Existing set of accounting records used

When an existing set of accounting records is used, it is necessary only to *adjust* the assets and liabilities to ***fair value***.

- A *revaluation account* is used to record the adjustments in the assets and liabilities to fair value.
  - For non-current assets, the accumulated depreciation is reversed, and the cost adjusted to reflect the fair value.
  - For accounts receivable, any decrease in value is recorded in a provision for doubtful debts account.
- The balance on the revaluation account is transferred to equity.
- The purchase consideration is settled by allocating equity in the new entity to the owners of the target entity. For example, when converting from a partnership

to a company, this is achieved by debiting the partners' capital accounts and crediting members' contribution.

- Pay any expenses on formation of the new entity.

Simon Smart is a commerce graduate and has always had an interest in, and aptitude for business ventures. As you know, he is involved in Smart Concepts, Sharp Moves, and Intense Sports. Simon has consulted with a number of business entities, and the examples in this chapter are case-studies based on his consulting experiences.

The following two examples illustrate the use of different sets of accounting records.

Example: Combination of two sole proprietorships into a partnership

On 1 January 20X6 Wood and Wedge, two sole proprietors, signed a partnership agreement. At that date their post-closing trial balances reflected the following assets and liabilities.

TRIAL BALANCES AT 1 JANUARY 20X6

	Wood		**Wedge**	
Description	**Dr**	**Cr**	**Dr**	**Cr**
Capital		65 000		109 500
Vehicles at cost	50 000			
Accumulated depreciation		5 000		
Land and buildings at cost			150 000	
Inventory	20 000		15 000	
Accounts receivable	8 500		10 000	
Allowance for doubtful debts				500
Bank	1 500		2 500	
Long-term loan				60 000
Accounts payable		10 000		7 500
	80 000	80 000	177 500	177 500

They agreed that the partnership would take over all the assets and liabilities of the two sole proprietorships, subject to the following conditions:

Wood:

- Vehicles are valued at R40 000.
- Inventory is valued at R17 500.
- The fair value of accounts receivable is R8 000.

Wedge:

- Land and buildings are valued at R160 000.
- The fair value of accounts receivable is R9 000.

All other assets and liabilities are considered to be fairly valued.

You are required to:

(a) enter the above assets and liabilities in the accounting records of the new partnership.
  (i) using Wedge's accounting records for the partnership
  (ii) opening a new set of accounting records for the partnership.

(b) prepare the statement of financial position of the Wedgewood partnership at 1 January 20X6.

Solution: Combination of two sole proprietorships into a partnership

(a) (i) Using Wedge's accounting records

GENERAL JOURNAL OF WEDGEWOOD PARTNERSHIP

Date	Description	Fol	Dr	Cr
01/01/X6	Land and buildings		10 000	
	Provision for doubtful debts			500
	Capital account – Wedge			9 500
	Revaluation of Wedge's assets and liabilities before introducing Wood's contribution			
01/01/X6	Motor vehicles		40 000	
	Inventory		17 500	
	Accounts receivable		8 500	
	Allowance for doubtful debts			500
	Bank		1 500	
	Accounts payable			10 000
	Capital account – Wood			57 000
	Wood's contribution to the new partnership			

Wedge's accounting records are to be used for the new partnership. Therefore the first journal entry adjusts Wedge's assets to fair value. The second entry introduces Wood's assets and liabilities into the accounting records.

(a) (ii) Using a new set of accounting records

GENERAL JOURNAL OF WEDGEWOOD PARTNERSHIP

Date	Description	Fol	Dr	Cr
01/01/X6	Land and buildings		160 000	
	Inventory		15 000	
	Accounts receivable		10 000	
	Allowance for doubtful debts			1 000
	Bank		2 500	
	Long-term loan			60 000
	Accounts payable			7 500
	Capital account – Wedge			119 000
	Wedge's contribution to the new partnership			

Date	Details	Fol	Debit	Credit
01/01/X6	Motor vehicles		40 000	
	Inventory		17 500	
	Accounts receivable		8 500	
	Allowance for doubtful debts			500
	Bank		1 500	
	Accounts payable			10 000
	Capital account – Wood			57 000
	Wood's contribution to the new partnership			

When using a new set of accounting records, the assets and liabilities of both Wedge and Wood are entered in the journal. For both partners, the excess of the assets over liabilities is credited to their respective capital accounts.

(b)

WEDGEWOOD PARTNERSHIP
STATEMENT OF FINANCIAL POSITION
AT 1 JANUARY 20X6

	R
ASSETS	
Non-current assets	200 000
Land and buildings	160 000
Motor vehicles	40 000
Current Assets	53 500
Inventory	32 500
Accounts receivable	17 000
Bank	4 000
	253 500
EQUITY AND LIABILITIES	
Capital	176 000
Capital Wood	57 000
Capital Wedge	119 000
Non-current liabilities	
Loan from bank	60 000
Current liabilities	
Accounts payable	17 500
	253 500

Example: Combination of a sole proprietorship and a partnership to form a company

Luca and Paciolli were equal partners in a firm of bookkeepers, providing bookkeeping services to small businesses in Johannesburg.

Their trial balance at 31 December 20X5 was as follows:

TRIAL BALANCE AT 31 DECEMBER 20X5

Description	Dr	Cr
Accounts payable		68 000
Accounts receivable	192 000	
Bank	27 600	
Capital – Luca		80 000
Capital – Paciolli		80 000
Current account – Luca		30 000
Current account – Paciolli		16 000
Motor vehicles at cost	74 800	
Accumulated depreciation		12 000
Allowance for doubtful debts		8 400
	294 400	294 400

On 1 January 20X6, Luca and Paciolli approached Francisco, who owned his own bookkeeping practice, with the idea of forming a private company, Debit and Credit Pty (Ltd). They all agreed to the idea and set out the following conditions relating to the formation of the company:

(1) They would continue to use the same set of accounting records as previously used by Luca and Paciolli.

(2) The assets and liabilities of Luca and Paciolli were agreed to be fairly stated on the statement of financial position, with the exception of accounts receivable, which were considered to be overvalued by R3 000.

(3) Work-in-progress of Luca and Paciolli at 31 December 20X5 was valued at R80 000.

(4) Francisco would contribute his assets and liabilities at the following agreed valuations:

Accounts receivable (net of a provision of R8 600)	R77 400
Motor vehicle (original cost R36 000)	22 000
Accounts payable	32 000
Bank	10 000
Work-in-progress	36 000

(5) The current accounts of Luca and Paciolli are to become short-term loan accounts in the company. An amount of R12 000 of the equity of Francisco is also to be established as a member's short-term loan account in the close corporation.

(6) There was no goodwill attributable to either of the two businesses.

(7) The company is formed with an authorised share capital of 500 000 shares of no-par value. Luca and Paciolli are to be allocated share capital according to the balances in their capital accounts in the partnership. Francisco is to be allocated share capital according to the balance on the capital account in the sole proprietorship. All the shares are issued at a price of R1 per share.

You are required to:

(a) provide the journal entries on formation of Debit and Credit (Pty) Ltd.
(b) prepare the statement of financial position of Debit and Credit (Pty) Ltd. at 1 January 20X6.

Solution: Combination of a sole proprietorship and a partnership to form a company

(a)

GENERAL JOURNAL OF DEBIT AND CREDIT CC

Date	Description	Fol	Dr	Cr
01/01/X6	Work-in-progress		80 000	
	Allowance for doubtful debts			3 000
	Revaluation			77 000
	Adjustment to the net assets of Luca and Paciolli			
	Revaluation		77 000	
	Capital – Luca			38 500
	Capital – Paciolli			38 500
	Transfer of the profit on revaluation to the partners' capital accounts			
	Current – Luca		30 000	
	Current – Paciolli		16 000	
	Loan – Luca			30 000
	Loan – Paciolli			16 000
	Transfer of current account balances to loan accounts			
	Capital – Luca		118 500	
	Capital – Paciolli		118 500	
	Ordinary share capital			237 000
	Allocation of equity in the company to Luca and Paciolli			
	Accumulated depreciation		12 000	
	Motor vehicles			12 000
	Accumulated depreciation on motor vehicles			
	Accounts receivable		86 000	
	Allowance for doubtful debts			8 600
	Motor vehicles		22 000	
	Accounts payable			32 000
	Bank		10 000	
	Work-in-progress		36 000	
	Ordinary share capital			113 400
	Assets and liabilities introduced by Francisco to the company			

(b)

DEBIT AND CREDIT (PTY) LTD
STATEMENT OF FINANCIAL POSITION
AT 1 JANUARY 20X6

		Cost	Accumulated depreciation	Carrying amount	R
ASSETS					
Non-current assets					84 800
Motor vehicles		84 800	–	84 800	
Current assets					411 600
Work in progress					116 000
Accounts receivable					258 000
Bank					37 600
					496 400
EQUITY AND LIABILITIES					
Equity					
Share capital	(237 000 + 113 400)				350 400
Current liabilities					
Accounts payable					100 000
Short-term loan	(30 000 + 16 000)				46 000
					496 400

20.2.2 Goodwill

You learnt about goodwill in Chapter 17, Accounting for Partnerships. In that chapter, goodwill was described as the excess of the value of a business entity as a whole (as indicated by the purchase consideration) over the fair value of its net assets. A distinction was also made between *internally generated goodwill* and *purchased goodwill*. Recall that internally generated goodwill is not recognised as an asset because it is not an identifiable resource controlled by the entity and its cost cannot be measured reliably. On the other hand, the value of purchased goodwill is based on an arm's length transaction between the seller and purchaser of a business entity (or, in the case of a partnership, part of a business entity).

An important principle of business combinations is that the acquirer of a business entity recognises the assets acquired and liabilities assumed at their ***fair values*** at acquisition date. Each *identifiable* asset and liability is measured at its acquisition date fair value. This has implications for the measurement of goodwill.

Goodwill is measured as the excess of the consideration transferred over the fair value of the assets acquired and liabilities assumed. Therefore, goodwill represents the future economic benefits arising from assets that are *not capable of being individually identified and separately recognised.*

The following two examples illustrate these principles.

Example: Conversion of partnership to company

Gavin and Paul decided to convert their partnership into a private company on 31 January 20X9. At that date the statement of financial position of the partnership was as follows:

GAVIN AND PAUL
STATEMENT OF FINANCIAL POSITION
AT 31 JANUARY 20X9

	Cost	Accumulated depreciation	Carrying amount	R
ASSETS				
Non-current assets				98 000
Plant and machinery	100 000	28 000	72 000	
Motor vehicles	40 000	14 000	26 000	
Current assets				90 000
Inventory				30 000
Accounts receivable				42 000
Bank				18 000
				188 000
EQUITY AND LIABILITIES				
Capital				160 000
Gavin				100 000
Paul				60 000
Current liabilities				
Accounts payable				28 000
				188 000

Gavin and Paul share profits and losses in the ratio of 2:1. The company, Gap (Proprietary) Limited, takes over all the assets and liabilities with the exception of the bank account. The agreed price is R200 000, to be settled by the issue of 200 000 ordinary shares of R1 each. In determining the purchase price, the company values plant and machinery at R80 000, the inventory at R26 000 and the accounts receivable at R36 000.

The shares are to be distributed to the partners in the profit-sharing ratio. A new set of accounting records is to be opened for the company.

You are required to:

(a) show the entries in the relevant ledger accounts to close the accounting records of the partnership
(b) prepare the journal entries to open the accounting records of the new company, Gap (Pty) Ltd
(c) prepare the statement of financial position of Gap (Pty) Ltd at the date of formation.

Solution: Conversion of partnership to company

(a)

LEDGER OF GAVIN AND PAUL PARTNERSHIP

Realisation account

Details	R	Details	R
Plant & machinery	100 000	Accumulated depreciation plant & machinery	28 000
Motor vehicles	40 000	Accumulated depreciation motor vehicles	14 000
Inventory	30 000	Accounts payable	28 000
Accounts receivable	42 000	Gap (Pty) Ltd	200 000
Profit – Gavin	38 667		
Profit – Paul	19 333		
	270 000		270 000

Bank

Details	R	Details	R
Balance b/d	18 000	Capital – Gavin	5 334
		Capital – Paul	12 666
	18 000		18 000

Gap (Pty) Ltd

Details	R	Details	R
Realisation	200 000	Shares in Gap (Pty) Ltd	200 000
	200 000		200 000

Shares in Gap (Pty) Ltd

Details	R	Details	R
Gap (Pty) Ltd	200 000	Capital – Gavin	133 333
		Capital – Paul	66 667
	200 000		200 000

Capital – Gavin

Details	R	Details	R
Shares in Gap (Pty) Ltd	133 333	Balance b/d	100 000
Bank	5 334	Realisation	38 667
	138 667		138 667

Capital – Paul

Details	R	Details	R
Shares in Gap (Pty) Ltd	66 667	Balance b/d	60 000
Bank	12 666	Realisation	19 333
	79 333		79 333

(b)

GENERAL JOURNAL OF GAP (PTY) LTD

Date	Description	Fol	Dr	Cr
01/02/X9	Plant and machinery		80 000	
	Motor vehicles		26 000	
	Purchases		26 000	
	Accounts receivable		42 000	
	Goodwill		60 000	
	Allowance for doubtful debts			6 000
	Accounts payable			28 000
	Gavin and Paul			200 000
	Recording the assets and liabilities of the partnership in the accounting records of the company			
	Gavin and Paul		200 000	
	Share capital			200 000
	Settlement of purchase consideration by issuing shares in the company to Gavin and Paul			

The newly formed company, Gap (Pty) Ltd, is using a new set of accounting records. The assets and liabilities of Gavin and Paul's partnership are entered at fair value in the journal of Gap (Pty) Ltd.

The goodwill of R60 000 is arrived at as follows:

Fair value of consideration		200 000
Fair value of assets acquired and liabilities assumed		140 000
Equity	160 000	
Bank not taken over	(18 000)	
Increase in plant and machinery	8 000	
Decrease in inventory	(4 000)	
Allowance for doubtful debts	(6 000)	
Goodwill		60 000

You should take note that the inventory of the partnership is recorded as purchases in the opening journal entry in the company's records. This is because it is not conceptually correct to have opening inventory in the first period of trading.

(c)

GAP (PTY) LIMITED
STATEMENT OF FINANCIAL POSITION
AT 1 FEBRUARY 20X9

	Cost	Accumulated depreciation	Carrying amount	R
ASSETS				
Non-current assets				166 000
Plant and machinery	80 000	–	80 000	
Motor vehicles	26 000	–	26 000	
Goodwill	60 000	–	60 000	
Current assets				62 000
Inventory				26 000
Accounts receivable (42 000 – 6 000)				36 000
				228 000
EQUITY AND LIABILITIES				
Capital				
Share capital				200 000
Current liabilities				
Accounts payable				28 000
				228 000

Example: Takeover of a partnership by a newly formed company

Russel, Andy and Darryl are in partnership as property owners, sharing profits and losses equally. All assets are considered to be fairly valued except for land and buildings.

RUSSEL, ANDY AND DARRYL
STATEMENT OF FINANCIAL POSITION
AT 31 DECEMBER 20X8

	Cost	Accumulated depreciation	Carrying amount	R
ASSETS				
Non-current assets				1 040 000
Land and buildings	1 040 000	–	1 040 000	
Current assets				180 000
Accounts receivable – for rent				60 000
Bank				120 000
				1 220 000
EQUITY AND LIABILITIES				
Capital				1 200 000
Russel				700 000
Andy				300 000
Darryl				200 000
Current liabilities				
Accounts payable				20 000
				1 220 000

The newly formed company, called RAD Properties (Pty) Limited, is formed with an authorised share capital of 1 000 000 ordinary shares of R1,50 each. The company is to take over the partnership as a going concern on the date of its formation.

The land and buildings have a fair value at acquisition date of R2 000 000. All other assets and liabilities are considered to be fairly valued.

The agreed purchase price is R2 160 000, to be settled by the issue of 864 000 ordinary shares. The shares are to be distributed to the partners to clear their capital accounts to zero.

You are required to:

(a) prepare the relevant journal entries to open the accounting records of the new company
(b) prepare the statement of financial position of the company at the date of formation.

Solution: Excess purchase price attributable to land and buildings

(a)

GENERAL JOURNAL OF RAD PROPERTIES (PTY) LTD

Date	Description	Fol	Dr	Cr
01/01/X9	Land and buildings		2 000 000	
	Accounts receivable		60 000	
	Bank		120 000	
	Accounts payable			20 000
	Russel, Andy & Darryl			2 160 000
	Recording the assets and liabilities of the partnership in the accounting records of the company			
	Russel, Andy & Darryl		2 160 000	
	Share capital			1 296 000
	Share premium			864 000
	Settlement of purchase consideration by issuing shares in the company to Russel, Andy and Darryl			

The newly formed company, RAD Properties (Pty) Ltd, is using a new set of accounting records. The assets and liabilities of the partnership are entered at fair value in the journal of RAD Properties (Pty) Ltd. There is no goodwill arising on this business combination, as shown in the following calculation:

The goodwill of R60 000 is arrived at as follows:

Fair value of consideration	2 160 000
Fair value of assets acquired and liabilities assumed	2 160 000
Equity	1 200 000
Increase in value of land and buildings	960 000
Goodwill	-

(b)

RAD PROPERTIES (PTY) LTD
STATEMENT OF FINANCIAL POSITION
AT 1 JANUARY 20X9

	Cost	Accumulated depreciation	Carrying amount	R
ASSETS				
Non-current assets				2 000 000
Land and buildings	2 000 000	–	2 000 000	
Current assets				180 000
Accounts receivable – for rent				60 000
Bank				120 000
				2 180 000
EQUITY AND LIABILITIES				
Capital and reserves				2 160 000
Share capital				1 296 000
Share premium				864 000
Current liabilities				
Accounts payable				20 000
				2 180 000

20.3 Conversions of incorporated entities

The examples in the previous sections dealt with the conversion or combination of unincorporated entities into incorporated entities. Although the accounting principles remain the same, there are certain legal provisions relating to the conversion of incorporated entities.

This section will only consider the conversion of a close corporation into a company. The Companies Bill of 2008 does not permit the formation of new close corporations.

20.3.1 Conversion of a close corporation to a company

The following provisions apply to the conversion of a close corporation into a company:[5]

- A close corporation may, with the written consent of all its members, apply to be converted into and be incorporated as a company, provided that every member of the close corporation becomes a member of the company.

- An application for conversion of a corporation into a company must be accompanied by:
  - a statement of the paid-up share capital. The paid-up share capital amount must not be greater than the excess of the fair value of the assets to be acquired by the company over the liabilities to be assumed on conversion. The company may treat any portion of such excess not reflected as share capital as a distributable reserve.
  - a statement by the close corporation's accounting officer that he is not aware of any contravention of the Close Corporations Act by the corporation or its members, or of any circumstances which may render the members of the corporation, together with the corporation, jointly and severally liable for the corporation's debts.

The conversion of a close corporation into a company has the following implications:[6]

- On the registration of a company converted from a corporation, the assets and liabilities of the corporation vest in the company.
- Any legal proceedings instituted by or against the corporation before the conversion may be continued by or against the company, and any other thing done by or in respect of the corporation shall be deemed to have been done by or in respect of the company.
- The juristic person which used to be the close corporation continues in existence, but in the form of a company.

Example: Takeover of a close corporation by a company

Anthony and David are the sole members in Polonius Promotions CC, a business enterprise which organises fun runs. They have an equal share in the profits and losses and they each contributed R2 500 to start the corporation in 20X5. On 1 March 20X8, Walk and Run Forever (Pty) Limited made an offer to take over Polonius Promotions CC. At that date the member's loan was payable to David. Anthony did not want to take up the offer so he asked to be paid out.

The statement of financial position of Polonius Promotions CC at 28 February 20X8 was as follows:

POLONIUS PROMOTIONS CC
STATEMENT OF FINANCIAL POSITION
AT 28 FEBRUARY 20X8

	Cost	Accumulated depreciation	Carrying amount	R
ASSETS				
Non-current assets				15 500
Land and buildings	12 500	–	12 500	
Motor vehicles	5 000	2 000	3 000	
Current assets				39 000
Inventory				22 500
Accounts receivable				7 500
Bank				9 000
				54 500
EQUITY AND LIABILITIES				
Members' funds				35 000
Members' contributions				5 000
Undrawn profit				30 000
Non-current liabilities				
Member's loan				15 000
Current liabilities				
Accounts payable				4 500
				54 500

Walk and Run Forever (Pty) Limited offered to pay Polonius Promotions CC R100 000 to take over the business as a going concern. The payment was structured as follows:

- R42 500 paid in cash – to pay Anthony for his share of the business.
- R42 500 by a fresh issue of ordinary shares in Walk and Run Forever (Pty) Limited at R1 each – to pay David for his share of the business.
- R15 000 by an issue of 150 10% debentures in Walk and Run Forever (Pty) Limited – to repay the member's loan to David in the CC.
- The land and buildings taken over were considered to be worth R37 500.

The statement of financial position of Walk and Run Forever (Pty) Limited at 28 February 20X8 was as follows:

WALK AND RUN FOREVER (PTY) LTD
STATEMENT OF FINANCIAL POSITION
AT 28 FEBRUARY 20X8

	Cost	Accumulated depreciation	Carrying amount	R
ASSETS				
Non-current assets				125 000
Land and buildings	100 000	–	100 000	
Motor vehicles	40 000	15 000	25 000	
Current assets				100 000
Inventory				15 000
Accounts receivable				25 000
Bank				60 000
				225 000
EQUITY AND LIABILITIES				
Capital and reserves				140 000
Ordinary share capital				100 000
Accumulated profit				40 000
Non-current liabilities				70 000
10% Debentures				50 000
Shareholder's loan				20 000
Current liabilities				
Accounts payable				15 000
				225 000

You are required to:

(a) prepare the journal entries to close the accounting records of Polonius Promotions CC
(b) prepare the entries in the journal of Walk and Run Forever (Pty) Limited to record the take-over of Polonius Promotions CC
(c) prepare the statement of financial position of Walk and Run Forever (Pty) Limited at 1 March 20X8.

Solution: Takeover of a close corporation by a company

(a)

GENERAL JOURNAL OF POLONIUS PROMOTIONS CC				
Date	**Description**	**Fol**	**Dr**	**Cr**
01/03/X8	Land and buildings			12 500
	Motor vehicles			5 000
	Accumulated depreciation		2 000	
	Inventory			22 500
	Accounts receivable			7 500
	Bank			9 000
	Accounts payable		4 500	
	Realisation		50 000	
	Transfer of assets and liabilities to realisation account			
	Walk and Run Forever (Pty) Limited		100 000	
	Realisation			100 000
	Purchase consideration			
	Shares in Walk and Run Forever (Pty) Ltd		42 500	
	Bank		42 500	
	Debentures in Walk and Run Forever (Pty) Ltd		15 000	
	Walk and Run Forever (Pty) Ltd			100 000
	Settlement of purchase consideration			
	Member's Loan		15 000	
	Debentures in Walk and Run Forever (Pty) Ltd			15 000
	Payment to David for member's loan			
	Member's contribution		2 500	
	Undrawn profit		15 000	
	Realisation surplus		25 000	
	Bank			42 500
	Payment to Anthony for share of business			
	Member's contribution		2 500	
	Undrawn profit		15 000	
	Realisation surplus		25 000	
	Shares in Walk and Run Forever (Pty) Ltd			42 500
	Payment to David for share of business			

(b)

GENERAL JOURNAL OF WALK AND RUN FOREVER (PTY) LTD				
Date	**Description**	**Fol**	**Dr**	**Cr**
01/03/X8	Land and buildings		37 500	
	Motor vehicles		3 000	
	Inventory		22 500	
	Accounts receivable		7 500	
	Cash		9 000	
	Goodwilll		25 000	
	Accounts payable			4 500
	Bank			42 500
	10% Debentures			15 000
	Application account			42 500
	Recording of assets and liabilities taken over			
	Application account		42 500	
	Share capital			42 500
	Issue of shares to pay David			

The goodwill of R25 000 is arrived at as follows:

	R
Consideration transferred (42 500 + 15 000 + 42 500)	100 000
Fair value of assets acquired and liabilities assumed	75 000
Goodwill	25 000

(c)

WALK AND RUN FOREVER (PTY) LIMITED
STATEMENT OF FINANCIAL POSITION
AT 1 MARCH 20X8

	Cost	Accumulated depreciation	Carrying amount	R
ASSETS				
Non-current assets				190 500
Land and buildings	137 500	–	137 500	
Motor vehicles	43 000	15 000	28 000	
Goodwill	25 000	–	25 000	
Current assets				96 500
Inventory				37 500
Accounts receivable				32 500
Bank				26 500
				287 000
EQUITY AND LIABILITIES				
Capital and reserves				182 500
Ordinary share capital				142 500
Accumulated profit				40 000
Non-current liabilities				85 000
10% Debentures				65 000
Shareholder's loan				20 000
Current liabilities				
Accounts payable				19 500
				287 000

20.4 Exam example

Chester was trading as a sole trader known as 'Backs', while Francois was also trading as a sole trader called 'Forwards'. Chester and Francois decided to combine their businesses with effect from 1 October 20X5 by forming a private company, Amaboko (Pty) Ltd.

The trial balances of the two businesses at 30 September 20X5 were as follows:

	'Backs'		'Forwards'	
	Dr	**Cr**	**Dr**	**Cr**
Owner's equity – Chester		275 000		
Owner's equity – Francois				345 000
Long-term loan		90 000		25 000
Land and buildings	300 000		100 000	
Vehicles at cost	90 000		125 000	
Accumulated depreciation		20 000		15 000
Accounts receivable	22 500		10 000	
Allowance for doubtful debts		2 000		500
Inventory	25 200		150 000	
Accounts payable		19 500		20 000
Bank		31 200	20 500	
	437 700	437 700	405 500	405 500

Chester and Francois met at the Touchdown Restaurant and decided on the following plan:

- ❑ Both sole traders would be dissolved.
- ❑ Chester would personally take over a vehicle from his business with a carrying amount of R20 000. The vehicle had cost R25 000 and R5 000 accumulated depreciation had been provided. Chester would also personally be responsible for settling the bank overdraft.
- ❑ All of the assets and liabilities of 'Forwards' would be taken over by the company.
- ❑ The accounting records of 'Forwards' would be used for the newly formed company.

The following information relates to the formation of Amaboko (Pty) Ltd:

- ❑ The company is formed with an authorised share capital of 1 000 000 ordinary shares of no par value.
- ❑ Assets and liabilities were taken over from **'Backs'** at the following values:
  - ☐ the long-term loan at face value
  - ☐ the land and buildings at a value of R337 500
  - ☐ the remaining vehicles at carrying amount
  - ☐ the accounts receivable at fair value of R20 500
  - ☐ the inventory at carrying amount
  - ☐ the accounts payable after Chester had personally paid R2 500 to a major supplier
- ❑ It was agreed that there was no goodwill value in 'Backs'
- ❑ The company settled its obligation to Chester by allocating to him shares equal to the amount owing by the company. The shares are issued at a price of R1 per share.

- All of the assets and liabilities of '**Forwards**' were taken over at their carrying amounts except for the following assets which were revalued before the combination and taken over at the revalued amounts:

	R
Land and buildings	187 500
Inventory	137 500

- The purchase consideration of R435 500 for 'Forwards' was settled by allocating shares to Francois in the new company equal to the amount of the purchase consideration. The shares are issued at a price of R1 per share.

You are required to:

show all the entries in the journal of 'Forwards'/Amaboko CC to record the formation of the company.

Solution: Exam example

JOURNAL OF 'FORWARDS'/AMABOKO CC

Date	Description	Fol	Dr	Cr
	Land and buildings		337 500	
	Vehicles (65 000 – 15 000)		50 000	
	Accounts receivable		22 500	
	Allowance for doubtful debts			2 000
	Purchases (inventory from partnership)		25 200	
	Accounts payable (19 500 – 2 500)			17 000
	Long-term loan			90 000
	(Thus . . .) Chester			326 200
	Assets and liabilities of 'Backs' taken over			
	Chester		326 200	
	Share capital			326 200
	Shares issued			
	Land and buildings (187 500 – 100 000)		87 500	
	Inventory (carrying amount)			150 000
	Purchases (valuation)		137 500	
	Capital – Francois			75 000
	Revaluation of assets of 'Forwards'			
	Capital – Francois (345 000 + 75 000)		420 000	
	Francois			435 500
	(Thus . . .) Goodwill		15 500	
	Purchase consideration entered			
	Francois		435 500	
	Share capital			435 500
	Shares issued			

Summary of concepts and applications

1. A business combination is the bringing together of separate entities into one reporting entity. The structure of a business combination requires consideration of the nature of the combination, the settlement of the purchase consideration and the legal form of the entities involved. A conversion refers to the situation in which a business entity changes its form of ownership.
2. The accounting issues to be considered in relation to an entity combination or conversion are, firstly, whether or not to open a new set of accounting records and, secondly, the treatment of any excess purchase consideration over the net asset value of an entity.
3. A close corporation may convert into a company, but, in terms of the Companies Bill, a company may not convert into a close corporation.

Notes

1. IFRS 3, Business Combinations, International Accounting Standards Board, (2008), Appendix A.
2. IFRS 3, Appendix A.
3. IFRS 3, Appendix A.
4. Close Corporation Act (1984), as amended, paragraph 27.
5. Companies Act (1973), as amended, paragraph 29C.
6. Companies Act (1973), as amended, paragraph 29D.

Part 6

Sundry Topics

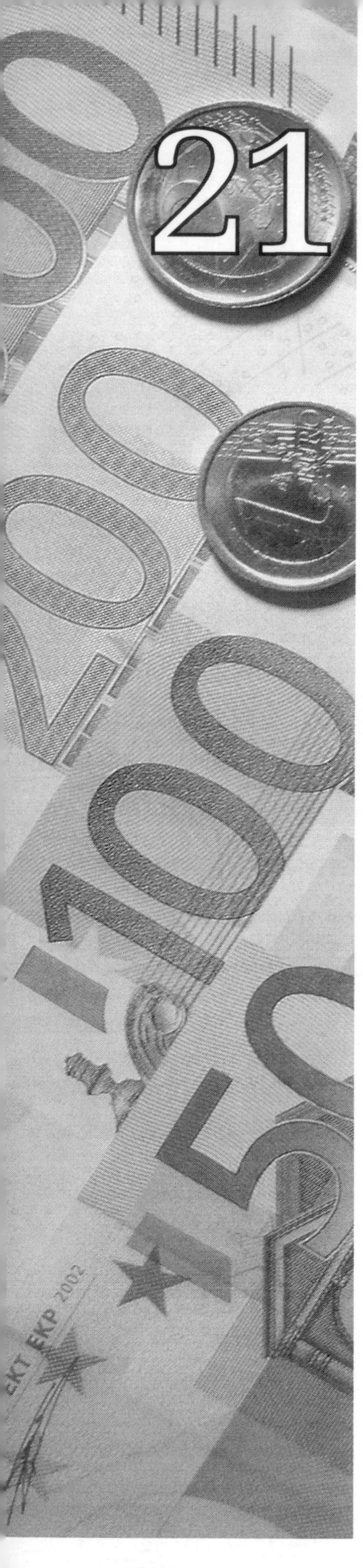

21 Statement of Cash Flows

'By making a comparison (of successive balance sheets) tabulating the increases and decreases of resources and liabilities, we can see from what sources all receipts came and to what destination all expenditure went. In making this tabulation, we may well give any one of three titles to each column. Let us call the first column credits, or receipts or "where got"; the second column we may call debits, or expenditure or "where gone".
(Cole, 1908)

Outcomes

- Describe the relevance of cash flow information.
- Define 'cash flows'.
- Classify cash flows by operating, investing and financing activities.
- Prepare a statement of cash flows.

Chapter outline

21.1 Importance of cash flow information
21.2 Meaning of cash flows
21.3 Classification of cash flows
21.3.1 Operating activities
21.3.2 Investing activities
21.3.3 Financing activities
21.3.4 Classification of specific items
21.4 Preparation of a statement of cash flows
21.4.1 Preparation of the operating activities section
21.4.2 Preparation of the investing activities section
21.4.3 Preparation of the financing activities section
21.5 Exam example

MTN Group Limited
Statement of cash flows for the year ended 31 December 2008

	(R Millions)
Cash flows from operating activities	
Cash generated from operations	33 334
Interest paid	1 013
Interest received	(3 589)
Dividends paid	(1 675)
Tax paid	(4 233)
Net cash inflow from operating activities	25 850
Cash flows from investing activities	
Acquisition of property, plant and equipment	(14 458)
Acquisition of intangible assets	(1 874)
Acquisition of other assets	(891)
Proceeds on disposal of non-current assets	71
Net cash outflow from investing activities	(17 152)
Cash flows from financing activities	
Proceeds from the issue of shares	60
Decrease in long term liabilities	(8 157)
Increase in short term liabilities	5 973
Decrease in other non-current assets	(11)
Net cash outflow from financing activities	(2 135)
Net increase in cash and cash equivalents	6 563
Cash at beginning of year	8 983
Cash at end of year	15 546

With over 40 million subscribers in Africa and the Middle East, MTN is one South Africa's most cash flush companies. The understanding of cash flow within an enterprise is essential from both an operational perspective and an investing perspective.

21.1 Importance of cash flow information

The accounting framework indicates that the objective of financial reporting is to provide information that is useful to a wide range of users in making economic decisions.[1] Information about the cash flows of an enterprise provides the users of financial statements with details of how the enterprise *generates* its cash flows and how it *utilises* those cash flows. To make economic decisions users require an evaluation of the enterprise's ability to generate cash flows as well as an evaluation of the timing and certainty of their generation.

An enterprise needs cash to conduct its operations, to pay its obligations and to provide a return to investors.[2] Cash flow information is uncontaminated by accounting allocations and adjustments which can have the effect of disguising cash flow from operations. Companies are permitted to pay dividends on the basis of accrual-based profits and therefore may pay cash dividends even though there may not be sufficient cash flow from operations to cover the dividend.[3]

It is important, however, that the statement of cash flows is used in conjunction with the accrual basis income statement and statement of financial position. This is necessary as the statement of cash flows includes cash flows from transactions that took place in an earlier period as well as cash flows which are expected to result in transactions in future periods. Disclosure of both cash flow information and accrual-based performance and financial position information provides users with a better understanding of the factors affecting cash flows. This enables users to assess the timing and certainty of future cash flows.[4]

The accounting standard dealing with cash flow information is IAS 7, entitled Statements of Cash Flows.

21.2 Meaning of cash flows

Cash flows are defined in IAS 7 as inflows and outflows of ***cash*** and ***cash equivalents***.[5]

Cash comprises cash on hand and demand deposits. Cash equivalents are short-term, highly liquid investments that are readily convertible to known amounts of cash. An investment normally qualifies as a cash equivalent only when it has a short maturity of approximately three months or less from date of acquisition.

For the remainder of this chapter, we will refer only to cash and cash flows in the interests of convenience.

21.3 Classification of cash flows

IAS 7 requires that the statement of cash flows reports cash flows during the period and that they are classified by ***operating***, ***investing*** and ***financing*** activities.

Classification by activity allows users to assess the impact of those activities on the financial position of the enterprise.[6] For example, it is relevant for an investor to know whether the cash flow from operating activities is sufficient for the enterprise to function or whether non-current assets may have to be sold to finance operations. Suppliers and lenders need to know whether there will be enough cash for the entity to pay its obligations as they become due.

It is important for you to know and understand what activities are regarded as either operating, investing or financing within the framework of the statement of cash flows. IAS 7 defines and describes each activity. We will examine this classification in detail before moving on to the computation and presentation of the statement of cash flows.

21.3.1 Operating activities

Cash flows from operating activities are primarily derived from the principal revenue-producing activities of the enterprise. Therefore, they generally result from transactions that are taken into account in the determination of profit or loss for a period.

The amount of cash flows arising from operating activities is an important indicator of the extent to which the operations of the entity have generated sufficient cash flows to repay loans, maintain the operating capability of the entity, pay dividends and make new investments without the need to obtain external sources of finance.

IAS 7 lists the following examples of cash flows from operating activities:[7]

- ❑ Cash receipts from the sale of goods and the rendering of services.
- ❑ Cash receipts from commissions and other revenue.
- ❑ Cash payments to suppliers for goods and services.
- ❑ Cash payments to and on behalf of employees.
- ❑ Cash payments or refunds of income taxes.

The figure reported as cash flow from operating activities is one of the most important figures for the user. It is often regarded as a key indicator of corporate success since cash flow from operating activities is usually the most important long-term source of cash to an enterprise.[8] However, as mentioned previously, cash generated from operating activities must not be considered in isolation from the profitability as determined by the profit on the income statement. It may happen that a profitable entity has cash temporarily tied up in inventory and accounts receivable, resulting in a poor cash flow from operating activities.

21.3.2 Investing activities

Investing activities relate to the acquisition and disposal of non-current assets. Cash flows from investing activities represent the extent to which cash has been utilised for resources intended to generate future profits and cash flows.

IAS 7 lists the following examples of cash flows from investing activities:[9]

- Cash payments to acquire property, plant and equipment, intangibles and other long-term assets.
- Cash receipts from sales of property, plant and equipment, intangibles and other long-term assets.
- Cash payments to acquire shares or debentures of other enterprises.
- Cash receipts from sales of shares or debentures of other enterprises.
- Cash advances or loans made to other parties.
- Cash receipts from the repayment of cash advances or loans made to other parties.

When reporting the cash paid for property, plant and equipment, we suggest that the amount be split between the portion that relates to *maintaining* existing operating capacity and that which relates to *expanding* the operating capacity. This is not required by IAS 7, but, if practical to do so, does provide useful information to users.

In a period of expansion, it is likely that the investing activities will result in a net cash outflow, referred to as cash utilised. The relationship between cash *generated* from operating activities and cash *utilised* in investing activities is useful information for the investor. The investor can assess whether the entity generates enough cash from operating activities to finance its investment in property, plant and equipment.

21.3.3 Financing activities

Financing activities are cash flows relating to the two forms of finance for any business entity, namely *equity* and *borrowings*. Information about cash flows from financing activities is useful in predicting claims on future cash flows by the providers of finance.

IAS 7 lists the following examples of cash flows from financing activities:[10]

- Cash proceeds from increases in equity, which, in relation to the four entity forms, implies:
  - for a sole proprietorship, cash invested as the sole proprietor's capital
  - for a partnership, cash invested as the partners' capital
  - for a close corporation, cash invested as the members' contributions
  - for a company, cash proceeds from issuing shares to shareholders.
- Cash paid to owners on repayment or redemption of the equity.
- Cash proceeds from long-term borrowings.
- Cash repayments of amounts borrowed.

21.3.4 Classification of specific items

There are a few issues arising from the discussion of operating, investing and financing activities that need clarification.

Gain or loss on sale of property, plant and equipment

The sale of an item of plant, for example, may give rise to a gain or loss, which is included in the determination of profit or loss for the period. However, the cash receipt from the sale of the plant is included in cash flows from *investing* activities.

Interest and dividends

Interest paid may be included as an *operating cash flow* as it enters into the determination of profit or loss. On the other hand, it may be argued that interest paid is a *financing cash flow* as it is a cost of obtaining borrowed funds.

Interest received can also be included as an *operating cash flow* as it enters into the determination of net profit or loss. Conversely, interest received could be classified as an *investing cash flow* as it is the return from investments. The same arguments apply to **dividends received**.

Dividends paid may be classified as a component of cash flows from *operating activities*, to assist users in determining the ability of an enterprise to pay dividends out of operating cash flows. The other alternative is to classify dividends paid as a *financing cash flow* because it is a cost of obtaining equity financing.

In this text, all of the above items are classified as cash flows from operating activities.

Taxation

Cash flows relating to taxation paid should be classified as cash flows from operating activities. You should bear in mind that the *taxation expense* on the income statement is unlikely to equal the cash paid in respect of taxation during a particular period. This is because of the estimates inherent in the calculation of the provisional tax payments and the time-lag between submission of an income tax return and assessment of taxes payable by the South African Revenue Service.

21.4 Preparation of a statement of cash flows

The data that you need to prepare a statement of cash flows is taken from the current and previous years' statements of financial position as well as the current year's income statement and statement of changes in equity. You need to examine the *movement* in each non-cash item on the statement of financial position, using relevant figures from the income statement and statement of changes in equity where necessary. Look at the following diagram:[11]

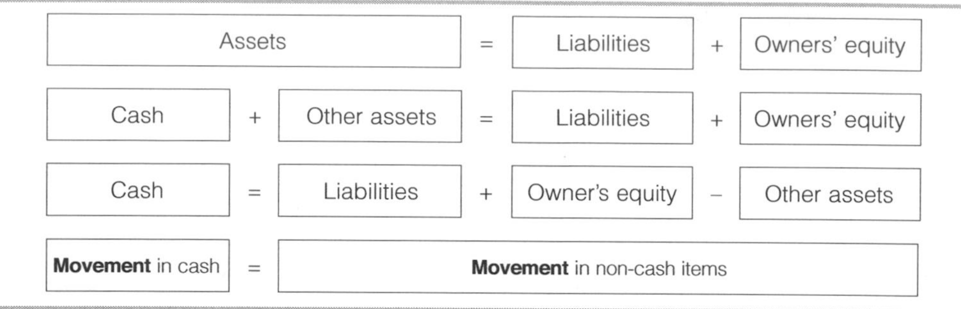

Diagram 21.1: Why an analysis of the non-cash items explains the movement in cash

If you examine the diagram above you will notice that, by a simple re-arrangement of the components of the accounting equation, cash can be isolated from the rest of the statement of financial position items. It then follows that, if you take into account the movement in all the non-cash statement of financial position items, you must be left with the movement in cash. To prepare a statement of cash flows, you need to:

- understand the procedure of examining the comparative statements of financial position to establish the movement in the non-cash items
- know the format of the statement of cash flows.

IAS 7 mentions two methods for presenting a statement of cash flows – the ***direct*** method and the ***indirect*** method – and encourages enterprises to use the direct method. In fact, it is only the *operating activities* section of the statement of cash flows that is affected by the choice of method. Irrespective of which method is used, the investing and financing sections of the statement of cash flows remain the same. The example that follows will illustrate the preparation of the statement of cash flows using both the direct and indirect methods. Each section of the statement of cash flows will be explained separately, and then the complete statement of cash flows using both methods will be shown for comparison.

Example: Preparation of a statement of cash flows

You will recall from previous chapters that Computer World Limited supplies computers to Smart Concepts. Due to the tremendous popularity of its brand, Computer World Limited has experienced significant growth over the last few years. The income statement, statement of changes in equity and statement of financial position of Computer World Limited for the year ended 31 December 20X8 are presented below:

COMPUTER WORLD LIMITED
INCOME STATEMENT
FOR THE YEAR ENDED 31 DECEMBER 20X8

		R 000's
Sales		30 650
Cost of sales		(26 000)
Gross profit		4 650
Other income		
Investment income		500
Operating expenses		(1 400)
Administration and selling		410
Depreciation		450
Insurance		500
Loss on disposal of equipment		40
Finance cost		
Interest on loan		(250)
Profit before taxation		3 500
Taxation		(300)
Profit for the period		3 200

COMPUTER WORLD LIMITED
STATEMENT OF CHANGES IN EQUITY
FOR THE YEAR ENDED 31 DECEMBER 20X8

	Share capital	Retained earnings	Total
	R	R	R
Balance at 1 January 20X8	1 250	1 380	2 630
Issue of share capital	1 150	–	1 150
Profit for the period	–	3 200	3 200
Dividends	–	(1 200)	(1 200)
Balance at 31 December 20X8	2 400	3 380	5 780

COMPUTER WORLD LIMITED
STATEMENT OF FINANCIAL POSITION
AT 31 DECEMBER 20X8

	20X8 R000's	20X7 R000's
ASSETS		
Non-current assets	2 430	850
Equipment at cost	3 880	1 910
Accumulated depreciation	(1 450)	(1 060)
Investments	3 440	2 500
Current assets	2 905	3 315
Inventory	900	1 950
Accounts receivable	1 700	1 200
Investment income receivable	100	–
Insurance paid in advance	15	5
Bank	190	160
	8 775	6 665
EQUITY AND LIABILITIES		
Capital and reserves	5 780	2 630
Share capital	2 400	1 250
Retained earnings	3 380	1 380
Non-current liabilities		
Loan from bank	1 800	1 040
Current liabilities	1 195	2 995
Accounts payable	130	1 880
Administration and selling expenses accrued	35	15
Interest payable	230	100
Taxation payable	400	800
Dividends payable	400	200
	8 775	6 665

Additional information

- Equipment which originally cost R200 000 was sold during the period.
- No loans were repaid during the period.
- No investments were sold during the period.

21.4.1 Preparation of the operating activities section

As mentioned above, there are two methods of reporting cash flows from operating activities. We will first explain and prepare the operating activities section using the direct method and then do the same for the indirect method. All amounts in the following explanation are R 000's, but are shown without the three zeros.

Direct method

When using the direct method, the starting point is the cash receipts from customers. The cash payments made to suppliers and employees are deducted from the cash receipts from customers in order to arrive at the *cash generated from operations*. Payments to suppliers include suppliers of goods for resale as well as all suppliers relating to operating activities. Amounts paid for all distribution, administrative and other operating expenses are therefore included. Note that amounts paid to employees for salaries and wages are often included in distribution or administrative expenses and are not shown separately.

The cash effects of non-operating items, dividends and taxation are then taken into account in order to arrive at the *net cash flow from operating activities*.

	Cash receipts from customers
–	(Cash payments to suppliers and employees)
=	*Cash generated from operations*
±	Cash effects of non-operating items, dividends and taxation
=	Net cash flow from operating activities

Diagram 21.2: Direct method of presenting cash flows from operating activities

Cash receipts from customers:

In order to calculate the cash receipts from customers, you need to examine the movement in the accounts receivable account together with sales for the year on the income statement. You can reconstruct the accounts receivable account as follows:

Accounts receivable

Details	**R**	**Details**	**R**
Balance c/d	1 200	***Bank***	***30 150***
Sales	30 650	Balance c/d	1 700
	31 850		31 850
Balance b/d	1 700		

The accrual basis sales for the year amounted to R30 650. The cash of R30 150 received from customers is calculated by starting with the opening balance of R1 200, adding the sales of R30 650 and subtracting the closing balance of R1 700. You can therefore calculate the cash received from customers like this:

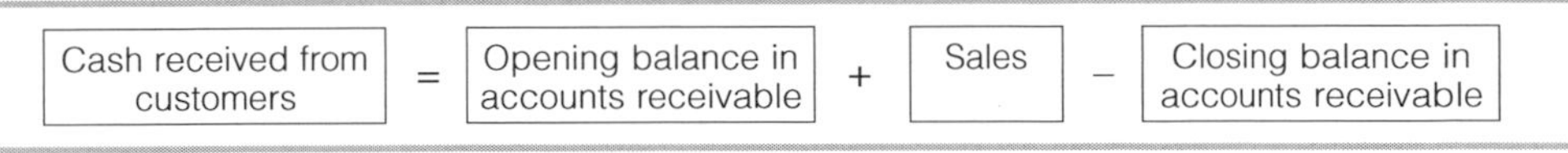

Diagram 21.3: Cash received from customers

Pause and reflect...

The calculation of cash received from customers in this example has taken the total sales of R30 650 all to be on credit. Would the amount of cash received from customers of R30 150 change if the total sales of R30 650 comprised credit sales of R25 000 and cash sales of R5 650?

Response

Following the logic of starting with the opening balance in accounts receivable, adding the credit sales and subtracting the closing balance in accounts receivable, the cash received from customers in relation to credit sales amounts to R24 500 (1 200 + 25 000 – 1 700). If we then add on the cash sales of R5 650, the total cash received from customers (in respect of both credit and cash sales) amounts to R30 150. Therefore, the cash received from customers does not change.

Cash payments to suppliers and employees:

IAS 7 requires the cash payments to suppliers and employees to be reported as one figure. Before examining the details of calculating this figure, it is important for you to understand what it comprises. The cash payments to suppliers and employees comprise cash paid to *suppliers of goods for resale* as well as cash paid for *operating expenses* (including salaries). This implies that the cash paid to suppliers includes all types of suppliers including suppliers of inventory (goods for resale) and suppliers of services (operating expenses). Salaries and wages paid to employees are also part of operating expenses but are not paid to an independent supplier. These payments must therefore be added in as well.

In order to calculate the cash payments to suppliers and employees, you need to examine a number of accounts. Firstly, you need to calculate the purchases for the year by inspecting the movement in the inventory account. Secondly, you combine the purchases figure with the movement in the accounts payable account to calculate the *cash payments to suppliers*. Thirdly, you need to examine the income statement and extract all the operating expenses, other than non-cash items such as depreciation. These expenses will include cash paid for all operating expenses as well as cash paid for salaries. If any of the operating expenses have a corresponding statement of financial position item, you will then also need to combine the income statement expense with the movement in the relevant statement of financial position account in order to calculate the cash payment.

To calculate the **cash paid to suppliers of goods for resale**, we begin with the movement in the inventory account, which you reconstruct as follows:

Inventory

Details	R	Details	R
Balance b/d	1 950	Cost of sales	26 000
Accounts payable	***24 950***	Balance c/d	900
	26 900		26 900
Balance b/d	900		

The purchases of R24 950 is calculated by combining the cost of sales for the year of R26 000 with the opening inventory of R1 950 and the closing inventory of R900. In general terms you can calculate the purchases like this:

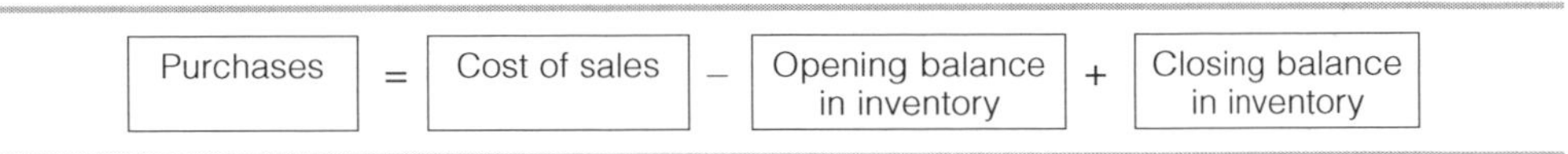

Diagram 21.4: Purchases

We then take the purchases figure and reconstruct an accounts payable account in order to calculate the cash paid to suppliers:

Accounts payable

Details	**R**	**Details**	**R**
Bank	***26 700***	Balance b/d	1 880
Balance c/d	130	Inventory	24 950
	26 830		26 830
		Balance b/d	130

The cash of R26 700 paid to suppliers is calculated by starting with the opening balance of R1 880, adding the purchases of R24 950 and subtracting the closing balance of R130. The principle used here is as follows:

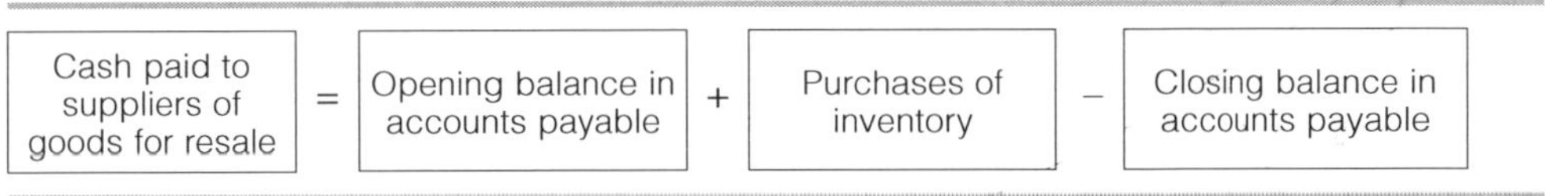

Diagram 21.5: Cash paid to suppliers

We now need to compute the **cash paid for operating expenses**, including salaries to employees. If you look at the income statement, you will notice that there are administration and selling expenses of R410 as well as an insurance expense of R500. If there were no corresponding statement of financial position amounts for the administration and selling expenses or for the insurance expense, we would simply add the R910 (R410 + R500) from the income statement to the cash paid to suppliers of R26 700, to arrive at the amount of cash payments to suppliers and employees. However, in this situation, there is a current liability on the statement of financial position for administration and selling as well as a current asset for insurance. The cash paid for administration and selling expenses can therefore be calculated as follows:

Administration and selling expenses accrued

Details	R	Details	R
Administration and selling expenses	15	Balance b/d	**15**
Balance c/d	35	Administration and selling expenses	35
	50		50
		Balance b/d	**35**

Administration and selling expenses

Details	R	Details	R
Bank	***390***	Administration and selling payable	15
Administration and selling payable	35	Profit and loss	**410**
	425		425

The cash paid for administration and selling expenses of R390 is calculated by starting with the opening liability of R15, adding the expense transferred to the income statement of R410 and subtracting the closing liability of R35.

The cash paid for the insurance expense is calculated as follows:

Insurance paid in advance

Details	R	Details	R
Balance b/d	**5**	Insurance expense	500
Bank	***510***	Balance c/d	15
	515		515
Balance b/d	**15**		

Insurance expense

Details	R	Details	R
Insurance paid in advance	500	Profit and loss	**500**
	500		500

The cash paid for insurance expense of R510 is calculated by starting with the closing asset of R15, adding the expense transferred to the income statement of R500 and subtracting the opening asset of R5.

The principles explained above can be summarised as shown in the following diagram:

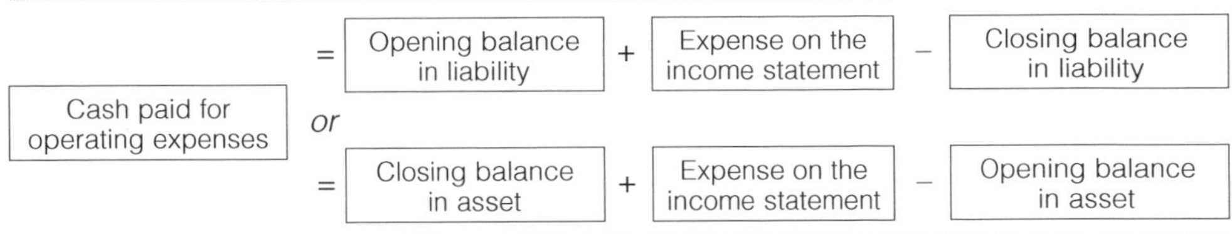

Diagram 21.6: Cash paid for operating expenses

In summary, therefore, the amount that appears on the statement of cash flows as cash paid to suppliers and employees is R27 600 (R26 700 + R390 + R510).

Pause and reflect...

What can you say about the operating expenses on the income statement and the cash paid for operating expenses if there are no accrued or prepaid expenses on the statement of financial position?

Response

If there are no accrued or prepaid expenses on the statement of financial position, then the operating expenses on the income statement must have all been paid for in cash.

Cash effects of non-operating items, taxation and dividends:

The non-operating items that typically need to be taken into account are the investment income and interest paid. It is again necessary to examine both the income statement item and the relevant statement of financial position amount, if applicable.

Looking at **investment income** first, the investment income receivable account is reconstructed like this:

Investment income receivable

Details	R	Details	R
Balance b/d	**0**		
Investment income	100	Balance c/d	100
	100		100
Balance b/d	**100**		

Investment income

Details	R	Details	R
Profit and loss	**500**	***Bank***	***400***
		Investment income receivable	100
	500		500

The cash of R400 received from investment income is calculated by starting with the opening balance of zero, adding the investment income of R500 and subtracting the closing balance of R100.

Turning our attention to the **interest expense**, the interest payable account is shown as follows:

Interest payable

Details	R	Details	R
Interest expense	100	Balance b/d	**100**
Balance c/d	230	Interest expense	230
	330		330
		Balance b/d	**230**

Interest expense

Details	R	Details	R
Bank	***120***	Interest payable	100
Interest payable	230	Profit and loss	**250**
	350		350

The cash of R120 paid for interest is computed by starting with the opening balance of R100, adding the interest expense of R250 and subtracting the closing balance of R230.

The cash paid for **taxation** and **dividends** (appearing on the income statement and statement of charges in equity respectively, with corresponding statement of financial position liabilities) is calculated in the same way as the cash paid to suppliers, the cash paid for operating expenses or the interest paid. The statement of financial position accounts are shown below for completeness:

Taxation payable

Details	R	Details	R
Bank	***700***	Balance b/d	800
Balance c/d	400	Taxation	300
	1 100		1 100
		Balance b/d	400

Dividends payable

Details	R	Details	R
Bank	***1 000***	Balance b/d	200
Balance c/d	400	Dividends	1 200
	1 400		1 400
		Balance b/d	400

Note that the cash of R700 paid for income tax during the year is different from the taxation expense of R300 on the income statement, and the cash of R1 000 paid for dividends is different to the dividend of R1 200 appearing on the statement of changes in equity.

Pause and reflect...

Can you answer the following questions by examining the dividends payable account?

a) What is the amount of the interim dividend declared in respect of the current year?

b) What is the amount of the final dividend declared and has this been paid?

Response

a) The R1 000 cash paid in respect of dividends during the current year comprises the cash paid in respect of the final dividend owing from the previous year of R200 as well as an interim dividend declared during the current year of R800.

b) The balance on the dividend payable account at the end of the current year of R400 must represent the final dividend declared for the current year. It has not yet been paid.

We have now considered each item in the *operating activities* section of the statement of cash flows using the **direct method**. This section of the statement of cash flows is presented below. The workings to arrive at each figure are shown in brackets:

Cash flows from operating activities				
Cash receipts from customers	(1 200 + 30 650 – 1 700)		30 150	
Cash paid to suppliers and employees	(1 880 + 24 950* – 130) + (15 + 410 – 35) + (15 + 500 – 5) (*Purchases = 26 000 – 1 950 + 900)		(27 600)	
Cash generated from operations			2 550	
Investment income received	(0 + 500 – 100)	400		
Interest paid	(100 + 250 – 230)	(120)		
Taxation paid	(800 + 300 – 400)	(700)		
Dividends paid	(200 + 1 200 – 400)	(1 000)	(1 420)	
Net cash inflow from operating activities				***1 130***

Indirect method

When using the indirect method, the starting point is the *profit before tax* on the income statement. As this is an accrual basis figure, it is first adjusted for the effect of non-cash items included in the determination of profit – for example, depreciation expense or the gain on disposal of a fixed asset. It is then adjusted for the effect of non-operating items also included in the determination of profit, for example, investment income and interest expense. This brings us to a sub-total, *operating cash flow before working capital changes.*

The next adjustment relates to the effects of working capital movements, that is, movements in accounts receivable, accounts payable and inventory to give the *cash generated from operations.*

Finally, the cash effects of non-operating items, dividends and taxation are taken into account to arrive at the *net cash flow from operating activities.*

	Profit before tax
±	Non-cash items
±	Non-operating items
=	Operating cash flow before working capital changes
±	Working capital changes
=	*Cash generated from operations*
±	Cash effects of non-operating items, dividends and taxation
=	Net cash flow from operating activities

Diagram 21.7: Indirect method of presenting cash flows from operating activities

Non-cash items:

There are some income and expense items included in the determination of profit which do not involve the receipt or payment of cash. Examples are the profit or loss on sale of non-current assets, and the depreciation expense. Bearing in mind all the time that the starting point for the indirect method is the profit before tax on the income statement, income items need to be subtracted from the profit before tax, and expense items need to be added. This is to reverse the effect of income items which have not resulted in the receipt of cash, and the expense items which have not resulted in the payment of cash. This can be summarised as follows:

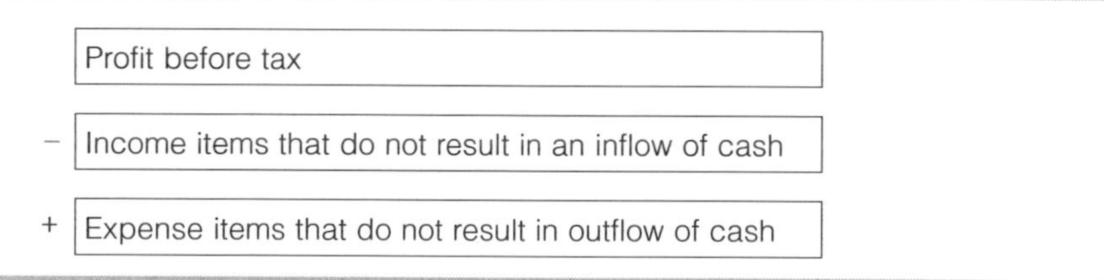

Diagram 21.8: Adjustments for non-cash items

The non-cash items on the income statement of Computer World Limited are the depreciation expense of R450 and the loss on disposal of non-current assets of R40.

Non-operating items:

As mentioned above, non-operating items of income and expense, included in the determination of profit before tax, need to be reversed in calculating the operating cash flow. This is a simple matter of subtracting the non-operating income items and adding the non-operating expense items. In this example, we need to subtract the investment income of R500 and add the interest expense of R250.

Working capital changes:

When calculating the working capital changes, it is again important for you to remember that the starting point for the indirect method is the profit before tax on the income statement. It is only the *non-cash* components of working capital that are adjusted as the movement in cash is the end result of the statement of cash flows.

Looking at **accounts receivable**, the balance increased from R1 200 to R1 700. This resulted from the *accrual basis sales of R30 650 being greater than the cash receipts from customers of R30 150.* As the accrual basis sales has been taken into account in the determination of the profit, the increase in accounts receivable of R500 (which is the excess of accrual basis sales over cash receipts), must be subtracted from the profit on the statement of cash flows.

Conversely, if the balance on accounts receivable decreased, it would result from *cash receipts from customers being greater than the accrual basis sales.* The decrease in accounts receivable is then added to the profit on the statement of cash flows.

Regarding **accounts payable**, the balance decreased from R1 880 to R130. This resulted from the *cash paid to suppliers of R26 700 being greater than the accrual basis purchases of R24 950* (which is part of cost of sales). As the cost of sales has been taken into account in the determination of the profit, the decrease in accounts payable of R1 750 (which is the excess of cash payments over accrual basis purchases), must be subtracted from the profit on the statement of cash flows.

Conversely, if the balance on accounts payable increased, it would result from the *accrual basis purchases being greater than cash payments to suppliers.* As the accrual basis purchases affects cost of sales, the increase in accounts payable is then added to the profit on the statement of cash flows.

Inventory will appear on the statement of financial position of all trading concerns. Any change in the closing inventory will have a direct effect on the cost of sales and therefore the gross profit and profit for the period. Increases in closing inventory increase profit, and decreases in closing inventory decrease profit. There is no cash effect in the inventory account, and therefore the decrease in inventory of R1 050 must be added to the profit. Conversely, an increase in inventory must be subtracted from the profit.

All changes in the non-cash working capital items must be taken into account. However, the non-operating items as well as taxation and dividends are excluded as they are reported separately. In the case of Computer World Limited, the only other non-cash working capital movements to take into account are the administration and selling payable and the insurance paid in advance.

As administration and selling payable is a liability, the principle is similar to the adjustment for accounts payable. The balance on the administration and selling payable increased from R15 to R35. This resulted from the *cash paid of R390 being less than the accrual basis expense of R410.* Therefore the movement of R20 must be added to the profit on the statement of cash flows. Conversely, if the balance on a current liability account decreased, it would result from the *cash paid being greater than the accrual basis expense*, and the movement would have to be subtracted on the statement of cash flows.

The insurance paid in advance is an asset and therefore the principle is similar to the adjustment for accounts receivable. The balance on the insurance paid in advance increased from R5 to R15. This resulted from the cash paid of R510 being greater than the accrual basis expense of R500. Therefore the movement of R10 must be subtracted from the profit on the statement of cash flows. Conversely, if the balance on a current asset decreased, it would result from the cash paid being less than the accrual basis expense, and the movement would have to be added on the statement of cash flows.

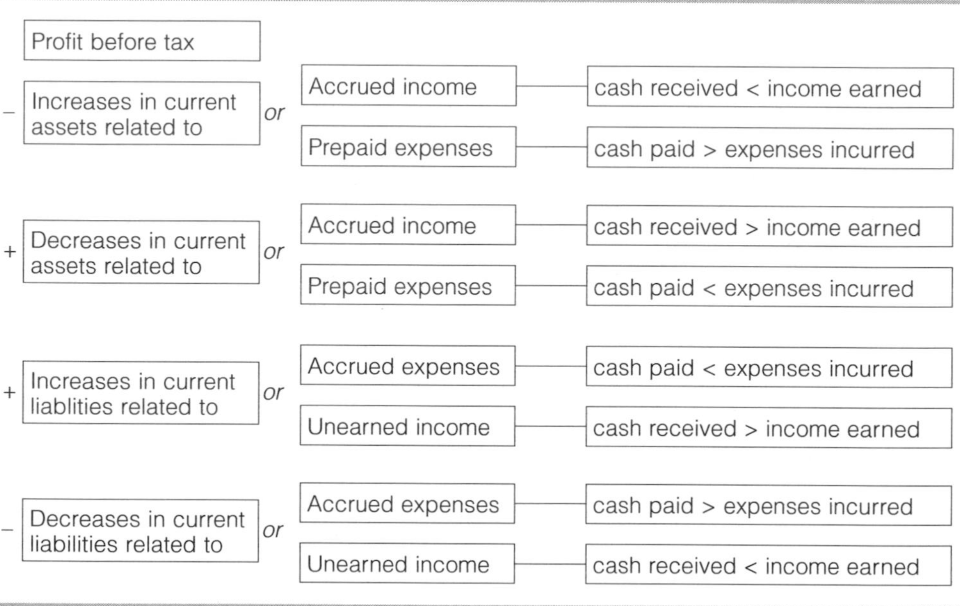

Diagram 21.9: Adjustments to non-cash components of working capital

The adjustments relating to the movement in the non-cash components of working capital are summarised in diagram 21.9. It is important for you to understand the reason for the adjustment, not only the mechanics of the adjustment.

Pause and reflect...

We have evaluated changes in working capital by comparing the amounts recorded in the income statement under the accrual basis to the actual receipts and payments. This comparison enabled us to calculate the appropriate adjustments to the profit before tax amount used in the indirect method. Can you think of an explanation for the accounts receivable and accounts payable working capital changes, that is based only on the movements in the statement of financial position?

Response

The accounts receivable balance increased by R500. Notwithstanding the sales recorded in the income statement, the R500 increase in accounts receivable indicates that the accrual-based sales are greater than the cash received from customers by an amount of R500. Therefore, the accrual-based profit is reduced by this amount in reconciling to the cash from operating activities.

The R1 750 decrease in accounts payable indicates that the amount paid to suppliers is greater than the accrual-based purchases by an amount of R1 750. This amount is not included in the cost of sales amount used to determine profit before tax. Therefore, the accrual-based profit is reduced by this amount in reconciling to the cash from operating activities.

Cash effects of non-operating items, taxation and dividends:

The treatment of these items is identical for both the direct and indirect methods. With regard to the non-operating items, the investment income and interest expense were reversed in arriving at operating cash flow before the working capital changes. Therefore, the cash effect is taken into account at this stage, as for the direct method.

The taxation is reported on the income statement *after* the profit before tax and the dividends are reported on the statement of changes in equity. There is thus no adjustment for these items, but rather the cash outflow relating to taxation and dividend is shown, again, as for the direct method.

The *operating activities* section of the statement of cash flows using the **indirect** method is shown below.

		R 000's	
Cash flows from operating activities			
Profit before tax (from I/S)		3 500	
Adjusted for non-cash and non-operating items			
Depreciation (from I/S)	450		
Loss on the disposal of equipment (from I/S)	40		
Investment income (from I/S)	(500)		
Interest expense (from I/S)	250	240	
Operating cash flow before working capital changes		3 740	
Working capital changes			
Increase in accounts receivable (1 700 – 1 200)	(500)		
Decrease in accounts payable (130 – 1 880)	(1 750)		
Decrease in inventory (900 – 1 950)	1 050		
Increase in admin and selling payable (35 – 15)	20		
Increase in insurance paid in advance (15 – 5)	(10)	(1 190)	
Cash generated from operations		2 550	
Investment income received (0 + 500 – 100)	400		
Interest paid (100 + 250 – 230)	(120)		
Taxation paid (800 + 300 – 400)	(700)		
Dividends paid (200 + 1 200 – 400)	(1 000)	(1 420)	
Net cash inflow from operating activities			***1 130***

Note that the cash of R2 550 generated from operations and the net cash inflow from operating activities of R1 130 are the same for both the direct and indirect methods.

21.4.2 Preparation of the investing activities section

The investing and financing activities sections of the statement of cash flows are identical for both the direct and indirect methods. This is because no accrual basis income or expenses are adjusted in these sections. Each section reports cash inflows and outflows that are not on the income statement.

Recall that the investing activities relate to the acquisition and disposal of non-current assets. You need to reconstruct the relevant statement of financial position accounts and establish the cash flows. Looking first at the **non-current assets**, the accounts are as follows:

Equipment at cost

Details	R	Details	R
Balance b/d	1 910	Disposal	200
Bank (additions)	***2 170***	Balance c/d	3 880
	4 080		4 080
Balance b/d	3 880		

You were told in the example that equipment which originally cost R200 was sold during the period. By entering the cost of the equipment disposed on the credit side of the equipment account, we can establish that the cash paid for equipment purchased during the period was R2 170.

Accumulated depreciation

Details	R	Details	R
Disposal	***60***	Balance b/d	1 060
Balance c/d	1 450	Depreciation	450
	1 510		1 510
		Balance b/d	1 450

The depreciation expense of R450, which is reported on the income statement, is entered on the credit side of the accumulated depreciation account. We can then deduce that the accumulated depreciation relating to the equipment sold amounts to R60. There is no cash flow implication in this number, but it is used to reconstruct the disposal account, as follows:

Disposal

Details	R	Details	R
Equipment at cost	200	Accumulated depreciation	60
		Cash (proceeds)	***100***
		Loss on disposal	40
	200		200

The cost and the accumulated depreciation of the equipment sold have been transferred from their respective accounts to the disposal account. The loss on disposal of equipment of R40 is known from the income statement, and therefore the cash inflow from the disposal of the equipment is R100.

 **Pause and reflect...**

Does the loss on disposal represent an outflow of cash?

Response

The loss on disposal is an accrual-based amount and does not represent any cash flow. The proceeds of R100 represent an inflow of cash.

Turning our attention to the investments, the balance increased from R2 500 to R3 440. As no investments were sold during the period, it is apparent that the cash paid to acquire new investments is R940.

The *investing activities* section of the statement of cash flows is shown below.

Cash flows from investing activities		
Purchase of equipment	(2 170)	
Proceeds on disposal of equipment	100	
Acquisition of investments (3 440 – 2 500)	(940)	
Net cash outflow from investing activities		***(3 010)***

21.4.3 Preparation of the financing activities section

As the financing activities section relates to the cash flows arising from changes in equity and borrowings, we need to examine the movements in the equity and non-current liabilities sections of the statement of financial position.

The share capital increased from R1 250 to R2 400. This means that there is a cash inflow of R1 150 from the issue of shares. The long-term loan from the bank increased from R1 040 to R1 800, implying a further cash inflow from long-term borrowings of R760.

The financing activities section of the statement of cash flows is shown below.

Cash flows from financing activities		
Proceeds from issue of shares (2 400 – 1 250)	1 150	
Proceeds from long-term borrowings (1 800 – 1 040)	760	
Net cash inflow from financing activities		***1 910***

Solution: Preparation of a statement of cash flows

For completeness, the full statements of cash flows prepared, using the direct and indirect methods, are shown on the following pages. The only section that is different between the two is the operating activities section. When the direct method is used, it is recommended that a reconciliation between the profit before tax as reported on the income statement and the cash generated from operations as reported on the statement of cash flows is presented. This reconciliation, although not required by IAS 7, is shown as a note to the statement of cash flows on the direct method as it provides information that is useful in understanding the statement of cash flows.

Although not required by IAS 7, a note reconciling the taxation and dividends paid, with their respective income statement amounts is also recommended. This provides users with additional decision-relevant information.

Direct method

COMPUTER WORLD LIMITED
STATEMENT OF CASH FLOWS
FOR THE YEAR ENDED 31 DECEMBER 20X8

			R 000's	
Cash flows from operating activities				
Cash receipts from customers	(1 200 + 30 650 – 1 700)		30 150	
Cash paid to suppliers and for operating expenses	(1 880 + 24 950* – 130) + (15 + 410 – 35) + (15 + 500 – 5)) (*Purchases = 26 000 – 1 950 + 900)		(27 600)	
Cash generated from operations			2 550	
Investment income received	(0 + 500 – 100)	400		
Interest paid	(100 + 250 – 230)	(120)		
Taxation paid	(800 + 300 – 400)	(700)		
Dividends paid	(200 – 1 200 – 400)	(1 000)	(1 420)	
Net cash inflow from operating activities				***1 130***
Cash flows from investing activities				
Purchase of equipment			(2 170)	
Proceeds on disposal of equipment			100	
Acquisition of investments	(3 440 – 2 500)		(940)	
Net cash outflow from investing activities				***(3 010)***
Cash flows from financing activities				
Proceeds from issue of shares	(2 400 – 1 250)		1 150	
Proceeds from long-term borrowings	(1 800 – 1 040)		760	
Net cash inflow from financing activities				***1 910***
Net increase in cash				**30**
Cash at beginning of period				**160**
Cash at end of period				**190**
Reconciliation of profit before tax to cash from operations				
Profit before tax (from I/S)			3 500	
Adjusted for non-cash and non-operating items				
Depreciation (from I/S)		450		
Loss on the disposal of non-current assets (from I/S)		40		
Investment income (from I/S)		(500)		
Interest expense (from I/S)		250	240	
Operating cash flow before working capital changes			3 740	
Working capital changes				
Increase in accounts receivable	(1 700 – 1 200)	(500)		
Decrease in accounts payable	(130 – 1 880)	(1 750)		
Decrease in inventory	(900 – 1 950)	1 050		
Increase in administration and selling payable	(35 – 15)	20		
Increase in insurance paid in advance	(15 – 5)	(10)	(1 190)	
Cash generated from operations			2 550	
Reconciliation of taxation and dividends paid		**Taxation**	**Dividends**	
Liability at beginning of the year		800	200	
Amount accrued		300	1 200	
Liability at end of the year		(400)	(400)	
Amount paid in cash		700	1 000	

Indirect method

COMPUTER WORLD LIMITED
STATEMENT OF CASH FLOWS
FOR THE YEAR ENDED 31 DECEMBER 20X8

		R 000's	
Cash flows from operating activities			
Profit before tax (from I/S)		3 500	
Adjusted for non-cash and non-operating items			
Depreciation (from I/S)	450		
Loss on the disposal of fixed assets (from I/S)	40		
Investment income (from I/S)	(500)		
Interest expense (from I/S)	250	240	
Operating cash flow before working capital changes		3 740	
Working capital changes			
Increase in accounts receivable	(500)		
Decrease in accounts payable	(1 750)		
Decrease in inventory	1 050		
Increase in administration and selling payable	20		
Increase in insurance paid in advance	(10)	(1 190)	
Cash generated from operations		2 550	
Investment income received (0 + 500 – 100)	400		
Interest paid (100 + 250 – 230)	(120)		
Taxation paid (800 + 300 – 400)	(700)		
Dividends paid (200 + 1 200 – 400)	(1 000)	(1 420)	
Net cash inflow from operating activities			***1 130***
Cash flows from investing activities			
Purchase of equipment		(2 170)	
Proceeds on disposal of equipment		100	
Acquisition of investments (3 440 – 2 500)		(940)	
Net cash outflow from investing activities			***(3 010)***
Cash flows from financing activities			
Proceeds from issue of shares (2 400 – 1 250)		(1 150)	
Proceeds from long-term borrowings (1 800 – 1 040)		760	
Net cash inflow from financing activities			***1 910***
Net increase in cash			**30**
Cash at beginning of period			**160**
Cash at end of period			**190**

Reconciliation of taxation and dividends paid	**Taxation**	**Dividends**
Liability at beginning of the year	800	200
Amount accrued	300	1 200
Liability at end of the year	(400)	(400)
Amount paid in cash	700	1 000

21.5 Exam example

PANCHENKO LIMITED
TRIAL BALANCE
AT 30 JUNE 20X4 & 20X3

	20X4 R 000's	20X3 R 000's
Non-current assets – cost	11 000	8 000
Investments	3 000	–
Accounts receivable	3 600	3 400
Inventory	5 000	3 600
Investment income receivable	400	–
Bank	1 200	800
Administration and selling expenses	24 200	–
Loss on disposal of investments	400	–
Interest expense	1 000	800
Taxation expense	2 000	1 400
Dividends declared	800	800
	52 600	18 800
Share capital	3 800	2 000
Dividends payable	400	800
Accounts payable	2 400	1 200
Accumulated depreciation	4 000	2 000
Taxation payable	600	200
Interest payable	200	800
Long-term loan	8 000	6 000
Gross profit	30 000	3 800
Investment income	400	–
Accumulated profit	2 800	2 000
	52 600	18 800

Additional information

- Depreciation of R2 400 000 was provided during 20X4.
- Non-current assets with a cost of R1 000 000 were sold during the year and a loss of R200 000 was incurred.
- An investment acquired for R600 000 during the year was disposed of before the year-end.
- Long-term loans of R2 000 000 were repaid during the year.
- Panchenko Limited marks up its goods for resale by 50% on cost to calculate its selling price.
- Gross profit for the current year was R30 000 000.

You are required to:

prepare the statement of cash flows for Panchenko Limited for the period ended 30 June 20X4, using the direct method. Notes to the cash flow are required.

Solution: Exam example

PANCHENKO LIMITED
STATEMENT OF CASH FLOWS FOR THE YEAR ENDED 30 JUNE 20X4

		R 000's	
Cash flows from operating activities			
Cash receipts from customers (3 400 + 90 000 (W14)* – 3 600)		89 800	
Cash paid to suppliers and employees (see W16)		(81 800)	
Cash generated from operations		8 000	
Interest paid (800 + 1 000 – 200) (W9)	(1 600)		
Investment income received (0 + 400 – 400)(W10)	–		
Dividends paid (800 + 800 – 400) (W11)	(1 200)		
Taxation paid (200 + 2 000 – 600) (W12)	(1 600)	(4 400)	
Net cash inflow from operating activities			***3 600***
Cash flows from investing activities			
Proceeds on disposal of fixed assets (W3)		400	
Proceeds on disposal of investments (W8)		200	
Acquisition of fixed assets (W1)		(4 000)	
Acquisition of investments (W7)		(3 600)	
Net cash outflow from investing activities			***(7 000)***
Cash flows from financing activities			
Proceeds from share issue (3 800 – 2 000)		1 800	
Repayment of long-term loan (W13)		(2 000)	
Proceeds from long-term loan (W13)		4 000	
Net cash inflow from financing activities			***3 800***
Net increase in bank			**400**
Bank at beginning of period			**800**
Bank at end of period			**1 200**
Reconciliation of profit before tax to cash from operations			
Profit before tax (W14)		4 800	
Adjusted for non-cash and non-operating items			
Depreciation (W2)	2 400		
Loss on disposal of fixed asset (W3)	200		
Investment income (Given)	(400)		
Loss on disposal of investments (Given)	400		
Interest expense (Given)	1 000	3 600	
Operating cash flow before working capital changes		8 400	
Working capital changes (W15)			
Increase in inventory	(1 400)		
Increase in accounts receivable	(200)		
Increase in accounts payable	1 200	(400)	
Cash generated from operations		8 000	

Non-current assets (1)

Details	R	Details	R
Balance b/d	8 000	Disposal	1 000
Cash – addition	***4 000***	Balance c/d	11 000
	12 000		12 000
Balance b/d	11 000		

Accumulated depreciation (2)

Details	R	Details	R
Disposal	***400***	Balance b/d	2 000
Balance c/d	4 000	Depreciation	2 400
	4 400		4 400
		Balance b/d	4 000

Disposal of non-current assets (3)

Details	R	Details	R
Non-current assets – cost	1 000	Accumulated depreciation	400
		Bank	***400***
		Profit & loss	200
	1 000		1 000

Inventory (4)

Details	R	Details	R
Balance b/d	3 600	Cost of sales (W14)	60 000
Accounts payable	***61 400***	Balance c/d	5 000
	65 000		65 000
Balance b/d	5 000		

Accounts receivable (5)

Details	R	Details	R
Balance b/d	3 400	***Bank***	***89 800***
Sales (W14)	90 000	Balance c/d	3 600
	93 400		93 400
Balance b/d	3 600		

Accounts payable (6)

Details	R	Details	R
Bank	***60 200***	Balance b/d	1 200
Balance c/d	2 400	Inventory	61 400
	62 600		62 600
		Balance b/d	2 400

Investments (7)

Details	R	Details	R
Bank	***3 600***	Disposal	600
		Balance c/d	3 000
	3 600		3 600
Balance b/d	3 000		

Disposal of investments (8)

Details	R	Details	R
Investment	600	***Bank***	***200***
		Profit & loss	400
	600		600

Interest payable (9)

Details	R	Details	R
Bank	***1 600***	Balance b/d	800
Balance c/d	200	Interest	1 000
	1 800		1 800
		Balance b/d	200

Investment income receivable (10)

Details	R	Details	R
Balance b/d	0	***Bank***	***0***
Investment income	400	Balance c/d	400
	400		400
Balance b/d	400		

Dividends payable (11)

Details	R	Details	R
Bank	***1 200***	Balance b/d	800
Balance c/d	400	Dividends	800
	1 600		1 600
		Balance b/d	400

Taxation payable (12)

Details	R	Details	R
Bank	***1 600***	Balance b/d	200
Balance c/d	600	Taxation	2 000
	2 200		2 200
		Balance b/d	600

Long-term loan (13)

Details	R	Details	R
Bank – repayment	2 000	Balance b/d	6 000
Balance c/d	8 000	***Bank – raised***	***4 000***
	10 000		10 000
		Balance b/d	8 000

PANCHENKO LIMITED (14)
INCOME STATEMENT
FOR THE YEAR ENDED 30 JUNE 20X4

		R 000's
Sales	(30 000 x 150/100)	90 000
Cost of sales	(30 000 x 100/50)	(60 000)
Gross profit	(Given)	30 000
Other income		
Investment income		400
Operating expenses		(24 600)
Administration and selling expenses	(Given)	24 200
Loss on disposal of investments	(Given)	400
Finance cost		
Interest expense		(1 000)
Profit before taxation		***4 800***
Taxation		(2 000)
Profit for the period		2 800

Working capital (15)

Increase in inventory (3 600 – 5 000)	(1 400)
Increase in accounts receivable (3 400 – 3 600)	(200)
Increase in accounts payable (2 400 - 1 200)	1 200
Decrease in working capital	(400)

Cash paid to suppliers and employees (16)

Cash paid to suppliers (W6)	60 200
Other expenses (W14)	24 200
Loss on disposal of non-current assets	(200)
Depreciation	(2 400)
	81 800

Summary of concepts and applications

1. Information about the cash flows of an enterprise provides the users of financial statements with details of the way in which the enterprise generates its cash flows and the way in which it utilises those cash flows. The statement of cash flows must be used together with the accrual basis income statement and statement of financial position. IAS 7, Statements of Cash Flows, deals with the presentation of cash flow information.
2. IAS 7 defines cash flows as inflows and outflows of cash and cash equivalents.
3. Cash flows from operating activities are primarily derived from the principal revenue-producing activities of the enterprise. Investing activities relate to the acquisition and disposal of non-current assets. Financing activities are cash flows relating to the financing of a business enterprise. The chapter also discusses the classification on the statement of cash flows of the gain or loss on the sale of property, plant and equipment and the payment or receipt of interest and dividends (included in cash flows from operating activities), as well as cash flows relating to taxation (included in cash flows from operating activities).
4. In order to prepare a statement of cash flows, one must first understand the procedure of examining the comparative statements of financial position of an enterprise so as to establish the movement in the non-cash items and, second, one must be aware of the format of the statement.

Notes

1. Framework for the Preparation and Presentation of Financial Statements, *International Accounting Standards Board*, (2004), paragraph 12.
2. IAS 7, Statements of Cash Flows, *International Accounting Standards Board*, (2004), paragraph 03.
3. Everingham, G. K. and Hopkins, B. D., *Generally Accepted Accounting Practice – A South African Viewpoint*, Cape Town: Juta, (1996), p. 368.
4. Everingham, G. K. and Hopkins, B. D., (1996), p. 369.
5. IAS 7 (2004), paragraph 06.
6. IAS 7 (2004), paragraphs 10 & 11.
7. IAS 7 (2004), paragraph 14.
8. Everingham, G. K. and Hopkins, B. D., (1996), p. 375.
9. IAS 7 (2004), paragraph 16.
10. IAS 7 (2004), paragraph 17.
11. Larson, K. D. and Miller, P. B. W., *Financial Accounting*, Chicago: Irwin, (1995), p. 545.

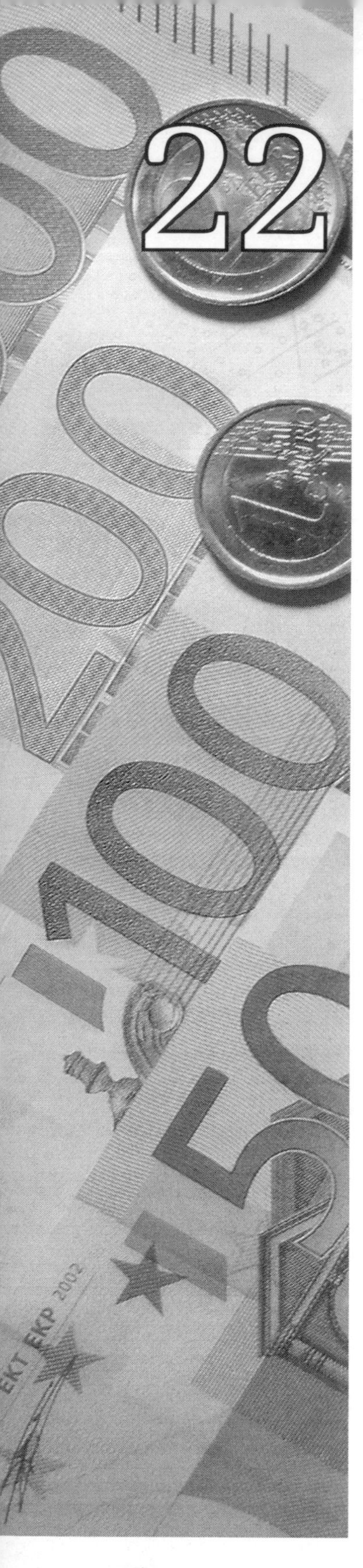

22 Analysis of Financial Statements

'Did not one of your fellow craftsmen, the late Sir Mark Webster Jenkinson, say only a few years ago that "backers of horses have better information available than speculations on shares"?'
(Jenkinson, c1930)

Outcomes

- Understand the objectives of financial statement analysis.
- Identify the external influences affecting a business entity.
- Use common-size and comparative financial statements as tools of financial statement analysis.
- Use ratios as tools of financial statement analysis.

Chapter outline

African Oxygen Limited
Statement of comprehensive income for the year ended 31 December

	(R Millions)	
	2007	**2006**
Revenue	5 849	3 914
Cost of sales	(3 663)	(2 424)
Gross profit	2 186	1 490
Expenses	(1 223)	(420)
Profit before tax	963	1 070
Tax	(350)	(284)
Profit for the period	613	786

From a quick glance of Afrox's 2007 results it seems the company has done admirably, producing a profit of R613 million. The purpose of this chapter is to examine the techniques of how to analyse financial statements. In order to provide useful information the financial statements must be compared to prior years and other similar companies.

22.1 Objectives of financial statement analysis

Financial reporting provides information about the financial position, performance and cash flows of a business entity. All the information is useful to a wide range of users in making economic decisions. The users need to evaluate the financial position of a business entity and the results of its business operations, when making economic decisions. This evaluation is the overall objective of financial statement analysis.

The analysis of financial statements may be used to predict future events, based on the past performance of the business and its financial position at a particular time.

Different users of the financial statements have different needs for information, and the specific objectives of the users will therefore depend on the use to which the user wishes to put the information.

The user may be a potential investor in the business entity who is concerned about the future performance of the business, such as the rate of return the business will achieve and its ability to make distributions to its owners.

The user may be a potential lender to the business entity. Such a user will be concerned that the business entity will have sufficient cash resources to be able to service its interest payments and to repay its debt when it falls due for repayment.

Management, in addition to wanting to assess past performance and financial position and to predict future performance and financial position of the business entity, will want to be able to identify potential problem areas, such as a shortage of cash resources, in order to take timeous corrective action.

22.2 External influences

A business entity is affected by many outside factors.

The state of the economy in which it operates has a major influence on the entity. If the economy is in recession it is likely to have an adverse effect on the financial position and performance of the business enterprise.

Changes in the particular industry in which the entity operates also impact on its financial position and results. A switch in demand from existing products, such as 35mm single-lens reflex cameras, to new products, such as digital cameras, can have a disastrous impact on entities which do not predict such changes.

When analysing the financial position and results of a business entity, it is important to be aware of these external influences and to incorporate their effects in the evaluation.

22.3 Tools of financial statement analysis

We are now going to consider the various tools which are commonly used in analysing financial statements.

Depending on the needs of the user, the analysis of the financial statements will focus on one or more of the following areas:

- Short-term liquidity
- Capital structure and long-term solvency
- Operational efficiency and profitability.

Let us consider particular interests of three typical user groups of financial statements. Potential lenders or suppliers to a business entity are interested in the short-term liquidity of the entity as assurance that it will be able to repay the amounts owing when these fall due.

Potential investors in a business entity are interested in the long-term solvency of the entity. The potential investors seek a return on the investment, on an on-going basis, as well as growth in the value of the investment. In order to achieve this, long-term solvency is vital.

Management as well as investors are interested in measuring the performance of the business entity and seek to measure both operational efficiency and profitability.

As well as looking at ratio analysis, which is a widely used tool of financial statement analysis, we will also look at other tools of financial statement analysis which provide valuable insight into the composition of the financial statements and of trends over time.

It is always important when interpreting the ratios or the results of the other tools of financial statement analysis, to 'look behind' the numbers. As we consider the various measures of performance and financial position, we shall see that a result which might be expected to be a warning of a problem or potential problem may be able to be explained satisfactorily, in a way that indicates that no problem exists.

We shall use the example which follows to explore the various tools of financial statement analysis.

We must always remember that an outside user of financial statements, such as a potential investor, is limited to published information regarding business entities and has to work with that information when analysing financial statements. This limitation can reduce the meaningfulness and effectiveness of the analysis.

Example: Ratio analysis of DiGold Limited

DiGold Limited is a manufacturer and distributor of components for the electrical engineering industry.

DIGOLD LTD
INCOME STATEMENT
FOR THE YEAR ENDED 30 SEPTEMBER 20X6

	20X6 R 000's	20X5 R 000's	20X4 R 000's
Sales	10 920	8 730	8 050
Cost of sales	(7 280)	(5 580)	(5 367)
Gross profit	3 640	3 150	2 683
Other income			
Investment income	35	22	20
Expenses	(2 645)	(2 762)	(2 014)
Operating expenses	1 490	2 162	1 264
Depreciation	1 155	600	750
Finance cost			
Interest expense	(365)	(215)	(215)
Profit before taxation	665	195	474
Taxation	(245)	(75)	(174)
Profit for the period	420	120	300

DIGOLD LTD
STATEMENT OF CHANGES IN EQUITY
FOR THE YEAR ENDED 30 SEPTEMBER 20X6

	Ordinary share capital	Share premium capital	Preference share	Retained earnings	Total
	R 000's	R 000's	R 000's	R 000's	R 000's
Balance at 30 September 20X3	1 000	2 000	500	310	3 810
Profit for the period				300	300
Dividends – preference				(60)	(60)
– ordinary				(100)	(100)
Balance at 30 September 20X4	1 000	2 000	500	450	3 950
Profit for the period				120	120
Dividends – preference				(60)	(60)
– ordinary				(20)	(20)
Balance at 30 September 20X5	1 000	2 000	500	490	3 990
Profit for the period				420	420
Dividends – preference				(60)	(60)
– ordinary				(150)	(150)
Issue of ordinary share capital	500	1 500			2000
Balance at 30 September 20X6	1 500	3 500	500	700	6 200

DIGOLD LTD
STATEMENT OF FINANCIAL POSITION
AT 30 SEPTEMBER 20X6

	20X6 R 000's	**20X5 R 000's**	**20X4 R 000's**
ASSETS			
Non-current assets	6 120	3 400	4 000
Property, plant and equipment	4 620	2 400	3 000
Investments	1 500	1 000	1 000
Current assets	3 450	4 130	2 470
Inventory	1 630	2 360	1 170
Accounts receivable	1 150	1 770	850
Bank	670	–	450
	9 570	**7 530**	**6 470**
EQUITY AND LIABILITIES			
Capital and reserves	6 200	3 990	3 950
Ordinary share capital	1 500	1 000	1 000
Share premium	3 500	2 000	2 000
Accumulated profit	700	490	450
Ordinary shareholders' interest	5 700	3 490	3 450
12% Non-redeemable preference share capital	500	500	500
Non-current liabilities	2 550	1 750	1 750
15% Debentures	1 750	750	750
Long-term borrowings	800	1 000	1 000
Current liabilities	820	1 790	770
Accounts payable	550	1 460	720
Taxation payable	70	20	50
Current portion of loan	200		
Bank overdraft	–	310	–
	9 570	**7 530**	**6 470**

Additional information

- Authorised ordinary shares – 3 000 000 of R1 each.
- Authorised preference shares – 2 000 000 of 50c each.
- 20X3 financial information available:
  - Sales R7 245 000
  - Cost of sales R4 830 000
  - Gross profit R2 415 000
  - Inventory R735 000
  - Accounts receivable R760 000
  - Accounts payable R612 000
  - Total assets R5 850 000
  - Ordinary shareholders' interest R3 310 000
- 500 000 ordinary shares were issued at a premium of R2 per share on 1 October 20X5.

- The market price of the ordinary shares at the end of each financial year was:
  - 20X4 – R4,50
  - 20X5 – R3,90
  - 20X6 – R5,50
- Tax rate for the company is 28%.

22.3.1 Common-size financial statements

Common-size financial statements are prepared using percentages for each item on the financial statements instead of showing the actual amounts.

In the case of the income statement, the sales are shown as 100%, with all other items shown as a percentage of sales.

In the case of the statement of financial position, the totals of both the assets and equity and liabilities sections are shown as 100%. Individual items are shown as a percentage of the total assets or of the total equity and liabilities. Interest-bearing and interest-free debt are often shown separately in a common-size statement of financial position.

The common-size financial statements reveal relationships between the various components of the financial statements. For example, the common-size income statement indicates the percentage of sales absorbed by each expense item, while the common-size statement of financial position indicates relationships, such as the percentage of the entity's financing which comes from debt, and the percentage which comes from equity or what proportion of total assets comprises cash.

Common-size financial statements are useful when users wish to compare different business entity. They can also be used to perform a trend analysis for the same business entity over a period of time.

The common-size financial statements of DiGold Limited follow.

COMMON-SIZE INCOME STATEMENT
FOR THE YEAR ENDED 30 SEPTEMBER 20X6

	20X6	**20X5**	**20X4**
Sales	100,00	100,00	100,00
Cost of sales	(66,67)	(63,92)	(66,67)
Gross profit	33,33	36,08	33,33
Investment income	0,32	0,25	0,25
Expenses	(24,22)	(31,64)	(25,02)
Operating expenses	13,64	24,77	15,70
Depreciation	10,58	6,87	9,32
Interest expense	(3,34)	(2,46)	(2,67)
Profit before taxation	6,09	2,23	5,89
Taxation	(2,24)	(0,86)	(2,16)
Profit for the period	3,85	1,37	3,73

COMMON-SIZE STATEMENT OF FINANCIAL POSITION AT 30 SEPTEMBER 20X6

	20X6 R 000's	20X5 R 000's	20X4 R 000's
ASSETS			
Non-current assets	63,95	45,15	61,82
Property, plant and equipment	48,28	31,87	46,37
Investments	15,67	13,28	15,45
Current assets	36,05	54,85	38,18
Inventory	17,03	31,34	18,08
Accounts receivable	12,02	23,51	13,14
Bank	7,00	0,00	6,96
	100,00	100,00	100,00
EQUITY AND LIABILITIES			
Capital and reserves	64,78	52,99	61,05
Ordinary share capital	15,67	13,28	15,45
12% Non-redeemable preference share capital	5,23	6,64	7,73
Share premium	36,57	26,56	30,91
Accumulated profit	7,31	6,51	6,96
Non-current liabilties	26,65	23,24	27,05
15% Debentures	18,29	9,96	11,59
Long-term borrowings	8,36	13,28	15,46
Current liabilities	8,57	23,77	11,90
Accounts payable	5,75	19,39	11,13
Taxation payable	0,73	0,26	0,77
Current portion of loan	2,09	0,00	0,00
Bank overdraft	0,00	4,12	0,00
	100,00	100,00	100,00

22.3.2 Comparative statements

Comparative financial statements show the financial statements for each of the required number of years, side-by-side, thereby highlighting changes in individual items from year to year. The percentage increase or decrease in an individual item is calculated as follows:

$$\frac{\text{Current year amount} - \text{prior year amount}}{\text{Prior year amount}} \times \frac{100}{1}$$

The usefulness of comparative statements is limited in that meaningful percentages cannot be computed when there is a movement from a positive to a negative or *vice versa*, or if the amount for the previous year was zero. If an item has a positive value for a previous year and is zero in the current year, the decrease is 100%.
The comparative income statement and statement of financial position for DiGold Limited follow.

COMPARATIVE INCOME STATEMENTS

	20X6	20X5	20X4
Sales	25,09	8,45	0,00
Cost of sales	30,47	3,97	0,00
Gross profit	15,56	17,41	0,00
Investment income	59,09	10,00	0,00
Expenses	(4,24)	37,14	0,00
Operating expenses	(31,08)	71,04	0,00
Depreciation	92,50	(20,00)	0,00
Interest expense	69,77	0,00	0,00
Profit before taxation	241,03	(58,86)	0,00
Taxation	226,67	(56,90)	0,00
Profit for the period	250,00	(60,00)	0,00

COMPARATIVE STATEMENT OF FINANCIAL POSITION ITEMS

	20X6	20X5	20X4
Capital and reserves	55,39	1,01	0,00
Non-current liabilities	45,71	0,00	0,00
Current liabilities	(54,19)	132,47	0,00
Property, plant and equipment	92,50	(20,00)	0,00
Investments	50,00	0,00	0,00
Current assets	(16,46)	67,21	0,00
Inventory	(30,93)	101,71	0,00
Accounts receivable	(35,03)	108,24	0,00

22.4 Ratio analysis

The financial statements of a business entity provide information which is used by investors, lenders, management and suppliers. The information is used to evaluate the performance and financial position of the business entity and the efficiency of management. Individual items in financial statements do not provide meaningful information when viewed in isolation. Ratios are therefore used to summarise financial data and to monitor trends in performance and deviations from past trends.[1] Ratios can also be used to evaluate the results of a business entity against the results of other business entities in the same industry.

You will notice that where the ratio incorporates an income statement amount in the numerator and a statement of financial position amount in the denominator, an average is used for the statement of financial position amount. Averages are used in an attempt to smooth out fluctuations between the current year and the prior year. However, it is important to note that the ratios can be satisfactorily calculated without the use of averages if prior year information is not available. The user then needs to take this into account when interpreting the ratios.

We shall use the information in the DiGold Limited example to illustrate the calculation of each ratio we discuss.

22.4.1 Short-term liquidity

There are several ratios which are used to measure whether a business entity has sufficient liquid resources to enable it to meet its short-term liabilities. This is an issue which is important to a variety of users, including the following: suppliers who seek assurance that they will be paid within agreed time limits, lenders who seek assurance that they will receive interest and loan repayments when due to them, employees who seek assurance that they will receive their remuneration regularly and investors who do not wish to see their investment jeopardised by the business entity experiencing a cash crisis, which could ring the death knell for the entity.

Current ratio

The current ratio measures the ability of the current assets to meet existing current liabilities and is calculated as follows:

$$\frac{\text{Current assets}}{\text{Current liabilities}}$$

A business needs to balance its ability to meet its short-term liabilities with its need to minimise those current assets that generate a low return. A current ratio of 2:1 is generally regarded as acceptable, but this assumption can be challenged.

The adequacy of the current ratio depends on the nature of the business, the composition of the current assets and the turnover rate of its current assets. A business which operates in a service industry and does not need to keep large inventories may have a low current ratio, but may be able to meet its short-term liabilities. If the current assets comprise mostly cash and accounts receivable, the business will be in a stronger position to meet its short-term liabilities than if its current assets comprise mostly inventories, which may take some time to realise in cash.

The current ratio for DiGold Limited for the 20X6, 20X5 and 20X4 years is calculated as follows:

20X6	20X5	20X4
$\frac{3\ 450}{820}$	$\frac{4\ 130}{1\ 790}$	$\frac{2\ 470}{770}$
= 4,21	= 2,31	= 3,21

Acid test or quick ratio

The acid test or quick ratio is a refinement of the current ratio in that the value of inventory and pre-payments is excluded from the current assets. Inventory is excluded from the calculation as it is the least liquid component of current assets and may take some time to be realised in cash. Pre-payments are excluded as they represent expenditure paid in advance and cannot be realised in cash. An acid test ratio of 1:1 is normally regarded as acceptable, although many enterprises operate with a ratio of less than 1:1. A business where the majority of sales are for cash and which, as a result, has a low level of accounts receivable, will normally have an acid test ratio of less than 1:1. The ratio is calculated as follows:

$$\frac{\text{Current assets} - \text{inventory} - \text{prepayments}}{\text{Current liabilities}}$$

The current ratio for DiGold Limited for the 20X6, 20X5 and 20X4 years is calculated as follows:

20X6	20X5	20X4
$\frac{3\ 450 - 1\ 630}{820}$	$\frac{4\ 130 - 2\ 360}{1\ 790}$	$\frac{2\ 470 - 1\ 170}{770}$
= 2,22	= 0,99	= 1,69

Inventory turnover ratio

The inventory turnover ratio is used to measure the rate at which inventories move through and out of the entity, and is an indication of the efficiency with which the business manages its inventory levels and its sales of inventory. The ratio is calculated as follows:

$$\frac{\text{Cost of goods sold}}{\text{Average inventory}}$$

The average inventory is the average of the opening and closing inventory.

The inventory turnover ratio for a business entity needs to be compared over a period of time in order for the ratio to convey meaningful information. It can also be useful to compare the inventory turnover ratio of a business entity with those of other entities in the same industry.

A high inventory turnover ratio can indicate efficient inventory management, but a ratio that is too high can also be indicative of inventory holdings which are too low. Low levels of inventories could lead to the business entity losing sales if particular inventory items are not available to meet customer demand. An inventory turn-over ratio that is low could be indicative of the entity holding excessive levels of inventory as a result of poor sales, or purchases of inventory for which there is little customer demand. However, it could also result from increasing levels of inventory in anticipation of increased customer demand or in anticipation of interruptions in normal supplies of inventory. It is therefore important for the analyst to explore the underlying causes of an inventory turnover ratio that is out of line.[2]

The inventory turnover ratio for DiGold Limited for the 20X6, 20X5 and 20X4 years is calculated as follows:

20X6	**20X5**	**20X4**
$\frac{7\ 280}{(1\ 630 + 2\ 360)/2}$	$\frac{5\ 580}{(2\ 360 + 1\ 170)/2}$	$\frac{5\ 367}{(1\ 170 + 735)/2}$
= 3,65	= 3,16	= 5,63

Inventory holding period

The inventory holding period is measured as follows:

$$\frac{365}{\text{Inventory turnover ratio}}$$

This calculation measures the number of days it will take to sell the average inventory in a given year. Looked at differently, it measures the average age of the inventory.

The following calculation shows the number of days it will take to sell the closing inventory.

$$\frac{365}{\text{Cost of goods sold/Closing inventory}} = 365 \times \frac{\text{Closing inventory}}{\text{Cost of goods sold}}$$

The inventory holding period for DiGold Limited for the 20X6, 20X5 and 20X4 years is calculated as follows:

20X6	20X5	20X4
$\frac{365}{3,65}$	$\frac{365}{3,16}$	$\frac{365}{5,63}$
= 100 days	= 116 days	= 65 days

The number of days it will take for DiGold Limited to sell its closing inventory for the 20X6, 20X5 and 20X4 years is calculated as follows:

20X6	20X5	20X4
$\frac{365 \text{ X } 1\ 630}{7\ 280}$	$\frac{365 \text{ X } 2\ 360}{5\ 580}$	$\frac{365 \text{ X } 1\ 170}{5\ 367}$
= 82 days	= 154 days	= 80 days

Accounts receivable turnover ratio

The accounts receivable turnover ratio is used to indicate how many times the average accounts receivable is generated or collected during the year. The ratio is calculated as follows:

$$\frac{\text{Net sales on credit}}{\text{Average accounts receivable}}$$

A high accounts receivable turnover ratio indicates that the collection of accounts receivable is being handled efficiently. On the other hand, it may be indicative of a credit policy which is too restrictive and which could be costing the business entity lost sales opportunities.

Most entities do not provide a breakdown between cash and credit sales on the income statement. It is therefore necessary to use the total sales amount and, depending on the estimated level of credit sales, appreciate that the ratio will be overstated.

The accounts receivable turnover ratio for DiGold Limited for the 20X6, 20X5 and 20X4 years is calculated as follows:

20X6	**20X5**	**20X4**
$\frac{10\ 920}{(1\ 150 + 1\ 770)/2}$	$\frac{8\ 730}{(1\ 770 + 850)/2}$	$\frac{8\ 050}{(850 + 760)/2}$
= 7,48	= 6,66	= 10,00

Collection period for accounts receivable

The collection period for accounts receivable is used to measure the number of days it takes, on average, to collect the accounts receivable. It is therefore a measure of the efficiency of the business enterprise in assessing credit risk when granting credit and in collecting its accounts receivable. The ratio is calculated as follows:

$$\frac{365}{\text{Accounts receivable turnover ratio}}$$

The collection period calculated should be compared with the terms of the credit policy of the business entity. If the collection period is higher than the policy allows, there may be problems with the collection process or there may be potential bad debts which may prove to be irrecoverable. On the other hand, a low collection period may indicate a credit policy which is too restrictive and which is costing the business entity lost sales opportunities.[3]

The collection period for accounts receivable for DiGold Limited for the 20X6, 20X5 and 20X4 years is calculated as follows:

20X6	**20X5**	**20X4**
$\frac{365}{7,48}$	$\frac{365}{6,66}$	$\frac{365}{10,00}$
= 49 days	= 55 days	= 37 days

Valuable information regarding the accounts receivable of the business entity can also be gained from an age analysis of the accounts receivable, in which outstanding amounts are aged, and shown as current, 30 days, 60 days, 90 days and 120 days and over. Such age analyses are extensively used by credit controllers.[4]

Accounts payable turnover ratio

The accounts payable turnover ratio is used to indicate how many times the average accounts payable is generated or paid during the year. The ratio is calculated as follows:

$$\frac{\text{Net purchases on credit}}{\text{Average accounts payable}}$$

The accounts payable turnover ratio for DiGold Limited for the 20X6, 20X5 and 20X4 years is calculated as follows:

20X6	20X5	20X4
$\frac{7\,280 + 1\,630 - 2\,360}{(550 + 1\,460)/2}$	$\frac{5\,580 + 2\,360 - 1\,170}{(1\,460 + 720)/2}$	$\frac{5\,367 + 1\,170 - 735}{(720 + 612)/2}$
= 6,52	= 6,21	= 8,71

Payment period for accounts payable

The payment period for accounts payable is used to measure the number of days it takes, on average, to pay the accounts payable. It is calculated as follows:

$$\frac{365}{\text{Accounts payable turnover ratio}}$$

It may seem beneficial if this ratio is high, indicating that the business entity is not paying out its cash resources too hastily. However, this must be balanced against the cost of losing early settlement discounts or even of having suppliers withdraw credit facilities to the business entity if normal settlement terms are not complied with.

The period it takes for DiGold Limited to pay its accounts payable for the 20X6, 20X5 and 20X4 years is calculated as follows:

20X6	20X5	20X4
$\frac{365}{6{,}52}$	$\frac{365}{6{,}21}$	$\frac{365}{8{,}71}$
= 56 days	= 59 days	= 42 days

22.4.2 Capital structure and long-term solvency

When assessing the capital structure and prospects for the long-term solvency of a business entity, we need to consider the level of debt in relation to the equity invested by the owners of the business entity, and also the ability of the business entity to service its debt. If the rate of return on the assets of the business is greater than the cost of debt, it is an advantage for the business entity to be funded by as much debt as possible, in order to maximise returns to investors. This must, however, be balanced with the inherent risk of being funded by debt rather than by equity. If a business entity is unable to service its debt or to repay amounts when due, it runs a real risk of being placed in liquidation.

A greater proportion of debt funding than equity funding can also be regarded by potential suppliers and lenders as a lack of commitment on the part of the owners of the business entity. It must be remembered that the equity funding provided by the owners of a business entity provides a margin of safety for the suppliers of, and lenders to, the business entity.[5]

The terms 'gearing' and 'leverage' refer to the use of debt in the capital structure of the business entity.

Debt and equity ratios

These ratios measure the relative contributions of equity and debt to the total funding of the entity and are measured in the following ways:

$$\text{Debt ratio} = \frac{\text{Total liabilities}}{\text{Total assets}}$$

$$\text{Equity rate} = \frac{\text{Total equity}}{\text{Total assets}}$$

$$\text{Debt equity ratio} = \frac{\text{Total debt}}{\text{Total equity}}$$

The sum of the first two ratios must equal one.

The debt ratio measures the extent of debt financing. If the extent of debt financing is too high, the business entity is at risk of not being able to meet its commitments. If the extent of debt financing is too low, the business entity may be losing opportunities to increase the return to the owners (through gearing or leverage) by taking advantage of a cost of debt that is less than the rate of return earned on the assets of the business entity.

The debt ratio for DiGold Limited for the 20X6, 20X5 and 20X4 years is calculated as follows:

20X6	**20X5**	**20X4**
$\frac{2\,550 + 820}{6\,120 + 3\,450}$	$\frac{1\,750 + 1\,790}{3\,400 + 4\,130}$	$\frac{1\,750 + 770}{4\,000 + 2\,470}$
= 0,35	= 0,47	= 0,39

The equity ratio for DiGold Limited for the 20X6, 20X5 and 20X4 years is calculated as follows:

20X6	**20X5**	**20X4**
$\frac{6\,200}{6\,120 + 3\,450}$	$\frac{3\,990}{3\,400 + 4\,130}$	$\frac{3\,950}{4\,000 + 2\,470}$
= 0,65	= 0,53	= 0,61

The debt : equity ratio for DiGold Limited for the 20X6, 20X5 and 20X4 years is calculated as follows:

20X6	**20X5**	**20X4**
$\frac{2\,550 + 820}{6\,200}$	$\frac{1\,750 + 1\,790}{3\,990}$	$\frac{1\,750 + 770}{3\,950}$
= 0,54	= 0,89	= 0,64

Interest cover ratio

The interest cover ratio measures the ability of the business entity to meet its interest charges. It is calculated as follows:

$$\frac{\text{Profit before tax and interest expense}}{\text{Interest expense}}$$

The higher the interest cover ratio, the better it is for investors in the business entity. This is because the business entity is at less risk of being unable to make its interest payments when due.

The interest cover ratio for DiGold Limited for the 20X6, 20X5 and 20X4 years is calculated as follows:

20X6	**20X5**	**20X4**
$\frac{665 + 365}{365}$	$\frac{195 + 215}{215}$	$\frac{474 + 215}{215}$
= 2,82	= 1,91	= 3,20

22.4.3 Operating efficiency and profitability

We are now going to consider several ratios which measure operating efficiency and profitability. These ratios can be based on either sales or investment.

Profit-margin ratios

Mark-up percentage

The mark-up percentage is used to compare the gross profit margin earned on goods sold with the mark-up used by the business entity. It is calculated as follows:

$$\frac{\text{Gross profit}}{\text{Cost of goods sold}} \times \frac{100}{1}$$

The mark-up percentage for DiGold Limited for the 20X6, 20X5 and 20X4 years is calculated as follows:

20X6	20X5	20X4
$\frac{3\,640 \times 100}{7\,280}$	$\frac{3\,150 \times 100}{5\,580}$	$\frac{2\,683 \times 100}{5\,367}$
= 50%	= 56,45%	= 50%

Gross profit percentage

The gross profit percentage measures the ability of the business entity to earn a gross profit from sales. It also represents how much of each sales rand is left over after paying for the cost of the goods sold.[6] The gross profit percentage is an indication of the efficiency of the management of the business entity in (a) controlling the costs of its inventory (which may be either purchased inventory or manufactured inventory), and (b) in recovering increased costs through its sales.[7] The gross profit percentage is calculated as follows:

$$\frac{\text{Gross profit}}{\text{Sales}} \times \frac{100}{1}$$

The gross profit percentage for DiGold Limited for the 20X6, 20X5 and 20X4 years is calculated as follows:

20X6	20X5	20X4
$\frac{3\ 640 \times 100}{10\ 920}$	$\frac{3\ 150 \times 100}{8\ 730}$	$\frac{2\ 683 \times 100}{8\ 050}$
= 33,33%	= 36,08%	= 33,33%

Profit percentage

The profit percentage measures the ability of the business entity to earn a profit from sales. It represents how much of each sales rand is left over after accounting for all expenses incurred in earning the profit during the year, and after accounting for the taxes due on the profit for the year. The ratio is calculated as follows:

$$\frac{\text{Profit after tax}}{\text{Sales}} \times \frac{100}{1}$$

The profit percentage for DiGold Limited for the 20X6, 20X5 and 20X4 years is calculated as follows:

20X6	20X5	20X4
$\frac{420 \times 100}{10\ 920}$	$\frac{120 \times 100}{8\ 730}$	$\frac{300 \times 100}{8\ 050}$
= 3,85%	= 1,37%	= 3,73%

Total asset turnover ratio

The relationship of sales to total assets is a measure of asset utilisation, and is a means of determining how effectively the assets are utilised in terms of sales generated. The ratio is calculated as follows:

$$\frac{\text{Sales}}{\text{Average total assets}}$$

Generally a high asset turnover ratio is an indication of effective asset utilisation. A low ratio may be indicative of an excessive investment in assets, or of poor sales, but there may be an acceptable reason for the low ratio, for example, a major new investment in assets just before the end of the year. In such a situation it is preferable to base the ratio on the weighted average of the total assets, if this information is available to the user who is preparing the analysis.

The total asset turnover ratio for DiGold Limited for the 20X6, 20X5 and 20X4 years is calculated as follows:

20X6	**20X5**	**20X4**
$\frac{10\ 920}{(9\ 570 + 7\ 530)/2}$	$\frac{8\ 730}{(7\ 530 + 6\ 470)/2}$	$\frac{8\ 050}{(6\ 470 + 5\ 850)/2}$
= 1,28	= 1,25	= 1,31

Return on total assets ratio

The return on total assets ratio (often referred to as the return on investment or ROI ratio), is used to assess the relationship between profit after tax and the resources invested in the business entity to generate that profit. The profit is adjusted to a 'before interest amount' in order to assess the return irrespective of the source of finance. The calculated return can then be compared by the user with the returns available on alternate investments. The ratio is calculated as follows:

$$\frac{\text{Profit after tax + interest expense (1 – tax rate)}}{\text{Average total assets}} \times \frac{100}{1}$$

The return on total assets ratio measures the efficiency with which the assets of the business entity are managed in order to generate a return on those assets.[8]

The return on total assets ratio for DiGold Limited for the 20X6, 20X5 and 20X4 years is calculated as follows:

20X6	**20X5**	**20X4**
$\frac{(420 + 365 \times 0{,}72) \times 100}{8\ 550}$	$\frac{(120 + 215 \times 0{,}72) \times 100}{7\ 000}$	$\frac{(300 + 215 \times 0{,}72) \times 100}{6\ 160}$
= 7,99%	= 3,93%	= 7,38%

Return on ordinary shareholders' equity ratio

The return on ordinary shareholders' equity ratio, or ROE ratio, measures the percentage of profit after tax and preference dividends which is available to ordinary shareholders. In other words, the return to ordinary share-holders. The profit after tax (which, by implication, is after interest) is used, as the return to ordinary shareholders can only be assessed after taking into account interest on debt. The ratio is calculated as follows:

$$\frac{\text{Profit after tax} - \text{preference dividend}}{\text{Average ordinary shareholders' equity}} \times \frac{100}{1}$$

The return on ordinary shareholders' equity for DiGold Limited for the 20X6, 20X5 and 20X4 years is calculated as follows:

20X6	20X5	20X4
$\frac{(420 - 60) \times 100}{(5\ 700 + 3\ 490)/2}$	$\frac{(120 - 60) \times 100}{(3\ 490 + 3\ 450)/2}$	$\frac{(300 - 60) \times 100}{(3\ 450 + 3\ 310)/2}$
= 7,83%	= 1,73%	= 7,10%

Earnings per share

The earnings per share measures the amount of profit after tax and preference dividends attributable to each ordinary share issued by a company. It is calculated as follows:

$$\frac{\text{Profit after tax} - \text{preference dividend}}{\text{Number of ordinary shares issued}}$$

The earnings per share ratio enables a user to compare the earnings of different sized companies. A comparison of the profit after tax and preference dividends of different companies will be less meaningful than a comparison of the earnings per share, as the number of shares issued by each company may differ substantially. The earnings per share ratios provide a common denominator by which the investment returns on different investments can be measured.[9]

The earnings per share for DiGold Limited for the 20X6, 20X5 and 20X4 years is calculated as follows:

20X6	20X5	20X4
$\frac{420 - 60}{1\ 500}$	$\frac{120 - 60}{1\ 000}$	$\frac{300 - 60}{1\ 000}$
= 24c	= 6c	= 24c

Dividends per share

The dividends per share measures the amount of dividends attributable to each ordinary share issued by a company. It is calculated as follows:

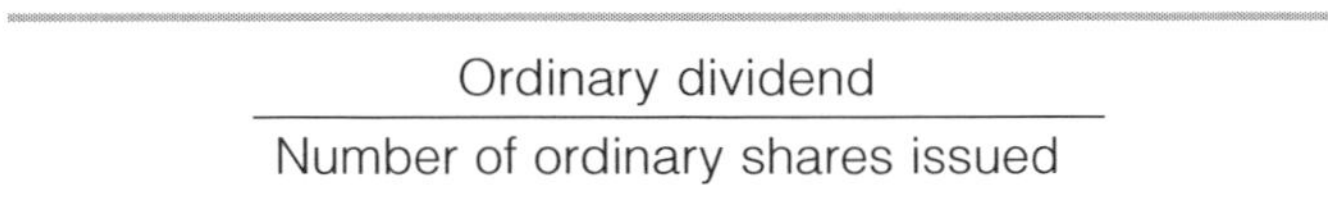

$$\frac{\text{Ordinary dividend}}{\text{Number of ordinary shares issued}}$$

The dividends per share for DiGold Limited for the 20X6, 20X5 and 20X4 years is calculated as follows:

20X6	**20X5**	**20X4**
$\frac{150}{1\,500}$	$\frac{20}{1\,000}$	$\frac{100}{1\,000}$
= 10c	= 2c	= 10c

22.4.4 Market measures

None of the operating efficiency or profitability ratios which we have considered is based on the amount which an investor pays for shares in a company. When making investment decisions it is important to measure performance against the cost, or against the value, of the investment. In the case of shares which are listed on a stock exchange, the investor needs to measure performance against the market value of the shares. We shall now look at various ratios which relate profitability to the market price of listed shares. As the market price fluctuates, so do the value of these ratios, which are often reported in the financial press alongside share prices.

Earnings yield

The earnings yield measures the earnings of the company in relation to its market value. It is calculated as follows:

$$\frac{\text{Earnings per share}}{\text{Current market price per share}} \times \frac{100}{1}$$

The average earnings yield for the JSE All Share Index at the end of 2008 was 10,8%.

The earnings yield for DiGold Limited, calculated using the market price at the end of the 20X6, 20X5 and 20X4 years is as follows:

20X6	20X5	20X4
$\frac{24c \times 100}{550c}$	$\frac{6c \times 100}{390c}$	$\frac{24c \times 100}{450c}$
= 4,36%	= 1,54%	= 5,33%

Price earnings ratio

The price earnings ratio, or P/E ratio, compares the market price of the share with the earnings per share, and is the reciprocal of the earnings yield. It is calculated as follows:

$$\frac{\text{Current market price per share at the end of the year}}{\text{Earnings per share}}$$

The price earnings ratio can be interpreted as being an indication of the number of years of earnings investors are buying. It provides a common point of reference for comparing one share with another, with the section in which that share is listed, and with the stock market as a whole. In addition, the P/E ratio serves as a yardstick, since it enables direct comparisons to be made between companies with high share prices and low share prices, and between shares with high earnings and low earnings.[10]

By comparing the price earnings ratios of different companies, investors are able to compare the performance of companies of different sizes, with substantially different numbers of shares issued. A high price earnings ratio is an indication of a fast-growing, popular company, whereas a low ratio is an indication of a slower growing, more established company.

The price earnings ratio is more useful as an indication of performance than the dividend yield, as it considers the total earnings of the company rather than just the amount which the directors have decided to distribute as dividends.

The average price earnings ratio for the JSE All Share Index at the end of 2008 was 9,2.

The price earnings ratio for DiGold Limited, calculated using the market price at the end of the 20X6, 20X5 and 20X4 years is as follows:

20X6	20X5	20X4
$\frac{550c}{24c}$	$\frac{390c}{6c}$	$\frac{450c}{24c}$
= 22,92	= 65,00	= 18,75

Dividend yield

The dividend yield measures the return in cash, by way of dividends, that investors can expect to receive on their investment. It is calculated as follows:

$$\frac{\text{Dividends per share}}{\text{Current market price per share at the end of the year}} \times \frac{100}{1}$$

While it does indicate to investors the return on their shares (which they receive in cash), it ignores earnings which have been retained in the company. This information could have a major impact on future earnings if returns were wisely re-invested to fund future expansion and replacement of assets.

The average dividend yield for the JSE All Share Index at the end of 2008 was 4,5%.

The dividend yield for DiGold Limited, calculated using the market price at the end of 20X6, 20X5 and 20X4 years is calculated as follows:

20X6	**20X5**	**20X4**
$\frac{10c \times 100}{550c}$	$\frac{2c \times 100}{390c}$	$\frac{10c \times 100}{450c}$
= 1,82%	= 0,51%	= 2,22%

Summary of ratios for DiGold Limited

	20X6	**20X5**	**20X4**
Short-term liquidity			
Current ratio	4,21	2,31	3,21
Acid test (Quick ratio)	2,22	0,99	1,69
Inventory turnover	3,65	3,16	5,63
Inventory holding-period (days)	100	116	65
Days to sell closing inventory (days)	82	154	80
Accounts receivable turnover	7,48	6,66	10,00
Collection period for accounts receivable (days)	49	55	37
Accounts payable turnover	6,52	6,21	8,71
Payment period for accounts payable (days)	56	59	42

	20X6	20X5	20X4
Capital structure and long-term solvency			
Debt ratio	0,35	0,47	0,39
Equity ratio	0,65	0,53	0,61
Debt: Equity ratio	0,54	0,89	0,64
Interest cover	2,82	1,91	3,20

	20X6	20X5	20X4
Operating efficiency and profitability			
Mark up %	50,00%	56,45%	50,00%
Gross profit %	33,33%	36,08%	33,33%
Net profit %	3,85%	1,37%	3,73%
Total asset turnover	1,28	1,25	1,31
Return on total assets	7,99%	3,93%	7,38%
Return on ordinary shareholders' equity	7,83%	1,73%	7,10%
Earnings per share	24c	6c	24c
Dividends per share	10c	2c	10c

	20X6	20X5	20X4
Market measures			
Earnings yield	4,36%	1,54%	5,33%
Price earnings ratio	22,92	65,00	18,75
Dividend yield	1,82%	0,51%	2,22%

22.5 Exam example

The Wits Finance Company is attempting to evaluate an applicant, Opium Ltd, for a short-term loan. The following table presents information concerning Opium Ltd and the corresponding industry average.

	Opium Ltd 31/12/X5	Industry Average 31/12/X5
	R 000's	R 000's
Cash	4 000	12 000
Short-term investments	5 000	8 000
Accounts receivable	58 000	72 000
Pre-payments	9 000	7 000
Closing inventory	72 000	96 000
Opening inventory	64 000	92 000
Accounts payable	36 000	50 000
Other current liabilities	22 000	30 000
Sales (all credit)	420 000	660 000
Cost of sales	320 000	500 000

You are required to:

(a) calculate the following ratios for both Opium Ltd and for the industry average:
   (i) current ratio
   (ii) quick ratio
   (iii) average number of days to collect accounts receivable
   (iv) inventory holding-period
   (v) average number of days taken to pay accounts payable

(b) consider the information provided and your calculations in part (a), and prepare a report for Wits's loan officer (Ms Nisbet), outlining those factors which might be useful to her in making her decision

(c) state what limitations you see in your analysis and what additional information might be helpful to the loan officer in making her decision.

Solution: Exam example

(a)

		Calculation	Ratio
(i)	***Current ratio*** Opium Ltd	$\frac{4\,000 + 5\,000 + 58\,000 + 9\,000 + 72\,000}{36\,000 + 22\,000}$	2,56
	Industry average	$\frac{12\,000 + 8\,000 + 72\,000 + 7\,000 + 96\,000}{50\,000 + 30\,000}$	2,44
(ii)	***Quick ratio*** Opium Ltd	$\frac{4\,000 + 5\,000 + 58\,000}{36\,000 + 22\,000}$	1,16
	Industry average	$\frac{12\,000 + 8\,000 + 72\,000}{50\,000 + 30\,000}$	1,15

(iii)	***Days outstanding in accounts receivable***		
	Opium Ltd	58 000 x 365 / 420 000	50 days
	Industry average	72 000 x 365 / 660 000	40 days
(iv)	***Inventory holding period***		
	Opium Ltd	72 000 + 64 000)/2 x 365 / 320 000	78 days
	Industry average	(96 000 + 92 000)/2 x 365 / 50 000	69 days
(v)	***Days outstanding in accounts payable***		
	Opium Ltd	36 000 x 365 / 320 000	41 days
	Industry average	50 000 x 365 / 50 000	37 days

(b)

Report on the short-term loan application of Opium Ltd

To: Ms Nisbet
From: Student
Date: 25 October 20X5

Based on the information provided, Opium Limited has been analysed on the following ratios in relation to the industry average:
(i) Current ratio
(ii) Quick ratio
(iii) Average number of days to collect accounts receivable
(iv) Inventory holding-period
(v) Average number of days taken to pay accounts payable

(i) Current ratio

The current ratio measures the company's ability to meet existing current liabilities.

Opium Limited has a ratio of 2,55 in comparison to the industry average of 2,44. This indicates that Opium Ltd is more liquid than the industry average.

(ii) Quick ratio

The quick ratio measures the company's ability to meet existing current liabilities by excluding inventory from the current ratio in its calculation, as this is the least liquid current asset. Opium Limited has a ratio of 1,16 in comparison to the industry average of 1,15.

The industry average for this ratio is similar to that of Opium Ltd, which indicates that Opium Ltd is not as liquid once inventory is excluded.

(iii) Average number of days to collect accounts receivable

This ratio measures the number of days it takes to collect the accounts receivable.

Opium Limited takes 50 days to collect their accounts receivable in comparison to the industry average of 40 days.

Opium Ltd is taking longer to collect its accounts receivable. In comparison to the industry average their collectability of accounts receivable seems to be a higher risk. I would question if the provision for doubtful debts is sufficient in this instance.

(iv) Inventory holding period

This ratio measures the number of days it takes to sell the average inventory in a given year. Opium Limited takes 78 days to sell their inventory in comparison to the industry average of 69 days.

Opium Ltd is taking longer to sell their inventory. This indicates that they are holding more inventory than the industry average. Opium Ltd's inventory-holding policy is more risky than the industry average since there is a greater chance of inventory becoming obsolete and unsaleable.

(v) Average number of days taken to pay accounts payable

This ratio measures the number of days it takes to pay the accounts payable.

Opium Limited takes 41 days to pay their accounts payable in comparison to the industry average of 37 days.

Opium Ltd is taking longer to pay their accounts payable. This indicates that they are not as liquid as the industry average since they have to extend their repayments to 41,06 days.

General

Even though Opium Ltd has a better current ratio than the industry average, the other ratios indicate that the company is not as liquid as the rest of the companies in the industry.

The current assets do not appear to be as liquid as the industry average. There is a greater risk that the accounts receivable will not be collected and that inventory is not saleable. As a result, Opium Ltd does not have the cash available to pay suppliers on time.

(c)

Limitations

- Need to compare Opium Ltd's results to previous periods.
- Ratios are calculated from historic cost, therefore not a good predictor for future performance.
- The industry accounting policies may not be the same as those applied by Opium Ltd (for example, inventory costing – LIFO vs FIFO).

Additional information

- Detailed income statement, statement of financial position and cash flow statement.
- Profitability ratios, e.g. GP%, return on total assets, return on equity, earnings per share
- Gearing ratios (long-term solvency), e.g. debt and equity ratios, interest cover.
- Knowledge of the industry in which Opium operates.
- Knowledge of Opium Ltd's operations, e.g. terms granted to customers, terms negotiated with suppliers, inventory-holding policies – in order to understand why the ratios differ from those of the industry.
- Changes in the business over the past period in comparison to prior periods.
- Plans for the future.
- Length of time in operation.

Summary of concepts and applications

1. Financial statement analysis may be used to predict future events, based on the past performance of the enterprise and its financial position at a particular point in time. The specific objectives of users depend on the use to which the user wishes to put information gathered from financial statements.

2. An entity is affected by a variety of external influences (for example, the state of the general economy and of the enterprise's industry) that ought to be considered when performing financial statement analysis.

3. Common-size financial statements firstly facilitate comparisons of different enterprises by revealing relationships between the various components of the financial statements and, secondly, they enable the performance of a trend analysis for a single enterprise. Comparative financial statements show the financial statements for each of the required number of years; consequently, the change in an individual item from year to year is highlighted.

4. Ratios are used in financial statement analysis to summarise financial data, monitor trends in performance and deviations from past trends, and evaluate the results of different enterprises operating in the same industries. Ratios used in ratio analysis provide an indication of the following with regard to an enterprise: short-term liquidity, capital structure and long-term solvency, operating efficiency and profitability, and market measures.

Notes

1. Bradshaw, J. and Brooks, M., *Business Accounting & Finance For Managers And Business Students*, Cape Town: Juta, (1996), p. 113.
2. Fraser, L. M. *Understanding Financial Statements*, Englewood Cliffs: Prentice-Hall, (1995), p. 153.
3. Bradshaw, J. and Brooks, M., (1996), p. 122.
4. Bradshaw, J. and Brooks, M., (1996), p. 122.
5. Bradshaw, J. and Brooks, M., (1996), p. 118.
6. Bradshaw, J. and Brooks, M., (1996), p. 123.
7. Fraser, L. M. (1995), p. 156.
8. Fraser, L. M. (1995), p. 157.
9. Fraser, L. M. (1995), p. 169.
10. Spira, J. and Matsheru, M., (1994). *Your Guide to Making Money on the Stock Exchange*, Johannesburg: Authors, p. 34.

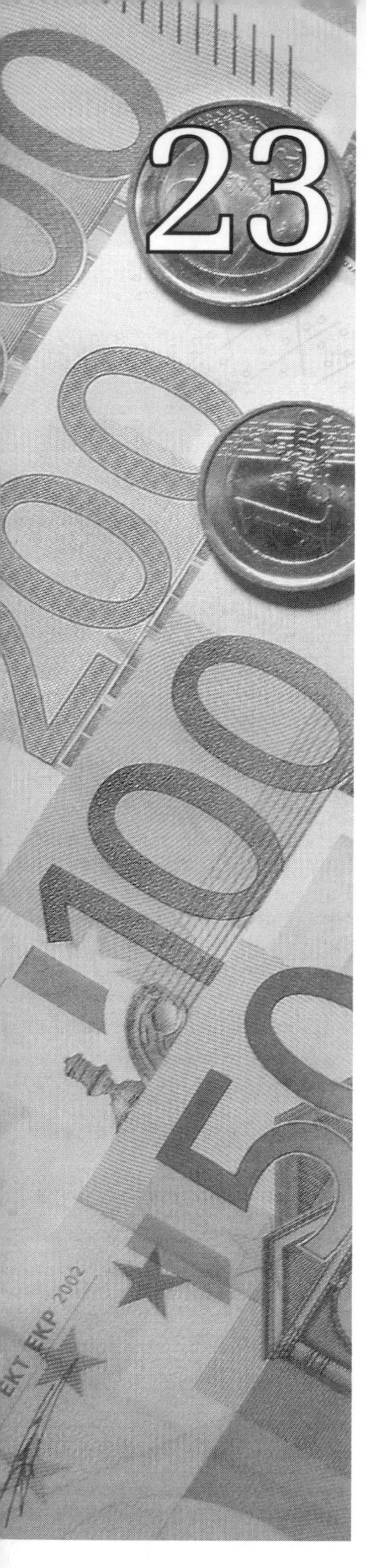

Accounting for Non-business Entities

'Recreations: reading who dunnits and balance sheets, light music'
(Lord Thomson of Fleet, 1972)

Outcomes

- Describe the characteristics of a non-business entity.
- Recall the sources of finance available to a non-business entity.
- Produce financial information for a non-business entity.

Chapter outline

Not all entities are established with the intention of profit. Many exist for the purpose of the furtherance of their concerned cause. Such entities include societies, clubs and public benefit organisations (PBO). Since they do exist to make a profit, the more traditional aspects of accounting, such as profit and loss, cannot be applied. The purpose of this chapter is to introduce the appropriate accounting methods for non-business entities.

23.1 Characteristics of a non-business entity

The primary focus of this text has been on the accounting and reporting requirements of business entities whose main objective is to earn profits. However, organisations exist whose primary objective is to provide services to their members. Examples of such organisations are sport and social clubs, welfare organisations and religious organisations. These types of organisation are known as non-profit or non-business entities.

The members of a non-business entity are not owners of the entity, and therefore do not expect to receive any distribution, either on an annual basis or on termination of the entity's activities.

A non-business entity does not exist to make a profit. However, in order to provide the service to members for which it was established, it needs to generate sufficient income to cover expenditure incurred. Income earned in excess of expenditure is regarded as a ***surplus*** and not as a profit. Similarly expenditure incurred in excess of income earned is described as a ***deficit*** and not a loss. Accordingly, the profit and loss account is referred to as an income and expenditure account and the income statement as an ***income and expenditure statement***.

The accounting records of a non-business entity are the same as those maintained by a business entity, except for specific requirements relating to the accounting for funds. Fund accounting is an important aspect of the reporting for a non-business entity because it provides control over the resources of the entity entrusted to management. It will be described in the following section.

Management of a non-business entity is entrusted to persons appointed by the members. For smaller entities such as a suburban tennis or bowls club, management is normally the responsibility of a committee comprising members of the club who provide their services on a voluntary basis. Larger clubs such as the country clubs which provide a range of sporting activities including golf, cricket, tennis and bowls and have facilities such as a restaurant, bar and a swimming pool operate with full-time managers and staff who are paid employees of the entity.

Non-business entities are not constrained by the requirements of International Financial Reporting Standards. We will therefore refer, in this chapter, to a balance sheet and, as seen above, to an income and expenditure account and not to the new terminology of IAS 1.

23.2 Sources of finance for a non-business entity

To understand the accounting implications relating to the sources of finance for a non-business entity, it is necessary to examine the accounting equation in a non-business entity.

A non-business entity does not have capital contributed by owners in the same way as a business entity does. Instead, it has an ***accumulated fund*** represented by entrance fees paid by members, the surplus retained from the entity's activities and *discretionary* donations or legacies. In addition to the accumulated fund, a non-business entity may also have a number of ***special funds***, established from *non-discretionary* legacies or donations. The accounting for the accumulated fund and the the special funds will be described in the paragraphs that follow. A non-business entity may also borrow funds from a financial institution. We can therefore restate the accounting equation for a non-business entity as follows:

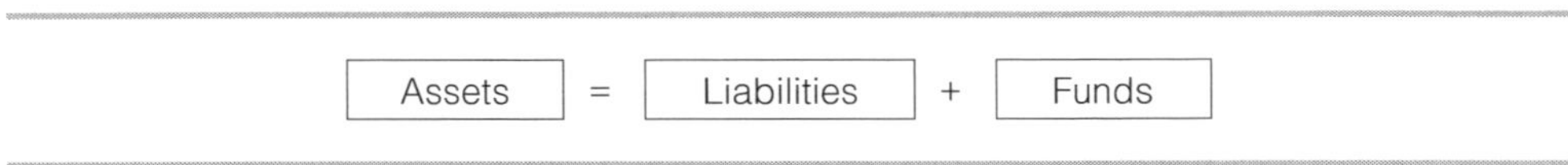

Diagram 23.1: Accounting equation for a non-business entity

23.2.1 Funds

As mentioned above, a non-business entity can have two types of funds, the accumulated fund and special funds.

Accumulated funds

The accumulated fund is equivalent to the capital of a business entity and comprises the entrance fees paid by members, the surplus retained from activities as well as discretionary donations. These aspects are discussed below.

Members of a non-business entity pay **entrance fees** when joining a club or association. As this is a single amount paid when joining and is non-recurring, entrance fees received are credited directly to the accumulated fund and do not comprise income earned during a period. This is similar in concept to capital invested by owners of a business entity, which is credited to owner's equity.

The **surplus retained** in a non-business entity is similar in concept to the profits retained in a business entity. However, a non-business entity is exempt from the payment of tax and does not distribute any amounts to members. The cumulative excess of income over expenditure therefore represents the surplus retained in a non-business entity and it is used to maintain and expand the services and facilities offered to members.

Discretionary donations refer to legacies or donations received where there is *no stipulation* on the use of the funds. These amounts are not regular sources of income and therefore should also be credited directly to the accumulated fund rather than included as part of income for the period.

Special funds

Special funds are accounted for separately from the accumulated fund. They arise from **non-discretionary** legacies or donations to a club or institution. These legacies or donations *stipulate* the use of the capital amount and any income earned from the possible investment of the capital amount. The terms of the legacy or donation could stipulate that:

- the capital amount is to be used to purchase or construct a specific asset

- the capital sum is to remain intact and that the income from the fund be used either for:
  - a specific expense, for example, coaching fees for the first team of a football club or a bursary to a student of an educational institution
  - general expenses.

We can summarise the funds of a non-business entity as shown in diagram 23.2.

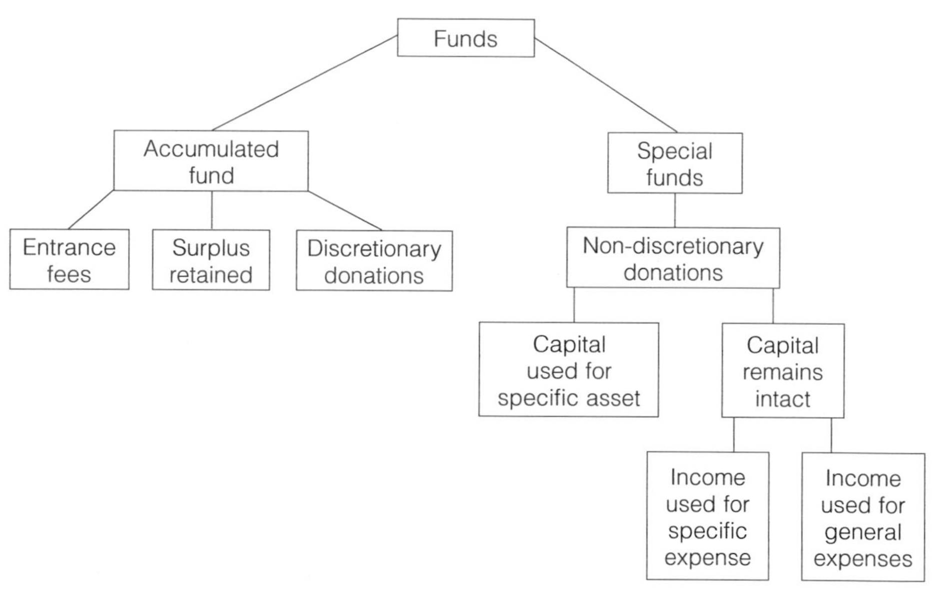

Diagram 23.2: Funds in a non-business entity

Example: Funds

During 20X5, Simon Smart joined the Cassey Country Club with the intention of socialising with potential customers. The Cassey Country Club received the following legacies and donation during the 20X5 year:

(1) R150 000 from the estate of P Fost on 2 January 20X5. The terms of the legacy stipulated that the capital sum should remain intact and be invested. The interest earned can be used to pay for coaching fees. On 2 January 20X5 the funds were invested in a fixed deposit at 18% p.a. During the sports club's financial year, ended 31 December 20X5, the club paid coaching fees of R35 000.

(2) R100 000 from the estate of J Daniels on 4 April 20X5. The terms of the legacy stipulated that the amount should be used to build new tennis courts. The tennis courts were completed on 15 September 20X5 at a cost of R100 000 and the estate paid the money over to the club. The contractor was paid by the club on 17 September 20X5.

(3) R200 000 donation from D Simpson, a well-known philanthropist, on 1 January 20X5. The terms of the donation stipulated that the capital sum should remain intact and be invested.

The interest earned could be used to pay for the general expenses to run the club. On 2 January 20X5 the funds were invested in a fixed deposit at 18% p.a.

Additional information

- Subscriptions earned and received, R250 000
- Other expenses incurred and paid, R258 000
- Accumulated fund balance at beginning of year, R14 000
- Bank balance at beginning of year, R14 000

You are required to:

(a) record the above transactions in the ledger of the Cassey Country Club.
(b) indicate how the legacies and the fund investments will be reported on the balance sheet of the club at 31 December 20X5.

Solution: Funds

(a)

Fost fund

Details	R	Details	R
Coaching fees	27 000	Bank	150 000
Balance c/d	150 000	Interest	27 000
	177 000		177 000
		Balance b/d	150 000

Fost investment

Details	R	Details	R
Bank	150 000		
		Balance c/d	150 000
	150 000		150 000
Balance b/d	150 000		

Daniels fund

Details	R	Details	R
		Bank	100 000
Balance c/d	100 000		
	100 000		100 000
		Balance b/d	100 000

Tennis courts

Details	R	Details	R
Bank	100 000		
		Balance c/d	100 000
	100 000		100 000
Balance b/d	100 000		

Simpson fund

Details	R	Details	R
		Bank	200 000
Balance c/d	200 000		
	200 000		200 000
		Balance b/d	200 000

Simpson investment

Details	R	Details	R
Bank	200 000		
		Balance c/d	200 000
	200 000		200 000
Balance b/d	200 000		

(Extract of) Bank

Details	R	Details	R
Balance b/d	14 000	Fost Investment	150 000
Fost fund	150 000	Tennis Court	100 000
Daniels fund	100 000	Simpson investment	200 000
Simpson fund	200 000	Coaching fees	35 000
Interest income	27 000	Other expenses	258 000
Interest income	36 000	Balance c/d	34 000
Subscriptions	250 000		
	777 000		777 000
Balance b/d	34 000		

Interest income

Details	R	Details	R
Fost fund	27 000	Bank	27 000
Income & expenditure	36 000	Bank	36 000
	63 000		63 000

Income and expenditure

Details	R	Details	R
Other expenses	258 000	Subscriptions	250 000
Coaching fees	8 000	Interest income Simpson	36 000
Accumulated fund	20 000		
	286 000		286 000

Coaching fees

Details	R	Details	R
Bank	35 000	Fost fund	27 000
		Income & expenditure	8 000
	35 000		35 000

Accumulated fund

Details	R	Details	R
		Balance b/d	14 000
Balance b/d	34 000	Income & expenditure	20 000
	34 000		34 000
		Balance b/d	34 000

The Fost fund is a non-discretionary legacy for which the capital must remain intact and the income can be used for coaching fees. In accounting for the fund, the bank is increased and the fund is increased. The cash is then invested into an income earning account. The income earned from the investment is added to the fund and the specific expense up to the amount of the income earned is written off against the income.

The Daniels fund is a non-discretionary legacy used to purchase a specific asset. In accounting for the fund, the designated asset is increased and the fund is increased.

The Simpson fund is a non-discretionary donation for which the capital must remain intact and the income can be used for the general expenses of the club. The income earned from the funds invested is treated as income in the income and expenditure statement and is not added to the Simpson fund

CASSEY COUNTRY CLUB
(EXTRACT FROM) BALANCE SHEET
AT 31 DECEMBER 20X5

			R
ASSETS			
Non-current assets			450 000
Tennis courts			100 000
18% fixed deposit investments			350 000
Current assets			
Bank			34 000
			484 000
FUNDS AND LIABILITIES			
Funds			484 000
Accumulated fund		34 000	
Balance at beginning of year	14 000		
Surplus	20 000		
Fost fund		150 000	
Introduced	150 000		
Interest	27 000		
Coaching fees	(27 000)		
Daniels fund		100 000	
Introduced	100 000		
Simpson fund		200 000	
Introduced	200 000		
			484 000

23.2.2 Loans

All entities, business and non-business, may finance part of their operations or activities by borrowing from a financial institution.

23.3 Producing information for a non-business entity

There are no statutory requirements relating to the financial statements prepared for a non-business entity. The information produced should meet the needs of members and be appropriate to the size and type of club, society or institution.

A ***receipts and payments statement***, prepared on the cash basis of accounting or an ***income and expenditure statement***, prepared on the accrual basis of accounting, can be prepared, depending on the nature of the non-business entity.

Example: Receipts and payments statement/Income and expenditure statement

Gary Good (Simon Smart's partner in Intense Sports) is a keen outdoor person. He has a dog that he trains at the Aquilla Dog Training Club. The following information is submitted in respect of the Aquilla Dog Training Club. Balance in the bank at 1 January 20X7, R5 570.

During the year ended 31 December 20X7, the club received:

	R
Subscriptions	30 600
Donations	3 200
Sale of raffle tickets	10 010
Proceeds of dog walk	3 250
Loan from W Katrigrah to pay for the new floodlights	15 000

The following amounts were paid:

	R
Rent for clubhouse	12 000
LIghts and water	4 000
Expenses for dog walk	2 080
Secretarial expenses	5 200
Stationery	2 200
Wages	3 000
Refreshments	4 000
Socials	2 400
Prizes	3 900
Dog-training equipment (expected life 5 years)	5 000
Trailer (expected life 4 years)	7 000
Floodlights (expected life 20 years)	15 000

In addition to the above, it was discovered that R700 was owing to the club in respect of subscriptions. Expenses in respect of the wages incurred but not yet paid totalled R220. The loan was taken out on 1 April 20X2, and interest is payable annually in arrears at 18% pa.

23.3.1 Receipts and payments statement

A receipts and payments statement is used for smaller non-business entities which have no significant assets other than cash resources. It reports all the cash received and paid by a non-business entity over a specific period of time. All receipts and payments, whether of an income or capital nature, are included.

The receipts and payments statement is simply a summary of the cash journals of the entity and can be compared to a cash flow statement. As such, this statement will not disclose gains or losses on the disposal of assets, nor will the effect of consumable stores on hand be recognised. Internal transactions are not taken into account.

Solution: Receipts and payments statement

AQUILLA DOG TRAINING CLUB
RECEIPTS AND PAYMENTS STATEMENT FOR THE YEAR ENDED 31/12/X7

	R
Cash received from:	62 060
Subscriptions	30 600
Donations	3 200
Sale of raffle tickets	10 010
Proceeds from dog walk	3 250
Loan from W Katrigrah	15 000
Cash paid for:	65 780
Rent for clubhouse	12 000
Lights and water	4 000
Expenses for the dog walk	2 080
Secretarial expenses	5 200
Stationery	2 200
Wages	3 000
Refreshments	4 000
Socials	2 400
Prizes	3 900
Dog-training equipment	5 000
Trailer	7 000
Floodlights	15 000
Net decrease in cash	(3 720)
Cash at beginning of period	5 570
Cash at end of period	1 850

The statement simply reflects the cash received and paid. This is consistent with Chapter 2 where the difference between the cash basis and accrual basis of accounting was explained.

23.3.2 Income and expenditure statement

An income and expenditure statement is normally prepared by larger non-business entities which require more detailed reporting because of the more complex nature of their activities. The income and expenditure statement is prepared on the accrual basis of accounting and thus performs the same function, and is prepared on the same principles as the income statement of a business entity.

There are a number of items on the income and expenditure statement for a non-business entity which need explanation. These are the members' subscriptions, results of trading activities and fund-raising activities.

Solution: Income and expenditure statement

AQUILLA DOG TRAINING CLUB
INCOME AND EXPENDITURE STATEMENT FOR THE YEAR ENDED 31 DECEMBER 20X7

		R
Income:		45 680
Subscriptions	(30 600 + 700)	31 300
Donations		3 200
Sale of raffle tickets		10 010
Dog walk	(3 250 – 2 080)	1 170
Expenses:		(42 445)
Rent for clubhouse		12 000
Lights and water		4 000
Secretarial expenses		5 200
Stationery		2 200
Wages		3 220
Refreshments		4 000
Socials		2 400
Prizes		3 900
Interest	(15 000 x 0.18 x 9/12)	2 025
Depreciation – dog training equipment	(5 000/5 years)	1 000
Depreciation – trailer	(7 000/4 years)	1 750
Depreciation – floodlights	(15 000/20 years)	750
Surplus		3 235

Members' subscriptions

Subscriptions received from members represent income earned, and for some non-business entities are the largest single source of income. Subscriptions must not be confused with entrance fees, which, as previously described, are allocated directly to the accumulated fund.

In accounting for subscriptions, the following aspects need to be considered:

- Subscriptions owing by members at the end of the *previous* period (an *asset* on the balance sheet, often referred to as subscriptions in arrears).
- Subscriptions received in advance from members at the end of the *previous* period (a *liability* on the balance sheet, often referred to as subscriptions in advance).
- Subscriptions received from members during the current period in respect of:
  - amounts owing from the previous period
  - amounts for the current period
  - amounts received in advance for the following period.

- The membership of some members may be terminated for non payment of their subscriptions.
- Subscriptions owing by members at the end of the *current* period.
- Subscriptions received in advance from members at the end of the *current* period.
- The subscription income earned during the current period and transferred to the income and expenditure account.

The following example illustrates the application of these items.

Example: Subscriptions

Simon Smart enjoys the finer pleasures in life and has a substantial wine collection. Simon joined the Stellenbosch Wine Tasters Club so as to indulge in his favourite pastime. At 1 January 20X7, the Stellenbosch Wine Tasters Club had 500 members. Annual subscription per member is R30. At 1 January 20X7, 50 members owed subscriptions for 20X6 and 31 members had paid 20X7 subscriptions in advance. 10 members who owed 20X6 subscriptions cannot be traced and their membership of the club has been terminated. During the year ended 31 December 20X7, R14 400 was received in respect of subscriptions. Included in this amount is R330 in respect of 20X8.

You are required to:

prepare the subscriptions account in the ledger of the club.

Solution: Subscriptions

Subscriptions

Details	R	Details	R
Subscriptions in arrear	1 500	Subscriptions in advance	930
		Bank	14 400
Income & expenditure	14 700	Bad debts	300
Subscriptions in advance	330	***Subscriptions in arrear***	***900***
	16 530		16 530

Workings

Opening members	500
Less bad debts	(10)
Total members for the year	490
Membership fees earned (490 x R30)	R14 700

Subscriptions in advance

Details	R	Details	R
Subscriptions	930	Balance b/d	930
Balance c/d	330	Subscriptions	330
	1 260		1 260
		Balance b/d	330

Subscriptions in arrear

Details	R	Details	R
Balance b/d	1 500	Subscriptions	1 500
Subscriptions	***900***	Balance c/d	900
	2 400		2 400
Balance b/d	900		

The balances in the subscriptions in arrear account and the subscriptions in advance accounts are transferred to the subscriptions account at the beginning of the period. These are typical reversing entries, previously explained in Chapter 5. The cash received during the year of R14 400 is entered in the subscriptions account as well as the bad debts. (Note that the entry to account for the bad debts is to debit bad debts expense and to credit subscriptions.) This is because the opening balance in the subscriptions in arrear account was transferred to the subscriptions account as one of the reversing entries. The subscriptions in advance at the end of the year is given at R330 and the income earned is calculated at R14 700. The subscriptions in arrear of R900 is a balancing figure.

Trading activities

Most clubs trade with their members by providing food and drink facilities. In larger clubs this often includes full restaurant and bar facilities. As these trading activities are not the main reason for existence of the club, the gross profit or loss from such activities are included as a line item on the income and expenditure statement, along with subscription income, investment income and any other income earned during the period.

The concept of gross profit is the same as for a trading entity. The details of the gross profit computation for the specific trading activity can be shown on the face of the income and expenditure statement or as a note.

Example: Trading activities in a non-business entity

The Stellenbosch Wine Tasters Club caters for its members in the club canteen. The following is an extract of the canteen trading information of the Stellenbosch Wine Tasters Club for the year ended 31 December 20X8.

STELLENBOSCH WINE TASTERS CLUB
(EXTRACT FROM) TRIAL BALANCE AT 1 JANUARY 20X8

Description	Dr	Cr
Canteen inventory	7 550	
Canteen accounts payable		3 500

Additional information

- Receipts from canteen sales were R24 900.
- Payments to canteen suppliers were R6 800.
- Canteen inventory at 31 December 20X8 was R4 800.
- Canteen accounts payable at 31 December 20X8 was R2 200.

You are required to:

prepare the canteen trading account for the year ended 31 December 20X8. (Include the canteen accounts payable, canteen inventory and canteen sales accounts in support of your answer.)

Solution: Trading activities in a non-business entity

Canteen accounts payable

Details	R	Details	R
Bank	6 800	Balance b/d	3 500
Balance c/d	2 200	***Purchases***	***5 500***
	9 000		9 000
		Balance b/d	2 200

Canteen inventory

Details	R	Details	R
Balance b/d	7 550	Trading	7 550
Trading	4 800	Balance c/d	4 800
	12 350		12 350
Balance b/d	4 800		

Canteen sales

Details	R	Details	R
Trading a/c	24 900	Bank	24 900
	24 900		24 900

Canteen trading account

Details	R	Details	R
Canteen inventory (opening balance)	7 550	Canteen sales	24 900
Purchases	5 500	Canteen inventory (closing balance)	4 800
Income & expenditure	16 650		
	29 700		29 700

In a non-business entity, trading activities are disclosed as income if a profit is made from the activity, or an expense if a loss is made.

23.4 Exam example

The following receipts and payments statement of the Greenfingers Gardening Club for the year ended 31 December 20X2 has been prepared by the club's treasurer.

GREENFINGERS GARDENING CLUB
RECEIPTS AND PAYMENTS STATEMENT FOR THE YEAR ENDED 31/12/X2

	R
Cash received from	13 084
Seed sales	1 684
Sale of tickets to non-members for national flower show	400
Lawnmower sales	3 800
Subscriptions received	
20X1	80
20X2	6 720
20X3	400

Cash paid to		(14 220)
Purchase of tickets & brochures for national flower show	3 600	
Seed purchases	1 900	
Lawnmower purchases	5 400	
Transport to national flower show	490	
Rent of clubhouse	500	
Gardening magazines for members' use	390	
Secretarial expenses	940	
Architect's fees for proposed new clubhouse	1 000	
Net decrease in cash		(1 136)
Cash at beginning of period		876
Cash at end of period		(260)

The club's executive committee has decided that members should receive an income and expenditure statement for the year ended 31 December 20X2 and a balance sheet as at that date. The treasurer has extracted the following additional information from his records:

(1) The assets and liabilities of the club (other than bank balances or overdrafts) are as follows:

	1 Jan 20X2	**31 Dec 20X2**
Plot of land for proposed new club building	2 000	2 000
Seed inventory, at cost	250	560
Accounts receivable		
– lawnmower sales	400	1 370
Members' subscriptions		
– in advance	240	400
– in arrears	120	160
Accounts payable		
– lawnmower supplier	800	170
– seed growers	110	340

(2) The club obtains lawnmowers from a supplier and sells them at cost price to members. The club never holds any stock of lawnmowers.

(3) Any member who had not settled his 20X1 arrears subscriptions by the end of 20X2 had his membership terminated on that date. Membership fees are R40 per year.

You are required to:

(a) prepare a trial balance for the club at 1 January 20X2.

(b) prepare an income and expenditure statement for the club for the year ended 31 December 20X2.

(c) prepare a balance sheet for the club at 31 December 20X2.

Solution: Exam example

(a)

TRIAL BALANCE AT 1 JANUARY 20X2

Description	Dr	Cr
Land	2 000	
Inventory of seeds	250	
Accounts receivable – Lawnmowers	400	
Membership subscriptions in arrears	120	
Membership subscriptions in advance		240
Accounts payable – Lawnmowers		800
Accounts payable – Seed growers		110
Bank	876	
Accumulated fund		2 496
	3 646	3 646

(b)

GREENFINGERS GARDENING CLUB
INCOME AND EXPENDITURE STATEMENT FOR THE YEAR ENDED 31/12/X2

	R
Income	
Subscriptions	7 120
Expenses	(5 696)
Loss on sale of seeds	136
Cost of flower show	3 690
Rent	500
Magazines	390
Secretarial expenses	940
Bad debts (120 – 80)	40
Surplus	1 424

GREENFINGERS GARDENING CLUB
BALANCE SHEET AT 31 DECEMBER 20X2

	R
ASSETS	
Non-current assets	3 000
Land at cost	2 000
Architect's fees	1 000
Current assets	2 090
Inventory of seeds	560
Accounts receivable – lawnmowers	1 370
Members' subscriptions in arrears	160
	5 090
FUNDS AND LIABILITIES	
Funds	3 920
Accumulated fund	
Balance at beginning of year	2 496
Surplus	1 424
Current liabilities	1 170
Accounts payable – lawnmowers	170
Accounts payable – seed growers	340
Member subscriptions in advance	400
Bank overdraft	260
	5 090

Workings

Subscriptions

Details	R	Details	R
Subscriptions in arrears	120	Subscriptions in advance	240
Subscriptions in advance	400	Cash	7 200
Income & expenditure	***7 120***	Bad debt	40
		Subscriptions in arrears	160
	7 640		7 640

Flower show trading

Details	R	Details	R
Cost of tickets	3 600	Sale of tickets	400
Transport	490	Income & expenditure	3 690
	4 090		4 090

Accounts payable – seed growers

Details	R	Details	R
Cash	1 900	Balance b/d	110
Balance c/d	340	***Purchases***	***2 130***
	2 240		2 240
		Balance b/d	340

Seed trading

Details	R	Details	R
Inventory	250	Sales	1 684
Purchases	2 130	Inventory	560
		Income & expenditure	136
	2 380		2 380

Accounts receivable – lawnmowers

Details	R	Details	R
Balance b/d	400	Cash	3 800
Sales	***4 770***	Balance c/d	1 370
	5 170		5 170
Balance b/d	1 370		

Accounts payable – lawnmowers

Details	R	Details	R
Cash	5 400	Balance b/d	800
Balance c/d	170	***Purchases***	***4 770***
	5 570		5 570
		Balance b/d	170

Lawnmower trading

Details	R	Details	R
Inventory	0	Sales	4 770
Purchases	4 770	Inventory	0
	4 770		4 770

Summary of concepts and applications

1. Non-business entities are organisations whose primary objective is to provide services to their members. Income earned in excess of expenditure is referred to as a surplus, while expenditure incurred in excess of income is referred to as a deficit. This information is recorded in an income and expenditure statement.

2. A non-business entity may be financed from its accumulated funds (the entrance fees paid by members, the surplus retained from the entity's activities, and discretionary donations or legacies), special funds (established from non-discretionary legacies or donations), and/or from funds borrowed from financial institutions.

3. Information may be produced for a non-business entity in the form of a receipts and payments statement or an income and expenditure statement. The chapter illustrates both methods through an example. Subscriptions received from members of non-business entities represent income earned.

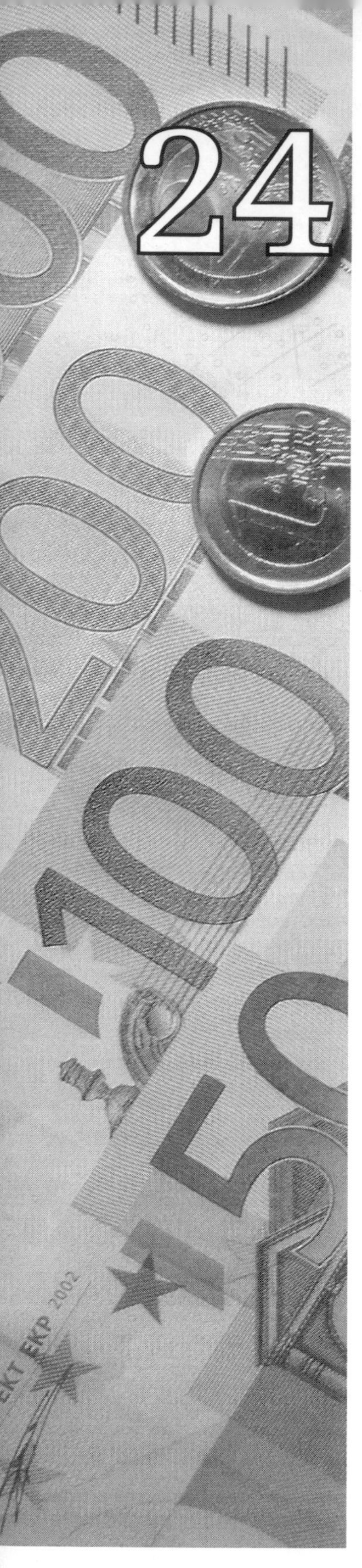

24 Incomplete Records

'It is an enormous advantage to be able to find your way about in a balance sheet and a profit and loss account. It must be most disconcerting never to know whether to look on the left or the right and to be continually surprised to find a trading loss included among the assets'.
(Mr Justice Salmon, 1959)

Outcomes

- Describe the situations giving rise to incomplete records.
- Prepare financial statements from incomplete records.

Chapter outline

Enron Corporation
Statement of financial position...

($ Millions)

In 2001 the world was rocked by the largest fraud ever. It was uncovered that Enron, one of America's largest corporations, had been grossly overstating revenues and understating liabilities, leading to the loss of billions of dollars in a very short period of time. It seems history is not without a sense of irony, because the company was ranked by Fortune magazine as America's most innovative company for six years, right up until it was liquidated. It now seems that the most innovative part of Enron was in fact its accounting.

24.1 Circumstances giving rise to incomplete records

No new concepts are taught in this chapter. However, an understanding of all the concepts taught in this book is required to solve a problem where the accounting records are incomplete.

There are varying degrees of incompleteness in accounting records. The procedures to be adopted when preparing financial statements will depend upon the nature of the records or data available.

There are various reasons for the records of a business entity being incomplete, for example:

- The person compiling the records has inadequate accounting knowledge.
- Financial data is not available because it has been lost, destroyed or stolen.
- Transactions are not recorded on a double entry basis and therefore the records may not directly provide the information necessary to determine:
  - the results of operations of the entity
  - the financial position of the entity.

It is often not feasible or practical for a small business to maintain accounting records using a full double-entry system of bookkeeping. Many small business enterprises are satisfied with the information they obtain from keeping a record of receipts and payments and a record of their accounts receivable and accounts payable. A large number of owners of such enterprises may not know how to correctly record transactions. They may record the details of a transaction once only, if at all! Many transactions may not be recorded, leading to incomplete information.

Section 56(1) of the Close Corporations Act 1984 requires a corporation to keep 'such accounting records as are necessary to fairly present the state of affairs and business of the corporation, and to explain the transactions and financial position of the corporation ...'. Section 284(1) of the Companies Act 1973 has a similar requirement for a company to keep 'such accounting records as are necessary to fairly present the state of affairs and business of the company and to explain the transactions and financial position of the trade or business of the company ...'.

There is no statutory obligation for a sole proprietorship or a partnership to keep such records. It is, however, necessary for such business entities to maintain adequate accounting records for the following reasons:

- The owners need to know if the business entity is profitable.
- It is necessary to determine the profits in order to submit information required by the Receiver of Revenue.
- In the case of a partnership, it is essential to know what profits have been made in order to allocate the profits to the partners.

Every set of circumstances that you will encounter, both in practice and in an exam, will be different. However, if the assignment is approached with the conceptual understanding that has been taught in this book, you should be able to reconstruct the information to produce a set of financial statements. A typical set of procedures to follow when preparing financial statements from incomplete records is given in the following section.

24.2 Preparation of financial statements from incomplete records

As mentioned above, the procedure for the preparation of financial statements from incomplete records will vary depending upon the circumstances. However, the following guidelines can be adapted to most situations:

- Establish, or reconstruct the financial position at the end of the previous period.
- Reconstruct information relating to the key areas of performance measurement
  - cash and credit sales
  - cash and credit purchases
  - other income and expenses
- Identify any capital contributions from owners and any distributions to owners.
- Determine any relevant adjustments at the end of the period.
- Prepare the financial statements.

24.3 Practical application

Donald, (a university friend of Simon's) assisted Michael and Minnie to form a private company called Euro Products Pty (Ltd) in October 20X5. They sell Disney products that are imported from America. Donald, who was an accountancy student, helped Michael and Minnie prepare the financial statements for the 20X6, 20X7 and 20X8 year-ends. However, he graduated from the Toon Town University at the end of 20X8 with honours and left the country to work in France. This left Michael and Minnie in a predicament and as a result no accounting records have been kept for the 20X9 year. They have now come to you, to ask for assistance in preparing the financial statements for the year ended 30 September 20X9. They have given you several boxes of papers from which you are able to ascertain the following:

(1) The opening balances per the trial balance as at 1 October 20X8:

Ordinary share capital	R350 000
Retained earnings	74 525
Loans from shareholders	100 000
Land and buildings	400 000
Motor vehicles – cost	200 000
Furniture & fittings – cost	65 000
Computer equipment – cost	34 000
Accumulated depreciation – motor vehicles	97 600
Accumulated depreciation – furniture & fittings	15 400
Accumulated depreciation – computer equipment	17 000
Inventory	84 256
Accounts receivable	25 022
Pre-paid insurance	3 546
Cash on hand	547

Accounts payable	55 262
Accrued expenses	
Lights & water	3 217
Telephone	654
Bank overdraft	98 713

(2) They banked their takings periodically after paying the following amounts in cash:

Salaries	R1 000 per week (each)
Staff wages (6 employees)	R456 per week (each)
Repairs & maintenance	R14 262

Cash on hand at 30 September 20X9 was R963.

(3) A loan was taken out on 1 March 20X9 from the Scrooge Bank in order to purchase the new motor vehicle. The loan bears interest at 18% per annum which is payable on 28 February each year in arrears. The loan is repayable in 5 years' time.

(4) Land and buildings were revalued during the year to R450 000.

(5) Depreciation is provided as follows:
Motor vehicles – 20% per annum on the reducing balance method.
Furniture & fittings – 10% per annum on cost.
Computer equipment – 25% per annum on cost.

(6) Bank account

6.1 The summarised bank statement for the year from Scrooge Bank showed the following:

	R		R
Balance at 30/09/X8	76 616	Deposits	2 280 559
Acquisition of motor vehicle	150 000	Deposit – Loan	150 000
Delivery charges outwards	134 876		
Insurance	14 940		
Advertising	43 798		
Lights & water	40 817		
Rent	54 000		
Repairs & maintenance	46 874		
Salaries	232 994		
Telephone	7 806		
Payments to suppliers	1 532 964		
Balance 30/09/X9	94 874		
	2 430 559		2 430 559

6.2 The bank balance at 30 September 20X8 did not agree with the balance in the 20X8 financial statements. There was an outstanding cheque for R22 097 (payable to the creditor) which only cleared the bank on 7 October 20X8. There were no outstanding deposits at 30 September 20X8.

6.3 The last three cheques made out on 28 September 20X9 did not clear the bank account until 5 October 20X9:

Cheque No. 1128	Accounts payable	R100 800
Cheque No. 1129	Advertising	R3 981
Cheque No. 1130	Repairs & maintenance	R2 121

6.4 An amount of R26 874 was deposited into the bank account on 30 September 20X9. This amount was processed by the bank on 1 October 20X9.

(7) An inventory count was conducted at 30 September 20X9. The total value of inventory on hand (at cost price) was R78 425. Included in inventory were items at a cost price of R26 896. According to Minnie, these items will only be able to be sold for R24 218. In addition to the inventory counted above, there was R12 658 of goods on consignment from Daffy Quack.

(8) In September 20X9, for the first time, Michael decided to import the goods directly from the overseas supplier, Marsoopalamy Distributors Limited. Goods to the value of R24 213 were ordered from the supplier in New York on 15 September 20X9. The terms of the contract were FOB New York. The ship left for Durban on 29 September 20X9.

(9) Michael and Minnie mark up their goods at $66^{2}/_{3}$ %.

(10) An accounts receivable listing was maintained on a monthly basis.

10.1 The list of accounts receivable at 30 September 20X9 was as follows:

Customer	Amount
	R
Pluto Toy Shop	17 623
Goofy's Toy Bar	35 241
The Dwarfs' Cabin	4 213
Beautiful Beasts	3 122
Daisy Toy World	24 125
Dark Wing Duck	22 525
Snow White Soft Toys	12 165
Total	119 014

10.2 At year-end Dark Wing Duck had gone insolvent and no cash was expected to be received from them.

10.3 Beautiful Beasts, on the other hand, had not paid their account for five months as they were experiencing financial difficulties.

(11) Apart from the goods purchased from Marsoopalamy Distributors Limited (see 8 above), Euro Products had only purchased their goods from Popeye Importers (Pty) Ltd.

11.1 The statement received from Popeye Importers (Pty) Ltd at 30 September 20X9 showed the following:

Date	Description	Doc	Debit	Credit
31/08/X9	Balance		252 400	
04/09/X9	Payment	R254		151 200
10/09/X9	Invoice	I4785	21 222	
12/09/X9	Credit note	C478		4 252
25/09/X9	Invoice	I4821	20 712	
30/09/X9	Balance			138 882
			294 334	294 334

11.2 On scrutinising the statement you discover the following:

- The payment made on 28 September 20X9 had not been credited on the statement.
- The credit note C478 should have been for R4 225.
- The August statement balance was overstated by R400. This had still not been corrected on the September statement.

(12) Michael informs you that they had failed to keep a record of inventory that they had taken as gifts for customers at Christmas. They are happy for you to determine the figure.

(13) The telephone account and lights and water account for September 20X9 were only received in October.

Lights & water	R3 536
Telephone	R732

(14) The amount paid for insurance was for a contract taken out on 1 January 20X9 in respect of insurance cover for the period ending 31 December 20X9.

(15) The taxation expense for the year is R39 170.

You are required to:

prepare the statement of comprehensive income and statement of changes in equity of Euro Products (Pty) Ltd for the period ended 30 September 20X9 and the statement of financial position at that date.

Solution: Practical application

EURO PRODUCTS (PTY) LIMITED
STATEMENT OF COMPREHENSIVE INCOME
FOR THE YEAR ENDED 30 SEPTEMBER 20X9

			R
Sales	(W1)		2 662 375
Cost of sales	(W4)		(1 600 103)
Opening inventory 01/10/X8		84 256	
Purchases	(1 594 114 – 2 520) (W3/4)	1 591 594	
Goods available for sale		1 675 850	
Closing inventory 30/09/X9	(W5)	(75 747)	
Gross profit			1 062 272
Operating expenses			(924 096)
Advertising	(43 798 + 3 981)	47 779	
Bad debts	(22 525 + 3 122)	25 647	
Delivery expenses	(note 6 given)	134 876	
Depreciation	(W6)	52 980	
Gifts	(W5)	2 520	
Insurance	(W7)	14 751	
Lights and water	(W8)	41 136	
Rent	(Note 6 given)	54 000	
Repairs and maintenance	(46 874 + 14 262 + 2 121)	63 257	
Salaries	(232 994 + (2 x 1 000 x 52))	336 994	
Telephone	(W8)	7 884	
Wages	(456 x 6 x 52) (W2)	142 272	
Finance cost			
Interest on loan (W8)			(15 750)
Profit before taxation			122 426
Taxation (Note 15 given)			(39 170)
Profit for the period			83 256
Other comprehensive income			
Revaluation			50 000
Total comprehensive income			133 256

EURO PRODUCTS (PTY) LIMITED
STATEMENT OF CHANGES IN EQUITY
FOR THE YEAR ENDED 30 SEPTEMBER 20X9

	Ordinary share capital	*Revaluation surplus*	*Retained earnings*	*Total*
	R	**R**	**R**	**R**
Balance at 1 October 20X8	350 000	–	74 525	424 525
Total comprehensive income		50 000	83 256	133 256
Balance at 30 September 20X9	350 000	50 000	157 781	557 781

EURO PRODUCTS (PTY) LIMITED
STATEMENT OF FINANCIAL POSITION
AT 30 SEPTEMBER 20X9

				R
ASSETS				
Non-current assets (Note 1,3,4 and W6)				716 020
	Cost	**Accumulated depreciation**	**Carrying amount**	
Land and buildings	450 000	–	450 000	
Motor vehicles	350 000	135 580	214 420	
Furniture and fittings	65 000	21 900	43 100	
Computer equipment	34 000	25 500	8 500	
Current assets				212 871
Inventory (W5)				75 747
Goods in transit (Note 8 given)				24 213
Accounts receivable (Note 10 = 119 014 – 22 525)				96 489
Allowance for doubtful debts (Note 10)				(3 122)
Pre-paid insurance (W7)				3 735
Cash on hand (Note 2 given)				963
Bank (W9)				14 846
				928 891
EQUITY AND LIABILITIES				
Share capital and reserves				557 781
Ordinary share capital (Note 1 given)				350 000
Revaluation surplus (Note 4 given: 450 000 – 400 000)				50 000
Retained earnings				157 781
Non-currrent liabilities				250 000
Loans from shareholders				100 000
Loan from Scrooge Bank				150 000

Current liabilities	121 110
Accounts payable – Popeye Importers (W3)	37 709
Accounts payable – Marsoopalamy (Note 8)	24 213
Accrued expenses (W8)	
Interest payable	15 750
Lights and water payable	3 536
Telephone payable	732
Taxation liability (Note 15)	39 170
	928 891

Euro Products (Pty) Limited – Workings

1 Sales

Accounts receivable

Details	R	Details	R
Balance	25 022	Cash (W2)	2 568 383
Sales	***2 662 375***		
		Bad debts	22 525
		Balance**	96 489
	2 687 397		2 687 397
Balance	96 489		

Accounts receivable listing	119 014
Bad debts	(22 525)
	**96 489

The accounts receivable figure for the statement of financial position is calculated from the information in point 10 of the example. The listing shows that, at the year-end, accounts receivable totalled R119 014. However, in 10.2, the information indicates that the amount owing by Dark Wing Duck needs to be written off as a bad debt. By reconstructing the accounts receivable account, the sales figure is calculated.

2 Cash receipts (from cash account)

Cash

Details	R	Details	R
Balance	547	Bank (actual deposits)	2 280 559
Accounts receivable (cash received)	***2 568 383***	Bank (outstanding deposit)	26 874
		Wages (52 x 6 x 456)	142 272
		Repairs & maintenance	14 262
		Salary (1 000 x 2 x 52)	104 000
		Balance	963
	2 568 930		2 568 930

In order to reconstruct the accounts receivable account, the total cash received from customers is required. To calculate this you need to reconstruct the cash account. The example gives the opening and closing balance of the cash account, the amount of cash banked, an outstanding deposit and amounts paid for in cash. The difference in the cash account is therefore the cash received from customers.

3 Purchases

Accounts payable

Details	R	Details	R
Bank **	1 510 867	Balance	55 262
Bank (cheques in transit)	100 800	***Purchases*** (including inventory for gifts)	***1 594 114***
Balance***	37 709		
	1 649 376		1 649 376

	R
* Payments – from bank	1 532 964
X8 outstanding cheque	(22 097)
Current year's payments	1 510 867

** **Supplier's reconciliation**	**R**
Balance per supplier's statement	138 882
Adjusted for:	
Payment not on statement	(98 280)
Mistake on credit note	27
Cast error from August not adjusted	(400)
Balance per accounting records	37 709

Summary of concepts and applications

1. There are various reasons for the records of a business entity being incomplete. In addition, there are varying degrees of incompleteness in accounting records. By applying the conceptual understanding as taught in this book, one should be able to reconstruct information to produce a set of financial statements.
2. The chapter recommends guidelines to be followed in the preparation of financial statements from incomplete records.
3. The chapter demonstrates the application of the recommended procedures through an extensive example requiring the reconstruction of information, as well as the preparation of financial statements from incomplete records.

To determine the purchases figure, you need to reconstruct the accounts payable account. The example gives an opening balance but no closing balance. Therefore the only way to determine the closing balance is to do a suppliers' reconciliation with the information from point 11 in the example. The rest of the information is supplied in the example, that is, payments made.

4 Gifts

Cost	100,00	
GP/MU	66,67	GP% = 66,67 / 166,67= 40 %
SP	166,67	

Therefore:

		R	
Cost	100,00	1 597 425 **	
GP/MU	66,67		
SP	166,67	2 662 375	(W1)

	R
Cost of sales ** (1 597 425 + 2 678)	1 600 103
Inventory 30 September 20X8 (opening)	84 256
Purchases (W3)	1 594 114
Inventory 30 September 20X9 (closing)	(75 747)
Gifts	(2 520)

Using sales and the GP%, cost of sales (before the inventory write-down) is first calculated. The cost of sales is then adjusted to the amount of the inventory write-down of R2 678. Then by using the opening inventory, purchases and closing inventory, the cost of gifts is calculated.

bank statement				67 854
Less: outstanding cheques	1128	Supplier	98 280	
	1129	Advertising	3 981	
	1130	Repairs & maintenance	2 121	(104 382)
Add: outstanding deposit				26 874
Balance per Euro Product's books				(9 654)

5 Inventory

	R
Inventory at cost	78 425
Inventory write-down (26 896 – 24 218)	(2 678)
Final inventory balance	75 747

6 Depreciation

				R
Motor vehicles – old	20%	R102 400	(1 year)	20 480
Motor vehicles – new	20%	R150 000	(7 months)	17 500
Furniture & fittings	10%	R 65 000	(1 year)	6 500
Computer equipment	25%	R 34 000	(1 year)	8 500
				52 980

7 Pre-paid insurance

Pre-paid insurance

Details	R	Details	R
Balance	3 546	***Insurance expense***	***14 751***
Bank	14 940	Balance*	3 735
	18 486		18 486

*14 940 x 3/12 = 3 735

By reconstructing the pre-paid insurance account and using the information in point 14 of the example, you can determine the insurance expense for the income statement and the pre-paid insurance asset for the statement of financial position.

8 Accrued expenses

Telephone liability

Details	R	Details	R
Bank	7 806	Balance	654
Balance	732	***Telephone expense***	***7 884***
	8 538		8 538

Lights and water liability

Details	R	Details	R
Bank	40 817	Balance	3 217
Balance	3 536	***Lights & water expense***	***41 136***
	44 353		44 353

Interest on loan	
R150 000 (18% for 7 months)	R15 750

Total accrued expenses	R
Telephone	732
Lights and water	3 536
Interest	15 750
	20 018

The telephone and lights and water expenses are calculated by reconstructing the respective liability accounts. Interest is calculated from the date that the loan was taken out.

9 Bank reconciliation

Balance per bank statement				94
Less: outstanding cheques	1128	Supplier	100 800	
	1129	Advertising	3 981	
	1130	Repairs & maintenance	2 121	(1
Add: outstanding deposit				
Balance per Euro Product's books				

To determine the bank balance for the statement of financial position, a bank reconciliati be performed using the information in point 6 of the example.

To determine the purchases figure, you need to reconstruct the accounts payable account. The example gives an opening balance but no closing balance. Therefore the only way to determine the closing balance is to do a suppliers' reconciliation with the information from point 11 in the example. The rest of the information is supplied in the example, that is, payments made.

4 Gifts

Cost	100,00	
GP/MU	66,67	GP% = 66,67 / 166,67= 40 %
SP	166,67	

Therefore:

		R	
Cost	100,00	1 597 425 **	
GP/MU	66,67		
SP	166,67	2 662 375	(W1)

	R
Cost of sales ** (1 597 425 + 2 678)	1 600 103
Inventory 30 September 20X8 (opening)	84 256
Purchases (W3)	1 594 114
Inventory 30 September 20X9 (closing)	(75 747)
Gifts	(2 520)

Using sales and the GP%, cost of sales (before the inventory write-down) is first calculated. The cost of sales is then adjusted to the amount of the inventory write-down of R2 678. Then by using the opening inventory, purchases and closing inventory, the cost of gifts is calculated.

bank statement				67 854
Less: outstanding cheques	1128	Supplier	98 280	
	1129	Advertising	3 981	
	1130	Repairs & maintenance	2 121	(104 382)
Add: outstanding deposit				26 874
Balance per Euro Product's books				(9 654)

5 Inventory

	R
Inventory at cost	78 425
Inventory write-down (26 896 – 24 218)	(2 678)
Final inventory balance	75 747

6 Depreciation

				R
Motor vehicles – old	20%	R102 400	(1 year)	20 480
Motor vehicles – new	20%	R150 000	(7 months)	17 500
Furniture & fittings	10%	R 65 000	(1 year)	6 500
Computer equipment	25%	R 34 000	(1 year)	8 500
				52 980

7 Pre-paid insurance

Pre-paid insurance

Details	R	Details	R
Balance	3 546	***Insurance expense***	***14 751***
Bank	14 940	Balance*	3 735
	18 486		18 486

*14 940 x 3/12 = 3 735

By reconstructing the pre-paid insurance account and using the information in point 14 of the example, you can determine the insurance expense for the income statement and the pre-paid insurance asset for the statement of financial position.

8 Accrued expenses

Telephone liability

Details	R	Details	R
Bank	7 806	Balance	654
Balance	732	***Telephone expense***	***7 884***
	8 538		8 538

Lights and water liability

Details	R	Details	R
Bank	40 817	Balance	3 217
Balance	3 536	***Lights & water expense***	***41 136***
	44 353		44 353

Interest on loan

R150 000	(18% for 7 months)	R15 750

Total accrued expenses

	R
Telephone	732
Lights and water	3 536
Interest	15 750
	20 018

The telephone and lights and water expenses are calculated by reconstructing the respective liability accounts. Interest is calculated from the date that the loan was taken out.

9 Bank reconciliation

Balance per bank statement				94 874
Less: outstanding cheques	1128	Supplier	100 800	
	1129	Advertising	3 981	
	1130	Repairs & maintenance	2 121	(106 902)
Add: outstanding deposit				26 874
Balance per Euro Product's books				(14 846)

To determine the bank balance for the statement of financial position, a bank reconciliation needs to be performed using the information in point 6 of the example.

Summary of concepts and applications

1. There are various reasons for the records of a business entity being incomplete. In addition, there are varying degrees of incompleteness in accounting records. By applying the conceptual understanding as taught in this book, one should be able to reconstruct information to produce a set of financial statements.
2. The chapter recommends guidelines to be followed in the preparation of financial statements from incomplete records.
3. The chapter demonstrates the application of the recommended procedures through an extensive example requiring the reconstruction of information, as well as the preparation of financial statements from incomplete records.